2395

D1085504

DEATH AND EXISTENCE

Contemporary Religious Movements:
A Wiley-Interscience Series

Edited by IRVING I. ZARETSKY

DEATH AND EXISTENCE

A Conceptual History of
Human Mortality

James P. Carse
New York University

A WILEY–INTERSCIENCE PUBLICATION

JOHN WILEY & SONS, NewYork Chichester Brisbane Toronto

For Alice

ἐὰμ καταβῶ εἰσ τὸμ ἄδημ

Library of Congress Cataloging in Publication Data:

Carse, James P.
  Death and existence.

  (Contemporary religious movements)
  "A Wiley-Interscience publication."
  Includes index.
  I. Death.   1. Title.

BD444.C37   128'.5   79-24830
ISBN 0-471-13704-9

Printed in the United States of America

10 9 8 7 6 5 4 3 2 1

SERIES EDITOR'S PREFACE

Of central importance in the life of every person is the confrontation of one's own mortality and thereby the development of an orientation or worldview toward life and death with which to shape the quality and content of daily conduct. Although every person's worldview is personally derived, it is not completely idiosyncratic; rather, it is culturally patterned and socially determined. Our socialization process, from infancy, provides us with only the initial raw material from which to develop our personal belief system.

Every human society has recognized the importance of orienting its members to the phenomenon of death, the process of dying, and death's aftermath. In providing belief and ritual systems dealing with human mortality a society gains a means of social control and provides its members with a source of social bonding and cohesion. But this was more true historically of traditional, homogeneous societies. In today's complex industrial societies, populations are not uni-ethnic, uni-cultural, or uni-religious communities. Rather, every society is composed of social groupings whose beliefs, even about the very basic issues of human mortality and the impact of death on human existence, are at great variance from one another. Therefore, to provide its members with a worldview that will engender social bonding and cohesion, a contemporary society has to provide not a unified, parochial belief system but the tools for learning about and comprehending the varieties of human belief systems and the legitimacy of each within its historical context. A unifying worldview in today's world is one that accounts for diversity, not one that excludes variation.

It is precisely on this point that this volume by Professor Carse makes a significant contribution. The book draws on historical, literary,

v

philosophical, and theological sources to portray systematically for us the evolution of human conceptions about mortality and our own understanding of our mortality as these affect human existence and the organization of societies and cultures. By beginning with the premise that to confront human mortality is a basic human need, and by providing us with a historical framework through which to view how societies answered such needs at various periods, Professor Carse allows us to share in a secular worldview that creates a bond of greater tolerance toward those whose beliefs might be fundamentally opposed to our own.

This volume appears at a time in our history when, as a society, we are struggling with the moral underpinnings of our conceptions of human mortality. Militarily we now have the capacity to kill instantaneously a vast portion of the world's population; medically we are able to abort human life with great safety; scientifically we have progressed remarkably in conquering human disease and prolonging human life; technologically and socially we are concerned with the quality of life, the quality of death, and the process of aging and dying. Our increased power over our mortality deserves our preoccupation with the moral underpinnings of our progress. And such present preoccupations have to be tempered and focused with a historical retrospective.

IRVING I. ZARETSKY

November 1979
New York, New York

PREFACE

"I signed up for this course because I knew there was absolutely nothing I could learn from it." These were the words of a student in the first class I was to teach on the subject of death, nearly ten years ago. Although the remark was received with considerable mirth by the other students, as the young man had intended, it now seems prophetically apt.

The student was perfectly correct. Neither I nor anyone else had anything to teach him about death *as such*. In itself death is nothing. When Hamlet referred to death as the distant land from whose shores no traveler ever returns, he starkly evoked the separation between ourselves and the dead, but, indirectly, he suggested that the dead are not just gone; they have gone somewhere else. We can imagine a great many states and locations in which the dead might exist, but if we do think of them *existing* there they are not truly dead for us. Indeed, we can no more think about the conditions persons are in when they are dead than we can think about where a candle flame is after it has been extinguished. The flame has not gone somewhere else; it has simply gone out.

In the years following that first class I have come to see that the deepest challenge of this subject is not to discover something about the nature of death that had hitherto lain obscured by centuries of oversight and ignorance. It is rather to integrate into the rest of our knowledge, and particularly into our self-understanding, the very fact that what death *is* will always lie beyond the scope of our comprehension. The fact that death is a subject about which nothing can be learned is itself exceedingly valuable to learn.

The absolute finality that death represents, and the consequent impossibility of having direct knowledge of it, constitute an acute issue in coming to understand what it means to exist as a person. On the one hand, the most intimate and at the same time most disturbing fact about ourselves is that we shall all die; on the other, death is a fact that almost perversely eludes our direct grasp. This is an acute issue, because no matter how clear and thorough the rest of our self-understanding might be, the incomprehensibility of death will remain coiled in its interior, quietly gnawing away at every one of its certainties. All knowledge, whether of the world or of ourselves, contains within itself a mystery it cannot extinguish. No matter how marvelously we might have constructed our schemes of thought, it is still true that each of us will vanish into the final darkness—along with our thought.

When the issue is put like this it appears, on the face of it, to present us with an insuperable dilemma. It may seem pointless to engage in thought at all, even to proceed with those ordinary projects of life that are fueled, as they must be, by visions of the future. It is by no means uncommon for persons to respond to their mortality by allowing a sense of futility to settle into every aspect of their existence.

This book celebrates the opposite point of view. It is written in the belief that if the young man in my first class on death has never lost his initial wisdom, and continues in that essential ignorance about himself, he will not have been crippled by despair, but, on the contrary, will have been elevated by wonder.

I do not offer this as a personal point of view, grounded nowhere except in the idiosyncracies of my own experience of my own experience and insight. I offer instead a critical study of the conception of death of several of the world's major thinkers and traditions; all of which have acknowledged the very essence of life to be the attempt to embrace the incomprehensibility of death.

Not one of the thinkers studied in this volume would deny that hopelessness waits like an anxious guest behind the door of every human heart. But they are, for the most part, unanimous in declaring that if we insist on holding that door shut—that is, if we continue to deny our mortality—we will only have locked ourselves into an airless spiritual trap. By denying death we will have denied life. Dare to build your cities under Vesuvius, Nietzsche declared, certain that those who would throw the door open to any of the dark guests whom mortality invites into their reflection would discover that life is far grander than they ever had believed.

The content and structure of this book have grown out of the adventure of teaching death to persons too intelligent and too serious about their personal journeys to accept facile answers to their questions. It should be read, therefore, not merely as a catalog of trenchant remarks on death by an assortment of quotable sages, but as a conversation of many voices. The attempt here is not to present what Hegel or the Islamic mystics or the Upanishadic rishis had to say about death—but to investigate how their thoughts illumine the critical and searching questions of contemporary persons concerning the nature of their own mortality.

During the time I have been occupied with the reflection, the research, and the composition of this book my own father and mother have died. So have several other deeply loved members of my family. Two grown children of families close to our own, Kelly Maguire and David Ware, persons we knew well and loved, have suffered accidental deaths. Several persons whom I first met when they were in the final stages of their illnesses are now dead. Their voices are also part of this conversation. For each of their lives I am grateful to a degree they could never have realized.

This is therefore a personal book, shaped partly by my own intellectual and spiritual quest and partly by countless discussions with students, colleagues, and friends. It is true that the book has nothing to teach about death as such; my only hope is that it, therefore, has much to say about life.

JAMES P. CARSE

Washington Square
Autumn 1979

CONTENTS

FOREWORD

Parallel to the conceptions of death, as delineated by Professor Carse in this text, are the pragmatic issues related to the process of dying; these are expressed and practiced by those involved in the new field of thanatology. Just as Professor Carse stresses the understanding that encompasses the more global concept of mortality, so the physician and other health-care givers stress psychosocial aspects of humanitarian and humanistic concerns.

Currently, our society is in the throes of a revolution in the training of those who will nurture our physical and emotional needs as our bodily functions start to fail. Perhaps it could be said that an attempt is being made to turn the clock backward to the time when health-care givers tried to effect cure without the support of the therapeutic "miracles" introduced over the past two decades in the form of new generations of drugs and techniques of biomedical engineering. Our present-day enlightment, for all of its benefits, has cast a shadow of still unknown dimensions on medical care and medical education, for, in the quest to achieve cure, the status of giving care has been diminished. Among medical educators concerned over this phenomenon, a search has been initiated to find ways of dispelling this shadow without endangering the mandated, nonpsychosocial components of the curriculum.

Within the educational setting, interdisciplinary relationships are altering the perspectives of those who must make decisions on the care of terminally ill patients, the members of their families, and other involved professional staff. The approaches to and expectations from therapeutic modalities are being broadened by new explorations into the ethics and values which should be automatically considered

whenever human lives are being cared for. Philosophical enlightenment adds indispensable historical clarification to scientific interven-
tions on behalf of the dying and the bereaved. Philosophy relates death
to human existence and the quality of life—the essential quality of
human existence itself that engages the consciences of those who
would offer us humanistic medicine. Compassion and knowledge are
the springs from which flow trust and faith, without which man can
live only a most deprived and barren existence. The task is to know
how and when decisions can be made, to proceed thoughtfully while
making them, to distinguish between what can and cannot be done and
what should and should not be done.

In analyzing death, in interpreting its every significant nuance, Professor Carse advances the cause of all who delve into the meaning of
life. Mere survival is not enough to provide nourishment for the soul of
man. The message to be read in Philosophy and in Thanatology is the
same: Life is a treasure which mankind must cherish, a treasure whose
value increases exponentially when one being bestows solace on and
acts to give love to humankind, collectively and individually.

AUSTIN H. KUTSCHER

Professor in the School
of Dental and Oral Surgery,
Columbia University, and
President of the Foundation
of Thanatology

INTRODUCTION

This book is a critical study of ten major conceptions of death. The task of the introduction is to outline the plan of the study and the reasons for undertaking it. We shall first therefore attempt to describe just what type of a phenomenon death is, and why it could be conceived in different ways—so different, in fact, that each is quite exclusive of the others. That is, what one tradition would consider death, others would not see as death at all.

An example of the difficulties involved in this subject can be found in a contemporary study of death that is organized around the assumption that in all the world's great religious and philosophical traditions there are only three major options for understanding death: complete extinction, preservation of the personality, and the continuing rebirth of the soul.[1] What I hope will become obvious in this volume is that this is indeed, only *one* way of conceiving death—it is an understanding of death that takes shape around the single conception of *survival*. This is a popular conception of death in our culture, and it has an auspicious origin in one of the West's great philosophical traditions—Platonism. Nevertheless, survival is an issue in only one of the ten ways of thinking about death to be examined in this study.

This example serves to indicate something of the reason for the present study. For all of us death unavoidably presents itself to our most concentrated reflection. There is no way we can ponder the course and the content of our lives without allowing for the possibility that death may cross our path at any point. Most of us are unaware of the array of alternative views of death that do not regularly appear within our cultural or educational horizons. Recent and widely read works have made much of the possibility of survival, even claiming to have empirical evidence that supports that possibility.[2] But such efforts reflect scarcely at all on the fact that the survival of a personality in death requires a specific conception of death and the nature of human existence. We shall discover that most of the world's major spiritual and intellectual traditions either do not consider survival a value—and some of them consider it something strenuously to be avoided—or do not see it as a possibility. The point is not to unseat a popular conception, and one in which many persons seem to have taken comfort, but to expand one's horizon in a way that could enrich personal reflection.

What is it, then, about the phenomenon of death that allows it to be so differently conceived?

"If we are, death is not; if death is, we are not," Epicurus declared in his famous formula. According to this view, the rift between life and death is so absolute that no experience can bridge it. Whatever we do experience must always be somewhere on life's continuum. We must be on both sides of it, anticipating it, recalling it, integrating it into a familiar sequence. But we can be on only one side of death. On this side, death is not yet; on the other, life is no longer.

Epicurus' formula requires us to clarify our terms at the outset, saving us from confusion later on. When one makes the distinction between life and death this total, we must understand death to be *the point where life comes to an end without remainder.* If something is left, whether it be a soul or a corpse or a fond memory, either what remains is not life or what occurred is not death. This is not an attempt to do away with the theory of survival by definition. Even advocates of that theory plainly concede that if one survives one does not die. It is only an attempt to be clear about the use of the term "death." Whatever dies comes to a definitive end and does not continue in any form. It may be, however, that there are living entities, or persons, that do continue and therefore do not die. We shall later examine that conception of death in detail.

Taking death as a state utterly exclusive of life, we find ourselves with a peculiar conceptual dilemma. We can no more experience death, Wittgenstein said, than we can see the end of our own field of vision. We do not *see* darkness in the total absence of light, we simply do not see at all. We do not experience death when life is over, we simply have no experience.

And yet, the field of vision does have its limit, and so does life. Even though we cannot experience death, death is nonetheless important to our experience. Indeed, it has been argued in a variety of ways, some of which we review later, that if there were no death, if life had no inviolable boundary, there could be no experience at all. If our vision had no limits, if by looking long and carefully enough we could see everything, we would see nothing. We do not see something that offers no resistance to our vision; we see *through* it. What cannot interrupt our sight is invisible. So with life: if we live long and carefully enough we will have experienced everything, but if everything then nothing. Whatever has no limits, no resistance, cannot be experienced. We pass through it unmoved, unchanged; we notice nothing.

The philosopher Charles Hartshorne observed in a trenchant essay that one can experience childhood only once.[3] Childhood, after all, is a state in which one is surrounded by much that is mysterious. One of the reasons it is such a charmed stage of life is that there is considerable resistance to its experience. There are many things adults can do that children cannot, and children are very soon aware that there will occur changes to their bodies and to their circumstances of which they can have at present no real knowledge. It would be impossible to have the experiences of the child, if only because much of what was withheld from the child has been lived through by the adult.

As we have acknowledged, not everyone would agree that if there is no final limit all other limits lose their importance. There are many sustained reflective efforts to show that death is not a final limit, that it can be surpassed, that it *is* an experience which can be survived. However, any argument for the survival of the *personality* must at least show that in its subsequent existence the personality is capable of having experience in much the same way as the personality is capable of experiencing at present. The experiences might be different, but they must come by way of some sort of resistance nonetheless. It is difficult to show that such resistance could continue for an infinite period of time, but, as we shall see, more than a few thinkers, some of them able indeed, have attempted to do so. Even if one proposes—seriously—that we sustain a massive technological effort to continue physical life indefinitely, as Alan Harrington does in his *The Immortalist,* there must be careful consideration of the problem of acute boredom. Scoffing at Alan Watts' vision of the "terrible monotony of everlasting pleasure," Harrington believes that the high appetite for life can be sustained technologically "by a system of *designed sleeps* and *programmed reincarnations.* Techniques of freezing or administered hibernation will permit us to rest for designated periods in between an endless variety of lives and careers."[4] What Harrington apparently wants is a forgetfulness between one "life" and another that makes new experience possible but does not eliminate the continuity of the conscious self. He wants a kind of death that is not a death.

Whether or not we believe death can be experienced, it is evident that death is important *to* experience. It was even important to Epicurus, and to Harrington in a strangely modified way. But how do we come to know of death? In what way does it manifest itself to us? A most obvious answer is that we experience the death of others. But this answer falls apart under scrutiny. What is it, for example, in the death of others that we experience *as death*? Can it be the fact that their vital physiological functions have come to an irreversible halt? Yes—and no. It is no doubt true that at least *some* crucial organs have ceased to function. But is this what we are saying when we report that someone has died? We are not talking about the organs, but the person; and persons are no more composed of their organs than symphonies consist of sound waves. True, persons cannot exist without physiognomies any more than music can be performed without sound; but then it is not the sound we listen to but Mozart's *Jupiter* or Beethoven's *Eroica*, and neither is it organic function we admire and love, but a husband, a wife, or a friend. Therefore, what we have experienced *as death* is the loss of a friend, a lover, a child. Let us look more closely at the kind of experience this is.

Just as the death of a person is not the death of an organism, neither is the life of a person merely an organismic phenomenon. To be a person we must exist in what for the moment we shall refer to as a web of connectedness with other persons. There is no doubt that if our goal were to extend our lives organically we could accomplish remarkable results by sealing persons into a germ-free environment, closely monitoring all vital systems, and providing them with a diet of maximum nutritional value—but this is no longer what we mean by human existence. It would assure continuity of the natural body at the expense of the continuity of the person.

Death therefore is primarily to be understood as the irreversible damage to the web of connectedness between persons. It is in this way that death is important to experience. What we experience is not the death of another *as death*, but the sudden tearing of the fragile web of existence.

Death has the immediate effect of *revealing* that interconnectedness of life. Often we do not know how closely our self-understanding is developed in relation to another person until that person has been taken by death. The severe disorientation of the bereaved is eloquent evidence that we are not only connected, but also that the web that holds us is so fragile. It is, in fact, torn away as though it were not ours at all, as though our very lives did not belong to us.

There is something else death reveals to our experience as no other event can. If it shows our dependence on the web of connectedness, it

also shows how simultaneously that web depends on us. Our relatedness to others is always reciprocal. As *persons* we are never inert objects at which others direct their actions. A personal relationship does
not exist until we *respond* to others, until we have entered into the
relationship out of our own freedom, even if that freedom is very slight.
A child, for example, is dependent on its parents, but the parents do not
raise the child *as a child* in the same way they might build a house or
cultivate a garden. The child must enter into the relationship with its
own freedom. If the parents got back in the child precisely what they
planted there, the child would scarcely be different from any other
object of manipulation for those parents.

What death reveals therefore is something of a paradox: *we have our
life from others, and with others, but only to the degree that we freely
participate in our relationship to those persons.* Death reveals our dependence, but also our freedom; *and* it reveals that we cannot have one
without the other. We can state the same paradox in other terms: our
life is not our own in the sense that it belongs exclusively to us; however, it *becomes* our own to the degree that we share it, make a gift of it
to others.

We have so far discussed life's web of connectedness in somewhat
spatial terms. As it will become increasingly evident in the course of
this study, what is far more constitutive for human existence is the
temporal continuity of life. Each human relationship is not only an
interdependence of shared freedom, it also points backward and forward in time, even beyond the moments at which the physical relationship begins and ends. The child comes to learn a heritage, a tradition,
something about the lives of its parents, and these things have great
meaning in the child's understanding of the future. Lovers know the
power of relating to each other experiences that they had had before
they met or of sharing their expectations of the future singly or together. In fact, the meaningfulness of their relationship varies directly
with how far it points backward and forward in time. Their immediate
dependence on each other is far less significant than their ability *jointly*
to find a way of extending the temporal continuity of their lives, regardless of the temporal limits of their physical existence. This is true not
only of the relationship between parents and children, or between lovers, but between persons in any communal context, even whole civilizations. One is an American or an Estonian or a Parsi not simply by
birth or by geographical location, but by a freely established connectedness with the history and the destiny of a people.

We should say here that life's temporal continuity is directly coordinated with its meaning. If nothing comes of our actions, if they have

no consequences for ourselves or others, they are quite obviously meaningless. Such actions are not even repeated, except as some sort of forlorn or mindless gesture. Whenever we begin to see that our lives as a whole have no issue, no outcome, no importance beyond themselves, we may find ways of concealing from oursleves the fact that we are truly alive in the sense of being both free and dependent in our relationships with others. We shall return to this point.

At this point in our discussion, it is necessary to stress the temporal connectedness of life, because the paradoxical union of freedom and dependence that death reveals is far more powerful in its temporal dimension. There cannot be a history that consists only of one person. My own history is a long series of exchanges with others, and, in fact, some of those exchanges, though extremely important to the perceived continuity of my life, did not even involve me and may even have occurred before I existed. So also is my future an anticipated sequence of relationships with others. This means quite simply that I cannot have any history I want, or any future I can imagine. *And yet*, it is still the case that my history is *mine*, and the future as well is *mine*; not because they simply happen to me as to an inert object, but because I have freely taken them as mine. There is no history and no future apart from the engagement of free persons with each other.

This is crucial for understanding the way in which death is important to experience, because death can take from me those persons in whose midst I have acquired the temporal continuity of my life; but *death cannot take away my freedom and cannot therefore destroy that continuity*. This means that death not only *reveals* my spatial and temporal interdependence, it also *challenges* me to sustain my personhood by freely sustaining the continuity that has become my own.

However, much of the discussion in this study will show how terrible this revelation of freedom is, and how threatening is the challenge to sustain the continuity of life. We noted above that continuity is directly coordinated with meaning. When we experience the loss of continuity in the death of another, we usually acknowledge it as something inherently meaningless. Why? is the open-ended, futile question that we repeatedly invoke before the fact of death. But the Why? sweeps more broadly than simply to the death of this person or that. It turns itself back on life, back toward our own personal existence. Finally, it is a question that can be directed at no one but the person asking it. *Why did this person die?* is at heart the question, *Why is there life at all?* And particularly, *What is the point of my life?* If I learn from this experience that my life will go out like a candle in the infinite night, then why live at all?

We refer to this kind of experience as *grief*. It is in grief that we feel most acutely the discontinuity, the meaninglessness, of life. The experience of grief is universal; it seems to vary hardly at all from culture to culture, or from one personality to another. The past seems to have come to naught. Even thought loses its force and impulse. There is nothing to say; words are replaced by silence or by incoherent wailing addressed to no one. In fact, wailing seems so appropriate an expression of the inner state of mourners that in many cultures persons unknown to the bereaved are engaged simply for the purpose of wailing. The fact that death seems to reach toward the grief-stricken themselves is widely reflected in funeral practices. In most European cultures the bereaved identify themselves by wearing black as the color of death. According to Jewish custom, the mirrors in the home of the bereaved are turned to the wall, as though the destruction of the soul, or the image of God, in the dead is shared by the grieving family and friends. No shoes are to be worn by the bereaved; they should not bathe, use cosmetics, or have their hair cut; they should be relieved of their ordinary business or household responsibilities—all of which reflects their isolation from the normal course of life, as though they were themselves dead.[5] In almost all cultures the bereaved are considered helpless, utterly dependent on others, even unable to feed themselves. They are regarded as having lost the essential capacities of life. Superstitions also surround the grieving. They are perceived to have a terrible power, the power of death itself. When the Egyptian goddess Isis discovered the corpse of her lover Osiris, her shrieks of grief caused a child standing near her to die of fright.

So far we have considered only the manifestation of death to experience as it occurs to others close to us. We had noted, however, that what we experience in this case is not the *death* of an other as such, but the discontinuity in our own lives caused by that death. It is implicit in this observation that death need not confront us in the loss of a person with whom we have shared much life—*death confronts us wherever we experience a radical threat to the continuity of our existence.* Anything that causes us to see that our lives come to nothing, and are essentially meaningless, has the power of death, since it has thrown across our path an impenetrable boundary, a terminus to all the lines of meaningfulness that extend outward from our vitality. Let us be as clear as possible on this point. The abrupt loss of meaning in life—the experience of irreparable damage to all the lines of expectation—is not the work of something like death; it is the very force of death itself. We had said it made no sense to speak of the death of persons as organic failure; death must in every case mean the end of personhood. And if we understand personhood in the most minimal sense as constituted by freely shared continuity, then whatever has the power of isolating us by way of shattering that continuity can only be death.

It follows that grief is not simply the reaction to the death of another. *We are in grief whenever the continuity of our lives has been destroyed.* The concept of grief appears prominently in all great systems of thought, although it does not always go by that name. We find it discussed under such categories as ignorance, despair, karma, yearning, neurosis, or the abandonment to history. Whatever the term, each of these shares the universal characteristics of grief: lack of effective speech, isolation from others, no interest in the future, abnegation of freedom—in sum, the contradictory state of living in a way that resembles death. Grief is our refusal to recognize the fact that death has *not* taken away our freedom to reconstitute the continuities it has destroyed.

If all great systems concern themselves with grief, it is not because they mean to argue that we are *condemned* to grief. Indeed, they are all of one voice in the conviction that no one need be forsaken to a life of ceaseless, if hidden, bereavement. Each in turn offers its cure, its way out of the contradiction, its strategy in bringing life back to life. The reason these systems are great, however, is that they have taken the power of death most seriously. They all assume it is impossible simply to walk away from the encounter with death. Death offers the kind of challenge that cannot be bypassed. The terms are either to persist in some form of grief, or to choose life.

The choice of life in the face of death is by no means simple. Death, after all, is powerful. It is a directed force and not to be compromised or bargained with. Because it is always experienced as an *imposed discontinuity*, it seems to act as an agent of something other than itself. Whether it be conceived as a personified will, a normal feature of the structure of things, the fated course of history, or the wages of sin, it is still an agent. It is therefore something alien to us and opposed. What is clear is that because of our impotence in relation to this agency we cannot meet death on its own terms. If death uses the weakness of the flesh, we will not win the struggle by strengthening the flesh. *Give the flesh to death* is the advice of thinkers holding this view, and *Go elsewhere with life*—to the mind, perhaps, or the spirit, or the All.

Whatever the agency of death, the strategy is always to go elsewhere with life, to reach for a higher willfullness that cannot be undone by the power of death. *In brief, the challenge of death will be met only by taking its threatened discontinuity into a higher continuity.* To take refuge in the present continuity of life is the reaction of grief. Since death is a power, what one achieves is not the elimination of death—it will not be compromised—but a higher form of freedom capable of establishing its continuity regardless of death. Ironically, then, in all great systems of thought the agency of death *is* alien and hostile, but it is *also* an invitation to new life. What first appears as the willful destroyer of meaning in human existence comes to be seen as the very point of access to a more durable meaning, one that can embrace all forms of meaninglessness in itself.

For that reason the most important intellectual and religious traditions have exceedingly vivid representations of the power of death, and the correspondingly firm clasp of grief. The greater the death, the more terrible the greif; but the greater the life to be won in struggle with it. History's grandest civilizations, religions, and intellectual movements have had the grandest conceptions of the damage death works in human life. The higher the thought, the more inclusive its vision of mortality. Whoever uncritically sees continuity everywhere, and thinks little comes to an end, thinks little—and finds little meaning in life.

Thus, the thesis of this book: *Death, perceived as discontinuity, is not that which robs life of its meaning, but that which makes life's meaningfulness possible.*

The plan of the book, accordingly, is to examine in sequence ten major conceptions of death. This requires us, first, to learn what the *agency of death* is for each of these traditions or thinkers; that is, how they describe the way we are threatened by discontinuity. This in turn brings us to the way they conceive *grief*, and its subsequent cure by the achievement of new life, a greater *freedom* to establish an inclusive continuity. Since one clue to the effectiveness of freedom is one's ability to act in such a way that something comes of those actions, we can in each case inquire into the consequentiality of that freedom; that is, we can look at the relationship of the person to *history*.

The two poles of this study are, therefore, death and freedom. We have observed that what death reveals is the paradox that although we are dependent on others for the very existence of our personhood, we can exist as persons only in the mode of freedom. Freedom in its highest form is the power to sustain continuity in the face of death—not to eliminate death. As we shall see, death presents itself to freedom not in the form of a single discontinuous event, or in several such events, but in a persistent, ongoing discontinuity—a condition we might most appropriately refer to with the term *becoming*. The challenge that grief represents to all free persons can therefore be described as finding a higher continuity capable of taking the condition of becoming into itself.

What follows is a study of ten distinct conceptions of death. Each conception has its corresponding view of the way in which persons may take the experienced discontinuity of death into a higher continuity; that is, the way one can freely contend with the fact that we relate to other persons, and to all existing things, only in the mode of becoming.

Each chapter heading will therefore contain an indication of the prevailing identification of death's *agency*, or the way its power is felt and perceived, and the form taken by the appropriate response of *freedom* in contending with death's persistent discontinuity, or becoming.

It is important for the reader to understand that while it is necessary to paint in a considerable amount of conceptual background for each of these ways of understanding death, it is not possible to offer a complete portrait of the traditions and thinkers studied. The approach in each instance will be to provide enough information for the distinctiveness of that view of death to emerge. In some cases this will mean that I must ignore large areas of interest, and even some of the alternative views of death, within the tradition. My task is to set out what is unique to each. The attention will be given more to the differences between traditions than to their likenesses. It is of course true that some Hindus are theists and have doctrines of the soul that resemble Plato's. It is also true that some mystics, some neoplatonists, and even some existentialists have considered themselves to be Christians. As I hope I can show, however, we can find in Hinduism, Platonism, mysticism, neoplatonism, Christianity, and existentialism singular views of death that cannot be found anywhere else, each of which is in fact irreconcilable with what is found elsewhere.

Finally, it will be evident enough that I have my own critical perspective. It is no doubt the case that pure objectivity in such a study is impossible. I can only say that my deepest intention is not to persuade readers but to invite, perhaps even provoke, them to reflections of their own.

Notes

1. John Hick, *Death and Eternal Life*, (New York: 1976), pp. 27 ff.
2. See especially Raymond A. Mooney, *Life after Life*, (New York: 1975).
3. Charles Hartshorne, "A Philosophy of Death," *Philosophical Aspects of Thanatology*, Vol. II, eds. S.M. Hetzler and A. H. Kutscher (New York: 1978) p. 83.
4. Alan Harrington, *The Immortalist* (New York: 1969), pp. 205 ff.
5. See Maurice Lamm, *The Jewish Way in Death and Dying* (New York: 1969), for a complete account of Jewish funeral customs.

ONE
DEATH AS CHANGE
—*KNOWLEDGE*

---

1 Plato and Platonism

At dawn on the day of his execution Socrates' friends gathered at the entrance to his prison. As soon as the jailer had awakened his prisoner and removed his chains, he admitted the small circle of friends. In sharp contrast to the manifest grief of his visitors, Socrates appears in high spirits. They find him rubbing his legs where the chains had been fastened, casually commenting on the relation between pleasure and pain. The friends seat themselves and in the next several hours engage in what is the most famous conversation in all antiquity.

Much of the singular force of this colloquy owes to the events immediately preceding and Socrates' response to them. The conversation is principally about death, but what is said has its appeal not only from the cogency of Socrates' arguments, but also from the way he acted in the face of his own impending death. Some thirty days earlier Socrates had been tried before a jury of 501 men on the vague charge that he was a religious heretic and had been corrupting the minds of the young with his teaching. His defense had been direct and simple. That he was a heretic, he said, was a lie. Indeed, he professed, he had a deep and compelling sense of the divine, and on frequent occasions was even visited by a supernatural presence in the form of a strong inner voice. As for corrupting the minds of Athenian youths, he admitted only to raising questions with anyone wishing to converse with him concerning the truth of their beliefs. For his own part, Socrates disavowed any exclusive possession of the truth. Such wisdom as he had was simply the wisdom that derived from his awareness that he had no privileged access to the truth. When a friend placed before the oracle at Delphi the question, *Is anyone wiser than Socrates?* he received the answer, *No.* Puzzling over this for some time, Socrates decided that the oracle was not referring literally to him, but, as he explained to the jury, "was merely taking my name as an example, as if he would say to us 'The wisest of you men is he who has realized, like Socrates, that in respect of wisdom he is really worthless.' "[1] There is no doubt that Socrates' searching examination of the professed wisdom of others not only exposed the errors of much of their beliefs, but also earned him considerable ill will.

It was this unpopularity of Socrates in the role of gadfly that inclined the jury to support the charges against him. By a majority of thirty votes he was found guilty. When his accuser asked the jury to approve the penalty of death for his crime, Socrates responded by saying that since he knew he was innocent of the charges it would be inconsistent of him to ask for any penalty whatsoever; in fact, since he was pursuing his task as gadfly for genuinely religious reasons, it would be more appropriate for the jury to award him a salary for his labors. Offended by the impudence of the accused the jury voted in favor of a death sentence by a still greater majority.

The verdict was something of an embarrassment to his highly placed accusers since they were aware the penalty was disproportionate to the crime. It was made clear to Socrates that a small bribe would win his release. To the anguish of his friends *and* his enemies he scoffed at the suggestion. His sole concern was whether his actions had been right or wrong—not whether he would be punished for them. He had already explained this to the jury before they reached their verdict. "You are mistaken" he said, "if you think that a man who is worth anything ought to spend his time weighing up the prospects of life and death. He has only one thing to consider in performing any action; that is, whether he is acting rightly or wrongly."[2]

There were other considerations. For one thing, Socrates was seventy years old. It is not such a tragedy, he suggests to the jury, for a man already near death to be put to death. For another, there is the problem of living in exile. Socrates had no thought of changing his profession and therefore knew that wherever he would wander he would attract young men, testing their wisdom and being tested in return, no doubt leading to the same conflict with the rulers of other cities. But most important of all is the fact that for a philosopher, that is, for one who has lived thoughtfully, death cannot be frightening. Socrates claims no special knowledge as to what will happen after death. In fact, he even says that "if I were to claim to be wiser than my neighbor in any respect, it would be this: that not possessing any real knowledge of what comes after death, I am also conscious that I do not possess it."[3] In spite of this ignorance he nonetheless insists that of all things death should be of the least concern to a philosopher. It was this teaching that occupied Socrates and his friends on the last day of his life.

At the beginning of the *Phaedo* conversation skips around a bit, waiting for a focus to develop. Socrates happens to remark that a true philosopher would hardly do himself violence. One of his friends quickly responds to this, pressing Socrates on the question of suicide: "Tell me then, Socrates, what are the grounds for saying that suicide is not legitimate?"

He seems to take this question somewhat casually. It is plainly not a personal or a philosophical issue for him; in fact, he says that it is "the one question that has an unqualified answer." The answer is no. His brief explication of this answer is rather un-Socratic. Suicide is an offense to the gods, he says, because we are possessions of the gods; and the gods, no less than humans, do not desire their possessions to be destroyed, much less destroy themselves. The answer is un-Socratic since it is not characteristic of Socrates to resolve any issue by consulting authorities that seem to stand above reason. Elsewhere all questions of thought or action are answered within the reasoning process. It may be that Plato added this brief discussion of suicide simply to lay to rest any suspicions that Socrates was moved by self-destructive intentions in accepting the sentence of death with such equanimity.

That he accepted his sentence on solid philosophical grounds becomes immediately apparent in the conversation. He moves straight to the point: "I want to explain to you how it seems to be natural that a man who has really devoted his life to philosophy should be cheerful in the face of death, and confident of finding the greatest blessing in the next world when his life is finished."[4]

He then makes what has come to be the most famous and most frequently quoted remark on the nature of philosophy:

> those who really apply themselves in the right way to philosophy are directly and of their own accord preparing themselves for dying and death. If this is true, and they have actually been looking forward to death all their lives, it would of course be absurd to be troubled when the thing comes for which they have so long been preparing and looking forward.[5]

A bit later in the discussion he puts it in even starker form: "True philosophers make dying their profession."[6]

The crucial term in this statement is "preparation." The Greek word has the sense of training for an athletic event or rehearsing for a theatrical performance. It is therefore preparation for a final event. Of course, if one has rehearsed or trained well enough, the final event is not a fearsome trial, but the manifestation of a properly disciplined life. For one properly trained it does not matter *when* that moment comes; in fact, by heightened anticipation well-trained persons live as though the final moment is already upon them. Socrates is suggesting that the discipline of philosophy prepares one to meet death at any moment. *When* death comes is not a question of any importance to the true philosopher.

What then is the discipline, or preparation, in which a philosopher engages? In Socrates' view the philsophical life gets its structure from what he believes is an absolute distinction between the soul and the body. The soul and the body are composed of altogether different substances that will not mix with each other. Ordinary persons have an incomplete and usually inaccurate understanding of the relation of the soul to the body. They do not understand that the body cannot affect the soul. For Socrates it was possible for the soul to move the body, but it was not possible for the body to have any effect on the soul. The difficulty arises in the improperly trained person who confuses the two. Such persons may then think that the highest attainments are those which satisfy the body: the use of food and drink, or sexual and other physical pleasures. But the true philosopher despises such physical pleasures. The uninterrupted concern of the philosopher must be to acquire a pure knowledge of the truth, and the truth is something that can be known by the soul alone.

The notion of a separable body and soul is such a commonplace that we easily overlook the subtlety in Socrates' appeal to it. There are three characteristics of the soul that are lost when one cannot keep a clear separation between them: independence, lucidity, and timelessness.

When ordinary persons confuse their soul with their body they in effect become dependent on their body, and in turn on the physical world of which their body is a part. When the body develops its appetite it will not always be the case that the world will produce what is desired. There is a difference between being thirsty and having something to drink. To be thirsty means that one must depend on the availability of water. There is the possibility of a dangerous illusion here: since water is usually available we think that it is there because we want it, and we forget the degree of our dependence. In sum, the soul that identifies with the body is no longer in control itself; the self is dominated by the nonself.

One reason that dependence on the physical world is to be avoided is that the physical world is always subject to change and is therefore always incomplete and imperfect. If we attempt to discern the nature of things from what we know of the world, we would have a most inaccurate understanding. Indeed, every time we look we will see something different, and we are therefore unable to have anything resembling reliable knowledge of the truth. We could never know what a triangle is, for example, if all we had were the physical triangles that present themselves to our senses, for no two of these triangles will be exactly the same. If we depended on our senses for knowledge we would have lost all possibility of *lucidity*, and would exist in a state of unrelieved confusion.

If the soul sacrifices its independence and lucidity when it identifies with the body, it will also give up its *timelessness*. The physical world changes ceaselessly; nothing endures, and all things that come into existence will pass out of it. Therefore, the soul that depends on the physical will have no understanding of its own timelessness. In addition to dependence and confusion, the soul will then be seized by anxiety and fear in the face of its own inevitable demise with the passing of all things physical.

Socrates offers us a very different vision of the soul: its pursuit of the truth is an inward pursuit; it is a search after something it already possesses. To find the truth is therefore to have a lucid insight into the soul's eternality. The philosophical life is thus a long and deliberate exercise of disentangling the soul from the body. The reason this is a "preparation for death" is that only the body is capable of death; the soul, properly purified, will be untouched by the body's passing. Indeed, the soul will now have a direct vision of the truth without any possible contamination of the body. "We are in fact convinced," Socrates said to his friends, "that if we are ever to have pure knowledge of anything, we must get rid of the body and contemplate things by themselves with the soul by itself."[7]

This remark tells us a great deal both about what the agency of death is and how it will be taken into a higher freedom. Death comes in the form of change. Changeability is a kind of powerlessness. It is to be at the mercy of external forces indifferent to our existence. In his later writings Plato shows a strong sense of the irrationality of natural events. He has nothing of Aristotle's conception of a causally ordered material universe. The forces of matter are capricious, and powerful. We are not only unable to control them, we are even unable to predict them. This quite clearly means that we will not win our struggle with death's agency *on its terms*—by preparing the *body*, the material element of human existence. Let time and death have the body, and let us find life elsewhere. Of course, holding on to the body, continuing the direct struggle with death, is the classical form of grief, and Plato, through Socrates, has already shown us the confusion and bewilderment that comes upon one who persists in living on the material level. It is a matter of woeful ignorance that can mean only bondage to the caprice of time-bound forces. If the philosopher's task is to rescue us from this bondage in misery, leading us to true life, Plato has announced that we shall find it in "pure knowledge."

So far the separation of soul and body has only been declared, not argued. When Socrates offers the first reasons for belief in this separation, we should take special note of the fact that he appeals to the nature of knowledge. The soul's independence, lucidity, and timelessness correspond to identical characteristics of knowledge. Socrates asks Simmias, one of those who came to share the last day of his life, the questions, "Do we recognize such a thing as absolute uprightness?" "And absolute beauty too?" Simmias agrees that we do. Then Socrates asks, "Have you ever seen any of these things with your eyes?" "Certainly not," Simmias replies.

Socrates concludes that all such qualities cannot be seen through the eyes, nor perceived through any bodily sense. We can have no sensory apprehension of the "real nature of any given thing," since its real nature is not something that changes and passes with time. The real nature of the statue is not the marble in which it is carved but, say, the idea of perfect humanity that it expresses through the marble. The idea will never change; the marble will become dust. The idea is therefore timeless and independent of the marble. It is also perfectly lucid. It can be clearly perceived as it is in itself—but only by that which is lucid, independent, and timeless.

Plato, through Socrates, is making two claims here that will have enormous impact on later philosophy in general and on thought about death in particular. The first is that the *real*, or the *true*, is changeless and therefore distinct from all temporality. Temporality, on this account, must be viewed as the region of the unreal, or the untrue. In order to perceive the truth we must look through all change for that which endures. The second assumption is that the soul must be *like the truth* in order to know it. Plato elsewhere will carry this so far as to suggest the divinity of the soul: "Of all the things which a man has, next to the gods, his soul is the most divine and most truly his own."[8] The soul, therefore, is not separate from the body merely because it is made of a different substance. It is separate because it has a different object. Whereas the body and all its senses respond to change, the soul responds to permanence. But what it responds to also somehow claims it. As the body goes to dust, the soul clings to its eternal objects and suffers no change. Plato is careful never to make an absolute identification between the soul and the divine, but the seeds for such a conception have been sewn and will flower later, as we shall discover. For Plato the soul may be divine in some sense, but it is always one's own. And the continuity that the soul has in the face of death is not mere existence, but *existence in knowledge*..

Socrates' friends are quite willing to accept the distinction between soul and body on the basis of knowledge, but some of them cannot see how this necessarily implies immortality, in spite of their desire to believe Socrates would survive his death and exist elsewhere in a sublime state. Cebes, for example, one of his closest friends, says that what Socrates has explained about the nature of the soul gives the average person no reason to think that the soul will not "be dispersed and destroyed on the very day that the man himself dies, as soon as it is freed from the body." Socrates responds by proposing to discuss the question: "Do the souls of the departed exist in another world or not?"[9]

Socrates then guides the discussion through a series of proofs for immortality. Perhaps the word "proof" is too strong. He is essentially elaborating his view of the nature of knowledge to show that, if it is properly understood, and if one carefully reflects on its consequences, belief in immortality is quite reasonable.

He begins with the weakest and perhaps the strangest of the "proofs." Citing the Orphic myth that souls do exist in another world before and after their earthly existence, he looks for an argument that will support such a belief. He finds his argument in the fact that all things seem to be generated out of their opposites. "For example," he asks rhetorically, "when a thing becomes bigger, it must, I suppose, have been smaller first before it became bigger?" They agree that it must have been. He offers a few other examples—beauty is generated from ugliness, right from wrong, the weaker from the stronger, the worse from the better—and then asks, again rhetorically, "Are we satisfied, then, that everything is generated in this way—opposites from opposites?" "Perfectly," they answer.

Socrates presses them on to the observation that death is the opposite of life; therefore death and life must come from one another. The conversation proceeds as follows:

"Then what comes from the living?"

"The dead."

"And what," asked Socrates, "comes from the dead?"

"I must admit," Cebes said, "that it is the living."

"So it is from the dead, Cebes, that living things and people come?"

"Evidently."

"Then our souls do exist in the next world."

"So it seems."[10]

If we were Cebes we might feel that Socrates had moved to the conclusion too quickly. There are a few questions that should be raised first. For example, is it true that *all* opposites are generated from opposites? Is the larger actually *generated* from the smaller, or is it not instead that for every object there already will be others both larger and smaller? It seems that Socrates has taken a term of comparison and has tried to draw from it something concerning the origin of the objects compared. To say that something is larger or smaller is to say nothing about its origin.

Moreover, is it true that death—as Socrates understands it—is really the opposite of life? When a man dies, according to what Socrates has taught earlier, he goes somewhere else—albeit without his body. He does not cease to exist. Therefore, the opposite Socrates is discussing is not actually between life and death, but between life on earth and life somewhere else. But such an opposite we cannot know to exist; indeed, this is just that which Socrates wants to prove. Had he taken death to mean ceasing to exist altogether it would be a genuine opposite, but it would also destroy the point he wanted to prove—that the souls of the departed exist in another world.

Having no objection from his friends, Socrates moves on to another "proof." This time he repeats in greater detail his theory that the knowledge of which the mind is capable could not possibly have been learned through its experience in the world; the mind must have been born already possessing its knowledge. Here Socrates uses the term by which this notion is best known: *recollection.* The learner does not actually acquire knowledge, but recollects what has already been known. In another of the early dialogues, the *Meno,* Socrates had proved to his friend that a young slave boy without the least education could do simple mathematical exercises. Socrates claimed this ability in the child could only have been possessed prior to his birth; therefore, the child's soul must have existed prior to his birth, *prior to all its births.* He makes a grand claim: "Seeing then that the soul is immortal and has been born many times, and has beheld all things both in this world and in the nether realms, she has acquired knowledged of all and everything . . . ."[11] The soul is eternal but continues, apparently indefinitely, to pass in and out of temporal attachment to successive bodies, carrying with it the "knowledge of everything." The reason we must *recollect* it and do not have this knowledge consciously is that, somehow, "we lost it at the moment of birth."[12]

When Simmias has pondered this teaching he finds himself unconvinced. He can clearly see the need for the soul's preexistence, but, "As for their existing after we are dead as well, I don't feel that has been proved, Socrates." Simmias can see no reason why the soul "at the moment of release," should not "come to an end and be destroyed."[13]

Socrates immediately points out that if one combines the argument concerning recollection with the argument for the generation of opposites one would see that the proof for continued existence has already been made. If the living come from the dead, then the soul cannot dissipate at death since then it could not be reborn from the state of death. But Socrates sees that the proof is not strong enough to eliminate the fears of death that some of his friends seem to possess. This gives occasion to a frivolous exchange in which Socrates advises the others that they should try to charm their fears away with magic spells—if philosophical reflection is not sufficient.

"But Socrates," Simmias replies, "where shall we find a magician who understands these spells now that you—are leaving us?"

Socrates soon returns the discussion to its topic and offers another "proof," but this time it is an argument of considerable philosophical power. Aware that his previous argument had left Simmias, and perhaps some of the others, unpersuaded, he takes up the problem of the soul being dispersed at the moment of death, like a puff of smoke in the wind. "What sort of thing is it that would naturally suffer the fate of being dispersed?" he asks.

He deals with this question by distinguishing between two kinds of substances: simple and compound. A simple substance or object is composed of only one thing and is therefore indivisible; it cannot break into smaller parts. A compound object is composed of several things and therefore, no matter how firmly bound they might be, it is always possible for the elements to be broken apart. It is also the case that a simple object is incapable of change. Nothing can be added to it or taken away. Obviously compound objects are always subject to variability.

Socrates next considers which types of objects are simple, and which compound. Does absolute beauty, of which we talked, admit of change? Clearly not, they all agree. "Well, what about the concrete instances of beauty—such as men, horses, clothes, and so on?" "With them, Socrates, it is just the opposite; they are never free from variation."

He then indicates that each of the objects which we determine simple, or incomposite, and therefore invariable, are not perceptible to the bodily senses. They cannot be seen by the eye, or heard by the ear, and so on. Now, he asks, how about the soul? Is the soul visible or invisible? It is not visible, they reply.

He reminds them of the earlier discussion in which they saw that the soul became confused the more it attached itself to the visible and variable compound objects of the world, and that by nature the soul should concern itself with that which is invisible, changeless, intelligible, and uniform. Therefore, are we to say that the soul, like the objects it beholds, is invariable as well as invisible? Certainly, they reply.[14]

Now Socrates wanders a bit, speculating on the fate of those souls that do make the mistake of attaching themselves to the visible and the variable compound objects of the world. Such souls, at the moment of death, are not completely liberated. They drag with them shades of their earthly existence and are held back from perfect union with the absolute and changeless reality. Socrates suggests that it is precisely these souls that we see in the form of ghosts or spirits, particularly in the neighborhood of tombs and graveyards. They "still retain some portion of the visible; which is why they can be seen." He then goes on to offer a theory of reincarnation by which "those who have cultivated gluttony of selfishness or drunkenness, instead of taking pains to avoid them, are likely to assume the form of donkeys and other perverse animals." At a somewhat higher level are those ordinary citizens who, without the help of philosophy, will exercise enough self-control to be reborn "into some other kind of social and disciplined creature like bees, wasps, ants; or even back into the human race again, becoming decent citizens."

But the soul that has practiced philosophy and is absolutely pure when it leaves the body will "attain to the divine nature. . . . This is the reason, my dear Simmias and Cebes, why true philosophers abstain from all bodily desires and withstand them and not yield to them."[15]

This brief excursus into speculation concerning reincarnation may be unwarranted by the argument concerning the incomposite nature of the soul, but it does have the value of telling us something more of Plato's understanding of the nature of knowledge. Knowledge has an actual effect on our encounter with death. It is not merely a matter of comfort that, in spite of death, we shall survive and enjoy indefinite existence. It is not simply the office of philosophy to *inform* us of the truth; it is also to *conform* us to the truth. *Philosophers teach the separation of soul and body in order that they might in fact be separated.* What Plato reveals here is that knowledge for him is something consequent; it makes a difference; it is powerful. It is only because it is powerful that it can be considered an antidote for death. Now, it is true that we survive our death regardless, but without the aid of true knowledge we suffer the possibility of surviving it at a less than human state. If so, we are to understand that it is a humiliation, a deserved misery. It is deserved not because we violated a moral dictum or disobeyed a god, but because we simply gave away our freedom to achieve the higher continuity and chose instead to exist at the level of change and temporality. In the terms of this study, Socrates' use of reincarnation in this context is a description of the nature of grief. It is the consequence of not rising to meet the challenge of death's threatened discontinuity.

This excursus serves as a kind of prefatory caveat for the argument from which he wandered: that the soul is incomposite, a simple substance and indivisible. He wants his listeners to see that what he is arguing with them is not something that may be of casual interest to them, but may have a direct effect on the nature of their existence. And, certainly, the argument he now offers has considerable force. To the present day, it has struck many thinkers as a solid base for the theory of immortality.

To begin with, the claim that the soul is simple and indivisible seems obvious. Were it compound and subject to change it would then be possible for me to wake up one morning to discover that I am no longer the person I was yesterday. It would even be possible to be a different person from moment to moment. In brief, I could not be a person at all unless there is both unity and continuity to my soul, or mind. Many things do change: we acquire new ideas or styles of living, we pass through different emotions, undergo varied experiences; but through all of this it is still "I" who know and experience all of this. The "I" cannot therefore be a creation of my previous experience, nor can it be an experience or combination of experiences in itself— because there must be an "I" before there can be experience.

Indeed, from this point it is a short distance to the conclusion that, since the soul is indivisible, not even death can cause it to break up; it will not change even in death.

Simmias and Cebes are obviously moved by this reasoning and are silent for some time; but we soon see they are not thoroughly convinced. They begin to whisper to each other while the others talk, and only with some hesitation bring their objection to Socrates. Like Socrates' argument, their objections have a distinctly modern ring to them. Simmias presents his objection first.

The soul might be compared to a musical instrument, he suggests, which is of course perfectly corporeal. The tune that is played on the instrument, however, is not corporeal. It is neither identical with the elements of the instrument, nor even with the sound by which it is heard. Just so might be the soul in the body: an "attunement" of the corporeal elements that make up the compound body. Now it happens that the attunement of a musical instrument, while not corporeal in itself, will cease to exist as soon as the instrument has been broken or has passed out of existence. Why then would the soul, if it is an attunement of the body, cease to exist when life has left the body?

Socrates concedes that Simmias has presented a strong challenge to his position, but withholds his response until he has heard from Cebes as well. Cebes has no difficulty with the argument that the soul might preexist the body, since he is convinced by the theory of knowledge as recollection; however, he still cannot believe that the same theory requires its existence *following* death. This is similar to his earlier argument against survival, although this time he has considerably strengthened it. When it is asked, Which is more durable, the soul or the body? it is clear that the soul can endure longer than the body, Cebes admits. But this is like asking which will last longer, the tailor or the coat he has made. Certainly the tailor will live longer than any of his coats. However, this does not mean that at the time of his death no coat will survive, since he may have sewn a coat a few weeks before that will outlast him many years. In the same way there is no reason to think that the soul will outlive *all* of the bodies it inhabits; it is just as reasonable to suppose that there will be one body, the last inhabited by the soul, that will outlast it. We should not be put off here by the quaintness of Cebes' argument, for there is a critical issue within it that Socrates does not fail to detect; if the soul is to exist freely and powerfully it must require significant energy to continue, and if that energy comes from itself will it not in time be exhausted?

These two objections have the immediate effect of shocking the gathered friends, since they had at first been persuaded by Socrates and now they have been dissuaded by Simmias and Cebes. But Socrates is not shocked. As Phaedo relates the discussion he effectively illustrates Socrates' unperturbed spirit by reporting that before he answered he leaned down to where Phaedo was sitting to play gently with his hair and tease him about his curls.

Socrates has two responses to Simmias' objection. First, he points out that if the soul is an attunement it cannot preexist the elements of which it is attuned; therefore the doctrine of recollection would have to be rejected. Knowing that Simmias has been convinced by prior arguments, Socrates simply says to him, "Make up your mind which theory you prefer—that learning is recollection, or that the soul is an attunement." Simmias responds, "The former, without any hesitation, Socrates."

The second refutation of the theory of attunement is subtler. Socrates leads Simmias to admit that an attunement is absolute and can permit no discord whatsoever; it is either an attunement or it is not. But can we say the same of the soul? Is it not the case that some souls are better than others? If so, how could a soul be like an attunement, since is it not true that something is either perfectly attuned or it is out of tune altogether? Simmias concedes the point. Socrates goes on to say that in fact the soul is just the opposite of an attunement. Whereas a tune is the result of a harmony of the elements that make up the instrument, the soul is constantly in tension with the elements of the body. All through life the soul must exercise control over these elements, "sometimes by severe and unpleasant methods like those of physical training and medicine, and sometimes by milder ones."[16] Simmias drops his objection.

There is actually a great deal at stake in Plato's refutation of the theory of attunement, though he has Socrates swiftly and painlessly undo it. It was extremely important to Plato that the soul be a *substance* and not, say, a principle or, much less, a metaphor. It is something quite real. We noted above that the soul's continuity is always a continuity *in knowledge* of the true, or real. What he is adding here is the insistence that the soul is something real itself in that knowledge, and not merely a free-floating piece of that knowledge. Platonists in subsequent centuries will, more than Plato himself, make much of the fact that the substantiality of the soul is in no way like the substantiality of worldly entities; there are, in fact, two quite distinct orders of reality—intimately associated but not mixed. Plato certainly points toward such a dualism in his firm belief that the soul cannot be an attunement because it exists independently of the body.

Before he takes up Cebes' argument concerning the possibility that the soul will eventually wear out, Socrates falls silent. Then, explaining to Cebes that "what you require is no light undertaking," he gives a long account of his own intellectual development. This account has given cause to considerable debate among scholars as to Plato's purpose in providing this glimpse into Socrates' youth; and there is wide disagreement over the actual meaning of some of the intellectual issues Socrates claims to have resolved.[17]

For our part it is enough to note that among the views of the world Socrates has rejected is one that explains all events mechanistically. Socrates does not want to reject the idea of causation, but he does not understand a cause to be some sort of physical mechanism. This is important in his discission of Cebes' objection because the younger man had in effect argued that the soul, though it might wear out a great number of bodies, will itself wear out; it will one day be exhausted an no longer able to move a body.

If Socrates is to show that the soul is inexhaustible, he must be able to show that the soul is capable of moving the body in a way that requires no sort of mechanical energy. He therefore introduces an idea that will have a profound effect on later philosophy, although an idea that is not altogether clear in itself. It is improper, Socrates avers, to think that a cause is a force that one object exerts on another. It is not physical objects, but intellectual forms, that provide causation. By "form" Socrates means the qualities of absolute beauty, or magnitude, or goodness—the kinds of knowledge the soul possesses at birth. A form cannot be directly viewed, and yet whatever is seen is identified according to one or another form. That we know this object to be a horse, that one to be a triangle, or that one to be a human being, is that we recognize the form of *horseness*, or *triangularity*, or *humanness* in the object under view.

To say that forms have the power of causation is a peculiar and difficult argument. What makes a body beautiful is not the arrangement of its physical elements, but the *form* of beauty that is not identical to any part of the object. What makes Socrates a man is not that he has two arms, two legs, a head, and so on; it is the form of *manness* that causes him to be a man.

There is no question but that this is a special use of the term "cause." What leads Plato's readers into confusion is that occasionally the same relationship will be expressed differently. For example, it might be said that what makes an object beautiful is that it *participates* in the form of beauty. Whether causation and participation are the same or different in Plato's philosophy is probably an unanswerable question.

Happily, there is no need to resolve the issue here, since Socrates' *point* in introducing the argument is clear enough, even if the argument remains obscure. He wants to be able to say that the soul is present in the body as beauty is present in an object. Just as the form of beauty causes something to be beautiful, the soul causes the body to be alive. We cannot think, of course, that the form of beauty will ever be exhausted; neither can we think that the soul will be spent. To make this point even stronger, Plato has Socrates argue that it is of the nature of a form never to admit an opposite (unlike objects that are actually generated from opposites). An object cannot be both beautiful and ugly. Of course, it can never be completely beautiful or ugly; only the forms themselves can be perfect. And so with the soul: it will never admit its opposite—death—into the body. Although the body will never be perfect in itself; it is only the soul that can be perfectly alive without the merest trace of death.

In the *Phaedrus*, another early dialogue, Socrates states this view somewhat more directly, by arguing that the soul is a self-moved mover. It is always in motion; when it ceases to move it ceases to live. But since it is its own source of motion, it cannot have been generated or begun by anything else—for this would make it an effect and deny its self-moving nature. "And since it is ungenerated, it must also be indestructible," he reasons. It is eternally its own beginning.[18] This does not really answer Cebes' question as to the source of the soul's inexhaustibility, but it does introduce into Plato's conception of the soul its essential *freedom*, because that which moves itself is by definition free. What we are to note here is that Plato associates freedom with immortality. We must be careful to see how he has done so. We saw earlier that the soul becomes like its object, that is, knowledge. Therefore, if knowledge is timeless so is the soul. But the soul is only *like* knowledge, it is not identical to knowledge. Thus the importance of its substantiality. But it must be a substance unlike material substances that are moved by other things. It must be able to move itself, which is freedom in its most perfect form. But how will it move itself in such a way that it will also be immortal? By attaching itself to timeless objects of knowledge. In other words, *the soul counters the agency of death, which is change, by freely becoming changeless.*

Returning to the *Phaedo*, we discover that he has persuaded Cebes of the soul's inexhaustibility by the outright rejection of mechanical causation. "Then it is as certain as anything can be, Cebes, that the soul is immortal and imperishable, and that our souls will really exist in the next world." Cebes replies that he has "no criticisms, and no doubt about the truth of your argument."

Although Cebes and Simmias are finally relieved of any doubt as to the truth of Socrates' teaching, these ideas will ferment in the minds of fully a hundred generations of philosophers. When we ask why they remain engaging, it cannot be that they are simply unclear. Instead, it is that they are addressed in an intensely thoughtful manner to matters of life and death, and bear the promise that further reflection will yield refreshing new insight into these mysteries.

The strength of Plato's thinking is that it evokes the human longing to surpass death and discusses it in terms of a directly identifiable quality of lived experience. To most persons the dual nature of human existence seems self-evident. The free, unrestrained movement of thought stands in such obvious contrast to the bound, caused character of the body. Plato's suggestion that it is one thing to see the horse, another its beauty, seems to describe our experience precisely. We know the beauty is "there," but we also know that it is not identical with the beast.

Dualistic thinking remains common in the Western world. It did not go long without challenge, of course—indeed, Plato's own student, Aristotle, offered a brilliant alternative—but with a multitude of refinements it has persisted as a major philosophic view to this day; and it still represents the major ground for the hope of surviving death. In fact, it is such a seductive argument for the immortality of the soul that it has been incorporated, though somewhat uncomfortably, into systems of belief that otherwise have nothing in common with Platonism. As we shall see, many Jews and Christians have been persuaded by the Socratic theory even though each tradition is quite antithetical to the sort of thinking attracted to the possibility that one may survive death.

One of the enduring problems in Platonic dualism has had to do with the substantial nature of the self. There is no doubt Plato favored the view that whatever is essential to the person would survive death *as that person*. It is not merely Socrates' soul, but Socrates, who will continue in the afterworld. In his concluding speech before the jury Socrates anticipates the pleasure of conversing with such great souls as Orpheus and Homer, and attempting to discover in that world, as he had in this, "who is wise, and who pretends to be wise, and is not."[19] But there is a serious difficulty here. We noted previously that Plato intends the soul to be substantial in order that it not simply be identical with its contents—knowledge. It must also be free, *but free to remain unchanged;* any other expression of freedom would send it back through another humiliating round of existence. The question is how Socrates could be immortal as the restless seeker after wisdom and still have a changeless, eternal, complete soul. By stressing the importance of the soul's perfect likeness to universal and timeless knowledge, Plato seems to have eliminated from the soul any particularity whatsoever, so that the soul of Socrates would be quite identical to all others, making it quite meaningless to refer to *this* soul as Socrates and *that* as Orpheus.

It may well be, of course, that my soul *will* survive my death even if it has lost all the particularity that makes it my soul—or makes it *me*. But this robs the theory of immortality of all its personal importance. "The information that my soul is to last forever," writes the philosopher Antony Flew, "could then be of no more personal concern to me than the news that my appendix is to be preserved eternally in a bottle."[20]

This difficulty comes up in another way. It would seem that dualists must have the most direct and unambiguous knowledge of their own selves as something quite distinct from passing phenomena. But this kind of knowledge has been powerfully challenged by David Hume in the eighteenth century, among other representatives of the Aristotelian tradition. "For my part," Hume wrote,

> when I enter most intimately into what I call *myself* I always stumble on some particular perception or other of heat or cold, light or shade, love or hatred, pain or pleasure, I can never catch *myself* at the time without a perception, and never can observe anything but the perception. When my perceptions are removed for any time, as by sound sleep, so long am I insensible of *myself*, and may truly be said not to exist.[21]

Hume's famous challenge drew a famous reply. Kant was so disturbed by Hume's skepticism that it drew him into an original and powerful philosophy of his own. Against this particular view of Hume's, he argued that, while we may not be able to perceive ourselves, there must nonetheless be a *perceiving* self, someone whose perception this is; otherwise it makes no sense to speak of perception and certainly none to speak of experience. Kant quickly admitted that this *transcendent* self can never be known or experienced, but this is no argument against its existence.

Kant was not a dualist, however, because he was not claiming the existence of a self that is distinct *in substance* from all nonself. In fact, he held that nothing whatsoever could be said about the transcendent self, except that it quite obviously must exist independently of its knowledge. This is not quite enough for true dualists who still want to claim the possibility of self-knowledge; if there is no self-knowledge, there is little weight to their assertion of a dual reality.

If I am to know myself I must have some awareness not only *that* I am, but *what* I am in my concrete particularity. This inescapably means what I am in relation to my body, and what I am in relation to others by way of my body. Responsible dualists would never argue that my particular character, or the present configuration of my thought, has nothing to do with my body. There is strong evidence indicating a direct influence of physiology on thought through the use of drugs or various kinds of technological stimulation. Moreover, that I am physically in New York means that I can have no direct knowledge of the weather in London. There are physical limitations and distortions of knowledge. Dualists do not resist this notion; on the contrary, they see it as an opening to self-knowledge. I can know myself as *this* person in *this* place because of the limitations of my physical nature.

This invites other, more serious difficulties for the dualist position, however. If I am not a universal and eternal soul merely taking temporary residence in a material body—as Plato believed—but am truly associated with it, how can it be understood that I am actually *connected* with my physical nature, especially when my soul is of a distinct substance? This is the familiar mind-over-matter question. How could one kind of substance—mind—have any causal relation to another kind of substance—matter? Many dualists fall into serious error here by treating mental reality as a kind of force, or collection of entities, that can be described as physical phenomena. This is an error because it gives away the radical distinctiveness of the two kinds of substance. A stronger defense of the dualist position can be made by evoking ordinary experience. Any number of times in an ordinary day we deliberate over our actions, reflect on alternatives, and carry out decisions. It seems certain that we possess a mental reality that is independent from the material and has power over it.

The materialist can respond that all of these so-called mental events are but subtle physiological processes, and that there is no need for a "mind hypothesis" to account for any of these experiences. At this point, however, the apparently stronger position of the materialist encounts its own insuperable difficulties. What does it mean to say that a thought *is* a brain process? It is of the nature of a thought to be *about* something. How could a process be about something other than itself? The notion is absurd. I might have a vivid picture of a friend in mind, but does the alleged brain process tell us who the picture is *of*? This relational or, as the phenomenologists call it, "intentional" aspect of consciousness cannot be captured in the materialists' explanation. We can put the same point a different way. If thoughts are processes, they can—at least in principle—be observed by others. What would it mean to observe a thought? We might have an elaborate track of synaptic patterns in someone's brain, but how could we tell from these patterns what the person is thinking? It is obvious we cannot anymore than we could discern what is passing through the mind of a fish by staring deeply into its eyes.

We must remember that what dualists are usually seeking as they assemble their arguments is strong support for the belief that they will survive their own deaths. In the centuries following Plato the dualist position has become increasingly sophisticated in its defense of survival. Summarizing the difference between contemporary dualists and Plato, we could say simply that they are now much more serious about *dualism* as such—that is, not simply that there are two natures, but two natures intimately associated with each other. We recall that Socrates explained to his friends the need to "get rid of the body and contemplate things by themselves with the soul by itself." Modern dualists are aware that the body cannot be so easily sloughed off. Indeed, because they know they must survive with their personality intact, and because they know their personality is not developed independently of a body, and therefore could not likely exist independently of a body in the next life, they must be prepared to offer a picture of something like an embodied existence after death. But more than embodied. A personality is also constituted by such qualities as memory, the ability to form relationships with others, and so on. In other words, dualists have attempted to defend themselves against the devastating criticism that, if we held to Plato's belief in the *likeness* between the mind and its proper object (eternal knowledge), Socrates could not have survived *as Socrates*.

However, eluding this problem they throw themselves into the lap of another. Can dualists describe a state in which one could exist in some sort of body, with a memory of the past, with others—*forever?* The task is manifestly difficult, and perhaps should not even be attempted, since all proposals stand the risk of banality, or the possibility of trivializing the issue and invite the inevitable question, "But could you do *that* forever?" Several philosophically sophisticated authors have nonetheless proposed such a continued existence, on the basis of the Christian doctrine of the resurrection, that seems to them to point toward some form of embodied and communal postmortem existence—though still quite mysterious as to detail.[21]

Whether any of these attempts succeed, or even could succeed, is a problem that need not detain us here. The reader is invited to follow the details of the argument by referring to the bibliography at the end of this chapter. What we clearly should do is indicate what the prevailing understanding of death is in the Platonic thought and the ensuing dualistic tradition. We had observed in the Introduction that death is addressed in systems of thought by proposing a continuity in the face of the discontinuity threatened by death. If no continuity is discoverable—or credible—the inevitable fact of death shatters the possibility of meaningful personal existence. *What Plato has proposed is a way of viewing life itself as indefinitely continuous.* Life, as such, has no opposite to itself. It is not life versus death. It is life and no death. In the Platonic conception of life can be *affirmed* only as death is *denied*. In fact, it can scarcely be said to happen. With the Platonists' emphasis on the survival of the personality, it is the case that nothing happens *to me*. I may enter into another region, but only as though I had passed quickly through a door, stepping from one room to another. Or it is like going to sleep and waking up in another place.

For this reason we have characterized Plato's classical conception of death as *change*, and the corresponding response to life *knowledge*. To "die" is only to let the body go. To "live" is to take timeless residence in "true knowledge." But the *true* is also the *real* for Plato. There is therefore no more reality to death than to the painted scenery on a stage. If we come to believe the scenery is real, we may also believe that we shall all perish with the last line of the final act. Plato was convinced that when the last line is spoken the scenery is removed and the conversation continues—on a different stage.

The question with which Platonists and Platonic dualists are inevitably left is whether life is possible without death, and consequently whether the denial of death is not in itself a distinctly antilife attitude. If the future is opened indefinitely, the pressure is taken off the present. There is nothing that cannot wait. If we continue into the next world with our personalities intact, we have in fact only extended this world, a gesture that would dramatically rob the meaning and significance of one's existence in the present. Like opening a sealed vessel to an infinite vaccuum, the elements of life would blow out in all directions. What does it matter how the first several acts of the drama develop when there is an endless number to come? How can it be a drama at all? Life would have no risk, nothing would be at stake. There could be no curiosity about a future in which anything could happen that one wishes to happen. History would have no fascination or importance. It is even quite likely that the personality itself would vanish into the vacuum, since its temporal structures would have become meaningless. A person's character is shaped by tragedy, suspense, hope, regret, an occasional victory over improbable odds, and an occasional irreversible defeat—but in an indefinite existence all this would be meaningless. Where then is the character? Where the person? The dualist is finally confronted with an especially poignant irony: *What is most deeply hoped for—the continuity of the personality—is precisely what is lost if this hope is realized.* In this sense, then, Platonic dualism, or the theory of the immortality of the soul, stands in acute contradiction to itself.

Why, then, we might ask, was a thinker the stature of Socrates oblivious to this aspect of immortality? We began this chapter by referring to the human situation of this most famous of conversations. Surely what gives the occasion its classic importance is the portrait of Socrates as he faces his death. The content of their discourse is facile and intelligent, but secondary to the drama of the occasion. Placing ourselves in that grieving circle of friends, we may not be surprised that Socrates is so convincing. It is not the credibility of the arguments but the credibility of the person that has the greater impact. What they beheld was a man whose high enthusiasm for life, whose moral and intellectual earnestness, whose affection for his friends and family are not the least diminished by the approaching hour of his death.

Crito, Socrates' closest friend, finally asks, "But how shall we bury you?" "Anyway you like," Socrates replies, laughing. "That is, if you can catch me and I don't slip through your fingers." He means by this jest to remind Crito that it is only Socrates' body and not Socrates that he will be burying. Then his wife returns, this time with all three of their sons, and they spend "a long time" together in private.

When the time comes for him to drink the poison, the prison guard expresses his anguish at carrying out his duty, saying to Socrates that "you are the noblest and the gentlest and the bravest of all the men that have ever come here." He breaks into tears as he speaks, turns quickly, and leaves. Then Crito begs Socrates to delay taking the poison since "the sun is still upon the mountains." With traces of laughter still in his voice, he chides Crito for thinking there is something to gain by waiting another few minutes. He takes a cup of poison, raises it with the prayer that his removal to the other world might be prosperous, and then "quite calmly and with no sign of distaste, he drained the cup in one breath." With this his friends begin to weep, some of them losing control in their grief. Socrates, still unperturbed, comforts them. The poison begins to take effect and Socrates lies down on the bed. As he dies his last words are an instruction to Crito to offer a cock to Asclepius, the god of healing. Even these final words have in them a trace of humor, and perhaps piety as well, for the offering of a cock was a gesture of gratitude for healing; it was as though he had been healed of death.

Crito asks if there is anything else to be done. There is no answer.

Notes

1. *Apology*, p. 52. Except where indicated all citations from Plato are taken from *The Last Days of Socrates*, tr. Tredennick.
2. Ibid., p. 59.

3. Ibid., p. 60.

4. *Phaedo,* p. 104.

5. Ibid., p. 107.

6. Ibid., p. 113.

7. Ibid., p. 111.

8. *Laws,* 959.

9. *Phaedo,* p. 116.

10. Ibid., p. 119.

11. *Meno* 81b.

12. *Phaedo,* p. 125.

13. Ibid.,p. 128.

14. Ibid., pp. 129 ff.

15. Ibid., pp. 134 ff.

16. Ibid., pp. 147 ff.

17. Vlastos, "Reason and Causes in the Phaedo," *Plato,* ed. G. Vlastos, pp. 132 ff.

18. *Phaedrus,* 245C−246A.

19. *Apology,* p. 75.

20. Flew, *Body, Mind, and Death,* p. 5.

21. See especially, H. D. Lewis, *Self and Immortality* and John Hick, "Theology and Verification."

TWO
DEATH AS DISPERSION
—DISREGARD

2 EPICUREANISM AND MODERN SCIENCE

The major philosophical alternative to Plato in the West was offered by Aristotle, a student in Plato's Athenian academy for twenty years. Aristotle developed a philosophy that essentially inverted his teacher's. Where Plato was convinced that true knowledge could be derived from the eternal realm of ideas that precedes and is independent of all changeable things, Aristotle taught that all knowledge originated in the senses and that the belief in eternal ideas was altogether unwarranted.

This, of course, meant that Plato's conception of the continuity of personal existence was flatly rejected. And, indeed, we find that Aristotle explicitly rejected any possibility of the soul's immortality. With this point of departure one might ask how Aristotle can find any continuity whatsoever. Why, in other words, would not knowledge be as chaotic and formless as the myriad events that stimulate our senses in their random manner? What protects Aristotle from this manifest absurdity is his introduction of "teleology" into the nature of things. "All men by nature have a desire to know," he declares at the beginning of the *Metaphysics*, and what we want to know of each thing is *why* it is as it is. That is, we want to know what caused it to be this way. It is this character of knowledge that discovers nature's teleology, or purposefulness. We learn that nothing occurs without a cause; that the universe as a whole is a vast assemblage of causal sequences.

Aristotle reasoned that each entity in the world has an underlying *substance*; it is something in itself. At the same time, it is part of a causal sequence and is therefore in the process of becoming something else. The acorn is in itself the substance it appears to be, but it is also, as that substance, a potential oak tree. To have true knowledge of the acorn is to know what it is in itself *and* to know the end for which it exists. Aristotle regarded the inherent tendency of the acorn to develop into an oak its *form*. He believed that knowledge of both substance and form was available through the senses alone.

What we discover through such knowledge is a most inclusive continuity indeed. By an ingenious definition of causation, a definition that would have a long influence on subsequent philosophy, Aristotle was able to show that for each entity to exist at all it must have not only substance and form, but also an originating agent capable of initiating the change *and* an end for which it exists. In one of his most famous arguments he shows that the universe as a whole cannot have a plurality of originating causes, but only a single *Unmoved Mover*. This uncaused cause does not simply bring the universe into existence and then ignore it. The Unmoved Mover sustains the universe in each movement of its existence. The universe, in fact, does not have a beginning in time, nor even a boundary in space. What is most important in Aristotle's understanding of causation and his theory of its single orginator, is that the Unmoved Mover, who is in the ultimate sense also the end toward which the universe is being moved, provides a coherence and a direction to all things that exist. The universe is fundamentally rational, since every part in it is ordered in relation to a single end. One could scarcely have a stronger sense of continuity.

This universal continuity includes each existing person as well. Just as each thing has its end, so each person. To Aristotle what this end is could hardly be in dispute: "The masses and the cultured agree in calling it happiness, and conceive that 'to live well' or 'to do well' is the same thing as 'to be happy.' "[1] Of course, they do not all agree on what happiness is. Aristotle's own famous definition is that *happiness is virtue*, by which he means, in brief, that we are truly happy when we are acting in a way that is in perfect agreement with the purpose of the universe. This requires that we act freely, and therefore with true knowledge of the nature of things, or that we be of one mind with the Unmoved Mover and the final end.

One might wonder, following these last remarks, why he would have so emphatically rejected the theory of immortality. The reason lies in the fact that causation is not transcendent to the universe but immanent in it. The Unmoved Mover does not inhabit a separate realm, mingling there with the eternal forms, as in the thought of Plato. In the same way, the soul does not have a mode of existence that is somehow separable from the material substance of the body. The soul is related to the body as the Mover is to the universe; the soul does not therefore transcend the body. The existing person is not the soul in itself, or the body in itself, but the body animated by the soul. When the body dies the soul ceases to animate it, and the person vanishes. We can say that the person is of one mind with the Unmoved Mover and the Final End, because the human soul, in contrast to the souls of other living things, is *rational* and can have clear knowledge of the end for which it and all things exist.

Aristotle's achievement was considerable. He described a dynamic association of the mind with a universe that did away with the antiworldly dualism of the Platonists, but still preserved a powerful continuity in the face of death. However, there is something bloodless, even detached, in the Aristotelian conception. For all its ethical sophistication there is a personal barrenness about it. Aristotle's universe is extremely tidy; everything fits. There are explanations for everything. All mystery has been swept away. The telic agreement of the soul is wonderfully rational, but it is also strangely passionless. There is no possibility here for ecstasy, or a flash of genius, or unthinkable tragedy. It is clear why his philosophy would serve as a model for those thinkers who reach for a comprehensive grasp of the whole, and why it especially would have been an enduring font for the great scientific labors of our own century. But even for scientific theorists its causal thoroughness is too consistent. If we are going to account for the possibility of such phenomena as life and death, its rigidities must be pried open. We must find some way of making space for the unpredictable and perhaps even the inexplicable.

We should not be surpised that Aristotle found considerable difficulty locating freedom in his metaphysical scheme. He certainly declares that unless a person freely and knowingly performs a virtuous action, that person cannot be said to be virtuous. Children, for example, no matter how well behaved, are not virtuous if only because they lack sufficient knowledge of their actions and of the nature of things. At the same time, he is troubled by a peculiar dilemma. If reason is made equivalent to the way events follow one another in causal sequence toward their proper end, then we not only have walked into a kind of determinism, but something more disturbing: it seems that what is *rational* to the mind is *necessary* to nature. If it is rational that Candidate A win the election tomorrow, Candidate A *must* win the election. Aristotle knew that this was far too strong a connection between intellectual reason and material necessity, since it sweeps away all possible ground for human freedom; it is in fact identical to the materialists' position that mind is merely one more entity swept along in the causal tide. Aristotle saw this dilemma in his thought, but never really resolved it.

This strange absence of any discontinuity and the resulting impersonal character of his thought are among the problems Aristotle left to succeeding generations of philosophers. As we look over the responses to Aristotle in the ancient world, we find two movements—Stoicism and Epicureanism—that uncannily prefigured important developments in modern thought. Epicurus' emendations of both Plato and Aristotle have a startling and oft-noted similarity to twentieth-century scientific thought, particularly as it concerns life and death. The Stoics took hold of some of the issues raised but not solved by Aristotle in a manner that has an unmistakable echo in existententialism. Since we shall examine some of the existentialists' understanding of death in a later chapter, a detailed discussion of Stoicism is omitted here. It is fitting, however, to look into the nature of Epicureanism since it deals with the problem of death in a way that serves as a useful focus for an examination of modern scientific thought pertinent to our understanding of the kind of discontinuity death represents.

Epicurus, an Athenian citizen, was born in 341 B.C.E., about six years after the death of Plato, and 42 years after the death of Socrates. Except for Socrates, there is probably no philosopher in antiquity who was more deeply venerated, as a person and as a thinker, than Epicurus. Although he and his followers were careful not to identify themselves with any religious sect or movement, Epicurus himself came to be revered in a way that was virtually religious. Two hundred years after his death the Roman poet Lucretius, in his monumental work, *De Rerum Natura*, said in praise of Epicurus that when he first beheld all the mistaken and superstitious errors of religion they only stirred the "eager courage of his soul." Rather than submit to error, "he passed far beyond the flaming walls of the world and traversed throughout in mind and spirit the immeasurable universe; when he returns a conqueror to tell us what can, what cannot come into being." Epicurus' work had the effect of trampling religion underfoot: "us his victory brings level with heaven."[2]

Epicurus lived in an age of vast intellectual and political chaos. While the assorted followers of Plato and Aristotle concerned themselves with an endless series of controversies, a rapid succession of tyrannical, and usually incompetent, rulers took control of Athens and other Greek cities. All remnants of effective democracy vanished; brief and costly wars between cities were common; the economic and cultural life of the cities was in shambles; poverty and slavery were widespread. Epicurus' reaction to this was not to offer his own political solutions, but to withdraw from public life. One of his most famous aphorisms is the brief injunction, "Live unknown."

It is of course gratifying irony that those who sought power were soon forgotten, but the modest and simple life of Epicurus was to become deeply appealing to the Greek and Roman world. He established his school in Athens in 306 B.C.E., scarcely leaving it until his death 35 years later in 271. The school consisted of a house, in which the philosopher lived with a group of his disciples, and a garden, some distance away, where they apparently spent most of the day. Epicurus intended that life in the garden be as pleasant and simple as possible. He taught and practiced a kind of frugality so thorough that he was able to say that when one has eliminated the desire for unnecessary delights, "bread and water produce the highest pleasure, when one who needs them puts them to his lips."[3] It is unfortunate that Epicurus would be characterized in the popular mind as an insatiable pleasure seeker, and that "epicure" would come to be the name used for person given to gluttonous, if somewhat refined, self-indulgence. He would have been appalled by this misunderstanding of his thought.

Sadly, of the approximately 300 volumes he is said to have written, only a small collection of fragments and brief works has survived. However, from this diminutive corpus, aided by Lucretius' long poem, we can put together a coherent, though incomplete, picture of what the whole must have been. For our purposes we shall take note of two aspects of his thought: his conception of the physical world, and his renowned attitude toward life and death, which follows from his conception of the universe.

The first principle of Epicurus' thought is that *nothing comes from nothing.* If something could come from nothing the world, he thought, would be hopelessly chaotic, since, as Lucretius put it, human beings might be born out of the sea, fish out of the earth, and trees might bear different fruit each season. It would even be possible for the entire universe to pass out of existence in the next moment.

In other words, Epicurus is clearly rejecting any possibility that there might be discontinuity within the physical nature of the universe. He presses this point even harder than Aristotle, who was satisfied to say that what provides continuity in physical nature is the persistence of forms. Instead, epicurus looked into the physical entities themselves for the source of continuity. This led him to the belief that the universe is made of discrete units of matter called "atoms" (literally, that which cannot be divided) that were incapable of change and therefore eternal. Epicurus is not the first to propose the existence of atoms, but of all the philosophers of the ancient world he makes by far the most comprehensive use of atomic theory.

Atoms are exceedingly small, invisible in fact, and infinite in number. He does not arrive at this latter point through observation, to be sure, but from his reasoning that the universe must be infinite in size. Lucretius defends this claim by asking us to imagine going to the edge of the universe and then throwing a javelin outward. Either the javelin will hit something, which shows we are not at the edge, or it will continue to travel outward, thus extending the boundary. If the boundary is infintely expandable, as it seems to show, then it is not a boundary at all. The universe cannot therefore have boundaries.

According to Epicurus, atoms vary in weight, size, and shape. The one feature they do share is velocity. They all move at the same speed, though not in the same direction. Objects are created when large numbers of atoms coming from different directions happen to collide and continue rebounding from one another in a mass that exhibits a momentary stability. The atoms never cease to move in this mass, but in the compacted space their impact on each other creates a subtle pattern of vibrations. All the objects that appear to the senses are so composed; they are all compounds of atoms trapped by a sequence of collisions.

We noted that one of the problems in Aristotle's thought was its apparently all-inclusive continuity; nothing was left out of its rational order, leaving no possibility for human freedom. If anything, Epicurus has the same difficulty, but in an even more severe form. His seems to be a universe of pure mechanical determinism, where all things are governed by necessity. Epicurus noted this difficulty and proposed a solution to the dilemma that was mocked by the Stoics as irrational to the point of absurdity. He argued that, without being caused from without or within, each atom will occasionally *swerve* in its path. This swerve can come at any moment, recur with any frequency, and be at any angle. Thereby the element of *chance* enters into physical events. Epicurus made certain that this unpredictable aberration in the atom's flight had no cause whatsoever. He thought, there can be no explanation for it. It must be taken simply as fact.

Now, to be sure, this spontaneity is not so extensive that it pulls the universe back into chaos, but it does mean that we cannot predict events with genuine accuracy and that there will be observable variations in identical series. Lucretius cites as evidence for this the fact that even in the regular cycles of nature there are such variations as make it possible for the cow to know her calf from all the others, or the ewe her lamb. Observe the cow when the calf has been sacrificed upon the altar, he writes, how she follows "the footprints stamped on the ground by the cloven hoofs, scanning with her eyes every spot to see if she can anywhere behold her lost youngling."[4]

We can see what Epicurus is attempting to do here. He wants an explanation of the world that will account for its impressive regularities, but one that will also allow for inexplicable deviations in otherwise stable configurations of phenomena. In essence, he is offering a view of the universe that will permit the appearance of life without having to take recourse in otherworldly explanations. The Stoics may have thought his solution reprehensible, but it does have the value of reflecting the phenomenon of life that seems most troublesome in other great rational systems: its spontaneity. As we shall see later in the chapter, modern scientific thought can do no better. The appearance of life, and particularly its evolution, is impossible to account for unless we acknowledge tolerable level of spontaneity in the behavior of the smallest units of matter.

We should include in this abbreviated account of Epicurean physical theory the considerable ingenuity in showing that the mind, or soul, is also a composite mass of atoms. Epicurus' proof is simply that the soul is capable of moving the body, and we cannot suppose that anything immaterial can influence the material. It is self-evident that only matter can move matter; therefore, the soul is material. But how the soul operates is not so simply described. He must show, of course, that sensory impulses, and even thoughts, are somehow composed of atoms. He reasons that, inasmuch as all objects are compounds of atoms in constant motion, there are small quantities of atoms always breaking free and flying away from each object. As they do they will strike the sensory receptors in the body and be received into the physical organism in a shape that maintains the physical characteristics of their previous body. In the rational part of the soul there is an accumulation of very fine atoms that can reflect images back and forth among themselves at extremely high velocities—thus thought.

What we have in this account is the almost total absence of what one could consider true *freedom*. We recall that Plato described the soul as a self-moving entity. He sidestepped the question of where the soul gets its energy to continue working its effects on the body by using an analogy that showed how forms are related to objects, but he made certain that all initiative was reserved for the soul itself. This would of course violate the fundamental axiom of Epicurus' thought, *nothing comes from nothing*. Plato's understanding of freedom means that *something comes from nothing*. This is as unthinkable to Epicureans as their atomic swerves are to Stoics. Epicureans are quite sure that nothing moves itself. All things are already in motion. There is no initiating of action anywhere; there are only collisions. What Epicurus has proposed as proof for sufficient variability in the universe—the fact that the ewe can recognize her own lamb—is not freedom, but *randomness*. Life is not a self-initiating phenomenon, as it is for Plato; nor is it an expression of the teleology of matter, as for Aristotle; For Epicurus it is an *accident*. It was essential to Plato that we seize control of change. For Epicurus nothing can rise above randomness. Since the swerving of the atoms can come at any moment, at any angle, and without any cause, there is no predictability possible. This means that knowledge altogether loses its efficacy for Epicurus. Plato thought knowledge could actually protect us *from change*; Epicurus teaches that knowledge can only be *of change*. However, knowledge does have a consoling function for Epicurus. Though it cannot make the soul eternal, philosophy can at least cure the soul of dread. In fact, this is philosphy's sole task: "For just as there is no profit in medicine if it does not expel the diseases of the body, so there is no profit in philosophy either," Epicurus wrote, "if it does not expel the suffering of the mind."[5]

But what is it that troubles the mind? We noted the social chaos of Epicurus' age. He saw everywhere that men and women were beset by terror and discerned that its chief source was their misunderstanding of the nature of death. Their misconceptions developed in several ways. Possessed by the fiction that the soul is immaterial and therefore does not perish with the body—the teaching of Plato—they believed that once dead they would be subject to punishments by the gods for their wrongdoings; or they believed that they would be reborn in a much less desirable state. These fears then grew from a kind of thinking that assumed a fundamental order to the nature of things—an order that holds us accountable for our actions and, therefore, expects us to pay for our violations. But in Epicurus' universe there can be neither gods to obey, nor universal order by which to abide. Life does not exist for a reason; it is accidental. It also serves no end and has no creator to which it is indebted. Moreover, just as it appeared by chance, with nothing causing it, so will it end, with nothing remaining and with no lasting effect on anything else. Since the soul, like the body, is material, it cannot survive the demise of the body. Its fine atoms will disperse into the air like smoke. Where then is the ground for fear?

But punishment for moral violation is not the only reason for fearing death. Death can also be seen as the thief that will eventually take from our grasp all that is pleasant and good. Epicurus' treatment of this problem is subtler and less direct. He indicates that, given the unpredictability of the future, one should never look ahead for the source of one's pleasure. Anyone who does so is bound to be unfulfilled in that desire and dissatisfied by the course of life. Whatever we hope for from the future stands under the constant threat of chance and death. For that reason, all our hopes are mixed with anxiety. By attaching ourselves to an uncertain future we have made the present miserable.

It is in this analysis of the fear and the misery of persons everywhere that we see the full force of Epicurus' conception of death. We note that he does not attempt to dissuade persons that death is inevitable, that it can come at any moment, and that it steals away all our hope. On the contrary, Epicurus underscores the uncompromising power of death. From what we have seen of his physical theory, it is obvious that *the agent of death is simply the inevitable dispersion of atoms.* The agent of death is not something outside matter, directing it this way or that; it is the very nature of matter itself. This is not only a powerful agency, it is so fundamental that there is no form of freedom or knowledge that can master it. Freedom is no more than randomness, and the mind is composed of matter. In fact, it is our desire to rise above the accidental that causes our misery, because it is a desire that both originates in our impotence before the power of death and confirms that impotence. It is engaging in a struggle we cannot but lose. The walking terror Epicurus sees in his contemporaries could hardly be considered life. It is in fact the kind of living death we have identified as *grief.*

To be sure, Epicurus has a cure for grief. He has a way of leading the living back to life. *Eliminate desire,* he urges repeatedly, since it is desire that throws us to the mercy of the future and its inevitable disappointment. Do not attempt to throw your order to randomness; you cannot succeed. Let death have your future: *Live in the present.* However, we should remember that Epicurus is not counseling resignation, grimly settling for a bad situation. Indeed, he promises that one feels a positive *pleasure* from the extinction of desire. He typically advises that "If you wish to make Pythocles rich, do not give him money, but diminish his desire."[6]

Epicurus applied this principle to even the most difficult of human circumstances. When one is in great physical want, as in hunger or disease, or in great pain, as in the cruelest torture, there is no obstruction to remembering past moments of pleasure to comfort oneself. No present distress can exceed in quantity the stored memory of past pleasures if one has truly lived well.

But how does one live well? How can desire be eliminated? Epicurus answers: by living simply, and by meeting the immediate needs of the flesh. This is no doubt that area of his thought that leads most easily to misinterpretation. "The beginning and the root of all good," he writes, "is the pleasure of the stomach; even wisdom and culture must be referred to this."[7] He does not mean by this to gorge oneself or to seek every manner of delectation. On the contrary, he means that one should in the simplest fashion *eliminate* the appetite and thirst. If one is saved from these elemental requirements, one "might rival even Zeus in happiness."[8]

He distinguishes between desires that are natural and necessary, and desires that are natural but not necessary. Sex is in the latter category. It is a natural desire, but it is not necessary. Hunger and thirst are the only natural *and* necessary desires. Epicurus enjoyed sex, apparently frequently, but he cautions others not to think it requisite. "The pleasures of love," he says, "never profited a man and he is lucky if they do him no harm."[9] As for such desires as success, he considers them neither necessary nor natural, but simply "due to idle imagination."[10] Beware of ambition and the pursuit of great ends, because "Nothing satisfies the man who is not satisfied with a little."[11]

Here, then, we have the essence of Epicurus' thought. Death is the inevitable, unpredictable dispersion of the atoms that coagulated by chance to constitute life. Life is in its ultimate nature a discontinuous phenomenon. There are no laws that lead to its appearance. It can have no lasting effect on succeeding masses of matter. It came without precedent; it will vanish without remainder. Since mind is also material and therefore subject to randomness, there is no hope of *control* through knowledge. Knowledge will change nothing. It can only give us an accurate picture of the nature of things, and thereby serve to comfort us. In fact, the proper understanding of death's inevitability *and* the unpredictability of the time of its arrival can afford us positive *pleasure*. But where is the continuity into which the discontinuity of death can be taken? How do we achieve a higher meaning that will embrace the meaningless discontinuity? We noted earlier that there *is* one absolute form of continuity: the atoms; however, they swerve, are timeless, and are constantly in motion. Epicurus is proposing that we let death have our future, and that we in effect learn to accept our atomic nature. Do not rise above change, but yield to it; do not strive to be free, but learn to accept randomness; do not rest your happiness on the temporally uncertain future, but release yourself to the eternal flow of matter.

Faced with death as simply the dispersion of matter, Epicurus responded by cultivating a serene *disregard*. Since the randomness of death is far more powerful than any agency of our own, disregard it; pay no attention to its effects, and turn instead to that which *precedes* death: the eternal motion of the universe. Do not contend with time: "Live unknown." Attend only to the most rudimentary function of your existence: thirst and hunger. There you are closest to your material existence.

We have seen that Epicurus is clearly not counseling resignation. He believes he is leading the living not back to something utterly mindless and dark, but toward a greater experience of life: "He who least needs tomorrow will most gladly go to meet tomorrow."[12] His writings have an unmistakable cheerfulness about them. Through them we have a vivid portrait of a man who finds deep enjoyment in the company of his friends and the sufficiency of his garden. His high encomium on friendship is probably the crowning piece of his philosophy. Once our minimal needs have been satisfied in the simplest possible way, and we have rid ourselves of fear and greed and the other fruits of ignorance, we are freed to share all that we have with our friends. He emphasized particularly the conversation among friends.

There is, however, something not quite convincing in his praise of friendship, at least not in the context of the whole of his philosophy. It is difficult to imagine a conversation in which there is nothing significant to be said about the future, but for Epicurus the wise person will have banished all interest in what lies ahead. Here conversation could be little more than the exchange of pleasantries and banalities. And what could friendship mean if it could have no bearing on the future? What is a friendship that has no transforming impact on one's life? Compare this to Socrates' conversation in which what was at stake was not passing time with Epicurean disregard, but the very *souls* of his friends.

From assorted biographical fragments we have good reason to believe that Epicurus himself did not live with such disregard; we can in fact conclude that he was a highly valued friend whose life and teaching transformed the lives of many others. If this is true, we must also conclude that it was not from his philosophy that he took the design of his life. The sort of disregard that would be a true response to death— conceived merely as random dispersion—is quite inimical to friendship; this view of death would create in the person an isolating detachment from all that is of consequence in human existence.

We can now turn to modern scientific theory, which in many interesting ways Epicurus had anticipated, and ask whether a more sophisticated understanding of the nature of life—and therefore death—represents an advance over the philosophical disregard that Epicurus recommended.

Before we begin, we must understand one crucial difference between Epicurus and modern scientific theorists. Epicurus took up philosophy not out of a detached interest in the truth, but out of a desire to "expel the sufferings of the mind." Because the fear of death is one principle cause of mental anguish, developing a conception of death was important to the function of his philosophy. Modern scientific theory is concerned with sufferings of the mind not as something to cure, but as one of many phenomena to be studied, and studied for no other reason than to understand them.

For this reason there is very little literature on death as such that can be properly considered scientific. Instead of hunting out these references, we shall come to scientific literature with the problem that developed in Epicurus' thought when he tried to find a place in his explanation of the universe for the concepts of life and death. Specifically, we shall inquire into the capacity of scientific theory to embrace the randomness or spontaneity that seems to make life distinct from other natural phenomena. We shall then ask what implications this has for understanding death and responding to its threatened discontinuity.

It would seem obvious that we should begin with biology, the "science of life." Biological research dates back as far as Aristotle himself who spent a great part of his life collecting and classifying specimens of plant and animal life. From his extant writings we know he had identified some 540 species of animal alone, many of which he had studied by dissection and behavioral observation. But it is not until the nineteenth century that biology became a broad collective effort, developing a consistent methodology. One of the most compelling interests among biologists of that century was to pursue the "secret" of life, a matter that had excited biological speculation from the time of the Renaissance. They were generally convinced that either the principle or the substance of life was discoverable by investigation.

One school of thought that had a broad influence on this discussion adopted a doctrine commonly called *mechanism*. This theory states that every event, living or nonliving, stands in a causal sequence; each event is to be understood as the direct effect of that which immediately precedes it and the cause of that which follows it. There are no exceptions whatsoever. This is Epicureanism without the swerves.

The mechanists· were regularly locked in debate with the *vitalists* over this question of the nature of life. Vitalism is a term loosely indicating a large number of solutions to the problem of finding the continuity between life and its natural environment; these solutions included unique substances, principles of behavior, and teleological structures reminiscent of Aristotle—anything except a direct mechanism. A classical conflict between vitalists and mechanists first erupted as far back as the seventeenth century when Anton van Leeuwenhoek discovered the spermatozoa. Mechanists, at a loss to suggest any other way in which the tiny mass could develop into an adult many thousands of times its size, came to the conclusion that the complete adult already existed, though in more compact size, within the body of the spermatozoa. This diminuitive being was referred to as the *homunculus*. For nearly a century biologists were so certain of this theory that they actually convinced themselves they could see the homunculus through their microscopes as it squatted in the tissue of the sperm. Of course, there was the embarrassing problem of the succeeding generations, and where they were residing. Some mechanists were not afraid to admit that in each homunculus there must be tiny reproductive cells which themselves contained still tinier homunculi, and in those homunculi . . . and so on.

In the meantime, the vitalists found the early breakthroughs in the field of embryology easier to embrace with their theory of the nature of life. They insisted, and were later proved correct by observation with subtler microscopes, that there are numerous organs and parts of the body that are not present in the embryo's earliest stages. Surely, they reasoned, these organs could not develop unless there was a guiding principle directing them toward a predestined end. If the mechanists' early attempt to account for the facts of embryonic development collapsed in absurdity, the vitalists attempt was thoroughly discredited by the new science of genetics. While mechanism, with a number of refinements, is still held by some scientific theorists, vitalism has all but vanished. The vitalists isolated no substances or processes that could be identified as life itself, and their other solutions proved either inadequate to account for the facts or were shown to be false.

This does not mean that all the enigmas concerning the phenomena of life have been resolved. There are many that continue to bedevil present theorists. Consider the case of the slime mold, for example.[13] In one variety the individual spores of the mold live as amoebas in large colonies of identical creatures, but each existing as an isolated individual. Responding to a signal still not understood, each of the single-celled individuals begins moving toward a center, gathering into a mass with 10,000 to 50,000 others. This collected mass, now visible to the naked eye and having the appearance of a stubby worm, moves to a drier place and undergoes a remarkable change. Depending on their location in the mass the individual cells perform one of three functions. The bottom layer shapes itself into a disk that securely holds the colony to its location. Other cells gather a stalk that supports a spherical mass to which the remaining organisms migrate, eventually forming a spore sack that will break open and release thousands of spores to the wind. Each of the spores is but a single individual that has dried and hardened, but each has also retained the biological ability to reproduce itself in a new colony.

What is remarkable about the behavior of the spore mold is not its complexity—in truth, it is one of the very simplest among its large species—but the fact that each cell can perform three entirely different functions in a way that seems as if they are mere mechanical operations. In addition, any one of the cells can take any one of the three functions, *depending on its relation to the other cells*. It seems that some become the base of the spore simply because they are at the bottom of the colony of individuals.

It may well be that an adequate mechanistic explanation of these phenomena can be found, but it is important to understand what is at stake in problems of this kind. Life seems in this instance to require a description altogether different from that appropriate to nonlife. It would therefore fall outside the province of scientific investigation and remain incomprehensible to the scientific theorist. The behavior of living organisms like the slime mold—and there are countless other examples—is an *anomaly*; that is, it is a phenomenon that does not conform to any of the known laws of behavior. Scientific theory cannot tolerate an anomaly. The reason for this is that explanations are intended to show continuities, or invariabilities, in the sequence of events: "the basic strategy of science in the analysis of phenomena is the ferreting out of invariants. Every law of physics, for that matter like every mathematical development, specifies some invariant relation."[14] If a phenomenon should occur that has no discernible cause, or effect, something intolerably invariable has confronted our analysis. This can be deeply disturbing to existing theory—sometimes causing a broad revision of knowledge, sometimes requiring a revision of the basic laws themselves. It was variabilities, or anomalies, of this sort that brought an end to Ptolemaic astronomy, for example, and Newtonian physics.[15] In the past several decades researchers in extrasensory perception and psychokinesis have warned of the potential danger of their work to existing theory.[16] In other words, *what is at stake in the discussion of the nature of life, and death, is the coherence of all present scientific knowledge.*

Here we are not concerned with the fact that life and death can be explained only by recourse to nonmaterial causation, but that life and death seem to have a quality that resists *all* explanation. Life is anomalous inasmuch as it appears to have a self-causing character that requires no preceding cause. Death is anomalous because it brings something to an end without remainder and therefore is an event that has no consequence.

Scientists are by no means unaware of this dilemma and they have not remained silent in the face of it. We shall look briefly at two important attempts to maintain the coherence of scientific knowledge without denying the observable peculiarities of living entities.

The first of these attempts is a sophisticated descendent of vitalism that has lately appeared under the term "organicism," or "organismic biology." In the case of the slime mold, for example, organicists would seriously consider the *organization* of the colony of cells. It is easy to overstate the importance of the organization, to regard it, say, as having a view of the purpose of the organism that none of the parts separately could have. The organization could then be presumed to give the appropriate commands to each of the cells. Organizations, however, do not *do* anything. Instead they are ways of *describing* what discrete entities do in a collective mass. Organization is a concept that can be used only to focus our attention on behavioral patterns; it cannot even be used as an explanation. That is, the individual spores of the mold do not act this way *because* they are organized; the fact that they act this way *is* their organization.

What this brings us to is the somewhat modest conclusion that organicism is simply a way biologists have of keeping their discourse distinct from other areas of science, such as chemistry or physics, where a concept like "organization" would be useless. In his defense of "organismic biology" Morton Beckner denies that it is the function of biology to describe the world "as it really is" and accepts the restriction on critical thinking imposed by Immanuel Kant nearly two centuries ago. Kant argued that there was no way the critical intelligence could know an object as it is in itself; therefore, the mind does not directly apprehend its knowledge but organizes its thinking in such a way that it can shape knowledge out of the mass of its unorganized perceptions of the world. Beckner is proposing that there is a "biological way of thought" that does not organize our perceptions in any privileged or advantaged way, but certainly in a distinctive way; that is, biological thought is not contradictory to other branches of science, but there are conceptual and methodological concerns biologists have for which other scientists find no use. He concludes his discussion with the suggestion "that for 'the whole determines the part,' and other such formulae, we read 'the concept of the whole determines the concept of the part.' "[17]

Beckner's comments are instructive in one important respect. They caution us from expecting to discover from biologists what we initially turned to them to learn: what life and death *are*. What we can learn is where the concepts "life" and "death" are to be found in academic discourse. He underlines the fact that the anomaly of life, and death, is not an anomaly *in fact*, but *in our discussion*. If the concepts "life" and "death" do not integrate into scientific discourse, we are not to assume that there *are* no such phenomena as life and death, but that when we speak of them we must do so outside the boundaries of that mode of discourse.

The question then is whether the concepts of life and death can be absorbed into the grammar of scientific language without distorting its basic lawfulness. This brings us to the second attempt to show how life can be explained in a manner consistent with the explanation of non-living phenomena. We might regard this attempt as a descendent of mechanism, but now much altered. We could refer to it as a refined materialism. Among its spokepersons we find some of the most distinguished theorists of the century.

Our refined materialist would by no means overlook the great improbabilities associated with the appearance of life in the universe. One scholar calculated the statistical likelihood that the leap from a nonliving molecule to the first unit of living matter had occurred *by change;* the probability was approximately one in 10^{308759}. If we were to write this figure out it would require more zeros than this book could contain.[18] This figure would still be more vast if we asked for the statistical probability of, say, the mind of Aristotle occurring by chance. This kind of cosmic guessing is often intended to show that a probability so exceedingly slight is equivalent to an impossibility, which brings us to the suggestion that life must have an extramaterial origin. We need not draw that conclusion, however, but only to ask our modern, refined materialist how such improbabilities can be explained without yielding to outright anomaly.

We have such a thinker in the great physicist, Erwin Schrödinger, who said of these staggering unlikelihoods that such facts "are easily the most interesting that science has revealed in our day."[19] Schrödinger's fascinating book on this subject is addressed to the question, "How can the events *in space and time* which take place within the spatial boundary of a living organism be accounted for by physics and chemistry?"[20] He begins by indicating that "the laws of physics and chemistry are statistical throughout."[21] When dealing with the smallest elements of which physicists have any knowledge, one must necessarily think in terms of probabilities. The reason for this lies in some of the surprises that emerged from the study of the atom in the early decades of this century. For one thing, the atom was discovered to be not the smallest possible unit of matter, as the Greek philosophers had supposed, but a complicated structure composed of particles incredibly small in size. The atoms themselves are already so small that if we were able to mark all the molecules of water (composed of several atoms) in a glass and then distribute them evenly through all the earth's oceans we could expect to find 100 of the marked molecules in any glass taken from any place on the seven seas.[22] How much smaller are the nucleus and the electrons that comprise the atom? Using another illustration, imagine an orange that has been expanded to the size of the earth. The atoms of which the orange is made would not be the size of cherries. The nucleus in the cherry-sized atom would still be invisible to the naked eye, but if we enlarged the atom until it was the size of the massive dome of St. Peter's Cathedral in Rome, then the nucleus would have the approximate size of a grain of salt and the electrons would be no larger than pieces of dust whirling around the nucleus at the speed of light.[23]

This is scarcely the hard substance physicists thought they would find. Relatively speaking, the enormous empty space within the atom seems to give matter an even less substantial quality. But there are still other surprises. The atom is composed of many other particles besides the electrons and nucleus; indeed, its structure is so complicated that we are far from knowing all of its component parts. Moreover, it has become clear that when we have found the smallest particle it will still not consist of something *substantial*. Nuclear physicists now know that there is absolutely nothing in the universe that can be regarded as an indivisible, indestructible grain of hard matter. All atomic particles, however small, are but accumulations of energy that have life spans as brief as millionths of a second or as long as millions of years.

Perhaps the most remarkable discovery of all is that these knots of energy behave in a way that is most unlike the gross objects visible to the naked eye. Through the work of Max Planck, Albert Einstein, and others, we know now that energy does not come in a smooth flow as it appears at the level of our perception, but in jumps, or what Einstein called "quanta," thus the term *quantum physics*. What is more, there seems to be a great deal of unpredictability in the appearance of quanta, enough that one cannot determine where in the atom any of the electrons are to be at any one time. They seem, in fact, to come in and out of existence without leaving a trace. One must speak of atomic particles not as existing here or there, but of having "tendencies" to exist at a certain place at a certain time. The peculiar behavior of quanta, and other paradoxes that emerged in the research of the physicists, such as "curved" space and "antiparticles," caused the famous physicist, Heisenberg, to ask himself repeatedly, "Can nature possibly be so absurd as it seemed to us in these atomic experiments?"[24]

These discoveries have obviously displaced the rigid mechanical view of the universe and have returned a great deal of the mystery to our knowledge of reality that seemed to be lost in Aristotle's tidy metaphysics. There is considerably more flexibility in modern scientific thought—a preparedness for surprise. This is the result not only of such perplexing facts as the passage of electrons in and out of existence, and the apparent bottomlessness of matter, but also the result of the expectation that whenever one mystery is solved others will present themselves. We can also see here how we have been thrown back into the philosophic lap of Epicurus whose swerving atoms introduced variability into a material universe. Both Epicurus and modern materialists affirm the existence of a region not dominated by causation. Like Epicurus, we are not left with a completely deterministic mechanism, but does it leave us with so little predictability that we are advised to have no confidence in the future? Not at all, Schrödinger says. While it is true that atomic particles are subject to unpredictable quantum leaps, it is also true that in extremely large numbers—as in living organisms—they collectively display highly ordered behavior. When we are concerned with the billions of particles that compose even the smallest organisms, we are speaking of very high probabilities. In such large numbers there is an extremely small divergence from causal sequence, so that living things are able to enjoy considerable continuity. We recall that one of the reasons Epicurus proposed his "swerves" was that without them there would be a tiresome sameness to existing objects. Schrödinger, too, must be able to demonstrate enough variability in causal patterns that the same physical laws, which account for life's continuity over long periods of time, will also allow for the sort of genetic changes that made evolution possible.

Schrödinger, turning to the science of genetics, considers the discovery that a single gene contains not more than a million, or perhaps several million, atoms: "That number is much too small . . . to entail an orderly and lawful behavior according to statistical physics—and that means according to physics."[25] While the organism itself is large enough statistically to correct the "lawlessness" of individual atoms, the genes are not. He then refers to studies in which it was learned that genetic change comes in "quantum leaps." Just as in the behavior of atomic particles, there seems to be no intermediate forms. For no reason at all, without apparent cause, a genetic change will appear. These changes are, of course, very rare, particularly the changes that cause permanent alteration of heredity. If mutations were not rare but common, life would soon have so little continuity that it could not exist at all; in Lucretius' phrase, human beings might be born out of the sea and fish out of the earth. Therefore, Schrödinger observes, "we must not be very much astonished that Nature has succeeded in making such subtle choice of threshold values as it necessary to make mutation rare."[26]

While Schrödinger introduces the discoveries of modern physics into the discussion of the nature of life, he leaves us only with a tentative, though confident, hope that the laws of physics can account for the phenomena of life in quite the same manner they can account for all other phenomena. It is his firm belief that atoms should display the same features whether they are in animate or inanimate matter; and at the level of atoms there can be neither life nor death, only the lawful play of energy. Writing several years later, after the epochal breakthrough in genetics, the biochemist and Nobel laureate, Jacques Monod provides firm support for Schrödinger's belief from within the science of biology.

Monod comes to the same phenomena with a much broader knowledge of the biology and chemistry involved, although he is quite as certain as Schrödinger that the laws of biochemistry are consistent with the laws of physics. Monod, in fact, makes the intellectual problem somewhat more difficult by noting that it is not simply the reproductive invariance of life that must be explained, but also what he calls its "autonomous morphogenesis" and its fundamentally "teleonomic" character. That is, Monod feels it is necessary to explain why living things can reproduce themselves *from within*, as it were, without the assistance of external agents (as even the subtlest of human-made machines would require), and why all living matter appears to be goal-seeking in its behavior. But all such explanations must satisfy the rigorous criteria of what Monod calls philosophical "objectivity." By this he means that we may not appeal to forces or elements that cannot be directly observed in physical matter. This places considerable burden on an explanation of the teleonomic character of life, especially since we must discover how the goal orientation of an organism is a property of its present chemical composition, even when that goal might be exceedingly distant in both time and structure. Where, in other words, can we see the physical factors in the recently fertilized single-celled ovum that will lead to a fully developed human adult many millions of times larger and so elaborately structured it is capable of writing a book like Monod's *Chance and Necessity*?

Monod follows a line of reasoning similar to Schrödinger's, although he has one advantage in his own work: the discovery of DNA by Watson and Crick, which along with Mendel's identification of the "gene as the unvarying bearer of hereditary traits," and the subsequent chemical identification of gene, "without any doubt constitute the most important discoveries ever made in biology."[27] In studies of the processes of heredity, where the teleonomic nature of life is most evident, the discovery of the substance DNA supplies an important piece of the puzzle that biochemists are attempting to resolve.

Scientifically speaking, the problem of accounting for teleonomy is a problem of accounting for the communication from one generation of organisms to another. The special function that DNA plays has chiefly to do with communication. It mandates a sequence of interactions among proteins that constitutes the contained growth and development of the body. To put it in the simplest possible terms, it is the function of DNA to prohibit certain chemical actions until others have occurred, but to do this with such precision that no variation in the sequence of actions is possible.

No sooner has the ovum been fertilized than the DNA sequence for the remainder of that organism's life has been determined. It is always possible, given the ultimate uncertainty of atomic behavior, that one of the proteins involved in the DNA sequence will be anomic, leading to a divergent characteristic in the organism. In identical twins, for example, even though the DNA sequence is the same for both, there will be a myriad of small physical differences, most of which are so minute as to be nearly undetectable; but given the statistical unlikelihood of variation in so large a mass as a human body, it would be extremely rare for any grossly visible differences to emerge.

This last point is important in the study of evolution. Early theorists were mistaken in thinking that the chance variations in the physical structure of the organism counted in the selection process, because the variations that arise within the DNA sequence are not inheritable. To put this in another way, DNA can mandate the sequence of protein interactions, but the lawless proteins cannot communicate back to the DNA in any manner that would cause a genetic change and affect succeeding generations. All genetic change must occur within the DNA itself. It is on this point that Monod can show the remarkable compatibility between the organism's reproductive invariance and its teleonomy. Its teleonomy, or goal-seeking behavior, consists in the highly precise manner in which the DNA mandates the sequence of chemical actions in the body—all by perfectly intelligible laws of physics, of course—and its invariance consists in the fact that the DNA can communicate only in one direction. In other words, there is nothing that can happen to the organism after its conception that can change its

DNA and, therefore, nothing that can affect what it can pass on to the next generation.

Where is there any space for change? If the system is that conservative, how can it be that Monod and Schrödinger are not as identical to each other as any two organisms of the slime mold? Or even: given such a conservative hereditary nature, why is not every manifestation of life identical to every other? How could evolution occur at all? Monod's answer returns us to quantum physics. The chemical action of the DNA involves such minute chemical quantities that it is statistically closer to the lawlessness of atomic particles. It is not so close, of course, that there will be changes in each generation, but close enough that in millions of generations some changes in the genetic code are inevitable.

Monod's detailed discussion of the genetic process and the role DNA plays in it has a clear philosophical intent: he wants to make it clear

> that chance *alone* is at the source of every innovation, of all creation in the biosphere. Pure chance, absolutely free but blind, at the very root of the stupendous edifice of evolution: this central concept of modern biology is no longer one among other possible or even conceivable hypothesis. It is today the *sole* conceivable hypothesis, the only one that squares with observed and tested fact. And nothing warrants the supposition—or the hope—that on this score our position is likely ever to be revised.[28]

Paradoxically, chance is simultaneously bound up with necessity in our theories of life. For one thing, from the study of atomic physics it is evident that chance is itself necessary; atomic particles are by nature unpredictable—within certain limits, to be sure. For another, through the offices of DNA what is originally wrought by blind chance becomes blind necessity—millions of perfect replications, until chance strikes again. This balance between chance and necessity that allows for high predictability in organic existence occasionally allows Monod to speak of living beings as "chemical machines,"[29] albeit self-constructing chemical machines. But there is no question that he means to destroy every foothold for mechanism, vitalism, or any other kind of "anthropocentrism" by introducing chance into biological theory.[30]

We turned to the work of Schrödinger and Monod with the question of whether life and death could find a place in the grammar of science. We saw that both of them were concerned that the description of physical matter display enough discontinuity that it could include the phenomena of life, along with the spontaneity, or the unpredictability, which it self-evidently possesses. We saw that the random variations in the atoms of DNA were the door by which life was admitted to scientific theory. With astonishing similarity to Epicurus, Monod argues that all phenomena, living and unliving, are subject simultaneously to chance and necessity. *Life is distinct from nonlife only in the fact that, by chance, it has evolved into a variety of structures that have the property of reproducing themselves, along with a tolerable level of randomness built into the reproduced structure.*

Monod does not discuss the place of death in human existence, but his theoretical description of life gives a clear indication of the role death plays in it. If life is fully material, untouched by any extramaterial influences whatsoever, death can only consist in the dispersion and redistribution of the tangible elements that had composed the organism. *Death itself offers no discontinuity since it brings nothing to an end.* All the constituent parts of the organism continue indefinitely. This continuity is not a requirement of the matter itself; it is a requirement of the theory. So far as the theory is concerned, what has come to an end is only the way these continuing entities are related to each other, but even this is a *lawful* change, that is, a *continuous* process.

We noted earlier in the discussion of organicism that when biologists speak of "organization" of matter peculiar to living bodies they are not referring to something extramaterial. Such references are only a way of speaking that distinguishes their mode of discourse from that of physicists and chemists. When we go to look for something corresponding to the concept of organization, there is nothing to be found. Organicists do not want to suggest they have found something that is invisible to physicists, nor even that biology and physics are not consistent with one another in every detail. While the concept of organization, as they use it, is not found in physics, they are quite prepared to give equal footing to physicists' descriptions of these same events. The point here is that *it is absolutely necessary to science to maintain a continuity in the description of phenomena.* Where the phenomena appear discontinuous, as in the slime mold or in the "stupendous edifice of evolution," scientific discourse must be adjusted to maintain its consistency.

If death is taken as an end without remainder, it is a perfect anomaly. In light of Monod's statement, quoted above, that it "is in fact impossible to analyze any phenomenon otherwise than in terms of the invariants that are conserved in it,"[31] it is obvious that death cannot be analyzed, for it is nothing but a variant. Does the same point apply to life? Beckner, Schrödinger, Monod, and countless other members of the scientific community are not in the least uncertain that living phenomena can be analyzed. But what is being analyzed? The phenomena as invariable physical entities, or life? Monod's answer is that we can study living entities *as* physical processes according to their invariants *and* as living processes according to their randomness. Monod, in short, is in perfect agreement with Epicurus. There is no place in scientific discourse for the phenomenon of *freedom*, that is, a self-initiating spontaneous action; there is a place only for randomness. To the end Monod, along with essentially all other theorists, would agree with the axiom we found central to Epicurus' thought: *nothing comes from nothing.* Accidents do happen, however, and life is one of them.

If we insist that death and freedom are true discontinuities, that one represents a beginning without precedent and the other an end without remainder, then we must conclude that *on the subject of life and death science remains silent.* Within the sciences persons neither live nor die; in fact, there are not even persons, only continuous entities. Therefore, the response to life and death is here what it was for Epicurus: *disregard.*

The Epicureans, we recall, retreated to their garden where they supplied their minimal needs and engaged each other in extended discourse, ignoring the rush of history beyond the garden wall. Not altogether facetiously, we could draw a parallel with what has happened in twentieth-century scientific discourse. Scientists are quite clear that their work must undisturbed by historical exigencies. Indeed, only in those universities and research institutions that have the means to provide for personal needs and the ability to prevent political and social events from breaking in on the free flow of reflection and inquiry will genuine scientific discourse occur.

It would be foolish to claim that science has no historical importance. For many centuries technological innovation and new insights into the nature of physical matter have had a profound impact on the course of public affairs. Scientists have not "lived unknown." However, it is also the case that although science has historical importance, *history has no scientific importance.* Indeed, it is a manifest contradiction to undertake a research project for historical reasons. Galileo did not investigate the heavens because he intended to bring down the papal hierarchy, or if he did that intention was irrelevant to his discoveries. The proper attitude of the scientific inquirer is to ignore history and be led by the flow of natural events. In fact, one must purge oneself of all historical influences, all unique needs and interests, in order to conform to what is happening outside oneself. One must not even *look for* something, but simply *observe,* and subsequently *report* what is observed in a way that bears no distinctive mark of the personal history of the observer. What is important about DNA is not that it was discovered by Watson and Crick, but that it was discovered *and* described in a way that anyone could observe the same phenomena.

There is, in other words, a strange inversion that occurs in science, quite similar to that which we saw in Epicurus. We noted that Epicurus' philosophy could not have been the source for the design of his life. His unique personal charisma and the way he was held in reverence for many centuries are hardly exemplary of the thorough disregard his philosophy seems to advise. Similarly, no scientists, as human beings, have their whole lives behind the laboratory wall. Even though history has no importance to science, that there is science at all is a phenomenon of history. It is the consequence of persons freely setting aside their personal freedom in order simply to conform to the nature of things. Science is an expression *of life,* but in no sense is it an expression *about life.*

What is discovered there does not then translate back into history. One cannot conduct one's affairs by passively conforming to the ceaseless flow of atomic phenomena. Monod has argued persuasively that the most dispassionate, objective scientific research can show that life is an exceedingly fine balance of necessity and chance. But this cannot be taken as a directly useful guide to life. As we have seen thus far, the continuation of the physical body (made possible by "necessity") has no real meaning for human existence. We have learned enough from physiological research to be able to isolate the body from all contaminating and injurious influences—that is, to reduce the possibility of accidental destruction—and to sustain its physical existence indefinitely. But this is not life as we live it, or even could live it. It is not *how long we live as a body,* but *how well we live with a body;* that is, how truly meaningful do our lives become. Similarly, randomness or chance has no real meaning for human existence. It is not what happens to me, but what I do that makes my existence genuinely human; not chance, but freedom. And freedom is important only to the degree that it has consequences beyond itself in time—that it affect others and, therefore, be historical. *The problem of death is not a problem of an accidental physical existence; it is a problem that can be understood only in the way we intentionally live through our physical existence with others.*

Through our review of the conception of death in scientific thought, we have found that if life is understood strictly in terms of invariants, or continuities, death is not a possibility, because whatever we call *death* can only be an event in which nothing comes to an end. As a result freedom is also impossible. Only where death is so conceived that its discontinuities cannot be disregarded can we understand what it means to be free.

We could put this in stronger terms by saying that adapting one's life to Epicurus' or the scientists' view of the universe is the very essence of grief. It is the contradictory attempt to live at a level of existence where we cannot be touched by death, and yet where we need not live by choice. It is to lose the power of effective speech, because the conversation of the Epicureans in their garden and the scientists in their laboratory cannot have any intention of engaging history, altering the future of the conversants, without violating the very genius of their respective philosophies. To place the garden, or the laboratory, above history is a manifestation of acute grief. The question of death has been sidestepped, but not answered.

We turn next to a conception of death that develops out of the experience of personhood as it emerges from its eternal matrix into an altogether unique and anomalous existence. We shall examine two of the most illustrious examples of this way of thinking: mysticism and psychoanalysis.

Notes

1. *Metaphysics*, I,i.
2. *De Rerum Natura*, p. 70. All quotations from the Epicureans are taken from *The Stoic and Epicurean Philosophers*, Ed. W. J. Oates.
3. "To Menoeceus," p. 32.
4. *De Rerum Natura*, p. 98.
5. Fragment #54.
6. Fragment #28.
7. Fragment #59.
8. Vatican Fragment #33.
9. Vatican Fragment #51.
10. *Principal Doctrines* #29.
11. Fragment #69.
12. Fragment #71.
13. Described in Sinnott, *The Biology of the Spirit*, ch. 3.
14. *Chance and Necessity*, p. 100.
15. See Thomas S. Kuhn, *The Structure of Scientific Revolutions*, for a detailed account of this process in the history of science.
16. Thus J. B. Rhine: "Here is a final and a venturesome reflection: It seems justifiable to expect to find underneath the surface of our somewhat arbitrary academic distinctions (physics, psychology, biology, etc.) a less de-

finable but more basic reality than has been known hitherto in natural science." The New World of the Mind p. 164.

17. The Biological Way of Thought, p. 188.
18. G. Blandino, Theories on the Nature of Life, pp. 307ff.
19. What is Life? p. 82.
20. Ibid., p. 3.
21. Ibid., p. 4.
22. Ibid., p. 7.
23. See F. Capra, The Tao of Physics, pp. 65 ff.
24. Physics and Philosophy, p. 42.
25. What is Life? p. 32.
26. Ibid., p. 68.
27. Chance and Necessity, p. 104.
28. Ibid., pp. 112 ff.
29. Ibid., pp. 45 ff.
30. Ibid., p. 113.
31. Ibid., p. 100.

Bibliography

Morton Beckner, The Biological Way of Thought (New York: 1959).

Giovanni Blandino, Theories on the Nature of Life (New York: 1969).

Fritjof Capra, The Tao of Physics (Berkeley: 1975).

Epicurus, The Extant Writings of Epicurus, tr. C. Bailey, The Stoic and Epicurean Philosophers (New York: 1946).

N. R. Hanson, Observation and Explanation (New York: 1971).

Werner Heisenberg, Physics and Philosophy (New York: 1958).

Dean H. Kenyon, Gary Steinman, Biochemical Predestination (New York: 1969).

Thomas Kuhn, The Structure of Scientific Revolutions (Chicago: 1970).

Lucretius, De Rerum Nature, tr. H. A. J. Munro, The Stoic and Epicurean Philosophers, (New York: 1946).

Jacques Monod, Chance Necessity, tr. A. Wainhouse (New York: 1972).

J. B. Rhine, The New World of the Mind (New York: 1968).

Jean Rostand, Human Possible, tr. Lowell Blair (New York: 1973).

Erwin Schrödinger, What is Life? The Physical Aspect of the Living Cell (Cambridge: 1969).

Edmund Sinnott, Biology of the Spirit (New York: 1955).

3 MYSTICISM

The difficulties of offering a satisfactory definition of mysticism are considerable. In 1899 William R. Inge, in his classical study, *Christian Mysticism*, needed an entire appendix merely to summarize the major definitions then available. If we eliminate at once the popular use of the term for a sort of religious befuddlement, or vague spirituality, we can say that scholars most frequently err by making the term too inclusive. In a well-known anthology[1] the editor collects passages from the *Tao te Ching*, the *Bhagavad-Gita*, the Gospel of St. John, and Dante's *Divine Comedy*, among others. It is difficult to know what is properly to be left out when the term is used to sweep so broadly. Similar excesses can be found in scholars as learned and discriminating as D. T. Suzuki and Thomas Merton.* In what is probably the finest study of the subject in this century, Rudolf Otto's *Mysticism East and West*, a careful comparison of the great ninth-century Hindu thinker Sankara with the Chris-

---

*In an enthusiastic essay Suzuki announces that the great German mystic Meister Eckhart "is in perfect accord with the Buddhist doctrine of *sunyata* (emptiness), when he advances the notion of Godhead as 'pure nothingness' (*ein bloss niht*)" (*Mysticism, Christian and Buddhist*, p. 18). There is no acknowledgment here of the enormous differences between the traditions out of which these concepts arise. In his *Mystics and Zen Masters* Merton discovers that the experience of the Zen adept has a trinitarian structure that shares deep similarities with the experience of the Christian mystic, but he fails to note the large number of irreconcilable differences between the two traditions (see pp. 3 ff.). A more balanced discussion of the differences between Zen and Christianity can be found in William Johnston's *The Still Point*, pp. 41 ff., 83 ff., et passim.

tian mystic Meister Eckhart (1250–1327), makes it obvious that for all the conceptual similarity one can find in selected doctrines the differences between East and West are deep enough to defy any facile identification of the two traditions. The major source of this difference lies in the essentially *theistic* nature of Western thought, in contrast to the *pantheism* of Hinduism and what we might provisionally refer to as the *atheism* at the heart of Buddhism.

We shall restrict our study of mysticism to Western sources and examine Hinduism and Buddhism separately in subsequent chapters, where it should become evident that their differences are far more revealing than their similarities. Our selection of sources in Western thought will take its basic cue from an observation of Gershom Scholem in his *Major Trends in Jewish Mysticism:* "Mysticism is a definite stage in the historical development of religion and makes its appearance under certain well-defined conditions." The first stage is that in which one experiences the world as full of gods whose presence and power are immediate and undisguised. In the second stage there is a distancing of the divine and the subsequent recognition of an abyss between human and divine existence. This stage "is the creative epoch in which the emergence, the break-through of religion occurs." The third is the stage of mysticism; it arises when there is a desire to cross the abyss, "a quest for the secret that will close it in, the hidden path that will span it."[2]

Our assumption here is that there is a unique region of human experience found only in the great theistic religions of the West—Judaism, Christianity, and Islam—in which there is a perceived abyss between the human and the divine, or between the part and the whole, and a consuming desire to traverse that immense intervening space. Whether this is an "accurate" definition of mysticism is really irrelevant; that it is a consistent body of thought and action distinct from all others will become clear in this chapter. We might at the outset offer a characterizing term that is most useful in pointing out the distinctiveness of this tradition. Commenting on Eckhart's famous sermon on the rage that seizes the soul when it discovers it cannot become God, Otto said that his was largely "the mysticism of numinous majesty." We shall be speaking of a tradition in which the *numinous majesty* of the divine is the single most dominating landmark in its broad terrain.

It could even be argued that the mystical tradition in the West has a specifiable origin. It would be an excusable exaggeration to regard the father of mysticism as an anonymous Syrian monk of the fifth century who composed a body of spiritual essays under the pseudonym Dionysius the Areopagite. Whether or not it was the author's intention, a legend quickly developed that Dionysius was a Greek who was present in Athens at the time St. Paul visited the city and gave his famous address on the "unknown God," after an inscription he had found there on one of the statues.[3] As a result of hearing this address, Dionysius was converted by the Apostle Paul and at once took up the intense spiritual life out of which these writings emerged.

It was not until the Renaissance that anyone doubted the authorship of this literature, and although it soon was apparent that it originated in the fifth century and not in the first century, the authenticity of the legend has even been defended by persons in the present century who persist in referring to the author as St. Dionysius. He is more commonly known as Pseudo-Dionysius. Certainly the belief that he was a convert of St. Paul gave great authority to his writings, but even if he had offered them under his own name they would have been widely influential, since they exhibit a wide range of original religious insight.

No doubt we can find examples of mystical insight prior to the fifth century. Augustine, writing a century before the nameless Syrian monk, displayed a strong mystical instinct, so much so that Dom Cuthbert Butler considered him the "Prince of Mystics."[4] But nowhere did Augustine assemble in a single work that array of theological and philosophical assumptions that were later to constitute the inner core of the mystical tradition. It is precisely this that Dionysius achieves. We can find in him, in lively expression, nearly all the major themes that emerge later in the enormous body of mystical literature found in Judaism, Christianity, and Islam. Probably no other source, apart from the Koranic and biblical material, is more frequently cited by mystics. To be sure, the influence on Jewish and Islamic mystics is indirect, passing first through the mysticism of medieval Christianity, but it is detectable.

For all their influence the works of Dionysius are rather brief. They are much more suggestive than exhaustive. Certainly the most arresting passages are those that seem to take their cue from Paul's reference to the unknown God. What Paul seems to have had in mind is the fact that the God who is revealed in Jesus Christ is a reality so compelling that it can only show the terrible emptiness of a religion that cannot even remember the identity of its idols. What Dionysius had in mind when he came across this phrase would have been deeply puzzling to Paul: the very unknowability of God.

Dionysius is obviously aware that the biblical literature has a great deal to say about God, applying names and attributes to him and

chronicling his actions in human history. But for Dionysius these are
not avenues of direct vision into the inner being of God: they are the
fragmentary and limited revelations about the divine nature that God
has adapted to the impoverished human capacity for knowledge of the
real. For this reason all that we have learned from the Bible and from
philosophers is an indication of the appalling limits of human intelligence, just as it is an indirect indication of the surpassing majesty of
God. This leads him to speak of the "hidden Deity" about whom we are
not permitted to say anything more than has been revealed to us in the
sacred oracles. This Deity, whom he does not even refer to as "he" but
only "it," is "elevated above all knowledge." Therefore, to none of
those

> who are lovers of the Truth above all Truth, is it permitted to
> celebrate the supremely-Divine Essentiality—that which is the
> super-subsistence of the super-goodness—neither as word or
> power, neither as mind or life or essence, but as pre-eminently
> separated from every condition, movement, life, imagination,
> surmise, name, word, thought, conception, essence, position, sta-
> bility, union, boundary, infinititude, all things whatsoever.[5]

This God, existing beyond all knowledge, separated from every
human condition, must therefore be said to dwell in a place that can
only be seen as darkness by the human intelligence. The only appropriate epithets for such a Deity are those such as Dionysius' "super-
unutterable and super-unknown Isolation."[6] Anticipating the powerful
preoccupation of later mystics, he makes frequent reference to the "Divine Gloom," the absolute emptiness, that is all the seeking mind can
find in its longing for direct vision.

The God beyond knowledge and the stark limitations of the human
intelligence are themes found in all mystics, but so is the paradox that
immediately follows this reasoning: the "gloom of unknowing" (ag-
nosia) is also a "super-bright gloom," since it opens us to the awareness
that "through not seeing and not knowing, to see and to know that not
to see nor to know is itself above sight and knowledge."[7] Here we have
the central problem in the life of every mystic: how to integrate the fact
that not to know is to know; how not to see is actually to see.

Dionysius' fictional placement of himself at the Areopagus in
Athens, precisely where Socrates was thought to teach, is testimony to
his desire to make contact between Platonic and Christian thought. We
can already see, however, that he has considerably distanced himself
from Platonism. Whether he also has moved away from Christianity is
less clear, although, as we shall discover, the subsequent mystical tra-

dition rarely found favor with official representatives of Christian orthodoxy and was equally troubling to the orthodox defenders of Judaism and Islam.

Dionysius makes an obvious departure from Platonism when he denies that the truth can be known directly. For Plato God was scarcely unknowable; on the contrary, knowledge of God (which is equal to the Idea of the Good) is the only true knowledge. It may well be that most persons are ignorant of the truth, but this does not mean that the truth is unknowable in itself. What is more, the paradoxical claim that this "gloom of unknowing" is itself a kind of knowing would be perfectly obscure to a Platonist who could imagine light entering the darkness and dispelling it, but could make no sense of the claim that the darkness is a kind of light. This is the fundamental division between mystics and Platonists; it has to do with radically different conceptions of the nature of the soul. For Plato there is a direct continuity between the human and the divine through the soul. This is the very continuity, in fact, that constitutes the soul's life over death, guaranteeing its immortality. The soul is immortal because it participates in the realm of eternal ideas. As Socrates argued, the soul cannot know beauty unless it has always known it. Knowledge is eternal for the obvious reason that what is true now is always true; and just as knowledge is eternal, so is the soul. Inevitably the soul begins to resemble its knowledge until it becomes essentially identical with it. As we noted previously, this close identification of the soul with eternal knowledge robs it of any personal particularities. There can be no such thing as Socrates' knowledge as distinct from Epicurus' knowledge. If what they know is true, they know the same thing. Their souls would therefore be identical.

The vast gulf that separates the mystic from the "numinous majesty" of the divine has the effect of isolating the soul, cutting it off from all identities. For this reason the mystic characteristically turns inward, studying at length the peculiarities of his or her own inwardness, but always as that inwardness stands over and against the transcendent Other. Because God is immanent, and not transcendent, for the Platonists they can comfortably speak of the divinity of the soul. As we shall see, mystics sometimes use similar expressions, but they have an altogether different sense. Where there is unity between the divine and the human it is not in knowledge, but beyond knowledge. Moreover, what unity the mystic speaks of can come only after the repeated and treacherous attempts to cross the abyss. For this reason Thomas Aquinas defined mysticism as *cognitio dei experimentalis*, the knowledge of God from experience.

In a preliminary way we can already see how the mystic's understanding of death must be decisively contrary to those we have studied. We have described the problem of death as the problem of restoring continuity to life in response to the threatened discontinuity of death. Plato proposed a continuity of the person through the moment of death. Epicurus and modern science proposed a continuity of the physical matter that constitutes life. Platonic dualism makes a nonevent of death, with the result that the temporal structures of selfhood are dispersed into the vacuum of an infinite future. Scientific materialism denies the discontinuity of death because it brings nothing to an end, and this results in the incapacity to comprehend life as anything distinct from the nonliving stuff of the universe. Plato's soul will necessarily continue at death. It could not choose to die. The scientists' human organism will necessarily disperse at death. It could not choose to live. For one, life is imposed; for the other, life is accidental. For neither is life itself a choice. It is precisely here that mysticism moves into a universe of its own.

Mysticism is distinct from both in its identification of personhood with freedom. Both Plato and Epicurus associated life with an unchanging *substance,* one psychic and the other material. Substance cannot choose; it simply is. Moreover, it *must* be, if it is. Atoms, or their smallest component parts, never cease to exist, neither does the Platonic soul. Mystics do not conceive of the soul as a substance, but as an *act.* The soul can *only* act. If it does not act it does not exist. Life's continuity is provided for the mystics not by self-existing substance, whether physical or psychic, but by one's own free act. Life is neither accidental nor necessary; it is voluntary. What stands behind this conception is a radical understanding of death. Where Plato took the agency of death to be temporal *change,* and Epicurus the *dispersion* of matter, mystics see it as the *separation* of the soul from its origin. What gives the mystics' conception its peculiar force is the distinctly voluntary nature of life. This has the result of understanding that separation to be one's own act. Death is not an accident that *happens* to me, according to this conception, neither is it a fate *imposed* on me; death can only be *chosen.* I do not die unless I choose to die.

We shall now explore these preliminary remarks by looking more closely at the way this view first takes root in an implausible soil: Western theism.

We have discussed, as the first major element of mysticism, the unknowability of the divine, indicating how this puts considerable distance between mystics and the two views examined earlier, Platonism and Epicureanism. It is already clear in Dionysius that we are not simply stranded in this unknowability, hobbled by our ignorance. It is a special kind of ignorance. Not only is it a lack of knowledge about something very great—the "numinous majesty"—it is a perfectly proper relationship to that most high Other. Our ignorance is not a sign of our limitation so much as an indication of the surpassing greatness of that from which we are separated. Not to know is a kind of knowing. The gloom of unknowing is really a "super-bright" gloom. For this reason mystics make much out of the *transcendence* of the divine.

Of the three major theistic religions of the West, Islam seems on the face of it to be the least likely place for mysticism to find a home, since Muslims commonly describe Allah in terms that make him utterly unapproachable. In the words of an Islamic scholar, Allah is "the One, Eternal, and Almighty God, far above human feelings and aspirations—the Lord of His slaves, not the Father of His children; a judge meting out stern justice to sinners, and extending His mercy only to those who avert His wrath by repentance, humility, and unceasing works of devotion; a God of fear rather than love."[8] The desire for union with such a Deity seems so unlikely that it is often suggested that Sufism, the major mystical tradition in Islam, can only be explained as the incursion of foreign religious influences. It is well known that in the early centuries of Islam there was extensive dialogue with Christian monastics and with Jewish Talmudists and Cabalists. Moreover, the rapid expansion of the Islamic empire to the East meant exposure to both Buddhism and Hinduism. Clear signs of each of these influences can be found in Islamic thought. And yet, "Even if Islam had been miraculously shut off from contact with foreign religions and philosophies, some form of mysticism would have arisen within it, for the seeds were already there."[9] We understand what those seeds are: the mystics commanding sense of the transcendence of the divine.

This great transcendence, this numinous majesty, however, is not a reference to the unbridgeable *distance* between ourselves and the holy; it also includes the infinite closeness of the Other. All mystical literature makes much of the paradoxical remoteness and nearness of the divine. A memorable use of this paradox occurs in a classical meditative work *The Vision of God,* by Nicholas of Cusa (1460–1460), who wrote it at the request of the monks in a Benedictine monastery who sought "an easy path unto mystical theology." Nicholas makes use of the metaphor of an icon or picture of God whose eyes follow one no matter at what angle or what distance one is standing from it. God is "omnivoyant"; he possesses "absolute sight." There is no way one can evade this vision. This metaphor has the effect of emphasizing the *thereness* of God, his irreducible transcendence and elevation above all things. We can detect here the strong influence of Dionysius on Nicholas, for the omnivoyant God is certainly above all knowing, since even our knowledge of this God falls beneath his gaze and cannot therefore reach up to seize the origin of that seeing itself. And yet, at the same time, the metaphor suggests the infinite closeness of God inasmuch as there is nothing in one which is not seen; there is no space in the self with which God is not completely intimate.

This could be said by any theist about God. But what makes Nicholas a genuine mystic is the way he carries the metaphor still further. "Thy vision, Lord, is Thine essence,"[10] he exclaims. God is not something that sees, but *is* that very seeing. Moreover, I am not a mere object that happens to fall under the glance of God; my existence is dependent on my being seen by God: "I exist in that measure in which Thou art with me, and since Thy look is Thy being, I am because Thou dost look at me, and if Thou didst turn Thy glance from me I should cease to be."[11] It follows from this that if I am held in existence by the sight of God the essence of my existence is my own vision. I exist only so far as I can see, but everything that I see God also sees. Therefore, though my vision is severely limited, all my seeing is nonetheless coincidental with God's sight. Paradoxically, by seeing what God sees I have a kind of vision of the invisible deity: "Thou, therefore, my invisible God, art seen of all and art seen in all seeing. Thou art seen by every person that seeth, in all that may be seen, and in every act of seeing, invisible as Thou art, and freed from all such conditions, and exalted above all for evermore."[12] I see God, but I do not see God; I see as God, but I am not God. This is the paradox we first met in Dionysius. It is ignorance, but a powerful ignorance.

Another widely cited expression of this same paradox is Augustine's declaration, "Thou wert more inward to me than my most inward part, and higher than my highest."[13] It is true that some mystics endeavor to cross over toward the transcendent by traveling outward. This is what is commonly called "nature mysticism."[14] But far more commonly the journey is inward. Here Augustine is typical. He knows that the only place in the universe where we can approach God "is the centre of our own soul. There He waits for us; there He meets us; there He speaks to us. To seek Him, therefore, we must enter into our own interior."[15] This is an instance in which the mystic *seems* to be saying that the soul is itself divine, as the Platonist would declare; but, in fact, what is never forgotten is that, though it dwells within the Divine, it is still absolutely transcendent and infinitely far from us.

If the mystic's single, most compelling desire is to pass over the separating void, it is therefore obvious at the very beginning that this can be achieved only by an emormous effort. Mystical literature frequently warns of the great trials that lie ahead for anyone taking up this path. There are no instant successes, no sudden and transporting visions, that end the quest on the spot; there is no virtuosic leap from here to there. We are in fact cautioned against the seductive quality of visions, for it is one thing to see the other side in a blinding insight, and it is another to be there. One can reasonably expect many years of disciplined prayer and meditation before even the first weak signs of progress appear. Indeed, once the awareness of the abyss has dawned and one is possessed of the desire to cross it, there is at first no understanding of how one might even begin. There is only a sense of one's own incapacity for the task.

A frequent teaching is that we are so distant from our goal that we are not able to search for it at all, despite what might be years of disciplined effort. One can seek only if one is first sought, we are instructed. In the words of the twelfth-century mystic, Bernard of Clairvaux (1090—1153), "every soul among you that is seeking God should know that it has been anticipated by him, and has been sought by him before it began to seek him."[16] And from the literature of the Sufis: "For thirty years I sought God. But when I looked carefully, I saw that in reality God was the Seeker and I was the sought."[17]

We are not to ignore the importance of the thirty years, for it underlines the degree to which one is separated from the divine at the beginning. If God is the seeker it can only be because we are lost, desperately lost, and it will take even God a great length of time to arrange our return. Mystics commonly describe the path of return as one of succeeding stages. In one of the most powerful metaphors for the stages of mystical progress, Teresa of Ávila (1515—1582), in her *Interior Castle*, says she began "to think of the soul as if it were a castle made of a single diamond or of very clear crystal, in which there are many rooms, just as in Heaven there are many mansions."[18] As one enters one's own soul with ordinary self-knowledge, one is only entering into the first mansion. With increasing meditation and ascetic discipline the second mansion can be entered, and onward toward the seventh that lies at the very center of the soul where God himself dwells. What has made Teresa's book a classic is the psychological perceptiveness and the astonishing personal candor with which she chronicles the long journey through the mansions of the soul. She likens herself to a butterfly who, once unfolded from its cocoon, attempts in its bewilderment and fragility to find its way back to its home.

Sufis speak variously of seven or eight stages as the soul ascends from that which passes away toward the eternal. When the soul has reached its goal and loses consciousness of all that is changeable, they speak of this moment as "the passing away of the passing away."[19] Augustine also speaks of seven stages, the highest of which is contemplation in which we behold "Ultimate Reality, Absolute Being—That Which Is."[20] The English mystic Richard Rolle (c. 1300–1349), like many others, follows Augustine in placing contemplation at the summit of mystical achievement. We reach this summit by following the path of reading, prayer, and meditation. "In *reading* God speaks to us; in *prayer* we speak to God. In *meditation* angels come down to us and teach us that we err not. . . ." The *contemplation* that follows is "the joyful song of God's love taken into the mind, with the sweetness of angel's praise."[21] St. John of the Cross, in his *Dark Night of the Soul,* likens the stages of ascent to "a ladder of love." The steps of the ladder "by which the soul mounts, one by one, to God, are ten."[22] On the final step the soul has "become wholly assimilated to God, by reason of the clear and immediate vision of God which it then possesses."[23] Although early Jewish mysticism did not develop any sense of an ultimate union with the divine, there was nonetheless an arduous and ecstatic ascent that each adept was expected to make through seven heavens.[24] Even St. Paul speaks of being carried away into the seventh heaven in an ecstatic experience,[25] certainly an early echo of the mystic's acknowledgment of the necessity of the soul's journey of return.

There are numerous attempts among students of mysticism to find some sort of scheme by which all the stages of mystical experience might be standardized, or by which we might find the inner essence of the experience.[26] This seems to be a mistaken approach simply because of the great variety of the pictured stages. Instead, what we should take notice of is the necessity of a journey to begin with. When mystics speak of the abyss, the infinite distance between themselves and the divine, when they speak of the God beyond knowledge, residing unseen in the soul and seeking them long before they know it, they are expressing their sense of being lost. They are in the wrong place; they are aliens in a homeless land without the merest knowledge of the manner of return. They belong somewhere else; they have a home from which they have been separated; they belong *to* someone else, but they have forgotten whom.

We can see here how far we have come from Platonism. Socrates' desire for immortality was the wish to continue the conversation with *these* friends or with similarly minded persons, a conversation in which he was already engaged. He longed for a continuation of his familiar world and therefore of his present self. It is safe to say that the popular appeal of the Platonic doctrine of immortality owes to its pro- mise that we can continue all of our present associations. Simply to exist forever in isolation hardly seems desirable. Therefore to look for- ward to survival is not the desire to take up a journey, but a desire to end one. It is not a longing to be changed, but to remain forever the same.

It is not immortality that the mystic desires. Mystics have no longing to continue anything, much less the present life in its alienated form. Instead, they have a passion to be transformed into something radically different from the familiar terms of earthly existence, something of which they have but the faintest intimation. For this reason biological death seems to have very little significance for any mystic. It is neither an evil in itself, nor is it something to be welcomed. It is not the point of entrance into another mode of existence, neither is it an end to this existence. The reason for this is that the transformation the mystic seeks is not to a way of being that lies somewhere beyond the present in a time that has not yet come, but a way of being that one already was and in fact still is. It is not a transformation from what one is to what one is not, but just the reverse—from what one is not to what one truly is. Therefore, the mystic is not attempting to be freed from mortality but from self-contradiction, not from limitations as such but from the ina- bility to be in fact what one is. Or, to preserve the proper mystical paradoxicality on this point, we could hardly do better than to quote the great Sufi teacher, Junayd, for whom the supreme aim was "to be as he was before he was."[27]

Starting with the paradoxical quality of the mystic's ignorance (not to know is to know), we saw that the mystic interprets this darkness as a sign of the distance one must yet travel to overcome the void that separates the human and the divine. The journey is not outward into a greater familiarity with the world, but inward toward a greater famil- iarity with the soul from which we are deeply alienated. The void between us and the divine, therefore, is a void between us and our- selves at the same time. The death of the body is irrelevant to this separation. In fact, biological death does not seem to be death at all. The mystic is unconcerned with the kind of struggle in which the Platonist engaged, between the soul and the body. The mystic's struggle is be- tween the soul and itself. It is the enormous effort of overcoming one's own existential self-contradiction inasmuch as one is not what one truly is. Where then is death, and how does the mystic conceive it? We must look more closely at the way in which mystics understand the interiority of their struggle.

This quality of existential self-contradiction, which the mystic experiences, shows itself in the heightened sense of sin that runs through mystical literature and in the resulting desire for penitence and self-mortification. If God is a great distance from us, both without and within, we not only have the sense of a long and treacherous journey ahead, but also find ourselves burdened with a self we do not want to be, and in fact are not. It is as if the possession of this self is a mortal burden, a cross, a condemnation, a constant reminder that *we are not who we are*. For such a condition mystics found traditional language about sin to be most appropriate.

However, consistent with the fact that mystics have no interest in immortality, they rarely consider sin in relation to some subsequent act of divine *punishment*.* There is something about sin that is already terrible in itself. Teresa of Ávila speaks of the way in which the favors of God are often not enjoyed because one is too mindful of one's sinfulness. "It is as if a mighty river were running through the soul and from time to time bringing these favours with it. But its sins are like the river's slimy bed; they are always fresh in its memory; and this is a heavy cross to it."[28]

But just what is that slimy bed of sin? Is it truly a matter of wrongdoing, or of violating commandments? Or is it something still more fundamental? It is noteworthy that while Allah, Jahweh, and the Christian God are all portrayed in sacred writings as jealous lawgivers demanding obedience under the threat of punishment, there is among mystics essentially no concern whatsoever with legal unrighteousness. The question is a little more complicated in the Christian mystics since in the Christian scriptures the face of God appears redemptive and loving. But that is only because Christ has suffered the punishment all persons deserve for their incurable unrighteousness under the law. The mystics have much to say about Christ, but it has much more to do with the union with God by way of Christ's suffering than it does with Christ's satisfaction of one's legal insufficiency before the Lawgiver.

Teresa herself offers a clue to what could be meant by the slimy bed of sin in her pronounced indifference to the welfare of the body: "Al-

---

*There are noteworthy exceptions to this observation. Thomas à Kempis, certainly a bona fide mystic, has this to say about sin and punishment: "What will the flames feed upon, but your sins? The more you spare yourself now, and indulge the desires of the body, the more severe will be your punishment hereafter, and the more fuel you gather for the flames. . . . Then will the slothful be spurred by fiery goads, and the gluttonous tormented by dire hunger and thirst" (*The Imitation of Christ*, pp. 59ff.).

though we get few or no comforts here, we shall be making a great mistake if we worry over our health, especially as it will not be improved by our anxiety about it—that I well know."[29] Teresa's unusual advice is not to take care of the body so that its illnesses will interrupt one's spiritual labors, but to ignore the body altogether whether ill or healthy. What we have here is not a simple renunciation of the flesh as something evil in itself, but a rejection of anything that will encourage us to maintain our residence as aliens in this foreign and homeless land. Indifference to the body is cultivated by all mystics, although almost never do they withdraw from active engagement in the human community. St. Catherine of Siena, for example, though she was a philanthropist, reformer, and politician, actually lived for years with no more sustenance than the consecrated wafer that she received daily at Holy Communion.[30]

When mystics speak of bodily pain and physical suffering, they are not complaining about their natural illnesses, nor even the evil corruption of the flesh; they are giving expression to the incommensurability between mystical experience and the mortal frame in which it occurs. The body simply cannot endure it. "Believe me, children," wrote the great German mystic Johannes Tauler, "one who would know much about these high matters would often have to keep his bed, for his bodily frame could not support it."[31]

Indifference to the body is, of course, not a sufficient end in itself; it actually belongs to the larger mystical desire to develop an indifference to selfhood altogether. Instead of indifference, one might even say that mystics are openly hostile to selfhood. The empirical self of concrete experience seems to be the very agent by which we become attached to the homeless region on this side of the abyss between the human and the divine. Therefore there is always the suggestion that if we can do away with the empirical self we shall have begun our journey, perhaps even found the way to the true self that we already are. "The whole of Sufism rests on the belief that when the individual self is lost, the Universal Self is found. . . ." Thus the Sufi injunction, "Die before ye die."[32]

Extreme acts of penitance, common among mystics, seem to have this intention. Scholem reports that among the Hasidim of medieval Germany there circulated the story of a simple and honest man who accidentally washed away the ink from a piece of parchment on which the name of God had been written. As penance for his offense against the honor of God's name he chose to lie down on the doorstep of the synagogue each day during the hour of prayer, forcing the worshippers to step over him, "and if one trod on him whether deliberately or by accident, he rejoiced and thanked God."[33] In Sufi literature there is the story of a shopowner who responded, when told that his shop had been destroyed by fire, that he was then free from the care of it. "Later, there came word that his shop was intact but that those around it had been destroyed. Then Sari gave all he possessed to the poor and took the way of a Sufi."[34]

Each of these stories evokes the image of persons who easily set their selfhood aside in order that the luminous majesty of the divine might be more fully displayed. More frequently mystics speak of the great difficulty of self-renunciation. If the slimy bed of sin is but one's attachment to the concrete self, we are more often than not deeply mired in it. To pull away and to drift freely in the transparent current of divine goodness is a work of spiritual virtuosity that far exceeds the capacities of ordinary seekers. The immensity of this labor and the poor progress in it lead mystics often to speak of despair and sadness. Theresa of Ávila would weep for days, developing terrible headaches. The anonymous author of *The Cloud of Unknowing* (written c. 1370) writes that "without God's very special and freely given grace, and your own complete and willing readiness to receive it, this stark awareness of yourself cannot possibly be destroyed. And this readiness is nothing else than a strong, deep sorrow of spirit." However, this important advice is then added: "Everyone has something to sorrow over, but none more than he who knows and feels that he is."[35] Again we must remember that *this sorrow is not moral, it is existential; it is a sadness that comes from the mere fact that one exists.*

Here we have a clear view of the mystics' distinctive understanding of death and the grieving response to it. Death is not *change* imposed on the mind or *dispersion* happening to the body, but *separation* of the soul from its divine ground. Now, since the divine dwells in the most interior parts of the soul, death is also separation from ourselves. This is why mystics typically describe their present life in terms of sorrow, gloominess, and hopelessness; it is a life of constant bereavement. It is as though the self we currently inhabit is dead and we are hopelessly cut off from the living soul, just as we are completely cut off from a loved friend whom death has taken. The indifference of mystics to the body resembles one's attitude to a corpse. The "dead" body is not evil; it is not a snare by which we are dragged into the excesses of the flesh, as it is often described by the dualist—even occasionally by Plato. It is simply a constant reminder that life lies elsewhere. What the true mystic seeks is not a resuscitated corpse or a reanimated soul in a once-dead body. This would only be an attempt to overcome grief by way of making the separation permanent—the classical strategy of grief, the attempting to achieve a living death. *What is desired instead is the complete death of that which is separated.* Leave the lost, isolated soul to death, and turn back to life. There is no other cure for grief.

But this cure is extreme. It means leaving much behind—everything in fact that belongs to us as separate persons, and that means everything we ordinarily consider our own, even our very selves. Initially we can only experience this as a terrible impoverishment. But just as our ignorance is a sign of God's surpassing majesty, so is our poverty a sign of God's exceeding richness. It is exactly to such a poverty that Eckhart urges us: "He is a poor man who wants nothing, knows nothing, and has nothing." To *want* nothing is, for Eckhart, not even to want to do the will of God; it is to will absolutely nothing at all, to allow the will to die. To *know* nothing is to be empty of all knowledge, even the knowledge of God; it is to be as empty as one was before one existed. To *have* nothing is to be so impoverished that one does not even have a place for God to act: "if God wants to act in the soul, he himself must be the place in which he acts—and that he would like to do."[36]

It is easy to understand why Eckhart, in spite of his enormous popularity as a preacher, was tried for heresy, for he pushed ahead until the paradoxicality of mystical instruction took on the appearance of intended sacrilege: "Thus we say that a man should be so poor that he is not and has not a place for God to act in. To reserve a place would be to maintain distinctions. *Therefore I pray God that he may quit me of god,* for [his] unconditioned being is above god and all distinctions."[37]

Other mystics are usually less inclined to use hyperbole than Eckhart, but they are often capable of vivid expression. In *The Cloud of Unknowing* this crucial moment in the mystical experience is described in metaphorical language:

> just as this cloud of unknowing is as it were above you, between you and God, so you must also put a cloud of forgetting beneath you and all creation. We are apt to think that we are very far from God because of this cloud of unknowing between us and him, but surely it would be more correct to say that we are much farther from him if there is no cloud of forgetting between us and the whole created world.[38]

There is no denying that the anonymous author of this classic is counseling us to regard our present selves as corpses; live as if dead to this world. Now, unfortunately, the cloud of unknowing separates us from God as well as the world, and there is no hope that it will be removed: "if you are to feel him or see him in this life, it must always be in this cloud, in this darkness."[39]

Because we are wrapped in ignorance, as completely as a corpse is wrapped in its shroud, we have entered into that awful space which Jan van Ruysbroeck (1293–1381) has called "the waylessness of God" and St. John of the Cross (1542–1591) has named "the dark night of the soul." Thus Ruysbroeck:

> The abysmal waylessness of God is so dark and so unconditioned that it swallows up within itself every Divine way and activity, and all the attributes of the Persons within the rich compass of the essential unity. . . . This is the dark silence in which all lovers lose themselves. But if we would prepare ourselves for it . . . we should strip ourselves of all but our very bodies, and we should flee forth into the wild sea, whence no created thing can draw us back again.[40]

St. John of the Cross speaks of a darkness that may last many years, convincing the soul that God has forever withheld his blessings, depriving it even of the ability to pray.[41] We are not to forget, however, that it is God who has brought us into the dark night, and that there are therefore great benefits that come from it even before we are aware of them: "This is the first and principal benefit caused by this arid and dark night of contemplation: the knowledge of oneself and one's misery." If we had continued in our former prosperity we should not have known the true lowliness of the soul.[42] Ruysbroeck advises that we contend with the waylessness of God by recklessly throwing ourselves into that "wild sea, whence no created thing can draw us back again." St. John of the Cross encourages us to expect that beneath all our misery God will have infused a "secret" contemplation, a secret that is "to be hidden from the work of the understanding and of the other faculties."[43]

After describing the "desert" into which one is led by complete poverty and emptiness of the soul, Eckhart also asserts that God has been at work in us, though invisibly—a God hidden in the core of the soul, while we have been looking outward to seek a God in the world and by way of ideas. The soul suspects "that something is afoot, even though it does not know how or what." We are coming to possess an "unknown knowledge"[44] that corresponds to what St. John of the Cross called "secret contemplation." It is a knowledge that comes exclusively from God and can be received only "by means of forgetting and losing self-consciousness. It is in the stillness, in the silence, that the word of God is to be heard." This loss of self-consciousness is a perfect igno-rance of all things worldly and divine, and it is this very ignorance that "will be ennobled and adorned with supernatural knowledge. It is by reason of this fact that we are made perfect by what happens to us rather than by what we do."[45]

This secret and unknown knowledge is obviously of a sort unavailable to the corpse of our present existence. It may not seem to be a knowledge at all. What we want, Eckhart says, is not "the God we have thought of, for when the thought slips the mind, that god slips with it. What we want is rather the reality of God, exalted far above any human thought or creature."[46] Merely to have thoughts about God is to have something adventitious intervening between the mind and its object; to have the reality of God is to be so flooded with a presence that one could know nothing else.

We have described the mystics' attitude toward the discovery of their existential isolation from the divine as one of sorrow, or grief. They do not attempt to cure this grief, but rather to yield to it and, recognizing their total spiritual poverty, to continue dwelling in their dark night of the soul. What is being sought here is acknowledgment of the fact that we are not grieving over someone else's death, but our own. We *are* the corpse that raises our sorrow—therefore we can only accept the fact that we have no more than what a corpse has. We have nothing—not even a place for God to act. This places absolutely all agency in the numinous majesty, infinitely distant, but infinitely close.

The metaphor of the corpse is useful here because it brings out what is easily the most problematical aspect of mysticism: the union of the soul with the transcendent Other. The mystic is not looking for a restitution of the now-expired soul, but for the entrance of God into the place of the soul. On the face of it, this is equivalent to arguing that one has vanished into God and no longer exists; god has *replaced* the soul. This is obviously the point at which orthodox theists find mysticism most unacceptable, for it certainly appears that they have rejected theism outright. That is, they have given away any possibility for saying that persons stand *over/against* the divine. They seem to have blown away all human limitations by making the soul divine.

There is no doubt that mystics do encourage this interpretation, since they have left a literature filled with rapturous, exultant exclamations of the union of the soul with God. The great Jewish mystic Abulafia (1240–c.1291) suggests that the dead soul is closed off from the divine by seals and knots, and that the mystic's task is one of breaking the seals and untying the knots. In what corresponds to guided meditation in the Christian tradition, he recommends focused reflection on the letters of the Hebrew alphabet and their configurations, particularly as they constitute the name of God. Abulafia filled books with descriptions of the proper discipline to follow in this meditation, all of which is but a preparation for the final transformation when the restraints on the soul suddenly give way: "The seals, which keep it locked up in its normal state and shut off from the divine light, are relaxed, and the mystic finally dispenses with them altogether."[47] While Abulafia does not attain the extremes found in other mystics in his description of the soul's union with the divine, it is clear that with all the restraints gone it is difficult to mark the point where the human ends and the divine begins.

The more extreme statements are found in the writings and stories of the Islamic mystics. Abu Ali of Sin once exclaimed that for "Thirty years the high God was my mirror, now I am my own mirror." He later offered an explanation of this puzzling remark: "That which I was I am no more, for 'I' and 'God' is a denial of the unity of God. Since I am no more, the high God is His own mirror." He concluded this explanation with a statement that can only appear outrageous to the traditional theist: "I went from God to God, until they cried from me in me, 'O Thou I!' "[48]

Abu Yazid of Bistam, a student of Abu Ali, described an experience of ascending to the throne of God and finding it empty. He took possession of it at once, proclaiming, "I am I."[49] There is also the story of Rabia, a saintly woman Sufi, whose servant called to her one day in the spring, "Come out and behold what God has made. But Rabia answered: Come in and behold the Maker."[50] Most notorious of all was the tenth-century mystic al-Hallaj who was crucified for uttering the supreme Islamic blasphemy, Ana 'l-Haqq: "I am god."[51]

No one in the Jewish or Christian mystical traditions has gone so far as to exclaim, "I am God," but in all great mystics there is an unmistakable flow in that direction. Consider Eckhart's statement:

> By nature the core of the soul is sensitive to nothing but the divine Being, unmediated. Here God enters the soul with all he has and not in part. He enters the soul through its core and nothing may touch that core except God himself. No creature enters it, for creatures must stay outside in the soul's faculties, from when the soul receives ideas, behind which it has withdrawn as if to take shelter.[52]

Elsewhere, when he speaks of that portion of the soul God enters, he often observes that "there is something in the soul so closely akin to God that it is already one with him and need never be united to him."[53]

However, for all this documentation, we still must come to terms

with the fact that essentially all mystics considered themselves orthodox, and no small number of them went through hopeless heresy
trials, imprisonment, and even death never admitting to a single
heterodox detail.

Here the key to the proper understanding of mysticism lies in a
subtlety unhappily overlooked by its orthodox tormentors. While mystics speak of the union of the soul with God, they scrupulously avoid
declaring that the soul *is* God. Even al-Hallaj's "I am God" has never
been renounced by his Sufi followers. In fact, they have defended it by
arguing that he had gone into an ecstatic state, and it was therefore not
al-Hallaj, but God himself, who was speaking through his selfless body.
In this same way Muslims have understood the God who spoke through
the burning bush to Moses.[54] What is implied here is that the mystic
does not have a *vision* of God from afar, but an *experience* of God
working through the soul—through the very center of the soul, closer to
us than we are to ourselves.

Eckhart is probably most helpful here, because he wants it made
clear that when he speaks of the *union* of the soul with God he does not
mean *identity*. He suggests that we understand union in terms of *likeness*. The soul, we are told, both hates and loves its likeness with the
divine. It loves the fact that likeness is established by God and not the
soul, but it hates the fact that it is *only* likeness and not unity. Remember Eckhart's sermon on the soul's rage that it is not God. Since
likeness is not unity it implies multiplicity, difference, and even opposition. The manifest desire of the fire to make the wood like itself presupposes a prior opposition of the two. Eckhart says of this "that as
long as there is mere likeness, as between wood and fire, there can be
neither true pleasure nor quiet, neither rest nor contentment." On the
other hand, this despised likeness, since it is begotten of the One that is
without beginning, is "the source of that glowing flower: love." To be
sure, "love's nature is such that it appears only where two are; but itself
turns out to be one and uniform and never twofold; for love cannot exist
divided. In love's nature, two function as one, and there is ardor, willing, and longing."[55]

The insight that in love two function as one tells us a great deal
about mysticism in its highest form. *The union of which the mystics
speak is not a conjunction of substances, but a congruence of action.* It
is always distorting to say that the soul *exists in* God; it may be more
correct to think that the mystics believe that the soul *acts with* God.
This discussion of the difference between likeness and identity in Eckhart's writings exposes two fundamental themes of mysticism. First,
the soul is conceived not as substance, but as *act*. Second, mystics

universally describe this act in its supreme form as *love. The union of which mystics speak is therefore not ontological but erotic.* The union with God must be a union in movement and not in being. When Teresa spoke of the slimy bed of sin along which the current of God's blessings flows, what makes the bed slimy is not what it contains in itself, but its inability to detach itself and to flow freely with the vitality of God.

Some of the most notorious distortions in the interpretation of mystical literature have to do with its erotic quality. It is common to caricature the passion, particularly in the writings of women mystics, or the ecstasy, which has been captured in their romanticized statues, as orgasmic rapture. The aspersion here is that mysticism is but the sublimated sexuality of virginal and self-denying women. Without question there are frequent expressions of surprisingly explicit erotic imagery, but these are by no means restricted to the women mystics. St. John of the Cross composed a series of verses, on which he then based his *Dark Night of the Soul,* among which are the following:

> Upon my flowery breast, kept wholly for himself alone,
> There he stayed sleeping, and I caressed him,
>   And the fanning of the cedars made a breeze.
>
> The breeze blew from the turret as I parted his locks;
> With his gentle hand he wounded my neck
>   And caused all my senses to be suspended.
>
> I remained, lost in oblivion;
>   My face I reclined on the Beloved.
> All ceased and I abandoned myself,
>   Leaving my cares forgotten among the lilies.[56]

Christian mystics particularly refer to the highest moment of spiritual ecstasy as the "spiritual marriage," speaking of Christ as the Spouse for whom one experiences a mounting and inexhaustible love. Bernard of Clairvaux is especially fond of this metaphor, speaking at length of the soul's matrimony with the Word (Christ). Practically the last words he wrote in his exceedingly eventful and accomplished life are concerned with the matrimonial embrace of the soul with the Word: "indeed, a mother has joy in her offspring; but a bride has greater joy in the embraces of her spouse. Dear are children, the pledges of affection; but kisses give greater joy. It is a good work to save many souls; but to be transported and to be with the Word, that is far more delightful."[57]

The erotic nature of union is found in all mystical traditions and may or may not contain sexual allusions. The Jewish Hasidim believe that afection and altruism follow from any genuine mystical experience.[58] The Sufis' love poetry is often indistinguishable from the expressions of worldly lovers, but their literature is also rich with examples of other forms of sacrifice and tenderness. Nicholson relates the tale of the Sufis Nuri and Raqqam who with several others had been sentenced to death for heresy:

> When the executioner approached Raqqam, Nuri arose and offered himself in his friend's place with the utmost cheerfulness and submission. All the spectators were astounded. The executioner said, "Young man, the sword is not a thing that people are so eager to meet; and your turn has not yet arrived." Nuri answered, "My religion is founded on unselfishness. Life is the most precious thing in the world: I wish to sacrifice for my brethren's sake the few moments which remain.[59]

This same affection extends to pity toward animals. A certain Sufi saint discovered when he returned home from a journey that the cardamon seed he had bought in a distant city contained a few ants. He immediately walked back to that city, a distance of several hundred miles, to return the creatures to their home.

The risk in interpreting such material, and the reason why it is so easily misunderstood, is that we are often inclined toward the kind of explanation we associated with Freudian psychoanalysis: we see all of this passion as something *sublimated*, assuming that if the impulses of these mystics were not restrained they would be directly engaged in acts of physical sexuality. Such an interpretation would not only cause us to overlook the true nature of mysticism, it is also a serious misreading of Freud. As we shall see in greater detail in the following chapter, Freud regards physical sexuality itself as something repressed; it is the result of severe limitations placed on the much more primitive and spontaneous flow of energy, or *libido*. What is more, the libido, the energizing source for all human actions, is fundamentally the desire for union. Instead of considering the erotic raptures of the mystic as a symbolic but failed attempt to be physically sexual, we should regard the sexual act as the symbolic, but tragically unsuccessful, effort to achieve true union.

The mystics speak of love, then, not because it represents something else, but because it is the one human act that *cannot* be reduced to something else. It is love that constitutes the original spontaneity, the irreducible *subjectness* of the soul. To quote St. Bernard again:

Love is sufficient by itself, it pleases by itself, and for its own sake. It is itself a merit, and itself its own recompense. Love seeks neither cause nor fruit beyond itself. Its fruit is its use. I love because I love; I love that I may love. Love, then, is a great reality. It is the only one of all the movements, feelings, and affections of the soul in which the creature is able to respond to its Creator, though not upon equal terms, and to repay like with like.[60]

What plainly emerges in this passage is the importance of *freedom* to mystics. It is not merely that the soul is understood as an act, and its union with God erotic rather than ontological, it is that this is a free act on the part of the soul. It can refuse the union; it can choose freely to remain separate; it can also freely choose to be its own corpse. The soul is a self-initiating entity, much like Plato's, with the important difference that Plato thought the soul to be a substance, where the mystics understand it to be an act. If the soul is a substance it must exist as it is regardless of its acts; if the soul is *act* it is what it does, and it does what it does for no reason or cause outside itself. "I love because I love," Bernard said, "I love that I may love."

However, it becomes immediately apparent that there is a difficulty with this emphasis on freedom; it raises the possibility of an inherent contradiction in mysticism. How can freedom be emphasized along with the self's complete incapacity to achieve the desired union? It is impossible to think of a corpse acting at all, much less acting *freely*.

Mystics are not, in fact, inconsistent here, and the reason lies in the fundamental conviction that the achievement of union is possible only by way of a *return*. The self's journey is always from its lost, isolated, existentially self-contradictory condition to its true condition; it is a passage from a dead present to the eternal origin of life. The importance of the spontaneity of the loving act alerts us to the fact that the mystic does not long to *vanish* into the immensity of the sublime All (as interpreters of mysticism frequently assert), but to recover the ceaseless spring of their own vitality, to enter into the jeweled center of the soul where one can live in perfect agreement with the very source of spontaneity of all that is. This inward journey into what Freud called the unconscious is not a spiral descent into an isolated cell, but a discovery of the manifold ways in which the individual self is connected to the whole, and consequently the discovery of the way one can abandon the ignorant and doomed attempts to preserve the self-contradictory existence of the individualized ego. But it is a journey that is also backward in time; it is a return to a prior state. The mystic can become what "I already am" only by way of being "what I was before I was." The logic of this backward movement is obvious: *if I am seeking the inexhausti-*

ble source of spontaneity it must be that, because my seeking is itself
an expression of that spontaneity, the source lies behind me and not
ahead. It precedes all that I do. I can only seek then for what I already
have. I can only know what I have already forgotten. It is precisely this
insight that Freud followed when he designed the psychoanalytic
method as an investigation of one's personal past.

We have observed that the mystic is indifferent to biological death
and never speaks of immortality in the usual sense as the survival of the
soul. The continuity that the mystic seeks to overcome the discontinuity of death is a dynamic union with the original spontaneity of all
that has being—a mode of existence that has no ending, but also has no
beginning. Why then does the mystic not speak of an immortal soul
that both preexists and succeeds this life? Because the mystic never
thinks of an eternal object, but only of an eternal act. It is not the
mystic's desire to become a being that has endless spontaneity, but to
be that eternal self-origination.

May we say then that there is no death at all for the mystic? The
answer to this is yes—and no. It is plain that the concrete, empirical
self, caught in its personal history, separated from its origin, must die.
The seals must be blown away; it must be left to wither on a deeper
psychic desert: "Die before ye die." But within the self-originating act,
within love, there is no death, for that which is its origin has no beginning and no end.

What does away with the apparent contradiction between the self's
utter helplessness and the emphasis on freedom is the fact that the
helpless, impotent self is the separate, cadaverous ego that has its being
in a specific historical context. That self is dead and must be left to its
death. The great struggle that emerges here, the reason there are many
stages to pass through, along with great sadness and gloom, is that one
must indeed live by way of dying. One deals with grief by yielding to it.
Because we are so completely stranded in our ignorance we cannot
possibly reach out for positive hope, rely on a guiding vision, or do
anything at all that will directly set ourselves on the journey. The only
thing that we can truly do is to burn out all such impulses.

We can now see why in sharp contrast to the Platonists and
Epicureans—and, as will subsequently become clear, all other religious
and intellectual traditions—the mystics conceive of death as a choice.
We have stressed the power of death that is common to everyone's
experience. Where is the power of death for mystics? The terrible force
of death does not owe to the willful agency of something outside ourselves, but from the very fact that we are inherently free. Nothing is so
difficult to alter as one's own free decisions. It is not a passage from

bondage to freedom, but from freedom to freedom. We must master one freedom with another. Having freely chosen separation as our existential condition, we must now take the inward step of freely choosing *that* choice. It is not only that we can do with the body what we like, but *we can do with what we like as we like.* That is what it means to *choose* our grief and not merely to suffer it.

We can see in this context why the mystics so frequently speak of *ascending* or *increasing* raptures. Overcoming one freedom with another is not a concluding or final act, it is only a stage that makes possible a still more fundamental freedom. It is a deepening movement that seems to increase exponentially, accelerating itself toward the speed of light, toward infinity. This is the quality of mystical experience captured in the following passage by Jan van Ruysbroeck, who speaks here of what happens when we first feel the touch of God's riches:

> the powers of the soul open themselves, and especially the desirous power; for all the rivers of the grace of God pour forth, and the more we taste them, the more we long to taste; and the more we long to taste, of the more deeply we press into contact with him; and the more deeply we press into contact with God, the more the flood of his sweetness flows through us and over us; and the more we are thus drenched and flooded, the better we feel and know that the sweetness of God is comprehensible and unfathomable.[61]

This brings us to the final portion of this portrait of mysticism—what we shall call here its *creative subjectivity.* The consequence of understanding both God and the soul as *act* rather than being is that neither can have objective existence; to exist at all they must exist as subjects. To be a subject is to be the origin of one's own actions. Consistent with the erotic quality of the dynamic union of the soul with its own origin, mystics are repeatedly drawn to the metaphor of birth. Thus Eckhart states: "It is of the nature of eternal birth that I *have been* eternally, that I *am* now, and *shall be* forever." It is a bit confusing, of course, to unite eternity with *birth,* since birth is always a beginning of something in time, and eternity could scarcely have a beginning. "In my eternal birth," Eckhart continues, clarifying the point, "everything was begotten. I was my own first cause as well as the first cause of everything else. If I had willed it, neither I nor the world would have come to be! If I had not been, there would have been no god."[62]

What happens in an eternal birth is not that *something*—namely, a soul—happens to have its beginning as an eternal object (which is the essence of the theory of immortality). Neither is it the moment in which *all* things have their beginning as objects (which is the theistic doctrine of creation). *Eternity for the mystics is not the beginning of an object but the beginning of a subject.* Eternal birth does not mean the beginning of something in time, but the beginning of time and all temporal things.

True subjectivity *is* eternity, for the simple reason that nothing can precede it in time. All temporally serial precedence is objective. All objects occur in a time that they did not make, but to which they belong. Each object is to be found *at a certain time.* But nothing can precede *me,* as a subject, in time; neither can anything succeed me, for the *before* and the *after* are both relative to my subjectivity. As a subject, I am not *in* a time, but am always the beginning of time. "I am what I was before I was."

The soul is therefore uncreated because it is by nature creative. It cannot be begotten, for it is itself the begetter. As subject the soul cannot be begun by something outside itself, because it would then be an object for that creator. *And most especially, the soul cannot be begun by God,* else it becomes an object to God—and, what is far worse, God becomes an object to the soul. They would then face each other as two objects that could be joined only in substance and not in act. But since God is the one subject that can never be an object the only possible union with him is the erotic union of creative subjectivity.

We must be careful to underscore the *creative* aspect of this subjectivity. Subjects do not spring from objects, but objects can be objects only where there is a subject. Subjectivity is therefore always the beginning of objects. Thus, one does not become subjective in a world of objects that are already created. One eternally begets the world—and, what is more, begets the temporality in which the world exists. Therfore Eckhart can say, "I am the first cause of everything."

This is a decidedly heretica' teaching. It is, of course, immaterial to our own appraisal of the mystics' understanding of death whether it is or is not in agreement with orthodox theism, but it is instructive in this setting to see *why* it diverges—and diverges sharply—from traditional theism. It should be apparent that one of the major charges against mystics—that they had claimed God and the soul to be identical in substance—is quite false, simply because they had done away with the category of substance. Another charge—that the soul is uncreated—seems valid, but in a way more serious than even the most earnest defenders of orthodoxy realized. What was important to them in this matter was the implication that, if uncreated, the soul exists independently of God whose majesty is thereby unacceptably compromised.

There is, however, a consequence of this teaching that is far more threatening to theism. It appears in the way Eckhart ties the soul's uncreatedness to its priority to both being and time. For Eckhart, and in fact for all mystics, the necessity of the soul's return—its journey back out of time into its eternal self-origination, out of objectivity into subjectivity—means that *death is understood not only as separation, but as temporal separation. We are dead insofar as we live in history.* To live truly is to renounce history. The corpse over which the mystic suffers is nothing less than temporally engaged personhood extended backward through a living memory and forward through expectation and hope.

It is the mystics' deep antihistorical impulse that is their real heresy. This runs directly opposed to the central current of all the major theistic religions of the West. This is not in itself an indication of any flaw in mysticism, only a sign of its distinctive conception of death. It is, however, a conception that is not restricted to mystics. We shall next consider another manifestation of the same kind of thinking: psychoanalysis.

Notes

1. F. C. Happhold, ed., *Mysticism: a Study and Anthology.*
2. Pp. 7 ff.
3. Acts 17:22 ff.
4. *Western Mysticism*, p. 20.
5. *The Works of Dionysius the Areopagite* pp. 8 ff.
6. Ibid., p. 17.
7. Ibid., p. 133.
8. Nicholson, *The Mystics of Islam*, p. 21.
9. Ibid., p. 20.
10. *The Vision of God*, p. 39.
11. Ibid., p. 16.
12. Ibid., p. 54.
13. *Confessions*, iii, 11.
14. As an example of this sort of mysticism see Happhold's selections from Richard Jeffries.
15. Quoted in Butler, *Western Mysticism*, p. 29.
16. *Library of Christian Classics*, Vol. XIII, p. 240.
17. Cragg, *The Wisdom of the Sufis*, p. 48.
18. *Interior Castle*, p. 28.
19. Nicholson, p. 60.
20. Butler, p. 24.

21. *Library of Christian Classics,* Vol. XIII, p. 240.
22. St. John of the Cross, *Dark Night of the Soul,* p. 167.
23. Ibid., p. 174.
24. Scholem, pp. 49 ff.
25. Acts 9:1 ff.
26. See, for example, W. T. Stace, *Mysticism and Philosophy,* Ch. 2.
27. Quoted by Zaehner, *Hindu and Muslim Mysticism,* p. 139.
28. *Interior Castle,* p. 170.
29. Ibid., p. 66.
30. Underhill, *Mysticism,* p. 59.
31. Quoted in Underhill, p. 61.
32. Nicholson, pp. 59, 41.
33. Scholem, p. 106.
34. Cragg, p. 41.
35. *The Cloud of Unknowing,* pp. 103 ff.
36. *Meister Eckhart, a Modern Translation,* pp. 227, 230.
37. Ibid., p. 231.
38. *The Cloud of Unknowing,* pp. 58.
39. Ibid., pp. 53 ff.
40. Quoted in Stace, p. 97.
41. *Dark Night of the Soul,* pp. 111, 113, 115.
42. Ibid., pp. 76 ff.
43. Ibid., p. 158.
44. *Meister Eckhart,* p. 100.
45. Ibid., p. 107.
46. Ibid., p. 9.
47. Scholem, p. 137.
48. Nicholson, pp. 17 ff.
49. Zaehner, p. 113.
50. Cragg, p. 85.
51. Nicholson, pp. 149 ff.
52. *Meister Eckhart,* p. 97.
53. Ibid., p. 205.
54. Nicholson, p. 152.
55. *Meister Eckhart,* pp. 56, 54.
56. *Dark Night of the Soul,* p. 34.
57. Quoted in Butler, p. 113.
58. Scholem, p. 92.
59. Nicholson, pp. 107 ff.
60. *Library of Christian Classics,* Vol XIII, p. 112.
61. Ibid., p. 313.
62. *Meister Eckhart,* p. 231.

Bibliography

Anonymous, *The Cloud of Unknowing*, tr. Clifton Wolters (Baltimore: 1961).

Raymond B. Blakney, ed. and tr., *Meister Eckhart, A Modern Translation* (New York: 1941).

Dom Cuthbert Butler, *Western Mysticism*, (New York: 1966).

James M. Clark, *The Great German Mystics: Eckhart, Tauler, and Suso* (Oxford: 1949).

T. W. Coleman, *English Mystics of the 14th Century* (Westport: 1938).

Kenneth Cragg, ed., *The Wisdom of the Sufis* (New York: 1976).

Dionysius, *The Works of Dionysius the Areopagite*, tr. John Parker (Oxford: 1897).

Erwin R. Goodenough, *By Light, Light: The Mystic Gospel of Hellenistic Judaism* (New Haven: 1935).

F. C. Happhold, *Mysticism: A Study and an Anthology* (Baltimore: 1973).

Georgia Harkness, *Mysticism: Its Meaning and Message* (Nashville: 1973).

Saint John of the Cross, *Dark Night of the Soul* (Garden City: 1959).

William Johnston, *The Still Point*, (New York: 1971).

Thomas à Kempis, *The Imitation of Christ*, tr. Leo Shirley-Price (Baltimore: 1952).

Nicholas of Cusa, *The Vision of God*, tr. Emma Gurney Salter (New York: 1969).

Reynold A. Nicholson, *The Mystics of Islam* (New York: 1975).

Rudolf Otto, *Mysticism East and West*, (New York: 1932).

Steven E. Ozment, *Homo Spiritualis* (Leiden: 1969).

Geoffrey Parrinder, *Mysticism in the World's Religions* (New York: 1976).

Ray C. Petry, ed., *Late Medieval Mysticism, Library of Christian Classics*, Vol. XIII (Philadelphia: 1957).

Gershom Scholem, *Major Trends in Jewish Mysticism* (New York: 1974).

Margaret Smith, *An Introduction to the History of Mysticism* (New York: 1930).

W. T. Stace, *Mysticism and Philosophy* (New York: 1960).

D. T. Suzuki, *Mysticism, Christian and Buddhist* (New York: 1971).

Saint Teresa of Ávila, *Interior Castle* (New York: 1961).

Evelyn Underhill, *Mysticism* (New York: 1961).

R. C. Zaehner, *Hindu and Muslim Mysticism* (London, 1960).

4 FREUD AND PSYCHOANALYSIS

No doubt Freud would have been puzzled as to why he would be paired in this study with the mystics rather than with the biologists. To the end of his life he was a strongly convinced materialist, certain that all the phenomena of the mind were but physiological processes in some part of the human anatomy. He was aware that his explorations were taking him into regions where no biologist had ever gone, where only a few poets had ventured, though only tentatively and without bringing any useful scientific light into that aspect of human existence. He did not, however, see himself as a Marco Polo of the inner world, going forth and returning with fascinating curiosities of an alien continent. He believed he was drawing up a map of the human psyche that any other scientist could just as well have done, a map that would be perfectly intelligible to any rational observer. In fact, what significantly added to the public shock at Freud's thought was the scientific authority in which it was clothed. If it had been offered as inspired or demented guesses, it may have raised a scandalized eyebrow or two, but would not have launched anything like the controversial psychoanalytic movement with its enormous impact on the twentieth-century person's self-understanding.

We shall discover here that what sets Freud most emphatically outside the circle of the empirical sciences is a distinction, integral to the full scope of his thought, between *instinct* and *stimulus*. Furthermore, we shall see that a structural tension in his system as a whole, which developed from his consistent differentiation of instinct and stimulus, led to the most radical of all Freud's ideas: the death instinct.

"An instinct," Freud writes, "is distinguished from a stimulus by the fact that it arises from sources within the body, that it operates as a constant force and that the subject cannot avoid it by flight, as is possible with an external stimulus."[1] This brief definition already shows how Freud departs from the sort of refined materialism we find in such persons as Monod and Schrödinger, whose thought we discussed in the Chapter 2. According to Freud's thinking, stimuli are intermittent, accidental in nature. They are always *from without* and can often be avoided. We need not, for example, put our hand in the fire. Instincts, however, come *from within;* they are constant and cannot be avoided. We cannot decide not to be hungry. What is surprising is that Freud would make a distinction here at all. Why is the instinct necessarily from within? What *contains* it? Why is the instinct steady, the stimulus accidental? The external and random nature of stimuli is a perfectly conventional piece of the materialists' view of things, but the internal and persistent "force" of the instincts is puzzling.

Freud did believe, as we indicated, that all human phenomena are of material origin and that the instincts must somehow be grounded in the body's substance. But how? Modern biologists have explanations that were unavailable to Freud. They can show that through subtle genetic coding each of us carries in our physiognomy a programmed set of reactions to certain stimuli. How far this genetic coding extends into "voluntary" behavior is still a subject of considerable debate, but there is no debate over whether these influences are all "external." They are perfectly normal causal relationships that can be accounted for by reference only to the external forces exerted on each entity. It is doubtful, though, that even if Freud had had knowledge of the great genetic discoveries of the last several decades, particularly the discovery of DNA, he would have been able to use them. In at least one important respect Freud's "instinct" does not consist with this way of thinking; genetic programming is something firmly established before the first cellular division of the zygote is formed in the embryo. Subsequent experience has no effect whatsoever on the genetic mechanism. In fact, no experience has any effect on the formation of the genetic heritage. Freud goes to great lengths to show the instincts *are* affected by experience, and in several conspicuous places in his thought speaks of the way in which we inherit, through the instincts, a residue of the experience of countless preceding generations.[2]

The simplest illustration of the alterability of instinct lies in the fact that Freud speaks of only two instincts—hunger and sex—but discusses only one of them. He seems completely disinterested in hunger simply because it cannot be tampered with. If we do not eat we die. If we do not love, on the other hand, we change our lives. We can do a lot more *with* the sexual instinct than with the hunger instinct. This is so important to Freud that he allows hunger to drop out of his theoretical structure altogether and takes the technical term for sexual instinct, *libido,* to stand for all instincts.

In brief Freud has created a space in human existence that is *causally discontinuous* with the rest of physical reality. By doing so he has opened the door, though not all the way as we shall learn, to a doctrine of self-causation in living things, but especially in human existence. The fact that libido can be tampered with at all can only mean that it must to some degree give away its blind, material absoluteness to individual autonomy. He has erected, in any case, a large and unavoidable *anomaly* as a principle support for his theory as a whole, thus leaving himself on the far side of the line that divides science from speculation, or observation from invention. He was himself quite aware that his treatment of instinct was irregular, and he occasionally expresses his misgivings: "The theory of the instincts," he writes, "is so to say our mythology. Instincts are mythical entities magnificent in their indefiniteness."[3]

The effect this distinction has on his thought can only be seen if we attempt a brief reconstruction of the central themes of his theory. In the course of assembling this theory Freud allowed a startling inconsistency to occur that he later mended with his proposal of a death instinct.

Freud's thought often seems to be under the influence of the metaphor of a machine, albeit a complicated machine, in his description of human existence. The body is a kind of mechanism whose energy source is the libido, or instincts. Freud uses the German word *Trieb* for instinct. *Trieb,* which can also be translated as "drive," has a telic quality; it is aimed at a goal. The goal in this case is described as *equilibrium*—a concept of nineteenth-century biology that had a strong appeal for Freud. Equilibrium here does not mean an equal balance of opposed forces as much as a state of perfect rest or the dissipation of all force. The steady approach of libido toward its goal obeys what Freud called the *pleasure principle.* The term pleasure in this instance is negative; it applies to the experience of the organism as the tensions within itself, and between itself and its environment, are being reduced. When perfect equilibrium is reached there is neither pleasure nor unpleasure.

The libido, however, is frequently interrupted. The pleasure principle often finds itself in conflict with *reality*, by which Freud means simply the world external to to the organism. Since the libido is constant and there is no way the organism can "avoid it by flight," a way must be found to reconcile the libido with reality. This becomes the task of the *ego*, which is that part of the self that has a direct, wide-awake perception of the external world. The ego must match up the libidinous impulses of the organism with realistic possibilities for their expression. Freud calls this the application of the *reality principle* to the libido. The only difficulty here lies in the weakness of the ego, which is possessed of little more than thought. It is by means of thought that it must "dethrone" the pleasure principle and erect the reality principle in its place.

Due to the inherent weakness of the ego, there are frequent moments in life when the uninterrupted current of the libido will cause the organism to crash on the disorderly terrain of reality. Freud's chief example of the dangers awaiting the human organism if it follows the pleasure principle exclusively is the Oedipus complex. The young child, almost always a male in Freud's account,* discovers extremely early in life, shortly after birth, in fact, that the path to equilibrium lies in the direction of immediate and constant contact with the mother. Birth, of course, is the archetypal instance of a disentropic, upward development of life, away from the less organized and toward the more organized level of existence. It is therefore a marked disturbance of equilibrium, and the child's manner of restoring that equilibrium is to *return to the state from which it has been torn.* This is the reason for the desire to be in ceaseless contact with the mother; it resembles the earlier state of the womb. Freud speaks of the child at this stage as being "polymorphous-perverse," by which he means that the child uses every part of its body for its libidinous pleasure, that is, the pleasure that comes with reducing the frustration of its instincts. Reality is unkind to this desire, however, and the child must then learn to seek another avenue of return. Since the mother is exclusively available to the child chiefly during episodes of nursing, the child learns to focus its libidinous desires on the oral contact with the breast: "He who sees a

---

*To be fair to Freud here we should cite a footnote in his *New Introductory Lectures*, a late body of writings which represent Freud's most mature views, in which he indicates that the father/son polarity of the Oedipal relationship should in fact be parent/child, but he uses the male pair only as a mode of simpler explanation. In that same essay he discusses the Oedipus complex in full, indicating an equivalency between men and women—an equivalency one cannot find everywhere in Freud's literature.

satiated child sink back from the mother's breast, and fall asleep with reddened cheeks and blissful smile, will have to admit that this picture remains as typical of the expression of sexual gratification in later life."[4]

It is pertinent to observe here that what has shocked so many readers and has led to silly caricatures of Freud's thought is what is in fact a serious misunderstanding of his view of the erotic nature of a child's experience. It is often thought that what Freud has in mind here is the presence of adult lust in an innocent child, with the consequent implication of a depraved infancy. On the contrary, what he is at great pains to make clear is that adult sexuality is itself the distorted and tragic remains of the polymorphous bliss of childhood, haunted by the indistinct memory of something still deeper and still more irenic. This is, by the way, a clear overlap with mystical thought, where the bliss was available only through a return to something that once was whole and is now isolated and lost.

Reality has other withering blows for this desired return to equilibrium. The most threatening of these is in the form of the father, who *also* wants the mother and is often in direct conflict with the desires of the child. The child now has two choices: it can engage the existing reality in battle for the mother, or it can offer the libido an alternative object of desire.

It is important to the understanding of Freud's theory to recall that there is one choice the organism does *not* have: the libido cannot be turned off, it cannot even be turned down. We have returned to the metaphor of the machine, which is driven by the libido like a powerful electric current. When all is normal the machine makes full use of the energy, but when some part of it breaks down, or when it cannot overcome some external resistance to its smooth functioning, it cannot make full use of the current that then has no place to go but into the machine—where it necessarily creates its own space.

The space created by the rejected energy is what Freud at first called the *unconscious*, and later the *id*. The unconscious has several extraordinary characteristics. Freud saw it as "a chaos, a cauldron full of seething excitations." Since it is the energy of the libido it is still dominated by one law only, the pleasure principle: "The logical laws of thought do not apply in the id, and this is true above all of the law of contradiction." Contrary desires exist side by side without diminishing each other in the least. In fact, nothing in the id is diminished; it exists there in all its original force. This means that there "is nothing in the id that corresponds to the idea of time; there is no recognition of the passage of time, and—a thing that is most remarkable and awaits consideration in philosophical thought—no alteration in its mental processes is produced by the passage of time." The rejected desires are "virtually immortal."[5]

Of course, this immortal and seething caldron has not lost its original power over the organism as a whole. The repressed material does not lie in the id like so many dead leaves, but rather like a continuing explosion that pushes at all parts of the mechanism at once. It cannot be resisted, and it raises a very great crisis within the organism. The libido must be released—but how? If it follows its original course it will cause the organism to be destroyed by the dangerous indifference and even hostility of the world to its existence. In the structure of the Oedipal triangle of mother, father, and child, if the child follows the prompting of the libido to maintain intimate physical contact with the mother, it will soon encounter the far superior and opposing force of the father. To avoid this hopeless confrontation the child, Freud explains, makes use of a subtle "dodge": *It identifies with the father.* The trick, in this case, is on the libido. The child pretends to be the father and therefore the mother's unchallenged lover. The trick succeeds in bypassing open conflict with the real father, but it fails to offer a satisfying release of frustrated libidinal power.

The consequence of failing to free the libido by way of the Oedipus complex is the creation of a new region of repressed energy. Freud called this the *superego* and assigned it a special function in human existence. The device of *identification* is essential here, for in effect the child has internalized the father who now takes a permanent, though still unconscious, place in the psyche. It is sometimes mistakenly held that the superego is equivalent to the conscience. In fact, the superego is described by Freud as the self-observing function of the ego and thus preparatory to the experience of judgment by the conscience. The superego observes, the conscience punishes.[6] This is important. Observation is always from the point of view of the internalized father; punishment however is self-administered. It is the *anxiety* one experiences for failing to reach the ideals of the father-observer. We shall return to this point later, asking why there should be self-punishment at all. Here we should note that the "super-ego applies the strictest moral standard to the helpless ego which is at its mercy. . . ." Freud was impressed by the fact that the superego is the "legitimate heir" to parental authority, but seems to have selected from the parents only their strictness and punitive qualities—even where the parents have been especially loving.[7] This is puzzling since the response of self-punishment to the failure to live up to the ideals of the superego is then unnecessary. There seems to be an unwarranted desire to carry within oneself all the values and goals of one's own mortal enemy, a desire that not only creates displeasure but anxiety.

It might be apparent from this brief account, as it in time became apparent to Freud, that the notion of the unconscious—without question the most famous part of his entire theory—has now acquired so many uses that it "begins to lose significance for us."[8] It is the function of the ego, for example, to repress dangerous desires, forcing them into a seething cauldron. If that cauldron is unconscious, so too is the act of the ego in placing frustrated desires into it. The ego cannot be equated simply with consciousness, since much of its essential functions are themselves unconscious. The same applies to the superego, for we cannot *consciously* be our parents. The distinction between conscious and unconscious therefore loses its force. In his later work Freud tended to replace *unconscious* with *id*. But sometimes id also seems to serve as the term for the whole psyche, and not just its hidden parts, so that the ego and the superego seem to be mere functions of the id. The reason for noting this apparent confusion is not to attempt a clarification of Freud's terminology, but to stress the fact that Freud did not have a conception of the psyche as a plurality, as is sometimes the appearance in his own thought as well as in some of the Freudians. Even the internalized father is not truly a foreign presence; it is the work of the id. When we are assailed by anxiety under the judgment of the conscience, it is not someone else or something else performing this action; it is an assault that comes solely from our own interior. Our self-condemnation has no external agency whatsoever.

This exposes another significant agreement with the mystics' view of selfhood. The self is not the ego. It is not the conscious, rational, awake, temporal person I seem to be to myself—that is only the most superficial mask of what I truly am, and, moreover, a thoroughly distorting mask. It is a mask made of "tricks" and "dodges" undertaken by the ego to reconcile its true desires with an indifferent world. It is therefore a distortion of the true self. In my experience as a whole I am not rational but boundlessly passionate, not temporal but outside all the limits of time, not isolated but an all-inclusive whole. The excessively weak ego, condemned by its own inwardness, faulted for its inevitable failures, is essentially the mystics' "slimy bed of sin." The ego of psychoanalysis, like the self of the mystics, is existentially self-contradictory. Furthermore, the ego's woeful, impotent, isolated, and ignorant existence is the very essence of grief. It has somehow come before the face of death and refused the challenge, turning away from life as well.

As we consider the manner by which the self can overcome its grief and restore itself to full and vital continuity, we observe a further parallel with the mystics: both have a fundamentally erotic conception of human existence. The unity sought by the self in a return to a prior wholeness is not a unity of being, but a unity of act. The identification with the father that results in the creation of the superego is an identification with what the father *does*; it is the adoption of his morals and ideals. What this tells us about Freud is that he is seeking a kind of equilibrium that is not ontological but voluntaristic. Freud was not truly seeking a *stasis*, else he would not have held so consistently to the distinction between instinct and stimulus; instead, it is implied in his thought that the person's deepest desire is to possess completely the sources of one's own spontaneity. How that is the case is most obvious in the way Freud was led to the proposal of the death instinct, and the cure for grief implicit in that proposal.

We had observed earlier that the death instinct grew out of an inconsistency in his thought that he knew had to be reconciled. That inconsistency is a major flaw in the structure we have just summarized, though perhaps it is has not become obvious. In the briefest possible formulation, we can consider it *the failure to make a clear difference between reality and the reality principle*. It is one thing to adapt one's libidinal energies to reality, it is another to adapt them according to a reality principle. The difference lies in the fact that external reality as it is in itself and reality as it is perceived are not necessarily the same, and may be the same only rarely.

Let us return briefly to the Oedipal triangle. We recall that Freud stressed the fact that the superego is distinct from the conscience; the one observes, the other punishes. While Freud has an explanation for identification with the father (the ego's attempt to trick the libido), he offers no reason for the self-punishment. We might say that there is a realistic fear that if the child actually does enter into open encounter with the father the child might be harmed. But the chances of this are exceedingly slight. No doubt children are occasionally treated painfully by their father, but so are they by mothers and siblings. The mortal danger the child feels before the father is far too universal to be explained this way. One of Freud's most notorious attempts at a naturalistic explanation of the ubiquity of Oedipal anxiety is the suggestion that what the (boy) child fears is castration (and what the girl child fears is "loss of love"[9]). But this fails, too, and for a fascinating, though by no means obvious, reason: *it is anxiety that causes repression, and not repression that leads to anxiety*. The reason the ego represses the libido's desires is not that they are inherently dangerous, but that they cause the ego to remember a truly painful experience. Obviously the little boy does not remember an earlier castration, because it did not happen. What is remembered is what *did* happen: the trauma (literally, injury) of birth, when the organism was violently separated from its amniotic bliss. What is terrifying the child is not its *death*, which the father is threatening, but a memory of its *birth*. It does not fear an injury that leads to *extinction*, but an injury that leads to *separation*.

The reality principle cannot therefore originate in reality. If it is true, as Freud believed, that the ego can perceive the external world without distortion, it cannot then be that the reality principle is the way the ego represents the demands of reality before the libido. The reality principle does not correspond to a world that is being *perceived*, but to a world that is being *remembered*. The father is real enough, and it may well be the case that the father competes with the child for the mother, but the child's resulting anxiety originates from within and not from "reality."

This inconsistency came to Freud's attention not through reflection on the theory itself, but through phenomena encountered in his practice and in the casual observation of the behavior of perfectly normal children. Those were reported in his *Beyond the Pleasure Principle*, which he began to write in 1919 and published the following year.

These phenomena contradicted a theory he had described in his *Interpretation of Dreams* (1900), the first properly psychoanalytic work. In that study Freud had argued that one of the chief purposes of dreaming is that, through symbolic wish fulfillment, the sleeper can trick restless libidinal urges into momentary release and therefore prevent being awakened. Dreams could be nicely explained, in other words, through the pleasure principle. If some unconscious method were not found to relieve the pressure of the libido, the organism would be so regularly disturbed that sleep would be impossible. However, this tidy theory was being repeatedly challenged by the reports of his patients of dreams that apparently did not, and could not, observe the pleasure principle. These were recurring dreams in which extremely painful events in the patients' past were being reexperienced. Freud could discern no pleasurable or constructive function in this sort of dream.

He noted the additional and suggestive fact that when a patient had suffered a massive *physical* trauma in the past there never was a dream in which this event was recalled—even in those patients who had suffered very serious and nearly mortal wounds during the war. It was only *psychic* traumas that were relived. Why is it, he wondered, that when the organism was confronted with very real, and physical, threats to its life it bore no scars from these moments, but when it was faced with merely psychic threats the scars were deep and troubling?

Freud reasons that the organism has so developed physiologically that it is capable of handling physical injuries. Quite simply, if they do not kill you they will heal. But the development of this physiological resiliency has no psychic counterpart. That is, there is no protection against assaults from within. What are these assaults? These can only be powerful psychic *desires* for self-destruction. But where do they come from if not from reality? They can only come from the instincts, Freud concluded. Here he describes instincts in a way with which we are already familiar: "*an instinct is an urge inherent in organic life to restore an earlier state of things* which the living entity has been obliged to abandon under the pressure of external disturbing forces."[10] We have already seen that the desire for equilibrium, which was the aim of the pleasure principle, was essentially a wish to move backward in time and toward a simpler form of existence. Now this desire is interpreted as something actually destructive. It is a drive that will *force* the organism backward into lower orders of organization. This is no longer a mere drift, or tendency, of things to seek comfort or rest. It is a powerful and destructive action that originates in the organism's secret interior. This is not a threat that life will be *taken away* from us; it is the threat that life will be *given away*. But given away by an act of life itself. Thus Freud's famous statement: "If we are to take it as a truth that knows no exception that everything dies for *internal* reasons— becomes inorganic once again—then we shall be compelled to say that '*the aim of all life is death.*' "[11] This is the so-called death instinct.

If it is the aim of all life to die, to become inorganic once again, why is there life at all? This question compelled Freud to offer an opposing force—the life instinct. He is far less detailed in his thinking about the life instinct, but on rather scant biological data he does feel justified in describing a drive inherent in organisms whose goal is growth and even increasing complexity.

We recall that Freud proposed the death instinct as an explanation for the inconsistency between reality and the reality principle or, more specifically, the psyche's punishment of itself without any external need to do so. We also recall that the form punishment takes is anxiety—which is the remembered injury of birth. In fact, the death instinct explains why there is self-destruction, but it is not clear so far why self-destruction should be considered punishment and should be anxiety provoking. Freud can have only one answer for this: the life instincts are persistently "emerging as breakers of the peace and constantly producing tensions whose release is felt as pleasure." The life instincts, in other words, are opposed to the pleasure principle: "The pleasure principle seems actually to serve the death instincts. It is true that it keeps watch upon stimuli from without, which are regarded as dangers by both kinds of instincts; but it is more especially on guard against increases from within which would make the task of living more difficult."[12]

Let us take particular note of several aspects of this reasoning. First, pleasure lies in the direction of death, and anxiety in the direction of life. Pleasure has to do with return, union, a distinct loss of individuality, a retreat from history and empirical selfhood. Anxiety is not *about* something, it is the very force of life itself, which is in the direction of isolation, individualization, time, hopeless relations with others. Second, we must not forget that both instincts rise out of our own existence, implying a division of self against self, and also implying that one is far more to be preferred than the other. The very fact that death represents pleasure means that this is the prevailing *desire* of the organism as a whole. We die because we choose to die.

What must be quite apparent by this point is that Freud has duplicated the mystics' view of death in virtually every detail. We can now see that the ego—the individualized, time-oriented, and outward-directed part of the self—is the manifestation of the life instinct, the corpselike worldly self of the mystics. The terrible gloom and ignorance one lives in is, of course, gloom and ignorance only for the ego, or the worldly self. Incredibly this ego hides from itself the fact that its anxiety is a mask drawn over a deeper and far more compelling desire. For anyone who has knowledge of the unconscious, or Eckhart's "unknown knowledge," it becomes apparent that the hidden desire represented by the death instinct is more nearly a desire for continuity, for a more perfect existence. What seems like death to the ego (union) is really life, and the ego's ignorant pursuit of its own increasing separation is really a desire for death. True death, in the mystics' vision, is not timelessness but separation, growth, advancing isolation. The ego's powerlessness is the impotence of a corpse separated from all its life-giving functions. We also recall that the mystics had little concern for biological death and were indifferent to what happened to their bodies. This is what Freud discovered with his dreamers; those whose bodies were injured quickly got over it, and the experience even slipped harmlessly into the past where it was forgotten.

Finally, most incomprehensible to his scientific colleagues and even the bulk of psychoanalytic theorists, is the presumption that the ego has separated itself freely. It can just as freely return. What holds us in our misery is not some force external to the organism; it is the autonomous choice of the organism. This is where we return to Freud's fateful but persistent distinction between *instinct* and *stimulus*. We find ourselves at an extraordinary juncture. We are free to go forward toward increasing separation or backward toward increasing union; we are free to choose history or to choose eternity. But in one crucial respect Freud departs from mysticism—in what is certainly the most truly controversial part of his theory: *we are free to choose either history or eternity, not in spite of our bodies, but by way of our bodies.* Freud's instincts are not psychic phenomena; they are organic phenomena. The psyche is not something that drifts epiphenomenally through the physical being like a ghost; it is the way the organism relates to itself. On the face of it, the consequences of this way of thinking are bizarre: on the one hand we find the possibility of organismic eternity, and on the other the indefinite historical existence of the organism. But are they bizarre?

Freud actually never seems to be able to reject either possibility, so they persist in the form of a conflict within himself. His personal reaction to his own theory is extremely revealing. We have seen that by holding to the distinction between instinct and stimulus he innocently opened the door to a radical voluntarism. But he proves a grudging host and attempts to slam his thought back against these outrageous options. In truth, he never succeeds. They keep their foot in the door to the end.

Two voices are speaking in Freud: in addition to the mystic calling us to eternal bliss, we can hear the unmistakable exclamations of the Hebrew prophet summoning us to history. We have listened to the mystic in him. It is a commanding presence, apparent not only in his identification of the death instinct, but also in his perception that it is the more powerful of the two—which is simply a way of saying that eternity is the deeper human longing.

But the prophet's voice cannot be ignored. It speaks for Eros, for time, for mastery of the hidden forces of history. Thus we find in the widely quoted statement from the late work, *New Introductory Lectures,* a declaration of the goal of psychoanalysis: "to strengthen the ego, to make it more independent of the super-ego, to widen its field of perception and enlarge its organization, so that it can appropriate fresh portions of the id. Where the id was, there ego shall be."[13]

This is an attempt to eliminate the id's eternality, to put stimulus in the place of instinct, reality in place of the reality principle, necessity in the place of freedom. Freud wants to abandon the autonomy of the id and float the ego on the temporal flow of the world, referring to the coherence between ego and world as *rationality*. There is something improbable in this, hopeless even. Since Freud has denied the ego any power of its own beyond thought, and knowing even that the energy required for thought must be "borrowed" from the id, we can hardly expect the ego to have any power over reality—beyond thinking in a manner that agrees with it. Freud seems to be offering the ego as a sacrifice to history. It is also puzzling that he would have thought the ego could expect any success in mastering the id. Since all power belongs to the id, the ego is left with nothing but its old tricks and dodges. In *Beyond the Pleasure Principle* he says that we must remember the past so that we can stop repeating it.[14] The suggestion is amazing. Can the seething cauldron of the immortal id be neutralized simply by looking into it? In short, assigning psychoanalysis the task of strengthening the ego is an advocacy for grief.

True, in another late work, *The Future of Illusion* (1927), Freud does speak with a rare optimism, predicting the ultimate triumph of reason over passion. But the optimism is rare. In another work of his late years, *Civilization and Its Discontents*, the pessimism returns. That the latter sentiment prevails in Freud's own life is evident from an observation of his biographer Ernest Jones:

> As far back as we know anything of his life he seems to have been prepossessed by thoughts about death, more so than any other man I can think of except perhaps Sir Thomas Browne and Montaigne. Even in the early years of our acquaintance he had the disconcerted habit of parting with the words, 'Goodbye; you may never see me again.' There were the repeated attacks of what he called *Todesangst* (dread of death). He hated growing old, even as early as his forties, and as he did so the thoughts of death became increasingly clamorous.[15]

Because Freud spoke with two voices, that of the mystic and that of the prophet, but listened to neither, his was a life of extended and intense bereavement.

It is worth stressing again that the options opened up by Freud's thought, as a consequence of the distinction between stimulus and instinct, are an eternal happiness and an indefinite history, not *apart from* the body but *with* the body. It is ironic, perhaps tragic as well, that Freud thought neither option was truly possible. Not all of his followers and students have been equally pessimistic. We shall consider two thinkers who have taken his conception of death and its implications most seriously indeed, and have been much more agreeable, perhaps even enthusiastic, hosts to what we have referred to as the mystical and prophetic voices.

Norman O. Brown, in his *Life Against Death,* takes as a cue for his study of Freud the mechanism of repression, which, as we have already seen, is the activity of the ego by which it turns back into the id those instinctual desires considered dangerous according to the reality principle. Brown is especially struck by the fact that the id therefore carries within itself all of the repressed desires of childhood. Each of us "has a lifelong allegiance (i.e., fixation) to the pattern of infantile sexuality."[16] Brown considers this condition to be filled with promise, in contrast to Freud for whom the great mass of human beings are doomed to suffer under the unresolved tension between the repressed desires of the child that lives within and the attempts of the mature adult to adapt to the realities of the world.

Brown characterizes Freud's understanding of infantile sexuality as the "pursuit of pleasure obtained through the activity of any and all organs of the human body. So defined, the ultimate essence of our desires and our being is nothing more or less than delight in the active light of all the human body."[17] Freud had strong theoretical reasons for the impossibility of reclaiming this pleasure. He provided a long chronicle of the way we suppress our original infantile desires by restricting their expression to increasingly restricted areas and functions of the body. Freud proposed for understanding this process a sequence of now-familiar "erotogenic" stages: oral, anal, phallic, and genital. The content and dynamic of these stages is less important to us here than the fact that they represent for Freud not so much an increase in our *control* of sexuality, but an increase in our *suppression* of sexuality. We have so successfully limited our freedom of sexual expression that there is no longer a possibility of playing this long symphony backward. No doubt Freud also had personal reasons for believing this avenue to happiness is sealed off. Freud, after all, was a Victorian, and the idea of adults resuming the polymorphously perverse behavior of infants was probably unthinkable.

Brown, however, is not a Victorian. Moreover, he seriously questions Freud's theoretical reasoning on this issue. He considers it unnecessary to conceive the life and death instincts as *dualistically* opposed to each other and suggests that they might be more correctly understood as *dialectically* opposed. When two forces are dialectically opposed it means that each requires the other in order to exist itself. It also means that they have arisen from an original unity, to which they still belong and to which they will in time be reconciled in a final union. When these two forces are life and death, we can say that without life there can be no death, and without death no life. To affirm one is to affirm the other. Where Freud foresaw the ultimate triumph of death, Brown offers a vision of life and death coming together in a reconciled whole that is greater than either.

By replacing dualism with a dialectic of life and death, Brown avoids the pessimism into which Freud fell with such personal anguish. The movement as Freud viewed it was from death to death, with a brief manifestation of life appearing and disappearing like a faint candle in the infinite night. Brown's revision has the effect of turning Freud's theory on its head, and in the place of pessimism there appears an ecstatic religious optimism. For Brown the movement is not from death to death, but from the perfect union of life and death through a momentary and pained separation of the two, back to the original union. Because Freud, like the mystics, understood death as separation, and because he did not have the mystics' confidence that one could return along the same path by which we increasingly isolate ourselves, he conjoined separateness with hopelessness. Brown, underscoring that understanding of death, restores hope in the certainty that we not only can return but inevitably will return to eternal wholeness.

Brown also reinforces Freud's rare vision that the path of that return is in fact through the body, something they do not typically share with the mystics. Brown does not forget that the path of union for Freud is love; it is an erotic wholeness that is being sought and sought organically: "close examination of Freud's own premises and arguments suggest that there is only one loving relationship to objects in the world, a relation of being one with the world."[18] Nor does he forget that death is integral to this organic return; it is in fact death that binds us to our bodies: "The precious ontological uniqueness which the individual claims is conferred on him not by possession of an immortal soul but by possession of a mortal body. Without death, Hegel argues, individuals are reduced to the status of mere modes in the one infinite and eternal substance of Spinoza."[19] To accept my own death is to accept the fact that I am my body and not an ethereal essence untouched by the brute concreteness of biological specificity.

The separateness of death has in it, for Brown, the same paradoxical quality it has for mystics. We are not separated *by our bodies* from life—as for the Platonists—we are separated *in our bodies*. Our bodies are not the agents of death that endeavor to take us away from life; the very distinction between life and death is something that occurs within the body. The life and death instincts are organic instincts. In spite of the fact that this seems contrary to much of the religious literature, Brown points to powerful religious visions that coincide perfectly with

the psychoanalytic insights. Chief among them is the Christian doctrine of the resurrection of the body, a doctrine that grows out of the
belief that a real death occurs and that life is restored not in a disembodied spirit, as in Platonism, but in a fully embodied reconstitution
of the self. There is, in fact, a surprising agreement between
psychoanalysis and religion on the question of the nature of death:
"Psychoanalysis comes to remind us that we are bodies, that repression
is of the body, and that perfection would be the realm of Absolute Body;
eternity is the mode of unrepressed bodies."[20]

Indeed, ultimately Brown's belief that the path to eternity is through
the body is in agreement with the mystics. The body, after all, is not the
terminus of the return. We return *with* the body, but not *to* it. We recall
that the mystics had a strong sense that once one set forth on the
journey one stage would give way to another, until something like an
eternal path opened up before one. Brown comes to the same way of
thinking. In a subsequent book, *Love's Body*, he acknowledges that the
body cannot be the point of arrival for our journey back through death,
since it is in itself merely symbolic of something still deeper. The
journey continues then until we reach the infinite creativity out of
which all else, including the symbols themselves, arise. This is the
same absolute subjectivity that we saw in the mystics, in which we
become "the first cause of everything" (Eckhart).

Brown has captured one side of Freud's thought as it develops
around the problem of death, but has neglected another. By insisting on
the dialectical relationship of the instincts, he underlined the deeply
desired backward movement of the psyche. He has therefore reversed
Freud's pessimism by showing how, on the basis of Freud's own
deepest insights, eternal bliss is truly available. But by doing so he
overlooked Freud's provocative belief that this movement must be
freely chosen. We do not follow the instinct to death; the instinct is our
choice of death. But if we choose death, we could also choose life. In
other words, if we understand the instincts to be dialectically related,
we shall regard them as *both/and, because one always entails the other.*
They are unified even before we can choose between them, thus our
choice is essentially meaningless. Dualistically related, however, the
instincts are *either/or, because one always excludes the other.* Their
opposition means that we *must* choose. What then are the implications,
never really discussed by Freud, of saying that we *could* choose life?

The Freudian scholar David Bakan provides an alternative reading of
Freud's thought concerning the death instinct. Where Brown em-

phasized that part of Freud's thinking that has to do with repression and the frustrated child that lives within each of us, Bakan exploits the possibilities implicit in Freud's insight that we all possess an autonomous desire for self-destruction.

He provides empirical support for this gratuitous opposition to our own well-being by citing recent studies of disease in which it is apparent that the occurrence of the illness cannot be wholly explained as the effect of an external agent such as a microbe or a toxic medium. There appear to be factors unique to each person that play a role in determining whether we will actually contract a disease after we have been exposed to it. The actual presence of the hostile agent is not in itself sufficient cause for the disease.

There is also a strong challenge to the belief that all of the organism's inherited internal biological mechanisms actually work toward its continued survival. It has been proposed, for example, that one significant cause of disease lies in the very biological mechanisms that ordinarily protect the organism from death. In order to survive, any higher organism must develop a great number of separate organs and functions that operate in close harmony with each other through an enormously complicated system of communication. It often happens that an organ will continue to function in a way that is consistent with its own development but that is destructive to the organism as a whole. The body may produce insulin or thyroid, for example, from healthy and active glandular action but in a quantity far greater than the rest of the body can endure, causing death or serious illness. Cancer is an even more vivid example of cells following a pattern of growth quite normal with respect to their own existence, but quite threatening to the host.

What happens in such illnesses is the breakdown of the system of communication. Communication is necessary to the well-being of the organism, since there must be a variety of ways of signaling the actions of certain organs or mechanisms when a change comes over the body that is threatening to the existence of the organism as a whole. There are many methods of communication within the human body, the best known and subtlest of which is the central nervous system. There are suggestive experimental data showing that cancer cells, for example, are much less receptive than other kinds of cells to the signals from other parts of the body that they cease dividing.

Bakan seizes on the importance of communication to offer a provocative definition of disease. If disease implies a failure of the organism to supervise the functions of its various parts in a way that strengthens its likelihood of survival, then we may consider disease as "telic decentralization." This term implies that in order to continue existing each organism must centrally coordinate all its functions. The term *telos* (plural *tele*) here refers to the forms, or functions, of the organism. If the various *tele* become independent of one another in the absence of clear communication, the organism as a whole will soon cease to exist. The brain, for example, cannot function unless the heart supplies it with blood. Disease may therefore be understood as the organism's failure to coordinate its assorted functions through effective communication from a controlling center.

So far we are concerned only with unconscious mechanisms. Up to this point there is no hint in Bakan's account that the body's tele are subject to *conscious* control. In fact, he wants explicitly to distinguish between "telos" and "purpose," with the latter term indicating some form of deliberative, conscious control. Telos is descriptive of the body's functioning without respect to the phenomenon of consciousness; purpose is descriptive of the acts of self-aware human beings.

Where does Bakan make a connection with Freud's discussion of the death instinct? It emerges in his remark that while telos and purpose are distinct they are also continuous: "it is evident that purpose is conscious telos."[21] This observation has the effect of placing consciousness within the hierarchical structure of the human organism, and so introducing purpose into the telic coordination of the body. Thus Bakan has arrived at the conclusion from which Freud had wanted to protect his theory: *instinct and freedom are identical.*

We are on uncertain ground here. A misstep will send us sprawling into absurdities. Bakan reduces the danger of stumbling by quickly adding that in addition to the tele that function in individual organisms there are apparently social tele that also exercise an influence over the fate of the individual. These, too, are subject to conscious control, though in this case the control must also be collective and therefore much more difficult to achieve. The free manipulation of instinct in the individual will always be tempered by the influence of social instinct. This brings Bakan to the conclusion that "Man may not be able to make himself, as an individual, immortal. But it is within his power to extend his life within the larger societal telos. By working to maintain the larger telos he may increase the number of his days as well."[22]

There are other factors that stand in the way of willfully choosing not to die. These emerge in Bakan's discussion of the nature of *pain.* Disease is accompanied in almost every case by the phenomenon of pain. It is through pain, in fact, that we usually discover a disease. But what is pain?

There is a curiously paradoxical quality to the phenomenon of pain. On the one hand, it is quite obviously physical—it is located somewhere in the body, very often with an easily identifiable point of origin. This characteristic of pain has frequently led theorists to propose that pain is a physiological process of one sort or another. However, such proposals have been notoriously inadequate, quite probably because pain is, on the other hand, a phenomenon of consciousness. It is plainly self-contradictory to say that I am in pain but am not conscious of it. Indeed, one of the classical ways of dealing with pain is either to eliminate or alter one's consciousness.

The paradoxical conjunction of consciousness and the physical body in the experience of pain leads Bakan to propose that we understand pain to be "*the psychic manifestation of telic decentralization.*"[23] Pain is the conscious discovery that a breakdown in the body's systems of communication has occurred. Since it is conscious, pain is an invitation to the person to restore the body to health out of one's ability freely to influence the physical instincts, or tele. We could put this in still somewhat stronger terms: since death is normally preceded by disease, and is the end of the line for telic decentralization, pain is a psychic message informing us we are free to undo the causes of our own death.

This is a message, however, we rarely, if ever, hear. Instead, we respond in a most inappropriate way. Failing to acknowledge that pain is a message to our freedom as persons, we exaggerate the physical nature of pain. We begin to regard pain as a physical process that must be stopped or driven from the body, and we often go even further to identify the pain with a certain part of the body. This in turn leads to the desire to cut away the diseased parts of one's own organism as though they are an alien presence. This results in a profound self-alienation in which the ego sets itself in opposition to the body, failing to see that it is a "body-ego."

Cutting away the diseased and therefore painful part of the body is equivalent to offering a sacrifice to the cause of the disease. Bakan suggests this as one of the roots of the universal religious ceremonies of sacrifice. In fact, it also provides a significant variation in the Freudian interpretation of the Oedipal conflict. We recall that as Freud saw it the child perceived a mortal danger in the father, which did not correspond to reality. Bakan claims that Freud did not recognize "that the Oedipus complex might itself be a reaction of the child to the infanticidal impulse in the father—Laius leaving Oedipus to die as a child—and a defensive response of the child against aggression."[24] The reason infanticide is a credible threat owes to the fact that sacrifice is symbolically most powerful when it is the offering of a part of one's self, and what living thing is more intimately connected to one's flesh than one's own child? Infanticide, in other words, is one of the deeply anchored responses to the (false) belief that we deal with the body's mortal faults by cutting out the offending member. Although there are such powerful contrainfanticidal influences on each of us that the wish is rarely carried out, it remains a wish and therefore leaves its symbolic mark on the psyche, as well as on myth and religious belief. The widespread infanticide in Greek mythology can be matched by such events in Jewish literature as the near sacrifice of Isaac by his father Abraham and the death of Job's children at the beginning of the narrative of his suffering. Christianity has a powerful infanticidal event at its very center: the death of the Son to appease the offended righteousness of the Father. These are veiled or indirect references, but they clearly point to a fantasy of the murder of children, Bakan insists, and, he adds significantly, "a fantasy of their being killed suggests a wish that they be killed."[25]

While the experience of pain should be an incitation to repair the disorder in the body's functions, we almost universally fail to accept it; we attempt instead only to get rid of the pain. The bitter reward for this failure is not only the abnegation of our personal freedom; it is also an increase in the amount of telic decentralization. Failing properly to understand the nature of its own disease and pain, the organism ironically increases both and unconsciously hastens its own journey toward death.

What is most striking in Bakan's analysis is that a clear line between instinct and freedom is never drawn. He shows convincingly why we choose to go with the regressive instincts in the direction of death, but he does not argue that we *must* go with them. Bakan's statement that "Man may not be able to make himself, as an individual, immortal" is most revealing. The word "may" contains in itself the implied but outrageous suggestion in Freud's thought that if we die for internal reasons we could have internal reasons not to die. Of course, Bakan, and Freud, *could* have argued that those so-called "internal" reasons are not internal at all, but stand in perfect causal continuity with the external world—effectively eliminating the distinction between instinct and stimulus. This is certainly the prevailing view of the biological community with which Freud had identified himself, and the philosophy that dominates the thinking of the scientific theorists we examined in Chapter 2 of this study. However, neither Bakan nor Freud took this option; they prefer to say that we die not because it *happens* to us, but because we *desire* it.

We have emphasized the fundamentally *erotic* character of mysticism and psychoanalysis. Their deepest desires are for an active, creative union with the source of their own existence. They place an exceedingly high value on happiness, bliss, and rapture. St. Teresa's face in the Baroque statue by Bernini has a striking similarity to Freud's "satiated child" who sinks back from the mother's breast with "reddened cheeks and blissful smile." It is this side of Freud that Brown encourages. Freud also made it clear that the life instinct is the mischief-maker; it repeatedly breaks up our rapture, deprives us of blissful union. Bakan, also pursuing this theme in Freud's thought, implies that if we choose life we choose to make pain the path to growth and independence. There is a manifest defiance in this. It is mysticism in reverse. Where the mystics yielded to grief, this side of Freud takes grief into itself in a vigorous willfulness. Where, at least in Eckhart's view, the absolute subjectivity of the mystic was equivalent to being the *creator of the universe*, the side of Freud that Bakan is encouraging desires to be *creative in the universe*. Where Brown reversed Freud's pessimism in the confident claim that we can have eternity through the body, Bakan counsels optimism, albeit a guarded optimism, concerning the ability of the person to take hold of history and impel it toward its own open-ended continuity. Freud, we said, became an advocate for grief. The positive side of this is that the pain that inevitably attends our separateness is also the signal that we can continue moving forward toward growth. Freud's own enormously creative life is eloquent testimony that the prophetic engagement with history cannot be had without pain.

Freud and his most inspired students understood the problem of death as a problem of making a fundamental human choice between happiness and history. We cannot have both. We must look elsewhere to learn whether we can be happy in our mortality and in the history to which mortality has confined us.

Notes

1. *New Introductory Lectures*, p. 96.
2. See especially *The Ego and the Id*, pp. 28, 45.
3. *New Introductory Lectures*, p. 95.
4. *Three Contributions to a Theory of Sex*, p. 43.
5. *New Introductory Lectures*, pp. 73 ff.
6. Ibid., p. 60.
7. Ibid., pp. 61, 62.
8. *The Ego and the Id*, p. 8.
9. *New Introductory Lectures*, p. 87.
10. *Beyond the Pleasure Principle*, pp. 67 ff.

11. Ibid., p. 70.
12. Ibid., p. 109.
13. *New Introductory Lectures*, p. 80.
14. *Beyond the Pleasure Principle*, p. 39.
15. *Life and Writings of Sigmund Freud*, Vol III, *The Last Phase 1919–1939*, p. 279.
16. *Love Against Death*, p. 28.
17. Ibid., p. 30.
18. Ibid., p. 42.
19. Ibid., p. 104.
20. Ibid., p. 93.
21. *Disease, Pain, and Suffering*, p. 39.
22. Ibid., p. 53.
23. Ibid., p. 59.
24. Ibid., p. 104.
25. Ibid., p. 105.

Bibliography

David Bakan, *Disease, Pain, and Suffering*, (Boston: 1971).

Norman O. Brown, *Life Against Death*, (New York: 1966).

Sigmund Freud, *Beyond the Pleasure Principle*, tr. James Strachey (New York: 1963).

———*Civilization and Its Discontents*, tr. James Strachey (New York: 1962).

———*The Ego and the Id*, tr. James Strachey (New York: 1963).

———*The Future of an Illusion*, tr. W. D. Robson-Scott (New York: n.d.).

———*A General Introduction to Psychoanalysis*, tr. Joan Riviere (New York: 1965).

———*The New Introductory Lectures on Psychoanalysis*, tr. James Strachey (New York: 1965).

———*The Problem of Anxiety*, tr. Henry Alden Bunker (New York: 1963).

———*Three Contributions to a Theory of Sex*, tr. A. A. Brill (New York: 1962).

FOUR
DEATH AS ILLUSION
—BEING

---

5 HINDUISM

The *Bhagavad-Gita* ("The Song of the Divine"), one of the most cherished works in all of the world's religious literature, is an appropriate gateway into the distinctive understanding of death found in the Hindu tradition. The *Bhagavad-Gita* is a conversation* between the god Krishna, here disguised as a chariot-driver, and the renowed Prince Arjuna, who is preparing to enter a battle he knows will bring unnecessary death to many thousands of persons. Arjuna is appalled by the prospect of such carnage, and saddened by the fact that on both sides he has many long and close friends, as well as brothers, cousins, and many other relatives.

Krishna addresses Arjuna's indecision concerning the battle by evoking most of the great themes of Hindu thought. For this reason the poem is often regarded as a condensed presentation of the essence of Hinduism.

"Omens of evil!" Arjuna cries out in despair to the divine charioteer. "Where is joy in the killing of kinsmen?" Arjuna's dilemma is in no way a lack of courage on his part. His valor as a warrior and his nearly

---

*The *Bhagavad-Gita* is actually a mere fragment of the world's longest poem, the *Mahabharata*. Consisting of nearly 100,000 stanzas, the *Mahabharata* tells the adventures of the descendents of the great King Bharata. It is an epic poem peopled by princes and warriors, forest demons and sublime deities, jealous lovers and saints. While it has always been a work of great popularity, the poem as a whole does not have the status of divine scripture, although it is understood generally to be an inspired interpretation of the authoritative sacred texts of the Hindus.

superhuman strength have been well demonstrated in earlier adventures. He was even reputed to have so thoroughly overcome laziness that he lived entirely without sleep. "Conqueror of sloth" is one of the epithets used by the epic writer to address him. His dilemma is that, being of the ruling caste and a party to the dispute whether he wanted to be or not, he is obliged to join the battle as a "caste duty." As the god Krishna stands before him in silence, Arjuna's pained monologue continues.

"Which will be worse, to win this war, or to lose it? I scarcely know." Finally the prince throws his weapons to the ground. "I shall not struggle, I shall not strike them. Now let them kill me, that will be better." Then, the *Gita* tells us, "his eyes filled with tears, and his heart grieved and was bewildered with pity."

With this Krishna turns and addresses him. His response comes almost in the form of a rebuke. "Your words are wise, Arjuna, but your sorrow is for nothing. The truly wise mourn neither for the living nor for the dead. There was never a time when I did not exist, nor you, nor any of these kings. Nor is there any future in which we shall cease to be." Krishna's words seem to have reached Arjuna's heart. The prince does not interrupt him. "That which is nonexistent can never come into being, and that which is can never cease to be. Those who have known the inmost Reality know also the nature of *is* and *is not*." Krishna then names this inmost "reality," which is both changeless and eternal: *Atman*. "Know this Atman unborn, undying, never ceasing, never beginning, deathless, birthless, unchanging forever. How can it die the death of the body?"

The unknown author of the *Bhagavad-Gita* put these spare sentences into the mouth of the god Krishna because they have for the Hindu the mark of indisputable truth. We should approach them with great caution, however, for the simplicity and elegance of their statement tend to hide from us the spiritual depth from which they have arisen. This is not the sort of truth that one comes upon casually or even the kind of truth that can be discovered by careful rational reflection. The words Krishna spoke to Arjuna carry in them centuries of intense spiritual experience. Hindu saints expected to spend most of their lifetime before they could come to a solid understanding of these truths. We can scarcely hope to comprehend them without looking back, if even briefly, at the history of their development.

We shall examine enough of the background of Hinduism as is necessary to show the truth distinctiveness of its thought about death. There is a notorious inclination on the part of many thinkers to look for parallels and identities between Hinduism and the religions and philosophies of the West. Hindus are as tempted to do this as Westerners. Our task here will be to show that if we look even slightly beneath the superficial likenesses we shall see important irreconcilable differences. We shall be concerned in particular to show that Hinduism, contrary to what it sometimes *appears* to be saying, views the continuity of life in the face of death in a way that ultimately has almost nothing in common with Platonism and mysticism. Hindus can speak of immortality, or of union with the divine, but what they mean by the terms is unique to Hinduism. Therefore, we must identify some of the sources of Hindu thought to establish its context and then attempt to draw out the complexities in such prominent doctrines as the One (Atman/Brahman), knowledge, karma, and transmigration—all crucial to the Hindu conception of death.

Some 1500 years prior to the composition of the *Gita*, roughly the same period in which the first great dynasties were flourishing along the Nile, a complicated and sophisticated civilization existed in the Indus Valley and along the Arabian Sea—a geographical area much larger than Egypt.

What we know of the Indus civilization comes chiefly from the archaeological exploration of two large, walled cities and the artifacts found in them. From the planned organization of the cities it has been concluded that the Indus people were firmly ruled. Their world appears to have been well-ordered and predictable. The architectural remains of large public baths and temples indicate a preoccupation with ritual purity and centralized, priestly worship. The frequency of phallic monuments and clay figurines of prominently masculine animals suggests further the importance of male authority in their religious worship. In contrast to most other early civilizations, there is a conspicuous absence of female symbols.

The Indus culture seems to have existed with relative prosperity and little challenge from without for more than 1000 years. Then in about 200 B.C., India was subject to the sudden but limited invasions of small groups of highly mobile and warlike people who moved down over the mountains from the north. Known to us as Aryans, they gradually came to replace the Indus civilization as the dominant culture in the Indian subcontinent. Whether the Indus culture was destroyed by the Aryans, or whether it died for internal reasons, we do not know. What is clear is that the Aryans were very different in racial background and cultural style. As a result the language of the Indus people vanished along with any memory of what must have been a long and fascinating history, and the urban nature of its culture was abandoned. It does appear, however, that the Aryans were affected by the dominant masculinity of the older religion and that traces of Indus worship survive in the Hindu tradition to the present, particularly where it is unabashedly polytheistic and where there is an emphasis on the aggressively sexual character of some of its male gods.

The earliest religious practices of the Aryans seem to center around a sacrificial ritual in which the symbolic meaning of the fire was focal. What had probably originated as a simple burnt offering to a nature deity developed in time into a tightly prescribed series of ritual observances under the supervision of a number of priests. It is apparent from what records we have of this earliest period of Hindu history that the sacrificial rituals virtually came to dominate the life of the people. They became enormously complicated and, of course, expensive. They not only involved many priests of varying authority, but in some instances the entire community. The most elaborate and costly of the rituals, the horse sacrifice, actually took a year to complete; consequently it came to be observed only by kings and then on very rare occasions.

The great emphasis placed on the sacrifice in these early centuries had two deep influences on later Hinduism, influences that seem at first to be contradictory. First, there was obviously considerable interest in the efficiency or power of the sacrifices. They were believed to be extremely effective in fulfilling the desires of the sacrificer for spiritual or material prosperity. The costlier and the more elaborate the ritual, the greater their power was thought to be. Therefore, the ritual had an element of magic, the external manipulation of forces of nature by way of symbolic action and speech. The words of the priests were expressions of power. Properly uttered they could alter the actual shape and sequence of events. This belief is, in fact, the origin of the most pregnant of all Hindu words, *Brahman*. At first *Brahman* probably meant nothing more than "sacred utterance," a recitation of the words of the ritual. As these words came to acquire great power their expression had to be carefully regulated. Indeed, only certain persons were privileged to use them. This, of course, meant the elevation of a superior class of priests who claimed exclusive access to the power of the sacrifice. In time the term *Brahman* came to be applied to the priests themselves. The significance of their office can be seen not only in their authoritative control of the ritual, but also in the fact that the Brahmans came to constitute the highest caste in Hindu society, of greater dignity and honor than even the ruling caste.

The rich ritual life of the Aryans had another, and apparently contrary, influence on the later Hindu tradition. As the sacrifice became

increasingly intricate, and as the number and variety of sacrifices mul-
tiplied, the presence of a genuinely learned priest was altogether indispensable to the correct, and therefore efficacious, completion of the
ritual. Absolutely no deviation was permitted in its performance. A
forgotten phrase or inept gesture could result in severe punishment. It
was the practice in most rituals that the supervising Brahman simply
observe the entire proceeding without participating in it at all, remaining in perfect silence. What was important was not his gestures but his
knowledge. Indeed, in time it was the knowledge possessed by the
priest, and not the actions of the peformers and celebrants, that came to
be all important. But this was no ordinary sort of knowledge. Since the
sacrifices from the beginning were intended to have an influence on the
deities who had the universe in their control, it was only logical that
the flawless enactment of the ritual would compel the gods to acquiesce in the designs of the priest. It is quite apparent in the more
refined sacrifices of this period that the gods have become quite accidental to the ritual itself, for the ritual has taken the place of divine
power. One can quickly see what this meant when the ritual's power is
thought to originate in the knowledge of the priest: *it is the knowledge
of the priest that then constitutes reality*. In this connection the term
Brahman takes on still another meaning. It is not only the sacred utterance, or the person who speaks it, it is also *what is uttered*. That is,
Brahman is the reality which the utterance was meant to influence.
Now we shall have an opportunity to develop more fully what Brahman
represents in this latter sense—as reality.

On the one hand, then, the sacrifice developed in the direction of
magical power; on the other, toward an exalted view of the nature of
knowledge.

These two tendencies are already evident in the oldest and most
authoritative of the Hindu scriptures, the *Vedas*. The *Vedas* survive in
four different collections, of which the *Rig Veda* is by far the most
important, because it is in this text that we have the most complete
assemblage of the hymns of praise used by the priests in the sacrifice.
The hymns are addressed to a large number of deities, most of them
scarcely distinct from the natural forces that they are intended to per-
sonify. There is a manifest preoccupation in these verses with influenc-
ing the actions of these deities. Their magical function, in other words,
is immediately apparent. This aspect of the sacrifice is even more pronounced in the *Atharva Veda*, which is a collection of the incantations,
spells, chants, and invocations more common with the people than
with the spiritually more refined and superior class of priests.

As one might imagine, the great antiquity of the Vedic literature makes it exceedingly difficult to interpret. They were written in an archaic form of Sanskrit and are, in any case, only fragments, probably accidentally gathered, of the ritual hymns. Nonetheless, there are unmistakable signs of the emergence of the priests' self-conscious use of the Brahmanic knowledge to which we have just referred. The priests are plainly not satisfied merely with knowing the names and the functions of the separate deities. Throughout the *Rig Veda* particularly there is a tendency toward the identification of one deity with another, a perplexing transfer of characteristics. It is as though they are looking for a singular essence in the divine that precedes all its individual manifestations. Occasionally there appears the abstract notion of the One, always written in the neuter gender that stands behind the discernible deities, as in these widely quoted verses:

> Holy Utterance is measured as four quarters; wise brahmans know these. The three (quarters) that are set down in secret they do not bring into movement. The fourth (quarter) of Holy Utterance is what men speak.

> They call it Indra, Mitra, Varuna, Fire (Agni); on it is the heavenly sun-bird. That which is One the seers speak of in various terms; they call it Fire, Yama, Matarisvan.[1]

There is in this passage the sense of a reality that transcends even the realm of the gods, a reality that is impersonal and without name or any other observable characteristic.

In the most celebrated passage of the *Rig Veda* there is a heady profusion of searching phrases in which the inspired but restless intelligence of the priests scattered the seeds of much that flowered later in classical Hinduism:

> Non-existent there was not, existent there was not then. There was not the atmospheric space, nor the vault beyond. What stirred, where, and in whose control? Was there water, a deep abyss?

> Nor death nor immortality (mortals nor immortals) was there then; there was no distinction of night and day. That One breathed without breath by inner power; that it verily was nothing else further.

> Darkness there was, hidden by darkness, in the beginning: an undistinguished ocean was This All. What generative principle was enveloped by emptiness—by the might of its own fervour That One was born.

Desire (creative, or perhaps sacrificial) impulse arose then in the beginning, which was the first seed of thought. The casual connection of the existent the sages found in the non-existent, searching with devotion in their hearts.

Who truly knows? Who shall here proclaim it—whence they were produced, whence this creation? The gods (arose) on this side (later) by the creation of this (empiric world, to which the gods belong); then who knows whence it came into being?

This creation, when it came into being, whether it was established, or whether not—he who is its overseer in the highest heaven, he verily knows, or perchance he knows not.[2]

There is much in the meaning of these words that will forever elude us, but there are several suggestive phrases that demand our reflection. These old priests were already projecting into that region *beyond being and nonbeing*. But they also felt the stupefying impact on the mind of such insights. What could be beyond being and nonbeing except that which was perfectly without form or even space? There is neither death nor life there, no light and no darkness. Indeed, even the darkness cannot be seen. It is an emptiness without boundary; yet, they can still refer to it as "This All." They seem to be suggesting something that even they feel is improbable—that the One, the All, has neither inside nor outside, neither content nor form. How then did that great emptiness arise? Perhaps the most interesting feature of this passage comes in response to that question. The immediate answer is out of *desire*, which can only mean *out of itself*. There is no God and no impersonal force standing behind the abyss or the All; it is utterly self-originating. But just as quickly the answer is cast aside and we discover a new question: *Who truly knows?* Just as surely as the Brahmanic wisdom led to the vision of an abysmal emptiness, it also insisted on the ineluctable mysteriousness of all that is, both in the mind and out of it.

More sublime religious reflections we are unlikely to find in any of the world's literature. The consuming question mark, which the Aryan priests posed before all the mind's certainties was not a gesture of cynicism or despair; it was an expression of undiminished wonder. It was evidently their way of acknowledging that there is no limit to knowledge, no quantity of wisdom that could ever sate the religious appetite. In all directions they could see only that they were surrounded by the infinite.

Vedic philosophy is, however, still unshaped by systematic reflection. It is a philosophy of insight rather than speculation. Their ideas have their own power; instead of stirring minds to thought they directly possess the thinker. This is quite evident in the Vedic attitude toward death. There appears to be an uncritical belief in some form of survival, though this is not stated with any detail. We do note that there seems to be no dread over the fact of death itself. Indeed, the prevailing spirit of the Vedic literature is quite robust and vigorously life-affirming, no doubt a part of the cultural heritage from the adventurous Aryan invaders. Instead of death itself the ancient Hindu fears what is called a "second death" or "re-death," a fate befalling those who have already died but whose lives were unworthy. Precisely how the recurrent "re-death" was pictured we are unable to tell, but we can clearly detect in the notion an early form of the endless wheel of death and birth associated with the well-known Hindu doctrine of transmigration that rises, as we shall see, out of the very core of classical Hinduism.

What is important to keep in focus here concerning Hindu thought in its earliest form is the combination of *knowledge* and *power*. The penetrating knowledge of reality and the sense of the infinite reaching beyond are not *mere facts or information* for the Aryan priests. This knowledge is direct involvement; it brings with it an *identity between knower and known* that took centuries to clarify conceptually. When Krishna spoke of the birthless, deathless Atman he was evoking thought whose origin was in the religious insights of the old priests, but which had undergone extensive refinement by *rishis*, or sages, through the intervening millenium or more.

The literature in which Hinduism finds its classical formulation is referred to collectively as the *Upanishads*. They are, for the most part, reflections of the rishis on the *Vedas*. Although all the books of the *Upanishads* could be gathered into one large volume, the latest composed about 1500 C.E. Like the *Vedas* they are considered by all sects and traditions within Hinduism to be an indisputed guide to religious truth. Unlike the *Vedas* they are adventurously speculative and philosophical. There is very little that is priestly about them. The rishis seem mostly indifferent to religious ritual. The *Upanishads* are, however, a clear extension of the Brahmanic knowledge mentioned above and do move out of the vibrant polytheism of the Aryan heritage toward an abstract pantheism, replacing the old interest in magic and ritual performance with an intense and often brooding inwardness. The Vedic life-affirming mood gives way in the *Upanishads* to a preoccupation with the brevity and darkness of life.

The pronounced inwardness of the rishis has the immediate effect of exalting a term that has only brief and obscure mention in the *Vedas: Atman*. We recall that Arjuna was instructed by Krishna that the inmost reality is "Atman unborn, undying, never ceasing, never beginning, deathless, birthless, unchanging forever." Westerners are put at an immediate disadvantage by the use of this word, for there is nothing equivalent in any major European tongue. It is sometimes translated as self, or soul, or psyche, but each of these words is bound to mislead the Western reader. As we shall discover there is almost nothing in common between the unborn, undying Atman described by Krishna and the immortal soul of Socratic, and subsequent Western, thought.

If such terms as self and soul tend to narrow the concept of Atman too much, there is another danger of misinterpretation that stems directly from the Sanskrit text: making the Atman too inclusive, as the following passage, typical of the *Upanishads*, seems to encourage:

> [Atman] is made of consciousness and mind: it is made of life and vision. It is made of the earth and the waters: it is made of air and space. It is made of light and darkness: it is made of desire and peace. It is made of anger and love: it is made of virtue and vice. It is made of all that is near: it is made of all that is afar. It is made of all.[3]

Indeed, in this passage and elsewhere in Upanishadic thought Atman is said to be identical to Brahman. This identification is evoked by Krishna when Arjuna asks to be instructed in the relation between Atman and Brahman: "Brahman is that which is immutable," the god replies, "and independent of any cause but Itself. When we consider Brahman as lodged within the individual being, we call Him the Atman. The creative energy of Brahman is that which causes all existences to come into being."

We seem here to have a hopeless conjunction of concepts. Atman is said to be all things, even identical to Brahman, and as such can be said to be the creative origin of all things as well. There appears no way of avoiding the absolute identification of Atman then with everything that exists, which has the consequence of draining the term of all its meaning. And yet, we do not need to read very far in these scriptures to find an expression that seems abruptly contrary to this unchecked inclusiveness. There is a fondness in the *Upanishads* for the formula, "Atman is not this and not that." (In Sanskrit, *neti, neti*.) While this looks at first to make matters worse, we might at least observe that the *neti, neti* has the effect of asserting that Atman is not a thing or an object of any kind. No sooner have we said what the Atman is than we must admit that, in truth, it is *not* this, and it is *not that* either.

What leads the inexperienced interpreter into difficulty here is the suspicion that the Upanishadic thinkers have a habit of obscuring the distinction between subject and object. We already noted that in the *Veda* there is a tendency toward the identification of one god with another. It is reasonable to think that this tendency recurs in the *Upanishads*. Just as one object might be confused with another object, so might a subject be confused with an object. This would explain the bald assertion that Atman is made of all things.

What has actually occurred here is an almost imperceptible philosophical shift that leads to bedeviling intellectual complexities. The simplest account of this shift is contained in the observation that the Upanishadic philosophers did not abandon the distinction between subject and object; on the contrary, *they introduced that distinction into the subject itself.* What they have discovered in their concentrated inwardness is the mind's infinite capacity for making an object of all its contents. The mind can look at its own thoughts, its own passions, as though they were objects that have been introduced from without. There is even the frequent presumption that we can look directly at ourselves. But such a presumption is absurd. The mind can no more think itself than the eye can see itself, or a finger touch itself, or the ear hear itself.

Recall the famous passage in the *Rig Veda* where the words of the priest pointed mysteriously into the emptiness that lies beyond the distinction between being and nonbeing. What we find in the *Upanishads* is that same adventure of thought, but now subtly refined. What the philosophers have discovered is the mysterious region that lies behind the distinction between subject and object. They have seen that there is something in the subject that can never become an object, not even for itself. This makes it absolutely irreducible—it can never be confused with anything else. It also makes it absolutely unknowable, because to know it would make it an object. Moreover, it cannot be subject to change; it can have no beginning and no end, for then it would no longer be identified with itself, but only an object among other changeable objects. The unbounded inclusiveness of the unchanging *beyond* means that there can be nothing beside it, or in addition to it; and in this sense it can be said to be all things. It is this irreducible and unknowable center that is comprehended in the term Atman.

The *Upanishads* can be read as one long hymn of effulgent praise for the Atman so conceived. This central, grand conception is held before the reader as one might examine a diamond of many facets, turning it slowly to watch the reflected light flash with ever changing nuances out of its interior. We shall take the time here only to look at those of this conception that add basic insight to the Hindu view of death.

Krishna identified the Atman with the creative energy of Brahman that brings all things into being. This gives the Atman a distinctly dynamic character. In the radical Upanishadic treatment of the subject/object distinction, as we have briefly described it, it is taken as self-evident that the eye cannot see itself, nor the ear hear itself. And yet, there is hearing and seeing. Who then is doing the hearing, who is seeing and knowing? In a variety of ways the Upanishads point beyond to the "ear of the ear, the eye of the eye, and the word of words, the mind of mind, and the life of life."[4] One often gets the impression from such locutions that the all-knowing and irreducible Atman resides in its keep beyond the scope of human comprehension, passively receiving the sensory data that floods in from without. We might even want to associate this metaphor with the famous Aristotelian image of the blank tablet or what Locke referred to as the tabula rasa—both represent the mind at birth, a mind on which each experience leaves its mark. If so, we have missed the point of the Upanishadic doctrine completely. In the Prasna Upanishad a sage asks a question that has a distinctly modern character: "What are the powers that keep the union of a being, how many keep burning the lamps of life, and which amongst them is supreme?" This is the question against which philosophers have judged the Lockean view of the self. Who or what will organize all these sense impressions that pile up like so many dead leaves into living thoughts? Who, if the mind is completely blank or passive, will actually do the thinking? The answer offered in the Upanishads is imaginative but philosophically forceful. It describes an occasion on which the separate sensory functions of the mind decide to act on their own without any guidance.

But Life, the power supreme, said to them: "Do not fall into delusion. It is I who, as Atman divided five ways, keep the union of this being and I am its foundation." But the separate powers believed him not.

Life was offended and rose aloft to leave the body, and all the powers of life had to rise, and, Life coming again to rest, all the powers had to rest. As when a queen-bee arises, all the bees with her arise, and when she comes to rest again, then all again come to rest, even so it happened to the powers of the voice, the mind, the eye, and the ear.[5]

Here the Atman does not merely receive what the senses bring to it, it actively coordinates all of these separate functions. The difficult expression "Atman divided five ways," which this Upanishad makes equivalent to Life (for which the Sanskrit word is *prana*, or breath), indicates the dynamic, but also unified and therefore unifying, presence of the Atman behind all five avenues of sensory knowledge. There simply could be no knowledge whatsoever if there were not a creative unifying force behind the perceiving functions of the mind.

In this connection we can see still another way of giving sense to the Upanishadic claim that *Atman is all*. It is not that Atman is to be literally identified with this object and that object, but that without the active, unifying presence of the Atman we could not even have an object. It would be as though the object were casting its sensory image onto a bare wall with no one there to see the projection, much less to recognize it. Therefore, all that the mind views, all that it comprehends, is a manifestation of the invisible Atman, a manifestation of the life that precedes our knowledge of life. Therefore, the characteristic Upanishadic humn:

> Concealed in the heart of all beings is the Atman;
> smaller than the smallest atom,
> greater than the vast spaces.[6]

The dynamic and creative nature of the Atman preserves the spirit of the great Vedic hymn, quoted above, in which the mystery of the origin of the universe is evoked but left open. There seemed to the Vedic mind no way of finding a true source of being that lay outside of being. In the *Upanishads* we find the thought that since the Atman is a subject that cannot be an object it must be self-originating. It is a thought, however, that is always expressed with the characteristic poetic grace of these scriptures: "from joy all beings have come, by joy they all live, and unto joy they return in death."[7] The word for joy, *ananda*, is often translated as bliss or happiness. In this context it has the effect of pointing to the inherent spontaneity of the Atman, or perhaps we should say of all that is.

With the notion that the Atman is the eye of the eye and the mind of the mind, we come to the unique core of Hindu thought that has no real counterpart in the West. This uniqueness gives us few familiar footholds as we try to make our way through the labyrinthine passages of Upanishadic thought. It might be helpful to draw contrasts with what lies ahead. The rishis could not have satisfied themselves with anything like the simple one-dimensional level of reality in Epicureanism and modern science, if only because there is one phenomenon that is left unexplained by both Epicureans and atomists: the phenomenon of knowledge. Not *thought,* but *knowledge.* The Greek atomists and twentieth-century physiologists have devised several accounts of the process of thought, but they have been conspicuously silent as to the phenomenon of knowledge. It is one thing for a thought to pass through a brain, it is another to *know* it. The rishis understood clearly that there has to be a knower distinct and prior to thought.

Plato, by contrast, was interested in knowledge at the expense of thought. For Plato thinking was participating in knowledge. Thinking was not a *process of the brain,* as it were, but the *presence in the mind* of the eternal ideas. This led to a contradiction, as we saw, inasmuch as in the *Phaedo* Plato is not concerned to argue that the ideas will survive, but that Socrates will survive—with *his* ideas. But if ideas are universal they alone can survive, but not as the ideas of Socrates or the ideas of Democritus. The rishis would have been delighted with Plato's eternal forms but would have insisted that they must have a knower who is not particular like Socrates, but eternal like the ideas. This knower, Atman, is always distinct from knowledge and the mind.

> That non-dual Atman, though never stirring, is swifter than the mind. The senses cannot reach Atman, for It moves ever in front. Though standing still, It overtakes others who are running . . . . It moves and moves not; It is far and likewise near. It is inside all this and It is outside all this.[8]

Plato was an immanentist since he believed that the ideas did not transcend the mind but were immediately present in it. The Upanishadists were extreme transcendentalists in their insistence that the mind always needs a mind—insofar as we are going to speak of *knowledge* and not merely of thought or reality.

Mystics are regularly confused with the Upanishadists because of the frequency with which both speak of *union.* The very great distance between the two is evident at once when we remember that mystics speak of what we have called an *erotic* union—that is, an identity not in being, but in act, and in a loving act. The *Upanishads* are completely oblivious to the erotic; it is just this quality that marks their divergence from the Aryan past. Where the mystics' ecstasy arises from the sublimity of a conjoint act, Upanishadic bliss, or *ananda,* is characterized by a total indifference to the act. Krishna explains carefully to Arjuna, for example, that it does not matter in the least whether he enters the battle or not, whether he kills or is killed, for he *is already* the Atman.

Looking ahead there is another contrast that can be briefly cited. The neoplatonists, following the second-century philosopher Plotinus, the greatest thinker to appear in the West since Plato and Aristotle, speak of the One that is utterly transcendent, similar to the rishis' Atman. The Neoplatonists, however, emphatically diluted this absolute transcendence by teaching that the One emanated itself outward into lower forms of existence. Since the soul is such an emanation it can be understood as substantially connected to the One, but nonetheless of fragmentary existence. There is no emanation of the Hindu's One. It simply is. What is real about us is not that we are a degenerated form of the Atman, but that we *are* the Atman.

We can summarize all of these contrasts under the categories through which we are discussing the problem of death, as follows: for Epicureans and modern science the continuity of life is in *matter*, for Platonists it is in *knowledge*, for mysticism it is in the *act*, and for the Hindus it is in *being*. We have also seen that each of these ways of dealing with the problem of death have left us with a problematic view of life. The materialists have so rigorously refused to allow an extramaterial ground for life that both life and death have vanished from their thought. The dualists have so separated life from its material limitations that the self loses all its structure to the vacuum of an endless future. The mystics so completely back into the eternality of the act that they deny the very history in which the act occurs. We must therefore look deeper into Hindu thought to discern the consequences of confronting the discontinuity of death with the continuity of being.

It is through their understanding of the nature of knowledge that the Upanishadic *rishis* came to the conclusion that there must be a knower behind the contents of the mind—since the mind cannot know itself. The transcendent nature of this sublime knower, or Atman, may now be clear. We can see in this conclusion the old priestly association of knowledge and power, for this knower is also the *origin* of the contents of its knowledge, and thus the origin of all that is. What is not so clear is how this transcendent Atman is actually connected to the wide-awake conscious mind.

When the Upanishadist speaks of the thoughts of the mind they are pictured as birds that venture forth, but always "return to their trees for rest," quite as "all things find their rest in Atman."[9] But the tree, or the Atman on which the birds alight, however necessary it might be for the birds does not itself require a ground on which to stand. It is perfectly unattached, and so is the mind that is purified and therefore identified with the Atman. Such a mind exists as in a state of deep sleep in which nothing is remembered; whatever it has seen in its travels does not follow it back, for there is nothing that can attach to it.[10] Another typically memorable metaphor is that of the Atman as the bridge between the eternal and the temporal: "Over that bridge there cross neither day, nor night, nor old age, nor death, nor sorrow, nor well-doing, nor evil-doing."[11]

Each of these metaphors offers a curious paradox; there is in every case a connection of the greatest importance, but a connection that never shows itself to the conscious self, to me. In this paradox is found the uniquely Hindu insight into the nature of selfhood and the very heart of its concept of death. The paradox is resolved by asserting *the fundamentally illusory nature of selfhood.* The term "illusory" is of critical importance here. What is real, what has true continuity, is *being*—the Atman. However real the birds of thought strike me, they always return to rest in the Atman. Insofar as I am "out there" I am a self that only seems to exist. "Whenever the soul has thoughts of 'I' and 'mine' it binds itself with its lower self, as a bird with the net of a snare."[12]

There are two philosophically important points inherent in this metaphor of the snared birds. First, the "I" and "mine" are referred to as *thoughts,* and not what is real. They are creations of consciousness like any other thoughts. Most emphatically this "I" is not to be confused with the author of consciousness, that is, with the Atman. The reason for this is quite simple: once we are able to think "I" or "mine" we have already made an object of ourselves, and we are living in the illusion that this "I," which is only a thought, is also the subject of itself—as if a thought could be the source of a thought. Thoughts, the *Upanishads* never tire of telling us, cannot think themselves.

Consider a second implication of this metaphor, somewhat more philosophically difficult. As the thought takes flight outward it is snared "out there" or away from the Atman. It is as though it has been caught somewhere in the world. This is another element in the illusory nature of selfhood; our ordinary self-understanding tells us that even though we are subjects to ourselves we are objects in the world. I am a person quite similar to other persons; I can be found in this place, at this time, and nowhere else. In this sense I know who (or what) and where I am. I can cite the hour of my birth, many details from my personal history, the precise location of my present activities. I am in those terms very much "in the world." But it is also in exactly these terms that, according to the Hindu master, I have also been snared, though I have not yet seen it—and this constitutes the illusion of selfhood.

Now it is precisely this illusory self, "out there" in the world, caught in the snare of its ignorance, that must die. Hindus do not deny death, but they do restrict it to that part of our existence that we have objectified. This is the self of our daily, waking existence, our three-dimensional living at a specific place and time. Our death is then connected to our ignorant assumption that this worldly context is both real and fixed.

> Whatever is here, is also there.
> Whatever is there, is also here.
> Whoever sees a difference between these
> wanders on from death to death.
>
> The mind is to attain the realization
> that there is no difference.
> Whoever sees a difference
> wanders on from death to death.[13]

There is a genuine danger in the way we become fascinated with the objective content of knowledge and fail to see the unified light of the Atman behind the diversity of the experienced world. But the danger in this case is not simply that we shall fall into ignorance, but that we shall be carried from "death to death" and be closed off from eternity. Knowledge, in the *Upanishads,* is not therefore simply the way the self looks on the world, it is the way the self actually goes out to the world, and there is always the high risk that the self will get caught there, like a bird in a snare, and never return to its eternal center.

This passage makes manifest the Hindu conception of the *agency of death as illusion.* It is our failure to know what is real. Again our lack of familiarity with the exalted Hindu teaching on the nature of knowledge is likely to obscure for us the enormous power of illusion. To live in illusion is not just to be mistaken or simply to stand in need of correction by new information. What is faulty is not something in our knowledge—but our knowledge itself. We send it out to the world, but overlook the fact that it must return. It becomes trapped by the world—and unaware we are captured as well. Quite simply, to think that our knowledge is always knowledge of something, and even to value our knowledge according to the accuracy and amount of its objective content, is to live in illusion. It is illusory to think there is something *there* about which I have knowledge. The power of this illusion lies in the supreme difficulty of stepping outside our knowledge to see the nature of our knowledge. When we are told that it is an illusion to think our knowledge is *about* the world, we are likely to shrug it off, assuming that what is meant is that the world is not quite what we think or that our knowledge should be about something higher than the world. The issue is not *what* knowledge ought to be about, but *that* our knowledge is about something at all. In truth, knowledge is never about something, it is what the thinker is thinking. *Knowledge does not have an object, but only a subject.* The only objects are objects *in* our knowledge, and not *for* it.

But why is illusion the agent of *death?* This has to do with the great power that knowledge possesses, a power discovered by the ancient priests. Knowledge is not something a thinker can turn on and off at will—knowledge carries the thinker with it. *We cannot believe or act on something we know to be untrue.* If we *know* the ice is too thin to walk on, we will not walk on it as if it is safe. We may be *mistaken,* but if we genuinely take something to be true we do not *believe* we are mistaken. Since knowledge does have this power, the kind of thinking that is tied to objects will cause us to consider ourselves as objects, vulnerable to the same inevitable demise to which all objects are fated. It is not because we think about these objects or those, but because we think *about* something at all that we are inescapably mortal.

Now, of course, we *are* mistaken about the nature of our knowledge. In fact, the mortal self is itself illusory. And since it is, we are not hopelessly lost. There is always the possibility that truth will break through the illusion and that we can allow the thoughts to return silently to their origin in the Atman. Because the Atman can collect these loose fragments of the worldly self, the *Upanishads* declare this as their highest teaching:

> When through self, by the suppressing of the mind, one sees the brilliant Self which is more subtle than the subtle, then having seen the Self through one's self, one becomes self-less. Because of being selfless, he is to be regarded as boundless, without origin— the mark of liberation. This is the supreme secret doctrine.[14]

What is assumed throughout is that if it is ignorance—or *false knowledge*—that got us into mortality it is only true knowledge that can get us out. "Whoever knows Brahman," the Upanishadist declares, "becomes Brahman."[15] This is plainly knowledge of a different sort. *It cannot be knowledge of an object* since that was the very sort of knowledge that snares our thoughts. A disciple asks his master: "Is anything higher than thought?" The master answers:

> Meditation is in truth higher than thought. The earth seems to rest in silent meditation; and the waters and the mountains and the

sky and the heavens seem all to be in meditation. Whenever a man attains greatness on this earth, he has his reward according to his meditation.[16]

The term *meditation* in this passage has the sense of a form of knowledge in which the subject and object are identical. The earth is said to meditate because it is simply itself and nothing else. Moreover, it is not even conscious of being itself. Meditation is sometimes said to be consciousness without an object. It is what happens to knowledge when it leads to the selflessness of the pure Self, or Atman. In meditation, or consciousness without an object, one reaches the end of the journey of knowledge. In the *Katha Upanishad* the metaphor of a chariot is evoked; its charioteer is reason, the horses the senses, the chariot itself the body, and the reins are the mind. Whoever drives the body with the wrong understanding will simply be riding behind the wild, runaway powers of sense, but whoever drives with the right mind "reaches the End of the journey, from which he never returns."[17]

It is the phenomenon of reaching the end of the journey, of having a knowledge of Brahman in which one becomes Brahman, that gave rise to the famed Upanishadic declaration, *Tat tvam asi*, usually translated, "That art thou." The *tat tvam asi* is characteristically uttered in those moments when one reaches levels of deep insight during instruction. When the master sees that the student has awakened to the eternal, changeless, deathless, boundless nature of the Brahman/Atman he may exclaim: *Tav tvam asi,* or That art thou!

Let us not overlook one crucial feature of this teaching—when the journey has been completed one *never returns.* One of the rishis, explaining to his students that when the Atman reclaims the fragments of the worldly self it is like salt disappearing in water, stresses the impossibility of getting the salt out again. He concludes from this metaphor that "there is no consciousness after death."[18] There is something in Socrates' anticipated conversation with ancient sages in the underworld that we can immediately understand, but it is usually deeply puzzling to the Western mind how the Upanishadic teaching could be taken as a great comfort. Where is the bliss or joy in the thought that the self can merge with the Atman without a trace of its former existence, quite as one might fall into a deep, dreamless sleep of which nothing could ever be remembered? In the *Bhagavad-Gita* the goal Krishna wants to achieve with Arjuna is not his entrance into battle, but his liberation from the "terrible wheel of death and re-brith." Krishna is certainly aware that this liberation will carry Arjuna beyond the borders of consciousness. Before we can come to an adequate understanding of the Hindu attitude toward death we must learn, therefore, why liberation is so deeply prized. Of what does the wheel of death and rebirth consist, and why is it so terrible? What, in other words, is the Hindu understanding of grief, or the state of existing in illusion?

Since the *Gita* is much more a song, or a poem, than it is a work of philosophy, we find no attempt there to explain why it is that death should be followed by rebirth and birth by another death, nor do we find why this succession should continue indefinitely as it would if it were on a wheel. With this question we have entered into the familiar Hindu conception of the transmigration of souls, a concept that appears often in popular religious thought in the West. However, in the Hindu setting transmigration is not an elaboration on the doctrine of immortality, for as we have observed in several ways the kind of continuity implied in immortality is unthinkable to the Hindu. Transmigration is not a teaching that takes its major force from the desire to escape death; it is not a signal of hope to the soul in dread of death. On the contrary, transmigration is the terrible fate that one must do everything possible to avoid. To the Western mind this teaching seems to offer a person another life, another chance to live through it all one more time but with less suffering and fewer mistakes. To the Hindu transmigration means not just another birth, but also another death. We noted earlier that in very ancient Hindu writings there is a pronounced fear not of death but of the "second death" that may follow. While this earlier notion remains vague, it shows that buried deep in Hindu tradition is the sobering spiritual insight that there is something far worse than death: the endless repetition of death and the rebirth that necessarily follows it. What is the source of the vision of an endless cycle?

We are somewhat at a disadvantage here in attempting to understand the Hindu mind, since in all the vast sacred literature there is scarcely a single clear argument that would make it apparent to a Western mind *why* life and death follow each other in this cyclical pattern. It was a fact so obvious to the Hindu that any argument for it would obviously seem superfluous. We must therefore look at several of the fundamental metaphysical beliefs held by all Hindus to find the clue to the great power of the idea of transmigration.

We note first that the circle of birth and rebirth has great power. We are swept along by it, overwhelmed and helpless. It is as though the whole past is still active as a force pressing against the unprotected self. The empiricial self seems like a mere straw borne on the torrent of a great river swollen with the runoff of snows that had fallen many seasons earlier. Hindus know this force as *karma*.

Sometimes karma is spoken of as though it is a kind of sin that places on its doer a burden or debt that must somehow be shed. Life appears in this case to be purgatorial, an extended labor of redemption by which one attempts to disburden oneself of the cumulative effect of former errors. Westerners seem to have no difficulty with this use of the term for it bears a strong resemblance to the sin/debt scheme found throughout Judaism, Christianity, and Islam. This similarity is quite superficial and misleading. In Western thought the burden of sin may well lead to punishment or the need for divine cleansing, but it does not lead to rebirth. For the Hindu karma is not only the consequence of the act; it is the act. The karmic burden one must bear is not the weight of demerits earned by disobedience of moral or divine law; the karmic burden is nothing less than the active self. One is liberated from karma not by a lifting of the weight by divine act, but by the achievement of tranquility, or nonaction, in which all karma is killed. That is, all deeds, both good and evil.[19]

In sharp contrast to the West we can say that the karmic burden is not the burden of a previous existence, but it is *existence itself*, that is, existence of a certain kind. According to the Upanishadic understanding of the nature of knowledge, what persons know is the way in which they engage the world, and when knowledge is concerned with the manifold diversity rather than the One that lies behind it all, there is a certainty of being snared by the world. "Thinking about sense-objects will attach you to sense-objects," Krishna explains to Arjuna.[20] The doctrine of karma arises from the insight that when we become occupied with the diversity of the world we begin to take our places in it as active agents. There is a merging here of action with misunderstanding or with false knowledge. What is it we do not understand about action? We do not understand that it is not action as such, but the *consequence of action*, that chiefly concerns us. "You have the right to work," Krishna says, "but for the work's sake only. You have no rights to the fruits of the work."[21]

When we become concerned with the diversity of the world and what is happening within it, we initiate actions designed to alter the outcome of events. We act *for* the consequences, in other words. But, we also act *because* of the consequences of previous actions. Our concern for the outcome of events has arisen in the past. The present is therefore only the point at which a nonexistent past directs the ignorant self toward a nonexistent future. The self has taken up the role of being a kind of broker between two great nonentities. But what is worse is that what the self recalls from the past never was truly existent, for what it sees looking backward is itself looking forward. Sometimes the *Upanishads* speak of this as a "shadow" that the self casts onto the next existence. The shadow created by one's ignorance in a previous existence falls into the present.[22] Of course, we must see here that the shadow cast by a previous self is not merely an influence on the present self, *it is the present self*. This results in the implausible situation that the present self that mediates by way of its action between a nonexistent past and a nonexistent future is not itself present, but dwells obscurely in the past as a shadowy being looking toward what it may be in the future. This may mean one's entire existence is so darkly shadowed that there is no light of consciousness in it. One might therefore be born as a "worm, or as a moth, or as a fish, or as a bird, or as a lion."[23] Some are even reborn "as rice and barley, as herbs and trees, as sesame plants and beans." In such a case the shadow of the past is so dense one has no hope of liberation unless "someone or other eats him as food and emits him as semen."[24]

The doctrine of karma represents another sharp difference with the religions and philosophies of the West. According to the sin/debt scheme in Western thought, we are loaded down with the weight of past misbehavior, but these punishable acts constitute violations of divine injunctions. There are no such divine ordinances in Hinduism (or in Buddhism). Moreover, these violations are made all the more serious, as Jews and Christians see it, by the fact that the sinner does not simply fail to live up the law, but aggressively breaks it out of the hidden *desire to become God*—the single most serious offense of human existence. Hindus, by contrast, consider the great human failure to be *the refusal to become God*: "To the Indian sage the only heresy there can be is the heresy of separateness, from which stems all the evil of the world."[25] In the West evil—including death—stems from the unwillingness to remain within the finite limits of human existence and, therefore, separate. What is more, the burden carried by the sinner is so great that it must be removed by a divine act. In the East karma can be evaded *only* by one's own act. Finally, since the karmic burden is not added to existence, but *is* existence, one has it from the beginning of life, automatically, by birth, as it were. The burden is removed by the free expression of the self. In the West the burden is *acquired freely*, and it is removed not when the sinner freely unloads it, but only when a perfect *obedience* between sinner and God is achieved—at which point God lifts the burden.

Drawing the contrast between Hinduism and Western theism in this matter helps to show why the *Upanishads* do not speak against the pain of life, and why Krishna should speak of the "terrible wheel of death and rebirth." If we regard karma as the psychic drag of the past on the present, and the present struggle of the self to escape that drag by flying into the future, thereby only increasing the karma, existence seems doomed to the continuing reinforcement of its unreality. What Hindus have in mind here is not some arcane mechanism, but a common feature of human existence evident in ordinary experience. The influence of the past is seen in very simple matters, such as the way we identify objects in the world: we see things in categories already familiar to us. We look at the world not to see what is there, but to see which of the things there we already know. What is this but bringing the past out of the past into the present? When this drag of the past confuses our relationship to the present, as it often does, leading to misunderstanding and frustration and error, we look anxiously forward to resolve the confusion, only weighting ourselves with more of a burden. To use the Upanishadic metaphor, existence becomes a prison of shadows, sealing us off from what is truly *real*. This is also why existence is a wheel: it endlessly *repeats* itself; and why it is terrible: it repeats itself *endlessly*. Hindus understand by karma what we have so far described as grief—a life that resembles death. Instead of restoring our living self to its true being, we repeatedly lead it to death.

We noted earlier that the *Upanishads* teach that since we get on this wheel by false knowledge we must get off by true knowledge—and this knowledge must take the form of meditation, which is knowledge without an object. Meditation alone can snatch us from the mouth of death and the inevitable rebirth. But how do we meditate? The great Hindu answer to this question is only named, and not discussed, by the *Upanishads:*

> When the five senses and the intellect are still, and the mind rests in silence, then begins the Path supreme. This is Yoga—the firm holding back of the senses. Here one becomes undistracted. Indeed, Yoga is the beginning and the end.[26]

Yoga is precisely the path that Krishna exhorts Arjuna to follow, in order that he might reach union with Brahman and be freed from the wheel of death and birth. A large part of the *Gita* is an eloquent description and praise of Yoga, as the following representative hymn shows us.

> The illumined soul
> Whose heart is Brahman's heart
> Thinks always: "I am doing nothing,"
> No matter what he sees,

Hears, touches, smells, eats;
No matter whether he is moving,
Sleeping, breathing, speaking,
Excreting, or grasping something with his hand,
Or opening his eyes,
Or closing his eyes:
This he knows always:
"I am not seeing, I am not hearing:
It is the senses that see and hear
And touch the things of the senses."[27]

Quite obviously for one to achieve this degree of nonattachment one must undergo rigorous and disciplined training. Classically, the path of Yoga is thought to have six stages, with two prior stages thought to be preparation. The preparatory disciplines of *yama* and *niyama* have chiefly to do with clearing one's personal life of distractions so that the necessary effort can be given the Yogic discipline proper. Yama focuses on one's social relationships and in particular, on the development of qualities such as compassion, truthfulness, chastity or sexual continence, and lack of greed. Niyama applies to one's own discipline and includes such virtues as cleanliness, contentment, studiousness, and an inclination toward the ascetic. We should not overlook the fact that yama and niyama, inasmuch as they are considered preparations for Yoga proper, presuppose that one must be in good physical spiritual health *before* taking up Yoga; one does not therefore make use of Yoga to achieve good health. Such a motive would constitute a serious misunderstanding of Yoga as a method to accomplish a goal or desire one has prior to entering onto the Yogic path. *One cannot properly enter onto that path until all such goals and desires have been set aside.* It is one of the deepest assumptions of the Yoga philosophy that when one has stepped onto the path with adequate preparation the path will lead to a place no one could have known in advance and, therefore, to a place no one could have desired to go.

The first of the six stages is *asana*, or posture. The famed lotus position is preferred by most Yogis, but some insist that any position will do so long as it frees one from any distraction that might come from physical discomfort. The second stage, *pranayama*, is the proper regulation of breath. There is much literature on this stage for the reason that in Hinduism, as in most religions, great importance is placed on the function of breathing. At the most elemental level breathing is the most obvious sign of life. It is nearly universally believed that death comes at the moment breathing ceases. It may still be the case that, for all the sophisticated devices and procedures developed for ascertaining the moment of death, the termination of breathing is the most reliable. At a deeper level, however, breath is seen as a rhythmic exchange of life-sustaining elements from the surrounding universe. The regularity, the pace, and the depth of one's breathing indicate the degree to which one is in congruence with the world around. Shallow, rapid breathing often means anxiety; deeper and more strained breathing usually attend sudden, physical exertion or sexual excitation. A sudden shock "takes one's breath away." Spiritual serenity is regularly accompanied by slow, evenly paced, very deep breathing. Words connected with "breathing" possess a range of nuances that we find in many religious traditions. The Latin term *spiritus*, the Greek *pneuma*, and the Hebrew *ruach*—all translated as "spirit"—have the common meaning "breath." The Yogic preoccupation with breath comes from the discovery that breathing not only indicates the state of one's inwardness, it also determines it.

When one has arrived at the stage of perfect harmony with the world by way of controlled breathing the third stage, *pratyahara*, has been reached. Here one withdraws one's sense from the world, severs all awareness of the physical world—both without and within one's body. This state is evoked in a poetic exclamation of Krishna's:

> The tortoise can draw in his legs:
> The seer can draw in his senses.
> I call him illumined.[28]

The next two stages, *dharana* and *dhyana*, are more difficult to describe and impossible to understand perfectly by one who has never been there. Very roughly the terms may be translated as concentration and meditation. "Concentration," wrote Patanjali, the great philosopher of Yoga, in the second century B.C.E., "is the binding of the mind to one place."[29] The mind can be thus bound to any object as concrete as the tip of the nose or as abstract as the "lotus of the heart." Meditation is an elevated form of concentration in which one holds the mind perfectly still, but without binding it to any object whatsoever. We saw earlier how one of the Upanishadic rishis spoke of the earth as meditating, suggesting that it had identified with itself in perfect concentration and thus had no object.

The sixth and final stage is *samadhi*, or perfect unification. Here the mind has so completely eliminated any trace of an object that it is merely One. It has left behind all of the activities of thinking and feeling, even concentrating and meditating. In his classic study of

Yoga, Mircea Eliade uses the suggestive term *entasis* to describe the state of samadhi. Entasis is to be contrasted with *extasis*, meaning literally to stand outside oneself. To be in a state of ecstasy is to be transported into another mode of existence; to be in entasis, or samadhi, is to abandon all transport and all alternative modes of existence, and merely to stand with perfect stillness inside onself.[30]

Although words can only point in the direction of this summit of the Yogic experience, we can see clearly enough along that path to know why Yoga is an indispensable part of the Hindu understanding of death. Previously we saw that, at least in the *Upanishads*, knowledge is given an exalted place in the spiritual life, so exalted that it can be said that faulty knowledge, or preoccupation with the diversity and ignorance of the One, can lead directly into the "mouth of death." However, a person does not escape death merely by acquiring more knowledge *about* the One, for this is still knowledge that has an object and is therefore the kind of knowledge that binds us to the world, holding us helplessly trapped between a nonexistent past and a nonexistent future. Whenever knowledge is *knowledge about* something beyond itself, we are swept along in the swirling torrent of karma, the unavoidable consequence of our worldly nature. Only when we have mastered the discipline of withdrawing all knowledge from its object and bringing it into itself so completely that all duality is burned away, leaving pure light, do we step off the terrible wheel of death and rebirth.

Hinduism then deals with the discontinuity of death by opposing it with the continuity of *being*, or the real—that which truly is. Death, in other words, is not opposed by *life*. The reason that continuity can be found only in being, and not in life, is quite simply that life has a beginning. It has come into existence and will pass out of it. Life therefore has a questionable metaphysical status that is described succinctly in this passage from the *Gita*:

> That which is non-existent can never come into being, and that which is can never cease to be. Those who have known the inmost Reality know also the nature of *is* and *is not*.[31]

Because life has come into existence it is, for the Hindu, not real. The reason life cannot oppose death is that there is in fact no such thing as life. What we usually regard as life is an illusion that has obscured Reality. But death is not real either, for the same reason. Life cannot oppose death, because there is nothing to oppose, because all oppositions are unreal.

Those who know the inmost Reality know that only that Reality is, and that it is One; they know therefore that *life is not* and that *death is not*. More importantly, those who truly know the inmost Reality *are* the inmost Reality. Only of them can it be said, *Tat tvam asi:* That art thou.

Notes

1. Rig Veda, 1.164.45,46 (tr. Edgerton).
2. Rig Veda, 10.129.1-4,6,7 (tr. Edgerton).
3. Brihad-Aranyaka Upanishad 4.4.5 (tr. Nikhilananda).
4. Kena Upanishad 1.2 (tr. Mascaro, altered).
5. Prasna Upanishad 2.3-4 (tr. Mascaro, altered).
6. Katha Upanishad 2.20 (tr. Mascaro, altered).
7. Taittiriya Upanishad 3.6 (tr. Mascaro, altered).
8. Isa Upanishad 4,5 (tr. Nikhilananda).
9. Prasna Upanishad 4.7 (tr. Mascaro).
10. Brihad-Aranyaka Upanishad 4.13.15 (tr. Nikhilananda).
11. Chandogya Upanishad 8.4.1 (tr. Hume).
12. Maitri Upanishad 3.2, (tr. Mascaro).
13. Katha Upanishad 4.10,11 (tr. Hume, altered).
14. Maitri Upanishad 6.20 (tr. Hume, altered).
15. Mundaka Upanishad 3.2.9 (tr. Mascaro, altered).
16. Chandogya Upanishad 7.6.1 (tr. Mascaro, altered).
17. Ibid.
18. Brihad-Aranyaka Upanishad 2.4 (tr. Mascaro).
19. See especially the long passage in the Maitri Upanishad 6.34.
20. *Bhagavad-Gita*, p. 42.
21. Ibid., p. 40.
22. Prasna Upanishad 3.1-3.
23. Kaushitaki Upanishad 1.2 (tr. Nikhilananda).
24. Chandogya Upanishad 5.10.6 (tr. Nikhilananda).
25. Feuerstein and Miller, *Yoga and Beyond*, p. 13.
26. Katha Upanishad 6.10,11 (tr. Hume, altered).
27. *Bhagavad-Gita*, pp. 57 ff.
28. Ibid., p. 42.
29. *Yoga and Beyond*, p. 30.
30. For a more complete discussion of these stages, along with the Patanjali philsophy of yoga, see Dasgupta, *Yoga as Philosophy and Religion*, Ch. xiii, et passim.
31. *Bhagavad-Gita*, p. 36.

Bibliography

Maurice Bloomfield, *The Religion of the Veda* (New York: 1969).

S. Dasgupta, *Yoga as Philosophy and Religion* (Delhi: 1973).

Franklin Edgerton, *The Beginnings of Indian Philosophy* (Cambridge: 1965).

Mircea Eliade, *Yoga: Immortality and Freedom* (Princeton: 1970).

Ainslee T. Embree, *The Hindu Tradition: Readings in Oriental Thought* (New York: 1972).

George Feuerstein, Jeanine Miller, *Yoga and Beyond: Essays in Indian Philosophy* (New York: 1972).

Thomas Hopkins, *The Hindu Tradition* (Belmont: 1971).

Robert E. Hume, tr. and ed., *The Thirteen Principal Upanishads* (Cambridge: 1965).

A. B. Keith, *The Religion and Philosophy of the Veda and Upanishads*, 2 vols. (Cambridge: 1925).

Juan Mascaro, tr. and ed., *The Upanishads* (Baltimore: 1971).

Swami Nikhilananda, tr., *The Upanishads* (New York: 1964).

Swami Prabhavananda, Christopher Isherwood, trs., *The Song of God: Bhagavad-Gita* (New York: 1951).

Swami Prabhavananda, Frederick Manchester, trs., *The Upanishads: Breath of the Eternal* (New York: 1957).

S. Radhakrishnan, *Indian Philosophy*, 2 vols. (New York: 1927).

Louis Renou, ed. and intro., *Hinduism* (New York: 1962).

R. C. Zaehner, *Hinduism* (New York: 1969).

FIVE
DEATH AS FICTION
—BECOMING

---

6 BUDDHISM

Tradition describes the Buddha as the son of a mighty ruler, who would have certainly mastered all of India had he not chosen the path of enlightenment instead. What we know from historical evidence is that the tradition is exaggerated. There is no record of his father's kingdom. Other details of his life remain obscure, buried in legend. We are not certain even what language he spoke. Scholars do generally agree on the years of his life as 563 to 483 B.C.E., but even in this trustworthy information is scanty.

The unreliability of the traditional narrative of the Buddha's life is, however, not important. It is not accuracy the tradition intends. The legendary biography of his life is meant to display the nature of his teachings, and the emphasis on his princely youth is especially revealing. Siddhartha Gautama—the family name by which he was known until his designation as the Buddha, or Enlightened One—was raised in a rare and widely envied opulence. His indulgent father spared nothing in providing for his pleasure. Prince Siddhartha took a woman of surpassing beauty for his wife and had a son whom he deeply treasured. He lived in this manner for thirty years.

Then, abruptly, accidentally, he was exposed to aging, disease, and death—phenomena from which his father had painstakingly sheltered him. It was a profoundly disturbing discovery that life was not thoroughly pleasurable, but was in fact everywhere in the grip of suffering and death. The serene continuity of his life was shattered. All he had valued, everything he had come to depend on for his happiness, proved to be ephemeral. The young prince's sudden experience of life's

136

discontinuity brought him to a personal crisis. He was compelled to find a higher meaning to life that could account for its irreversible contingencies.

Secretly he resolved to take up the life of a mendicant monk. One night, rising silently from his bed, he looked briefly at the sleeping faces of his wife and son, knowing he would never see them again, and fled into the forest. For the next six years he put himself under the guidance of a series of spiritual masters, following their assorted regimens with unrelenting ardor. He starved and tortured his body until his skin became leathery and covered with sores. He ate only enough to keep himself alive, but little enough that the fires of passion would cease to burn in his flesh. He became so emaciated that, as one of the ancient texts put it, the mark of his seat where he had sat on the ground looked like the footprint of a camel.

But, for all his efforts, these strategies were no more effective in shielding him from the anguish he experienced in the face of suffering and death than his father's protective extravagance had been. When he came finally to see that neither extreme would lead him to life's higher meaning, it struck him that if such a meaning existed at all the path to it must lie somewhere else. In a decisive moment Siddhartha sat beneath a great tree, placed his hand on the earth, and vowed he would not rise again before he had attained the liberation from the suffering he sought.

The historical details of his life are far less important to later tradition than *the character of his interiority at the moment of his enlightenment* that occurred as he sat under the Bodhi tree. "In a word, what constituted the life and spirit of Buddhism," D. T. Suzuki, the eminent Buddhist interpreter and historian, has written, "is nothing else than the inner life and spirit of the Buddha himself; Buddhism is the structure erected around the inmost consciousness of its founder."[1]

Legend preserves a charming account of the way in which Prince Siddhartha passed into Buddhahood. A woman who had come to offer food to the spirit of the tree mistook the gaunt, motionless figure for the demon she wanted to appease, and set the food before him. This innocent gesture awakened in Siddhartha the realization that he must henceforth follow a middle way between the two extremes of pleasure and deprivation. He ate the modest portion of rice that had been placed before him. The bare simplicity of this event, the rude humanity of a starved man eating a mistakenly offered sacrifice, easily masks the profound depth of this moment that has attracted the many followers down through the centuries. For them this was the true entrance into what has traditionally been called the religion of the Middle Way. To the Western reader the notion of the Middle Way seems disappointingly flat, a sort of compromise, at best a reflection of the Greeks' Golden Mean. However, we must discover how the Middle Way has essentially nothing in common with the Greeks' sense of mean or compromise; the Middle Way in fact reveals a path to a spiritual realm never known in the West.

After Siddhartha realized he must abandon his extremes, and after he had taken the offering, he remained under the great tree meditating with increasing intensity. It is said that his enlightenment came in three stages, or during three "watches of the night." During the first watch, or evening, he had a vision of his previous existences, in perfect detail, one after the other, numbering into many thousands. During the second watch, which was the middle of the night, he had a similar vision, but this time he saw all other creatures as he had seen himself—passing through an endless cycle of rebirths. He also had a clear view of the law of karma by which each subsequent birth is determined by the quality of the previous life: those whose lives were filled with good deeds were born higher than those whose lives had been evil.

During the third and crucial watch, between midnight and dawn, he discovered the principle of "dependent origination" and understood at once how suffering was to be eliminated.

The principle of dependent origination is really a way of viewing the causal interrelatedness of all that exists. It is an extension of the cyclical pattern of rebirth that Gautama had perceived during the second watch. According to this view every existing entity comes into being as a consequence of a prior entity. Nothing arises out of itself alone, or out of nothing by its own agency. In order to exist at all, it must depend on something other than itself. What is most important in this view is that the entities included in the principle of dependent origination are not merely physical entities, but absolutely everything that can be said to exist—such as emotions, thoughts, all possible sensory data, even suffering and death.

To state it in its simplest form, Siddhartha's search for a release from suffering came to an end with the discovery that *one must free oneself from every sort of causal relatedness.* The discovery was abrupt, instantly clear, and irreversibly effective. Indeed, the discovery as to how he was to be liberated was itself the liberation. What is more, it was an awakening so final and deeply convincing that everything that had gone before suddenly looked different, and there was no possibility of returning to a prior moment in his spiritual journey. Indeed, there was no more possibility of a journey at all. Siddhartha had become what would later be called an *arhant,* one whose enlightenment had reached the stage from which there is no forced return, where there is no longer the danger of rebirth.

By the time dawn had broken after the third watch of the night Siddhartha knew that he was now the Buddha, a term indicating the supreme accomplishment of perfect enlightenment. He is said to have remained under the Bodhi tree for forty-nine days, speaking to no one. He did receive offerings from two itinerant merchants who acknowledged him as the Buddha. Evidently even in his physical appearance one could see that he had wiped away every trace of suffering.

All his life and teaching, all 2500 years of Buddhist tradition, have been directly concerned with making clear how the Buddha overcame the crippling perception of life's utter discontinuity—which is death in its most powerful form. No one of the figures or traditions included in this study began with a clearer view of the force of death or were more conscious of a resolve to contend with that force. Like all the other great systems of thought, in facing the problem of death there is no attempt to meet it *in kind* and to overpower it. There is no suggestion that we should endeavor to lengthen our lives, find kingdoms of health and pleasure more securely protected against suffering and death—nor even that we should, like the Hindus, take flight from this world as though it were illusion and pass into the real. When the Buddha took the offered rice it was a gesture that put him decisively outside the Hindu strategy for coping with death's threatened discontinuity. The Buddha did not question the world's *reality*.

As we begin to look at what the Buddha *did* intend in this moment, we must take seriously the fact that 2500 years of explication in dozens of languages, and scores of schools of interpretation, have preceded us. All we can hope to do here is to allow the Buddhist conception of death to begin to emerge in some of the most distinctive features of its spiritual profile. As in Hinduism the simplicity of expression can be deceiving if we take it from its intellectual and cultural context. In the pages that follow we shall attempt to discover some of this context, but to do so is inevitably to introduce arguments and paths of reasoning as difficult as any to be found in this study. Buddhists have an apparently endless capacity for splitting hairs and searching out paradox where none seems evident.

A paradox appears at the moment of the Buddha's enlightenment with the question as to whether he should say anything at all about it. Since he had reached the end of his journey he was *in need* of nothing more—not even of announcing he had achieved it. Nonetheless, after the forty-nine days under the Bodhi tree he rose and went forth to proclaim his *dharma*. The term, dharma, translates only with distortion. It can, in various contexts, mean doctrine, or teaching, or truth, or even reality. Perhaps we come closest to its original sense if we take it to refer to *that which is actually the case.* To proclaim the dharma is to state the way things are. This is not to say, however, that the dharma is a dispassionate account of objective reality. Neither may we take it as a prescribed list of doctrines that functions like a creed. The dharma has no content in the static sense. What the Buddha achieves in the proclamation of the dharma is not a description of the world "out there," not a psychological analysis of consciousness, and not what his consciousness contains; it is the communication of his consciousness itself. What the Buddha offers in his dharma is not what we are to look at in the world, or in ourselves; he offers us sight itself, the true sight that brings liberating enlightenment. If the dharma has to do with that which is actually the case, we can say that the Buddha's consciousness is that which is actually the case.

The importance the Buddha gave to the place of the dharma is well-illustrated in the story that shortly before his death, at that moment when he might have appointed a successor or when he might have invested a certain institution with his authority, he simply announced to his followers that the dharma would be their leader. This is a clear difference between the Buddha and Jesus. It is not Jesus' teaching, but Jesus, who is the foundation of the Christian's faith. It is not so much what Jesus said, or did, that counts for Christians, as it is the fact that he is the incarnate deity. In Buddhism the humanity of its founder remains unmixed with divinity. Unlike all the other great religions of the world, there is no great emergence of the divine into the human sphere, there is no sudden bestowal of a godly proclamation on a selected human agent. There is only a physically and spiritually exhausted monk who had set aside all known religious resources and achieved his own liberation. In the words of a distinguished scholar of Buddhist thought, "we must note that within the sphere of Buddhism one finds no story of Creation, no Creator, no God, no First Cause, no monotheistic idea. Nor do we have any trace of materialism, hedonism, or extreme asceticism."[2] The centrality of the dharma, in other words, reflects the spiritual accessibility of Buddhism. One need not depend on the will of a deity, or the possession of supernatural gifts, or membership in a certain caste or profession, to achieve enlightenment. One need only seek it; nothing is required but the desire to have it.

It is important to our understanding of Buddhism to take special note of the fact that the Buddha *did* choose to teach the dharma. This is important because it is obvious that he thought it could be communicated by way of discourse. Many centuries later, however, it seemed to many Buddhists that the true nature of the Buddha's consciousness would forever elude verbal description, and one should therefore eschew all attempts to state what *it* is. There is a sense in which that is true. We have already seen that it is not the role of the dharma to describe enlightenment as such, but to communicate it. It is the communication, or the passage from one person to another, of liberating consciousness that is at stake here, not the ability to define precisely what that consciousness is. This is confusing to students of Buddhism and was even confusing to the Buddha's own followers, for they, like we, are often impatiently led to ask what, after all, the Buddha is talking *about* when he speaks of release, or enlightenment. We shall, therefore, have widely missed the mark in our own discussion of Buddhism here if we assume we can talk about what enlightenment is. What we can talk about is why one would wish to attain it, and how it could be attained. In doing so, we would only be following the Buddha's own approach, for he steadfastly refused to answer any direct questions concerning the nature of enlightenment—and a number of other "imponderables" on which he maintained a "noble silence."

The dharma has developed over the centuries, therefore, around the questions and puzzlements raised by the powerful impact of the Buddha's consciousness. Like the itinerant merchants or like his former monastic companions, when they first beheld him after his enlightenment, the fact that something extraordinary had occurred was obvious, but what it was and what it meant was in no way as easily perceived. As we examine the dharma with special attention to the way in which it has integrated the experienced discontinuity of death, the themes that most significantly inform it are the following: *dukkha*, the suffering or sorrow that can always be heard as the deep background chords; *samsara*, the wheel of birth, death, and rebirth much like that found in Hinduism; *anatman*, the doctrine of the nonself that represents a complete rejection of the Hindus' central emphasis on Atman; *Sunyata*, the void or emptiness of all things, quite probably the most difficult of all Buddhist teachings; *prajna*, the rare wisdom that emerges from the persistent affirmation of the primacy of mind; and finally *nirvana*, the ultimate liberation in which the experienced discontinuity of death is finally extinguished.

What is suffering, and why is its occurrence so universal? The Buddha made clear the cause of suffering in his first address after his enlightenment. Having resolved to proclaim the dharma, he left his place under the tree and walked several hundred miles to the city of Benares where he found the five monks who had been his companions up to the time he renounced the discipline of extreme asceticism—to their scorn. They quickly acknowledged his Buddhahood and declared themselves followers. His first instruction to them was a discourse on the truths discovered in the course of his enlightenment. He first states flatly that existence is everywhere characterized by suffering:

> birth is painful, old age is painful, sickness is painful, death is painful, sorrow, lamentation, dejection, and despair are painful. Contact with unpleasant things is painful, not getting what one wishes is painful. In short, the five *skandhas* [all the elements that make up an individual's human existence] are painful.

The Buddha then proceeds at once to the origin of human suffering:

> Now this, monks is the noble truth of the cause of pain: the craving, which tends to rebirth, combined with pleasure and lust, finding pleasure here and there; namely, the craving for passion, the craving for existence, the craving for non-existence.

The conclusion of this analysis is self-evident: one overcomes suffering by wiping away all craving, by achieving total "abandonment, forsaking, release, non-attachment."[3]

That first address to the five monks offers little interpretation or explication of the "noble truths," but even in their simplest presentation certain distinctive features come into view. For one thing, all of existence is painful. It is not as though we are to understand existence as a combination of sorrow and happiness, sometimes more one, sometimes more the other. To exist is to suffer. Suffering is not, therefore, some sort of damage that is done to one, it is not a matter of disfunction or privation or misfortune. It is an unrelenting existential condition.

This analysis becomes even more forceful when the Buddha insists that the *cause* of this condition is "craving." The cause is not, in other words, external to one's existence, but is to be found at the very center of existence. We do not suffer because we have been compelled to accept the burden of existence; instead, it is the *way we exist* that has made existence a burden. To crave is to desire to possess something we do not currently possess. Craving arises from a keen dissatisfaction with what we have and where we are in the present; it is a serious form of self-rejection. Since suffering is existence in itself, and not some externally originating incursion into existence, it follows that what we most deeply crave is to have another existence. Suffering, we can say without distortion, begins in the desire not to *have* something else, but to *be* something else. *The true cause of suffering is quite simply the desire to be.* The contrast with Hinduism here is particularly conspicuous. Hindus sought release from the wheel of death and rebirth *by way of being,* reaching the perfect center of all that is—Atman.

Since it is of the nature of desire that it originates entirely within oneself, it is the very essence of freedom. Whatever it is that we desire we can freely cease desiring. This is the driving insight of the sermon at Benares: we can stop craving as easily as we continue to crave. In sum, if suffering arises with the desire to be, it is because we have freely chosen to be, and to be as we are. A typical instance of the Buddhist sense of self-sufficiency in all matters spiritual is the memorable line from the *Dhammapada:* "Well-makers lead the water wherever they like; fletchers bend the arrow; carpenters bend a log of wood; wise people fashion themselves."[4]

But what can we actually do with this freedom? If dukkha rises from the desire to be, can we escape it by choosing *not to be?* The Buddha speaks to this point by observing that the craving for nonexistence is no more liberating than the craving for existence. In other words, the suffering that makes itself evident in human existence as the consequence of encountering the phenomenon of death is not to be solved by death itself. One does not escape the pain of life by dying, for dying too is a choice. The solution is not to choose one thing rather than another, but *to stop choosing.*

The question raised by this analysis of dukkha is how it could be possible to live without making any choices at all, including the choice to exist or not to exist. The answer to this question lies in the distinctive Buddhist teaching on the nature of causation, which brings us to the subject of *samsara.*

There are few doctrines in Buddhism that have been more discussed or are more laced with fine distinctions than what is sometimes called the "formula of causal origin," or the "chain of causation," or even the "twelve preconditions." Some ancient scriptures claim that the Buddha discovered the twelve preconditions during the time he sat in meditation under the Bodhi tree, since it is a clear implication of the principle of dependent origination. Our task here is not to explore this doctrine in all its nuances but to see what it intended, to grasp its function in the larger sweep of Buddhist thought, and particularly to give us an insight into the *samsaric* nature of things.

The twelve preconditions are sometimes represented as a chain, sometimes as a wheel. In either case, the first of the series is ignorance and the last are aging, dying, and death. It is said that the Buddha, meditating on the causes of aging and death, found that neither would exist unless there were birth. Nothing would be born, of course, if it were not for the process of becoming. There would be no becoming unless there was something that got appropriated and consumed by the process, as a fire consumes fuel. Continuing in a similar manner to seek the prior condition of every causal event, the Buddha perceived the sequence after appropriation to be craving, feeling, contact, the six sense fields, name-and-form, consciousness, karma, and finally ignorance.

Later Buddhist philosophy gave volumes of analysis to the ways in which each condition was related to the next and to the precise sort of causation that was meant to pertain to the entire chain. For our purposes it is enough to make the following three observations. *First*, aging and death are actually *caused*; they are not phenomena that stand by themselves, neither are they causes that have their effects but are themselves uncaused. They are also not some sort of universal metaphysical condition that affects everything but their own existence, such as gravity, or motion, or resistance. *Second*, we can discover what it is that causes aging and death. Most immediately, of course, it is birth; nothing dies that is not first born. Ultimately, however, we must say that the true cause is ignorance. As we are increasingly reminded, this is a most distinguishing element in Buddhism. To say that death is caused ultimately by ignorance is very different from saying that it is introduced into human reality by a god, or that it originates in human disobedience or arrogance, or that it is an accidental quality of existence. To say that it is ignorance is consistent with the exalted doctrine of freedom we have already discovered in the discussion of dukkha, and it is an indication of what we shall presently discuss under the term "primacy of mind." The way one ceases to move back and forth on the chain of causation—and, therefore, the way one demolishes the suffering that appears with the discovery of death—is to replace ignorance with wisdom. Precisely what this wisdom is we shall see more completely in the discussion of *prajna*.

The *third* and final observation to be made about the twelve interrelated preconditions is that they are entire in themselves. That is, while no one stage on the wheel can exist without the others, the wheel as a whole needs no cause outside itself. There is no prime cause, no unmoved mover, no enduring entity that prevents the chain of causes to empty into the void, and no eternal matrix in which all change is suspended. In sum, we can now see that the doctrine of dependent origination, elaborated in the theory of the twelve preconditions, blocks all access to the absolute in any form and catapults us into complete relativism. It is this complete relativism that is meant by "samsara."

At first glance Buddhism may not seem altogether unusual in this respect, for its emphasis on universal causal relatedness shows an obvious resemblance to Epicureanism and modern science. Both systems, as we have seen earlier in this study, held that all entities are to be understood as caused. Nothing is exempted from causal sequence. The contrast with Buddhism comes not in the Epicurean and atomistic insistence on universal causation, but in its affirmation of a primordial freedom in human existence. Both Epicureans and modern scientific theorists have allowed for *randomness* in the behavior of atoms— enough to account for variety, though not enough to permit outright lawlessness—but they have also made it clear that randomness is not to be mistaken with freedom. The question then arises as to how Buddhism can commit itself to both universal causation *and* freedom. The question is an important one because, as we observed in the discussion of science, nothing can be said to be alive if it is not also free. Among Epicureans and biologists this had the result of engendering an attitude of disregard toward death—and life. Does Buddhism provide sufficient weight to its affirmation of freedom to justify anything more than the attitude of disregard?

The ingenious way in which Buddhism has combined causation with freedom can be put quite simply. In both Epicureanism and modern science there is the implicit assumption that there is a world that is truly "there," external to the observer, and that it can be described as it is in itself. This, of course, implies in turn that the observer is, at the very least, able to rise above the flux to a point of observation that is not part of the flux itself. In Buddhism samsara is far more radically conceived. *The theory of dependent origination applies not only to all that one may observe; it applies to the observer as well.* Epicureans and scientific theorists are unwilling to throw their systems open by declaring the causal status of the theory itself. They would not deny, of course, that mental events are caused and that, therefore, the theory of causation *as mental event* has causal antecedents. But this is very different from saying that the theory *as theory*, or that the theorist *as theorist*, is caused, because then the theory could not be the *theory of* anything, only the effect of something; furthermore, the theorist could not be distinct from what is being observed. One could not observe sound while listening to it, nor the process of aging while aging.

Recall that the Hindus found a serious omission in scientific theory, because in science there is no discussion of the nature of knowledge;

not thought, but knowledge. It is one thing to think, and another to know that one is thinking. The Buddhists expose this omission from another perspective. From their doctrine of absolute causation the scientific thinker does not go far enough, but holds back just enough from the flux to allow for the existence of the consciousness of the observer. In Hinduism nothing really changes, but only appears to; in Buddhism nothing remains the same, nothing is immune to the flux. Not only is there no knowledge behind the thought, there is no thinker behind the thinking.

We introduced this "step beyond" into the flux, characteristic of Buddhism, to show how Buddhists can simultaneously affirm universal causation and freedom. The possibility of doing so derives from the fact that when the theory of dependent origination is considered to be an instance of dependent origination, all phenomena are granted the same mode of (non)existence. There is no mental reality exempt from causal sequence; but by the same token there is no causal sequence that is not simultaneously mental reality. This curious interchangeability of the two is sometimes referred to by Buddhists as the "primacy of mind." (It follows that all phenomena could be regarded as nonmental and, indeed, one tradition of Buddhist thought, known as the No Mind School, maintains such a position. Fortunately, our understanding of the problem of death would not be advanced by a review of the arguments of these thinkers.)

The primacy of mind in Buddhism is precisely the freedom of which we have been thinking. The conceptions of ourselves and the universe are essentially what we think they are, and if we ask *why* we think in this way or another about ourselves and the world, we can look only to the preceding thought or thoughts. One thought seems to follow necessarily from another in a process we usually do not question. However, there is no necessity here. Collectively all our thinking is spontaneous and therefore subject to abrupt alterations at any moment. This uniquely Buddhist sense of the primacy of mind is elegantly put in the following passage from the *Dhammapada* ("Path of the Dharma"):

All that we are is the result of what we have thought: it is founded on our thoughts, it is made up of our thoughts. If a man speaks or acts with an evil thought, pain follows him as the wheel follows the foot of the ox that draws the carriage.

All that we are is the result of what we have thought: it is founded on our thoughts, it is made up of our thoughts. If a man speaks or acts with a pure thought, happiness follows him, like a shadow that never leaves him.[5]

The self is the residue of what has already been thought: it is a gathering of mental habits; everything we are is dependent for its origination on what has passed. But, at the same time, all of this can be changed in a second. This is the great presupposition that lies behind all Buddhist teachings: nothing is preventing you from altering the flow of your thoughts but your own free choice.

However, there are still many obstacles to achieving the freedom implicit in the primacy of mind. Although one is absolutely free to alter one's thoughts in any way and at any time, the habits of past thinking exercise great influence on the present. They do not actually compromise or diminish one's freedom, but only obscure it. We are so accustomed to thinking in one way or another that it may never occur to us that it is not in the least necessary to think in those ways. In other words, no matter how aware we might be of the samsaric nature of our existence we may not believe we could alter it by way of thought. We may not believe in the true primacy of mind. It would seem, then, that one could properly comprehend this crucial fact only by first developing an appropriate respect for the power of the mind. If it is the case that "all that we are is the result of what we have thought," then respect for the mind is fitting; for just as it is powerful, it is also dangerous. On one occasion the Buddha likened the mind to an elephant: the creature can stampede out of fear, dragging its helpless master along behind, or it can be led so deeply into a mire by a careless trainer that it may not be able to extricate itself. Of course, the great power of the beast can also be properly disciplined to do precisely what its master wishes.

A sure sign that the mind has gotten loose and is dragging its impotent master in its circuitous tracks is that it has begun to ask metaphysical questions; that is, it has set off to discover what is the nature of things, to learn what lies behind visible reality. This was commonly occurring to the Buddha's own disciples. While they listened to his discourse they were at once struck with its truth, but when they reflected on it later they thought they had discovered inconsistencies. They could not determine, for example, whether the Buddha was teaching that the soul is deathless and therefore will survive the passing of the body, or whether we are mortal through and through. One of his closest disciples came to him one day exclaiming that if the Blessed One would not explain such mysteries as to whether the world is eternal or finite, or whether the saint does or does not exist after death, "I will abandon religious training and return to the lower life of a layman."

The Buddha's first reply to this demand was to remind his disciple that he invited him into the religious life to find enlightment and not the answers to such questions. For the disciple *now* to press these queries indicates that he does not understand the nature of enlightenment, for the answers he seeks do not move him any closer to the goal.

He then compared the inquisitive disciple to a man who had been struck with an arrow heavily smeared with poison. The wounded man refused to have the arrow removed by a physician until he could learn the name of the archer who had wounded him; he wanted also to know whether this archer was tall or short of stature; what the color of his skin was; whether he was from this city or another. These questions are plainly irrelevant to the fallen man's health, and so are the metaphysical questions that preoccupy the mind of the disciple. "The religious life," the Buddha explained after telling this parable, "does not depend on the dogma that the world is eternal; nor does the religious life depend on the dogma that the world is not eternal." No matter how such questions are to be answered, "there still remain birth, old age, death, sorrow, lamentation, misery, grief, and despair, for the extinction of which in the present life I am prescribing."[6]

The mind can also get away from us by a subtler, but equally effective, breaking of its tether. It can drift into the habit of what Buddhists call "I-making" and "mine-making." Even though one has no ego and no self, one nonetheless drifts into the mental mire of fashioning an "I" and, what is worse, fashioning a world that is in some sense "my" world. The warning against letting the mind run off in this direction exposes us to the full force of the Buddhist doctrine of *anatman*, or nonself. We recall that in Hinduism the Atman was positively required as the timeless, boundless self that was the seer behind the seeing and the hearer behind the hearing; this is "I-making" in its boldest form; when carried to its metaphysical extreme, it leads to the Upanishadic affirmation that the *Atman is all*. Buddhist teaching makes it quite clear that if we are to take seriously the samsaric nature of all reality, then we must not look for the reality *behind* the passing world, but for the reality *of* the passing world—and this utterly eliminates any possibility of a transcendent self in Atman. For Hindus the danger in thinking is in the risk that thoughts will get "snared" in the world and not return to the Atman, as birds return to their nests. For Buddhists there is nothing that can snare thoughts and nothing to which they could return. There are simply thoughts—with no thinker and no objects to which they could refer or be attached.

Here we can state that *the agency of death* for Buddhists has become clear: death is the force that causes reality to be a *fiction*. What death reveals, what the Buddhist experiences in a first encounter with suffering and death, is that life and the world are not what we thought they were. They are falsehoods, inventions, fabrications. A fiction is utterly different from an *illusion*. An illusion is also false, but a falsehood that hides a truth. If the world is illusory it is because it masks what is truly the case. There is always the possibility we can see through it or behind it into the truth. A fiction has no corresponding reality whatsoever; there is no truth to be concealed by it. It does not even speak of reality or concern itself with what is true. It simply offers itself as something complete.

The response of grief to death in this form is extremely powerful. It is the craving to find something real, a truth, being. It is to find a continuity that does not have the absolute limits of a fiction, or perhaps one should say the absolute emptiness of fiction. So grieving, we fall into the habit of thinking there is something corresponding to the thoughts. But nothing corresponds to thought—nor is there a thinker of thoughts. The *belief* that I am thinking my thoughts is only another thought: "I am thinking my thoughts." Indeed, I cannot even think about my own thoughts: "as the blade of a sword cannot cut itself, as a fingertip cannot touch itself, so a thought cannot think itself."[7]

It is evident that, just as the Buddha has an extremely powerful conception of death, there should also be a powerful form of grief. Of course, there will be a solution to the dilemma more powerful than either death or grief and it is a solution based on the freedom we have already uncovered in the Buddhist notion of the primacy of mind. Let us then turn to a consideration of the way Buddhists propose to take the discontinuity of death into a higher meaning, thereby overcoming the acutely bereaved pursuit of truth, or of being.

We opened the previous section with the question as to how Buddhists connect a radical doctrine of causation with freedom, instead of with randomness, as we found it in modern science. By taking to its extreme the notion that the mind itself is caused, and not somehow hovering above the flux observing its passage without being affected by it, the Buddhists may seem in one respect to *reduce* the mind to a physical process in which it is helplessly batted about by one force or another. In another respect, however, physical process is *elevated* to mind, since there is no difference between the two, and therefore possesses all the spontaneity of thinking, particularly a thinking that is not *about anything* and not *by anyone*. But this abandonment to the flux, whether free or not, is the experience of the discontinuity death introduces into life. If death reveals this sort of freedom, how can we freely contend with death?

Since the mind is the beast that can break its tether in grief and run off into the mud pit of reality, the first task is to put it under a careful discipline. Observing that "as rain breaks through an ill-thatched house, passion will break through an unreflecting mind,"[8] the Buddha urges a proper sort of reflection, a precise kind of mindfulness. Buddhism develops a great variety of strategies for this training, ascribing many of them to the Buddha himself. An early and famous device was called the "fourfold denial." This was a way of answering questions of a metaphysical type that abruptly altered the mindfulness of the inquirer. For example, on the question of immortality the Buddha would typically respond:

> A saint is after death,
> A saint is not after death,
> A saint both is and is not after death,
> A saint neither is nor is not after death.[9]

The fourfold denial was later modified into the *koan,* a meaningless question asked by a master of a disciple in Zen Buddhism. The purpose here is also to awaken disciples to the nature of the mind and not to send them off looking for answers.

Awareness of the mind as mind: this is the essence of the meditative discipline required to prevent the mind from carrying us off into spiritually blind alleys. Just such an awareness is the goal of the following instruction the Buddha was said to have given his followers:

> And how does a monk live contemplating the mind in the mind? He comprehends the mind which has passion and that which has none as such, which has hatred and that which has none as such, which has confusion and that which has none as such; he comprehends the collected mind, the distracted mind as such; the mind which has some other or no other (mental state) superior to it; the mind which is concentrated or that which is not as such; he comprehends the mind which is freed or that which is not freed as such. . . . It is thus that a monk lives contemplating the mind in the mind.[10]

There is no analysis here, no desire to show the structure of the mind; only an instruction that the monk comprehend or behold the mind *as it is.* In this connection Buddhists commonly use the word "suchness," *tathata.* They intend simply to see things *such as they are.* This term is of such importance to Buddhism that one of the highest titles given to Siddhartha after his enlightenment was *Tathagata,* or "he who is such as he is." We can more deeply note the force of this notion if we compare it to Hinduism, which has sometimes been called the religion of "thatness" rather than "suchness." When the Hindu utters the famous *tat tvam asi*, "that art thou," what is meant is that one is identical with the transcendent reality of Atman/Brahman. Thatness always refers, therefore, to *that being*. Suchness always refers to the way that entity is at this moment in its samsaric existence. When a monk "contemplates the mind in the mind" it is not in order to do somethingwith it or for it, or to train it into one condition or another, or even to send it to deeper levels; it is simply to become aware of the mind as mind however it is found, which is equivalent to saying that all concern for the substance, or the content, of the mind has been dropped. To call the Buddha *Tathagata* is to pay him the recognition that he has completely eluded all substantive existence and has succeeded in being simply as he is.

But why does arriving at *suchness* have the effect of liberating the mind from its spiritual grief? When the mind contemplates the mind as it is, it offers no resistance to its movement whatsoever. Now, we recall that in grief the impulse of the mind was to leap off the wheel of ceaseless change in the desperate attempt to find something immovable. It is this desperation that gives rise to suffering. This is what Buddhists call attachment. Attachment leads inevitably to suffering because nothing is exempt from change and to think that something is, that one is oneself, is to be in profound contradiction to one's own samsaric existence. Therefore, one does not look for a way to get off the wheel, and certainly not for a way to stop the wheel, for the only true release from pain comes when one *freely moves with the wheel.*

We have come back, therefore, to a point touched on earlier—that the choice the enlightened person makes concerning attachment or nonattachment is not to choose at all. One chooses freely not to resist the causal flow; that is, *one chooses freely not to be free.*

The highest act of the mind, in other words, is to eliminate mind. This is why along with the primacy of mind Buddhists can attempt to achieve the perfectly mindless act. This is the act in which one neither *chooses something* nor *is someone* who is doing the choosing. The grand effect of this is that *one overcomes the absolute discontinuity of life, that is, the experience of acute grief, by becoming absolutely discontinuous.*

This is the achievement of the state Buddhists call *nirvana*. In Sanskrit the word nirvana means something close to "extinction," in the sense of being snuffed out as a flame. It is bringing to a complete stop all the striving and discipline used to get there. However much one might have desired the attainment of this state, or struggled to reach it, the state is completely empty of desire and striving. We must remember from an earlier discussion that Buddhists are not attempting to achieve nonbeing. Their desire is not to bring being to an end, but to bring desire to an end. Therefore, nirvana is not properly to be understood as a state of *being*, but a state of *acting*, although acting in the very special sense of doing nothing and being no one. It is because of this special sense of acting that we can characterize the Buddhist response to death as *becoming*. In this study the term, becoming, will mean the overcoming of mind with mind and its consequences of freely turning with the wheel of endless change.

Nirvana is a familiar term, but when it is taken in the rather paradoxical sense of an act without subject or object, one is easily confused. What sense does it make to talk of freedom where there is no one to be free? How can *anatman*, or nonself, be free without being a self? Also what can it mean to talk about freedom when there is nothing to be chosen?

We are left with two questions. First, what sense does all this make? Second, how does one actually live according to these insights? In other words, how shall we *understand* this, and how shall we *act* on it? Fortunately, Buddhists do not bring us to the doorstep of nirvana and leave us there. They have a great deal still to offer for both comprehension and practice. They do not simply *declare* grief to have been ended. On the contrary, Buddhists never lose sight of the great power of bereaved attachment.

We shall trace only one of the many paths of understanding in Buddhism: *Madhyamika* philosophy and one of its most famous practical disciplines: what the Chinese called *Ch'an*, and the Japanese *Zen*.

The principle source of Madhyamika, or the philosophy of "the middle way," is the thought of Nagarjuna, a philosopher who is thought to have lived in the second half of the second century C.E. Nagarjuna was concerned that Hindu thinkers were putting thoughtful Buddhists at a disadvantage by their superior philosophical skills. The Hindus, whose tradition we have termed the Religion of Being, were coming to see Buddhism as the Religion of Nonbeing. Nagarjuna knew that this was false, but Buddhists did not have the sufficient conceptual resources to clarify this misunderstanding. Nagarjuna's genius appeared in his ability to develop a *philosophy of becoming* that represented a middle way between being and nonbeing.

The reigning concept in this philosophy is *sunyata*, void or emptiness. We can get a preliminary idea of what Nagarjuna means by sunyata if we consider the way in which he argues that the concept of causation, so fundamental to Buddhist thought, is actually quite empty. He acknowledges the importance of causation by opening his major work, *The Fundamentals of the Middle Way*, with the observation:

1. Never are any existing things found to originate from themselves, from something else, from both, or from no cause.

The first phrase of this opening sentence sounds quite like a standard expression of the theory of dependent origination, but when he continues with the statement that existing things do not originate from something else, and in fact have no cause at all, we move into another way of thinking. What this way of thinking is can be more completely seen in the five concluding arguments of the same chapter:

10. Since existing things which have no self-existence are not real, it is not possible at all that: "This thing 'becomes' upon the existence of that other one."

11. The product does not reside in the conditioning causes, individually or collectively, so how can that which does not reside in the conditioning cause result from conditioning causes?

12. Then the "non-real" would result from those conditioning causes. Why then would a product not proceed also from non-causes?

13. On the one hand, the product consists in its conditioning causes; on the other hand, the causes do not consist of themselves. How can a product resulting from conditioning causes not consisting of themselves be consisting of those causes?

14. Therefore, that product does not consist in those causes; yet it is agreed that a product does not consist of non-causes. How can there be a conditioning cause or non-cause when a product is not produced?[11]

We could offer a compressed paraphrase of Nagarjuna's argument here by saying that, for him, to be real is to be self-caused. Nothing in the mode of becoming could cause itself, for it could not *become* what it is; it would already *be* what it is. Insofar as it is in the mode of becoming it must be caused, but by what? It could not be caused by something real, for the real is only the cause of itself. It could not be caused by something that is itself in the mode of becoming, for that would mean being caused by that which is nonreal. Conclusion: anything existing in the mode of becoming can neither be caused by, nor be the cause of, another thing. It is therefore causally unrelated to everything else.

Nagarjuna develops a similar view concerning time. In the nineteenth chapter of the *Fundamentals* he opens with the following propositions:

1. If *the present* and *future* exist presupposing *the past, the present* and *future* will exist in *the past*.

2. If *the present* and *future* did not exist in *the past*, how could *the present* and *future* exist presupposing that *past?*

3. Without presupposing *the past the present* and *future* could not be proved to exist. Therefore neither present nor future time exist.[12]

Nagarjuna's strategy here is simpler than it may seem. He is playing with the fact that there can only be a past insofar as there is a present and a future. To be past something may not be present; yet it is past in relation to the present. There can be a present, therefore, only because there are things that are no longer present. The present then has its origin in the past. But how could the present come from the past when the past is not present? Similarly, how can the present pass into the future and still be present? The three divisions of time depend on each other to be what they are, but since they cannot be either of the others they cannot be related at all. Conclusion: anything existing in the mode of time can neither be before nor after another thing. It is therefore temporally unrelated to everything else.

It is most important to the understanding of Nagarjuna's Madhyamika philosophy to see that in neither of these passages has he made an outright rejection of the existence of causation, or of time, or even of things. Instead, he is systematically eliminating any possibility that a thing could be *intelligibly* related to any other thing. The word intelligibly is emphasized here because, when one truly understands the way things are, one would see that there are no connections between things, and one would also see that things come in and out of existence by no constraint whatsoever and in no necessary order. This has a powerful intellectual consequence. Because the only way of thinking about the world is to take note of the connectedness of its myriad part, *doing away with connectedness means that one cannot think about things at all*. There is literally nothing to think about. In an early sutra the Buddha is quoted as saying: "In what is seen there must be just the seen; in what is heard there must be just the heard; in what is sensed there must be just what is sensed; in what is thought there must be just the thought."[13]

What Nagarjuna has offered us is a mental discipline that provides us with the intellectual ability of knocking away the connections between things—temporal, causal, spatial, emotional, imaginary, and so on—until we are able to simply behold an object independent of its relations. The question here, of course, is whether it is in fact possible to behold entities in their pure unrelatedness. Essentially every way we have of identifying objects makes use of descriptions of their relatedness to other objects. If something is seen as heavy, round, swift, multicolored, and in motion, it is seen exclusively in terms of its relative properties, for all of these terms are relational. Something is heavy only in relation to something less heavy; so also with the other terms. How could we then pay attention to an object without identifying any aspect of it that could be considered relational? How could we look at the famed Bodhi tree and not see that it is green, or massive in size, or penetrated with golden shafts of light; how could we ignore the fact that it was here that the Buddha achieved release? What is a tree that has no color, no size, no history, no shape, and not even any discernible distance from the observer? Nagarjuna's classical answer is that this does not mean that the Bodhi tree does not exist, but only that it is perfectly *sunya*, or empty.

Sunyata is therefore not properly to be taken as a metaphysical term. That is, it is not descriptive of the world, but of the way the world is understood by the purified consciousness. Something is not empty *in relation to something else;* it is empty just because *it is not in relation to something else.* Nagarjuna is not proposing a kind of mental trick here. He is not saying that if you squint your mind's eye you can almost see something without its color, even when you know that in truth it has a color. He is quite seriously urging us to acknowledge that when the mind is truly clarified the relations between things will drop away and entities will be seen in their original emptiness. This is the way the mind works when it is not clouded by ignorance. This is tantamount to saying that the perceived relations are not there at all, but are inventions of the mind that is still caught in the web of ignorance and is still, therefore, resisting samsara by trying to find an absolute place outside itself from which it can be seen in its comprehensive relatedness. If the relations are not there and are invented, then the self lives in a fictional world and, moreover, is also a fiction insofar as it is related to a world at all.

We observed earlier in our discussion of Hinduism that the Upanishadic rishis regarded the world as *illusory*. In contrast, the Buddhist arhant knows the world to be *fictional*. Hinduism does not deny the existence of the real, only asserts that the ignorant mind does not see it for what it is. Buddhism most emphatically denies that there is any reality behind the apparent and argues that what we do see is not there at all. This, to be sure, includes the self. This leads to a solution to the problem of death, as stated above, in which its threatened discontinuity is overcome by becoming absolutely discontinuous. Nagarjuna's philosophy has the force of showing that to be discontinuous is not to be nonexistent; it is to be *empty*. Things are empty when they are regarded independently of their relations. Nagarjuna's great contribution to Buddhism is not that he offered *an intellectual restoration of the prior continuity, but an intellectual method of affirming discontinuity*. What we find in Nagarjuna is an extremely sophisticated philosophical support for Buddhism's deepest spiritual insights.

This solution to the problem of death has a decisive influence on the way one approaches the phenomenon of death in practice. To say that life and death are fictional does not have the effect of eliminating either—which was one of the goals of Hinduism. On the contrary, it supposes that the shocking encounter with death can bring a salutary revision to one's understanding of the disconnectedness of life. It was after all the Buddha's perception of aging and death that led to his enlightenment. The most pronounced example of this use of death to teach one the nature of things is the monastic practice of requiring students to meditate for long periods of time in the presence of corpses in various stages of decay. A similar point is made by the well-known Buddhist parable of the woman whose infant son had died. In her grief she came to believe that she could find a medicine that would cure the child of his affliction and restore his life. Unable to find the medicine anywhere else she came to the Buddha. He instructed her to go about the city collecting mustard seeds. She was to go to each house, inquiring whether a death had recently occurred in that house, and, if not, she was to request a single mustard seed. After searching through the entire city she at last returned to the Buddha to report that she had not found one house in which there had not been a recent death and that she had, moreover, cast away the stiffened body of her child with the certainty that there was no cure for death. The Buddha surprised her by acknowledging her freeing spiritual growth, for she had learned that no matter how deeply and passionately attached one is to the things of this world death will carry that person off "as a flood carries off a sleeping village."[14]

The kind of wisdom the grieving mother acquired, the kind of understanding of the nature of things impressed upon the young monks in meditation before decaying corpses, is what is known in classical Buddhism as *prajna*. Prajna is not simply an increased knowledge about the inevitability of death, nor is it the result of shocking or painful experience; it is a way of knowing about the samsaric quality of things that is so complete that one has actually become one's own thinking. We noted above in our discussion of the primacy of mind that we are the result of all that we have thought. Prajna is the transformation that occurs when we cut loose all mental attempts to find the enduring or the permanent in the midst of the passing; it is the kind of wisdom we have acquired when we have ceased trying to step off the wheel of samsara and simply turn with it. In the words of Buddhist scholar, Frederick J. Streng, author of a study of Nagarjuna, wisdom in the Madhyamika philosophy "was not an ultimate view, nor was it an assertion about absolute being. Wisdom was the practice of dissolving the grasping-after-hoped-for-ultimates either in the phenomenal world or the realm of ideas."[15]

In light of the Madhyamika philosophy we can see why Buddhists would come to conceive of *nirvana*—which is the supreme goal of all striving and the state one achieves with the acquisition of prajna—as identical with samsara itself. *Nirvana is the state of pure becoming,* the state where one thing follows another without the slightest causal necessity, and therefore without any relation to any other entity, the state of perfect emptiness. Nirvana is not, therefore, like the Hindus' *samadhi,* a state of being in which nothing actually happens; nirvana is a state of action in which all being has vanished, an act without a doer and without an object. We indicated earlier that Buddhists are faced with the two problems: first, developing a way of addressing their radical spiritual insights to the *understanding* and, second, designing an appropriate way of *acting* in response to that understanding. If Madhyamika philosophy with its doctrine of sunyata is a major Buddhist attempt to express its philosophy, the corresponding effort to make that philosophy practical is Zen. We shall place Zen Buddhism in its historical context and show its inventive and effective manner in dealing practically with what we have described in this study as the problem of grief.

The legendary monk credited with taking Buddhism north into China in the latter part of the fifth century C.E. is known by the honorific name Bodhidharma. The stories told of this redoubtable personage are illustrative of the vibrant religious practice Nagarjuna's philosophy inspired. In his temple in the Chinese mountains he is said to have meditated for nine straight years seated before a blank wall. He sat in a lotus position so long that his legs fell off. On one occasion he became so furious with his inability to fight off sleep through long meditations that he cut off his eyelashes, throwing them to the ground where tea plants immediately appeared. Thereafter tea was used by monks everywhere as a preventative against sleep. The young monk who was later to become his successor approached him with great ardor desiring instruction, but Bodhidharma ignored him and on subsequent appeals from the monk took no notice of his existence. Once, after waiting for hours in the accumulating snow, the desperate monk cut off his arm and presented it to Bodhidharma as a sign of his earnestness. Finally Bodhidharma asked what it was the younger monk sought.

"I have no peace of mind," said Hui-k'o. "Please pacify my mind."

"Bring your mind here before me," replied Bodhidharma, "and I will pacify it!"

"But when I seek my own mind," said Hui-k'o, "I cannot find it."

"There!" snapped Bodhidharma, "I have pacified your mind!"[16]

One of the greatest of the Chinese Ch'an* masters was Hui-neng, known as the Sixth Patriarch in direct descent from Bodhidharma. Hui-neng was an illiterate boy when he happened to overhear someone reciting the *Diamond-Cutter Sutra*, a prominent Chinese spiritual document. He was so touched by the words that he resolved later to take up the life of a monk. When he came to the monastery the Fifth Patriarch immediately saw that the boy was spiritually gifted, but so illiterate and uninformed that he did not permit him to associate with the other monks, assigning him to the kitchen instead. Shortly afterward the Fifth Patriarch announced to the monks that he was ready to pass on the mantle of leadership. His successor would be selected on the basis of a verse he asked all the monks to submit. One of them, widely thought by the others to be the most deserving for the honor, posted the following verse:

> The body is the Bodhi Tree,
> The mind is like a bright mirror-and-stand.
> At all times wipe it diligently,
> Don't let there be any dust.

*The term, *Ch'an*, which became *Zen* in Japanese, was the Chinese translation of the Sanskrit word, *dhyana*, or concentration—one of the highest stages in Yoga. The discipline of dhyana required an undistracted focusing of one's attention on a single object, either external or internal. If one could eliminate all sense of the relatedness of the object then it would cease to be an object as such, and the distinction between the viewer and the viewed would disappear.

The illiterate Hui-neng heard a boy reciting the verse and instantly composed his own which he then asked someone to write out for him:

Bodhi really has no tree;
The bright mirror also has to stand.
Buddha-nature is forever pure;
 (or: Really no thing exists)
Where is there room for dust?[17]

The Fifth Patriarch knew at once that the unidentified author of the second verse was alone worthy of succession, and he also knew who had composed it. He called Hui-neng to his room in the middle of the night, passed the mantle over to him, but urged him to flee at once that he might escape the jealous reaction of the other monks. In time Hui-neng was widely acknowledged as the Sixth Patriarch, although the rejected candidate claimed his own succession, giving rise to a school that lasted many generations. However, we can see that Hui-neng was far closer to the tradition that begins with the Madhyamika philosophy of Nagarjuna and continues through Bodhidharma. His verse displays a keen understanding of the nature of emptiness, and his illiteracy, always given great importance in the later tradition, shows that one need not be learned or even wise in the manner of the world to achieve perfect nirvana. It is this true innocence, combined with sudden insight, that most directly characterizes the method of Zen. What Hui-neng had seen so clearly, and what he was able to teach with great effectiveness, was what D. T. Suzuki has called direct seeing into self-nature: "The Mind or Self-Nature was to be apprehended in the midst of its working or functioning. The object of dhyana [Ch'an] was thus not to stop the working of Self-Nature but to make us plunge right into its stream and seize it in the very act."[18]

It was the teaching of Hui-neng that had the most decisive influence on two great Japanese monks, Eisai (1141–1214) and Dogen (1200–1254), who came to China within a few years of each other in the attempt to understand Buddhism at a place closer to its source. Although Buddhist teachers had reached Japan many centuries before, and even though Zen was already known and taught as a spiritual method, neither Eisai nor Dogen were satisfied with what they had learned. Two schools of Zen later developed around the insights each brought back from the mainland of China. While there are several important differences between these schools (known as Rinzai and Soto), we shall in this brief examination of Zen be concerned with only those areas in which they are in substantial agreement.

Although Hui-neng had reached an instant enlightenment as an illiterate child, and virtually by accident, it is widely acknowledged that the repetition of his achievement is extremely rare. Instead, most persons must spend years in discipline. The basic element in Zen training is what is known as *zazen*, from the words, *za* (or sitting) and *zen* (or concentration). In its narrowest sense zazen is a seated concentration, although there are forms of mobile zazen that may involve prescribed movements, chanting, or even engagement in ordinary activities. All the great Zen masters, however, stress the importance of learning the proper way of sitting with the legs folded in front, the eyes open and looking slightly downward, the arms resting easily on the thighs, hands loosely cupped in each other. The erectness of the spine is absolutely necessary, since only then can there be an effortless interpenetration of mind and body.

Once one has assumed a proper position the concentration usually begins with a simple counting of the breath. When one has reached the point where the counting can continue by itself, then the mind is brought to a concentration on the breathing until there is harmony between the rhythm of breathing and thinking. So far it is important that the concentrating mind have an object. In effect, the mind by doing so is giving up the control of itself to a perfectly mindless process. In some cases particularly gifted students can follow a method known as Shikan-taza in which the mind does away with all objects; no attention is paid to anything. This is, however, rarely recommended by the master to beginning students, since its great difficulty is often discouraging.

If one has followed the discipline of zazen this far with sufficient energy there will already be important spiritual consequences. One will see, for example, the disconnectedness of all things. It will be evident that one thing followed another without being forced, like one breath follows another, or like the thoughts come in succession without any intervening agency. What may also be evident by now is the deep grip of suffering in which we are all held, because one can detect the persistent tendency of the mind to take back its control, to place some thoughts over others, to attempt to play the intervening causal function, forcing thoughts to go as we wish. It is here that the Zen masters often refer to the mind as "the stream of life and death," because there is essentially no difference between our thinking and ourselves, and, insofar as our mind resists the eternal flux, we begin to reach out desperately for life out of the fear of death. Death is terrifying because it seems to be swallowing the stream of life, and life is therefore only the bitter prelude to death. If one has taken up zazen with the proper effort, one will soon see that both life and death are part of the stream— neither its beginning nor its end.

But this is not the final achievement; this is not the liberation, or *kensho,* sought by the Zen student, for the mind is still far too active even when it is concentrating on nothing more than the rhythm of breath. The master is likely at this point to assign the student a *koan,* an unanswerable question or an apparent contradiction, to which the student will now be expected to give complete attention. There are many famous koans known to readers of popular literature on Buddhism, such as "What is the sound of one hand clapping?" or "What was the appearance of your face before you were born?"

It is a mistake to assume that there is some sort of hidden answer to these questions. The object of the koan is to concentrate on it so intensely that one's entire mental existence has been penetrated by the question. One's mind is therefore in the state of radical doubt, insatiable puzzlement, incapable of containing any answers whatsoever. This is spiritually necessary to Zen, for only in this way can one discover that the mind is properly the container of nothing permanent—and answers assume permanence. When the master asks for an "answer," therfore, he is looking for evidence that the student has discovered this aspect of his existence and is no longer looking for something to hold on to with the mind.

One of the most famous koans concerns the Zen master Joshu, who was aksed by a monk, "Has a dog Buddha-nature or not?" Joshu's classical response was simply, "Mu!" The word *mu* in Japanese has the meaning of the simple negative, "not," or "is not," or "nothing." Joshu was not using this simple negative to answer the question, as though saying that a dog does *not* have Buddha-nature. Mu cannot be taken that way. It is rather a non-answer, a way of recognizing the question but not bringing the monk's mind to rest with an answer that will free his mind from continuing doubt.

The doubt must continue until the very act of thinking is transformed. In his commentary on Joshu's koan another great Zen master, Mumon, says, "To realize this wondrous thing called enlightenment, you must look into the source of your thoughts, thereby annihilating them." If you are unable to "exhaust the arising of thoughts, you are like a ghost, clinging to the trees and grass."[19] We might ask why looking into the source of thoughts has the effect of annihilating thought. The classical view, with which Zen is perfectly consistent, is that thoughts arise from an inner craving, from one's desire to take flight from suffering by striving for the permanent—the very way suffering originates. If one sees that thinking is a form of craving, the thinking will cease. This does not mean that there will be no thoughts, or no mind. Instead, it implies that both will become fluid, and like water they will always take the shape of their container, but without exerting any force of their own. And if the container, the thinker, steadfastly refuses to disturb the mind, it will come to a perfect rest, reflecting the "moon of truth" off its surface without the merest distortion.

In place of the thinker there will be only a void. This void will not, however, be something of a gap, a place of emptiness, a space of nothing somewhere in the midst of being. It will be a void that will precede all things. Indeed, "with enlightenment, zazen brings the realization that the substratum of existence is a Voidness out of which all things ceaselessly arise and into which they endlessly return."[20] The void is not *my* void, neither is it *my self* emptied of its craving; it is the void that stands at the beginning and the end of every existing thing. We used earlier the figure of the stream of samsara through which the Hindu rishi sought to pass. We then found that the Buddhist has no wish to reach the further shore, which does not exist in any case, but only to yield to the stream. Even here one might hold back from the radical Zen view of the stream. Recall Suzuki's description of Huineng's method, that is, to plunge into the "stream and seize it in its very act." Strictly speaking, Suzuki falls short of the true Zen view here. To seize the stream in its very act is still to be distinct from the stream; it is still holding on to some sort of separate existence. A more accurate use of the metaphor here would be that we are not only to yield to the stream, we are to cease existing apart from the stream. We are to *become* the stream in its infinite changeableness, but not in any sense as an object that goes with the stream. Therefore, just as the shape of the water changes with every new instant of its passing, so do we. It is this metaphor that most accurately captures the essence of *becoming* in Buddhist thought and practice as we have been referring to it in this chapter.

This extreme view of human existence as becoming has a distinct impact on the way Buddhists regard time and history. If we have become identical with the stream, it is then the case that we no longer *are* apart from time. The distinction between our existence and time has been wiped away. This was already seen in the works of early Chinese monks, one of whom authored these words:

> Being-time stands on the topmost peak and in the utmost depths
> of the sea, being-time is three heads and eight elbows, being-time
> is a height of sixteen or eighteen feet, being-time is a monk's staff,
> being-time is a fly swatter, being-time is a stone lantern, being-
> time is Anyone, being-time is earth, being-time is sky.

Dogen, probably the greatest of the Japanese Zen masters, quotes this passage in his own thirteenth-century work, to support his own understanding that being and time are inseparable. He then comments: "Time must needs be with me. I have always been; time cannot leave me." There never was a time when I was not in time; therefore, I can never be understood as distinguishable in my being from time. Dogen states further: "Do not regard time as merely flying away; do not think that flying away is its sole function. For time to fly away there would have to be a separation between it and things."[21] It is probably the case that we ordinarily think that it is *time* that passes, when in fact it is *we* who are passing.

The Buddhist view of history makes its unique mark apparent in this line of thinking. Inasmuch as we are not distinguishable from time, we are utterly historical. We cannot stand on the bank and watch history pass as though we are not in it. On the other hand, history in itself is perfectly empty. It means nothing beyond itself. It is merely change. Our historicity is merely becoming. The stream in fact goes nowhere; indeed, there is no such thing as a stream apart from the ceaseless shaping of the unresisting water by the banks of the channel that contain it. We are perfectly historical when we choose not to interrupt the flow of thought and action, but history does not take us somewhere; history has no point, no end, no reason outside itself.

It is on this point precisely that the Buddhists find themselves most equipped in coping with the threatened meaninglessness of death. An example of the power of this view occurs in a series of letters sent by a young woman dying of tuberculosis to her Zen master. Only a few days before her death does she actually achieve liberation. In one of her final letters she describes the result of her liberation:

> I am in the center of the Great Way where everything is natural, without strain, neither hurried nor halting; where there are no Buddhas, no you, no nothing; and where I see without my eyes and hear without my ears. Not a trace remains of what I have written. There is neither pen nor paper nor words—nothing at all.

This is the great void of which we have spoken, and for many it may read as though death itself were being described. Instead, this experience led to joy in the face of death:

> I can't tell you how joyous I am and how thankful for my present state. This is all the outcome of zazen, of a determination never to stop with a small success but to go on no matter how many lifetimes elapse. Now I can commence the unending task of rescuing every living being. This makes me so happy I can scarcely contain myself. All is radiance, pure radiance.[22]

The joy she expresses is not simply the result of her being snatched from the dreadful maw of oblivion. It is a sense of effulgence that sweeps life and death into itself. It is, moreover, the evocation of a desire to rescue "every living being." This does not point to some survival or transformation into a saving deity. It is rather that her joy can no more be restrained than light can be withheld by the flame. And love seems to attach to that joy quite as much as warmth belongs to the light.

With these remarks we have come as close to the center of the Buddhist conception of death as we can come. What we notice in this young woman is that no part of her spiritual triumph is constituted by a victory over death as such. Death is not even an enemy. Instead, death is the very goad that brought her to see the nature of her true liberation, exactly in the way the Buddha was led to the Bodhi tree and to his release. Death enters as a dilemma, but the solution is so much grander than either life or death that both essentially disappear from the attention of those liberated. To use the familiar Buddhist metaphor, death is an event no more substantial than the act of cutting the air with a knife. But the function of death as a prod to reflection may not be dismissed. One famous monk, in a gesture similar to Siddhartha's resolve when he took his place under the tree, held a knife in one hand and a stick of burning incense in the other, exclaiming that if he were not enlightened by the time the incense burned down he would plunge the knife into his breast. Enlightenment came as the incense began to burn his fingers.

In other words, what is won in liberation is not a victory over death that gives one more life, but a victory over the craving that originally made life painful and death fearsome. We have spoken of the Buddhist understanding that life and death are fictions. This is because one can be concerned with life and death only when one has been possessed by craving and, therefore, the desires to become something permanent and untouched by the eternal flux—*when craving leads one to see something and to be something that is not there.*

Buddhism deals with death by making it the ultimate koan. It is the source of the endless self-questioning that brings us at last to deny the causal connectedness between all things, even between our thoughts that led to this conclusion. Its answer to the koan of death is to say Yes to the disconnectedness with which death threatens us and to wipe away any experience of distance between our own existence and the eternal, unconditioned spontaneity of all that is.

Notes

1. *Zen Buddhism*, p. 40.
2. J. Takakusu, *Philosophy East and West*, p. 70.
3. *The Teachings of the Compassionate Buddha*, p. 30.

4. Ibid., p. 57.
5. Ibid., p. 52.
6. Ibid., pp. 33 ff.
7. *Buddhist Texts through the Ages*, p. 163.
8. *The Teachings of the Compassionate Buddha*, p. 53.
9. *Death and Eastern Thought*, p. 130.
10. *Buddhist Texts through the Ages*, p. 58.
11. Streng, *Emptiness*, p. 98.
12. Ibid., p. 205.
13. Kapleau, *The Three Pillars of Zen*, p. 71.
14. *The Teachings of the Compassionate Buddha*, 44 ff.
15. *Emptiness*, p. 98.
16. Suzuki, *Essays in Zen Buddhism*, Vol. I, pp. 170 ff.
17. Robinson, *The Buddhist Religion*, pp. 90 ff.
18. *Zen Buddhism*, p. 76.
19. *The Three Pillars of Zen*, p. 71.
20. Ibid., p. 116.
21. Ibid., pp. 297 ff.
22. Ibid., pp. 278 ff.

Bibliography

E. A. Burtt, ed., *The Teachings of the Compassionate Buddha* (New York: 1955.)

Witter Bynner, *The Way of Life According to Laotzu* (New York: 1962).

Chuang Tsu, *Inner Chapters*, trs. Gia-Fu Feng and Jane English (New York: 1974).

Edward Conze, I. B. Horner, D. Snellgrove, A. Waley, eds., *Buddhist Texts through the Ages* (New York: 1964).

Heinrich Dumoulin, *A History of Zen Buddhism*, tr. Paul Peachey (Boston: 1969).

H. Byron Earhart, *Japanese Religion: Unity and Diversity* (Belmont: 1974).

Helmut von Glasenapp, *Buddhism: A Non-Theistic Religion*, tr. Irmgard Schloegl (New York: 1966).

Eugen Herrigel, *Zen in the Art of Archery* (New York: 1971).

Frederick Holck, ed., *Death in Eastern Thought* (Nashville: 1974).

Philip Kapleau, ed., *The Three Pillars of Zen* (Boston: 1967).

Lao Tzu, *Tao te Ching*, tr. D. C. Lau, (Baltimore: 1970).

Richard H. Robinson, *The Buddhist Religion: A Historical Introduction* (Belmont: 1970).

Nancy W. Ross, *Three Ways of Asian Wisdom*, (New York: 1972).

Frederick Streng, *Emptiness: A Study in Religious Meaning* (Nashville: 1967).

Beatrice Lane Suzuki, *Mahayana Buddhism* (New York: 1969).

D. T. Suzuki, *Essays in Zen Buddhism*, 2 vols. (London: 1927).

———*Zen Buddhism* (New York: 1956).

J. Takakusu, "Buddhism as a Philosophy of Thusness," *Philosophy East and West*, ed. Charles A. Moore (Princeton: 1946).

Edward J. Thomas, *The Life of the Buddha* (New York: 1927).

Laurence G. Thompson, *Chinese Religion: An Introduction* (Belmont: 1969).

Arthur Waley, *The Real Tripitaka* (London: 1952).

Alan Watts, *The Way of Zen* (New York: 1957).

Guy Richard Welborn, *The Buddhist Nirvana and Its Western Interpreters* (Chicago: 1968).

SIX
DEATH AS INEVITABILITY
—HISTORY

---

7 JUDAISM

The Jewish conception of death is pivotal to our study for two reasons: first, it has had a far-reaching influence that has affected our way of thinking about death in the Western world; second, the Jews' experience with death in their own history, and particularly that twentieth-century chapter of their history that includes the Holocaust, has placed that very way of thinking under severe judgment.

With some exaggeration, though not much, we can say that Judaism offers the major alternative mode of thought to Platonism in the West. For our purposes the signal difference between the two lies in the attitude toward history. As we have already seen in Plato—and will see from another perspective in Neoplatonism—the result of looking for the continuity of human existence in knowledge is a retreat from history. The Jews have done precisely the opposite. *Their salvation is not from history, but for history.* This is why the Holocaust is so deeply disturbing. It is not only a terrible tragedy in itself; it also raises for Jews and non-Jews alike the question as to whether the history is saving or damning.

Because a large part of the modern thought about death turns on the questions raised with such critical force by the intellectual and personal history of the Jews, this chapter will have a proportionately greater length.

"In the beginning God created the heavens and the earth." This simple declaration, the first sentence of the Hebrew scriptures, contains in itself all the distinguishing marks of the religion to the Jews. Everything that makes the Jewish people unique among the religions and cultures of the world can be traced directly back to it.

"In the beginning . . . ." That there *was* a beginning is already a distinctive belief. Such a remark would be unintelligible to Hindus and Buddhists, and could have found a place nowhere in their scriptures. To the modern scientific mind such a claim would fall so completely outside the limits of meaningful discourse that it could in no way even be argued. We have seen in an earlier chapter that scientific discourse tolerates no anomalies; it exists in fact to eliminate all discoverable anomalies and, consequently, to establish a uniform lawfulness in all our descriptions of the world. With the claim that there was an absolute beginning we abandon all appeals to uniform lawfulness, which become meaningless. For something to be lawful it must stand in a sequence of events coming before and after it according to a discernible pattern. Such lawfulness makes it possible, therefore, both to predict what will come as a consequence of any given event and to discover its origins. By declaring an absolute beginning the ancient Jews closed all avenues of inquiry into the ultimate cause and the ultimate end of all that exists. As we shall see, this has made it impossible for faithful Jews to explain the world *in terms of the world.*

It later became fashionable among philosophers, and particularly Christian philosophers, to think of the *creatio ex nihilo*, or creation out of nothing. Strictly speaking this phrase does capture the literal sense of the opening declaration of the scriptures. But religiously and intellectually it is misleading. The phrase comes from the reflective person's curiosity about what it was that might have preceded the creation; if it is nothing, then it is out of that nothing that the creation arose? Inescapably the nothing becomes a kind of something that serves as a precedent to the appearance of the heavens and the earth, giving some comfort to the mind impatient with the thought of an absolute beginning. We cannot stress firmly enough that this impatience was not evident in the author of this passage.

It must be admitted at once, of course, that not infrequently the Jews themselves felt it impossible to abide the stark sense of these words. A Talmudic rabbi, writing many centuries later, offered the following alternative version:

> In the beginning, two thousand years before the heaven and the earth, seven things were created: the Torah written with black fire on white fire, and lying in the lap of God; the Divine Throne, erected in the heaven . . . Paradise on the right side of God, Hell on the left side; the Celestial Sanctuary directly in front of God, hav-

ing a jewel on its altar graven with the Name of the Messiah, and Voice that cries aloud, "Return, ye children of men."[1]

Many similar elaborations on the creation legend can be found in Jewish literature, but still we must note what this author, and others like him, do not do. They are not denying the creation itself, and while they are suggesting that something did in fact precede the creation of the heavens and the earth, they are always perfectly clear that whatever that was it too was created. There are only two terms in this declaration: God and his creation. There was no medium out of which God created, no preexisting space in which he could place the earth, no principle or idea according to which God was required to assemble the universe. Therefore, we know nothing of God except through his creativity. "God never ceases from making something or other," the great Jewish philosopher of the first century C.E., Philo Judaeus, exclaimed, "but, as it is the property of fire to burn, and of snow to chill, so also it is the property of God to be creating."[2]

Philo has made something of a positive principle out of the creation with respect to our ability to have knowledge of God. But God's incessant creativity strikes most Jewish thinkers as a screen for the speculative mind. We cannot see through it into the mind of God; we know nothing of his plan or intention in creating. "All we hear about is the mystery of God's creative act," the twentieth-century philosopher Abraham Heschel has written, "and not a word about intention or meaning. The same applies to the creation of all other beings. We only hear what He does, not what He thinks."[3] Moses Maimonides (1140–1205) argued that the doctrine of the creation, given the stark absoluteness of its beginning in the will of God, makes it impossible for us ever to ask God the question, Why? "Accepting creation, all miracles become possible," he wrote, and we need not attempt an explanation. To all questions Why? there is only the answer, "He willed it so; or, His Wisdom decreed it."[4] Just as the world cannot be explained in terms of the world, neither can God be explained in terms of the world—nor the world in terms of God. The doctrine of the creation suggests the view that since nothing can be explained all that exists is a miracle. The universe in its entirety is miraculous.

Although the universe is miraculous as a whole, it cannot be stressed too much that it is not for anything in itself that its mystery arises. It is a miracle only because its origin lies outside itself and in that which is radically unlike itself. This perception has momentous consequences in Jewish life—and inasmuch as Jewish religion is one of the primary shaping elements of Western culture, momentous consequences for all of Western civilization. Because of the absolute distinction between God and the world, the world is utterly emptied of any trace of divinity. It has not the merest fragment of its own sacred power. The world is without any design or willfulness of its own, independent of its creator. Nothing earthly—and, for that matter, nothing human—is worthy of worship. No demons, no magical powers, no dark secrets belong to the earth.

There is only one indisputable order of authority and power within the creation: the lordship of men and women over all the rest of the earth. This authority was established at the time of the creation:

> Then God said, "Let us make man in our image, after our likeness; and let them have dominion over the fish of the sea, and over the birds of the air, and over the cattle, and over all the earth, and over every creeping thing that creeps upon the earth [Genesis 1:26].

All other orders of authority however are subject to challenge and abrupt termination. There is no priesthood, no kingship, no familial relationship that gives one person the privilege of absolute dominion over others. In the relation of human nature to animal and physical nature, however, authority is beyond question. It is, in fact, analogous to God's relationship to the creation: we may dispose of it as we wish, for no other reason than our own pleasure.*

The nontechnical terms "image" and "likeness" have, of course, drawn a swarm of technical interpretations. Philo, typical of those thinkers under the influence of Greek philosophy, explained that the image and likeness of God have "reference to the most important part of the soul, namely, the mind."[5] Following another verse from the Genesis account of the creation in which "the Lord God formed man of dust from the ground, and breathed into his nostrils the breath of life" (2:7), he even goes so far as to say that it was nothing less than the "divine spirit" itself that God breathed into the creature of dust, as though this creature did in fact share some part of divinity.[6] This compromise of the division between the human and the divine appears frequently in Jewish literature. Even a careful scholar like Theodor Gaster can refer to

---

*This is not altogether true. There is in the Bible, and in the succeeding Jewish tradition, an occasional expression of abhorrence of cruelty in the treatment of animals. "Whether the mother is a cow or a ewe, you shall not kill both her and her young in one day," we are enjoined in the Book of Leviticus (22:28). There are also carefully specified methods of slaughter, ranging from the shape of the knife to the manner in which it is to be inserted in the throat, that have developed in sacrificial ritual and have the manifest intention of sparing the animal unnecessary pain (Ausubel, *The Book of Jewish Knowledge*, p. 68).

one's "divine spark which is always and innately within him but which usually lies smothered beneath the dust of his mortality."[7] Heschel seems closer to the center of the tradition with his remark, "The image is not in man; it is man."[8] Image has not primarily to do with the relation of the person to something within oneself; neither does it have primarily to do with the person's relation to God. The great tenth-century rabbi Saadia (892–942) seems more accurately to have evoked the original sense of this verse by asserting that in making us in his image God bestowed on us the superiority of wisdom. It is by virtue of this wisdom that one

> is able to subdue the animals so that they may till the earth for him and bring in its produce. By virtue of it he is able to draw the water from the depth of the earth to its surface; he even invents irrigating wheels that draw the water automatically. By virtue of it he is able to build lofty mansions, to make magnificent garments, and to prepare delicate dishes. By virtue of it he is able to organize armies and camps, and to exercise kingship and authority for establishing order and civilization among men.[9]

I have given emphasis to this point because, as we shall see, it has a substantial bearing on the Jewish understanding of the nature of death *and* on the great tragedies that are a part of Jewish history. In a searing critique of Jewish religion the modern scholar Richard Rubinstein argues that the doctrine of creation, by emptying the earth of its sacred powers and by authorizing men and women to "subdue" it to their own ends, has led to the secularization and the bureaucritization of the modern world. In an analysis of recent history, which we shall summarize later in this chapter, Rubinstein shows that the Nazi death camps represent a triumph of bureaucracy in a secularized world. It is "crucial that we recognize that the process of secularization that led to the bureaucratic objectivity required for the death camps was an essential and perhaps inevitable outcome of the *religious* traditions of the Judeo-Christian West."[10] Rubinstein does not, of course, deny that there have been profound changes in the culture of the West in the twenty-five centuries between the biblical age and the present. However: "In the biblical world, all of human activity stands under the judgment of a righteous and omnipotent deity; in the modern world, the righteous and omnipotent deity has disappeared *for all practical purposes*. Man is alone in the world, free to pursue whatever ends he chooses. . . ."[11]

Before we can have a clear understanding of the biblical mind, we must know what it means to live in a desacralized world, but "under the judgment of a righteous and omnipotent deity." It would be an inexcusable distortion of Saadia's high praise of wisdom, which includes the ability "to organize armies and camps," to assume that what he had in mind was a world that lived free of God's terrible judgment. Our question therefore concerns the way in which God's judgment is experienced in a world over which we have unchallenged lordship.

There are, in fact, two creation stories in the book of Genesis, one following the other so uninterruptedly that the casual reader may not see the break in the narrative. In the first story God creates an unnamed male and female on the sixth day, after all else has been made. In the second story God fashioned a man out of dust, breathed life into him, and placed him in a garden. God gave this man a single commandment: You may freely eat of every tree of the garden; but of the tree of the knowledge of good and evil you shall not eat, for in the day that you eat of it you shall die" (2:16–17). Later, the woman whom God had made, since it "is not good that the man should be alone," was approached by a serpent who urged her to eat of the forbidden tree, assuring her: "You shall not die. For God knows that when you eat of it your eyes will be opened, and you will be like God, knowing good and evil" (3:5). The serpent had lied. God held to his threat. The two were driven out of the garden, and at its boundaries God "placed the cherubim, and a flaming sword which turned every way, to guard the way to the tree of life" (3:24). For their disobedience they were punished with pain in childbirth, the burden of toil for their well-being, and mortality.

Mortality, however, is more than simply punishment. The serpent had promised that they would not die *for they would be like God, knowing good and evil.* Deathlessness and the knowledge of good and evil are precisely what separates the divine from the human. *The arrangement in the garden was simple: the man and the woman could have either knowledge or immortality, but not both.* They chose to have both, and by driving the two from the garden God did nothing more than restore the original arrangement. Now, however, instead of immortality they possessed the knowledge of good and evil. It is conspicuous that God did nothing to erase that knowledge from them. He certainly could have acted otherwise. He could have removed the tree of knowledge, allowing them to live forever, but unconsciously, in the darkness of ignorance.

This decision of God's has two great consequences. The first is that mortality, although certainly a punishment, is more importantly to be understood as the one irreducible fact of human existence that forever

separates the human from the divine; it is a reminder that we are creation and not creator. The second consequence is that we still possess
the knowledge of good and evil. The punishment does not consist in
depriving us of knowledge. This is a point of some importance in the
later tradition and therefore worth examining more closely here. Note
that the offense of Adam and Eve against God was not mere disobedience, but disobedience that took the form of acquiring knowledge. The
fact that it is knowledge *of good and evil* is of less weight than the fact
that it is knowledge as such. The expression "of good and evil" does
not have an explicit ethical reference, but rather indicates a broad inclusiveness. What is meant here is that by eating of that tree Adam and
Eve came to have a knowledge of "practically everything." But nothing
more emphatically marks the difference between the human and the
divine than knowledge. God alone may know everything. Human
knowledge is strictly limited, and any attempt to exceed those limits
must be understood as a presumption of divinity on the part of the
human. Repeatedly the Bible reminds us of the inability of human
knowledge to comprehend the things of God.

The fact remains, however, that we are not altogether without
knowledge, however much it is limited. We are not dumb or mindless
like the beasts. The knowledge that we *do* possess can be distinguished
from God's by noting that once the original pair became knowledgeable
they lost their immortality and were expelled from paradise. With
knowledge came death and the necessity of caring for themselves. They
could no longer live in a mindless and eternal present with no anxiety
before the uncertainties that lay in the future. When God forced them
from the garden he drove them into *time. In exchange for this
deathlessness he made them historical—and knowledgeable.* They are
forever to be wanderers, forever to be drawn ahead by the vision of a
future they can never finish and bring into the present; following them
is a past whose meanings are endlessly changing. In the garden they
lived in eternity, but unconsciously. Outside the garden they are to live
in memory and hope.

Stressing the fact that death is the way God has chosen to keep clear
the boundary between the human and the divine has the effect of diminishing the *punitive* nature of death. It is certainly the case that the
Hebrew scriptures abound with references to death, apparently applied
by God as a kind of punishment. If we look carefully at those instances,
however, we find that the penalty for crimes is death only where one
has stepped across the limitations of humanness. God destroyed the
Tower of Babel because the builders displayed an exceeding skill not
only in their engineering genius but in their social organization, for

they had become one people, speaking one language. What otherwise seems to be a commendable human society is shattered by God because "this is only the beginning of what they will do; and nothing that they propose to do will now be impossible for them" (Genesis 11:6). It is only God for whom all things are possible; it is only God who is not subject to the vagaries and relativities of an unfinished history.

In the other direction, persons may no more live as animals than they may live as deities: "Whoever lies with a beast shall be put to death" (Exodus 22:19). Capital punishment for sexual violations seems particularly severe. Adultery, incest, and homosexuality are punishable by death: "If a man takes a wife and her mother also, it is wickedness, they shall be burned with fire, and both he and they" (Leviticus 20:10−14). But not all sexual deviations are capital crimes. If a man lies with a slave who is betrothed to another, "they shall not be put to death, because she was not free" (Leviticus 19:20). We can take a narrow view in our interpretation of these perplexing verses, saying simply that the ancient Hebrews were excessively vindictive in their protection of conventional morality, particularly when persons maritally attached could somehow be understood as *possessions* of their partners. A broader view would account for the fact that only those sexual acts were considered completely reprehensible that threatened the fundamental institutions of the society, institutions that can be weakened only at the cost of weakening the society as a whole. Since what bound that society was the compelling vision of its historical destiny, these crimes all delivered a shuddering blow that affected the very roots of the people's historicity. Their cruelty is undeniable, but their intent does not seem in doubt.

The same point can be made concerning the more obvious acts on God's part to dash the enemies of Israel. God is uniformly expected to be vengeful in the protection of his people from the wicked. Thus the psalmist:

> Keep me as the apple of the eye;
> > hide me in the shadow of thy wings,
> from the wicked who despoil me,
> > my deadly enemies who surround me.
>
> They close their hearts to pity;
> > with their mouths they speak arrogantly.
> They track me down; now they surround me;
> > they set their eyes to cast me to the ground.
> They are like a lion eager to tear,
> > as a young lion lurking in ambush.

> Arise, O Lord! confront them, overthrow them!
>> Deliver my life from the wicked by thy sword,
> from men by thy hand, O Lord,
>> from men whose portion in life is of the world.
> May their belly be filled with what thou hast stored up for
>> them;
>> may their children have more than enough;
>> may they leave something over to their babes [Psalms
>> 17:8−14].

It is not enough that the enemies be defeated, they must be violently done in, and their innocent children must suffer with them. The passions are excessive, but the logic behind them is nonetheless clear: what is of supreme importance is that our history continue, that the ground of hope never vanish.

God is the author of death, but death is the ground of history. Even when death seems to be viewed primarily as punishment, as mere vengeance, it is always in the interest of keeping the way open for the forward movement of the people of Israel into their unfinished future. The most sacred relationship between God and his people, therefore, is not that in which death is removed or prevented, but that in which history is guaranteed. This guarantee is proclaimed at once in the opening narrative of Genesis. If history begins with the expulsion from the garden, the first event in that history is a murder. In a fit of jealousy, Cain, the son of Adam and Eve, slays his brother Abel. Immediately following this narrative, Eve conceives and bears another son: "God has appointed for me another child instead of Abel," she says, "for Cain slew him" (4:25). Some generations after Adam and Eve, God covers the earth with a flood, saving only Noah and his family. After the waters have receded God announces to Noah: "I establish my covenant with you, that never again shall all flesh be cut off by the waters of a flood, and never again shall there be a flood to destroy the earth" (Genesis 9:11). The convenant, or agreement, that God establishes has the force of a promise both from God and from his people that they commit themselves to a continuing history. Therefore, the fundamental relationship to God is an agreement made in the past, binding into the future. "To believe is to remember," Abraham Heschel has written.[12] And however anguished or distressing history might become, the loyalty of the Jewish people to God's promise will always be "an anchor of meaning" in that history. [13]

The way God exercises judgment over his people, then, is basically by sustaining the distinction between the human and the divine. It is death that establishes that distinction and enforces it. But death, it should be emphasized, it not to be understood as a punishment for being human, but is punishment only when we refuse to live within the limits of our humanness. Death, then, is not a burden placed capriciously or vindictively by an evil diety on the whole race. It is one of the essential characteristics of humanness. To be human is to be able to die. This means that death need not be understood as an evil, or as the fated disaster that cuts us off from the blessings of this life. On the contrary, the Hebrew scriptures make it clear that it is not in spite of death, but through death, that God promises his richest blessings. It is *by means of death,* in the sense that it is death, that makes history possible, and it is history that is God's greatest blessing to his children. We must therefore examine more closely the relationship between death and history.

Death comes from the hand of God—and only from the hand of God. Death has no power of its own. There are no agents of death independent of God. But since God has unequivocally committed himself to history through the covenant—repeatedly renewed in the course of the biblical narrative—each death has the effect of recharging the dynamic of history. For nearly all of the personal deaths noted in the biblical literature there is the sense of something completed, a life lived out to its appropriate limits: "All the days that Adam lived were 930 years; and he died" (Genesis 5:5). The biblical author seems indifferent to the immense length of Adam's life, and those of his immediate ancestors. The force of this sentence is rather the suggestion that Adam had satisfied his commitment to history, *and then died.* Similarly, the account of Joshua's eventful life, during which he led Israel out of the wilderness into the promised land, is concluded with an almost casual locution: "After these things Joshua, the son of Nun, the servant of the Lord, died, being one hundred and ten years old" (Joshua 24:29). Death comes characteristically "after these things." The vision of tragic death is largely absent in the Bible. Although instances can be cited, we are far from, say, the mind of the ancient Greek, for whom death was not only tragic but inherently antihistorical. The killing of Hector in Homer's great epic was tragic because a person of exceeding nobility and courage was destroyed at the zenith of his heroic career. But it was also the effective end of the narrative, the final act in a piece of finished history. Neither do we find anything similar to the towering grief of Gilgamesh over the death of his companion Enkidu that impelled the mythic Assyrian hero to undertake an epic journey in search for the secret of immortality. We also note that there is a curious absence in the reflections of the Hebrews of any anguish over the death of children or the loss of persons to disease or natural disaster. Death was not viewed as an evil in itself. Indeed, nowhere in the Bible is death *as such* isolated and discussed as a subject or issue.

This does not mean, however, that death passes unnoticed in biblical narratives or that the dead are not mourned. When the aged Jacob "breathed his last, and was gathered to his people," his son "Joseph fell on his father's face, and wept over him, and praised him" (Genesis 49:33 – 50:1). The description of David's grief over the death of his son Absalom, though he had fought on the side of his father's enemies, is one of the most poignant episodes in world literature. When he learned of Absalom's death, "the king was deeply moved, and he went up to the chamber over the gate, and wept; and as he went, he said, 'O my son Absalom, my son, my son Absalom! Would I have died instead of you, O Absalom, my son, my son!' " (2 Samuel 18:33).

These instances of grief are never answered with words of comfort or with assurances of compensation. The loss is absolute. The dead are never replaced or recovered; they are forever beyond the reach of our affection; they are also beyond the reach of our retributive anger. *Nonetheless*, the deeper theme is not obscured; what God has promised will not be annulled by death. Whatever we may expect from God we *can* receive only in the context of life, and we *shall* receive it there. To be sure, this often leads to a curious compromise or qualification in the promise, for death may well come to those to whom the promises are made before God has fulfilled them. But they will be fulfilled all the same. While already advanced in age, the patriarch Abraham, whose wife was still embarrassingly barren, was told by God: "I will make of you a great nation, and I will bless you, and make your name great, so that you will be a blessing. I will bless those who bless you, and him who curses you I will curse; and by you will all the families of the earth bless themselves" (Genesis 12:2 ff.). The extraordinary promise to an old man went ignored for twenty-five years. When Abraham was ninety-nine years old the Lord announced that his ninety-year-old wife Sarah would bear a son. Incredulous, the old man laughed. Sarah nonetheless conceived, and Abraham was later to die with this single issue as the only firm sign that God intended to complete the promise. There was no doubting, however, that his descendents were to be as great in number as "the dust of the earth" (Genesis 13:16).

The Jews were certain that, just as Adam and Eve were assured of their progeny by the birth of another son after the murder of Abel, God would guarantee that the labors of the righteous would bear fruit in succeeding generations, but the situation with the wicked was not so clear. On the one hand, there was a confidence in God's vindictiveness, characteristically evoked by Ezekiel who wrote that God instructed him no longer to preach that judgment would bypass the wicked in their lifetimes, falling later on their descendents: "Behold, all souls are mine; the soul of the father as well as the soul of the son is mine; the soul that sins shall die" (Ezekiel 18:14). More commonly, however, it was believed that God was not demanding a full measure from the wicked for their evil.

> Righteous art thou, O Lord, when I complain to thee;
>> yet I would plead my case before thee.
> Why does the way of the wicked prosper?
>> why do all who are treacherous thrive?
> Thou plantest them, and they take root;
>> they grow and bring forth fruit . . . [Jeremiah 12:1 ff.].

Jeremiah's plea is echoed throughout the Hebrew scriptures. The case made against God is severe: not only do the wicked seem to experience no punishment in this life, they actually thrive. This is doubly perplexing since they have been "planted" by God himself. God seems flatly contradictory in this matter.

Jeremiah's question is never really answered in the Bible. The best that Jeremiah can get from God is another promise: "if any nation will not listen, then I will utterly pluck it up and destroy it, says the Lord" (12:17). In later centuries rabbinic interpreters will provide a strong doctrine of immortality to allow God an occasion for redressing these imbalances, but in the biblical literature all notions of the afterlife remain inchoate. The common biblical term, "Sheol," *appears* to name a kind of place to which the dead go. When Jacob (mistakenly) believes his son Joseph has been devoured by wild beasts, "he refused to be comforted, and said, 'No, I shall go down to Sheol to my son, mourning' " (Genesis 37:35). The thought of joining his son in Sheol was certainly of no comfort. It is plainly not a place where they could dwell together. Job refers to Sheol as

> the land of gloom and deep darkness,
> the land of gloom and chaos,
>> where light is as darkness [Job 10:21 ff.].

Job describes it as a place from which one cannot return, where there is no hope (17:13 ff.). What seems primary to Job is not his distress over what Sheol is like or what happens there; his distress is that nothing happens there. His references to Sheol are not to another life, but to the end of this life and to the staggering thought that a person lives but once. A tree can be cut down and its roots will sprout again.

But man dies, and is laid low
   man breathes his last, and where is he?
As waters fail from a lake,
   and a river wastes away and dries up,
So man lies down and rises not again;
   till the heavens are no more he will not awake,
   or be roused out of his sleep [Job 14:10−12].

Nowhere in the Bible does Sheol appear as an abode of immortals. It is no Tartarus filled with moaning shades and shrieking faceless divinities; it is no Inferno where the wicked undergo tortures ingeniously fitted to their sins. Rather than exciting the imagination it seems to confound it, binding one's reflections about death to thoughts of vanishing without a trace into the dust. Sheol is not an image of after*life*, but of after*death*. It is a brutal reminder that to be dead is to be cut off—not only from those whom we love, as Jacob from his son, but from God himself.

Turn, O Lord, save my life:
   deliver me for the sake of thy steadfast love.
For in death there is no remembrance of thee;
   in Sheol who can give thee praise [Psalms 6:4 ff.]?

Not only may one not return, as the psalmist laments, but God himself could not bring us back. Sheol, then, is not conceived as a *consequence to life,* but as a *contrast to life.* Allusions to Sheol consistently have the spiritual impact of directing our attention back to the fact that we are, after all, still alive. More than that: it is the dark screen against which the brilliant profile of life appears in its manifold richness.

Sheol, then, is obviously not an answer for the repeated biblical question as to why the wicked prosper. It would be incorrect, however, to conclude from this that the prophets felt God was truly contradictory, or at least flawed in his justice; neither did they satisfy themselves with mere empty promises. The answer to this dilemma lies deeper. We can find it by looking more closely at the way in which death, particularly in the image of Sheol, causes life to stand out in spendor—for all its incompleteness. To look directly at death, in other words, is to find our gaze returned at once to life. A proper understanding of the biblical view of death requires us, therefore, to discover how life appears in the face of death. At first we might well be perplexed, for what immediately appears is a greatly varied surface, often contradictory in its details.

Certainly, the darkest passages concerning the nature of life occur in Job. After losing his flocks, his children, and then his health, Job curses the day of his birth with a passion probably unequalled in the Bible:

> Let the day perish wherein I was born,
>   and the night which said,
>   "A man-child is conceived."
> Let that day be darkness!
>   May God above not seek it,
>   or light shine upon it.
> Let gloom and deep darkness claim it.
>   Let clouds dwell upon it;
>   let the blackness of the day terrify it. [Job 3:3−5].

"I loathe life," Job cries out later (7:16), as though existence itself has become a burden. Certainly Job carries the biblical view to an extreme. Taken out of context, these exclamations have a distinctly Buddhist quality, since their preoccupation with suffering seems to echo the Buddhist equation of life and suffering. There is, however, a manifest difference. For the Buddhist it is not as though the living are burdened with suffering; they are burdened with existence that consists of suffering. The only release is a release from existence. Job, for all his loathing, still expects comfort *within* the context of life. "Let me alone," he begs God, "that I may find a little comfort before I go whence I shall not return" (10:20 ff.). The astounding contrast between Job's suffering and the simultaneous affirmation of existence no doubt account for the fact that Job and the equally doleful book of Lamentations are the only selections from biblical literature that a mourner is permitted by Jewish law to read in the period of most intense grief.[14] It may also explain why, alone of all the books of the Bible, Job is the only scripture the rabbis thought one could directly doubt.

Ecclesiastes also offers a renowned observation on the quality of life, but one that represents a palpable contrast to Job's:

> Vanity of vanities, says the Preacher,
>   vanity of vanities! All is vanity.
> What does man gain by all the toil
>   at which he toils under the sun?
> A generation goes, and a generation comes,
>   but the earth remains for ever [Ecclesiastes 1:2−4].

It is not suffering that animates the unknown author of this brief work; it is the familiar biblical fact that all things have their season, that nothing endures. If Job's plaint rises from a life from which too much has been taken away, the anguish found in Ecclesiastes arises from a life to which too much has been given. After recounting how he had built great houses, owned many slaves, planted vineyards, hired singers, acquired concubines, and "became great and surpassed all who were before me in Jerusalem," he then stopped to consider "all that my hands had done and the toil I spent in doing it, and behold all was vanity and a striving after wind, and there was nothing to be gained under the sun" (2:9–11). But it is not just the tangible objects of this world that vanish with the passage of time. Wisdom also, and even the wisdom that comes from this realization, is of no comfort.

> I perceived that this also is but a striving
> after wind. For in much wisdom is much vexation
> and he who increases knowledge increases sorrow
>   [Ecclesiastes 1:17 ff.].

One need not search long through the pages of the Bible before finding sentiments contradictory to Ecclesiastes:

> Happy is the man who finds wisdom,
>   and the man who gets understanding,
> for the gain from it is better than gain from silver
>   and its profit better than gold.
>
> She is a tree of life to those who lay hold of her;
>   Those who hold her fast are called happy [Proverbs
>   3:13–14, 18].

The Song of Solomon, a work of resplendent praise for the pleasures of the worldly life, and roughly contemporary to both Job and Ecclesiastes, seems oblivious to such attitudes toward life.

> How graceful are your feet in sandals,
>   O queenly maiden!
> Your rounded thighs are like jewels,
>   the work of a master hand.
> Your navel is a rounded bowl
>   that never lacks mixed wine.
> Your belly is a heap of wheat,
>   encircled with lilies.
> Your two breasts are like two fawns,
>   twins of a gazelle [Song of Solomon 7:1–3].

The manifestly erotic quality of this entire book has not infrequently put its interpreters in an awkward position, compelling them to read it as an allegory of disguised spiritual secrets. We, however, should have no difficulty in seeing how perfectly this coheres with what has preceded. The same stark view of death that leads to Job leads to poetry of this kind. Job and Ecclesiastes, Proverbs and the Song of Solomon offer an inconsistent characterization of the surface of life, but, still, in one significant respect they are cut from the same spiritual cloth. They are all enormously busy with life. They live at its limits, mount its summits, and spring back at its tumults.

There is something else that binds these authors to a single point of view: confronted by the vagaries of life, its treacheries, and its fundamental unpredictability, they did not look for a continuation of life after death either as a way of requiting its losses or sustaining its joys. It was not *more life* but the *source of life* that commanded their attention. If existence was not for them a burden from which one must somehow be relieved, neither was it a possession one could endeavor to increase in quantity. Life, or existence, was not what they *had*; it was what they *were*. To be precise, we may not even speak of their being busy *with* life. They were busy *living*. The biblical Jew could not have imagined standing before God bargaining for more life, for the simple reason that the bargaining was already an expression of life. We saw earlier that death as such was not a subject in the Hebrew scriptures; it is now apparent that neither is life such a subject.

Here we have a glimpse of some of the deeper elements in the creation story. God created a certain, concrete human being, from whom we are all directly descended—by blood and along an unrepeatable history. He did not create humanity as an abstract entity or the laws of chemistry and physics in such a way that they could allow for the random rise of life out of the barren ocean of the primitive planet. God is not the source of my *life*, but of *me*. This accounts for the intensely *personal* quality of the Jew's God—in sharp contrast to, say, the highest being of the Hindus or the Neoplatonists. Since God is the immediate source of all that we have and do, he is closer to us than hands and breathing.

> For thou didst form my inward parts,
>   thou didst knit me together in my mother's womb.
>
> Thy eyes beheld my unformed substance,
>   in thy book were written, every one of them,
> the days that were formed for me,
>   when as yet there was none of them [Psalms 139:13,18].

It also means that any separation from God is unthinkable. In the words of the same psalmist:

> Whither shall I go from thy Spirit?
>> Or whither shall I flee from thy presence?
> If I ascend to heaven, thou art there!
>> If I make my bed in Sheol, thou art there!
> If I take the wings of the morning
>> and dwell in the uttermost parts of the sea,
> even there thy hand shall lead me,
>> and thy right hand shall hold me [Psalms 139:7 ff.].

Taken in its true biblical sense, the recognition that each human person stands in relation to God—not as to an object, or to an idea, or even as to an experience, but as to one's own source—is the recognition that none of the questions directed to God could ever receive an answer. *The answer always precedes the question.* The answer to the question is nothing less than the possibility of asking the question.

It is for this reason that the biblical Jews could demand that God explain why the righteous suffer, why the wicked prosper, or why all things pass—but never notice they were not answered. It is also for this reason that we find unlikely juxtapositions in the biblical texts. For example, after Job has repeatedly pressed God for an explanation of his apparently undeserved suffering, God finally speaks, but his answer is quite plainly a nonanswer:

> Gird up you loins like a man,
>> I will question you, and you shall declare to me.
> Where were you when I laid the foundation of the earth?
>> Tell me, if you have understanding.
> Who determined its measurement—surely you know!
>> Or who stretched the line upon it?
> On what were its bases sunk,
>> or who laid its cornerstone,
> When the morning stars sang together,
>> and all the sons of God shouted for joy [Job 38:3 ff.]?

In some of the scripture's grandest poetry God continues to place before Job a sequence of unanswerable questions, all referring to God's essential identification as creator and cutting off all access to the mind of God by human understanding. At best, God's questions are rhetorical. "Where were you when . . ." has the effect of exclaiming, "You were not here until I placed you here." It is the poet's way of reminding us that the answer always is prior to the question.

An essential clue to the Hebrew mind lies in the fact that this radical unknowability of the divine does not cause one simply to turn away from its reality. On the contrary, the overwhelming majesty of God irradiates the biblical literature as a whole, and particularly those passages where the brevity or the uncertainty of life are most poignantly evoked.

> A voice says, "Cry!"
>   And I said, "What shall I cry?"
> All flesh is grass,
>   and all its beauty is like the flower of the field.
> The grass withers, the flower fades;
>   but the word of our God will stand forever [Isaiah 40:6,8].

Job, at the very height of his miseries, and under the merciless assault of his friends, even before God has given his rhetorical "answer," cries out, "I know that my redeemer lives" (19:25). This declaration has often been cited by interpreters in later centuries as the supreme moment of the Job story. Ecclesiastes, in spite of all the weariness and futility he has expressed, rises to the same recognition: "There is nothing better for a man than that he should eat and drink, and find enjoyment in his toil. This also, I saw, is from the hand of God; for apart from him who can eat or who can have enjoyment" (2:24 ff.)?

In sum, what we have before us is a view of death unique among the philosophies and the religions of the world, a view we might state in the following formula: when the Jews looked at death they saw life; and when they looked at life they saw God. The God they saw was the immediate source of all they were and did. This exultant God-centeredness is a quality that remains at the very center of Jewish religious life. It bespeaks a sense of the perfect sufficiency of God. Baal Shem Tov, the charismatic founder of the Hasidic movement in eighteenth-century Poland, exclaimed, "If I love God, what need have I of a coming world?"[15] It was told of Rabbi Zalman, one of the subsequent leaders of Hasidic Jews, that he once "interrupted his prayers and said, 'I do not want your paradise. I do not want your coming world. I want you, and you only.' "[16] Before the spiritual force of this recognition of God's enormous sufficiency, human existence is not an objective fact, it is a miracle.

We have attempted in this book to discern the way in which distinct religious and intellectual traditions have established a sense of continuity in the face of death. The continuity that has so far emerged in the Jewish tradition is filled with paradox. To begin with, it rests on the acceptance of death as an indisputable fact. Sheol is a place where absolutely nothing happens, where the dead are forever cut off from the living and even from God, and from which there is no hope of return. Since birth is a beginning as absolute as death is an ending, life can be properly characterized as a journey from "dust to dust." Continuity is not then achieved by the elimination of death; indeed, it is not *achieved* at all, but *given*. Just as God has given death, he has provided human existence with a continuity in the form of history. Paradoxically, death is not an impediment to history, but its very ground. But human existence is historical, as we have seen, not simply because it passes through time, but because it is characterized by the possession of the knowledge of good and evil; that is, a knowledge that has to do with what a person does, with what comes of one's actions. We are historical because we can look forward; we can forsee the consequences of our actions. This means, of course, that the future is not a point in time somewhere still beyond us; more precisely, the future is the fruit that time bears from the seeds we nourish in the present. *The future is not something that will happen to us, but what will come of the way we are currently living.*

We saw that what constitutes the evil character of the wicked is their fundamental antihistoricity. The threat of Israel's enemies was not merely the threat of death; it was rather that they seemed occasionally to have the power of bringing the history of Israel to an abrupt end. God's failure to punish the wicked seems only to increase this danger. But overriding this perplexing inconsistency on God's part is the promise. Essentially it is a promise to keep history from dying, though never a promise to keep these persons, or any others, from dying. Abraham's descendents are more than could possibly be counted, but Abraham is not promised immortality, not even a life a second longer than is necessary to conceive his solitary legitimate heir. Because Abraham is confident that God will keep his promise, he dies fulfilled, though he has seen nothing of this vast history but the birth of a single child. Abraham, moreover, had no desire to view this great progeny, no desire to live into his own future, because he understood implicitly that the future already existed in his present life. *It was not necessary for Abraham to experience the history whose seeds lay in him; it was sufficient for him to experience his historicity.* We have offered the formula that for the Jews to look at death is to see life, and to look at life is to see God. What is perfectly clear in the story of Abraham, and elsewhere in the Bible, is that each time God appeared to him it was to announce a future event. We can then add to our formula that to see God is to see an open future.

The contrary to this is that evil does not enter history with death, but with the inability to see God present in it. If to see God's presence is to see an open future, then *to see history without God is to believe that the future is ours to do with as we like.* When Saadia said in the tenth century that by virtue of wisdom we are "able to organize armies and camps," he knew that it was God who had given that wisdom, and that he had given it as part of his guarantee to keep history open. When Hitler, in the twentieth century, used his own peculiar intellect to organize armies and camps, it was in a declared rejection of God's lordship over history. Hitler intended to make history his own and to bring the history of the Jews—and ultimately the rest of the world—to an end, *his* end.

It is precisely concerning this point that the most damaging criticism of Judaism has been raised, namely, that the radical separation of the creator from the creation led to the very secularization and bureaucratization of the modern world that made the Holocaust possible, and perhaps inevitable. In other words, there may be a supreme irony in the fact that it was the ideology of an open future that led the Jews into what came tragically close to destroying that future altogether. The Holocaust forcefully begs the question concering the presence of *God* in history. The twelve terrible years of Nazi rule call the bluff on 3000 years of promise. Is God faithful to his word, or is it the Babylonians, Romans, Cossacks, nazis, and other oppressors of the Jews who rule the world? If the vision of an open future is the genius of Judaism, it has also come to be its chief crisis.

Our task here is to look at the history of the Jews, both as it occurred and as it was interpreted, in order to see whether the claim of an open future is truly credible, and not simply an empty though dangerous ideology. If it is not credible, the Jewish understanding of death is incoherent, for it would mean that the paradoxical affirmation of historical continuity in the face of personal death collapses into a direct contradiction.

How do we look for the presence of God in history? From the opening sentence of Genesis we have been told that God cannot be historical, and that we cannot be anything *but* historical. Therefore, it makes no sense to find a particular historical phenomenon we could point at and designate as God. We have already seen that the *effect* of God's presence is an open future. We must then attempt to discern the way in which that future is opened and kept open—by God.

The earliest centuries of Jewish history, as they are remembered in the biblical narrative, offer a somewhat naive view of the way in which God prevents the future from closing in on the children of Israel. Beginning with the murder of Abel by his brother, the first event after the expulsion from the garden, there is a long sequence of episodes filled with the sort of concrete detail and personal color that assure a rapt audience for the oral retelling of these stories. We note quickly a common narrative development in these separate but sequential tales: the people of Israel are suddenly threatened by an enemy from without or by dissension from within, but no matter how outnumbered or how faithless they have become God does not abandon them. These accounts are simplistic only because their perspective on this history is untroubled; there are no events that challenge God's repeated promise to keep the future open for his people. The continuing growth of Israel, both religiously and politically, seems to have an irresistible force behind it. Extraordinary figures arise at critical moments. Moses proves a dynamic leader for the daring escape from Egypt and the bitter sojourn in the wilderness. Moses received the law directly from God, holding before his fractious followers the ideal of becoming "a nation of priests and a holy people." At a time of civil war David appeared, possessed with a military and political genius that made him the greatest of all the kings of Israel. Jerusalem became a splendid royal city and the site of a grand temple that gave the religion its first cultic center.

In 586 B.C.E. an event occurred that utterly confounded this simple view of history, marking the end of the Jews' naive understanding of their relation to God: Jerusalem was taken by a greatly superior force, the temple destroyed, and the priesthood, along with many of the people, driven into exile. The destruction of the temple not only brought the cultic life of Israel to an end, with its ritual sacrifices and elaborate priestly ceremonies, it required an altogether new way of understanding how God was providing the continuity in the life of his people. So devastated were the basic institutions of the nation that it was beyond reason to expect a leader of the genius of Moses or David to rise from its scattered people. According to the previous view it would seem obvious that the God of Israel had proved helpless against the gods of the Babylonian conquerors. Where then is the continuity of the history that God had repeatedly promised the patriarchs? The events of 586 B.C.E. had the effect of giving authority to a new vision of continuity that had already been evoked by a series of inspired preachers, or prophets. The fact that God seemed indifferent to the enemy's conquest of the city of David, and even more important seemed unmoved by the fierce religious hatred that defiled the high altar and pulled the temple down around it, struck the prophets as a clear message that

"Israel had been punished for her sins, and it was God who had carried out the punishment. God was not conquered but vindicated. The pagans were merely his instruments."[17]

For centuries the prophets had been warning Israel of God's impending judgment for their unrighteousness. More than 200 years earlier Amos had offered his bitter condemnation of the cult in God's name:

> I hate, I despise your feasts,
>   and I take no delight in your solemn assemblies.
> Even though you offer me your burnt offerings and cereal
>   offerings,
>   I will not accept them,
> and the peace offerings of your fatted beasts
>   I will not look upon.
> Take away from me the noise of your songs;
>   to the melody of your harps I will not listen.
> But let justice roll down like waters,
>   and righteousness like an ever-flowing stream [Amos
>   5:21 ff.].

Religion was not a matter of ceremonial observance, but a passion of the heart that leads one into a life of justice and compassion. What God wants is not a powerful royal or priestly hierarchy that can manipulate human affairs by external force, but a renewed sense of the limits of human existence and the knowledge that history begins from within.

> For thou hast no delight in sacrifice;
>   were I to give a burnt offering, thou wouldst not be
>   pleased.
> The sacrifice acceptable to God is a broken spirit;
>   a broken and contrite heart, O God, thou wilt not de-
>   spise [Psalms 51:16 ff.].

While the exile had the immediate effect of elevating the role of the prophet, and the long-range effect of assuring that the prophetic spirit would never lose its influence in the shaping of Jewish religion, it is still the case that when the Jews returned from exile almost a century later they restored the temple and with it cultic worship. Over the next 500 years the fortunes of the people tumultuously rose and fell. In 70 C.E. there occurred one of the most decisive events in all of Jewish history: the second and final destruction of the temple.

The year 70 marks the end of any significant political or religious prsence of the Jews in Jerusalem until the establishment of the state of Israel in 1948. Although there was an obvious parallel with the destruction of the first temple 650 years earlier, this time there were no prophets to raise the people's hopes to the high promise of a glorious return, nor to identify in the Romans' thorough profanation of religious places and institutions the punishing hand of God scourging Israel for her faithlessness. This time the disaster yielded to no such explanation. It was an undeserved and meaningless evil. Even the prophetic understanding that history would be kept open by God if only his people were contrite in heart and loved justice, made no sense. It seemed as if the future were closing itself to the children of Israel.

That the destruction of the second temple did not mean the end of Jewish history altogether owes to a development that had begun inconspicuously and quite by accident centuries before. After the return of the Jews to Jerusalem from their exile in Babylonia in the fifth century B.C.E., and the subsequent reconstruction of the temple, the priest Ezra came into possession of a written copy of the Torah, or what now comprises the first five books of the Hebrew scriptures. Ezra's giving the Torah ritual significance had the effect of attracting a group of scholars and teachers whose primary interest was reading and interpreting the written text. The most assiduous among these teachers, or rabbis, eventually formed a party known as Pharisees—a term meaning "separatist." Since the Pharisees placed the study of the Torah above all other religious duties, they were obviously less dependent on the temple and eventually were even alienated from its priestly functions. The destruction of the second temple and the dispersion of the people were therefore to have the immediate effect of bringing the institution of the temple priests to an abrupt and final end. The rabbis, however, regardless of their terrible suffering, were able to keep their tradition vigorously intact. The Torah, after all, can be read and studied *anywhere*, and its laws apply to the whole of life in *every* setting.

Although the rabbis saw no meaning in the destruction of Jerusalem by the Romans, it is important to note that in no way did they conclude that God had withdrawn his presence from history. Indeed, even in the ceremonial structure of the religion, which developed out of rabbinic Judaism, all the festivals and holy days have a directly historical significance. *Passover*, for example, commemorates the flight of the Jews from their Egyptian bondage. *Succoth*, or the Feast of Booths, recalls the perilous sojourn in the wilderness on the way out of the Promised Land. The fasts, or "half-holidays," which have largely fallen into neglect, recall those occasions when God had shown his displeasure with Israel. Even the popular, and less religiously important, celebrations,

Purim and *Hannukah*, serve as reminders to significant historical moments when Israel was delivered from its oppressors. *Rosh Hashanah*, or the celebration of the new year, and *Yom Kippur*, the day of atonement, have no explicit reference to historical occasions. Each does, however, have a distinctly personal spirit, intended to evoke an awareness of god's presence in every aspect of our lives. Yom Kippur, the holiest day of the year, emphasizes the importance of repentance to religious life. Genuine repentance is not only the recognition that one's behavior in the past has been inadequate; it is also the desire to achieve a complete relationship with God by an inward transformation, by a realization that in the encounter with God we are active participants and not merely swept along in the current of external events: "To put it another way, God works *within* man, not *upon* him. . . ."[18]

In each of these festivals there is the clear understanding that these were events that have occurred but once and will not occur again. At the same time, it is affirmed that the God whom Israel met in history remains unchanged. Contemporary celebrants are not, therefore, to examine their lives to see how the historical circumstances of, say, the Jews' bondage in Egypt have repeated themselves in the present; instead, they are to attempt to be open within their own historical circumstances to the presence of God, just as when they were slaves in Egypt and found the future opening before them. *What remains constant is not the content of history, but the fact of history.*

The festivals rest on the firm vision of the unrepeatability of history. This is a vision that has a strong double effect. Looking backward, it means that we cannot define Israel as a transcendent phenomenon, such as an eternal priesthood, or an unchanging principle of social organization, or even a recurrent pattern of human events, which remain constant while all else changes. Israel is, in fact, nothing more nor less than the persons who have voluntarily chosen to live in its history. Israel is these particular people. This is why the Bible is so careful to maintain a clear record of the lineage from Abraham to the present. It is not that one is specially privileged to be born into this lineage and therefore has a preferred relation to God, but that God is always the God *of these people*, the "God of Abraham, Isaac, and Jacob." Looking forward, the unrepeatability of history has another effect: it prepares us for surprise. The festivals do not point toward their recurrence, but toward the new and unforeseen events for which God is preparing us.

We entered this most recent discussion with the question as to how we look for the presence of God in history—for if God is absent then there is no continuity through the absolute terminus of death. Death would not then be what God has given us, but the very thing that cuts

us off from God, leaving God helpless to provide the promised blessings. We have seen that the early, naive view of God's presence as a
superior tribal deity was altered by the prophets who knew God
through an intense inwardness and the desire to live justly on the earth.
Although the second destruction of the temple meant the absolute end
of the prophetic age, the rabbis were nonetheless so filled with the
sense of continuity that they understood themselves to be the heirs of
the prophets. Indeed, they even considered Moses the first rabbi and, in
some cases, spoke of God himself busy with rabbinic activities. However, looking backward we can see marked differences between the
prophetic and rabbinic ages, differences caused by placing the Torah at
the center of religious life. In no way was the Torah understood by the
rabbis to be a linguistic record of past events; it was the living address
of God to an an ever-changing human situation. God is no longer present in the form of spectacular historical deliverances, such as the
tower of fire that led the children of Israel out of Egypt. Neither is he
present in the form of cultic and political power. God is now present in
the form of language, *his* language. Insofar as they considered this
language God's living address to them, *the rabbis no longer had a
history; they had become the history.* The continuity apparently lost in
the Roman destruction of Jerusalem is restored by way of rabbinic religion, and God's guarantee of an open future is now by way of his Word.

The term "torah" has the meaning of "teaching" or "instruction"
and not, as it is often thought, "law."[19] If the Torah is not a code of law
to be obeyed, neither is it simply a book that can be read or learned, as
though it were a compilation of theological treatises or dogmas. What
makes the Torah a unique phenomenon in human history is that while,
on the one hand, it represents God's direct address to his believers, it
includes, on the other, the response of his listeners. It is not an accumulation of heavenly dicta uttered in the distant past to which all subsequent history is to be held accountable. It is not past at all; it is the
very point of contact between God and his believers in the living present. Now, it is true that the rabbis were quite certain that God communicated directly to Moses and that Moses wrote down precisely
what God had said. This was the same written document that came into
the possession of Ezra in the middle of the fifth century B.C.E. What
assured the Torah its place in the living present was the added belief of
the rabbis that along with the written Torah God had given Moses an
oral Torah, the latter containing a vast store of wisdom that had its roots
in the written word. The reasons the oral Torah was not written down
are, first, that it has the character of an investigation and exploration
into an endless sea of knowledge and, second, that it is in fact a conver-

sation and not an address. In other words, the written Torah is so vast in its meanings that one could never exhaust it, not even God; and so important is this constant interpretation of it out of the living situation that a properly conducted exegesis has the same authority as the words of scripture. "God himself, studying and living by the Torah, is believed to subject himself to these same rules of logical inquiry."[20] It is in this latter sense that the whole Torah, written and oral, constitutes a genuine conversation between God and his created children.

This radical understanding of the way in which God remains present in history, guaranteeing its open future, did not spring fully developed from a single inspired intelligence; it developed over centuries and thus acquired a remarkable ability to adapt itself to changing human situations and, even more important, gained the power to shape history itself. The "Talmudic Age" extends over more than eight centuries, from Alexander the Great (330 B.C.E.) to 500 C.E., just before the rise of Islam. Because of the stability of the Talmudic community structure through these centuries, it is even possible to speak of a "Talmudic Civilization."[21]

The power of the Torah actually to shape history can be seen by looking more closely at the actual form the verbal or dialogical relationship to God took for the ancient rabbis. When Rabban Johanan ben Zakkai founded the first center for the study of the Torah in a small Palestinian city, in the year 70 C.E.—the very year in which the temple was destroyed by the Romans—it had the effect of assuring that the oral tradition would continue to exist in the memory and the lively imagination of those rabbis who survived the Roman persecution with him. In 200 C.E. Rabbi Judah, called "the Prince," organized the oral tradition concerning the law into a form known as the *Mishna* (from a Hebrew word meaning "to repeat"). Although the Mishna was at first committed to memory and not wirtten down until some time later, it had the effect of providing an agreed on body of laws that were beyond question but that nonetheless required constant reinterpretation. By 400 C.E. the Jews still living in Palestine had written down the Mishna and its interpretations in a single document known as the *Talmud*. By 500 another Talmud, much greater in length and differing in many of its interpretive contents, was published in Babylonia. Although each Talmud was completed by these dates there has been no interruption to the present day in the cumulative task of getting at the hidden meanings and finer points of distinction in scripture as a whole.

There is one other aspect of the Talmud important to include in this account. In addition to the Mishna and the commentaries directly concerned with the law, known as the Halakah, the Talmud includes an enormous amount of investigation and explanation of nonlegal matters that fall under the collective term, *Haggadah* (or Agada). The Haggadah consists of

> legends, folklore, ethical and "philosophical" and theosophical and theological speculation, homilies, parables, prayers, gnomic sayings, historical reminiscence, old wives' tales too: in other words, that large unbounded expression of the human imagination reacting to the universe, in anguish, in wonder responding to the here and now and to what was and to what will be in the end of time.[22]

Of the two, Halakah, or commentary on the law, is by far the more important in the Talmud, for the familiar reason that what was always the greatest concern of Jews was the translation of the words of Torah into the actual lives of its students. What we meet here is an obvious and powerful echo of that distinctive Jewish understanding of knowledge, which we first met with in the story of the Garden of Eden with the forbidden tree of the knowledge of good and evil. The knowledge that God gave the first pair in exchange for their immortality was the knowledge as to how they were to comport themselves in the human community; it was not knowledge about the secrets of the universe. It is one of the triumphs of the Talmudic rabbis that they succeeded in keeping Halakah—or that form of knowledge that is always identified with action—at the center of Jewish life. However, we should not underestimate the enormous appeal of Hagada. It is in the Hagada that we see the human setting in which the law was learned and pursued; it is here also that we see that there is also in the Jewish tradition a love of knowledge as such, for whatever is known can only be of God's creation and, therefore, worthy in itself. If law for the Talmudic rabbis was the heart and body of Judaism, Hagada "was its lifeblood and marrow."[23]

Therefore, the Talmud was neither a document that was written about the past, nor a chronicle *about* the present lives of the rabbis and their people—it was the lives of those rabbis. They did not point to some external authority, to the dignity of an office, to validate their teachings, as the temple priests had done when they claimed their authority from the prophets. They had so completely integrated the tradition with their lives they needed only to allow others to see the Torah in them. This, to be sure, created a class of remarkable and charismatic persons, some of whom abused their considerable personal power by converting it to magic. For the most part, however, they were radiant, God-centered persons. Since the rabbis were in conversation with God, they understood the Talmudic labors to be nothing less than the imitation of God. But this did not produce an arrogance in them; instead, it engendered in their lives a strong sense of the nearness of God. They felt such an intimate relation to the words of scripture that it could be said that God's revelation to Moses at Sinai "was to them not a mere reminiscence or tradition, but that, through their intense faith, they re-witnessed it in their own souls, so that it became to them a personal experience."[24] This intimacy in the rabbis' experience of God never in the least diminished their respect for God's utter transcendence. For that reason the heart of rabbinic Judaism is probably best expressed by the liturgical declaration known as the "Shema", the opening lines of which are: "Hear, O Israel: the Lord Your God is one Lord; and you shall love the Lord your God with all your heart, and with all your soul, and with all your might" (Deuteronomy 6:4). God is one God, there is none beside him; but your relationship to him is one of the heart, and your heart and soul are to be filled with nothing but rapt devotion to him.

The rabbis were to have many occasions, under heavy persecution, to demonstrate the depth of their piety. After a failed rebellion in 132–135 C.E. to wrest control of Palestine back from the Romans, among those executed in the retaliatory persecution was the famed Rabbi Akiba. As the Romans tore his flesh with iron combs he began to recite the Shema, "and the breath of life left him while he was saying the word 'One' ".[25]

The devotion to God had the further effect of filling the rabbis with love for the world and their fellow creatures. This love is often cited in both the teachings and the life of Hillel the Elder (c. 60 B.C.E.–c. 10C.E.), one of the greatest of all the rabbis. A certain heathen once taunted him, daring Hillel to teach him the entire Torah while standing on one foot. Hillel's famous reply: "What is hateful to you, do not do to your neighbor; that is the entire Torah; the rest is commentary; go and learn it."[26]

Hillel's answer once more evokes the familiar theme that one cannot have a knowledge of God apart from action: "Now how can a man be wise enough to understand the Lord? This is impossible" declares one of the Talmudic interpreters. "But we know him by exercising justice and righteousness, for the Lord is the author of these."[27] Always present in any discussion of the knowledge of God is the absolute difference between the human and the divine, with the consequent fact that any direct knowledge of God would require stepping over the mandated limits of the human: "You cannot see my face," God told

Moses, "for no man shall see me and live" (Exodus 33:20). A fifteenth-century rabbi, Joseph Albo, said succinctly: "If I knew Him I would be Him."[28]

The great Haggadic literature of the Talmud that speaks of the nearness of God rests on the belief that when "the words of the Torah enter and find the chambers of the heart unoccupied, they make their home in the person."[29] This means a yielding from within, setting aside one's own will to create space for God. In the words of Judah the Prince, "if thou hast done His will as though it were not thy will, then thou has done His will as He wills it."[30] The Torah should become a preoccupation, crowding out all other concerns: "If one wakes in the night and the first words out of his mouth are not words of the Torah—it might have been better for him if . . . he had never been born and beheld the world."[31] Such all-consuming attention to the Torah led one Talmudist to make the playful observation that "This round world is suspended in space and has nothing to rest on except the breath of Torah study from the mouths of students—just as a man may keep something up in the air by the blowing of his breath."[32] It is not only the hearts of men and women, but the whole creation that is addressed by the Torah: "When God gave the Torah we read that the creatures of the firmament paused in their flight, those of the earth ventured not to lift up their voices, the waves of the boisterous seas ceased to roll," and even the angels stopped their singing—all for the sake of listening as God spoke.[33]

We have here, then, a vision both of the great sufficiency and the necessity of the Torah: "Nothing of the Torah, God assures Israel, was kept back in heaven."[34] And there is no aspect of life that is not regulated or illumined by it. Hillel often said that everything he did was to fulfill one commandment or another. When asked whether even his going to the privy fulfilled a commandment, he would reply, "Indeed, so that the body do not deteriorate."[35] Moreover, there is a perfect congruity between the Torah and nature: "Whoever says the words of Torah are one thing," explained the Hassidic Rabbi Pinhas, "and the words of the world another, denies God."[36] A passage from the Talmud speculates that "Had the Torah not been given us, we could have learned modesty from the cat, the command not to rob from the ant, chastity from the dove, and propriety from the cock."[37]

The rabbis were so deeply engaged in the study of the Torah that a life without it was scarcely life at all to them: "He who has not studied at all is like a beast, for he was created solely for the purpose of learning and studying Torah, whose ways are ways of pleasantness."[38] When one does not study even food is useless.[39] The distinguished modern

Talmudic scholar Solomon Schechter summarized the rabbinic notion of religion with the remark that, for them, "if religion is anything, it is everything."[40]

If the "whole Torah," oral and written, as it takes shape in the Palestinian and Babylonian Talmuds and in the ongoing interpretive work of subsequent generations, is to be understood as a *conversation* with God in which he keeps history open in the face of death, then we can see that that conversation does indeed involve everything, our private as well as collective lives, even nature. The Talmud, we noted, is not a document written *about* the past, or even the present, lives of its people; it is their lives. Taken in its most comprehensive sense, what we have then in rabbinic Judaism is not only the experience of history continued, but the emergence of a new understanding of what history is. The vital nerve of rabbinic religion is not in the belief that one day God will rearrange the nations of the earth, placing the children of Israel above its oppressors; instead, it is the certainty that whatever God could promise for the future he makes available immediately. For the rabbis one does not wait for the promise, one takes it up at once. And what *is* it that God is promising. It is the extraordinary privilege of answering to his word. He is not only a God who speaks, as the prophets had portrayed him, but one who listens as well. History is open, therefore, to the extent that there is always something to say. This does not mean, of course, that it is open simply because there is still time for us to speak, to utter one more cry of joy or grief into the uncomprehending void. It means that we are still able to speak words that will be heard, that will make a difference to the future, that will even have the power to keep the future open.

This, of course, implies that God is *affected* by what we say and that he is not indifferent to what happens in history. He is as moved by its tragedies, and is sometimes just as helpless before them, as we are. A frequently cited midrash reports that when the children of Israel had successfully crossed the Red Sea and the water behind them poured in on the Egyptian army the angels wanted to sing for joy, but God forbade them, saying, "My children lie drowned in the Red Sea, and you would sing?"[41] To be in genuine conversation with God our freedom is essential; we must be able to alter the course of affairs even against God's will. Our disobedience must be a genuine dilemma for God: "How could Divinity be actually present as commanding unless obedience and disobedience made a real, ultimate difference?"[42]

The reciprocity inherent in this conversation, the vulnerability of God, has been described by Martin Buber in his famous use of the metaphor of the "eclipse of God." Buber describes as a religious dilemma for modern persons the acute overconsciousness of oneself *as* praying or worshipping, a preoccupation with one's inwardness as it turns toward God. It is this "gigantically swollen" self-awareness that has stepped "between our existence and his" just as something can come between the earth and the sun.[43] God has been eclipsed by us, and his light cannot get through. God is not, however, permanently shut out, for the relationship is, after all, historical and therefore ever-changing. This leads Buber to conclude, "The eclipse of the light of God is no extinction; even tomorrow that which has stepped in between may give way."[44]

The fact that neither we nor God can effect an utter eclipse, or sustain an absolute silence, means that history is not to be understood as that which provides the possibility of a conversation; *history is the conversation.* What the Talmudic rabbis came to understand is that history is not the *place where* men and women *meet* with God, it is *what happens when* men and women *speak* with God.

We have come to this conclusion by way of the question as to how the presence of God is to be seen in history. God is present in the conversation that constitutes history. But how do we know that? How do we know we are not talking to ourselves? We still cannot *see* God. The implied rabbinic answer is that as long as the future is open it is with God that we are in conversation. If history is what happens when we speak with God, then it is the openness of history that validates God's listening presence to our speaking.

The rabbis contributed a rare understanding to the history of religion, as well as to the understanding of death, when they found a way of integrating the transcendent otherness of God with the finite, time-bound limitations of human existence. Not only is it possible to engage God in history, it is possible to engage him *only* there. The engagement with God *is* history. For this reason, the continuity of human existence in the face of death does not mean indefinite longevity, but ceaselessly creating an open future. When the rabbis perceived the discontinuity that death represents, they understood it not simply as the concealing pit from which there is no hope of return, but as a final silence in which there is nothing to say and no reason to listen. Indeed, if one were to exist forever, but not be able to live a creative life toward an open but unfinished future, it would not be life as such, but mere existence; it would be the eternal mindlessness of Adam and Eve before the expulsion. When one is, however, living creatively toward an open conversation with God, one neither needs nor wishes to live forever—any more than Abraham needed to know each of his numberless progeny. The continuity inherent in the Talmudic conversation does not eliminate my death; it includes my death.

In other words, it is not my life that is carried into the future, but my death. To create a future is to turn our history over to others, to relinquish the claim that the future belongs to us as much as the present does; indeed, it is to grant others dominion over our creation with all the authority God has given all men and women over his creation. To create a future is to give it away. If we create it to keep it, it is not a future we have created, but only an extension of our own present. Although the future receives its life from those of us in the present who live openly into it, it will only be lived by those who come after us— just as we do not live the life of Moses, but the life that became ours through Moses' discourse with God at Sinai, which opened the future to include us. It is not the continuity of the man, Moses, but the history begun in him that undoes the power of death.

We have admittedly been discussing the nature of rabbinic Judaism in a way that would have seemed most peculiar, and perhaps even outrageous, to the rabbis themselves. We have been looking at it as a *verbal event*, seeing in the phenomenon of rabbinism as a whole the original and seminal understanding of language that made it possible. In other words, we have been reflecting on the fact that rabbinic Judaism can be understood as a conversation with God, but not as the actual contents of that conversation. If we look at what the rabbis *actually said* about death, and drop for the moment our interest in the fact that they were speaking with God, a sharply different picture of death emerges.

We observed earlier that the rabbis enjoyed a relationship of intimacy with God. The God who most frequently appears in their writing is "the warm and protecting Father, whose chief concern is over the welfare of His children."[45] However, they also had a strong belief in his perfect justice, knowing that the wicked were most certainly to be punished and the good rewarded. When death was viewed from the perspective of God's justice it developed two great themes in the Talmud.

The first theme is that whatever suffering and death we undergo must be regarded as punishment: "whoever does evil and introduces violence and corruption, is himself the victim of the harms caused by those very evils he introduces. . . . [Mi]isfortunes are a punishment, they are not accidental events. Evil deeds boomerang."[46] Therefore, "When man sees that suffering comes upon himself, he has to examine his actions," to see where he might have sinned.[47] But death and suffering can also have a positive function beyond mere punishment; they may be viewed "as an atonement, bringing pardon and forgiveness and reconciling man with God."[48] And when suffering has been self-inflicted it has the effect of a sacrifice offered to appease God.[49] This same notion can be extended to the belief that the "atonement of suffering and death is not limited to the suffering person. The atoning effect extends to all the generation." This is particularly true in the suffering of the innocent, and especially of children.[50]

It is this latter aspect of death that creates the possibility for martyrdom. Jewish literature is filled with the heroic gestures of martyrs. In the Second Book of Maccabees, an account of the resistance to the enforced Hellenization of the Palestinian Jews in the second century B.C.E., the story is told of seven brothers who were arrested with their mother for refusing to violate the law against eating the flesh of swine. Each of the brothers in turn was horribly tortured to death before their mother, who to the end steadfastly refused to relent, causing her own death under the lashes and flaying instruments of the heathen king.[51] Similar stories are preserved from other periods of Jewish history. After the Roman conquest in 70 C.E., the last Jewish military fortress at Masada refused to surrender and turn themselves over to the Romans for slavery and fates even worse, choosing rather to commit mass suicide: "Including women and children, nine hundred and sixty perished on this occasion."[52]

The suffering that one endures, the suffering of the innocent, and the heroic gestures of the martyrs, all have one intended effect: *repentance*. Earlier we noted the importance of repentance inasmuch as it was the recognition of the fact that history always begins from within. It is not enough simply to suffer; one's life must be transformed by it, filled with the resolve to live justly and walk humbly before God. Repentance is not just remorse, then, but a moral renewal. The importance was so great to the rabbis that it was said to be "one of the things which preceded creation, as a preliminary condition to the existence of the world."[53] Great moral catastrophes, such as David's sin of adultery or Israel's worship of the golden calf at Sinai, are preserved in scripture for the sole reason of convincing us that "no sin is so great as to make repentance impossible."[54] The rabbis were convinced that all repentance would be accepted by God, and at once. A mystic once declared that even if a voice should come from heaven telling us not to repent, we should not obey it.[55] While God will always accept repentance, even in the final moments of one's life, deathbed confessions are ill-advised, for one never knows when death will come: "let him repent today lest he die on the morrow; let him repent on the morrow lest he die the day after: and thus all his days will be spent in repentance."[56]

A life spent in uninterrupted repentance not only involves the recognition that God works within us, rather than on us, in keeping history alive, but also the belief that evil too comes from within. The Talmud occasionally ties evil so closely to human existence it can be declared that "the first seminal drop a man puts into a woman is the evil impulse! And the evil impulse lies verily at the opening of the heart . . . ."[57] Here evil is not an external agent, but something belonging to the person—an impulse, or imagination. The evil imagination is invited quickly into the heart by way of vanity, or idolatry, or adultery.[58] This understanding of evil, of course, does limit its range to personal existence, making it easy for the rabbis to believe that, for all its ubiquity and power, it was God himself who placed the evil impulse in men and women. Therefore, it was not without reason that we came to be evil: "The Lord created the evil impulse, but he created Torah and repentance as its remedy."[59] From all such evil the study of Torah will be a sufficient protection.[60] It is almost as though we were given an evil impulse *in order* that we might also have the Torah. There are also social reasons: if it were not for the evil impulse we would not marry, or build houses, or assemble a civilization.[61]

This, then, is one of the great themes of suffering and death in the Talmud: death is a punishment for our sins; therefore, since sinfulness comes from an evil impulse within each of us, we are expected to undergo the moral renewal of repentance. But there is a second theme, often contradictory to the first, but recurrently pursued with great feeling: the evil that brings death and suffering upon us does not come from within but from without, and it is undeserved. We are all innocent sufferers, and not martyrs but victims. This second approach to death in the Talmud is raised by the same enduring question of scripture: How is it possible that such suffering could go without recompense, and such evil without retribution? "The initial premise of Talmudic as of all subsequent monotheistic thought is that God rewards justly. To deny retribution is to deny divine justice. And to the Rabbis the denial of God's justice is the essence of atheism."[62] The notion that reward and punishment are sure had worked itself deeply into the biblical mind: "Honor your father and your mother," reads one of the Ten Commandments given by God to Moses, "that your days may be long in the land which the Lord your God gives you" (Exodus 20:12). It was certainly obvious that the reward following the commandment could not be counted on for this life. God's promise of long life must therefore be fulfilled in some other way.

The Talmudic rabbis, pressed with this issue, gave great weight to the prophetic vision of a world to come in which "the wolf shall dwell with the lamb, and the leopard shall lie down with the kid" (Isaiah 11:6). It will be a time when the people

shall beat their swords into plowshares,
    and their spears into pruning hooks;
nation shall not lift up sword against nation,
    neither shall they learn war any more;
but they shall sit every man under his vine and under his
        fig tree,
    and none shall make them afraid [Micah 4:3 ff.].

It is evident that the prophets were thinking of a historical age into which the present would open. With the promise now too long delayed, the rabbis were thinking only of a time following death, not preceding it, and a world made possible only by a resurrection of the dead.

The doctrine of resurrection has few scriptural texts to support it,[63] and only once is there any suggestion that both the wicked and the righteous will be raised to face the judge—and this is in the very late Book of Daniel: "And many of those who sleep in the dust of the earth shall awake, some to everlasting life, and some to shame and everlasting contempt" (12:2 ff.). But the Talmud offers abundant references to the resurrection and the life to come. In the words of one of the rabbis: "The end purpose of everything our Mishna has described is the life of the world to come."[64] One Mishna puts the matter so tersely it reads like a formula: "The ones who were born are to die, and the ones who have died are to be brought to life again, and the ones who are brought to life are to be summoned to judgment." The same Mishna adds later: "Know thou that everything is according to the reckoning."[65]

A lengthy midrash on the birth of the soul describes how God selects a soul to be joined to the seed of a mortal. The soul then objects to entering into the seed, "for I am holy and pure." God replies that the "world into which I would have you enter is better than the world in which you find yourself now." He then appoints a messenger to take the recalcitrant soul before it is born to the Garden of Eden, where the righteous dwell in glory, and to the place of the damned, where the sinners burn in eternal anguish. Following this the soul is shown all the places it will dwell as a mortal, "and the place in which it will be buried at last." Later, when the soul is born, its crying shows that the messenger had struck it just below the nose, causing it to forget all that it had known, so that it comes forth unwilling. When the messenger comes at the end, the soul cries again, forgetting that it was destined to die, "and at last will give account and reckoning before the King over king of kings, the Holy One, blessed be he."[66] We are a long way here from the dusty pit of Sheol, which as we have seen is more an after-*death* than an after*life*.

What is most important in this story is not that there is an afterlife, but that the attitude of the soul is consistently one of resistance to its own future. It is dragged first into conception, then into birth, and finally into death, protesting at each stage, having forgotten what God had prepared for it. The afterlife, like history, is available only because God has opened it. In time, however, particularly under the influence of Greek philosophy, the doctrine of resurrection yields to the Socratic doctrine of immortality. A Venetian rabbi, Leone Modena (1571–1648), in an essay representative of the rabbinic view, admits it is "frightening" that "we fail to find in all the words of Moses a single indication pointing to man's spiritual immortality after his physical death, or the existence of any world beside this one." Even in the prophets the relevant passages that we can find "are only vague hints concerning immortality; and all such supposed hints might just as well be interpreted as having reference to physical life." Nevertheless, Modena argues, even if the scriptures are silent, "reason inclines us (if it does not altogether compel us) to believe that the soul continues on after our physical death." The decisive proof lies in the fact that man "has been created for the purpose of giving God pleasure by his wide range of intelligent actions." How could such a creature, possessed of such gifts, be allowed to "perish entirely like a horse, or a dog, or a fly?" It is only reasonable to believe that "this Creator has made it possible for a man at this death to have his soul separated from his body, so that the soul may remain to receive the pleasure or the pain of which, in his lifetime, the man was judged deserving, in accordance with his deeds."[67]

The rabbis took refuge in the theory of immortality, or the resurrection and the life to come, out of the strong conviction that God is just. In doing so, however, they fell away from the vision of historical continuity that is apparent when we take the phenomenon of rabbinism as a whole to be a history engendering conversation with God. The theory of immortality is antithetical to this particular experience of continuity, but only when it is represented as a belief and not as the sort of discourse that will keep the future open. Instead of presenting a direct contradiction to the experience of historical continuity, we should rather say that it presents a challenge, or even a threat, to it, for it is the sort of theory that can lead one to final belief instead of continuing, creative action. What the belief threatens is historicity itself. It encourages indifference to the issues of this world, because it offers a hope that, in spite of the poverty of our temporal existence, God will restore what we want *somewhere else*. In his *Judaism as a Civilization*, written in the ominous year 1933, Mordecai Kaplan wrote with considerable passion concerning the historically weakening effect of otherworldliness that seems to have been born of the Jews' sense of hopelessness in the course of human affairs. Jews have traditionally thought salvation, Kaplan observed, as "the fulfillment of their destiny in the life beyond the grave. Men and women were so dissatisfied with their lives, with the imperfections of the physical order and of human nature, that they despaired of ever attaining salvation in this world."[68] Kaplan's prophetic warning was that unless Jews turned away from the hereafter and faced the historical realities of the present, that history would only magnify their sufferings.

The thesis of this chapter is not that the rabbinic understanding of history as a continuing conversation with God is the essence of Judaism. It is only a theme within Judaism, though a prominent theme. Judaism is far too rich and complicated a movement, with roots far too deep in the past, to organize around any single motif or principle. Instead, our thesis proposes that in classical rabbinism there rises to maturity an understanding of the nature of death that originates deep in the biblical mind and that can be found in no other religion or philosophy. It does, however, have a far-reaching impact on modern civilization and its collective disposition toward death, as we shall see in subsequent chapters.

We have attempted to show that within Judaism this view of death is theatened by the theory of immortality. When Jews speak of an immortal soul, or of raising those who are asleep into the world to come, they have lost their distinctiveness on the question of the meaning of death. There are other threats to this rare understanding. We shall briefly discuss two of them: messianism and the Holocaust. Our intent is not to offer a more complete historical portrait of rabbinic Judaism, but to show how fragile this view of death is, and how easily it can be led onto paths that look similar or at least parallel. With a clearer picture of the Jewish conception of death in relation to the modern world, we shall be in a better position to assess its extensive influence on the contemporary mind.

The term Messiah, or "Mashiah," means simply "the annointed one," indicating a ritual act that confers kingship. The earliest references to a Messiah in scripture are in Amos and Hosea, prophets who lived about 200 years after the reign of David and Solomon. In 930 B.C.E., following the reign of Solomon, the kingdom that David had united fell into strife and divided again. Amos and Hosea predicted a disastrous "day of the Lord," in which Israel would be punished for her iniquities. They also dreamed of a new kingdom that would come when the children of Israel will have dwelt "many days without king or prince," after which they "shall return and seek the Lord their God, and David their king." (Hosea 3:5). In these early prophecies the kingship of David is taken as the model for the one still to come, and consistently through the long history of messianism it is necessary that the Messiah belong to "the stump of Jesse," or lineage of David. Nowhere in scripture is the image of the Messiah more eloquently drawn than in Isaiah who spoke of the glory to which the children of Israel will come "in the latter days."

> For to us a child is born,
>   to us a son is given;
> and the government shall be upon his shoulder,
>   and his name will be called
> "Wonderful Counselor, Mighty God,
>   Everlasting Father, Prince of Peace."
> Of the increase of his government and of peace,
>   there will be no end,
> upon the throne of David, and over his kingdom,
>   to establish it, and to uphold it
> with justice and with righteousness
>   from this time forth and for evermore.[Isaiah 9:6 ff.].

Occasionally there is a vision of a messianic kingdom without any reference to the Messiah; it will be a time of peace when the wolf will lie down with the lamb, when nations shall beat their spears into pruning hooks. The speech of the peoples will become a "pure speech, that they may call on the name of the Lord and serve him with one accord" (Zephaniah 3:9). The Lord in that time "will feed his flock like a shepherd, he will gather the lambs in his arms" (Isaiah 40:11).

After the restoration of the temple in 520 B.C.E. there is a long silence concerning the Messiah. It is during this time that Ezra had succeeded in placing the Torah at the center of the religious life of the people. In the tumultuous period that followed the conquest of Palestine by Alexander in 331 there was a vivid renewal of interest in the Messiah. According to the Psalms of Solomon, composed in the middle of the first century B.C.E., a Messiah of pronounced military qualities will appear. He will be pure from sin, will bless the people of the Lord, and then will destroy or enslave all the enemies of the Lord. "All nations shall be in fear before him, for he will smite the earth with the word of his mouth for ever.[69] From the Ethiopian Book of Enoch (c. 95 B.C.E.) we have a strong image of God raising the dead out of Sheol, then appointing a Messiah to "choose the righteous and the holy among them." In those days the mountains will leap like rams, the faces of the angels will light up with joy, and the earth will rejoice.[70] The Fourth Book of Ezra, written after the fall of the second temple in 70 C.E., looks ahead to a messianic age in which a radically different world is established. Even nature will be altered: "Then shall the sun suddenly shine forth by night and the moon by day: and blood shall trickle forth from wood, and the stone utter its voice."[70]

There are several patterns that emerge here. The messianic expectation, while never altogether forgotten, is clearly more prominent during the times of great historical uncertainty, such as exile, woeful defeat, or forced profanation. As the actual circumstances turn worse the visions become decidedly apocalyptic, forseeing dramatic reversals in the historical fortunes of Israel, effected by a vague figure of cosmic powers. Apocalypticism moves far beyond the visions of the prophets who "know only a single world, in which even the great events at the End of Days run their course. Their eschatology is of a national kind: it speaks of the restoration of the House of David, now in ruins, and of the future glory of Israel. . . ."[72]

That the messianic expectations of the people is a function of circumstances is evident in two tragic episodes in later Jewish history. Following the expulsion of Jews from Spain in 1492, and the Polish uprising in 1648 when many thousands of Jews were killed, there was a veritable flood of fanatical messianism. The troubled Sabbatai Zevi, a Polish Jew who declared himself the Messiah at the height of the massacre of 1648, appeared to have the charismatic power necessary to persuade all of Jewry he was indeed the Anointed One—until his forced conversion to Islam.

We have spoken of messianism as a threat to the view of death that emerges in rabbinic Judaism. Just as the theory of immortality was widely espoused by the rabbis, so do nearly all of them look forward to the messianic age. They say the Messiah will be a human figure whose arrival is preceded by widespread woe. According to one legend he would be found among the poor and the sick at the gate of Rome. Some of them envisioned a marvelously reconstructed Jerusalem, "the Temple rebuilt in splendor and magnificence, the sacred vessels of the Tabernacle restored, and Aaron and his descendents ministering under the direction of Moses."[73] The effect of this vision is similar to that of the belief in immortality: it breeds an indifference to history, or a serious distortion of its events. For example, the widely held notion that the appearance of the Messiah would be preceded by terrible suffering (so grievous, in fact, one rabbi begged God to send no Messiah at all) meant that many of the faithful would take flight into the fantasy of what was to come, only to be confronted with increased misery when seeing the hard fact of what had already come. The mass dislocations and abandonment of personal property that occurred during the frenzy of the Sabbatai Zevi affair were felt for many generations.

It is true that messianism was often tempered and rationalized by the rabbis. Moses Maimonides (1140–1205), one of the greatest of all Jewish thinkers, strongly rejected the apocalyptic element of messianism and denied that "anything of the natural course of the world will cease or that any innovation will be introduced into the creation." What is of supreme importance to Maimonides is that the Messiah will "restore the kingdom of David to its former might." This means a gathering of the dispersed peoples and the reestablishment of the central place of the Torah. The Messiah will not need to perform miracles or raise the dead in order to prove his authenticity. If he is "successful in rebuilding the sanctuary on its site and in gathering the dispersed of Israel, then he has in fact proven himself to be the Messiah." What is most telling in Maimonides' vision of the future is that the messianic age will not be one of the military or administrative superiority of Israel over the rest of the earth; all that the sages longed for in the days of the Messiah, "was to have time for the Torah and its wisdom with no one to oppress or disturb them."[74] In other words, the coming of the Messiah will not bring history to an end, but only assure the indefinite continuity of rabbinic Judaism. Maimonides plainly wanted to sustain the elevation of rabbinism over messianism.

Maimonides was not alone in his distrust of fanatic messianism. Those rabbis for whom Halakah, or the legal material in the Talmud, was primary saw in messianism the threat of self-destructive anarchy, for it was generally believed that the Messiah would not only fulfill the present law of the Torah, thus making it void, but would bring a new mystical Torah. In a bizarre confirmation of this fear, Jacob Frank, a self-proclaimed Messiah of the eighteenth century, was said to have torn parchment from the Torah and given it to his friends to wrap around their feet as shoes.[75] The rabbis concern that messianism was essentially antihistorical is evident in their consistent warning against predicting the arrival of the Messiah; they knew such knowledge could discourage one's active engagement with history, causing one simply to wait. Although the Messiah is a servant of God, and sent by God, all Talmudists were "agreed that the Messiah's date of arrival depended on man."[76]

We can see, therefore, that the rabbis were concerned that messianism not exempt one from living creatively toward an open future.

Messianism, for all its promise and attentiveness to the coming age, is essentially antihistorical. Ultimately it reduces to the belief that the future is closed. "Jewish Messianism," Scholem has written, "is in its origins and by its nature—this cannot be sufficiently emphasized—a theory of catastrophe."[77] It is a theory that emerges when history is thought to be so far beyond control that personal continuity is possible only if history is concluded by forces external to it.

In Scholem's estimation, "the price which the Jewish people has had to pay out of its own substance for this idea" is far too high:

> The magnitude of the Messianic idea corresponds to the endless powerlessness in Jewish history during all the centuries of exile, when it was unprepared to come forward onto the plain of world history. There's something preliminary, something provisional about Jewish history; hence its inability to give of itself entirely. For the Messianic idea is not only consolation and hope. Every attempt to realize it tears open the abysses which lead each of its manifestations *ad absurdum*. There is something grand about living in hope, but at the same time there is something profoundly unreal about it. It diminishes the singular worth of the individual, and he can never fulfill himself, because the incompleteness of his endeavors eliminates precisely what constitutes its highest value. Thus in Judaism the Messianic idea has compelled a *life lived in deferment*, in which nothing can be done definitively, nothing can be irrevocably accomplished. One may say, perhaps, the Messianic idea is the real anti-existentialist idea.[78]

The theory of immortality threatens the Jewish conception of historical continuity by offering *an escape inward*. It is the belief that human existence is at its center not subject to history. When Adam and Eve were expelled from the Garden of Eden, it was only their bodies that were driven into time. Their minds, or souls, never left; they dwell still in the eternal paradise in which they were made. Messianism threatens historical continuity by offering *an escape outward*, to a space safely beyond all possibility of temporal reversal. According to this view Adam and Eve were not driven into time as such, but into *a limited period of time* that they are compelled to endure rather as a punishment. When that time has elapsed they will either return to the original paradise or arrive at the entrance to another.

As serious as these threats are, they are insignificant in comparison to the Holocaust. The experience of the Jews under the Nazis not only destroys the religious value of the theory of immortality and messianism, it does something worse: it threatens to make history itself unbearable—while cutting off every possibility of stepping out of history. The Holocaust suggests that when Adam and Eve were forced to leave their unconscious paradise, they were driven not into time but into a nightmare.

We find that "The Nazi genocide of the Jewish people has no precedent within Jewish history. Nor, once the necessary distinctions are carefully made, will one find a precedent outside Jewish history."[79] Indeed, Richard Rubinstein declares flatly that "Their story is one of the most terrible in the annals of the race."[80] It would be strangely comforting if we could say of this event that it was an awful *accident* of history. The fall of the temple in 70 C.E., the expulsion of the Jews from Spain in 1492, and the massacre of Polish Jews by Cossacks in 1648, are all enormous and unnecessary tragedies, but whose origins can be traced to the ignorant and largely capricious passions of a small number of persons. The same point cannot be made about Nazi Germany. It is true that shortly after Hitler's rise to power there were spradic attacks on Jews by small groups of Nazi thugs, but Hitler quickly eliminated this sort of action and, in fact, executed a number of those who had espoused it. What is most important here is that the government's decision to eliminate the Jews could only be done through an exceedingly efficient and extensive bureaucracy.

> The destruction process required the cooperation of every sector of German society. The bureaucrats drew up the definitions and decrees; the churches gave evidence of Aryan descent; the postal authorities carried the messages of definition, expropriation, denaturalization, and deportation; business corporations dismissed their Jewish employees and took over "aryanized" properties; the railroads carried the victims to their place of execution, a place made available to the Gestapo and the SS by the *Wehrmacht*. To repeat, the operation required and received the participation of every major social, political, and religious institution of the German Reich.[81]

A particularly painful part of this story, as Richard Rubinstein relates it, is the participation of the Jews themselves in their own destruction: "Wherever the extermination process was put into effect, the Germans utilized the *existing leadership and organizations* of the Jewish community to assist them."[82] The point here is not the inherent self-destructiveness of the Jews, but the power of bureaucratic organization.

As we indicated earlier in this chapter, Rubinstein makes a strong case for the fact that, although there have been efficient bureaucracies in other civilizations, "the full development of bureaucracy in the Christian West came about as the result of the growth of a certain ethos that was in turn the outcome of fundamental tendencies in occidental religion."[82] We have discussed these tendencies as they become apparent in the story of creation in the scriptures, where the distinction between an infinite God and the finite earth is absolute, with the consequence that the earth is emptied of its own sacred power. The subsequent assignment of dominion to Adam and Eve over all the rest of creation laid the ideological ground for an unrestrained exploitation of the earth. Bureaucracy is the social institution developed to make this exploitation most efficient.

There is, of course, nothing evil in bureaucracy itself. There are several historical factors that have brought the governmental policy of genocide together with modern bureaucratic skill. Rubinstein cites the serious problem of overpopulation in the twentieth century as the chief of those factors. The existence of "superfluous" people has led repeatedly in the first half of this century to the systematic elimination of many millions of persons—possibly as many as *one hundred million!*[83] The fact that Jews were declared superfluous is only a function of Christian anti-Semitism—though it was not until this century that the elimination of the Jews, rather than isolation or expulsion, became an official policy. Certainly another factor is that the process of secularization that begins with biblical religion finally succeeds in vacating any sense of God's judgment from historical process. As we have observed previously, this has the effect of closing history off to one's own ends. The Holocaust may be interpreted as the act of a modern society to close the future to the Jews—the very people who authored the notion that the future can be endlessly opened to the whole human race.

We have said that the Holocaust is not an accident of history; instead, it was the deliberate act of an entire society. That society was not itself an accident of history, but had its roots deep in the 4000-years tradition generated by biblical religion and was, moreover, responding to experienced pressures of overpopulation. We must add one more fact: the Germans could not have carried the Holocaust as far as they did without at least the implicit cooperation of other modern societies. It is well documented that the Germans, until the beginning of the war, had pursued a policy of expulsion and not extermination. In a memorandum to Hitler, the German Foreign Minister, von Ribbentrop, reported in December of 1938 that France would receive no more Jews and, in fact, had already to ship some 10,000 somewhere else. He explained to the French foreign minister "that we all wanted to get rid of our Jews but that the difficulties lay in the fact that no country wished to receive them."[84] When informed in 1944 that Eichmann would exchange one million Jews for trucks and other equipment, Lord Moyne, a high British official, replied, "What shall I do with those million Jews? Where shall I put them?"[85] Furthermore, there were considerable commercial interests at stake in the question. With an almost endless supply of slave labor available, large German industries were encouraged to locate their plants adjacent to some of the camps. Most all of the largest German corporations built sizable installations, particularly at Auschwitz, with investments running into billions of dollars. One of the factories at Auschwitz had important financial connections with Standard Oil of New Jersey, the largest corporation in the United States, that extended into 1942 with damaging effects on the ability of American industry to produce synthetic rubber.[86]

On December 13, 1942, Goebbels wrote into his diary a remark that the facts seem strongly to support: "At bottom, I believe that both the English and the Americans are happy that we are exterminating the Jewish riffraff."[87]

The Holocaust, far from being an *accident* of history, seems rather to be an *expression* of history. It is to this that history has brought us, and impelled by forces of such scope history will continue to offer up other disasters of equal horror or worse. The war in Vietnam, the waves of mass starvation in Asia and Africa, the widespread use of random terror in suppressing popular opposition to the totalitarian governments of Latin America—each of these seem inevitable products of a history that is now out of hand. We are living in a century of catastrophe.

For many this makes an irrefutable case against the Jewish belief that God is present in history. All the traditional ways in which Jews have accounted for human suffering, finding ways of integrating it into God's deepest intentions for human existence, are rendered absurd by the Holocaust. To say that the Holocaust is God's punishment for the sins of his own people makes absolutely no sense. No sins could possibly deserve such indiscriminate punishment, particularly when it involved so many who were obviously innocent—one million children perished in the camps. To say that the suffering of the innocent represents an atonement for the rest of humankind makes only a mockery of the suffering of these children.

If one were to argue that the Jews were being tested by the Holocaust like Job was tested by God, one must overlook one crucial difference: the biblical Job, deeply wounded physically and spiritually, nonetheless *survived to ask his pained questions.* At Auschwitz the destruction was so complete that even the question was silenced: "There was no question because there was no Job. Job went up in smoke. His question went with him."[88] If we were to call on the ancient rabbis' glorification of martyrdom as an explanation, we still could not account for the fact that there were countless Jews who went to their death not for religious belief but for the accidental fact that one of their grandparents had been a Jew. Shall we then say that the Holocaust was the very suffering that had been foreseen as the opening into the messianic age? The answer to this is simple: no Messiah has come, neither has a new world in which the study of the Torah can proceed without interruption.

If the Holocaust is not an accident of history, but an expression of it, and if Jews are participants in the present shaping of history, then each Jew stands before the question: "If the Exodus led to Sinai, then where does Auschwitz lead?"[89] One possible answer is that the question is unanswerable. Elie Wiesel, who as a child witnessed the death of his own father in a Nazi camp, speaks with unforgettable eloquence to the persistent force of this question:

> As for the scholars and philosophers of every genre who have had the opportunity to observe the tragedy, they will—if they are capable of sincerity and humility—withdraw without daring to enter into the heart of the matter; and if they are not, well, who cares about their grandiloquent conclusions? Auschwitz, by definition, is beyond their vocabulary.
>
> The survivors, more realistic if not more honest, are aware of the fact that God's presence at Treblinka or Maidenek—or, for that matter, his absence—poses a problem which will remain forever insoluble. . . .
>
> Perhaps someday someone will explain how, on the level of man, Auschwitz was possible; but on the level of God, it will forever remain the most disturbing of mysteries.[90]

Rubinstein's response to the question as to where Auschwitz leads is to reject Judaism outright, declaring death to its God. In his judgment Judaism was deeply flawed by the very development we have referred to in these pages as its genius: rabbinism. The Roman destruction of the temple in 70 C.E. opened a period of nearly 2000 years in which Jews were not only deprived of a homeland, but forced to live in a Christian civilization that treated them as "the rejected of God." Although they displayed admirable skills of surviving during this period, rabbinic religion was essentially a self-protective retreat that had the effect of making them the victims and not the agents of history. The destruction of the temple alienated the rabbis "from direct sensuous contact with life and death in the religious act." Their religion became verbal and abstract, "scholars and their disciples studied and debated the laws of a defunct sacrificial order. Instead of offering real sacrifice, Jews prayed that their ritual recitations of the laws of sacrifice be accepted as a surrogate. A book—the Torah—became the center of Jewish life."[91] This retreat into the abstract could not prepare them for Hitler: "The Jewish reaction to the Nazis was one of the most disastrous misreadings of the character of an opponent by any community in all of human history. In the face of the Nazi threat, the Jewish community trusted its ancient adaptive instincts and failed totally."[92]

The question raised by the Holocaust, however, is not simply a question for Jews, for the very reason that it was *not* an accident of history. It is a question for all of us. Is history a nightmare, are we all its victims, some of us merely more fortunate than others? Or can it still be said that continuity in the face of death is truly historical?

Another distinguished Jewish thinker has written that the answer to this latter question is—yes. Acknowledging the appeal of secularism to the contemporary Jew, Emil Fackenheim invokes the experience of Auschwitz as a reminder to the secularist that, if God is dead, the devil certainly is not. This puts the secularist in the peculiar position of viewing history in which there is no presence of the divine, but in which satanic forces of evil are irresistibly active. The flaw in this position is that "Opposition to the demons of Auschwitz cannot be understood in terms of humanly created ideals." The ideals of reason and progress fail; they are too abstract to deal with the terrible realities of history. Those demons can be opposed only by something both concrete and absolute; such an opposition can be grasped only in terms of "an *imposed commandment*." The secularist, as well as the believer, are "*absolutely singled out* by a Voice as truly *other* than man-made ideals—an imperative as truly *given*—as was the Voice of Sinai."[93]

What does this voice say, and whose voice is it? Fackenheim puts the matter in brutal terms: Hitler did not only want to destroy the Jews, but the Jewish religion as well. He wanted to make martyrdom meaningless. The question for Jews then is whether Hitler should be allowed "to dictate the terms of our religious life."[94] If the Holocaust has made Judaism meaningless, then Hitler has won his war. The voice that speaks from Auschwitz has a clear command:

> Jews are forbidden to hand Hitler posthumous victories. They are commanded to survive as Jews, lest the Jewish people perish. They are commanded to remember the victims of Auschwitz lest their memory perish . . . . A Jew may not respond to Hitler's attempt to destroy Judaism by himself cooperating in its destruction. In ancient times, the unthinkable Jewish sin was idolatry. Today, it is to respond to Hitler by doing his work.[95]

But whose voice is this? If it speaks from Auschwitz can it also be the voice of God? The reason many Jews have turned away from God is that they have seen Auschwitz either to be his own work or the evidence of his impotence to prevent such tragedy. If this is understood as God's voice, it must be of a God understood in some radically different way. Fackenheim's surprising suggestion is that we listen to the same God who spoke to the ancient rabbis. We recall that for them history remained open so long as there was still something to say—and someone to listen. God had become one who listens as well as speaks. And, most important, what is being said matters to God. God is himself affected by history. He refuses to let the angels sing for joy when the Israelites escape across the Red Sea because of his grief for the Egyptians that were drowned. As Rabbi Akiba had said after the destruction of the temple, God had gone into exile with his people. The God we engage in history is therefore not the caricatured God who tosses off Holocausts with serene indifference, but one who can be no more indifferent to history than we are. Religious Jews therefore find themselves at a place in their conversation with God where their next words are words of protest, but with a seriousness unknown in Jewish history, "for there is no previous Jewish protest against divine Power like [their] protest." Jews are now forced to invoke God against God in ways so extreme as to dwarf the protesting cries of Abraham, Job, and Jeremiah.[96]

However extreme this outcry is, it is nonetheless necessary that God not be so eclipsed that he cannot listen: "If *all present* access to the God of history is *wholly* lost, the God of history is Himself lost."[97] But how will we know that it is God who listens, or if there is any listening at all? Fackenheim's implicit answer to this question recalls a theme discussed earlier in this chapter. It is God who is listening if the future remains open. It is God who is listening if the Jews endure: *"The Jew after Auschwitz is a witness to endurance. . . .* He bears witness that without endurance we shall all perish. He bears witness that we *can* endure because we *must* endure."[98] To be sure, enduring means more than simply continuing to exist. It means enduring in order to utter the words that will keep history open. There is only one reason to endure history; it is the same reason Jews had to attempt an almost impossible escape from the murder camps: "Why must one escape? To tell the tale."[99] If the tale is not told the world may forget and, forgetting, repeat its history; the suffering would then have been pointless, and God would have vanished. Having escaped, having endured, the tale must be told: "for a Jew hearing the commanding Voice of Auschwitz the duty to remember and to tell the tale, is not negotiable. It is holy."[100]

Jews are not telling this tale merely for themselves, however, any more than Auschwitz was an isolated event within the limits of Jewish history: "Jews after Auschwitz represent all humanity when they affirm their Jewishness and deny the Nazi denial."[101] The rabbis believed that in the Talmudic Age Judaism became a universal religion. That belief has now been challenged as never before. Jews must now decide whether their supreme tragedy will require them to bury rabbinic religion under the dust of historical irrelevancy or to speak through it with a new voice, calling the world to the discovery of an endlessly open future.

The experience of death is the experience of a perceived discontinuity that robs life of its meaning. Meaning is restored only to the degree that we have been able to discern continuity in the face of death. The Jews' unique understanding of the meaning of death begins with the affirmation that death marks an absolute end to the existence of a person. Therefore, continuity does not consist in extending the temporal length of life, but instead in the creation of a future by means of speech. It is central to Jewish understanding that this discourse be an exchange between themselves and their creator from whom they are as distinct as the finite from the infinite. Their future will be open then only insofar as the infinite God enters into that conversation as a genuine listener, responding whenever he is addressed.

The heart of this view is that death, far from being the phenomenon that cuts us off from God, provides the very possibility for the creative discourse. But there is a risk in this view as well. We might discover that we have been speaking only to ourselves. This could be either because we have been trying to mold history to our own ends, or because there is no God there to listen. Unfortunately, there is no simple or rational method we can use to arrive at an intellectually satisfying answer to this dilemma. There are no data we can call forth that will settle it. The Jews, it is now evident, did not offer us *a way of knowing* whether it is truly God with whom we are engaged in our personal and collective histories. They did, however, offer us *a way of speaking* by which we are able to introduce the dynamic of infinite openness into the finite reality of history. If there is any answer, therefore, it will not be in what we say, but the consequences of our saying it.

Notes

1. Ginzberg, *Legends of the Jews*, Vol. I, p. 3.
2. *The Essential Philo*, p. 43.

3. Riemer, ed., *Jewish Reflections on Death*, p. 60.
4. Glatzer, ed., *The Judaic Tradition*, pp. 322 ff.
5. *The Essential Philo*, p. 19.
6. Ibid., p. 29.
7. Gaster, *The Festivals of the Jewish Year*, p. 136.
8. *Jewish Reflections on Death*, p. 62.
9. *The Judaic Tradition*, p. 320.
10. *The Cunning of History*, p. 30.
11. Ibid., pp. 28 ff.
12. *Israel: an Echo of Eternity*, p. 60.
13. Ibid., p. 66.
14. *Jewish Reflections on Death*, p. 22.
15. Buber, *Tales of the Hasidim*, p. 52.
16. Ibid., p. 267.
17. Neusner, *The Way of Torah*, p. 5.
18. *The Festivals of the Jewish Year*, p. 136.
19. Schechter, *Aspects of Rabbinic Theology*, p. 117.
20. *The Way of Torah*, p. 35.
21. Schwarz, ed., *Great Ages and Ideas of the Jewish People*, p. 147.
22. Goldin, ed., *The Living Talmud*, p. 26.
23. *Great Ages and Ideas of the Jewish People*, p. 180.
24. *Aspects of Rabbinic Theology*, p. 24.
25. *The Judaic Tradition*, p. 177.
26. Ibid., p. 197.
27. *The Living Talmud*, p. 44.
28. Jacobs, *A Jewish Theology*, p. 2.
29. *The Living Talmud*, p. 51.
30. Ibid., p. 85.
31. Ibid., p. 123.
32. Ibid., p. 47.
33. *Aspects of Rabbinic Theology*, pp. 130 ff.
34. Ibid., p. 134.
35. *The Living Talmud*, p. 111.
36. *Tales of the Hasidim*, p. 34.
37. *The Judaic Tradition*, p. 222.
38. *The Living Talmud*, p. 68.
39. Ibid., p. 149.
40. Ibid., p. 142.
41. Fackenheim, *God's Presence in History*, p. 25.
42. Ibid., p. 24.
43. *The Eclipse of God*, pp. 127 ff.
44. Ibid., p. 129.
45. *Great Ages and Ideas of the Jewish People*, p. 192.

—

46. *The Living Talmud*, p. 93.
47. *Aspects of Rabbinic Theology*, p. 307.
48. Ibid., p. 304.
49. Ibid., p. 308.
50. Ibid., p. 310.
51. *The Judaic Tradition*. pp. 58 ff.
52. *Quoted from Josephus*, Ibid., p. 159.
53. *Aspects of Rabbinic Theology*, p. 314.
54. Ibid., p. 317.
55. Ibid., p. 334.
56. *The Living Talmud*, p. 105.
57. Ibid., p. 108.
58. *Aspects of Rabbinic Theology*, pp. 252 ff.
59. *The Living Talmud*, p. 142.
60. Ibid., p. 125.
61. *Aspects of Rabbinic Theology*, pp. 266 ff.
62. *Great Ages and Ideas of the Jewish People*, p. 194.
63. Psalm 88:11−13; Job 14:12; Ecclesiastes 7:14 are commonly cited as resurrection texts.
64. *The Living Talmud*, p. 146.
65. Ibid., p. 179.
66. *The Judaic Tradition*, pp. 332 ff.
67. Ibid., pp. 329 ff.
68. Ibid., p. 6.
69. *The Judaic Tradition*, p. 71.
70. Ibid., p. 65.
71. Ibid., p. 167.
72. Scholem, *The Messianic Idea in Judaism*, p. 6.
73. Greenstone, *The Messiah Idea in Jewish History*, p. 100.
74. *The Messianic Idea in Judaism*, pp. 28 ff.
75. Bakan, *Sigmund Freud and the Jewish Mystical Tradition*, p. 106.
76. *Great Ages and Ideas of the Jewish People*, p. 209.
77. *The Messianic Idea in Judaism*, p. 7.
78. Ibid., p. 35.
79. *God's Presence in History*, p. 69.
80. *The Cunning of History*, p. 96.
81. Ibid., pp. 4 ff.
82. Ibid., p. 27.
83. Ibid., p. 7.
84. Ibid., p. 18.
85. Ibid., p. 17.
86. Ibid., pp. 58 ff.

87. Ibid., p. 18.
88. Rubinstein, The Religious Image, p. xix.
89. The Way of Torah, p. 56.
90. Jewish Reflections on Death, p. 38.
91. The Religious Image, p. xv.
92. Ibid., p. xvii.
93. God's Presence in History, p. 83.
94. Ibid., p. 74.
95. Ibid., p. 84.
96. Ibid., p. 88.
97. Ibid., p. 79.
98. Ibid., p. 95.
99. Ibid., p. 85.
100. Ibid., pp. 85 ff.
101. Ibid., p. 86.

Bibliography

Leo Baeck, God and Man in Judaism (New York: 1958).

David Bakan, Sigmund Freud and the Jewish Mystical Tradition (Boston: 1958).

Martin Buber, The Eclipse of God (New York: 1957).

———Tales of the Hasidim: The Early Masters (New York: 1947).

Arthur A. Cohen, The Natural and Supernatural Jew (New York: 1962).

Lucy S. Dawidowicz, ed., The Golden Tradition: Jewish Life and Thought in Eastern Europe (Boston: 1968).

Terrence Despres, The Survivor (New York: 1977).

Emil Fackenheim, God's Presence in History (New York: 1970).

Theodor H. Gaster, Festivals of the Jewish Year (New York: 1962).

Louis Ginzberg, Legends of the Jews, 7 vols. (Philadelphia: 1913).

Nahum Glatzer, ed., The Judaic Tradition (Boston: 1969).

Judah Goldin, ed. and tr., The Living Talmud (Chicago: 1957).

Julius H. Greenstone, The Messiah Idea in Jewish History (Philadelphia: 1906).

A. J. Heschel, Between God and Man, ed., Fritz A. Rothschild (New York: 1959).

———God in Search of Man (Philadelphia: 1955).

———Israel: An Echo of Eternity (New York: 1969).

———The Sabbath: Its Meaning for Modern Man (New York: 1951).

Raul Hilberg, The Destruction of the European Jews (Chicago: 1961).

Louis Jacobs, A Jewish Theology (London: 1973).

Mordecai Kaplan, Judaism as a Civilization (New York: 1967).

Maurice Lamm, The Jewish Way in Death and Dying (New York: 1969).

Moses Maimonides, The Guide of the Perplexed, tr. Schlomo Pines (Chicago: 1974).

Jacob Neusner, *Invitation to the Talmud* (New York: 1975).

————*The Way of Torah: An Introduction to Judaism* (Belmont: 1970).

Philo Judaeus, *The Essential Philo,* ed. Nahum Glatzer (New York: 1971).

Jack Riemer, ed., *Jewish Reflections on Death* (New York: 1975).

Cecil Roth, *A History of the Jews* (New York: 1970).

Richard Rubenstein, *After Auschwitz* (Indianapolis: 1960).

————*The Cunning of History* (New York: 1975).

————*The Religious Imagination: A Study in Psychoanalysis and Jewish Theology* (Indianapolis: 1968).

Hayyim Schauss, *The Jewish Festivals* tr. Samuel Jaffe (New York: 1938).

Solomon Schechter, *Aspects of Rabbinic Theology* (New York: 1961).

Gershom Scholem, *The Messianic Idea in Judaism* (New York: 1971).

————*On the Kaballah and its Symbolism* (London: 1965).

Leo W. Schwarz, ed., *Great Ages and Ideas of the Jewish People* (New York: 1956).

Hermann L. Strack, *Introduction to the Talmud and Midrash* (Philadelphia: 1931).

D. Zlotnick, tr., *The Tractate "Mourning"* (New Haven: 1966).

SEVEN
DEATH AS TRANSFORMATION
—FAITH

---

8 CHRISTIANITY

An essential insight into one aspect of the Christian conception of death can be found in the opening verses of the Christian scriptures. The Gospel of Matthew begins with the genealogy of Jesus. He is traced by direct descent through forty-two generations back to Abraham. Many names on this list are well-known figures in the Hebrew scriptures, some are of minor importance, and some occur nowhere else at all and are therefore utterly unknown to us.

What this tells us of the Christian conception of death is quite simply that Jesus is thoroughly human, born to a long line of mortals of the most ordinary strengths and weaknesses. There is nothing in his lineage itself to suggest that he should be born an exceptional human being; and anyone tracing his lineage back far enough would likely find among his forbears quite as many heroes as villains, along with those who left no memory whatsoever of their lives. It seems evident that Matthew is approaching his subject with the assumption that Jesus is a mortal quite like the rest of us, subject to all the limitations of human existence, including suffering and death; and, moreover, that the birth, life, and death of Jesus has a once-and-for-all character.

It is as though the Christian scriptures intend to make it clear at once that the messianic titles such as "Christ," "Son of God," and "Son of Man" do not in the least diminish the essential humanity of Jesus. In no way does he resemble, say, the Greek gods who could assume human form—or any other form for that matter—and move about on earth without the least possibility of harm from mortals. Nor is he to be confused with the frequent incarnations of Hindu gods, like Krishna who once was human, having lived a quite natural life, before he became divine. Unlike Jesus, Krishna was thought to reappear frequently in assorted disguises long after the termination of his human life.

As we shall discuss later, there are aspects of several dramatic appearances of Jesus after his death, but they were not disguises and they had the effect only of confirming his resurrection. The portrait of Jesus that emerges in the synoptic Gospels,* while often extraordinary, is nonetheless that of a person who lives entirely within the limits of human mortality. These are not the stories of an invulnerable superman untouched by ordinary weakness and capable of astounding deeds. It is sometimes thought that the performance of miracles was a manifestation of his superhuman or divine power, but in no instance does Jesus make that claim himself, nor does the Bible draw such theological conclusions from the miracles. They seem only to have the design of winning persons to faith or showing the depth of Jesus' love for others. In any event, the alleged power to perform miracles is so common among spiritually distinctive persons that it can hardly be considered unique to Jesus.

If we focus our attention on the synoptic Gospels as a way of getting at the Christian understanding of death, we see the way Jesus himself looked at death and the way he is reported to have died. But there is more to the Christian scriptures than the synoptic Gospels. Elsewhere, chiefly in the letters of Paul and the Gospel of John, the concern is less with the content of Jesus' historical life and his teachings than with the meaning of his death and resurrection. And, of course, there is more to Christianity than the scriptures. Indeed, the entire Christian tradition can be understood as a continuing interpretation of the life, death, and resurrection of Jesus.

The following discussion will center on three questions: (1) What did Jesus say about death during his own lifetime? (2) What conclusions do Paul and John draw from the death of Jesus? The letters of Paul, the Gospel of John, and the synoptic Gospels do not make up the entire Christian canon, but they are by far the most influential part of it. (3) How has the Christian tradition interpreted the death and resurrection of Jesus?

---

*Matthew, Mark, and Luke are referred to as the synoptic Gospels because they consist primarily of a collection of stories and homilies that had been circulating orally among believers for two or three decades before being written down. The Gospel of John, often referred to simply as the Fourth Gospel, has a distinctly different quality; written by a single author it shows a sophisticated theological perspective and a refined narrative skill which is lacking in the first three gospels.

If we begin our examination of Jesus' teaching about death by attempting to determine whether he believed in some sort of survival of death, we find numerous references that indicate he held such a belief. He speaks of the "outer darkness" where the condemned will "gnash their teeth." He enjoins his disciples not to "fear those who kill the body but cannot kill the soul; rather fear him who can destroy both body and soul in hell." Jesus clearly has an image of a *place* to which the unfaithful will *go* and be properly punished. From what scant references he makes to such a place, there is no reason to think he is doing anything more than expressing assumptions common in the Jewish tradition at the time.

Whether Jesus has a developed view of a contrary place—where the faithful are rewarded—is not as clear. It seems implied by what is said, though he offers us little of his thinking on the matter. The most complete reference occurs when the Sadducees attempt to corner him with a trick question: a woman is married seven times; each of her husbands has died; when she dies which of the seven will be her husband in heaven? Jesus answers: "When they rise from the dead, they neither marry nor are given in marriage, but are like angels in heaven." Then he adds, as though to press the point further, God "is not the God of the dead, but of the living" (Mark 12:25 ff.). He seems to concede that there is a *place*, but what it is like he does not say. The expression, "like angels," is quite vague. He certainly does not mean that the raised *are* angels, but what it is to be like angels is open to speculation. However, it is just such speculation that Jesus rebukes in the Sadducees with the remark that God is not the God of the dead. This has the effect of saying that such questions show ignorance about God; furthermore, Jesus is interested in matters of life, not death. This is reminiscent of his instruction to one of his disciples who had stated his desire to follow Jesus, but only after he could bury his father who had recently died: "Follow me," Jesus responded with obvious annoyance, "and leave the dead to bury the dead" (Matthew 8:22).

It is this last remark that seems most characteristic of Jesus' teaching on death. Quite simply, death is not a central question and may not be a question at all for him and most of his followers. From the synoptic Gospels we get the impression that his whole ministry is oriented toward issues of life—as though all issues of death should be left to the dead.

In the most extended collection of his teachings in the first three Gospels—the collection known as the Sermon on the Mount—there is no teaching about death whatsoever. There are several indirect allusions to "hell" and "destruction," but they cannot be taken to be teachings as such. They are the same vague asides we noted above. The Sermon on the Mount is concerned solely with the relation of the living to a living God and to their living neighbors. It summons its hearers to a vigorous, open life of a very special sort: "Do not be anxious about your life, what you shall eat or what you shall drink, nor about your body, what you shall put on. . . . [Y]our heavenly Father knows you need these things. But first seek his Kingdom and righteousness, and all these things will be yours as well" (Matthew 7:25 ff.). The two great themes that run through this scattered assemblage of sayings are the *sufficiency of God* to provide all that is necessary for those who faithfully seek righteousness and the *unconditioned love* appropriate to the relationship between persons. So far will Jesus enjoin his hearers to unconditioned love that he will dare a radical reinterpretation of an ancient teaching:

> You have heard that it was said, "An eye for an eye and a tooth for a tooth." But I say to you, Do not resist one who is evil. But if any one strikes you on the right cheek, turn to him the other also; and if any one would sue you and take your coat, let him have your cloak as well; and if any one forces you to go one mile, go with him two miles. Give to him who begs from you, and do not refuse him who would borrow from you" [Matthew 5:38 ff.].

Nowhere else in the synoptic Gospels do we find Jesus addressing the question of death itself. Neither does he deal with the themes so common in the religions of the East that set life in the context of suffering and that regard all things under the category of the ephemeral. The reason for this is clear. Jesus is concerned with the way persons relate to each other and to their God. Death is not therefore a primary concern. He is obviously aware of death; he diminishes it no less than he magnifies it. Death is an inevitable event that befalls us all, but in the full range of the life of a religious person it is an event far less important than obedience before God and love for the neighbor. It is for this reason that Jesus' references to heaven and hell are so indirect and incomplete. *Of course*, life is greater than death, he seems to be saying; therefore, what happens in life has consequences that carry beyond the grave—but don't wander into pointless speculation concerning *what* is beyond the grave.

In sum, the synoptic Gospels describe a Jesus moved by the same kinds of this-worldly concerns that we discovered in classical Judaism. Where Socrates said that the philosopher's task is to meditate on death, Jesus might have said that the believer's task is to get on with the difficult business of living in such a way that the future remains open.

In one respect, however, one does find many statements of Jesus that do refer to death—those that have to do with his own impending death. These statements fall into a repeated pattern. Their form even suggests a kind of ritualistic or liturgical repetition that would more likely have originated in the early church than in Jesus' own speech. In these sayings Jesus refers to himself as the "Son of Man," a term of varied meaning. He seems usually to use the term in a way that reflects the Jewish expectation of a Messiah who comes in glory to judge the unrighteous and set them apart from the righteous. There are several recurring features in these passages: "The Son of Man is to be delivered into the hands of men, and they will kill him, and he will be raised on the third day" (Matthew 17:22 ff.). To the details of a violent death at the hands of men and Jesus' resurrection by an act of God, the writers frequently add the exaltation of the Son of Man and the unknown hour of his appearance:

> the sun will be darkened, and the moon will not give its light, and the stars will fall from heaven, and the powers of the heavens will be shaken; then will appear the sign of the Son of Man in heaven, and then all the tribes of the earth will mourn, and they will see the Son of Man coming on the clouds of heaven with power and great glory; and he will send out his angels with a loud trumpet call, and they will gather his elect from the four winds, from one end of heaven to the other [Matthew 24:29 ff.].

And in Luke, "the Son of Man is coming at an hour you do not expect" (Luke 12:40). There is almost always a judgment motif: when the Son of Man comes, "he will repay every man for what he has done" (Matthew 16:27).

Curiously, in each of these Son of Man statements Jesus refers to himself in the third person singular. This gives his remarks a strange kind of distance. It is not only that he seems to be talking about someone else, but he seems to be voicing an expectation that arises less from his personal experience than from a developed tradition that looks forward to an apocalyptic event that will change the course of history. Like the references to death discussed earlier, Jesus never elaborates on these prophecies, nor talks about them as such. They have the quality of an announcement, and not an explanation, and seem to leave his listeners confused. On at least one occasion the disciples, after Jesus' reference to the Resurrection of the Son of Man, are said to have kept the matter to themselves, questioning what the rising from the dead meant" (Mark 9:10).

Looking backward in time it can be seen that Jesus was referring to his own resurrection or at least this seems to be what the authors of the first three gospels want the reader to assume. In spite of the formularistic, third person singular, he does plainly mean that he will himself appear as the Son of Man. Again it is curious that, while Jesus is speaking of his death, these sayings are not properly *about death itself*. In the synoptic Gospels Jesus never speaks of anyone else being raised from the dead. He is not announcing a general resurrection, only his own. Since this resurrection is so closely associated with judgment, with separating the sheep from the goats (Matthew 25:32), with repaying each person for good works, it is the case that his discourse is still in the context of love and obedience. Jesus continues to address the relationship of persons to each other and to their God; he is not concerned with death as such.

More curious still is the fact that, for all the references to his future resurrection, the synoptic Gospels picture Jesus facing his own death with a range of emotions we might expect in any ordinary mortal. In addition to fear he is possessed in the final hours with a sense of the betrayal and abandonment of his friends. Contrary to Socrates, who seemed almost to look forward to his death and who blithely refused the offer to escape, Jesus seems driven into an experience he views as one of pain and loss. As it is recounted in the Gospel of Luke, Jesus, moments before he was betrayed by his disciple Judas and arrested by the soldiers of the chief priests, uttered the telling prayer: "Father, if thou will, remove this cup from me; nevertheless not my will, but thine, be done." It is certainly not his will to die, and he asks even to be spared the necessity of dying, but he is above all obedient and will go to his death regardless. Luke obviously wants to reinforce the reader's perception of Jesus' internal revulsion to death and adds the following: "And there appeared to him an angel from heaven, strengthening him. And being in an agony he prayed more earnestly; and his sweat became like great drops of blood falling down upon the ground" (Luke 22:42 ff.).

In reading this passage we can imagine Jesus, like any other human being, merely recoiling from the pain of what he knows will be a violent and cruel death. However, in the Gospel of Matthew this reading is made rather unlikely by what he reports is the last cry of Jesus from the cross on which he died: "My God, my God, why hast thou forsaken me" (Matthew 27:46). This is more than the fear of death; it is the fear that his very life has been lived in vain.

Here is no Socrates comforting his grieving friends, jesting with his jailer, and conversing dispassionately on a number of abstract issues. Jesus is a tormented man. It is surprising that the anticipations of his own resurrection, so much grander than Socrates' speculations about the continued existence of the immortal soul, did not give him the strength to face death with equanimity. What has happened, we might ask, to his confidence in the God who will raise him from the dead and return him to judge the earth on clouds of glory?

There are serious incongruities in this account of Jesus' life and death that are not easily removed. The safest interpretation seems to be that the references to his resurrection are later additions to the narrative by those who accepted the resurrection as a fact and could not help but think that Jesus had foreseen it. However, the authors of the Gospels will still not suppress the obviously powerful narratives of Jesus' revulsion to the experience of death. This seemed to them to be a fitting and even necessary piece of their portrait of Jesus' humanity.

It is certainly unfair to think that there might have been any conscious effort to distort the historical record on this point—as though the Son of Man and Resurrection themes had been gratuitously added to the earlier and more accurate memory of what had actually occurred. It is no doubt the case that Jesus had made frequent references, however indirect, to Jewish eschatological expectations, and natural that, thirty or forty years later, believers would have remembered these as references to himself. If we read the Son of Man passages in this way the earlier impressions of a man consumed with the issues of life reemerge. Here is a person for whom death is real, marked with true loss and despair, but a man who nonetheless says: leave the dead to bury the dead, for your God is the God of the living. Jesus' suffering in the face of death has the effect of emphasizing the importance of life.

One might assume that these impressions of Jesus could be modified by the accounts of his resurrection in the synoptic Gospels, but, in fact, they are strengthened; here, too, we find a person focused entirely on life and not at all on death. Although there are several narratives, contradictory to each other in some of their details, they share a basic structure and make the same theological point. On the morning of the third day after his death two (or three, depending on the account) women went to see where he had been laid in the tomb only to discover that it was empty. An angel appeared who instructed them to inform the others that Jesus had been raised from the dead. Their astonishment at this and the subsequent surprise and joy among the disciples indicates that their own anticipation of his resurrection had been forgotten.

Shortly after the women announced what the angel had told them Jesus began to appear to the disciples. These appearances seem intended to prove that he had indeed arisen. To prove further that he was not an apparition, he is reported by Luke to have eaten a piece of broiled fish in the presence of his apparently doubtful disciples.

What is crucial in these narratives is not merely that he has risen from the dead, but what he now says to them before he departs again. His final words are exceedingly brief. According to Matthew his entire address was the following:

> All authority in heaven and on earth has been given to me. Go therefore and make disciples of all nations, baptizing them in the name of the Father and of the Son and of the Holy Spirit, teaching them to observe all that I have commanded you; and lo, I am with you always, to the close of the age [Matthew 28:18 ff.].

Luke records as his final words the injunction that "repentance and forgiveness should be preached in his name to all nations" (24:47).

These last remarks are consistent with his earthly ministry. Jesus is sending his disciples into all the world to baptize the nations and to preach repentance and forgiveness—that is, to do what he had done: to teach persons the proper relationship to God (repentance) and the proper relationship to each other (forgiveness).

What is conspicuously missing in these stories is any reference to a general resurrection. It seems appropriate that if Jesus had wanted to promote the hope that the faithful would be raised he would take this occasion to do so, but the authors of the Gospels omit any word of it. There is not the least suggestion that others will be raised as Jesus was raised. Of course, the possibility that this might occur is not *denied*. It is simply not a proclamation, at least according to the synoptic Gospels. When Jesus has a last chance to summarize and continue his ministry, it has nothing to do with a personal victory over death.

Clearly we can see that in these three Gospels, which are nearly the only sources of knowledge of Jesus' life and teaching, there is nothing resembling a doctrine of immortality as we find it in Plato. For one thing, a dualistic conception of human existence—in which the mind or soul is separable from the body—is quite foreign to these authors. Although they wrote in Greek and were not altogether unfamiliar with some of the terms of Greek philosophical thought, they are writing out of a Jewish intellectual context in which human existence is regarded primarily in terms of *actions* and not states—the actions of *whole persons* and not of their separate faculties. Moreover, the emphasis on history in these pages is far more Jewish than Greek. Salvation here is not from history but in it. There is a strong sense of continuity with the whole history of the Jews, as we can see in the genealogy of Jesus which is meant to connect him to Abraham by blood descent. Finally, there is no hope, or even interest, in the possibility of *surviving* death. There is only one interest: the victory of life over its enemies.

Death, for the synoptic evangelists, has the same historical inevitability it has for the Jews. The continuity offered in the face of this death is not the survival of a purified soul, but *a moral style of life, a way of living with others*. It is a continuity with the past and with a concrete body of persons—for the synoptic writers, the historical continuity is with the Jews. Death is not described as an evil, as an unjust fate, as a distortion of nature, or even as a human tragedy. What is most important here is that death is not seen as the *opposite to life*. Life has its enemies, not in any metaphysical sense or even in its destruction, but in *those persons* who break the continuity of history through their disobedience—which for the evangelists is seen largely in the moral terms of advancing oneself at the expense of others. The opposition to life lies in those actions that tear apart its delicate fabric of affection, of common caring.

Jesus' death was an event of great physical and psychic pain, but it was an experience he did not hesitate to undergo for the sake of the continuity in the moral life of his friends—he did not hesitate even though he was deeply troubled that his life would not have the effect of continuity. The resurrection narratives make the point of assuring us that Jesus' death was successful in extending his life into the life of his friends; it was because of his death that his friends would take up his life, understanding that the very purpose of his life was to make a gift of it to others. The utter absence of a reference to an afterlife in the resurrection narratives and the emphasis on preaching repentance and forgiveness to the world indicate that the disciples understood that Jesus' gift of life to them was to be a gift of life through themselves to the world.

The synoptics deal so prominently with the events of Jesus' life that they have in fact little to say of the way the restored continuity in the face of death is experienced. Their portrait of Jesus is indispensable, but they report almost nothing except indirectly concerning the impact that these events had on the internal life of Jesus' disciples and friends. Their interpretation of what they report is accidental and unreflected. John and Paul, on the other hand, come to these same historical observations out of a greater theological sophistication and with carefully focused interpretive designs based both on their own experience and the perceived needs of the primitive Christian community.

The letters of Paul were written in the first several decades after the death of Jesus, and the Gospel of John (or the Fourth Gospel) toward the end of the first century, or fully three generations after the crucifixion. Both bodies of literature make clear departures from the view of Jesus, and the consequent view of death, we found in the synoptic Gospels.

Although the writings of Paul precede John's in chronology, they show a greater difference from the synoptics; therefore, we shall begin with the Fourth Gospel.

The most obvious difference in the Fourth Gospel is its style and structure. Although we know nothing about John himself, it is apparent he is a well-educated and gifted writer, possessed of rich theological insights into the events he is describing. The book has a highly poetic, sometimes majestic quality, and in contrast to the synoptics a guiding sense of its narrative unity. The Fourth Gospel uses its narrative events to illustrate consciously developed theological motifs.

The grandeur of John's theological conception, as well as his prose style, is apparent in the opening passage:

> In the beginning was the Word,
> and the Word was with God,
> and the Word was God.
> He was in the beginning with God;
> all things were made through him,
> and without him was not anything made that was made.

Making an obvious allusion to the opening verse of the Hebrew scriptures ("In the beginning God created the heavens and the earth . . ."), John introduces us at once to a very different way of thinking about Jesus. Now he is placed squarely in the godhead, not in any minor way but as equal to God in power and dignity. Moreover, he refers to him as the "Word," or in Greek, *Logos*, a term that has a long and varied philosophic use meaning several things at once: the spoken word, the logic or the reason with which all things exist, and the divine presence in all that is.

The reader is informed at once that what is important is the original intention of the godhead that underlies the fact that the "Word became flesh and dwelt among us, full of grace and truth." Where Matthew began by citing Jesus' lineage—in effect proving he was descended from Abraham—John begins inside the being of God himself. His design is to give force to the conviction that Jesus is a true revelation of God: "No one has ever seen God; the only Son, who is in the bosom of the Father, he has made him known"(1:18). Jesus not only makes God known, he *is* God. Therefore, the presence of Jesus among men is the presence of God himself. Whatever one is to know of God can be received from Jesus: "And from his fulness have we all received, grace upon grace"(1:16).

There is, of course, an acute difficulty in the manner in which God has chosen to reveal himself. Not only has no one ever seen God, but, because all have fallen and their sight has been clouded by sin, they *cannot* see God. Therefore, to the unknowing, sinful mind Jesus will not be seen for what he is: "The true light that enlightens every man was coming into the world. He was in the world, and the world was made through him, yet the world knew him not"(1:9 ff.). It is not enough merely to *look* at Jesus or to *hear* about him (or *read* about him); one must have a clarified vision. One must be remade into a new kind of person, "born not of blood nor of the will of the flesh, but of God"(1:13).

Having started at a high level of abstraction in the prologue to his Gospel, John sharply switches to a most human account of the history of Jesus' ministry. It is, however, unlike the synoptic Gospels in both tone and content. It is a unified, progressive narrative. The fact that John composed his Gospel more than a half-century after the events he describes has allowed him to unify and simplify the drama of Jesus' encounter with his world. Where the synoptic Gospels spoke of the Sadducees and Pharisees, implying that they were but two sects among Jews, John makes a few distinctions between the Jewish religious bodies, seeing them collectively as enemies of Jesus. The synoptics see Jesus as a Jew; John sees him against the Jews. No longer is he described as a rabbi or a prophet announcing that the Kingdom of God is at hand. It is apparent that by the time John wrote his account the followers of Jesus no longer saw themselves as a Jewish sect, nor were they so regarded by the Jews. John simplifies the plot of his narrative by setting the Jews against Jesus in the conflict that leads to his death.

There is, however, a deeper theological point that John wants his readers to discover in Jesus' conflict with the Jews. It is important to John to show *how* Jesus has gone beyond Judaism. In a typical encounter the Jews accused Jesus of healing on the Sabbath. (Since healing is a "labor" it is forbidden on the Sabbath along with all other labor.) Jesus' answer was doubly provocative to his accusers: "My Father is working still, and I am working." Then John explains: "This was why the Jews sought all the more to kill him, because he not only broke the Sabbath, but also called God his Father, making himself equal with God"(5:17 ff.).

It is not mere opposition to the Jews that John wants us to see in Jesus, but that he has risen above the law and, moreover, has made the unthinkable claim that he is one with the Father and equal with him. Both themes are prominent throughout the Fourth Gospel: "I and the Father are one," Jesus states flatly (10:30). His abrogation of the law is emphatic. He even speaks of the law in conversation with officers of the chief priests as "your law"(8:17). There is a conspicuous absence in the gospel of ethical injunction. In contrast to the other Gospels there is virtually no instruction on Jesus' part concerning the behavior of his followers. The closest we get to this is the oft-quoted statement: "A new commandment I give to you, that you love one another." But Jesus makes no association between this commandment and the law; its basis lies elsewhere. Just after he told his disciples that he would be with them only a little while, knowing that they would seek to find him, he added: "Where I am going you cannot come." The commandment to love one another is given to make up for his absence—and in two ways. They are to love each other "even as I have loved you." In their fellowship with one another they will receive what Jesus had given them. And they are commanded to love for a second reason: "all men will know you are my disciples, if you love one another"(13:33 ff.). They are enjoined both to *continue* the love of Jesus within their own body and to *display* that love to others.

What lies beneath this "new commandment" is the unity of Jesus with his followers. Just as Jesus made manifest the love of God for the world by virtue of his unity with the Father, his disciples will manifest that same love by virtue of their unity with him. John offers little by way of speculation on the nature of this unity. His vision of it is most completely expressed through metaphor: "I am the true vine," he has Jesus say to his disciples, "and my father is the vinedresser . . . . I am the vine, you are the branches. He who abides in me, and I in him, he it is that bears much fruit, for apart from me you can do nothing"(15:1 ff.).

Not only does Jesus set himself above the particular requirements of the law; he goes even further—to the Jews, an inexcusable step—by making himself the basis of the new commandment. This is indeed a radical departure from classical Judaism. But still more offensive to the Jews are Jesus' claims to equality with God. This, too, is expressed primarily in Johannine metaphor:

> I am the bread of life;
> he who comes to me shall not hunger,
> and he who believes in me
> shall never thirst [6:35].

> I am the resurrection and the life;
> he who believes in me,
> though he die,
> yet shall he live [11:25]

Truly, truly, I say to you,
before Abraham was I am [8:58].

I have come as a light into the world,
that whoever believes in me
may not remain in darkness [12:46]

Here we have one of the sharpest contrasts with the synoptic Gospels. The content of Jesus' teaching is not the religious life, not the trials of discipleship, and not the nature of the world. The very close identification of Jesus with the Father in John's theology, and the claim that Jesus is himself a manifestation of God, means that *the content of his teaching is himself.* "I bear witness to myself," he says quite directly, "and the Father who sent me bears witness to me"(8:13). Therefore, because of the unity of Jesus with the Father, and the unity of the disciples with Jesus, what is of paramount importance to the Christian life is the relation of the person of the believer to the person of Jesus. He who believes in *me*, Jesus says, shall live. The most complete statement of this view occurs in Jesus' prayer for his disciples shortly before his death:

Father, the hour has come; glorify thy Son that the Son may glorify thee, since thou hast given him power over all flesh, to give eternal life to all whom thou hast given him. And this is eternal life, that they know thee the only true God, and Jesus Christ whom thou hast sent [17: 1 ff.].

The fact that John could not possibly have heard Jesus utter this prayer, and the additional fact that it has a strongly formularistic and even liturgical quality, makes it seem contrived and unreal. But we should not assume that John was intending historical authenticity here; instead, he was using this dramatic moment to put into Jesus' own words what John took to be the very heart of the gospel. And in those words we find a distinctive view of death. To *know* Jesus as the Son of the Father is to have eternal life. It is a life shared with the Son, as the Son shares it with the Father. What kind of knowledge this is John leaves as unspecified as what sort of unity there exists between Jesus and his followers. And the eternal life of which he speaks is also left unexplained.

What we *can* say is that this knowledge is directly opposed to the ignorance of those who dwell in darkness, under the dominion of the "ruler of this world"(12:31; 16:11). John uses this term as a euphemism for the devil, but we do not elsewhere in his writings find a satanic agency in evil. Persons are not sinful because they are driven into falsehood by the devil; they do not *want* to see the light. They "loved darkness rather than light, because their deeds were evil"(3:19). The evil of their deeds consists in the fact that they do not *see* that the world is created by God through the Logos, by the Father through the Son. In the First Letter of John, probably by the same author, it is said that whoever does not see this light, that is, that Jesus is the Son of the Father, is a "liar"(1 John 2:22).

In sum, those who live in the darkness blind themselves to the truth of the world—that it is created by the Father—and are therefore in bondage to the world, which means *bondage to death.* Jesus declared to the Jews, "you will die in your sins" for not accepting him as the "true light"(8:21,24). It would be easy to confuse John's thought here with Platonism because he seems to be identifying evil and death with worldliness. That this is not the case has already been affirmed in the prologue where it is announced that *all things* were made through the Logos *by God.* God would not have made something to oppose himself. As in the Jewish tradition the world is good in itself and not evil. Evil comes from (willful) false knowledge about the world. The truth about the world will set us free (8:31), releasing us from the bondage to death to enter eternal life. *Eternal life, then, is not a liberation from the body, or from the world, but from ignorance. It is living in the world as it truly is.*

For John we do not possess eternal life as we might possess a death-less soul. We have eternal life only so far as we *know* the only true God and the Son he has sent. For Plato the soul's immortality is the result of its own given divinity. For John there is not the merest shred of divinity in the native possession of men and women; they can only be the recipients of grace from the divinity of the only true God, and even then not all will receive grace; not all will have eternal life. Plato has Socrates speak of the possibility of conversing with the dead of previous ages in his immortal state. John does not refer in any detail whatsoever to the postmortem state of the believer. In fact, he seems profoundly unconcerned with what will happen *after* death. Almost all of his Gospel is concerned with the present living unity between believers and their Lord.

Each aspect of John's view of death emerges more vividly in his narration of the events surrounding the death and resurrection of Jesus. The unity of Jesus with the Father is reflected in the absence of any sense of terror, or failure, or abandonment, on the part of Jesus as he approaches his own death. He does not sweat blood, nor pray for strength to endure his death, as in the synoptic Gospels, and he does not cry out in despair from the cross. According to John his last words were: "It is finished." (In Greek, the language in which John wrote, this is but a single word.) There is in this expression a confidence that what was necessary to do has been done in his earthly existence; his mortal life was complete.

The absence of a theory on the immortality of the soul is apparent in John's account of Jesus' appearance to his disciples after the resurrection. To make it clear it was a resurrection of the *body*, and not simply a continuation of the disembodied soul, John reports the scepticism of the disciple Thomas who refused to believe that it was the raised Jesus who stood before him until he could touch the wounds Jesus suffered at his death.

The unity of Jesus with his disciples is a theme John continues to use by stressing the intimacy of his appearances. For example, he comes to them in the privacy of their homes where they are hiding from the Jews. On one memorable occasion he appears to them in the midst of their labor. Simon Peter and several other disciples had been fishing, but without success, though they had fished all night. Just as dawn was breaking a stranger was seen standing on the shore. He called out to them to cast their nets on the opposite side of the boat. They did so, "and now they were not able to haul it in, for the quantity of the fish." One of the disciples recognized the stranger and cried out "It is the Lord!" At once Simon Peter sprang into the sea and swam to the shore in his joy (21:1 ff.).

The intimacy and the affection of these meetings bear nothing whatsoever of a cosmic or universal event. Jesus does not appear to the nations, only to a few of his friends. In no way does John speculate on the consequences or meaning of these appearances apart from the joy of the disciples in being reunited with their lord. And, as in the synoptic Gospels, there is no mention of a general resurrection. Earlier Jesus had referred to *himself* as the resurrection and the life, but that was more directly in reference to the knowledge of him or the belief in him: "whoever lives and believes in me shall never die" (11:25 ff.). In the resurrection narratives themselves, however, there is no reference to death in any way. Here, too, the emphasis is on life. After Jesus had eaten breakfast with the disciples who had been fishing, he asked Simon Peter three times, in an obviously symbolic exchange: Do you love me? Each time Simon Peter answered that he did. Jesus' successive responses were: "Feed my lambs." "Tend my sheep." "Feed my sheep." Shortly after that he rose and before leaving spoke his final words: "Follow me." Certainly this last encounter, as John reports it, is enigmatic. Perhaps the safest interpretation is that which stays closest to the literal sense of Jesus' remarks. To follow him does not mean to go bravely into death, but to "feed his sheep," that is, to continue life among the living. Here, too, the question of death vanishes before a pressing concern for life.

In the Johannine literature there is a conception of continuity significantly different from that found in the synoptic Gospels—no longer that of the moral community connected with a rabbinic tradition, but a spiritual community connected by a mystical union with a risen Lord. Although Jesus is absent after his death, they are still bound to him and to one another in the Spirit of Truth (16:13) and in the Spirit of Love: "All who keep his commandments abide in him, and he in them. And by this we know that he abides in us, by the Spirit which he has given us" (1 John 3:24). The community is no less loving than in the synoptics, but in this case the loving relationship is the very presence of the spirit of Jesus in his disciples' lives, and not a response to ancient law. There are also areas of substantial agreement in this matter between the Fourth Gospel and the first three. Here, too, the opposite of life is not death. Life has its enemies in those who are unable to see the eternal bond between Jesus and those that love each other in his spirit, and those who therefore attempt to destroy that bond as religiously false and dangerous. John, no less than the other evangelists, speaks of a genuine death—an event that brings life to a biological, physical, and psychic end. Human existence has nothing imperishable in its natural composition. The resurrection of Jesus does not here, any more than in the synoptics, promise a general resurrection. There is no indication that the separate histories of individuals will be made indefinite; there is only the declaration that the living presence of the Spirit will never abandon the historical existence of those who "know" Jesus.

John's understanding of the life and death of Jesus was influenced by the events that had occurred in the intervening half-century. Paul's understanding was influenced by his own dramatic encounter with the risen Christ. Although a contemporary of Jesus, Paul never saw him in the flesh. Within what was probably only a few years after Jesus' death, Paul was converted to the Christian faith through a sudden and astonishing vision of the resurrected Lord. In spite of the fate that Paul's writings are generally the earliest of the Christian scriptural literature, his focus is almost entirely on the meaning of Jesus' death and resurrection, and not on the content or the events of his life. Only once does he refer to anything in the life of Jesus and that is the Last Supper, which the disciples had with him before his death. Paul's description of this event has a distinctly ritualistic quality—as though the young church had already developed a liturgy for the sacramental repetition of this final meal.

Even more than John, Paul takes considerable pains to show that the law has been abrogated by Jesus. Paul has a far more negative view of the law. He directly associates it with death. He can even refer to it as "the law of sin and death." The reason for this is that when Adam first sinned, therefore committing all his descendents to sinfulness, God provided the law by which righteousness might be regained. So deep is the sinfulness of each of us, however, that the law, far from helping, has only increased our unrighteousness. Paul's attitude toward the law is basically psychological. He knows that to say the law is death is to condemn God who gave the law. Therefore, it is not the law itself but our reaction to it he is discussing.

> What then shall we say? That the law is sin? By no means. Yet, if it had not been for the law, I should not have known sin. I should not have known what it is to covet if the law had not said, "You shall not covet." But sin, finding opportunity in the commandment, wrought in me all kinds of covetousness [Romans 7:7 ff.].

Paul's point seems to be that our sinfulness is too deep for the law to help. Hearing the law we only add to the scope of our disobedience. Since disobedience of God is punished by death, the law virtually guarantees our death. This means that God, if he intends to give us life, must do so apart from the law. Of course, since God *made* the law, he cannot, or will not, merely set it aside as though it were pointless or as though he had made a mistake in instituting it. The law must still be answered to: the offenses against it must be paid for. It is such a payment that Jesus made with his own death. Departing from the synoptic and the Johannine views, Paul speaks of the death of Jesus not as an historical as much as a theological event. The death of Jesus is sacrificial; it was offered for our sins, and we are therefore *justified* by it. But it does more than justify sinners; it also redeems them for a new life of faith. Justification removes the sentence of death; redemption is the gift of renewed life.

The question arises immediately: Are *all* sinners justified and redeemed by the death of Jesus? Jesus died for all those, Paul says, who receive him by faith. By faith Paul does not mean an *action* of the sort the law might enjoin; he means just the opposite of an action. Faith has much more the sense of acknowledging one's helplessness, one's utter inability to save oneself by the law.

If we are justified by such faith it is only because God has acted and not us. But, once justified, and excused from the condemnation of the law, are we also free from death? Yes and no. Like John, Paul never denies human mortality; yet he also speaks of a new sort of life. The paradox in this view easily leads to confusion. There is no question that Paul wants his readers to see that death has been vanquished. Quoting from the prophets, he announces:

> Death is swallowed up in victory.
> O death, where is thy victory?
> O death, where is thy sting [1 Corinthians 15:54 ff.]?

Although death has been *overcome*, it has not been *eliminated*. Nowhere in Paul's writing is there a suggestion that we can elude our death. But far more clearly than in the other biblical literature we have so far considered, Paul promises a new, resurrected life for the faithful. As in John this new life is grounded in the unity of the faithful with Christ. But for Paul our identity with Christ includes our death as well as our life. Therefore, he can say:

> Do you not know that all of us who have been baptized into Christ Jesus were baptized into his death? We were buried therefore with him by baptism into death by the glory of the Father, we too might walk in newness of life [Romans 6:3 ff.].

For John the believers' unity with Jesus was to be expressed in his absence by their love for each other. Paul pushes this a step further. The unity with Christ means that the believer bears in himself the death and life of Jesus:

> We are afflicted in every way, but not crushed: perplexed, but not driven to despair; persecuted, but not forsaken; struck down, but not destroyed; always carrying in the body the death of Jesus, so that the life of Jesus may also be manifested in our bodies [2 Corinthians 4:8 ff.].

Paul is convinced that the faithful are raised with Jesus, but that resurrection is not something that will occur *only* after they have died. With what some biblical scholars have regarded as elements of mysticism, Paul asserts that insofar as believers are already united with Christ by faith they are *at present* living a kind of resurrection life. There is certainly a difference between their condition now and their condition after death.

Paul shows no hesitation in referring to the difficulty of the present condition: "We know that the whole creation has been groaning in travail until now, and not only the creation, but we ourselves," who are waiting for the "redemption of our bodies" (Romans 8:22 ff.). But there is no real complaint against this condition. On the contrary, our "bondage to decay," our manifold sufferings, have the positive aspect of a sign of the coming redemption: "We have this treasure in earthen vessels, to show that the transcendent power belongs to God and not to us" (2 Corinthians 4:7).

However, while we are still inhabiting our mortal bodies, and while the flesh is still under the condemnation of the law, we require a special kind of guidance. In the physical absence of Jesus, God is still present in the comfort and guidance of the Holy Spirit:

> if Christ is in you, although your bodies are dead because of sin, your spirits are alive because of righteousness. If the Spirit of him who raised Jesus from the dead dwells in you, he who raised Christ Jesus from the dead will give life to your mortal bodies also through his Spirit which dwells in you [Romans 8:10 ff.].

It seems that some of the early believers were confused by this notion and argued with each other about what sort of body they would be raised with after their earthly death. Paul addressed himself to this question with a careful explanation in one of his letters to the young Church in Corinth. At the beginning of this passage he attaches the resurrection of Christ to the resurrection of the believers: "Now if Christ is preached as raised from the dead, how can some of you say that there is no resurrection of the dead" (1 Corinthians 15:12). He then provides a narrative sequence of the saving acts connected with the death and resurrection of Jesus. First, Christ reverses the effects of Adam's sin: "For as by a man came death, by a man has come also the resurrection of the dead. For as in Adam all die, so also in Christ shall all be made alive" (15:21 ff.). But not all will be made alive at the same time. Christ himself will rise before anyone else, then "those who belong to Christ." Finally, there will be a grand judgment when Christ delivers the kingdom of his believers to the Father and puts "all his enemies under his feet. The last enemy to be destroyed is death" (15:25).

When Paul comes to the specific question—With what kind of body are the dead raised?—he develops his answer around the metaphor of a seed. "What you sow does not come to life unless it dies," he says, meaning that the seed dies after it is sown, and a new plant grows in its place. (There is no thought here that the seed might contain the mature plant in itself in some unknown way—as we know now to be the case.) The body we now inhabit is, in death, sown like the seed, and like the seed, it perishes. In its place a new body is raised by God—a very different body.

> What is sown is perishable,
> what is raised is imperishable.
> It is sown in dishonor,
> it is raised in glory.
> It is sown in weakness,
> it is raised in power.
> It is sown a physical body,
> it is raised a spiritual body [15:42 ff.].

If we should wonder what is meant by "spiritual body," Paul tells us very little; only that "as we have borne the image of the man of dust, we shall also bear the image of the man of heaven" (15:49). The question is left in the air. What we can say is that Paul's emphasis here is much more on the *body* than on the *spirit* of the body. It is extremely important to him that we be raised in our full human nature and not simply by one of our faculties, like the mind, or the animating spirit. This is the point he wants most to communicate to the Corinthians who have some difficulty over the idea of a raised *body*. Paul's word for body here *(soma)* should be distinguished from the word for flesh *(sarx)*, inasmuch as the former indicates the complete person; but we should also note that the person we truly are *(soma)* includes our flesh.

Paul concludes this discussion with a statement that has the form not of explanation but of announcement:

Lo! I tell you a mystery.
We shall not all sleep, but we shall all be changed,
in a moment, in the twinking of an eye,
at the last trumpet. For the trumpet will sound,
and the dead will be raised imperishable, and we
shall be changed. For this perishable nature must
put on the imperishable, and this mortal nature must
put on immortality [15:51 ff.].

As we have seen, for Socrates immortality means an imperishable soul that remains unchanged through death—with its memory and personality intact. The whole point of the doctrine is continuity, and not change. For Socrates one is immortal by nature—whether or not there is a God. For the evangelists and for Paul one's life *and* death are entirely in the hands of God. There is no continuity from one life to the next; there is an absolute discontinuity, after which God will do that which a sinful nature is incapable of doing. In the same way, all the biblical writers understand Jesus to have died a natural death and to have been raised by an act of God. They differ on the significance they attach to the resurrection of Jesus. Neither John nor the synoptic Gospels see in it the promise of a general resurrection; Paul takes the promise to be implicit, almost to the extreme of saying the resurrection of Jesus is meaningless if believers are not raised with him.

Neither in Paul nor elsewhere in the Christian scriptures is there further speculation on the nature of the resurrected life or on the resurrection body with which the faithful are raised. The question is left open: "Lo! I tell you a mystery," Paul exclaimed. "We shall not all sleep, but we shall all be changed." This is a mystery that need not be explained to make faith possible. It is a mystery that faith takes into itself, knowing all will one day be shown in full: "For now we see in a mirror dimly, but then face to face" (1 Corinthians 13:12).

There is no question that death as such has a more prominent place in Paul than in the synoptics and John. Death is a direct enemy of life. However, because Paul connects death with the law, and the law with God, the opposites of life and death have no ultimate significance. It is true that death is vanquished, but it is not life that wins the struggle: it is God who wins it for life. Death, as the loser of this contest, however, continues to exist. Life can only continue on some ground other than its own; it must be transformed. *Our life is therefore not our own; it is Christ's. But then neither is death our own—it too is Christ's.* We carry the death of Jesus in our bodies in order that the life of Jesus might also be there. Paul allows us no escape from history—we must suffer all its inevitabilities, including death; but our true life, our transformed existence, is no longer historical. The struggle between life and death was not won in history. It was a cosmic event that did not occur in time as we know it; however, it did change the time in which we live. As Christians experience it they are saved *in* the context of their personal history, but, in sharp contrast to Jews, they are not saved *for* history. The "rulers of this age" are doomed to pass away (1 Corinthians 2:6), and shortly, for the time of the end is not far off (1 Corinthians 7:29). Paul refers to this as the "day of the Lord Jesus" (1 Corinthians 1:8; 5:5), "when he delivers the kingdom to God the Father after destroying every rule and every authority and power" (1 Corinthians 15:21). This means that the history we now live in has lost its finality—and therewith its drama. It does not matter what happens here. Our true, transformed life is elsewhere: "From now on, therefore, we regard no one from a human point of view; even though we once regarded no one from a human point of view; even though we once regarded Christ from a human point of view, we regard him thus no longer. Therefore, if any one is in Christ, he is a new creation; the old has passed away, behold, the new has come" (2 Corinthians 5:16 ff.). We are living in an interim period, merely waiting for great events of the end; what we are now in faith we shall be then in full.

Paul has by far the greatest influence on the subsequent Christian tradition of any of the writers collected in the Christian canon. It is Paul who established the unique view of death's discontinuity as *transformation*. What ruptures the course of life is not its biological demise, neither is it the moment when the flesh drops away from the immortal soul; it is the transformation of this life into another. It is a transformation we shall resist if we cannot see that the death of our bodies is the death of Jesus and, therefore, that the temporal life we now live could be the eternal life of Jesus. But seeing that Jesus has died, our death is not an ordinary vision or piece of knowledge; it can be seen only by *faith*. It is in the work of Paul that the Christian doctrine of faith has its most substantial foundation; in Paul, therefore, we can see most clearly that it is faith that restores the continuity of human existence destroyed by death. For it is with faith that we can live a life that is not ours and suffer a death that is not ours.

This novel conjunction of ideas had the effect of challenging two millenia of thinkers who sought to clarify, expand, or reject Paul's singular picture of the religious life. We shall explore the development of these ideas in some of the major Christian thinkers.

The centrality of death to the Christian faith is shown most emphatically in the fact that the fundamental symbol of Christianity is the cross. It was of course Jesus who died on the cross, but there is a close bond between his death and ours, so that the cross stands for our own death as well and the victory Jesus won through his death. What happened on that cross is characterized in the title of an essay by a Puritan divine: "The Death of Death in the Death of Jesus."

In Christian orthodox teaching, death has its cause in *original sin*. It was evident from the beginning that death could not be a natural evil of the sort described by extreme dualists. Since all things have been made by God, all things must be inherently good. There is nothing evil or flawed in the basic substance of the flesh. As Augustine, one of the most seminal Christian thinkers, wrote, it was not the body that corrupted the soul, but the soul that caused the body's corruption by losing control over it.[1] But what caused the soul to corrupt the body? Christians have been for the most part quite clear that this evil did not enter human existence through the direct will of God or through a satanic agency capable of resisting the creator's omnipotence, although frequently enough the devil has been represented as a *tempting* influence, as in the story of the original fall in the Book of Genesis.

The very essence of the doctrine of original sin is that the first created pair *freely disobeyed God and were punished by death*. Death therefore originates in a free decision, and though it is imposed by God it is a perfectly fitting payment for our offense. The nature of this offense is clear enough from the biblical account of the first sin: it is the desire to be like God. Here Christianity is in agreement with Judaism, for death is understood both as the line that separates human from divine existence *and* the punishment for trying to cross that line.

There are two immediate difficulties that arise with the doctrine of original sin. The first is the possession by Adam and Eve of a personal freedom so extensive that they could have worked such a disaster on the succeeding thousands of generations of descendents in direct contradiction to the intentions of their creator. The second is the manner by which the original act of freedom communicates itself to the descendents. If death is the consequence of a free act in our first parents, how can it befall every human person without exception and still be considered a free choice?

So far as the latter, and least controversial, of these two difficulties is concerned, it can be said that Christians have decided to live with a doctrine that is clear to faith but obscure to reason. The sixteenth-century reformer John Calvin speaks for the prevailing view of the Christian tradition when he pairs one fact—that our first parent Adam could have chosen eternal life but instead freely rejected it—with another—that we have contracted from him a "hereditary taint."[2] Now, of course, this taint must be strong enough to include all persons in all of human history and yet limited enough that we cannot say that nature itself is flawed; moreover, our own free consent to this taint must not be diminished. Calvin does not hesitate to say "even infants themselves, while they carry their condemnation along with them from the mother's womb, are guilty not of another's fault but of their own."[3] However implausible this all seems, for our purposes here it is enough to note that it is a fundamental belief of Christians that *all* persons are *freely* sinful to the degree that they *deserve* death as a punishment. Death is a natural event, but it is not caused by nature—it is caused by sin.

As to the other of these difficulties—the power God gave Adam and Eve to spoil his creation—it must frankly be said that here, too, no adequate *explanation* is available. Christians have simply had to accept what amounts to a contradiction; namely, that God through his all-powerful will created a possibility for that power to be compromised. We should stress this contradiction at the outset because it gives Christianity its most distinctive shape in contrast to the other major ways of conceiving the discontinuity of death. The question is always how far Christian thinkers can tolerate the contradiction. They have in fact gone to considerable lengths to trim its rough edges without altogether eliminating it.

Thomas Aquinas, another of the church's most influential minds, held firmly to God's power to destine all events, while affirming Adam's freedom to sin. He even taught that God knew precisely how many persons, and which ones, would be saved and which would be damned before the creation.[4] At the same time, however, he stressed that a person is predestined to salvation *conditionally*; that is, one may freely sin thus relinquishing salvation. Those who are damned are also free, though they are not free to choose salvation; they may only choose *which* sins they will commit and freely enough that they are condemned to death for them.[5] Elsewhere Aquinas seems to soften the contradictions of this account by arguing that death was actually not desired by our first parents; instead, it was an *accidental* result of their disobedience. Their act "took away original justice, which not only kept the lower powers of the soul in subjection to reason, without any disorder, but also kept the whole body in subjection to the soul, without any defect." The loss of original justice so deranged the powers of the soul that death occurred.[6] This bends the contradiction a little by suggesting that God did not actually ordain death, but only allowed it to happen indirectly through the way he had structured the nature of things. The distinction between God's *ordaining will* and his *permitting will* finds widespread use in classical Christian thought by those authors who see the importance in the doctrine that death is chosen freely.

Certainly another path to a less contradictory understanding of the relation of death and freedom was opened when the powerful influence of Platonic philosophy began to be felt. Most Christians found the theory of immortality, in particular, to be irresistible. It had the advantage of limiting the effect of death. The soul was not now *destroyed* by sin, only *damaged* by it. Calvin, who uncritically accepted the doctrine of natural immortality, said that the "perfect excellence" of Adam's soul before the Fall "was subsequently so vitiated and almost blotted out that nothing remains after the ruin except what is confused, mutilated, and disease ridden."[7] God seems less compromised here because what he created with the possibility of immortality does continue to exist even if in a state of confusion and disease. However, it has a much more serious disadvantage. The risk in accepting the theory of immortality is that it sharply diminishes the force of the biblical teaching that "the wages of sin," in Paul's phrase, "is death." There is still a punishment for sin, but it is no longer death as such.

Augustine's attempt to reconcile immortality with the biblical account illustrates the dilemma. He suggests that the death which follows sin be regarded as a state in which the soul is "forsaken" by God. He refers to this as a "second death," for the first the soul is forsaken by the body, and then by God. In this second death we are not just dying, as we are while in the body, but *endlessly* dying: "in striking contrast to our present conditions, men will not be before or after death, but always in death; and thus never living, never dead but endlessly dying. And never can a man be more disastrously in death than when death itself shall be deathless."[8] When immortality is introduced death itself ceases to become a punishment; it is rather that the death of the body simply changes the nature of the punishment, which can only be understood as *a life of suffering*, even if it is a postmortem life. Thus, we find the widespread reference in Christian thought to scenes of eternal punishment where the dead are not really dead; they are only unable to take flight from the misery that they have earned for themselves in their earthly existence.

Another risk in incorporating the theory of immortality into Christian doctrine is that the soul would come to represent an entity that was essentially independent of God. If we are truly immortal we shall continue to exist regardless of what God wishes. Some thinkers, among them the profoundly gifted third-century teacher Origen, came to believe, like Plato, that if the soul could survive its death it should also preexist its birth. This view, along with another teaching of Origen that *all* souls would in time be restored by God to their sinless purity, was declared heretical in 553 at the Council of Constantinople. For the most part, Christians want immortality, but only so much of it; and they do not deny death, but they want to deny its absoluteness.

More recent theologians have seen the fundamental anti-Christian nature of the Platonic influence on the understanding of death. It not only has very little, if any, biblical support; it also obscures the line between life and death. Life does not actually come to an end, it is moved to another setting. This not only encourages a deep otherworldliness that has plagued Christianity not infrequently over the centuries, it also opens the future to an infinitude that in turn erodes all the temporal structures of selfhood. As the twentieth-century theologian Karl Barth has put it, we do indeed have souls, but they are not something separable from our bodies. Our soul is the way we live with our body. This presupposes that the soul is temporal quite like the body. If a person "lives at all, he lives in his time. His life is a series of the acts of his own movement, enterprise, and activity. . . . If man had no time, if his existence were timeless, he would have no life."[9]

Another contemporary, Paul Tillich, attempts to reduce the traditional Christian contradictoriness in relating death to sin by drawing into question the assumption that death is not a natural phenomenon. Because God has created all things, including human persons, and because all created things are contingent, "Christianity must reject the doctrine of natural immortality."[10] Death must be understood as a natural inevitability: "The idea that the 'Fall' has physically changed the cellular or psychological structure of man (and nature?) is absurd and unbiblical."[11] Therefore, sin is not for Tillich the cause of death, but its "sting": "It transforms the anxious awareness of one's having to die into the painful realization of lost eternity."[12] By taking this point of view, Tillich threatens the precarious association of death and freedom from another side. If the doctrine of natural immortality leads to a kind of timelessness in which history becomes meaningless, the doctrine of natural mortality leads to a kind of "time-boundedness" in which history becomes hopeless. Tillich does make a strong claim in his thought for the experience of "eternal life" in history, but he is never convincing in his attempts to show that the events of history make a difference to the experience of eternal life, or that such an experience has an effect on history—which, like all other things, must come to an absolute end.

If Tillich ameliorates the contradictory association of sin and death by making death natural and interpreting sin as a way of responding freely to death's necessity, Karl Barth softens the contradictoriness in a fashion much more consistent with Christian orthodoxy as a whole (minus its entanglement with the Platonic theory of the survival of the soul). Barth takes the birth and death of human persons to be the absolute beginning and end of their natural existence. These are not just natural limits, they are limits also set by God. As such, they reflect "the two great acts of God at the beginning and the end of all things, the creation and the consummation."[13] God has established the outer boundaries for all that exists, for all human history, and for the natural history of the universe in its entirety.

We have no freedom over these limits; we can choose neither the beginning nor the end. We are "first called to the sphere of spontaneity, and then called away from it; first kindled as a self-illuminating light, and then extinguished." The stress here is on the fact that one is *made* free; freedom is not its own origin. This means for Barth that it "is I who live, but in doing so I do not belong to myself; I am indebted to the power which ordained that I should live within the limits laid down not by myself but by that power."[14] Life is everywhere characterized by the fact that it extends between birth and death; in each human act we are moving away from one limit and moving toward another. Thus, "my life becomes my history—we might almost say drama—in which I am neither the author nor the producer, but the principal actor."[15]

Barth holds back from the direct statement that death is the *result* of sin in the sense that if we had not sinned we would be immortal. He is unambiguous concerning the claim that sin is the desire to become God and is therefore a clear violation of divine law: "All evil consists in the fact that we do what we do under this desire. And when it is misused in this way the Law itself can only prepare death for us." What is important about death here is not that it simply brings life to an end—for that is no evil in itself—but that we are thereby excluded from the house of the Father and all his goods.[16] Death itself is not the punishment, but the means by which the punishment is expressed. Barth follows Paul in his belief that Jesus has suffered this punishment for us and that God is no longer withholding his abundant goodness. This does not mean we cease to die, but that death takes on a new significance. Birth and death now point directly to God's goodness, and the primary reason is that Jesus has shared in our death: "Living in this limitation we are like him. That is why the limitation declares to us a great freedom."[17] What we are free from is the nothingness of death; we need no longer live as though all that is good in life will vanish into the vast emptiness of death, for God is the Lord of death as much as the Lord of life. Barth can say that death is not only an act of God, but also a gift of God. It is a free action on his part:

> God is not obliged to act this way. It is His gift. It is grace which He shows to man but does not owe to man; grace by which he binds us but not Himself. This is revealed in human death. He is still the God from whom man is, even when He lets man die. Thus in death and above death, He is still the hope of man.[18]

Barth speaks for the mainstream of Christian orthodoxy in the consistency with which he defends God's utter omnipotence against any erosion, even at the occasional expense of rationality or clarity. It is true that all persons rebel against the very God who made them, but he made them free to do so as well. It is also true that they all will die, but God fashioned the death of his children along with their freedom. Barth captures the essence of the orthodox view when he describes life in the metaphor of a drama in which we are neither author nor producer, but performers. But this metaphor also raises the question as to how seriously Christians can take history. It is not possible for God simply to be the producer of this drama. He cannot erect a theatre and turn it over to the performers—he must also write the script. How free are we if we are held only to the performance of an already finished script? Refusing to compromise God's omnipotence seems to have the effect of compromising history.

There are considerable differences of opinion among Christian thinkers on how specifically God has scripted our lives; that is, on the amount of freedom we have within the established plot. Thomas Aquinas can go so far as to argue that it is "fitting that his providence should permit certain defects in particular things, lest the perfect good of the universe should be impaired." It seems to be a defect in the script, for example, when some persons are allowed enough freedom to become cruel tyrants, but without them there would be no martyrs to show the glory of God.[19] It is an inviolable requirement on all Christian doctrine to show that the final scene is God's. However badly we might have confused the plot, God will right all things just before the final curtain. No matter who plays what role or how well it is performed, the scripted denouement cannot be in the least bit altered. "Even the enemies of God," Barth declares, "are the servants of God and the servants of his grace."[20] On the same point Aquinas quotes with approval from Augustine's *Enchiridion* (Book Two): "God omnipotent would not allow any evil thing to exist in his works, were he not able by his omnipotence and goodness to bring good out of evil."[21] Christian thinkers have always been clear on the fact that we are saved *in* history, as we noted earlier, but they also have insisted that since all things ultimately belong to God, we are not saved *for* history.

Orthodox Christianity has never permitted a retreat from history by entering into a prior unity with the divine, as it has been described by mystics. Neither is there any possibility of treating historical existence as an illusion and seeking union with the All, as in Hinduism. And certainly there is essentially nothing in common with the Buddhist teaching that both life and death are fictions. On the other hand, Christians also believe that the object of salvation is not to continue history, as Jews have conceived it, but to return history to its maker. *God is the agent of death, and it is through this agency that he keeps all things for himself.*

Christians understand the *discontinuity* of death as a transformation: "Lo! I tell you a mystery. We shall all be changed." The corresponding *continuity* is not immortality, as we have seen, but faith: "whoever believes in me shall never die." The role of faith is central to the complete Christian understanding of death. Faith is not a matter of knowledge merely, for the resurrection is consistently understood as a mystery and beyond human comprehension. This is all still "wrapped in obscurities." Calvin wrote, but the day is coming when we may behold it all "face to face."[22] Until that day, however, we can have only faith in its reality. But what *is* faith, and how could it possibly be the way in which God restores the continuity of our lives in the face of death?

The doctrine of faith is one of the most difficult and most controversial in all of Christian thought. To have an adequate grasp of its nature we must look briefly at the complications that are necessarily a part of it in the context of the theological account of God's relationship to history.

Christian doctrine is under the difficult requirement of showing how God has acted in history, but without taking history away from meaningful human experience. That is, if we are human only to the extent that we have a genuine history (Barth), how can God act in his own production in such a way that he does not dominate the stage, giving us only bit parts?

First, it must be clear that since we are condemned to history by our sin God can approach us only through history—thus the incarnation of God in Jesus. There have been frequent challenges to the orthodox view here by persons who found it quite reasonable to have knowledge of God from sources other than the historical event of incarnation. Such challenges have never prevailed, however, largely because they have the result of allowing us to transcend our historical limitations, if only by the exercise of a purified reason. This means that the orthodox doctrine of the incarnation must assert that Jesus was perfectly human without the faintest element of divinity mixed with his humanity. In Paul's phrase, "Christ Jesus, who, though he was in the form of God, did not count equality with God a thing to be grasped, but emptied himself, taking the form of a servant, being born in the likeness of men" (Philippians 2:5 ff.). Having established his perfect humanity, Christians must then show how Jesus' actions within the limitations of that humanity, were sufficient to restore the continuity of life. The most common theological interpretation of Jesus' historical life—what theologians refer to as the "work of redemption"—is that Jesus offered himself as a blameless sacrifice to satisfy the divine justice that requires payment for the sins of all humankind against their maker.

It often happens that the work of redemption is described in suprahistorical terms—as an exchange of merits, earned by the Son in his perfect obedience even unto death, an obedience between the Son and the Father on behalf of sinners. Since the Son has enough merits for all of us, we are thereby justified in God's sight; that is, God lifts his condemnation and declares us righteous. All of this can happen behind our backs, as it were, without our knowing it and without any discernible effect on history. It is effectively an exchange between God and himself that does not involve his creatures. But traditionally the doctrine of *justification* is conjoined to the doctrine of *sanctification*. Justification is an act of God concerning us; regeneration is our response to that exchange.

The relation between justification and sanctification has led to a number of famous disputes in Christian history. Since we cannot reestablish the continuity of life from out of our own history, it has seemed necessary to most Christian thinkers to argue that we can have nothing whatsoever to do with our own justification. Our inherited sin is so complete that we can no longer justify ourselves before God. This position has struck many Christians, however, as too extreme, too abstract, and they have wanted to say that there must be *something* we can do to earn our salvation, even if it is very little. In the great flourishing of Christian thought in the Middle Ages the doctrine evolved that *prior* to our justification each of us must do whatever lies in us, *facere quod in se est*, to work toward justification. We cannot complete the task, but God's grace is sufficient to carry the willing penitent on to righteousness. This seemingly sensible advice struck the Protestant reformers as a profound offense to the omnipotence of God and a serious misunderstanding of the power of sin and death. We are justified not by what we *do*, but by *faith alone*; as Luther declared this in the sixteenth century he broke Christendom into apparently irreconcilable divisions.

The understanding of faith that Luther rejected may not seem so very different at this distance. Faith, Aquinas taught, is "to think with assent," where that which one thinks about one knows to be true.[23] It was important to Aquinas that faith be connected to action, that it not be *merely* assent. He therefore understood it as a *habit*, which allowed him to connect intellect and will in the act of faith. This means that faith has for its object both things that are *true* and things that are *good*.

Although one *knows* the true and *wills* the good, faith is nonetheless a unity since God is at once the Truth and the Good. Aquinas certainly did not believe one could earn salvation by one's faith. God's assistance is altogether necessary: "When a man gives his assent to the things of faith, he is raised above his own nature, and this is possible only through a supernatural principle which moves him from within."[24]

Luther did not attempt to split will and intellect in the matter of faith. Instead, he stressed the fact that righteousness can in no way be something we are *doing*—even with God's assistance. "He is not righteous who does much," Luther argued in a famous disputation at Heidelberg, following his first public break with official Christendom, "but he who without work, believes much in Christ."[25] For Luther belief, or faith, is not an act, much less a habit, in the Thomistic sense. It is the bare recognition that righteousness must be given, or imputed, and cannot therefore be our own. Luther refers to it as an *"alien righteousness, that is, the righteousness of another instilled from without."*[26] He was accused by the contemporary defenders of traditional Christianity of leaving good works altogether out of faith, but he went to some lengths to show this was not the case. "We are not made righteous by doing righteous deeds," he argued in the "Disputation against Scholastic Philosophy" (1517), "but when we are made righteous we effect righteous deeds."[27]

Luther's desire to protect the omnipotence of God in the matter of faith is clearly consistent with the prevailing views of all major Christian thinkers. He took his thought to extremes, however and made it appear outrageous to the partisans of medieval Christianity, although those extremes are nothing more than the consistent working out of Pauline thought. Luther held strictly to the view that since Christ died our death for us, taking the punishment due us, the righteousness Christ imputes to us is not a justification of our present life, but the establishment of a new life—Christ's. "Through faith in Christ, therefore, Christ's righteousness becomes ours; rather he himself becomes ours . . . he who trusts in Christ exists in Christ; he is one with Christ, having the same righteousness as he."[28] This identification with Christ now means that we live the life of Christ in the world: "Just as he himself did all things for us, not seeking his own good but ours only— and in this he was most obedient to God the Father—so he desires that we also should set the same example for our neighbors." This is a most radical reversal of our usual mode of life. Commenting on the passage from Paul quoted above, concerning the act of Christ, though he was in the form of God, to give up his divinity, Luther says, "Paul's meaning is that when each person has forgotten himself and emptied himself of

God's gifts, he should conduct himself as if his neighbor's weakness, sin, and foolishness were his very own."[29]

The fact that we now live the life of Christ in the world means that we have begun *to live a new history in the context of the old.* According to the old we are condemned to death. According to the new we are brought back into life, although it is still a *vita extranea,* a life outside our own. Since God did not change the old world—did not make our present bodies immortal, our present lives righteous—our new life is *invisible* to those still living in the old. In the Heidelberg disputation Luther states as a thesis that only that person is a Christian theologian "who comprehends the visible and manifest things of God seen through suffering and the cross."[30] To all others what is seen as God is not God; evil and good are confused. They do not understand that God is a hidden God, *deus absconditus,* visible only to the "alien" eyes of fath: "This is clear: He who does not know Christ does not know God hidden in suffering. Therefore he prefers works to suffering, glory to the cross, strength to weakness, wisdom to folly, and, in general, good to evil."[31]

Like Paul, Luther in no way wants to deny the absoluteness of natural mortality. We shall most certainly die—all that we are will perish. Our personal history will come to a definitive end. But, while it is a natural end, it is *also* an end established by God—and thus is no evil in itself. Also like Paul, Luther views suffering, weakness, and death as the elements of human existence that do not separate us from God but bring us into his presence due to his exceeding goodness through which he shared in our condition. In other words, *we already live at the end of the present history.* We are not waiting for the final scene; we are living in it now, *through faith.* The present history has not only lost its force, it is essentially over.

Since only those who are righteous by faith know that history has ended—that we are all dead regardless of the number of lines we have yet to recite in the theater of this world—the faithful live a new history in the context of the old. The new history is not an *escape* from the old; it is a way of *showing* the old that it is dead. *The history of the faithful is an antihistorical history.*

For Luther and Paul, and indeed most all Christians, the resurrection is an event that did truly occur in time, but an event that changed the nature of all time. It made worldly time theatrical—not fictional, not unreal, not evil, merely provisional. It is a time that will be set aside like so much costumes and scenery. Christians call the new time the

Life Eternal, or the Resurrection Life. It is a life off the stage, that we live while even on the stage, though quite invisible to the other players.

Neither Paul nor Luther have much to say about the nature of the Resurrection Life after the curtain has fallen on all worldly time. They seem to have Jesus' attitude of leaving the dead to bury the dead. But this is not true of all Christian thinkers. Augustine, though he accepted the Platonic theory of immortality without the slightest hesitation, gave considerable space to speculation on the nature of the *bodies* with which we are resurrected—a question Plato could only have considered irrelevant, if not silly. It was important to Augustine that the Resurrection Life be both bodily and perfect. The righteous will be restored to their most comely possible appearance. Unseemly blemishes and deformities will be corrected. Fetuses will be mature, monsters made normal, each having some "recognizable likeness to their former self." However, the thin will not be raised thin, nor the obese in their former obesity.[32] Such bodies "shall need neither any fruit to preserve them from dying of disease or the wasting decay of old age, nor any other physical nourishment to allay the cravings of hunger or of thirst."[33] Calvin, like Augustine and most other orthodox Christians, wanted it clearly understood that there would be a *continuity of substance* from this life to the Resurrection Life. "Since God has all elements ready at his bidding, no difficulty will hinder his commanding earth, waters, and fire to restore what they seem to have consumed."[34]

This is not an attempt to revive the Egyptian theory of physical continuity. For Egyptians death is a nonevent; one continues through it. For Christians death is real, but life is lived in two places and in two ways at once. We are in essence the same persons in both, and inasmuch as we are the persons who are only with this body and this particular history, there must be some kind of physical continuity— even if reconstituted—and some kind of historical continuity—even if it means living in two histories at once.

We observed in the previous chapter that the deep commitment in Judaism to keeping history open was eroded by the rise of messianism, along with the belief in immortality. Periodic movements or the appearance of messianic personalities caused a sudden lack of concern for the facts of present history among Jews. It is clear that this has happened in Christianity with an attitude toward history we have characterized as theatrical. We also found that messianism flared in those times of catastrophe when the Jews were under severe persecution. Christians also associate the messianic role of Jesus with catastrophe, but they have escalated its scope, seeing it not as historical misfortune but the end of history itself. But since the end has already been scripted by the Author of the whole, those who know the plot have internalized the catastrophe. They are constantly living at the end. The world is real but dead. Life has been restored but it is invisible to worldly audiences.

For Christians, then, death is a historical and natural reality, and there is nothing in history or nature that can save us from it. Only the Author of both can save us. Our salvation is *in* history, but since our Author transcends it, we are not saved *for* history, but *against* it.

Notes

1. *City of God*, p. 424.
2. *Institutes*, I,xv, 8.
3. Ibid., II, i, 8.
4. *Summa Theologica*, I, Q. 23, Art. 7.
5. Ibid., I, Q. 23, Art. 3.
6. Ibid., I, Q. 85, Art. 5.
7. *Institutes*, I, xv, 4.
8. *City of God*, p. 421.
9. *Church Dogmatics*, III.2, p. 437.
10. *Systematic Theology*, I, p. 188.
11. Ibid., II, p. 67.
12. Ibid., II, 68.
13. *Church Dogmatics*, III.3, p. 230.
14. Ibid., p. 230.
15. Ibid., p. 232.
16. Ibid., II.2, p. 590.
17. Ibid., III.3, p. 236.
18. Ibid., III.2, p. 348.
19. *Summa Theologica*, I. Q. 2, Art. 22.
20. *Church Dogmatics*, II. 2, p. 92.
21. *Summa Theologica*, I. Q. 2, Art. 22.
22. *Institutes*, III, xxv, 10.
23. *Summa Theologica*, 22ae, Q. 2, Art. 1.
24. Ibid., 22ae, Q. 6, Art.1
25. "Heidelberg Disputation," #25, *Luther's Works*, Vol. 55.
26. "Two Kinds of Righteousness," *Luther's Works*, Vol. 31, p. 297.
27. # 40, *Library of Christian Classics*, Vol. XVI, p. 269.
28. "Two Kinds of Righteousness," p. 298.
29. Ibid., p. 300.
30. # 20, *Luther's Works*, Vol. 31, p. 52.
31. # 21, Ibid., p. 53.

32. *Enchiridion*, xxiii, 89f., *Library of Christian Classics*, Vol. VII.
33. Ibid., xiii, 22.
34. *Institutes*, III, xxv, 8.

Bibliography

Augustine, "Enchiridion," *Augustine: Confessions and Enchiridion*, tr. and ed., Albert C. Outler, *Library of Christian Classics*, Vol. VII (Philadelphia: 1955).

Rudolf Bultmann, *Theology of the New Testament* (New York: 1951).

John Calvin, *Institutes of the Christian Religion, Library of Christan Classics*, Vols. XX, XXI, ed. John T. McNeill, tr. Ford Lewis Battles (Philadelphia: 1960).

Hans Conzelmann, *An Outline of the Theology of the New Testament* (London: 1969).

————*Jesus* (Philadelphia: 1973).

Reginald Fuller, *The Foundation of New Testament Christology* (New York: 1965).

————*Formation of the Resurrection Narratives* (New York: 1971).

Friedrich Gogarten, *Christ the Crisis* (Richmond: 1970).

Justin, The Martyr, "The First Apology," *Library of Christian Classics*, tr. and ed., Cyril Richardson, Vol. I (Philadelphia: 1953).

John Knox, *The Death of Christ* (Nashville: 1958).

————*Jesus: Lord and Christ* (New York: 1958).

Martin Luther, "Disputation Against Scholastic Theology," *Library of Christian Classics*, Vol. XVI, tr. and ed. James Atkinson (Philadelphia: 1962).

————"Heidelberg Disputation," *Luther's Works*, Vol. 31, tr. Harold J. Grimm (Philadelphia: 1957).

————"Two Kinds of Righteousness," *Luther's Works*, Vol. 31, tr. Lowell J. Satre (Philadelphia: 1957).

Willi Marxsen, *The Resurrection of Jesus of Nazareth* (Philadelphia: 1970).

Origen, "Exhortation to Martyrdom," *Library of Christian Classics*, Vol. II, tr. and ed., J. E. L. Oulton, Henry Chadwick (Philadelphia: 1954).

Jaroslav Pelikan, *The Shape of Death* (Nashville: 1970).

Norman Perrin, *The New Testament: An Introduction* (New York: 1974).

Paul Tillich, *Systematic Theology* (Chicago: 1967).

John Calvin, *Institutes of the Christian Religion, Library of Christan Classics*, Vols. XX, XXI, ed. John T. McNeill, tr. Ford Lewis Battles (Philadelphia: 1960).

EIGHT
DEATH AS THRESHOLD
—*VISION*

---

9 JUNG AND
ANALYTICAL PSYCHOLOGY

In his autobiography, dictated to an associate when he was in his eighties, Jung makes the notable statement, "All my work is about the interplay of the 'here' and the 'hereafter.' "[1] This disclosure is striking to anyone who has read a good deal of Jung's work if only because the theme of death, and more particularly the theme of life after death, or the "hereafter," is so rarely addressed in this wide-ranging body of literature. Indeed, there is marked absence of reflection on mortality. In one respect, it could be thought that Jung was bored by the subject; in another, one might suppose that, in sharp contrast to Freud, the great Swiss analyst had somehow come to terms with his own death. As we shall see, the phenomenon of death is central to everything Jung wrote, giving credibility to the suggestion that he had found a way of making the fact of death integral to his own self-understanding—integral enough that it does not repeatedly appear in his writing as a matter of intellectual confusion or personal anguish.

There is something still more puzzling in this autobiographical statement. The use of the terms "here" and "hereafter" seem to refer to the ordinary belief in immortality, or the continuation of the individual into a life or existence following the present one. However, Jung did not hesitate to explain to inquirers that "I could not say I believe in [personal survival after death], since I have not the gift of belief. I only can say whether I know something or not."[2] He prided himself on being an "empiricist," regularly denying that he was a philosopher, much

254

less a believer. The question of surviving death could not be resolved by an appeal to experience, as the empirical method would require, and therefore cannot be resolved at all, short of exercising what he curiously called "the gift of belief."

To make the matter even more confusing, there are a number of instances where phenomena that point toward personal postmortem existence, or at least disembodied existence, are accepted as hard fact. In his autobiography he reports that

> When I began working with the unconscious, I found myself much involved with the figures of Salome and Elijah. Then they receded, but after two years they reappeared. To my enormous astonishment, they were completely unchanged; they spoke and acted as if nothing had happened in the meanwhile.

Jung goes on to explain that important things had been happening in his life at this time. Since in the two years of their absence Elijah and Salome were out of contact with Jung's conscious existence, they had to be brought up to date on the "latest."[3] Is this the discourse of an empiricist, a nonbeliever, a careful scientist reporting plain facts? Or has Jung made use of a kind of empiricism broader in scope than that of the traditional scientist who admits as relevant data only careful measurements of publicly observable phenomena?

After receiving a letter from a German pastor who reported a long conversation with his brother at the very time his brother was dying in Africa, hundreds of miles away, Jung replied by strongly encouraging the pastor to believe that the conversation had in fact occurred, and that such phenomena are not unusual. They are not to be dismissed as phantasms of the imagination. He justifies this view by noting that the psyche is not bound to space and time. We might even consider space relative to the psyche. Spatial distance could be said to be "physically contractive." "It is probable," he adds, "that only what we call consciousness is contained in space and time, and that the rest of the psyche, the unconscious, exists in a state of relative spacelessness and timelessness."[4]

We find other examples of Jung's apparent inconsistency on the issue of death, and particularly life after death, in letters of condolence he wrote late in his life. "The dead are not to be pitied," he wrote the widow of a close friend, "they have so infinitely much more before them than we do—but rather the living who are left behind, who must contemplate the fleetingness of existence and suffer parting, sorrow, and loneliness in time." He would prefer to offer his compassion to the living who

> in the darkness of the world, hemmed in by a narrow horizon and the blindness of ignorance, must follow the river of their days, fulfilling life's task, only to see their whole existence, which once was the present brimming over with power and vitality, crumbling bit by bit and crashing into the abyss.[5]

Whose voice does Jung take in remarks such as these? Is it still that of the critical empiricist, or is it that of an old man who has temporally put aside his objectivity to comfort a friend or indulge in a fantasy? Jung would have most certainly taken offense at the suggestion that he had suspended his scientific temperament in these instances. How then was it possible for him simultaneously to proclaim his empiricism and to assert that *all his work* is about the relation of the here to the hereafter?

On one occasion Jung did address the issue of death in a formal lecture, responding to an invitation to speak on that topic. It is in this lecture that we find the clue to his thought on death and glimpse the deeper consistency lying beneath the remarks already cited. He likens the passage of life to a parabola, an arc of 180°, that is divided into four quite distinct sections. The arc begins with birth and childhood, the first quarter. The child is carried upward, toward adulthood and the zenith of the arc, by the natural flow of energy, what Jung calls "instinct." The "dynamic" advance of life is not perfectly coincidental with the rise of consciousness, for during the period of childhood consciousness lags behind physical development and does not catch up until early adulthood. Then, at the beginning of the second quarter, a person begins to focus on the zenith and now strives upward, driven not by the physical energy of instinct, but by "psychic energy." At midlife the zenith is met and passed; the arc turns downward, and "in the secret hour of life's midday the parobola is reversed, death is born. The second half of life does not signify ascent, unfolding, increase, exuberance, but death, since the end is its goal."[6]

When the descent begins, when "death is born," there is very often a crisis in one's life that arises from the unwillingness to accept the geometry of the curve. It is common that old age is resisted in the desire to continue the path ever upward toward a grander zenith. But the path of physical energy is clear; it had a teleology from the beginning; what started with birth must end with death: "Waxing and waning make one curve."[7] However ardently one struggles against the descent it cannot be checked. The fourth stage is finally reached, a stage resembling the first: the person is childlike, no longer in conflict with instinct: "Willy-nilly, the aging person prepares himself for death."[8]

Jung observes that we encourage the young to prepare for the zenith, and, "of course, with the zenith one has obviously reached something." The goals of adulthood are largely attainable; one knows where the zenith is and when it has been reached. But can we prepare for death? Do we know what it is? Do we know "what is attained with death?" With this question the empiricist steps directly before us, assuring us that we are mistaken if we expect him

> suddenly to pull a belief out of my pocket and invite my reader to do what nobody can, that is, believe something. I must confess that I myself could never do it either. Therefore, I shall certainly not assert now that one must believe death to be a second birth leading to a survival beyond the grave.[9]

Now, a curious move occurs in Jung's argument. He says nothing about his own view of death as the physical goal of life, but turns instead to what he calls the *consensus gentium,* or the universal agreement among cultures and religions on the issue of death. The great consensus of these traditions is that life "actually has no significance except as a preparation for the ultimate goal of death. In both the greatest living religions, Christianity and Buddhism, the meaning of existence is consummated in its end."[10] Jung makes no effort to defend the truth of this consensus, but rather vigorously commends its "psychological" significance. That is, Jung regards the great religions not as the receptacles of hard-won empirical truths, but as manifestations of the psyche.

Suddenly Jung is not talking about death, but about the psyche. When he says that the religions see fulfillment in death, it is equivalent to saying that the psyche sees in the experience of death its own completion, the goal of its journey. This, of course, is a death that does not coincide with the death of the body. It is not indifferent to the death of the body, for it is the psyche that recognizes that "death is born" with the descent from the zenith of life's curve. "Dying, therefore, has its onset long before actual death."[11]

Are we then to assume from this that the psyche dies at a different time or in a different way from the body? In this essay Jung makes the same point concerning the timelessness and spacelessness of the psyche we noted above. Being timeless, it obviously cannot therefore reach an end in time as the body must. And yet, we are to suppose from this same essay that psychic death is exceedingly important to the meaning of life. "From the middle of life onward," Jung wrote, "only he remains vitally alive who is ready to *die with life*."[12]

This is a puzzling remark, for how can one speak of the death of that which is timeless? Moreover, that which is truly timeless in the way in which Jung means it here cannot be said to be existing in an unending linear history, but must exist in a mode that is altogether outside of time. Therefore, it makes little sense to talk of the "hereafter" as though it were a place where our personal history continues. What does Jung mean by *death* in this case?

As stated above, he makes very few references to death throughout the long course of his writing. These references are, as we have seen, extremely suggestive, even if they remain unclear. It has been left to the best of Jung's students—particularly Erich Neumann, Joseph Campbell, Edgar Herzog, and James Hillman—to draw out the full significance of the experience of death that is implicit in Jung's thought.

It should be emphasized in this context that what interests Jung, as well as his most distinguished students, is not the *theory*, but the *experience*, of death. "*Death and existence* may exclude each other in rational philosophy," writes James Hillman, former director of the Jung Institute in Zurich, "but they *are not psychologically contrary*. Death can be experienced as a state of being, an existential condition."[13] In his book on suicide Hillman actually takes the daring position that suicide is to be understood as the psyche's bid for fulfillment: "The impulse to death may not be conceived as an anti-life movement; it may be a demand for an encounter with absolute reality, *a demand for a fuller life through the death experience*."[14]

So far, then, we have a description of the human body following its predictable course from birth to death. Somehow connected to, or contained in, the body is the psyche, which is both nontemporal and nonspatial. We know that the death of the body is important to the psyche, and that the psyche can reach a "fuller life" only through its own experience of death, only through "dying with life." But how did the psyche get there to begin with? Jung never really answers this question, for it is far too speculative for his empiricist temperament. He does have much to say about the way the psyche is *related* to the body and how it can *experience* death, as we discover through inquiring more deeply into his analysis of the psyche as such.

Any reader not familiar with the basic structure and terminology of Jung's thought is certain to be dismayed by the array of words and concepts he uses to discuss personal existence. In addition to *psyche*, perhaps the most frequent term, one is likely to find in any single work of Jung or the Jungians such (usually undefined) terms as *anima, soul, unconscious, ego, consciousness, persona, self, spirit,* and *collective unconscious*. In spite of this apparent confusion, Jung is reasonably clear on what these terms mean and, with occasional moments of carelessness, manages to keep them distinct from one another. We need not discuss all of them here,[15] but it is necessary to make clear Jung's understanding of the psyche, the ego, and the relation of consciousness to unconsciousness. Later in this chapter we shall examine his notion of the self and the rather obscure references to the spirit, since they show quite clearly how Jung can be distinguished from other thinkers who have also viewed death as presenting discontinuity in the form of a *threshold*.

The term *psyche* refers to all those elements of personal existence that have the possibility of becoming conscious. Psyche quite obviously therefore includes both the conscious and the unconscious. We shall look first at the realm of consciousness because, in any case, this is where we stand. Of what does consciousness consist? Jung is quite willing to admit that he is puzzled by the phenomenon: "The nature of consciousness is a riddle whose solution I do not know." While it cannot be explained, it is certainly possible to describe it. It is evident that "anything psychic will take on the quality of consciousness if it comes into association with the ego. If there is no such association, it remains unconscious." This is an observation that can be made on the basis of a common experience: "Forgetfulness shows how often and how easily contents lose their connection with the ego." Jung is intentionally making use of metaphor here and thus is discussing a mental process as though it were no different from the physiological phenomenon of eyesight: "We could therefore compare consciousness to the beam of a searchlight. Only those objects upon which the cone of light falls enter the field of perception. An object that happens to lie in the darkness has not ceased to exist, it is merely not seen."[16]

If we pursue this metaphor we will note that, in addition to the beam of the searchlight, there is that which the light illumines and that which makes use of, or directs, the searchlight. What is it that holds the searchlight? It is the ego. And what does the ego see by way of the light? Images. Let us first look at the nature of the ego.

Jung has three ways of picturing the ego in its relation to the illumined images: it is the "*centrum* of my field of consciousness,"[17] or the *subject* to which all images are objects, or it is itself a *complex* of images. In some cases, Jung runs all three of these notions together, apparently assuming that there is no difference between them. Can we make a coherent concept of the ego out of them? We can if we recall the metaphor of the searchlight.

A searchlight has a directed beam that extends outward from a single point. That single point constitutes the center of the sphere of perceptible objects. To have a center means to have a single perspective, an exclusive point of view shared with no other center. Furthermore, it means to have one's own consciousness, or view of things, which is quite distinct from any other. I do not deny that you have a center to your consciousness, but it is certain that it is somewhere else than mine. You might be conscious of the same objects as I, but your consciousness of them is utterly different. What you can see with your searchlight I might be able to see with mine, but from where I am standing everything looks rather different to me.

Moreover, having a center means having a structure. If I could see from all perspectives at once, I might be able to see how the chair was arranged in relation to the table and the door, but I would not know where I was in relation to them. Being centered, or having an ego, means to Jung that I am able to see a structure and at the same time to see where I am in that structure.

To refer to the ego as the *subject* has a slightly different sense. It is a way of acknowledging a fundamental division between that which sees and that which is seen. What the ego sees is not simply a structure of things that somehow exist separately in themselves. The ego sees only those things that are objects to itself as *subject*. The ego sees only that aspect of a thing that is in relation to the viewing subject. Jung is quite prepared to accept the consequences of this argument, namely, that there is no way the ego can go beyond the limits of consciousness to see what it is on which consciousness rests, or from what it has arisen. So far as the psyche is concerned (and here we are speaking strictly of the conscious psyche, although the same point can be made of the unconscious), there is no "outside," no Archimedean point. Jung says, "only the psyche can observe the psyche."[18] But it is also true that the psyche can see only the psyche.

Now we must ask how it is possible for Jung to regard the ego as a *complex* as well as a centrum and a subject. There is a problem here because a complex implies a manifold object, something composed of parts and therefore without the singularity that is implied by the concepts of centrum and subject. It appears that Jung comes to the notion of *complex* at this point out of a difficulty that follows from his view that only the psyche can observe the psyche or, more pointedly, that the ego can be conscious only of those objects already in consciousness. There is a damaging circularity here. It makes no sense so say that we are conscious of those things of which we are conscious, and yet how could it be otherwise if the ego cannot step outside the circle of consciousness? Jung sees this dilemma himself. He formulates it by saying that consciousness "seems to be the necessary precondition for the ego. Yet without the ego, consciousness is unthinkable."[19] He proposes the notion of the complex as a resolution of this dilemma.

He suggests that we consider the ego not as something transcending consciousness but as a kind of "reflection" of the many processes that make it up. The use of the word *reflection* here seems to have the force of keeping the ego distinct from the processes themselves; that is, the ego is not to be considered a process of consciousness. When we look at the nature of those processes what we see is that "their diversity does indeed form a unity," for in their relation to each other there is "a sort of gravitational force drawing the various parts together." "For this reason," Jung concludes, "I do not speak simply of *the* ego, but of an *ego-complex*, on the proven assumption that the ego, having a fluctuating composition, is changeable and therefore cannot be simply *the* ego."[20] In other words, the ego is not a free-floating entity, self-identical, with only accidental relations to the objects of its sight.

What Jung has attempted to do through the three-way definition of the ego is to connect it with the objects of its sight and simultaneously to maintain its own unique structure and separateness from other egos. We noted earlier that the psyche is nontemporal and nonspatial. This would seem to make it impossible to speak of *this* psyche or *that*, since such references would at least suppose *location* in space and time. Earlier in our discussion of Hinduism we examined the Upanishadic analysis of the perceiving self in which seeing and knowing were actually the function of the Atman, the infinite and all-inclusive self: "Atman is all." For Hindus the individual self is only an illusion one should endeavor to be rid of. Jung is strongly attracted to Hindu thought, frequently citinb agreement with Upanishadic teachings, but on this point he holds back. The ego is not illusory for Jung. It is not the whole psyche either, but for all the distress it causes the psyche, neither Jung nor the Jungians will abandon it like the Upanishadic rishis.

What may be said then about the objects that are illumined by the ego's "cone of light?" Jung's usual term for the object of the ego's sight is "image." It is a word he seems to have chosen quite carefully. The ego sees nothing but images; consciousness has no content except images. Accordingly, we cannot see *things*; we cannot look at something without seeing it as an image. Even the most rudimentary sensory experiences such as "the activities of seeing, hearing, etc., create images of themselves which, when related to the ego, produce a consciousness of the activity in question."[21] This brings Jung to the formulation: "We live immediately only in the world of images."[22]

This point closely resembles the one made above concerning the absence of an "outside" for the psyche; it differs only in Jung's introduction of the term "image." The choice of this term strongly influences the way in which basic mental processes are regarded. If Jung had spoken of "neural reaction," or "electrical impulse," or even of "sense impression," we might have been led to think of the mind as little more than the *locus* for these activities. The *mind* would have been essentially identical to the *brain*. But when the basic content of the mind is image we are led to regard the activity of the mind as *imagination*. The ego, or conscious psyche, is for Jung enormously inventive, alive, and, most important of all, possessed of its own source of nearly inexhaustible energy or *libido*. Jung takes libido to be the self-initiating "intentionality" of the psyche, and not the purely sexual instinct of Freud. It is a highly variable energy source "able to communicate itself to any field of activity whatsoever, be it power, hunger, hatred, sexuality, or religion, without ever being itself a specific instinct."[23] It is the *spontaneity* of the psyche, a mysterious spring of vitality that flows at its own impulse, that seems deeply to have impressed Jung.

There is a second consequence that is inherent in the choice of the word "image" to describe that which the searchlight of the ego has illumined. An image is essentially a reflection, a likeness. When we "see" an image we are not seeing an object that is momentarily veiled by an illusion or an obscurity; we are seeing an object as though it were something else, as though it were a reflection that has another and hidden source. Here something has been added to the searchlight metaphor. What is being illumined is not a darkened space of hitherto unseen objects; what the ego sees in the bright light of its dynamic intentionality is a great palace of mirrors in which images of unknown origin are cast from one reflecting surface to another.

Before we can discover where it is that these images originate, we must take note of another feature of the ego's reflective consciousness. Jung often refers to the psyche as an *opus contra naturam*, a work against nature, an antinatural creation. He considers instinct to be the steady, irresistible push of natural energy—a source of energy quite distinct from and, indeed, opposed to psychic energy. "Instinct is nature and seeks to perpetuate nature," he says. "It is just man's turning away from instinct—his opposing himself to instinct—that creates consciousness. . . . As long as we are still submerged in nature we are unconscious, and we live in the security of instinct which knows no problems.''[24] To be unconscious, then, is to be swept along in the dark currents of instinctual compulsion; to be conscious is to rise above that current and to resist its terrible force. This resistance will eventually fail, as Jung indicates in his metaphor of the parabola of life. However powerfully the psyche struggles against the blind force of nature, the body will in time be carried down the descending arc to death and dissolution. But for an extraordinary season of light and vision consciousness knows itself to be free from natural necessity. This means that every act of imagination, every use of an image, is a kind of struggle, a conflict with dark powers, a defiant repulsion of the natural instinct. Therefore, the vast screen onto which the illumined images of ego-consciousness have been reflected is nothing less than the opaque wall of nature's hostile and deadly power. Every act of the imagination is an attempt to keep the walls from closing in on the ego's palace of mirrors.

Here we have Jung's basic conception of freedom. *Freedom is the ability to keep the imagination alive in the face of instinct.* What is noteworthy in this conception is that what instinct threatens is not the death of the body, but the death of the imagination. Earlier we asked about the relation of the psyche to the body. Its timeless and nonspatial character seemed to make its location in a time-bound organism unnecessary, if not illogical. Here we find that the psyche's presence in the body is at least *contrary* to its nature, which is defined by Jung as an *opus contra naturam*. However, what the psyche is opposed to is not the body as such, but the natural instincts that hold the body in their certain grip.

Grief, in these terms, is not over the threatened loss of the body, but over the threatened loss of the imagination. Indeed, grief can be understood as existing in the mode of a natural body that is in perfect agreement with its natural surroundings. The psyche adjusts all its resources to follow precisely the parabolic path of life's rise and fall, with no attempt on the part of the psyche to flee upward and away. It is revealing that Jung, who very rarely takes space in his writings to attack opposing views, releases an emotional fusillade against Friedrich Nietzsche for his high celebration of instinct over the imagination. Jung obviously not only felt that Nietzsche was wrong, but that such a view is dangerously encouraging to the psyche to give up its struggle and to throw away its freedom.[25]

Natural instinct is powerful. It is an agent of death that cannot be compromised. The psyche must clearly see that in its struggle it is not going to change the geometry of the arc of physical life to the merest degree. The psyche's freedom does not consist in its ability to lengthen physical existence. The psyche must see that it can only "die with life" and that its freedom consists in taking that mortality into a higher continuity.

What are the psyche's resources that enable it to embrace its bodily death in a more inclusive life? Jung's famous answer is that the psyche must turn to its *memory*, but memory of a special sort. We asked, Where did these images come from that are reflected in the ego's palace of mirrors? *We remember them.* Jung finds that when we observe small children in the process of becoming conscious what we see is that "when the child recognizes someone or something—when he 'knows' a person or a thing—then we feel that the child has consciousness." The operative term here is *recognition.* We cannot re-cognize something we have not already cognized. "We speak of 'knowing' something when we succeed in linking a new perception *to an already existing context*, in such a way that we hold in consciousness not only the perception but parts of this context as well."[26] Consciousness is, then, a matter of making connections between things separated by time. It is, in fact, a way of denying the passage of time altogether, for when we re-cognize something we are acknowledging that which has recurred, that which has never ceased to be regardless of the passage of time. Consciousness then opposes instinct by opposing time. Its palace of mirrors is not a doomed ephemera that will presently be carried away in the flood; it is a place absolutely secure against the entrance of temporal necessity in the form of natural instinct.

Now we have a new difficulty. If it is the phenomenon of memory that shows us the atemporality of the unconscious psyche, where, we must ask, do the contents of that memory come from? If what the ego "sees" with its searchlight are the images reflected out of the past by the memory—or, to state it more forcefully, if what the ego sees is the past in the mode of an eternal present—what gives rise to this apparently limitless sea of images that *presents* itself to the conscious psyche? This question carries us into a consideration of Jung's theory of the unconscious, certainly the most original and powerful aspect of his thought.

We began this discussion of Jung's thought by noting several paradoxes: although he had written little about death, he said at the end of his long career that everything he had written is about the interplay between the "here" and the "hereafter." While the hereafter seems to suggest the continuation of a separable soul, Jung stoutly denies any belief in such a theory. He clearly indicates that the body, in which the psyche is enclosed, will die. The psyche, however, is timeless and would seem therefore to be immortal. But the psyche must "experience" death before it will reach its fulfillment. In an effort to make sense of these apparent inconsistencies and obscurities we have looked into the structure of the psyche, beginning with the ego, or the region of the psyche's consciousness. The ego is quite real, and not illusory as in Hinduism, but the objects of its sight are images, not things. Images point beyond themselves. When we ask where, we find they point backward in time. To know what they are images *of* we consult the memory. The memory is in truth a timeless region in which all things exist simultaneously, though to the ego they seem to be distant in time.

Jung also understands the psyche as a whole to be an *opus contra naturam*, that is, in a basic struggle with natural instinct. It cannot succeed in this struggle at the temporal, physical level. That is, the psyche cannot lengthen our bodily life. It can, however, call on the timeless reservoir of images by way of memory. It is only by that strategy that the psyche can die with life as an act of its own life, that is, take natural death into a higher continuity. What we shall discover is that the psyche's journey into the memory is not a flight from death, it is an entrance into its own inmost existence. The fact that the psyche *originates* in the unconscious was the most outrageous of Jung's thought to the Freudians, and the point at which the two schools of thought are most distant from each other.

Why did Jung think that the images of ego-consciousness came from the unconscious? This, too, he insists, came from empirical observation and not from mere guesswork. At the simplest level of consciousness he finds mysterious elements that point beyond the boundaries of consciousness. "We are so deeply impressed," he reports, "with the truth of our imprisonments in, and limitation by, the psyche that we are ready to admit the existence in it even of things we do *not* know: we call them 'the unconscious.' "[26] What kind of unknown things does Jung mean? In general, there are two categories of phenomena that seem to have the kind of obscurity that points beyond them to the existence of the unconscious: one category is associated with what Jung refers to as the "shadow" aspect of the psyche, the other with his well-known concept of the "archetype." We shall look first at the psyche's shadow.

We noted previously that the ego's "imaging" had the character of struggle or conflict with the relentless force of natural instinct. But how is the ego to identify these opposing powers, particularly if all that the psyche can observe is the psyche itself? Clearly, in order to contend with these powers they must be given images; they must be *personified* and therewith assumed to have their own vital center quite as the psyche has its center in the ego. Once this is done the ego can then assemble its own images, taking itself to be the fair young knight in mortal combat with the subterranean dragon, or the soldier of righteousness always prepared to locate and destroy any lurking agents of an evil enemy.*

Jung introduces the metaphor of the shadow to this action of the ego to show that the images which the ego sees in opposition to itself are nonetheless its own projections. Thus, it happens that the psyche divides against itself, for the true conflict is not between the ego and a hostile world, but between the ego and its unconscious. Therefore, the ego is at every moment both what it thinks it is and the "shadow," or opposite of its images for itself. If the ego is a knight, it is also the dragon the knight attempts to slay, and in this sense the dragon is the "unknown thing" within the "prison walls" of consciousness.

Jung discovered the existence of the shadow from years of experience with his patients and also discovered how powerfully the ego is trapped by the projections of its shadow self onto the world. Since these projections are unconscious, the ego has no way of knowing that they are projections at all; they seem to be firm elements of the world itself. As Jung puts it, "*one encounters projections, one does not make them. The effect of a projection is to isolate the subject from his environment, since instead of a real relation to it there is now only an illusory one. Projections change the world into the replica of one's unknown face.*"[28]

The most significant example of the projection of the shadow onto the world is found in Jung's discussion of the *anima* and the *animus*. Anima is the Latin word for soul and is of the feminine gender. Jung observed that any person, male or female, who projected strong qualities of femininity onto others while seeing oneself in distinctly male images was being unconsciously possessed by the anima or feminine soul. Jung is quite obviously suggesting, through the pairing of the anima and the animus, that each person is, psychically speaking, *both male and female to an equal degree*. Of course, each person is always both one's conscious self and one's unconscious shadow to an equal degree.

The shadow, then, is not only unconscious, it is severely limiting to

---

*This common Jungian metaphor should not be understood to harbor a male bias. Jung regarded the psyche as a whole to be androgynous, but in both men and women the conscious ego appears in dreams and the imagination as an aggressive male hero searching for its own hidden female half.

the ego; it constricts the space in which the ego can freely move—only because the ego is unaware that it is restricting itself. It follows from this that the ego's freedom enlarges only as it takes its shadows into its consciousness, only as it directs the searchlight of its understanding onto the world and finds it composed of its own projected images. As we shall see presently, it is the conscious reconciliation of these opposites within the psyche that occurs in the experience of death.

But there is another and far mor insuperable limit set against the ego by the unconscious—in the form of the archetypes. Jung discovered the existence of the archetypes through his work with patients' dreams. For years it had been his practice to encourage them to elaborate on the images in the dreams "in any number of ways, dramatic, dialectic, visual, acoustic, or in the form of dancing, painting, drawing, or modeling."[29] As he looked back over the results of this work he found there were

> certain well defined themes and formal elements which repeated themselves in identical or analogous form with the most varied individuals. I mention as the most salient characteristics, chaotic multiplicity and order; duality; the opposition of light and dark, upper and lower, right and left; the union of opposites in a third, the quaternity (square, cross), rotation (circle, sphere), and finally the centering process and a radial arrangement that usually followed some quaternary system.[30]

It will be noticed at once that these are not images, but a variety of ways in which images can be organized. An archetype, therefore, cannot be viewed directly any more than one can see the light apart from that which it illumines.

The exceedingly broad range of his reading, and the inclusiveness of his interests, brought the existence of archetypes to his attention in another way. He noticed the recurrence in ancient literature and sacred or mythological texts of what Jacob Burckhardt called "primordial images." Jung considered it a "truly amazing phenomenon that certain motifs from myths and legends repeat themselves the world over in identical forms."[31] In fact, the archetypal patterns in this literature duplicate precisely what he had discovered in the dreams of his patients. He felt compelled by this, not only to argue that the unconscious had a certain universal shape, but to take the next step into the assertion that *there is one unconscious universally shared by all individual psyches.* He refers to this as the *collective,* or *impersonal, unconscious.*

Jung leaves open the question of the metaphysical status of the collective unconscious (that is, ascertaining the nature of its contents, or determining how it can be present in diverse psyches and unified in itself), but he does say a great deal about the effect it has on the conscious ego. He observes, for example, that "To the extent that the archetypes intervene in the shaping of conscious contents by regulating, modifying, and motivating them, they act like the instincts."[32] They have the same all-or-nothing character, and the same incorrigibility, as the instincts. They are therefore experienced by the ego in a manner similar to the instincts: they are powerful and they threaten the ego with diminishment; they rise before the ego like gods of uncertain benevolence. Indeed, in the primitive mind they are personified as gods.

On the other hand, the archetypes are quite different from those aspects of the unconscious that belong to the psyche's shadow. It is not simply the mirror world of the conscious ego, neither is it the repository for all those items repressed or forgotten. (Jung uses the term "impersonal" unconscious to distinguish it from those psychic elements that are related to the ego's own experience.) The evidence plainly shows "that the unconscious also contains components that have not yet reached the threshold of consciousness."[33] The fact that the archetypes are to be found throughout the ancient religious and mythical traditions—as well as in the dreams of contemporary patients—shows that they are not only timeless, but also innate. Not only is it obvious that they do not originate from one's own personal experience, it is also apparent that they are the shaping elements of that experience. They precede experience in every case.

This might seem a strange position for an empiricist, particularly when it has been a firm part of the empiricists' approach to human nature since the time of Aristotle to insist that the mind at birth is a blank page, a *tabula rasa*, on which experience leaves its cumulative record. Jung can say flatly that "in everything the psyche is preformed."[34] The newborn infant "is not an empty vessel into which, under favorable conditions, practically anything can be poured. On the contrary, it is a tremendously complicated, sharply defined individual entity which appears indeterminate to us only because we cannot see it directly."[35]

Just how the archetypes got into the mind prior to its birth cannot be known precisely. Occasionally Jung assumes that they are the "deposits of the constantly repeated experiences of mankind,[36] almost as though there is a single mind in which we all participate and on which all psychic events leave an indelible mark. We receive the archetypes, therefore, by heredity.[37] For this reason, the "true history of the mind is not preserved in learned volumes but in the living mental organism of everyone."[38]

One consequence of this view, of great importance to Jung and the Jungians, is that collective unconsciousness, while it is often experienced by the conscious ego as a threatening limitation, actually brings to the boundary of the ego a possibility for experience and knowledge far more profound than one could acquire in a single conscious lifetime. "Looked at in this way, the unconscious appears as a field of experience of unlimited extent."[39] The unconscious with its vast store of archetypes is "anything but an incapsulated personal system; it is sheer objectivity, as wide as the world and open to all the world."[40] What the ego perceives as a threat is nothing more than the beckoning infinitude of the archetypal unconscious offering an adventure into the region of the unknown and the unimaginable. It is an invitation to endless growth and to discovery—which is in every case self-discovery.

We should take note briefly of the relationship of the archetypes to the images. Jung does not spell this out explicitly anywhere in his writings, but from what has been said about the nature of them we can see how they are connected. As we noted, an archetype cannot be seen; we cannot look straight at it as we do an image; it always constitutes the form, and not the content, of that which the ego's searchlight illumines. In fact, if it were not for mythologists and analysts we would not know of the archetypes at all, for it is not possible, from Jung's account, to detect them in ourselves. However, we should not conclude from this that there is a fixed quality to the archetypes, as if one could describe them and set them down in a catalogue. Jung steadfastly refuses to do this. There are certain archetypes to which reference is frequently made, such as mother, hero, quaternity, divinity, father, and anima. But as Jung and his students approach each of these and others we find that it is characteristic of the archetypes constantly to be shifting their appearance. It is as though whenever we reach out to grasp its pure form it presents us only with an image, while the form recedes. The archetype of the daughter will, when one looks directly at its form, yield to the archetype of the female lover, then perhaps the wife, and behind the wife we see the archetype of the mother emerging, and behind the mother . . . perhaps the bottomless unconscious itself.

We might put all this another way. We observed previously that the images are in fact reflections, but we left unresolved *that which they reflect*. Certainly, they could not have been simply reflections of each other, any more than a mirror can be a reflection of another mirror. Indeed, each image is a reflection of that which lies out of the line of the ego's conscious sight. Now when the ego discovers this reflection of the unconscious and turns the light of its waking attention on it, what is seen is then a reflection of something still deeper, something of which the ego is again unaware. I would suggest that what Jung means by archetype is not a protoimage, or a primordial pattern that maintains its static form, but rather *a sequence of yielding images that carries the visioning ego ever deeper into the unconscious.* It is not a reproducible form that we could re-cognize as we do an image, but the royal way of access to the limitless sea of the collective unknown and, therefore, also into ever-renewing self-discovery. To "see" an archetype then, whether in oneself or in another, is not to have identified a familiar form, but to have proceeded on the journey that leads into one's own hidden self. In a strict sense, we never see the archetype of *another*; for all archetypes emerge from the *collective* unconscious and therefore are ours as well. It is in this sense that Jung and the Jungians are quite insistent that the participation of the analyst in the healing of the patient is not that of a mere observer, for the analyst cannot confront the archetypal unconscious of the patient without confronting his or her own.[41]

The metaphor of the searchlight now takes on an alluring emendation. As we light up the objects before us, they appear as images; images are reflections and, when we realize that, we turn with the illumining focus of our conscious ego to discover what it is they reflect. If we then discover how it is that one image is the reflection of another that is itself a reflection, and if we then proceed down that lengthening corridor of self-exploration, we find what seems to be an endless sequence of reflected light. The palace of mirrors is nothing but the central hall of a vast network of dazzling passages. Now something else happens. We find that the light of consciousness, the directed beam of the ego's attention, is no longer the only source of illumination. It seems to be coming in from all sides. It is as though we are no longer set off by our private view of things but share in the collective wisdom of the ages. We no longer see objects in the light of our personal experience: we no longer illumine, but are illumined; we no longer look, but are seen; we no longer are the subjects of our actions, but the objects of an eternal movement.

This continuing expansion of the consciousness, this deepening of the vision into one's unconscious psyche, is a great deal more than a therapeutic strategy or an entertaining flight of imagination. It is the very destiny of human existence to create more and more consciousness. In his autobiography Jung refers to the advance of the conscious into the unconscious as the primary task of being human. Elsewhere he regards the synthesis of the conscious and the unconscious as the climax of psychic effort.[42] Although there are always risks to the ego along this road—the ego can at any point be overwhelmed and carried away by the unconscious, resulting in great danger both to oneself and to others—Jung believes it is possible to maintain what he calls a relationship of "critical understanding."[43]

Critical understanding presupposes a fully conscious awareness of the point at which the ego meets the nonego, but now with deepening consciousness it also entails the recognition that the nonego is not something foreign and hostile. In fact, the ego finds that the nonego is within the boundaries of the psyche and does not stand in opposition to the ego but is complementary to it.[44] It is when we are able to see our relationship to our own unconscious with critical understanding that we first become aware of our *self*. Self is quite distinct from ego, and, psychically speaking, enormously superior to it. It is to the entire psyche what the ego is to the conscious psyche alone; it is the absolute center of our psychic existence, it is the point of unity around which all else rotates.

We observed above that as the ego journeys outward into the unconscious there is a strange transformation in the nature of the light. No longer does it come from the single source of the focusing ego; instead, it now seems that the ego is illumined by a source deep within itself. It is the self that is this deeper source of light. The self is the sun around which the ego revolves.[45]

> The ego stands to the self as the moved to the mover, or as object to subject, because the determining factors which radiate out from the self surround the ego on all sides and are therefore superordinate to it. The self like the unconscious is an a priori existent out of which the ego evolves. It is an unconscious prefiguration of the ego. It is not I who create myself, rather I happen to myself.[46]

If the self is an unconscious prefiguration of the ego, there is the suggestion that the ego moves steadily closer to the self as it enlarges the region of its vision. While that is the case, it is also true that the ego and the self will never become identical, for to do so would mean that the ego has penetrated the entire universe of the unconscious, and this, Jung believes, is impossible in any single lifetime.[47] Although the ego will never become identical with the self, and will never have a direct view of the self, it can nonetheless exist in an open and receptive relationship to the self by acknowledging that the boundary of ego and nonego is precisely that point at which the self is exerting its influence on the conscious ego. Therefore, the mode of existence appropriate to the ego's true nature is one of highly imaginative and continuing self-discovery and creativity. Anyone who looks to that boundary as the source of revelation, or the point of departure for astounding new adventures, will find the ego transformed by the self. Anyone who ceases regarding the boundary of the ego as a point of conflict, as a meeting place of hostile power, and who therefore no longer sees the ego as the center of control will find that boundary transformed into a horizon. Horizons mark the end of the field of vision; they exist because we cannot see everything. But a horizon is infinitely extensive; as we elevate our perspective the horizon recedes and our vision enlarges. Our field of vision will always have its horizon, Jung is telling us, but there is no time in our lives when we cannot elevate our sight.

Where does death belong in this account?

In the preceding discussion we introduced the notion of the transformation of the ego by the self. It is in the phenomenon of *transformation* that we encounter most directly the manner in which the Jungians deal with the issue of death. If we turn back for a moment to Jung's use of the metaphor of the parabola, we recall that the geometry of the line carried us from organic birth to organic death and that there was absolutely no resisting the force of this movement. The psyche however did not always coincide with the arc in its movement. At first it dragged, then it rose beyond, then it held back on the descent. When the psyche first takes note of the downward movement of the organism it reacts with fear. What is the origin of this fear?

In his book *Psyche and Death* Edgar Herzog speculates on the cultural origin of the fear of death, which he assumes to be analogous with the psychic origin. Death is a disturbing phenomenon to the child or the primitive because it is a transformation of a person into something hidden. The person disappears. The earliest understanding of this, judging from mythology, is that death is a deed committed by an alien force; death begins with murder. It is an act by which something present is taken away and hidden. Herzog gives considerable emphasis to the "hiding" function of the agent of death. Among the most prevalent symbols of death are the dog, the serpent, and the bird. Dogs, like Cerberus the fearsome guard of Tartarus, the Greek underworld, are possessed of powerful jaws. They tear at flesh and crush bones. Elusive coyotes and wolves are often taken to be the messengers or the symbols of death. Serpents have very different but powerful symbolic qualities. They live in the earth and appear and disappear with great suddenness. Moreover, they regularly shed their skin, suggesting immortality or eternal youth. Birds also appear and vanish quickly, ascending abruptly into the empty air like souls departing the body of the recently dead. The soul is therefore often pictured as a bird or winged creature, such as the Ba-bird in Egyptian mythology, or as an immortal being, such as an angel or cherub. But birds can also kill with both stealth and savagery; thus birds of prey are frequently taken as totemic symbols by warfaring or militaristic groups.

All of these symbolic representations of death have the quality of devouring or taking away, both acts of hiding. Significantly when we combine all the characteristics of these animals into a single beast we have a *dragon*. Dragons appear with striking similarity in a number of cultures that have had no contact with one another—an indication of their symbolic power. Dragons are serpentine, scaly beasts with bone-crushing jaws and wings. Their great psychic importance is shown in the fact that they are thought to have great wisdom, are usually feminine in gender, stand guard fiercely over an inexhaustible treasure or a young virginal woman, and feed on themselves. What these facts tell any Jungian is that the dragon, combining the characteristics of dogs, snakes, and birds, is nothing but the limitless wisdom of one's own unconscious that is complete in itself. The treasure and the virgin represent an endless wealth of knowledge and experience. As Neumann emphasized, virginity has nothing to do with sexual purity, but is an indication of openness to the divine. It is a state of readiness that awaits the entrance of the power of the unconscious into the conscious.

We should not overlook the fact that dragons are not only terrifying, *they invite conflict*. Whenever the hero hears of a dragon he prepares himself for battle; whenever he learns of a treasure or a captive maiden he should immediately suspect the presence of a guarding dragon. What the hero desires, in other words, he can have only by dreadful conflict. What is it that the hero desires, and why must it be fought for? At the most obvious level what the hero fears is the loss of life, but why must he fight the dragon for his life? Jung does not omit the detail that the dragon is female, as a rule, and feeds on herself, for these are the characteristics of the self-inclusive unconscious. However, he explicitly reminds the reader that fear of life is not fear of the mother— on the contrary, the maternal symbol here is itself a reference back to instinct. It is instinct, the blind directionality of his physical nature, that the hero fears. As we noted earlier the psyche for Jung is always an *opus contra naturam*; it must oppose nature simply to exist. The hero's struggle with the dragon is nothing less than the ego's attempt to free itself from instinct, to oppose the powerful forces of nature in the hope of releasing the vast treasure of an inexhaustible imagination.

I have examined these symbols briefly to indicate that the fear of death that arises from the "hidden" feature of the recently dead is in fact not a fear of being taken off somewhere else, but a fear of one's own unconscious. What one fears is not the death of the body before external forces, but the death of the ego from internal forces; that is, the reclamation of the *ego* by the *self*. To be sure, death first appears as the death of *another,* and as such a *physical* occurrence. Indeed, in mythology death usually enters into human culture in the form of murder, quite as the first death in Hebrew mythology is the murder of Abel by his brother Cain. But this only shows the hiddenness of the unconscious and not the hiddenness of the dead.

However, this is a misunderstanding of no small importance. As Jung puts it, the confusion of organic with psychic death causes one to identify death with the increasing demise of the physical body. There then arises a longing for earlier stages of life, for the abundant health and energy of youth. The fear of death causes one to look back "for something that used to be on the outside," and to ignore that which is within—and timeless.[48] This confusion, and its resolution, is nowhere more vividly portrayed than in the story of Gilgamesh, one of the world's oldest narratives. After the death of his friend Enkidu, Gilgamesh first perceives his own mortality and sets off on a long adventure in search of the secret of immortality. The narrative tells of extraordinary encounters with supernatural beings—clear evidence to the Jungian interpreter that Gilgamesh is struggling against his unconscious. When a serpent steals the herb of eternal youth (not immortality) from Gilgamesh, given to him earlier in the adventure, the snake sheds its skin as it disappears into a pond; only then can Gilgamesh accept his mortality and return to the full daylight of the conscious world.

When Jung discusses the hero's (the ego's) acceptance of physical mortality and the consequent acceptance of the wisdom of the hidden psyche, he uses the term *sacrifice.* Sacrifice seems to Jung the proper term here not only because we are concerned with the destruction of the ego, but also because there is a deeper question as to whom the ego belongs. Sacrifice always has the peculiar character of giving up something that is one's own, with which one can in fact identify, and simultaneously giving up that which belongs to the gods. The ego is sacrificed because it is *mine,* and yet, the gods—or the unconscious—to whom the ego is offered are themselves the very source of that ego.[49] It is important that the sacrifice be voluntary. The gods do not take the sacrifice before it is offered; the unconscious does not take the unaware ego back into itself. It is a choice, an act of self-understanding. *The ego can die only in an act of freedom.*

The conscious sacrifice of the ego to the unconscious, or more accurately to the *self,* which constitutes the *centrum* of the unconscious, is precisely the experience of death that Jung has declared necessary to the psyche's fulfillment. It is the way the psyche can take the death of the body into itself and move in into a higher continuity. We have entitled this view of death as *threshold*. The true discontinuity threatened by death is in the form of an elevation to a higher mode of existence, which the ego at first strongly resists. The ego first perceives natural instinct as an enemy to be opposed. It therefore engages in a conflict with instinct in the only way it can—through images of it. The misunderstanding here is in the ego's belief that the *image* of natural instinct *is* natural instinct and not something the ego itself has invented. It becomes divided against itself, struggling not with instinct but with its own projected shadow, with the result that the true path of its freedom—the imagination—is closed off altogether. This is why what instinct threatens is not death as such, but a death of the imagination.

When the ego (the hero) encounters the projected dragon (the unconscious), it must see that it is not the defeat of the dragon that will overcome death, but the defeat of the hero-image by a deeper self-understanding. The conflict is won only when the ego sees that it is both sides of the conflict. Doing so the ego moves closer to the self and more consciously acknowledges its own nonspatiality and nontemporality.

Jung speaks of this self-enlargement of the ego as "transformation." What is meant is not a transformation of being, but a *transformation of energy* that now flows out of the unconscious into the conscious. The result of this is a great burst of imagination in the conscious ego. In none of the Jungian literature is this view of death more fully expressed than in the work of James Hillman.

Accepting as pivotal Jung's distinction between organic and psychic death, Hillman insists that the understanding of death as an organic, or natural, event is nothing more than "a fantasy of the ego," and he refers to the ego as that "great literalist, concretizer, realist."[50] Taking his primary cues for the proper understanding of death from Greek mythology, Hillman distinguishes between death as a natural, or *underground*, event and death as a psychic, or *underworld*, event. The difference between underground and underworld is decisive. The Greeks understood the earth quite as we do—as the tangible ground, the very soil beneath our feet. It is true that the body will return to the soil. It is not true, however, that the psyche will go with it, for the psyche has a synchronous existence in the underworld, the region over which the dark-faced Hades presides. To say that the psyche has a synchronous underworld existence is not to say that it will *eventually* go there—*it is already there*. The psyche exists simultaneously in the "upperworld" of the conscious mind and the chthonic underworld of the unconscious.

Hades, the Lord of Tartarus, is the brother of Zeus, the reigning deity of the upperworld. The underworld is a complete counterpart to the upperworld; its darkness indicates that it is the shadow side and that the "shades" who exist there are but the shadows of the egos who dwell in the light. How do we know this? Through the imagination, and particularly through that most vivid source of imagination: dreams. Hillman vigorously assaults the notion that the fantasy world of dreams is *unreal* and the rational world of the ego is *real*. This is another trick of the ego. To catch the ego in this trick we must teach it how to release the imagination—the means by which we can "see" into the shadow world below. "If our therapeutic job is to walk the ego back over the bridge of dreams, to teach the ego how to dream, we must reverse our usual procedure and translate the ego into dream-language rather than the dream into ego-language. This means doing a dreamwork on the ego, making a metaphor of it, seeing through its reality."[51] Here is Jung's argument that the ego is the creation of the psyche, the view that so distressed the Freudians who understood the unconscious strictly in terms of that which the ego has repressed into it.

As Hillman shows, the translation of the ego into dream-language means an abandonment of one's self-understanding as a hero.

> Through dream-work we shift perspective from the heroic basis of consciousness to the poetic basis of consciousness, realizing that *every reality of whatever sort is first of all a fantasy-image of the psyche*. . . . Thus, *we work on dreams not to strengthen the ego but to make psychic reality, to make souls by coagulating the imagination.*[52]

The shift from the heroic to the poetic means that the ego no longer rules over the unconscious by reason as though in a monotheism, but is ruled by the unconscious through the imagination as in a polytheism.

Hillman summons us to "a polytheistic consciousness, whether that of Greek religion or of archetypal psychology." Emphasizing the parallel between Jungian, or archetypal, psychology and the Greek world view, he observes that "while we begin always with an ego, the Greeks always began with the Gods."[53] This has a startling consequence. Since the archetypes (gods) exist quite independently of our egos, it follows that the origin of our psyche is not personal but impersonal. The human task, as the Greeks understood it, was to draw the soul

> closer to the Gods, who are not human but to whose inhumanity the soul is inherently and priorly related. To neglect or forget

these powers—to believe one's life was one's own, or that one's feelings were personal, or that personal relationships alone could provide community or substitute relations with Gods—meant loss of humanity. The human was unthinkable without its inhuman background. To be cut off from personified archetypal reality meant a soul cut off.[54]

Here we have it then: Death is the sacrifice of the ego to the unconscious; it is the recognition that the ego belongs to the lower world of the shades. The transformation that comes with this sacrifice releases enormous quantities of psychic energy that visits consciousness in the form of imagination—but an imagination of such poetic power that we recognize it to be the creator, and not the creation, of the soul. To die is to return to the impersonal, and immortal, origins of the psyche. But to die is not an antilife movement, as Hillman put it, but "a demand for a fuller life through the death experience."[55]

We have characterized Jung's view of death under the metaphor of threshold. We can now see how the metaphor applies to the full scope of his thought. The threshold in this case marks the point of separation between the conscious and the unconscious. To cross the threshold from life to death is to cross from the "upperworld" of the conscious mind into the underworld of the hidden psyche. Is this, properly speaking, death? There is no doubt for the Jungians that there is a true death of the ego in this transformation. Indeed, unless the ego is sacrificed in the full freedom of conscious recognition of the emerging but still hidden unconscious, there will be neither death nor life. Of course, the body will vanish into the earth leaving no trace whatsoever. But this is an event that is utterly indifferent to the psyche—insofar as the psyche has fought with the dragon of its instincts and has opened itself to the poetic presence of the gods.

One aspect of death that is shared by all "threshold thinkers" is that the soul does not simply continue, it *ascends*. Death marks the point at which the soul moves to higher orders of being. This ascent is not, of course, the simple elevation of the selfsame ego. It is the growth or expansion of the ego toward ever-increasing inclusiveness. We noted above the fact that an archetype is not itself the object of sight but instead a sequence of yielding images that carries the seeing ego even deeper into the unconscious. There is an infinitude that opens before the psyche's expansion, something endlessly opening. It is now plain why Jung could not assent to a simple theory of the immortality of the soul, and yet why he could, at the same time, speak of the psyche's amazing powers of defying even the spatial and temporal powers of death.

As we shall see, Jung also shares with other threshold thinkers the priority of *vision* as a mode of existing. Once death has been understood as a threshold to a higher level, it is always the case that the method of crossing the threshold is that of sight. *Whoever sees the higher level already exists there.* For Jung, to see is everything. This is the real force of his prominent use of "image" in his thought. An image *always* presupposes the existence of a beholder. It is also significant that Hillman should call his major book, an effort to go beyond what we have called Freudian mysticism, *Revisioning Psychology.* All of life is to be given to the task of extending the field of vision, even though it must proceed through those media others find so obscure or unrealiable—dreams and the imagination.

Earlier, we stressed the difference between Jung and Upanishadic Hinduism that is apparent in Jung's refusal to take the ego as an illusion. This difference might now seem to be diminished, if not eliminated, by the infinite expansiveness of the ego. In truth, Jung—and the Jungians—maintain a sharp difference with Hinduism, both in the content of their thought and in temperament. This is memorably illustrated by a vision Jung had during a critical illness that he thought (mistakenly) would be his last. This vision must have made a deep impression on Jung, for he gives it prominence in his autobiography and refers to it at length in several of his letters. Writing to Dr. Kristine Mann in 1945 he refers to the experience as "a glimpse behind the veil." In his dream he found the only difficulty was to get rid of the body, but when you can "give up the crazy will to live and when you seemingly fall into a bottomless mist, then the *real* life begins with everything you were meant to be and never reached. It is something ineffably grand. I was free, completely free and whole, as I never felt before." In the vision he found himself rising above the earth, about 15,000 kilometers above the southern tip of India. He suddenly had the feeling he was about to reach "full knowledge." He saw at a distance a great black stone that proved to be a temple. Seated in the temple was an Indian wise man, a personification of the wisdom of the East. He describes this moment as a

> silent invisible festival permeated by an incomparable, indescribable feeling of bliss, such as I never could have imagined as being within reach of human experience. Death is the hardest thing from the outside and as long as we are outside it. But once inside you taste of such completeness and peace and fulfillment that you don't want to return.[56]

Presently a messenger arrived and announced that his time had not yet come, and that he must return to earth, which he did with great reluctance.

Jungians must always return to the earth. No matter how perfect the bliss that lies beyond one's earthly death, the messenger comes, representing the ego's reluctance to drop the searchlight of its vision. Although Hillman writes enthusiastically of the polytheism of the psyche and the death of the literalist ego, it is still the case that the archetypes (gods) that rise in the soul are archetypes *for someone;* that even though the soul is "coagulated imagination," *it is someone's imagination.* The soul, the imagination, the archetypes, and all the other phenomena of the psyche do not occur disconnected in a boundless chaos—they all occur to someone. Hillman's psyche may be a polytheism, but it is not a pantheism. The Olympian divinities are, after all, performers; their lives are not pure essences, but dramatic plots, and their heavenly dwelling is not the clear light of the All, but a colorfully illumined theater. The Greek gods exist to be acknowledged *by* the seeing self, not to *become* that self.

What none of the Jungians will abandon here is the notion of a *centered* being. If there is going to be a vision, there must always be someone who sees; the vision will not consist simply of unseen light. We should not forget that for Jung the discovery of the unconscious came primarily with the discovery of the self—which is the *center* of the unconscious, quite as the ego is the center of the conscious psyche. Earlier we examined the powerful metaphor of the searchlight. However, what we did not observe is what is always missing in Jung's use of this metaphor—but what is always implied—the existence of someone *who can see the images* which the light exposes. We found that the light came from the deeper levels of the psyche, perhaps from the psyche itself. Still, there must be someone holding the light, or beholding the images. It is not simply reflected light without a center. Jung steadfastly refused to give up what he called "critical understanding."

The Jungians know that to let go of individuality is to fall into an uncentered and unseen universe of infinitely reflected images. But who is the unnamed, undesignated, unseen viewer holding the light and comprehending the images? The Jungians are clear that it is not the ego. Who, then, or what, is it? Can it be the self? But finally even the self is seen as a projection, an archetype.

We are dealing here not with a minor omission, but with a far-reaching difficulty in thinking through the issue of death. There are essentially two directions in which one can go from this point. One can either identify and name the center of the vision, or one can move into the deeper and boundless region of the spirit, unafraid of losing the boundaries of individual existence. The former option is taken by the existentialists whom we discuss later in this study. The latter position is taken by a most remarkable assemblage of thinkers whom we examine next.

Notes

1. *Memories, Dreams, and Reflections*, p. 299.
2. Letter of 12 October, 1956, *Collected Works*, Vol. II, p. 333.
3. *Memories, Dreams, and Reflections*, p. 306.
4. *The Letters of C. G. Jung*, Vol. I, p. 256.
5. 22 December, 1950, *The Letters of C. G. Jung*, Vol. I, pp. 568 ff.
6. "The Soul and Death," in Feifel, ed., *The Meaning of Death*, p. 6.
7. Ibid., p. 6.
8. Ibid., p. 10.
9. Ibid., p. 7.
10. Ibid., p. 8.
11. Ibid., p. 10.
12. Ibid., p. 6.
13. *Suicide and the Soul*, p. 60.
14. Ibid., p. 63.
15. A useful guide to the definitions and function of these terms in Jung's thought may be found in Jolande Jacobi's *The Psychology of C. G. Jung*.
16. "Spirit and Life," *Collected Works*, Vol. VIII, p. 323.
17. *Basic Writings*, p. 246.
18. "Phenomenology of the Spirit in Fairy Tales," *Psyche and Symbol*, p. 61.
19. "Spirit and Life," p. 323.
20. Ibid., pp. 323 ff.
21. Ibid., p. 325.
22. Ibid., p. 328.
23. *Collected Works*, Vol. V, p. 137.
24. "Stages of Life," Ibid., p. 388.
25. "On the Nature of the Psyche," *Basic Writings*, p. 40.
26. Ibid., p. 39. My italics.
27. "Psychological Commentary on 'The Tibetan Book of the Great Liberation,'" *Collected Works*, Vol. IX, p. 479.
28. "Aion," *Psyche and Symbol*, p. 8.
29. "On the Nature of the Psyche," *Basic Writings*, p. 72.
30. Ibid., p. 73.
31. *Two Essays on Analytic Psychology*, p. 75.
32. "On the Nature of the Psyche," *Basic Writings*, p. 75.
33. *Two Essays on Analytic Psychology*, p. 137.

34. "Psychological Aspects of the Mother Archetype," *Basic Writings*, p. 332.
35. Ibid., p. 330.
36. *Two Essays on Analytic Psychology*, p. 79.
37. *Psychology of Religion*, p. 64.
38. Ibid., p. 41.
39. *Two Essays on Analytical Psychology*, p. 194.
40. "Archetypes of the Collective Unconscious," *Basic Writings*, pp. 305 ff.
41. See Hillman's discussion of this issue in *Suicide and the Soul*, Part Two.
42. "On the Nature of the Psyche," p. 81.
43. *Two Essays on Analytical Psychology*, pp. 173 ff.
44. Ibid., pp. 186 ff.
45. Ibid., pp. 250 ff.
46. "Transformation Symbolism in the Mass," *Psyche and Symbol*, p. 209.
47. "Aion," p. 22.
48. *Symbols of Transformation, Collected Works*, Vol. V, p. 404.
49. *Psyche and Symbol*, pp. 206 ff.
50. "Dreams and the Underworld," p. 278.
51. Ibid., p. 285.
52. Ibid., p. 304.
53. *Revisioning Psychology*, p. 192.
54. Ibid., p. 193.
55. *Suicide and the Soul*, p. 63.
56. *The Letters of C. G. Jung*, Vol. I, pp. 157 ff.

Bibliography

Herman Feifel, ed., *The Meaning of Death* (New York: 1959).

Edgar Herzog, *Psyche and Death*, tr. David Cox (New York: 1967).

James Hillman, "The Dream and the Underworld," *Eranos Jahrbuch 1973* (Leiden: 1974).

———*Re-visioning Psychology* (New York: 1975).

———*Suicide and the Soul* (New York: 1964).

Jolande Jacobi, *The Psychology of C. G. Jung* (New Haven: 1973).

C. G. Jung, *Answer to Job*, tr. R. F. C. Hull (New York: 1970).

———*The Archetypes and the Collective Unconscious, Collected Works*, Vol. IX, Part One, tr. R. F. C. Hull (Princeton: 1968).

———*The Basic Writings of C. G. Jung*, ed., Violet S. de Laszlo (New York: 1959).

———*C. G. Jung Letters*, ed. Gerhardt Adler and Aniela Jaffe, tr. R. F. C. Hull (Princeton: 1973).

———*Memories, Dreams, and Reflections*, trs. Richard and Clara Winston (New York: 1963).

————*Psyche and Symbol*, ed. Violet S. de Laszlo (New York: 1958).

————*Psychology and Religion* (New Haven: 1938).

————*Structure and Dynamic of the Psyche, Collected Works, Vol. VIII*, tr. R. F. C. Hull (Princeton: 1969).

————*Symbols of Transformation, Collected Works, Vol. V*, tr. R. F. C. Hull (Princeton: 1967).

————*Two Essays on Analytic Psychology*, tr. R. F. C. Hull (New York: 1969).

Erich Neumann, *The Origins and History of Consciousness*, tr. R. F. C. Hull (New York: 1964).

10 NEOPLATONISM AND HERMETIC PHILOSOPHY

In 1460 a monk returned to the city of Florence from Macedonia whither he had been sent by Cosimo de' Medici to collect manuscripts. Among his purchases was a large book, written in Greek, that was to have an enormous impact on the Renaissance and subsequent intellectual history, and may even be considered a significant influence in the development of modern science. The book, later to be known as the *Corpus Hermeticum*, was widely believed to have been written by the legendary Hermes Trismegistus, a figure of immense wisdom who was to have lived in a time prior to Moses.

Cosimo, the quintessential Renaissance ruler, adept at the use of power and astute in intellectual matters as well, considered the book a great treasure and ordered it translated into Latin at once. This task fell upon Marsilio Ficino, the brilliant young scholar and philosopher, who had recently been assigned by Cosimo to translate all the works of Plato. Ficino was instructed to set the Plato aside and take up the *Corpus Hermeticum* without delay. The labor was completed several months before Cosimo's death. The text of the manuscript was of great solace to the old ruler who had it read to him at his bedside.

The *Corpus Hermeticum* served a remarkable role in the fifteenth and sixteenth centuries. To an intellectual world already in eager pursuit of the sources of all fields of knowledge and in hope of finding the unifying principle that held it all together, the book was received with great enthusiasm. Indeed, sixteen separate editions were to appear before the end of the century. What gave the book its rare authority was not only its presumed antiquity; it was also regarded as a compendium of all the intellectual and religious traditions that were to develop in the two millenia that lay between Moses and the Medicis. It was seen therefore as the very origin of traditions as divergent as Judaism, Christianity, Islam, and Platonism, and the clue to reconciling their differences.

Our interest here is not with the text of the *Corpus Hermeticum* itself but with the philosophical insights it engendered in the diverse but brilliant Renaissance figures who fell under its influence. As history amply shows, the *Corpus Hermeticum* failed to lay the ground for a common religion as it was expected to do, or to expose the unifying principles by which all philosophical disputes might be resolved. It did, however, gather into a single focus a broad spectrum of intellectual schools and spiritual practices that, subsequently, emerged with a unique and compelling conception of the place of death in human nature. As we shall see presently, the Hermetic tradition offers a view of the self that does not stop at the psychic line over which Jung refused to step. It is especially telling that Jung turned repeatedly to aspects of the Hermetic tradition—particularly alchemy, astrology, and parapsychology in general—and heavily mined it for data supporting his own theories, but failed to see that at the very center of that body of thought is a vision of the boundlessness of the self, or what the Hermetics called variously the mind, the spirit, or the intellect. We should, however, not take Jung's restraint lightly. There is an appropriate sense of danger, a deserved alarm, one should have while approaching this region. The uncanniness that attaches to occult phenomena is but a superficial reflection of a greater danger: a loss of self altogether, not to the malevolent agency of the demonic but to the deeper powers of one's own soul. A study of the concept of death in the Hermetic tradition will give us a direct perception of these threatened dangers, but also of the ecstasies its adepts report.

We shall largely ignore the text of the *Corpus Hermeticum* itself for several reasons. In 1614, nearly a century and a half after Cosimo obtained his copy, a humanist scholar named Isaac Casaubon showed beyond all question that the *Corpus* could not possibly be dated before Moses. Internal and historical evidence showed that it could not have been composed before the second century C.E. Casaubon speculated that it was the fraudulent work of early Christians and had nothing to do with Egypt, its claimed place of origin. Moreover, it is of a multiple authorship as its variations in style and acute inconsistencies betray.

Just where the document originated is now impossible to say. There is some reason to think that some of its material was drawn from late

Egyptian, probably Alexandrian, sources, since Gnosticism and other esoteric practices were heavily concentrated there. But that Hermes was an ancient Egyptian, whose honorific title "Trismegistus" or "thrice-great" was earned by his supremacy as a philosopher, priest, and king, cannot be believed. His identity was acknowledged as mysterious even by his Renaissance believers, some of whom identified him with the Greek god of the same name, or with the Egyptian divinity Thoth. Ficino even speculated that, given their common Egyptian origin, Hermes and Moses could be the very same person.

What we have in the document then is not an original, primal statement of the truth, but a largely derivative and uneven collection of verities authored by mediocre and forgotten thinkers. What is of greater interest to us is the intellectual environment that led to such a high appraisal of the *Corpus*. We must take seriously the fact that thoughtful persons were looking passionately for a philosophical structure that would integrate all of thought and history into a single whole. What is apparent to us now is that this very search was itself the expression of a philosophical view that had been shaped centuries before in the work of Plato and Plotinus. Although Plotinus may have been contemporary to the composition of the *Corpus*, or may even have lived after it was completed, his distinctive interpretation of the Platonic tradition is similar to the Hermetic literature and is, of course, both more lucid and original. We shall therefore isolate the distinctive elements in Plato and Plotinus and then show how they provide the inner core of the Hermetic tradition that awakens in the Renaissance and flows into such diverse phenomena as astrology, the occult, magic, alchemy, phrenology, parapsychology, and later into Romanticism, Rosicrucianism, theosophy, and anthroposophy.

It seems necessary here to explain to the reader that the return to Plato and Plotinus is undertaken not out of a merely antiquarian impulse. There is an important reason for examining these sources. It is common among scholars to expose the naiveté, if not the ignorance or deceptiveness, of the occult arts. Alchemy is often seen as the misinformed predecessor to chemistry, astrology a superstitious distortion of objectively observable astronomical phenomena, and so on. If we look first at Plato and Plotinus we shall see that the Hermetic tradition and the occult arts are by no means premature versions of physical sciences. They arise from a view of human nature that is quite different from that which is associated with contemporary science. What they seek to achieve is nothing like what scientists seek. It is a genuinely alternative view with a very different conception of human freedom and therefore of human mortality.

We have met Plato before in these pages. We listened in on his classic dialogue, the *Phaedo*, where Socrates talked with his friends on the last day of his life, calmly explaining the reasons for believing the soul to be immortal. The Plato we now meet is very different. The document in question is the *Timaeus*, probably the best known of Plato's works during the Renaissance, but among the least studied now. The *Timaeus* was written many years after the *Phaedo*. Some years after the Socratic dialogues, Plato wrote the famed *Republic* (also a dialogue, but the Socrates that appears there seems unrelated to the very real historical personage we meet in the *Phaedo*) in which he laid out the structure of an ideal state. No doubt Plato would have been happy with Cosimo de' Medici, for he seems to have come close to what he had in mind with his philosopher king. In his own lifetime Plato was not so lucky. His attempts to find such a ruler and his labors at founding such an ideal state met with bitter frustration. It is therefore a much sobered, less hopeful philosopher we find in the author of the *Timaeus*. Still, the quest after a rational and orderly society continues to occupy his reflection, though now his concerns are much less practical than theoretical.

The *Timaeus* is Plato's attempt to show that the rational in human nature is not something that rises from one's social setting, neither is it the result of instruction. Reason in the human intelligence is identical to the reason that provides the orderliness in the universe itself. The search after rational forms of human association is identical with a study of the rational structure of the whole of being. I have introduced this point to indicate how far Plato has come from the simpler wisdom of the *Phaedo*. There it was enough for Socrates to show how the soul and the body were separable, and how, in fact, the body even holds the soul back from its purest happiness. What emerged there is an uncomplicated dualism, a kind of thinking that has had an enormous impact on subsequent theories of the soul, and therefore on conceptions of death. In the *Timaeus* no such dualism is apparent. Here Plato is not separating the soul from its material location, but showing its fundamental congruence with the sensory stuff of the universe. As a result a very different conception of death—along with a very different view of human freedom—emerges.

Timaeus, the fictional philosopher through whom Plato speaks in this essay, is giving his view of the origin of the universe and its contents—as a kind of preface to the subsequent discussion of the ideal political organization of the human community (a discussion Plato never actually wrote). He begins by making a distinction between "that which is always real and has no becoming," and "that which is always becoming and is never real.''[1] The basis of the distinction between the real and the becoming is then stated by Timaeus in a terse sentence that comes from the very center of Plato's thought and from which all strands in his philosophy can be unraveled: ''That which is apprehensible by thought with a rational account [meta logou] is the thing that is always unchangeably real; whereas that which is the object of belief together with irrational sensation is the thing that becomes and passes away.''[2]

Here, at the very beginning, Plato makes a connection between thought and being that will have a far-reaching impact on subsequent thinkers. Thought does not infer the existence of something, it directly apprehends the real. Things in a state of becoming, which are not real, affect the mind by way of sensations; but sensations are not thoughts. They pass away like objects without leaving a trace. It is the nature of thought to find the enduring patterns in the passing sensations. Whatever endures without change is the real, and, properly speaking, thought can have no object but the real, the eternal. Here Plato is very careful to have Timaeus say that that which comes into being and passes away ''is the object of *belief* together with irrational sensation.'' The mind can only presume (in its ignorance) to have knowledge of passing objects.

In this key passage we should pay special attention to what Plato is saying: the rational is not the merely logical; to be rational is to be real, to be enduring. The reasoning intelligence does not give itself to analysis or inference, but to the direct apprehension of the unchanging. To reason for Plato is to *behold*. Reasoning is a way of seeing the eternal.

Timaeus proceeds at once to the assertion of another fundamental principle of the Platonic intelligence: ''everything that becomes must of necessity do so by the agency of some cause; without a cause nothing can come to be.''[3] This seems to contradict ordinary experience, for it is usually the case that the cause is indeed a passing phenomenon that vanishes as soon as the effect has come into being. Plato does not deny this common experience, and later in the *Timaeus* he refers to it as ''secondary causation.''[4] However, he quite clearly intends by this phrase to indicate that secondary causation is merely a matter of irrational sensation and not the apprehension of true causation. Things only appear to cause each other. We know from other works of Plato that true causation can be achieved only by the real, by the unchanging. He frequently cites forms as causes, for example. But how can this be so? How can the unchanging cause change? Plato's answer to this difficult question is complicated and not altogether satisfying. It seems that temporal objects *participate* in the eternal forms. He never offers a complete explanation of what he means by "participation," largely because, for all its importance to his thought, it was never really clear to him.[5] The relationship is not one of force or influence, but one of being. Each passing object has its existence within one form or another. In the state of becoming they pass through the real. It is because of this that the reasoning mind can *see* the eternal in the midst of the passing.

Timaeus wonders about the existence of the world as a whole—for the world is certainly changing and therefore must have been brought into existence. Plato introduces a term here that has had a notorious history in subsequent interpretations of his thought. He has Timaeus suppose that the universe is being brought into existence by a "demiurge" or artificer. Jews have taken the reference to mean Jahweh; Christians have identified the demiurge as the second person of the trinity through whom the Father created; Gnostics regarded Plato's artificer as a rather imperfect divinity. In light of the preceding remarks about causation, it seems plain that Plato means by the demiurge the creative aspect of the eternal and unchanging Real. Nowhere is there a suggestion in the *Timaeus* of personal qualities in reference to the demiurge.

What we are to take particular note of here is that whatever the demiurge, or the creative Real, brings into existence, it will display what Timaeus refers to as the "likeness" of its creator. If the world's relationship to its creator is one of participation, then the eternal Real will be shining through every aspect of it. Put in another way, the rational will be everywhere visible in the passing phenomena of the universe. This way of conceiving of the relationship between *becoming* and the *real* has a startling consequence, perhaps even bizarre to the comprehension of the modern reader, but a consequence that nonetheless has a deep formative influence on later thought. If the world is created in the likeness of the demiurge, then it, like its creator, will have its own rational intelligence and its own soul. "Thus then," Timaeus concludes, "we must declare that this world came to be, by the god's providence, in very truth a living creature endowed with soul and reason."[6]

To conclude that the world is a living creature is not a momentary excess on Plato's part, but a serious and indispensable feature of his overall thought that bears several important implications for the spiritual life. To begin with, it is an abrupt rejection of the view that the universe is made up of disparate and independent parts that have only an accidental and external relation to each other—a view similar to that held by the Epicureans and by contemporary science. The universe is an organic whole, each part belonging directly to a center and therefore under firm guidance. Everything is pregnant with meaning.

A more important spiritual implication has to do with the self-sufficiency of the universe. The world's body is perfectly round and smooth on the outside. While it is both penetrated and enveloped with soul, there is nothing beyond the edges of its sphere for it is in need of nothing beyond itself: "it was designed to supply its own waste as food for itself and to act and be acted upon entirely by itself and within itself; for its constructor thought it would be better self-sufficient rather than dependent on other things." Like reason itself it turns "uniformly in the same place and within its own bounds."[7]

The spiritual significance of the self-sufficiency of the world is more evident when we consider a third implication of the doctrine that the world is a living creature. We have examined Timaeus' remark that the world body contains reason and a soul. If reason has to do with the unchanging real, and if material bodies exist in the mode of becoming, it is the office of the soul to take an intermediate position between the two extremes. It is through the soul that the changeless forms have their effect on the passing phenomena of the world. Although Plato never works the obscurities out of his doctrine of the soul, one has the strong impression that it is the source of the body's vitality; an agency that integrates the forms of the mind (nous) into the material aspect of the world.

The world soul also has an intermediate position between the divisible and the indivisible, allowing it to be both at the same time. Thus, the world soul divides itself into discrete souls that attach themselves to material bodies, while simultaneously sustaining its basic unity. Plato has an extravagant scheme for the division of the souls: he has the demiurge divide the world soul into as many separate parts as there are stars, then distribute the souls to their respective stars. From the stars they descend, incarnate, to spend a length of time among the mortal creatures of the world. Depending on their activity, there they will either return to the heavenly bodies "and there spend a happy and congenial life" or they will continue to descend into lower forms of existence—apparently as a kind of punishment for failing to live by the rule of reason.[8]

The outcome of this notion is not only that the world soul is identical in form to the demiurge, but that individual souls are themselves ingredients in the world soul. We can easily see here how far we have come from the simple proposal of personal immortality offered by Socrates in the *Phaedo* and the *Apology*, for in those earlier dialogues Plato seems content to say that Socrates' soul will survive his death and continue to exist *as Socrates*. The personal identity and distinctness of the soul are not in question. Socrates can even be imagined discoursing with the great men of the past in some invisible region of the dead. In the *Timaeus* the emphasis is not on survival but participation, not on the continuity of the personality but on the merging of the personality with a higher form of existence. It is not the permanence of the soul with which Plato is now concerned, but its intermediary status between the divisible and the indivisible, or between the becoming and the real. The soul is not the form in which we shall eternally exist, but the means by which we shall ascend from lower forms of being to pure and unchanging Reality.

We can now identify the later Plato with a different conception of death: instead of *continuation* his thinking points toward death as a *threshold*, as the point from which the soul undertakes ascent to higher and more inclusive modes of being. When death is regarded as continuation, it cannot really be death at all. The proposed continuity of life must simply deny any death as such, close out any possibility of true discontinuity. If Socrates is to continue as Socrates he must clearly deny that death has any effect on his life—or whatever it is about him that makes him Socrates. This late work of Plato's offers an altogether different conception. What causes the discontinuity of death now is the falling away of all bodily restraints, and this allows the soul to be taken up into a higher mode of existence. Death is the soul's elevation toward a more perfect participation in the all-inclusive world soul. It is a threshold in the sense that it is not merely a changed status, but an opening into a new kind of life for the soul. This new life is not really visible to the worldly intellect that is still absorbed in particulars—to such intellects death can only be discontinuous; there is no continuity in sight. What Plato's later thought proposes as a continuity we shall characterize as *vision*. To understand this vision we turn to other arguments of the *Timaeus*.

We have already seen that reasoning for Plato is very much like beholding, or seeing, the changeless. The distinctive power that belongs to the act of seeing is most evident when we consider the difference between reason and what Plato calls "necessity." Ordinarily we would take the term necessity to be congruent with reason; that is, the necessary would seem also to be the rational. Plato uses the term in just the opposite way, implying a meaning similar to what we mean by "change." The necessary is that which lies outside reason and therefore beyond control. It is that which occurs through an agency, free from the influence of mind or reason. The experience of necessity is therefore the experience of fate: being subject to events that are unaffected by our own will. Put most simply, the necessary is the irrational.

It is of course problematic that necessity could coexist with reason, particularly in view of the fact that the world is a living creature so perfectly resembling the demiurge that Plato can refer to it as "a blessed god."[9] He does not give us a metaphysical explanation for the emergence of necessity (and with it the presence of evil in the world), but he does offer a mythic account. The generation of the universe, he has Timaeus explain,

> was a mixed result of the combination of Necessity and Reason. Reason overruled Necessity by persuading her to guide the majority of those things that become towards what is best; in that way and on that principle this universe was constructed in the beginning by the victory of rational persuasion over Necessity.[10]

Although we do not learn from this account *why* there is necessity, we do learn that reason is the superior element, since it is by reason that necessity is allowed to exist at all.

The distinction is important to our understanding of Plato's conception of death—and the role vision plays in relation to death—because the mortal element in human nature (that is, the body) is compounded of necessity.[11] Death occurs by necessity; it is fundamentally irrational. But if reason is a greater power than necessity, we can only assume that death occurs because reason permits it. Does it also follow that death can be eliminated by reason? In one respect it does not follow, since the body—the irrational part of our earthly existence—has already been turned over to necessity and cannot be reclaimed. But, then, there is no need to reclaim it, for human nature is compounded of the necessary *and* the rational. Since the rational is unchanging, it is immortal; indeed, it is divine.

Our approach to death therefore is not to deny it, but first to acknowledge what is necessary and then to direct our vision to the unchanging. It is here that we feel the full force of the Platonic conviction that thought and being are intimately connected. *What reason beholds, reason is.* In the concluding passage of the *Timaeus* Plato exclaims that if a man "has set his heart upon learning and true wisdom, and has exercised that part of himself above all others, he is surely bound to think thoughts immortal and divine, if he lay hold upon truth, nor can he fail to possess immortality in the fullest measure that human nature allows."[12]

We should emphasize in conclusion that what Plato is offering here is not properly a mysticism; it is not a retreat to a universe hidden within. The vision by which our immortality is assured is directed outward at the universe where, properly informed, it can behold the profound agreement between what is one's own and what is the whole.

Following the motions of the divine mind, we can "recognize the harmonies and revolutions of the world," thereby bringing our intelligent part into the likeness of that which it beholds, achieving "the best life set by the gods before mankind both for this present time and for the time to come."[13]

The highly speculative *Timaeus*, with its curious and often obscure ventures into numerology, astronomy, and the science of the elements, may well be one of the most influential works of all antiquity; but it does not for that reason answer all the questions it raises. The originality of the work, along with the epic scope of its intentions, left to centuries of interpreters the task of clarifying Plato's meaning and reconciling his descriptions of the universe with known fact. There can be little doubt that one of the most original and subtle of those interpreters was Plotinus, who appeared in Rome as a teacher somewhere near the middle of the third century C.E. 600 years after the *Timaeus* was written.

Both Plato and Plotinus lived in turbulent eras, but Plato, at least for a large part of his life, was far more active in public affairs than Plotinus. Third-century Rome was marked by severe political and social unrest, but we would scarcely know it from the writings of Plotinus. Only indirectly, by his consistent emphasis on the higher orders of being, do we sense the philosopher's disbelief that any improvement in earthly life is possible. It is probably because Plotinus was so successful in finding a spiritual mooring in the transcendent that his thought so deeply appealed to his own age and to many subsequent ages.

Plotinus' philosophy, a great deal of it written down by his students, following his own habit of translating thoughts into highly condensed prose, presents a number of difficulties in interpretation. In several important respects, however, his clarifications and extrapolations of Platonic thought add greater force to some of its central themes. Plato left largely undiscussed the complicated relationship between the one and the many. It is clear that the human soul is a part of the world soul, for example, but in what way, if any, can it be said to be separate? The metaphysical status of the one, or unity, is also left unexplored in the dialogues; and while Plato plainly affirms several levels of being, he leaves us uninstructed on the relations between them. Each of these problems is addressed in the body of Plotinus' work.

Near the end of the *Enneads*, the single volume that constitutes the whole known corpus of Plotinus' writing, he enunciates a simple principle that we can take as a clear starting point for the development of his thought:

> All beings, both the supreme beings as well as those who are called beings on any pretext whatsoever, are beings only because of their unity. What indeed would they be without it? Deprived of their unity, they would cease to be what they are. An army cannot exist unless it is one. The same holds for a chorus or a flock. Neither a house nor a ship can exist without unity.[14]

Of course, it is impossible for unity to arise from the component parts. It is not a soldier, or a group of soldiers, that gives the army its unity. From what then does unity derive?

Plotinus answers that it is the soul that gives unity to otherwise disconnected things. Does this mean that the soul is itself the unity? The soul *has* unity, to be sure, but that is for Plotinus different from *being* unity. The soul cannot be unity for two reasons: it has its unity over other beings, that is, its singularity is distinct from other single things such as armies and choruses; and it is composed of component parts "such as discursive reason, desire, and perception—all of them faculties joined together in unity as if by a bond."[15]

What then *is* unity? Plotinus' famous answer to this question is simply "the One." When we survey his thinking on the character of the One we enter into an area that is entirely Plotinian. Although he goes to great lengths to cite the authority of Plato for all of his major doctrines, it is still the case that the One, as Plotinus discusses it, makes no appearance in the metaphysics of Plato, though it could be argued that what Plotinus has to say on this subject is not inconsistent with Platonic philosophy. What makes Plotinus distinctive here is the extreme to which he takes the notion of unity. Although subsequent religious thinkers have made attempts to identify the God of the Jews or the Christians with the Plotinian One, it can easily be shown that they have misjudged the stark exclusiveness of the doctrine as it appears in the *Enneads*.

To begin with, it cannot even be said that the One has being; "As the being of each thing consists in manifoldness, and the One cannot be manifoldness, the One must differ from being." Consider human beings, for example. They *have* unity, but what is being unified is a vast accumulation of separable entities: "There is therefore a difference between man and unity. Man is divisible while unity is indivisible."[16] To be one, to be unity itself, means to have no other. Furthermore, it means to have no internal structure, no movement, no thought or will, and no attributes whatsoever. Since the One is utterly without distinction within itself, or between itself and any other, we are brought to the surprising conclusion that the One is incapable not only of knowledge, but of self-knowledge as well. It cannot be conscious of itself.

This strong doctrine has several marked advantages. It eliminates the possibility of dualism. Although Plotinus occasionally seems to regard the body as a kind of prison from whose evil grasp the soul must seek liberation, there never is a possibility of supposing that earthly existence stands against the divine, since the One has no opposite whatsoever, else it could not be perfect unity. At the same time, the doctrine of the One rules out pantheism. The One could not be said to be identical with the totality of Being, for that would make it manifold and violate its unity.

This skillful avoidance of pantheism and dualism is a legacy Plotinus leaves for the Hermetic tradition. It allows adepts to speak of the divinity of their souls and even the divinity of nature without diminishing or limiting in the least the transcendence of the source of all that is.

But the doctrine of the One also leaves Plotinus with a difficult philosophical problem: how can the One be related to the Many without compromising itself? Plotinus' treatment of this difficulty is not strictly philosophical. It makes use of the metaphor of emanation or radiation. While the One is truly beyond all distinction, it nonetheless emanates its pure light outward, quite as the sun radiates light and heat without diminishing itself, without any regard to any other beings, and without motive. The sun does not need a motive to shine; it *is* radiance. Similarly, the One "is the power that begets the things while remaining within itself without undergoing any diminution. It does not pass into the things to which it gives birth because it is prior to them."[17] Altering the metaphor he asks us to "imagine a spring which has no further origin, which pours itself into all rivers without becoming exhausted by what it yields, and remains what it is, undisturbed."[18]

As anyone can plainly see, the sun's brilliance decreases with distance. So also with the One. At the origin of the light there is faultless unity, though as we follow the emanations outward there is increasingly less unity. The metaphor of emanation therefore permits Plotinus to establish levels of existence, one distinguished from the other by the character of its unity. Closest to the One is the level of being Plotinus calls *mind*, or intelligence (*nous*); he regards it as roughly equivalent to Plato's demiurge. Mind is indivisible, but it is also manifold, for it contains within itself all the forms and figures by which lower orders of being are shaped.

The emanation closest to mind is *soul* (*psyche*). To understand its nature we must first see that it stands in an intermediate place between mind and the lowest emanation: the material world. Its essential function, in fact, is to mediate the creative power of the mind, communicating the forms that exist in mind in a state of pure unity to the inert and shapeless matter at the nether range of being. "The soul gives the four elements (earth, air, fire, and water) their cosmic form, but it is Intelligence (or mind) that provides her with her forms, just as an artisan receives his instructions from his art as it is handed to him."[19]

When we examine Plotinus' theory of the soul more closely, we find that it seems to have its own levels of being. At the upper range there is the world soul, quite similar to Plato's in the *Timaeus*. At the lower range there are the individual souls located in physical bodies, though certainly not separate from the world soul. A problem arises here as to the relation between the individual souls and the soul in its higher unity. If we follow the metaphor of emanation, there should be an unbroken continuity of existence between the two such that each human soul is a direct participant in the world soul. Plotinus affirms this continuity, unwilling to compromise the soul's collective unity, and yet he also wants to preserve the reality of personal identities (else our ethical behavior in our earthly existence would be irrelevant to our eternal existence). He asks whether we may "suppose that the Soul is to be appropriated on the lower ranges to some individual, but to belong on the higher to that other sphere (that is, the world soul)? At this there would be a Socrates as long as Socrates' soul remained in the body; but Socrates ceases to exist precisely on attainment of the highest." This strikes Plotinus as the correct way to put the matter, but he leaves out a philosophical discussion of the problem by simply asserting (in agreement with Plato) that each soul is simultaneously identified with and distinct from the world soul: "each soul is permanently a unity [a self] and yet all are, in total, one being."[20] We should note here that with this indecisive conclusion Plotinus keeps tantalizingly open the question of personal immortality. Quite obviously, the weight of his entire philosophy favors its impossibility, but his refusal explicitly to deny it has left an ambiguity in the Platonic tradition that surfaces regularly in the Hermetic literature where there are often references, side by side, to both personal immortality and a merging with the divine whole.

In any case, we are not to lose sight of the fact that the human soul, residing in the material body, which is the lowest level of emanation from the One, has an extraordinary capacity for ecstatic communion with higher orders. Plotinus looks at the relation of the soul to the One and compares it to the relation between earthly lovers whose desire to possess the other must ever be frustrated, for the two remain separate from each other in their earthly forms. "Only in the world beyond is the real object of our love, the only one with which we can unify ourselves, which we can have part of, and which we can intimately possess without being separated by the barrier of the flesh." Here Plotinus is speaking about a union that is immediately available to the human soul; it is uncommon but possible in this life: "He who has had this experience will know what I am talking about. He will know that the soul lives another life as she advances toward the One, reaches and participates in it, and in this condition recognizes the presence of the dispenser of the true life. Then she needs nothing more." Plotinus reported to his disciples that several times in his own lifetime he has had this experience himself. Each time it was brief, but it was sufficient to give him a taste of the ecstasy that awaits each properly contemplative person; these experiences kindle the desire to abandon bondage to this lower existence and to embrace the true object of love. Reflecting on his own experience, he writes of the ecstatic union:

> Then one can see it and oneself, as far as it is permitted to see. One sees oneself shining brilliantly, filled with intelligible light. Or rather one is oneself pure light, that is, subtle and weightless. One has *become* divine, or rather one *is* part of the eternal being of the divine that is beyond becoming. In this condition one is like a flame; but if later one is weighted down again by the sense world, one is like a light that is extinguished.[21]

What we have, then in the Neoplatonic philosophy of Plotinus is a breath-taking vision of the soul's ascent along an infinite expanse of being, at each stage of which one attains a clearer comprehension of the fundamental oneness of all things. Although Plotinus thought this world incapable of improvement and sought eagerly to escape its bondage, he nonetheless regarded it as a luminous manifestation of the truly real. Unlike the Hindu's view, there is nothing illusory about this world. And certainly the classical Buddhist assertion of its nonexistence is far from the Plotinian vision. When we have become properly armed with this vision by disciplined engagement in the contemplative life, we can make our way through the limitations of life toward the ecstatic ascent that is beyond the threshold of death.

Marsilio Ficino completed his translation of the *Corpus Hermeticum* in 1463 in a villa near Florence, which Cosimo de' Medici had provided him. Its immediate and enthusiastic reception in the intellectual world of the Renaissance should really not be surprising. The interest of the

Renaissance in original sources and the fascination with exotic traditions and phenomena are well-known. What made the Corpus so especially influential was the Neoplatonic cast of its doctrines. The works of Plato and Plotinus had been the reigning philosophical texts through nearly the whole of Western intellectual history. During the fifteenth century there was a particularly vivid interest in Platonic studies. In fact, Cosimo had established an "academy" precisely to advance the study of Plato and Plotinus, some two decades before he acquired his copy of the Corpus. The Platonic Academy, not a school in the proper sense of the term, but an informal gathering of learned men, was presided over by Ficino.

Cosimo died in 1464, leaving the rule of Florence to his ailing but scholarly son Piero. During the five years remaining in Piero's life the Academy prospered handsomely. In 1469 Piero's twenty-year-old son Lorenzo (later to be called "il Magnifico") assumed the rule of the city. Like his grandfather he proved to be skilled in both government and the arts. He not only considered himself a member of the Academy, but took part enthusiastically in its proceedings. Each November 7, he presided over a ceremony at his villa in Coreggi, celebrating the traditional birthday of Plato. Lorenzo was accomplished enough in his Platonic studies to have engaged the young Pico della Mirandola, Ficino's most gifted protégé, in a debate concerning whether the One and Being are in fact the same in Plato's thought.

The generous patronage of such powerful figures and the intellectual virtuosity of its members accounts for the profound impact the Medician Platonic Academy had on the intellectual life of Europe. In many places similar academies were founded, the most successful of them in France.[22] We can well imagine, then, the force of Ficino's widely believed claim that he had in the Corpus Hermeticum uncovered an original source of human wisdom, authored in Egypt, the wisest and most ancient of civilizations.

Ficino's own extensive and masterful volumes found their way into virtually all centers of learning in Europe. Traces of Ficinian Platonism can be found in several centuries of scholarship.[23] But Ficino did not mind the great eclectic possibilities opened up by the Corpus. His student, Giovanni Pico della Mirandola, a young aristocrat whose brief life was uncommonly productive, had by the age of twenty-four already indicated the almost limitless inclusiveness of the Hermetic/Neoplatonic tradition. In that year of his life Pico had composed 900 propositions, which he offered to defend in a public disputation in Rome. The disputation never occurred, but we have the text of the theses. They are wonderfully inclusive. Obviously convinced he would

be defending a thoroughly consistent system of thought Pico had assembled material from Plato, Aristotle, Orpheus, Pythagoras, Zoroaster,
Plotinus, the Greek and Latin church fathers, the major philosophical
and theological figures of Medieval Scholasticism, the *Corpus Hermeticum,* and, most significantly, the Hebrew *Cabala.*

If anything signaled the vigorous eclecticism of the Hermetic tradition it was Pico's knowledge of Hebrew, along with his deep interest in
the Hebrew religious tradition, and even an impressive facility in
Arabic and Aramaic. Pico would not be alone in this interest, and for
good reason.[24] The Hebrew term *Cabala* originally meant "tradition."
In time it came to mean a specific tradition within Judaism, namely the
search for a way to unity with the divine. Gershom Scholem in his
Major Trends in Jewish Mysticism shows that the Cabala includes literature written over a period of nearly 2000 years. In spite of the enormous variety in that literature, its common denominator can be characterized as follows: "The consensus of Kabbalistic opinion regards the
mystical way to God as a reversal of the procession by which we have
emanated from God. To know the stages of the creative process is also
to know the stages of one's own return to the root of all existence."[25]
The similarity of this to Neoplatonic teaching, particularly in its Plotinian form, is obvious.

We might add that there were other features of the Cabala attractive
to the Hermetics. It contains both an oral and a written tradition, implying that there are matters of such subtle meaning, and teachings so
difficult to understand, that learners must be instructed in them
through intimate association with a spiritually adept master. Pico cites
the Jewish belief that when Moses received the law from God he also
received a secret interpretation of the law "under the holy seal of silence" that was to be revealed only to those high priests who were to
succeed him. The reason for the silence was simply the general wickedness of the people: "to disclose to the people the more secret mysteries, things hidden under the bark of the law and the rough covering
of words, the secrets of the highest divinity, what was that other than to
give what is holy to dogs and to cast pearls among swine?" Pico also
believed that the secret interpretation of the law was a practice observed by all the ancient philosophers. However, Pythagoras wrote
down very little. The Egyptians carved enigmas on their temples. Plato
often wrote elliptically. Even "Jesus Christ the master of life revealed
many things to his disciples which they did not want to write down,
lest they become common to the vulgar."[26] The esoteric communication of wisdom would become a prominent characteristic of the Hermetic tradition, particularly in the occult sciences such as magic and
alchemy. (The Latin term *occultus* means *hidden.*).

There is also a fascination with number mysticism in the Hebrew tradition. This was shared by the Hermetics who saw great importance in the symbolic numerology of Pythagoras. Indeed, Pythagoreanism entered prominently into the Platonic tradition through Plato's extensive use of Pythagorean principles in the *Timaeus* to explain the rational composition of the world. It was also believed by Ficino and many others that Pythagoras was a student of Orpheus, who in turn was a student of Hermes Trismegistus.

Although Pico is more expansively eclectic than his great teacher Ficino, they equally share an interest in one occult science that was to play a critical role in the Hermetic tradition: magic. In his address, "On the Dignity of Man," Pico writes, referring to his 900 theses,

> I have proposed theorems about magic, too, wherein I have signified that magic is two-fold. The first sort is put together by the work and authorship of demons, and is a thing, as God is true, execrable and monstrous. The other sort is, when well explored, nothing but the absolute consummation of the philosophy of nature. When the Greeks mention these, they call the first sort, γουτείαν, not dignifying it in any way by the name magic. They call the second sort by its proper and peculiar name, μαγείαν, the perfect and highest wisdom as it were."[27]

The distinction between these two forms of magic has been variously termed "white" and "black," or "natural" and "demonic." The basis of the distinction is crucial to our proper understanding of the Hermetic philosophy.

White, or natural, magic arises from the Neoplatonic conception of the connectedness of all things. We recall Plato's peculiar doctrine that the universe is a living being with its own soul and body, and that we are likenesses of the universal being. This establishes an integral organic relationship between all the parts of the universe, so that what happens to one area of its body, however remote from the rest, will have its effect throughout the whole—quite as a light injury anywhere on the human body will affect the stasis of one's entire physical disposition. Natural magic has to do with the recognition of the influences of actions in the universe, near and distant, on one's own individual being. There is no intention in natural magic of manipulating or altering the movements of the universal being; its primary design is to achieve an aligment or harmony between oneself and the universe. Such magic presupposes a continuing effluvium of powers pouring down through the heavens, powers which can be canalized by those who have learned their paths, that is, the correspondence between stars, planets, stones, metals, and humors of the body. The magician is simply that person who understands the workings of the organismic universe and knows where to enter it in order to share maximally in its powers.[28]

Ficino himself had much to say about magic. As Yates characterizes it, Ficino

> bases the theory of how we are to 'draw down the life of heaven' upon the *spiritus* as the channel through which the influence of the stars is diffused. Between the soul of the world and its body there is a *spiritus mundi* which is infused throughout the universe and through which the stellar influences come down to man, who drinks them in through his own spirit, and to the whole *corpus mundi*. The spiritus is a very fine and subtle substance. . . .

In fact, it is very much like a fine air or heat. Ficino apparently intends it to be quite palpable.[29]

Drinking in the stellar influences by way of a tangible spiritus, and thereby connecting with the powers that organize the entire universe, requires the use of subtle activities and devices. There quickly appeared numerous manuals recommending detailed practices. Ficino himself proposes many. He notes, for example, that the human heart, using the medium of spiritus, distributes energy throughout the body in precisely the same way that the world soul makes use of a special medium or "fifth essence" (*quinta essentia*) to radiate the energy of the sun into the physical universe. We would therefore greatly increase the effectiveness of the heart if we could locate those substances that are rich in this fifth essence. He suggests that we should make use of those foods that have a "warm, damp, and clear quality, such as wine or white sugar, particularly when they are mixed with cinnamon or even gold."[30]

Other common practices of white magic include wearing symbolic talismans, taking note of certain arrangements of numbers and letters, repeating prescribed incantations, and humming melodies thought to be identical to the "music of the spheres." The primarily intellectual nature of white magic is evident. As Pico observed, the Greek word for this magic bears the implication of wisdom or knowledge. The user of white magic is perhaps more appropriately referred to not as a magician, but a "magus," the traditional designation of a person thought to be possessed of special wisdom. One must take care, of course, particularly when considering the practices of white magic, not to confuse it with black, or demonic, magic.

Demonic magic involves actual manipulation of natural forces by way of evil agencies toward ends that are one's own and therefore not in agreement with the universe as a whole. The possibility for such manipulative magic in the Neoplatonic scheme arises only because, in their desire to show the reality of evil, the Neoplatonists argued that there must be regions of nonbeing or utter darkness not penetrated by the emanations of the One. Those who make use of black magic are therefore engaging directly in works of evil. Although it is not only Neoplatonism that is responsible for the deep dread of (and attraction to) witchcraft throughout the centuries of the Renaissance, it is not surprising that philosophers and academics influenced by the Hermetic tradition should have kept perfect silence in the face of the appalling imprisonment, torture, and execution of persons (usually older women) accused of witchcraft. In the sixteenth and seventeenth centuries, the same period that saw the greatest flowering of the Hermetic tradition, there were probably a quarter of a million persons executed for this "crime."

If Hermetic thinking leads one toward magic in one direction, passing eventually into witchcraft, it points in another toward astrology and alchemy, for the omnipresent world soul is constantly making use of the substantial bodies of the heavens, no less than the substances of the earth, in its creative engagement with the souls of living persons. Before we look more closely at these aspects of the Hermetic tradition, it is necessary here to appraise the consequences of what we have discussed thus far and to relate this thinking to death.

In the thought of Plato and Plotinus, death is not to be understood as the survival of the personality, as in the doctrine of immortality, but as the point at which the individual soul drops all traces of its individual isolation and merges with the world soul. The Hermetic thinkers of the Renaissance add to this understanding a heightened awareness of the location of the thinker in a universe of space and time. Those who hold the simple doctrine of immortality as the continuation of a completed and self-enclosed personality saw the world only as a place of imprisonment and unnecessary suffering. The Hermetics' attitude toward the world is radically different. Even if they see it as a kind of bondage, as some did, their chief interest was in the connectedness of all things: the pregnant unity by which the most basic and remote levels of physical existence may be seen as continuous with the human soul in their common manifestation of the One. Therefore, the earth and the heavens are studied not so that one might escape entrapment by them, but so that one's soul might be elevated toward its proper unity. Death, from this perspective, is neither a tragedy nor a release. Although black magic often trafficked with the powers of death, natural magic and the contemplative labors of the Hermetics never sought to manipulate death itself; their goal was always the achievement of the soul's higher unity.

To be sure, the use of white magic, even though it was chiefly meditative and serenely intellectual, brought with it the possession of favorable power. Henry Cornelius Agrippa of Nettesheim in his widely influential volume, *On Occult Philosophy*, speaks of the magical powers one acquires by spiritual ascent: "no one has such powers but he who has cohabited with the elements, vanquished nature, mounted higher than the heavens, elevating himself above the angels to the archetype itself, with whom he then becomes co-operator and can do all things."[31] Whoever has the gift of ascending to the level of the "archetype," or what would correspond to the *mind* in Plotinus' system, would scarcely be concerned with the death of the body.

One way of sharpening the distinctiveness of the Hermetic view of death is to note its relation to traditional Christian thinking. As we have seen, the Hermetics were eclectic enough to have believed that there was one body of wisdom into which all religions could comfortably find their place and that, as a result, at their center, they were all in agreement. While such persons as Ficino and Pico—and following them such intellects as Giordano Bruno and Agrippa—were always of the opinion that they were faithful Christians, the official organs of the Church became increasingly suspicious of the entire Hermetic phenomenon, finally declaring it heretical. This was true not only of Roman Catholicism but, after the Reformation, all the major branches of Christianity (and, of course, also Judaism and, less explicitly, Islam).

Ficino and Pico were both under severe attack during their lifetimes, though both were lucky enough to have died natural deaths in their own beds—Ficino because he had the protection of powerful men and Pico only because he died at the age of twenty-nine. Such was not the fortune of the greatest of all the Hermetic thinkers, Giordano Bruno. Giordano's impact on the sixteenth century was vast. He traveled and lectured widely, wrote a number of learned and provocative volumes, and never restrained his voice or pen when he thought truth was an issue. The truth and its goal for Giordano were taken directly from classical Neoplatonism: the unity of the soul with the One; and among the means by which he undertook this pursuit was magic. Giordano had a great dread of black magic, but he brilliantly advanced his own magical methods; Yates describes his pursuit as "the conditioning of the imagination or the memory to receive the demonic influences through images or other magical signs stamped on the memory." Imagination for Giordano—and here he anticipates the major later development of the Hermetic tradition—was the source of psychic energy when joined to cogitative power. "This magically animated imagination is 'the sole gate to all internal affections and the link of links,' " Yates writes, quoting Giordano.[32]

There are good reasons why the Church should have found Giordano heretical. The identity of the human soul with the divine, the central role of the imagination, and the pious appeal to magic, all are an affront to traditional Christian thought in which the division between the human and the divine is absolute, and in which the divine is the exclusive effective agent in matters of salvation. Giordano found plenty of space for Christians in his system; indeed, he considered himself a true believer to his last anguished breath; but the Church repaid this inclusiveness by sending him to his death by burning at the stake.

Although—possessing our historical distance from the Renaissance and a vastly altered view of human affairs—we could scarcely endorse the Church's action in Giordano's case, we would be misinformed to agree with him that the Hermetic tradition and Christianity are not exclusive of each other. Nowhere is this more evident that in their views of death. For Christians the primary conception is that of *transformation* occurring simultaneously with one's resurrection. Since the resurrection is in no sense a human act, and cannot even be earned by human acts, it can be the work of God alone; and since there is such a radical discontinuity between present historical existence and the Resurrection Life, there can be no knowledge of what that life is. Therefore, the appropriate attitude toward life in the face of death is *faith*. Christians understand faith to be not a form of knowledge, but a belief that rests on what non-Christians can only consider inconsequential or even absurd historical events. The Hermetic's conception of death as threshold and the consequent appeal to vision is in quite another spiritual and intellectual realm.

There is probably no single text that displays the radical difference between the Christian and Hermetic traditions more effectively than the following passage from the *Corpus Hermeticum:*

> If then you do not make yourself equal to God, you cannot apprehend God; for like is known by like. Leap clear of all that is corporeal, and make yourself grow to a like expanse with that greatness which is beyond all measure; rise above all of them, and become eternal . . . dream that you too are immortal, and that you are able to grasp all things in your thoughts . . . find your home in the haunts of every living creature; make yourself higher than all heights, and lower than all depths; bring together in yourself all opposites of quality, heat and cold, dryness and fluidity; think that you are everywhere at once, on land, at sea, in heaven; think that you are not yet begotten, that you are in the womb, and that you are young, that you are old, that you have died, that you are in the world beyond the grave.[33]

Giordano was by no means the last of the Hermetics to be executed

304 DEATH AS THRESHOLD—VISION

for their spiritual generosity and for their admirable, if naive, hope that all religious differences can at last be removed. Many more were to be imprisoned, scorned, and driven from their homes and academies. Some of the greatest among them, such as Cornelius Agrippa and the alchemist Paracelsus, would spend most of their lives in flight, traveling from one refuge to another, often conducting their research, healing, and teaching in secret. But the Church and other powerful groups in society have failed to suppress the tradition, which is still alive in the present century. In the Renaissance can even be found a fascination with all the occult phenomena among the rich and the powerful. The Hapsburg Emperor Rudolph, for example, moved the imperial court from Vienna to Prague—a city then famous for its open intellectual atmosphere, where Jewish Cabalists worked without interference and the vigorous Bohemian church of the earlier reformer John Hus still thrived. Rudolph turned away from the troubling affairs of his realm and absorbed himself in esoteric and scientific studies. As Frances Yates observed in her history of these events, "Prague became a Mecca for those interested in esoteric and scientific studies from all over Europe."[34] The great English Hermetic John Dee, Giordano Bruno, and the astronomer Johannes Kepler were among those attracted to the city. After Rudolph's death in 1612 there was even an attempt to establish Frederick of the Palatinate, after his marriage to Elizabeth the daughter of England's James I, as his successor. Frederick and Elizabeth both had avid interests in Hermetic subjects, and the hope was that under them the whole empire could be opened to a new spiritual age. It was a hope that was quickly crushed by the League of Catholic Princes in an outpouring of religious hatred that led to the devastating Thirty Years War.

In Pico della Mirandola's address "On the Dignity of Man," there occurs a remarkable and oft-cited passage in which he offers an exceedingly free interpretation of the creation story as he found it in the testimony of "Moses and Timaeus." After God had fabricated the house of this world, adorned the supercelestial region with minds, animated the stars with souls, and filled the lower world with animals, he knew there was something missing in the intermediate position; therefore, he created a man, and as he placed him at the midpoint of the world, he addressed him as follows:

> In conformity with thy free judgment, in whose hands I have placed thee, thou art confined by no bounds; and thou wilt fix limits of nature for thyself. I have placed thee at the center of the

world, that from there thou mayest more conveniently look around and see whatsoever is in the world. Neither heavenly nor earthly, neither mortal nor immortal have We made thee. Thou, like a judge appointed for being honorable, art the molder and maker of thyself; thous mayest sculpt thyself into whatever shape thou dost prefer. Thou canst grow downward into the lower natures which are brutes. Thou canst again grow upward from the soul's reason into the higher natures which are divine.[35]

Pico exposes in these words a distinctive view of freedom. Here the issue is not whether one is free to *do* what one chooses, but to *be* what one chooses. Pico is not concerned to establish a *freedom of the will,* but is proposing an *ontological freedom.*

Ontological freedom has been implicit in the platonic/Neoplatonic tradition all along. Plato's identification of thought with being has the consequence of implying that as one's thought is progressively cleansed of ignorance it comes closer to an identification with the very summit of intellectual reality—the Idea of the Good. The generative nature of the Idea of the Good is vastly expanded in Plotinus' doctrine of the One from which all things mental and material emanate. Therefore, as one's understanding of the true nature of reality is clarified, it brings one ever closer to an identification with the center of origin of all being. When the Neoplatonists speak of the "divinity" of the soul, it is this possibility that they have in mind: its creative relation to all that is.

This conception of freedom is the animating genius living at the heart of the Hermetic tradition. Since one's own origin is simultaneously the origin of all being, it is inevitable that the Hermetics would believe that they had in their intellectual labors the key to all the differences that separated persons and traditions from one another. Since it also implies a direct participation in the generative powers of the universe, it is also inevitable that Hermetism would encourage such occult arts as magic, alchemy, and astrology. The popular occultism that continues into the present is what becomes of Hermetism when its animating Platonic genius has fallen asleep.

But throughout history that genius still made a number of striking appearances. The sweeping sense of harmony and universal congruence characteristic of Hermetic Neoplatonism, what the French came to call the "musical philosophy," was to have an enduring influence on England in particular: "by the beginning of the Jacobean period the traditional symbolism, based upon the descent of ancient wisdom from the East, especially from hidden Hebrew lore, had been gladly welcomed by those intellectual circles gathered around the English throne."[36] Hermetic symbolism and concepts can be seen in the poetry of Edmund Spenser and in the plays of Shakespeare. In fact, Shakespeare's last play, *The Tempest*, is essentially a Hermetic allegory. A great number of English philosophers, theologians, artists, and even scientists found themselves deeply informed by Hermetic thought, establishing a tradition that was kept alive by such figures as Wordsworth, Coleridge, W. B. Yeats, and most especially William Blake.

The Hermetic influence was also powerfully felt in German intellectual history. One of the visitors to Prague during the time of Rudolph II, who was in the midst of his esoteric studies, was a modest German wool merchant, possessing almost no formal academic training, by the name of Jakob Boehme. Before he had become exposed to the discussions of the Cabalists, astrologers, alchemists, and assorted magi, he had already written several meditative religious works of uncommon originality, though deeply troubling to the orthodox Lutherans in his native city of Gorlitz. His mind was remarkably open to these influences, particularly the alchemical and occult philosophy of Paracelsus. By the time he died, in 1624, at the age of forty-nine, he had authored a body of literature that severely increased the persecuting vengeance of the orthodox Lutherans; however, he also introduced the world to a radical new insight into the nature of human freedom.

Boehme's style is almost hopelessly symbolic and turgid, forcing the casual reader to conclude prematurely that it contains little sensible thought. This and the subtlety of his doctrines make his thinking difficult both to characterize and to summarize. It is sufficient for our purposes here to indicate where he was touched by the Neoplatonic philosophy, and how he transformed it under the driving force of his own originality. Recall that, according to Plotinus, one cannot say that the One exists, for then it would place the One in a relation with non-Being, thereby diminishing its perfect unity. The non-Being of the One has an uneasy and generally unexplored place in the development of Neoplatonic thought. However, Boehme, whether he got the doctrine from the writings of Plotinus or reinvented it himself, quickly seized it, took it to an extreme, and made it the conceptual center of his later works.

Boehme did not hesitate to adopt the characteristic Hermetic vision of the "musickal" interrelatedness of all things, but he was also thoroughly persuaded of the reality of both freedom and evil, and knew that both had to have a central place in that sublime oneness. He also perceived that freedom and evil belong insolubly to each other. One cannot assert the reality of evil with any seriousness if it is taken to be but a momentary rise of darkness far from the perfect source of being, where it does not appear with its own ineluctable power but seems to be a restorable lapse in the otherwise omnipresent goodness of being. If one is not originally free to be evil, one is not free to be good; goodness therefore arises with necessity and has nothing to do with freedom. If that were the case, the good could never be chosen; or, nothing but the good could be chosen. The universe would be emptied of value; human existence would merely be a playing out of the necessary.

What marks the radical distinctiveness of Boehme's approach to this problem is his incapacity to accept the usual Neoplatonic solution by which evil is taken to be a mere absence of being, but the sort of absence that does not compromise the perfection of the source of being. Boehme's own solution was to propose an *Ungrund*, or *Nonground*, that precedes the very existence of God and all else. The Nonground is the absolute origin of freedom; it is Boehme's attempt to explain the fact that nothing whatsoever can come before an act of true spontaneity. If there is true freedom, then that which is free can have absolutely no antecedent. If we are talking about the sort of ontological freedom which Pico described, in a way characteristic of Neoplatonists, we are obliged to say that a free being is one that has no basis whatsoever, no ground, no prior stage or existence. We are also carried to the next reflection: there is no way a free being can be constrained toward one action rather than another. True freedom then introduces the reality of an original and ineradicable evil. We must be careful to note that Boehme is not proposing that evil originate in *another being*, which is opposed to the divinity of supreme benevolence. He is most definitely not a dualist. Evil arises from the same freedom out of which the "Most High God Himself" is born.

Boehme's basic conception of the universe is therefore tragic. He replaces the Neoplatonists' certainty that the universe is finally a comedy with the vision that the deepest drama of life is a tragedy. Since Boehme understood that we participate in, and perfect our likeness of, the divine—as a "microtheos and a microcosmos"—we are even more profoundly free than Pico supposes, and certainly much more intimately associated with evil.

Following Boehme's death and the quick translation of his writings into English, there appeared a movement that called itself "Behmenism" in England; it consisted of small learned groups who gathered for the study and interpretation of his obscure and provocative texts. He was studied with great avidity by William Blake, who responded particularly to the concept of freedom in Boehme's thought: "Perhaps Blake's importance as an artist and prophetic writer rests more than anything else on his achievement in giving form to Boehme's vision on precisely this point."[37]

Of his influence on German thought we can be even more extravagant. Debts to Boehme's stunning insights into the living center of Platonic thought, not to mention mysticism, Christianity, and the Cabala, are quite visible and often gratefully acknowledged in such thinkers as Fichte, Schelling, Hartmann, Hegel, Goethe, Nietzsche, and Heidegger.

The primary reason for examining the Hermetic tradition is to display more vividly its distinctive view of death and freedom. If, as we have been arguing throughout the volume, there can be no death if there is no freedom, the Hermetic tradition declares that freedom is related to death insofar as *we are free to die, but we are also free not to die.* Life is not something that is imposed on us, but is that which we have only by choice. We do not live unless we freely choose to do so.

We have found that the Plato of the *Timaeus* is certainly not the youthful Plato who wrote the *Phaedo* and the *Apology*. In those early dialogues life was something given; we were immortal whether or not we chose to be. In that sense, we are not free with respect to death; thus, the attitude toward death is simply one of *denial*. The philosophical life, Socrates said, is truly a preparation for death, but that preparation consists in learning how it is that the soul cannot perish—that there is in fact no death at all.

Vision takes the place of denial in the tradition that begins with the later work of Plato, but in the thought of Plotinus that vision acquires a distinctive character. With Plotinus *beholding* becomes equivalent to ascending. The reason we are free not to die is that the enlightened exercise of our freedom brings us into identity with higher levels of being, on which the shadow of death never falls. Death is surely real; something that is free actually dies. However, as the alchemists in particular were wont to demonstrate, death is simply a dissolution that allows a higher recombination. What dies is our isolation from the rest of the cosmos; it dies when we see that isolation is something we have freely imposed on ourselves, and just as freely need not impose. In that sense death is fittingly seen as a threshold.

We recall Jung's hesitation to enter into the infinitude of the spirit, his inability to abandon the individuality of the self. Looking back we can see that the empirical scientist in Jung discouraged him from losing *control.* He knew that once the self was released to the boundless spirit there was no way the conscious ego could again master it. From Jung's perspective, that seemed to be the very maw of incurable and desparate madness. Lost in an imagination that had no guiding center, we would be tossed chaotically about by the unconscious archetypes that dwell in the lower reaches of the psyche like so many blinded Titans. This was a danger the Hermetics were willing to risk, but they went forward with the hopeful conviction that the infinite sea of the spirit, or mind, was in fact a living unity that was thoroughly benevolent. More than anyone else in the Hermetic tradition Jakob Boehme sought to remind us that because of our ontological freedom we live in a universe that is finally tragic. Such freedom leaves no possibility that in the last weighing of human history neither good nor evil will completely prevail; each will be mixed with the other. This is a metaphysical condition even God could not improve. There can be no hope that the forces of good will prove superior to evil and purge human experience of its suffering. Our losses will go unrestored, our ill-seeking hearts will be incapable of correction. *Nonetheless*, Boehme called us to the vision of the eternal drama between good and evil—a drama found even in the heart of the divine—as though it is precisely this that makes life thrilling.

It remains for the reader to judge which is the preferred option: Jung's ultimate refusal to enter into the drama of the unbounded spirt or the Hermetics' incautious desire to release the powers of the *Ungrund* within themselves, a desire aptly expressed in Blake's famous line: "Excess is the palace of wisdom."

Both Jung and the Hermetic tradition understand death to be a threshold. They differ greatly, however, in their willingness to step across it. As we saw in the previous chapter, Jung will not give away the autonomy of the ego—if only in the interest of preserving it as an *observer* of the drama of the psyche, with the result that ego does not take part in the drama; it cannot be both audience and actor. Jung refuses to step across the threshold of death into Blake's "excess" in the wish to rescue the ego from the boundless spirit, and is consequently denied the poet's "palace of wisdom."

Notes

1. *Timaeus*, p. 13.
2. Ibid., pp. 13 ff.
3. Ibid., p. 14.
4. Ibid., p. 46.
5. See Gregory Vlastos, "Reasons and Causes in the Phaedo," *Plato*, p. 142.
6. Timaeus, p. 19.
7. Ibid., p. 24.
8. Ibid., p. 39.
9. Ibid., p. 25.
10. Ibid., p. 51.
11. Ibid., p. 98.

12. Ibid., p. 132.
13. Ibid., p. 132.
14. *Enneads, VI. ix. 1.*
15. Ibid., VI, ix. 1.
16. Ibid., VI. ix. 2.
17. Ibid., VI. ix. 5.
18. Ibid., III. viii. 10.
19. Ibid., V. ix. 3.
20. Ibid., IV, iii. 5.
21. Ibid., VI. ix. 10
22. See Frances Yates, *The French Academies of the Sixteenth Century.*
23. See P. O. Kristeller, *Philosophy of Marsilio Ficino.*
24. See Leon Blum, *The Christian Interpretation of the Cabala.*
25. P. 20
26. *On the Dignity of Man*, pp. 29 ff.
27. Ibid., p. 26.
28. See Yates, *Giordano Bruno*, p. 45.
29. Ibid., pp. 68 ff.
30. See Wayne Shumaker, *The Occult Sciences in the Renaissance*, pp. 108 ff., for a detailed discussion of natural magic.
31. Quoted by Yates, *Giordano Bruno*, p. 241.
32. Ibid., p. 266.
33. Volume I, p. 221.
34. Yates, *The Rosicrucian Enlightenment*, p. 17.
35. *On the Dignity of Man*, pp. 4 ff.
36. Desiree Hirst, *Hidden Riches*, p. 82.
37. Ibid., p. 99.

Bibliography

Henry Cornelius Agrippa von Nettesheim, *Occult Philosophy or Magic*, tr. Willis F. Whitehead (New York: 1975).

Owen Barfield, *Romanticism Comes of Age* (Spring Valley: 1966).

Jacob Boehme, *Six Theosophical Points*, tr. John Rolleston Earle (Ann Arbor: 1958).

Titus Burckhardt, *Alchemy*, tr. William Stoddart (Baltimore: 1974).

Desiree Hirst, *Hidden Riches* (New York: 1964).

P. O. Kristeller, *The Philosophy of Marsilio Ficino*, tr. Virginia Conant (Gloucester: 1964).

Pico della Mirandola, *On the Dignity of Man, On Being and the One, Heptaplus*, tr. Charles G. Wallis, Paul J. W. Miller, and Douglas Carmichael (Indianapolis: 1965).

Plato, *Timaeus*, tr. John Warrington (London: 1965).

Plotinus, *The Enneads*, tr. Stephen MacKenna (London: 1957).

——*The Essential Plotinus*, tr. Elmer O'Brien (Indianapolis: 1975).

Friedrich Schelling, *On Human Freedom*, tr. James Gutman (Chicago: n.d.).

Wayne Shumaker, *The Occult Sciences in the Renaissance* (Berkeley: 1972).

Rudolf Steiner, *Christianity as a Mystical Fact* (New York: 1972).

——*An Outline of Occult Science*, trs. Maud and Henry B. Monges (Spring Valley: 1972).

——*The Philosophy of Freedom*, tr. Michael Wilson (Spring Valley: 1964).

Frances Yates, *The French Academies of the Sixteenth Century* (London: 1947).

——*Giordano Bruno and the Hermetic Tradition* (New York: 1969).

——*The Rosicrucian Enlightenment* (London: 1972).

Gregory Vlastos, "Reasons and Causes in the *Phaedo*," *Plato*, ed. G. Vlastos (Garden City: 1970).

11 TEILHARD DE CHARDIN

Books and articles dealing with the thought of Teilhard de Chardin commonly begin by taking note of the remarkable confluence between his life and his thought. With great intensity he attempted to design a life that would be consistent with his deepest reflections. Where unplanned events, disappointments, and tragedies crossed his way, he did not retreat from them into some safe and undisturbed chamber of mind, but integrated them into his thought. In reading Teilhard one has the impression that the man was profoundly moved by almost everything that was happening around him—everything from current social crises and the latest discoveries in astronomy to the continuing geological evolution of the earth and the spiritual welfare of his friends. He was a man who found himself in the middle of a living universe pulsing with excitement and promise. In all his writings he seems to be transported on the grand vision of the continuity of all things.

Mare-Joseph-Pierre Teilhard de Chardin was born in 1881 at Sarcenat in the province of Auvergne, France, the fourth child in a family of eleven that could find both Pascal and Voltaire in their ancestry. The warm piety of his mother seems to have been the decisive influence on his early choice to enter the priesthood. In 1899 he was enrolled in the Jesuit seminary at Aix-en-Provence. Continuing an interest in geology he had developed as a child, he went to the island of Jersey in 1902 to study that subject along with philosophy, completing his scholasticate in 1905. During the next several years, while teaching physics and chemistry at the Jesuit college in Cairo, he extended his interests into the field of paleontology. Teilhard was ordained into the priesthood in

1911, and shortly after that began doctoral studies in paleontology. Following France's entrance into World War I in 1914, he was drafted into the army where he served as a stretcher-bearer and was cited three times for exceptional courage in battle. At the age of forty-one, in 1922, he completed work on the doctorate and traveled to China where he studied several important fossil deposits.

Teilhard's ability and daring in integrating widely diverse bodies of knowledge first became known to persons outside his immediate circle of friends in 1924, when he returned to Paris to lecture on evolution. The content of these lectures, and their theological implications, were so disturbing to his Jesuit superiors that he was forbidden to publish or to lecture in the area of philosophy and was confined to research only in his proper academic field. In 1926 he was sent back to China where he remained until 1946. He returned from the Orient with two completed manuscripts: The Divine Milieu, which he was refused permission to publish shortly after he had written it in 1927, and the major work of his life, The Phenomenon of Man. He personally went to Rome to seek approval for the publication of the latter manuscript and was again refused. Teilhard would not live to see either book in print.

The last years of his life were spent chiefly in New York, where he died on Easter Sunday in 1955. Although hundreds of scientific articles had appeared under his name, principally from his extensive paleontological research, the suppression of his theological and philosophical work meant that he died in relative obscurity. Scarcely a dozen persons attended his funeral. Within several years the sudden appearance of these withheld books and articles excited considerable enthusiasm and controversy in the academic and intellectual world—a reaction appropriate for the discovery of a genuinely original mind.

Certainly it is misleading to consider Teilhard a paleontologist. To call him a "scientist" in a more general sense—the designation with which he would probably have been most satisfied—also distorts the awesome inclusiveness of his work. The terms mystic, theologian, philosopher, visionary, all are equally inadequate because they obscure the "this-worldliness" of the man. One Teilhard scholar has chosen to refer to him as a "Christian humanist."[1] This has the gracious effect of associating him with the open inquisitiveness of a Renaissance scholar. Still, there is something too pallid in the term "humanist." It lacks the element of fire; it does not suggest his all-consuming desire to see into the nature of things—the characteristic quality evident on every page of his writings. The difficulty of categorizing Teilhard arises not merely from the limitations of our vocabulary, but from the fact that he was engaged in a singular quest for which there is no contemporary role.

Teilhard was himself acutely aware of this. We find his questioning in these lines, written less than a month before he died:

> How does it happen that, still intoxicated by my vision, I look all around me and find myself practically alone? How is it that I alone should have *seen*? How is it that I am incapable, if someone asks me, of citing a single author, a single work, where there is to be found clearly expressed that marvelous "diaphany" which in my eyes has transfigured everything? . . . May I not after all be simply the victim of some mental delusion? That is what I often ask myself.[2]

We shall suggest here that there is a role by which the work of Teilhard may be appropriately characterized: that of the *Renaissance magus*. It will become apparent here that what he sought was a unified vision of the universe, the very quest that compelled the greatest minds of the Hermetic tradition. Indeed, what we see in Teilhard is the animating genius of that tradition now standing boldly and in full view before us, but clothed in modern scientific learning.

Our interest in Teilhard in this volume, however, is not in proving the case that he was a *magus redivivus*, but in exploring how he placed the problem of death at the center of his thought and dealt with it in a way that is both novel and disturbing. Although, as we shall see, he quite obviously views death as a threshold, he brings to this venerable concept an extensive knowledge of the very discoveries that exposed how mistaken these old "philosophers of nature" had been. In order properly to assess the importance of his understanding of death, we must first look briefly over the major contours of his thought.

We find in Teilhard what one comes across at every high moment in the Platonic/Neoplatonic tradition: the supreme importance of *seeing*; in Teilhard's words, "there is one point no one will context, and that is my preoccupation to unify an interior vision. . . . It is a terribly painful thing not to be able to see enough."[3] He says of his major work, *The Phenomenon of Man*, that it "may be summed up as an attempt *to see* and *to make others see*" what happens when we consider man as a phenomenon. And why should we want to see?

> *Seeing*. We might say that the whole of life lies in that verb—if not ultimately, at least essentially. Fuller being is closer union; such is the kernel and conclusion of this book. But let us emphasize the point: union increases only through an increase in consciousness, that is to say in vision.[4]

And if we ask *what* he wishes us to see, we find in his answer much of the reason for the disquiet Teilhard's work has aroused in the scientific community.* In *The Divine Milieu* he describes himself as "a man who, because he believes himself to feel deeply in tune with his own times, has sought to teach how to see God everywhere, to see him in all that is most hidden, most solid, and most ultimate in the world."[5] There are doubtless many who would respond to this remark by suggesting that if he were truly in tune with his own times he would try to see the world without imposing the concept of God into any rational account of natural process. But such a response would miss the force of his observation, for he was firmly resolved not to compromise in the least the hard-won data of empirical research. Indeed, he gave the great balance of his life to painstaking research, often under hazardous and trying circumstances. The singularity of Teilhard's vision is that it is precisely on the basis of such knowledge that one may be able to "see" God.

His grandest complaint against modern science is not that it had gone too far in its claims to have eliminated any need to appeal to the transcendent, but that it had not gone far enough in accounting for all the data available to the objective observer. At the beginning of *The Phenomenon of Man* he declares that if the "book is to be properly understood, it is to be read not as a work on metaphysics, still less as a sort of theological essay, but purely and simply as a scientific treatise. The title itself indicates that. This book deals with man *solely* as a phenomenon; but it also deals with the *whole* phenomenon of man."[6] What the whole phenomenon includes, and what science systematically excludes, is consciousness, or what he sometimes calls *soul* or *mind*. And if consciousness is inherent in the phenomenon of man, any scientific treatise that leaves it out or denies it has gravely compromised itself.

*As an example of the divergent reaction Teilhard has found among the learned, compare the judgments of his work by two distinguished scientists: "Teilhard's beliefs as to the course and the causes of evolution are not scientifically acceptable because they are not in truth based on scientific premises and because to the moderate extent that they are subject to scientific tests they fail those tests" (George Gaylord Simpson, *This View of Life: The World of an Evolutionist*, p. 232). "What made Teilhard's views novel and controversial was that he refused to pattern his thinking to fit it into any one of the recognized academic or intellectual categories. He was too much a scientist to set forth his conclusions in a manner wholly to please the theologians, and too much a theologian to make himself altogether a scientist. . . . He defied those who regarded science and mystical vision no more blendable than oil and water. In an age of analysis he dared to essay a synthesis" (Theodosius Dobzhansky, *Teilhard's Letters to Two Friends: 1926–1952*, pp. 221 ff.).

The exclusion of consciousness as a datum to be studied and explained results in what Teilhard calls the "impersonalization" of nature. He cites two reasons for this tendency: "The first is *analysis*, that marvelous instrument of scientific research to which we owe all our advances but which, breaking down synthesis after synthesis, allows one soul after another to escape, leaving us confronted with a pile of dismantled machinery, and evanescent particles. The second reason lies in the discovery of the sidereal world, so vast that it seems to do away with all proportion between our own being and the dimensions of the cosmos around us."[7] One can include the phenomenon of soul, or mind, in the study of human existence only if one does not so dissolve the whole into discrete units that its unity vanishes. Teilhard is also suggesting here that the appearance of consciousness is most definitely related to the incredible immensity of the physical universe—an improbable claim we shall presently have the chance to examine.

Teilhard's strong preference for synthesis does not grow out of a desire to conceal the results of analysis; instead, it rises from his belief in the connectedness of all things, including especially the most primitive elements of the universe discoverable only by thoroughgoing analysis. The connections are lost if one looks only at the separable units at the lowest orders of physical existence. Here we might note that Teilhard is in basic compatibility with the Hermetics who also stressed the connectedness of things, particularly the continuity of the soul with the world. However, his ardor on this point carried him to extremes no Neoplatonist ever reached. When he discusses the "super-eminent nature" of our dependence on matter he even speaks of it as a "*mystical* union" with the material. He uses that term here "to mean the strengthening and purification of the reality and urgency contained in the most powerful interconnections revealed to us in every order of the physical and human world."[8]

These dependent interconnections range from the infinitesimally small orders of subatomic reality to the endless reaches of stellar space. What seems to move Teilhard in the contemplation of these orders is the sheer marvel of their existence. Merely to behold them is to be carried toward deeper reflection: "when the world reveals itself to us it draws us into itself: it causes us to flow outward into something belonging to it, everywhere present in it, and more perfect than it."[9]

The marvel of the universe that tends to draw us into itself springs not from its mere existence, and not even from its breathtaking plurality and scope, but from the fact that it is *systematic* and *unified*. To say that the universe is a system is, for Teilhard, to assert that its many parts, though they often do appear or develop accidentally and independently, are actually functions of something higher. They are not merely connected, they are in the service of greater powers and, simultaneously, have within their own unity lower orders of things.

> Each element of the cosmos is positively woven from all the others: from beneath itself by the mysterious phenomenon of "composition," which makes it subsistent through the apex of an organized whole; and from above through the influence of unities of a higher order which incorporate and dominate it for their own ends.[10]

This structure of the universe means that we cannot take a part of it, isolate it from the rest, and properly understand it. We must always be able to see how that particular entity, whether it be an electron, a glacier, or a super nova, is the unity of entities smaller than itself and a function of a still higher unity.

To add a further, but crucial, subtlety to this account, we should observe that Teilhard, in sharp contrast to the Hermetics, leaves no place for analogy in our understanding of the universe. That is to say, once we have learned how the "system" of the atom works, we will not have learned how other "systems," such as viruses, or souls, or comets, work. He explains, "These multiple zones of the cosmos envelop without imitating each other in such a way that we cannot pass from one to another by a simple change of coefficients. Here is no repetition of the same theme on a different scale. The order and the design do not appear except in the whole."[11] The consequence of this observation is that, although we cannot understand what something is unless we know the system in which it exists, we cannot know the system of the universe from its parts, but only from its whole. "All around us, as far as the eye can see, the universe holds together, and only one way of considering it is really possible, that is, to take it as a whole, in one piece."[12]

What we have here, then, is a most original vision indeed. Beginning with the ancient wisdom that "the whole of life" lies in our ability to see, Teilhard, as if speaking for the Platonic tradition, asserts that *what* we are to see is nothing less than God himself. And when he comes to saying *where* we are to see God, he would have dazed even the Platonists: in the very heart of matter itself. Genuinely to look at matter, however, is to be drawn into it, to find our vision being carried upward and downward along the lines of its comprehensive system. Each system in turn points beyond itself to one more inclusive; so our vision is not complete until we have seen the system of the whole. What then shall we have seen? A systematic *totum* that includes the fact of our seeing; indeed, the final system *is* the act of seeing, an absolute consciousness.

In order to explicate this last remark we must now introduce into our account of Teilhard's thought the one element that most clearly distinguishes him from the Hermetic tradition and leaves his scientific critics in numbed silence: *time*. The total system of the universe "only takes on its full significance when we try to define it with regard to a concrete natural movement—that is to say, in *duration*."[13]

We recall that in Plato a sharp contrast was drawn between becoming and the real. The genuinely real was not subject to change, much less the kind of change time might work on it. When Plato addresses the question of time in the *Timaeus*, he passes over it in a brief passage, noting that time came into existence with the living being of the cosmos, but in a most peculiar way. Since the creating demiurge was making the cosmos according to a model that was perfectly eternal in itself, and since the cosmos was *in motion*—and therefore in the process of temporal change, the demiurge made it "as it were a moving likeness of eternity." This "likeness" is present in its numerical perfection. This perfection is found in the movements of the heavens that were created by the demiurge "for the definition and the preservation of the numbers of Time." Time is therefore a kind of calibration imposed on the movement of things from without. Plato has no capacity for imagining the internal transformation of entities, or for describing the unceasing metamorphosis that time works on all things—a notion without which Teilhard could scarcely have written a page. For Plato a thing could be identified by that which endured within it, untouched by time. In sharp contrast Teilhard could say that the very roots of our being "plunge back and down into the unfathomable past. . . . In each one of us, through matter, the whole history of the world is in part reflected."[14] The same point can be made with regard to the future: "Not a single thing in our changing world is really understandable except insofar as it has reached its terminus."[15]

The Renaissance thinkers saw no need to improve on Plato's doctrine of time. Unlikely as it may seem, they had no true philosophy of history. They were renowned for their interest in the origin of things, thus their fascination with the claimed antiquity of the *Corpus Hermeticum*; but this was only because they thought that if they went *ad fontes*, to the source, they would have the thing in its pure, and eternal, form. Insofar as there is a history, it is detectable only in the corruption of timeless verities, and if one could have those verities in their pristine condition, the effect of history could be canceled out. Teilhard comments on the absence of an adequate understanding of time, noting that less than 200 years ago the past was hardly imagined at all and the future was thought to hold no more than a few thousand years: "An incredibly short time; and what is even more disturbing to our minds, a span of simple repetition during which things were conserved or reintroduced on a single plane, and were always of the same kind."[16] However much thinkers attempted to ignore history, it is manifestly the case that history did not ignore them: "And then, by insensible gradations, came one of the greatest intellectual events that history has ever recorded: the revelation of time to the human consciousness."[17]

We showed above how perfectly connected Teilhard thought we were with the physical universe; we can see now that in terms of time, as well as space, there is an unbroken continuity in each existing thing. Just as nothing can be isolated from the total system of space, nothing can be isolated from the full reach of time before and after it. It is this thoroughgoing vision of spatial and temporal connectedness that gives Teilhard's theory of evolution its radical—and controversial—cast.

Teilhard does not find inadmissible any of the facts of evolutionary development that have surfaced in direct investigation of the evidence. He does not even hold out against what one might consider one of the most damaging theories for Teilhard's thought: the second law of thermodynamics. According to this law every physicochemical change causes a loss of energy in the form of heat. The overall effect of this phenomenon is the entropy, or increasing disorganization, of the universe. True, there is a constant transformation of simple compounds into those more complex, however, as Teilhard said: "Quantitatively, this transformation now appears to us as a definite, but costly, operation in which an original impetus slowly becomes exhausted. Laboriously, step by step, the atomic and molecular structures become higher and more complex, but the upward force is lost on the way." The second law of thermodynamics is designed only to describe what transpires within physicochemical actions, and not how the world will end. However, if one wished imaginatively to extend the collective effect of energy loss into an indefinite future, one might see the universe descending into eternal darkness: "A rocket rising in the wake of time's arrow, that only bursts to be extinguished; an eddy rising on the bosom of a descending current—such then must be our picture of the world."[18]

Teilhard takes no issue with the accuracy of the second law, but, predictably, he demurs on drawing such a conclusion. On the very face of it, one cannot deny the powerful evidence that evolution has a *direction*. If we look, for example, at the chordate branch of the tree of life, of which we are a part, "an outstanding characteristic is apparent, one which has for long been emphasised in paleontology. It is that we find from layer to layer, by massive leaps, the nervous system continually developing and concentrating."[19] But this is true for other branches, even the insects that "display, like ourselves, the influence of cerebralization. The nerve ganglions concentrate; they become localized and grow forward in the head. At the same time instincts become more complex; and simultaneously the extraordinary phenomena of socialization appears . . . ."[20] The universal drift of evolution is toward a more and more complex nervous system, toward consciousness. Teilhard finds this evidence strongly resistant to the metaphor of time's arrow rising only to burst and then vanish. Perhaps it is true that matter, acting by the second law, tends to pull the process backward, but he also argues that the tendency toward consciousness cannot be accidental. It is quite reasonable to believe that just as matter conservatively holds us back, something else is creatively pulling us ahead. Out of this argument arises the notion of *orthogenesis*, the most misunderstood element of Teilhard's thought.

The term orthogenesis has a rather imprecise definition, and fortunately Teilhard uses it only rarely—though enough to identify him, in the view of some critics, with the very shoddiest episodes in evolutionary theory. It suggests to those critics an external pressure on the evolutionary process that impels it toward a predetermined end. Instead of the subtle balance between chance and necessity, which we found in the scientific theory of Jacques Monod (see Chapter 2), one suspects the introduction of a divine power eliminating all possibility of chance. This is by no means Teilhard's own view of the matter. He is, in fact, at great pains to rule out all external influences on physical process—one of the reasons for the disfavor showed to him by the Vatican. Teilhard's own version of orthogenesis stands on a most improbable ground: *freedom*. This is a point that is overlooked by nearly all of his detractors, as well as many of his defenders, even though he never tires of reminding the reader that evolution is unthinkable without freedom. And, as will become evident, it is an understanding of freedom that has directly to do with death.

Recall that Teilhard consistently demands that the empirical scientist study the *whole* phenomenon of human existence—including consciousness. This means that when we look backward in time, and downward into increasingly more primitive levels of the organization of matter, we must be able to see the possibility for everything that came later. *What* developed, and *when*, through those vast reaches of

time and space can be plausibly shown by science, whether it be inanimate matter or living organisms. Nothing occurred unlawfully.
There are no anomalies in the ceaseless evolution of matter. Not even
life is anomalous. *It is no accident.* The empirical scientist takes it as a
fact that there is "a *physical connection* between living beings. Living
beings *hold together* biologically. They have organic command of their
successive appearances, so that neither man, the horse, nor the first cell
could have appeared earlier or later than they did."[21]

How, then, are we to account for the appearance of consciousness
within that sequence of physical connectedness? It is Teilhard's conten-
tion that consciousness is ignored by science because it is concerned
only with the external, mechanical relations between physical objects.
Consciousness from that perspective is an epiphenomenon, a sport,
that occurs by chance; or perhaps it is a by-product blindly produced
by an otherwise unexceptional survival mechanism: the central nervous system. Certainly there is no impulse here to see consciousness as
the "way out," as the alternative to the universe's inevitable physical
demise by way of the second law. The rocket of life will surely therefore
burst and pass into the eternal darkness. Teilhard responds, "So says
science: and I believe in science, but up to now has science ever troubled to look at the world other than from *without?*"[22]

Teilhard's novel suggestion is that we not only look at things from
without but also from *within.* If consciousness is truly part of the
natural process, then it has its spatial/temporal roots in the very beginning of time and in the most infinitesimal regions of subatomic reality.
Since physics, biology, astronomy, and the other sciences cannot see
consciousness there, because they are looking from without, Teilhard
feels himself pushed to a conclusion "pregnant with consequences":

> It is impossible to deny that, deep within ourselves, an "interior"
> appears at the heart of beings, as it were, seen through a rent. This
> is enough to ensure that, in one degree or another, this "interior"
> should obtrude itself as existing everywhere in nature from all
> time. Since the stuff of the universe has an inner aspect at one
> point of itself, there is necessarily *a double aspect to its structure*,
> that is to say, in every region of space and time—in the same way,
> for instance, as it is granular: *co-extensive with their Without
> there is a Within to things.*[23]

This vision implies that in each order of being beneath the human, or
prior to the human in time, there is a kind of consciousness. Even in the
smallest units of matter we should expect to find "grains of thought."

There is something almost quaint, perhaps even wishful, when it is put this way, and no doubt this opens Teilhard to bemused ridicule on the part of anyone possessed of an empirical temperament. One could imagine that a porpoise or a dog has a sort of primitive consciousness, but an oyster? Or an electron? But this is a mistaken reading of Teilhard. He is not projecting a human consciousness into the subhuman orders. He explains, for example, in a footnote, that "the term 'consciousness' is taken in its widest sense to indicate every kind of psychism, from the most rudimentary forms of interior perception imaginable to the human phenomenon of reflective thought."[24] It is, in other words, a kind of *seeing*. A close reading of Teilhard's literature on this point suggests that consciousness is an object's capacity for *responding* to its environment rather than erely *reacting* to it. An object is not merely knocked about by external forces, but *anticipates* those forces in some sense. Indeed, what constitutes the superiority of one level of being over another is its ability to see better. Seeing and consciousness then can also be considered equivalent to freedom: "The *within, consciousness,* and then *spontaneity*—three expressions for the same thing."[25]

This way of looking at reality gives to the physical universe a powerful internal dynamic: "*Nothing really exists in the Universe except myriads of more or less obscure spontaneities, the compressed swarm of which gradually forces the barrier separating it from liberty.*"[26] This enthusiastic remark introduces us to the next step in Teilhard's theory of evolution. If the universe is composed of myriads of spontaneities, where does its order arise, and why should it move constantly in the direction of less obscure spontaneity? We learn now that there is a lawful interdependence between the within and the without. To describe this interdependence Teilhard proposes that we regard all energy as having two components: "a *tangential energy* which links the element with all others of the same order (that is to say, of the same complexity and the same centricity) as itself in the universe; and a *radial energy* which draws it towards ever greater complexity and centricity—in other words forwards."[27]

Tangential energy accounts for the way in which entities are related to each other externally, or mechanically. Radial energy accounts for the internal spontaneity. It is not always clear whether Teilhard wishes us to think that there are two kinds of energy, or simply two ways the same energy manifests itself. In either case, it is clear that there is an *economy of energy* within each discrete thing. The primary demand on its limited quantum of energy is external; it has to do with the relatedness of the entity to others like it. Unless it is connected with them in ways that guarantee its safety and reproductiveness, it will not continue to exist. At first, the spontaneity of the thing is of no value to itself, and may in fact destroy it. It is only when it has succeeded in attaining an external association with other similar entities sufficient to protect itself against the vagaries of the environment without, and its own spontaneity from within, that the economy of the entity allows a portion of its quantum to be expressed radially.

In slightly different terms, this means that the individual has begun to express itself in ways that are independent of its collective identification with the species. It is certainly conceivable that, due to the sheer spontaneity of radial energy, it may result in a too severe isolation of the individual from the group and lead to its demise. On the other hand, it might also allow the individual to remain in the group and change at the same time. This could have the effect of requiring an altogether new adjustment of the external relations between entities. The appearance of cleverer apes might cause an abrupt alteration in the accessibility of the most desirable food supplies and mating partners. This behavior in turn will produce a new social organization that is capable of sustaining individuals with greater vision, or freedom, without allowing a breakdown to the point where no individuals can survive.

The kind of internal change that gives the individual an ability to "see" in a way that is superior to the other members of the species is what Teilhard means by the term "centricity," or sometimes "centration." It is a condition in which energy emerges more from one's center—that is, from one's consciousness or spontaneity. In every case, this development is in the direction of a more complex physical organization. Radial energy, then, works in the direction of increasing complexity and consciousness. Teilhard often speaks of the "law of complexity consciousness."

What we have so far described is a kind of rhythmic advance of evolution through the interdependent relationship of radial and tangential energies. Teilhard means this economic interplay of energy to constitute the universe at every level of its existence. Even the formation of the stars and the planets can be understood in these terms. Once the tangential energies of the whirling matter that constitutes the planet earth, for example, had achieved a kind of stasis, a radial transformation from within could begin. This stasis was reached when it attained a spherical shape, that is, when it reached around and contained itself. Teilhard refers to this attainment of stasis as the *geosphere*. For many millions of years the radial transformation of the geosphere was geological, but with an increasing complexity in physicochemical development. And then at the proper moment of physical and chemical balance, there was a radial change, a new centering, that marked the appearance of life and the resulting creation of the *biosphere*. The simplest forms of life were, of course, enormously dependent on their species behavior; the radial element in those first living molecules was exceedingly small. It cannot be said then that there were living individuals on the surface of the inaminate earth, as much as there was a *living film* that covered the face of the earth in its own spherical tangential profusion.

What marks the line between the animate and inanimate, or between what Teilhard preferred to call life and "pre-life," is not the insertion of something spiritual into what had been a purely physical process. It is a change so minute and subtle that it could scarcely be detected. It is, in any case, a change no different in kind from that which had already occurred billions of times in "pre-life." As the climb toward greater centration steadily continues, Teilhard proposes that we draw another line at the point where organisms achieve a kind of psychic distinctiveness, where they exhibit a degree of liberty inconceivable at lower levels. Beyond this line lies the *psychosphere*.

There is still another sphere. The highest stage discernible to the evolutionary scientist is that in which the process of psychic centration has turned in on itself. Teilhard calls it the *noosphere*, from the Greek word *nous*, or mind. (We recall that Plotinus considered the *nous* as the first emanation of the One.) Just as the threshold between life and "pre-life" was marked by an external change of the smallest sort, so is the threshold into human consciousness: "Morphologically the leap was extremely slight, yet it was the concomitant of an incredible commotion among the spheres of life. . . ."[28] Once the hominids had reached the kind of spherical equilibrium that allowed them a guarantee that the species would exist, there began to appear the phenomenon of mind. In human beings consciousness reaches a new level; Teilhard calls it *reflection*. He means by it "the power acquired by a consciousness to turn in upon itself, to take possession of itself *as of an object* endowed with its own particular consistence and value: no longer merely to know, but to know oneself; no longer merely to know, but to know that one knows."[29] In other words, in reflection, consciousness itself becomes spherical just as matter had in its original sidereal form.

Because Teilhard wants to insist on the unbroken continuity of the process from pre-life to life to reflection, he is in substantial agreement with the materialistic monism of contemporary scientific theory. Up to his introduction of the notion of reflection, what we find here is not markedly different from the view of modern geneticists who maintain that the exceedingly small degree of unpredictability in subatomic events is sufficient to explain all the observed variations between species and even between individuals within species. Geneticists speak of this, however, as the exercise of chance, and certainly not as a "law of complexity consciousness." The rise of consciousness is not a violation of known physical law, but it is certainly not an inevitable development of matter as it is for Teilhard.

Perhaps the clearest way of showing the distinctiveness of Teilhard's view of evolution is to say that other scientists regard spontaneity as the essentially disordering element in the relations between things; spontaneity is therefore identical with their inability to be able to predict what will occur. Teilhard, on the other hand, sees spontaneity infecting the entire universe with itself—not by carrying everything back to chaos, but by creating an interior region that is increasingly shielded from the patterns of necessity comprehended by the "science of the without." It is a region that increases in power while it increases in complexity, as it becomes simultaneously more aware of itself and more perceptive of its environment. Indeed, there is scarcely a better example of this power than the rise of science itself. Science is, of course, an enormously refined attempt to *see* what is there; but seeing in science is joined to *predicting*, and predicting leads to *control*. In Teilhard's terms science has greatly magnified the freedom of the individual by moving us away from being mechanically knocked about by tangential forces. Or, to put it in terminology used earlier, instead of being a blind, and therefore impotent, and part of a larger system, science puts in the hands of individuals the capacity to control massive physical systems.

We noted above that evolution and freedom are associated with each other in such a way that we cannot have one without the other. The radical consequences of that observation now come into full view. If it is the case that through science we are able to control massive systems, what shall we say of the most immense system of all, the system that includes all the other: evolution? Can it be the case that the complete history of evolution has come to the place where it turns itself over to us? Teilhard's astounding answer to this question is not just, Maybe, but Yes! Enthusiastically endorsing Sir Julian Huxley's opinion, Teilhard wrote, "Man discovers that *he is nothing else than evolution become conscious of itself.*"[30] This has been the secret dream of science all along: to understand the physical process so completely that "by grasping the very mainspring of evolution," we can seize the "tiller of the world."[31] Elsewhere: "By reflecting on itself in man, evolution does not therefore merely become conscious of itself. It becomes at the same time to some extent capable of directing and accelerating itself also."[32]

By introducing time into his sythesis, Teilhard takes a step beyond the Neoplatonists: "Man is not the centre of the universe as once we thought in our simplicity, but something much more wonderful—the arrow pointing the way to the final unification of the world in terms of life."[33] Unlike the Neoplatonists we do not, in Teilhard's conception, rise *above* the physical nature of the world, but rise *with* it.

We have stressed throughout this study the relationship between freedom and death on the basis that, since death always appears as an agency, a focused and alien power, to embrace its disruption in a more inclusive continuity is to attain a higher degree of freedom. In Teilhard's thought we have seen that the agency of death is not simply the force of physical matter, but *evolution*. What causes incessant change, the repeated destruction of one stage to make way for another, is the lawful evolving of matter toward a distant end. Teilhard's amazing claim is that our freedom can take even this vast force into itself. This raises two questions: Now that we have the tiller of the world in our hands where do we go with it? And, closely related, How do we take our own death into this grand voyage?

In this irreversible movement toward consciousness of an ever higher order it might seem that the reality of death has been overlooked. But anyone who has read a great deal of Teilhard, including his letters and especially the various pieces written mostly for himself during his service in the war, will find that the thought of death was never far from his mind. Even at the theoretical level, he could certainly not ignore the fact that our profound attachment to matter will inevitably tie our fate to the material dissolution of our bodies. Although we might look with hope to the future, we cannot help but notice that as we look inward there is a steady diminishment of our physical capacities by the forces of matter: "And all these lines of rigidity have a common integument: the fundamental obligation imposed on us of living without having wished to do so; and they all converge upon one and same inescapable centre, Death."[34] So far we have stressed the dynamic, active aspect of life; but much of life is passive as well. Even growth is a form of passivity, though growth is finally overcome by the "passivities of diminishment."

> In death, as in an ocean, all our slow or swift diminishments flow out and merge. Death is the sum and consummation of all our diminishments: it is *evil* itself—purely physical evil, insofar as it results organically in the manifold structure of that physical na-

ture in which we are immersed—but a moral evil too, insofar as in the society to which we belong, or in ourselves, the wrong use of our freedom, by spreading disorder, converts this manifold complexity of our nature into the source of all evil and all corruption."[35]

Furthermore, there is no doubt that death will come not only to individuals. As we reflect on the whole course of evolution there begins to take shape in our reflection a fantastic "event which comes nearer with every day that passes: the end of all life on our globe, the death of the planet, the ultimate phase of the phenomenon of man."[36]

With death such an inevitable and inclusive event, what shall we then say of evolution, particularly since it now depends on our own spontaneous energies? How could it possibly continue in the face of such eventualities? On one point Teilhard is most emphatic: unless we can see a way out and be persuaded that it exists, we shall not move ahead. "An animal may rush headlong down a blind alley or towards a precipice. Man will never take a step in a direction he knows to be blocked." What then can convince us that the way ahead is open, that there will be no barrier to the utmost development of humankind? This is, Teilhard concedes, a "stupendous demand." But it is a demand that can be met within the very nature of consciousness itself, for it is inconceivable that we could ever place a limit against the growth of consciousness. "There are innumerable critical points on the way, but a halt or a reversion is impossible, and for the simple reason that every increase of internal vision is essentially the germ of a further vision which includes all the others and carries still farther on."[37] This open-endedness of consciousness is something that must be convincing to us; moreover, it is something we should desire: *"without the taste for life*, mankind would soon stop inventing and constructing for a work it knew to be doomed in advance."[38] In the terms we have been using, this is equivalent to saying that unless we can have a clear vision of a higher continuity into which all discontinuity can be embraced, we would lose all desire to move forward—and this is the desire that is life itself. We would be stupefied with *grief*. We would close off the openness presented to us in consciousness and become mindless passengers on the vessel of the world, unaware that the tiller is there to be seized.

But how is consciousness open-ended? Is it enough to say that one vision leads to another? Does this sequence of penetrating visions actually undo the bonds of death? There are times when Teilhard seems to be suggesting that the soul possesses a kind of immortality of the sort we first found in the dialogues of Plato. Instead of death he sometimes says there will be a new breakthrough, "an escape on the physical level through an excess of consciousness."[39] With remarkable similarity to the Socrates of the *Phaedo*, he can insist that once the center of reflection (or soul) has formed it cannot change: "To outward appearance, admittedly man disintegrated just like any animal. But here and there we find an inverse function of the phenomenon. By death, in the animal, the radial is reabsorbed into the tangential, while in man it escapes and is liberated from it."[40] Here is an apparent image of the soul taking flight, sustaining its own independent existence separate from the world and from other souls.

Perhaps, like the Neoplatonists, Teilhard resists now and then the thought of giving up a personal center, but when we place these remarks in the total context of his work another image emerges. Death's final power is undone not by the continuity of the individual soul, but by the unity of that soul with that which is higher. Also like the Neoplatonists, Teilhard draws a clear connection between thought and being. When he speaks of increasingly greater visions, he is speaking of greater existence; when he speaks of the unity of thought, he means also the unity of being.

> Within the cosmos all the elements are dependent upon one another ontologically in the ascending order of their true being (which means of their consciousness); and the entire cosmos, as one complete whole, is held up, "informed," by the power energy of a higher, and unique, Monad which gives to everything below itself its definitive intelligibility and its definitive power of action and reaction.[41]

The Neoplatonists spoke of death as that which marks the transition from one level of being to another. What dies is the disorganized manifold of our existence. So too for Teilhard: unification means a detachment from that which holds us apart from the whole. Until we can be carried into a grander unity, a deeper center, we must first "*lose all foothold within ourselves* . . . ." And what will be the agent of this definitive transformation? Nothing else than death.[42]

With *what*, or *whom*, are we unified through the transformation that comes with death? Teilhard answers this question several ways. Quite often he speaks of a unity with God. These are the passages that seem to arise from the spatial metaphor and encourage some interpreters of Teilhard to regard him as a proper mystic:

> God must, in some way or other, make room for himself, hollowing us out and emptying us, if he is finally to penetrate into us.

And in order to assimilate us in him, he must break the molecules of our being so as to re-cast and re-model us. The function of death is to provide the necessary entrance into our inmost selves. It will make us undergo the required dissociation. It will put us into the state organically needed if the divine fire is to descend upon us. And in that way its fatal power to decompose and dissolve will be harnassed to the most sublime operations of life. What was by nature empty and void, a return to bits and pieces, can in any human existence, become fullness and unity in God.[43]

In another exultant passage, written when he was on an extended expedition into the Ordos desert in China, Teilhard speaks of a collective unity with God:

The world can never be definitely united with you, Lord, save by a sort of reversal, a turning about, an *excentration*, which must involve the temporary collapse not merely of all individual achievements but even of everything that looks like an advancement for humanity.

If such exclamatory sentences, of which a great many can be found in Teilhard's literature, are not explicitly Christian, they are certainly not offensive to the Christian sensibility. But they might fall just as comfortably into the Neoplatonic tradition. It is not until he introduces the factors of space and time that Teilhard's thought becomes distinctive, until we see the force of his observation that space-time "penetrates to our soul; it fills it and impregnates it; it blends itself with the soul's potentialities to such an extent that soon the soul no longer knows how to distinguish space-time from its own thoughts."[45]

Once we introduce this kind of thinking into the discussion of the higher unity of consciousness through the transformation of death, we find ourselves moving into a unique conceptual region. Teilhard wants us to see that

by structure, the noosphere (and more generally the world) represents a whole that is not only closed but also *centered*. Because it contains and engenders consciousness, space-time is necessarily *of a convergent nature*. Accordingly its enormous layers, followed in the right direction, must somewhere ahead become involuted to a point which we might call *Omega*, which fuses and consumes them integrally in itself.[46]

In other words, thinking is not *about* space and time, it *is* spatial and temporal. When Teilhard speaks of a vision that carries in itself the germ of a further vision, when he insists on the open-endedness of consciousness, he is not saying that consciousness *has a future* somewhere outside itself, but rather that it carries its future within itself. What will happen is already happening. For this kind of thinking the traditional concept of God will not do; therefore, he offers the term *Omega*, the last letter of the Greek alphabet, as that toward which all is moving. He does not mean to abandon the concept of God, but only to reinterpret it in the light of space-time consciousness. Often he speaks of "God-Omega," indicating the two terms are identical.

One striking feature of this way of thinking is the heightened value one must now place on history. We are not freed from space-time, we are penetrated with it; thus human history—and the history of the whole cosmos as well—is the manifestation of an emergent consciousness. History displays the convergent lines of radial energy, transporting us to a more inclusive unity. The rise of science, the appearance of mass social movements, the invention of sophisticated communication systems, the crowding population of the earth, the steady erosion of local isolation, the cosmopolitanism of racial inclusiveness, the oft-expressed desire for an effective world government—all such phenomena are, in Teilhard's philosophy of history, signs of the rise of global consciousness. So powerful is this tendency that massive human conflict is taken into it: "Every new war, embarked upon by the nations for the purpose of detaching themselves from one another, merely results in their being bound and mingled together in a more inextricable knot. The more we seek to thrust each other away, the more do we interpenetrate."[47] What is happening on a worldwide scale is what happened at the level of the individual human organism in the achievement of reflection when thinking became aware of itself, when consciousness became self-consciousness enclosing itself in a sphere.

> Mankind, born on this planet and spread over its entire surface, coming gradually to form around its earthly matrix a single, major organic unity, enclosed upon itself; a single, hyper-complex, hyper-centrated, hyper-conscious arch molecule, co-extensive with the heavenly body on which it was born. Is not this what is happening at the present time—the closing of this spherical thinking circuit?[48]

We recall that Jung, when he faced the yawning openness of the psyche where there seemed to be no bottom, no defining limitations, held back to insist on the irreducibility of the singular self. This leads us at this point to ask of Teilhard, What happens to the "I," the personal center of one's earthly existence, the psychic identity that develops in the space-time region between physical birth and physical death? If his thinking does not lead to the doctrine of personal immortality, what then is the mode of deathlessness as it applies to our present self-understanding? In response to what he takes to be the Marxist teaching that the true worth of personal existence is what it bequeaths to succeeding generations in the way of ideas, discoveries, and art, Teilhard concedes the importance of such a heritage, but says that we cannot stop with an assessment of our earthly works:

> Our works? But even in the interest of life in general, what is the work of works for man if not to establish, in and by each one of us, an absolutely original centre in which the universe reflects itself in a unique and inimitable way? And those centres are our very selves and personalities. The very centre of our consciousness, deeper than all its radii; that is the essence which Omega, if it is to be truly Omega, must reclaim. . . . The conclusion is inevitable that the concentration of a conscious universe would be unthinkable if it did not reassemble in itself *all consciousnesses* as well as *the conscious*.[49]

Teilhard is describing a spiritual phenomenon that appears to most minds to contain a straight contradiction: the more we are unified, the more we are uniquely ourselves. The closer we get to Omega, the more clearly we are distinct from all the others. He is appealing to the principle that "*union differentiates*. In every organized whole, the parts perfect themselves and fulfill themselves."[50] A center cannot dissolve; it can only "supercentralize itself" by an ascending spiral of reflection in which the universe itself is reflected in its being. The "grains of consciousness" do not then lose their individual contours but only "accentuate their death." The most definitive statement we will have from Teilhard on the nature of the unity with Omega is the following one, in which he assures us

> it would be mistaken to represent Omega to ourselves simply as a centre born of the fusion of elements which it collects, or annihilating them in itself. By its structure Omega, in its ultimate principle, can only be a *distinct Centre radiating at the core of a system of centres;* a grouping in which personalization of the All and personalizations of the elements reach their maximum, simultaneously and without merging, under the influence of a supremely autonomous focus of union. That is the only picture which emerges when we try to apply the notion of collectivity with remorseless logic to a granular whole of thoughts.[51]

If the *philosophical* intention of these observations is to find a way of combining perfect unity with perfect uniqueness, the *spiritual* intention is to counteract what Teilhard feels is a serious danger in the way of thinking: impersonalism. To speak of a more inclusive union is obviously to approach the impersonal, and, to be sure, this was a view strongly espoused by Plotinus. As one ascends the orders of being toward the One, the personal is left behind. Plotinus strictly purges the higher orders of any of the limitations usually associated with personality. Jung, too, stressed the impersonal character of the unconscious. For Teilhard precisely the opposite is the case. As one draws toward the Omega it is not *what* but *who* that is approached. This is one place where Christian language is particularly useful in expressing Teilhard's singular vision. He regards the *who* as the Incarnation of God in the man Jesus that brings God as close to us as matter itself. We recall that matter is not alien to the soul but the very matrix of its existence, related to us essentially as a living entity.

> What name can we give to his mystical Entity, who is in some small way our own handiwork, in whom, eminently, we can enter into communion, and who is some small part of ourselves, yet who masters us, has need of us in order to exist, and at the same time dominates us with the full force of his Absolute being?

> I can feel it: he has a name and a face, but he alone can reveal his face and pronounce his name: Jesus![52]

But is this the familiar Jesus of the Gospels, an itinerant rabbi moving through the hills of Galilee, putting into the vernacular of the people a personalized interpretation of traditional Hebrew wisdom, and dying an ignominious death on the cross? Teilhard raises the question himself, quite obviously aware of the distance humanity has come in 2000 years: "Is this the Christ of the Gospels, imagined and loved within the dimensions of a Mediterranean world, capable of still embracing and still forming the centre of our prodigiously expanded universe?"[53] Although Teilhard's answer is emphatically in the affirmative, explicit references to this Jesus are scanty. This is not to say, however, that he dismisses the importance of Jesus' earthly existence. On the contrary, the fact that God became incarnate and personally shared in the life of matter is of the greatest spiritual importance to Teilhard. Christianity

> unveils to our eyes and hearts the moving and unfathomable reality of the historical Christ in whom the exemplary life of an indi-

vidual man conceals this mysterious drama: the Master of the world, leading, like an element of the world, not only an elemental life, but (in addition to this and because of it) leading the total life of the universe, which he has shouldered and assimilated by experiencing it himself.[54]

God did not enter the elemental universe simply for the sheer theater of it; he shared it with us because he wanted to show that *there is a way out*. Strangely, while we might expect Teilhard to emphasize the resurrection at this point, it is the cross that appears to him as the supreme symbol of the life of Christ. The physical suffering and death of Christ indicate that he had run the full course of matter, that he too was emptied out and had given up his foothold in the biosphere. The fact that God should undergo this suffering can only mean that the way ahead, which is the way of death, is also the way of God and is therefore open.

In its highest and most general sense, the doctrine of the Cross is that to which all men adhere who believe that the vast movement and agitation of human life opens on to a road which leads somewhere, and that that road *climbs upward*.[55]

The cross is a symbol in an exemplary sense—it shows how we are to suffer and yet have hope. But Teilhard wants to describe a relationship between each individual and Christ that is more than merely symbolic; he describes a relationship rooted in consciousness itself. Because of the Incarnation, because Christ had "sprung up as man among men," he

put himself in the position (maintained ever since) to subdue under himself, to purify, to direct and superanimate the general ascent of consciousnesses into which he inserted himself. By a perennial act of communion and sublimation, he aggregates to himself the total psychism of the earth. And when he has gathered everything together and transformed everything, he will close in upon himself and his conquests, thereby rejoining, in a final gesture, the divine focus he never left. Then, as St. Paul tells us, *God shall be all in all*.[56]

We opened this discussion of Teilhard's Christology, or doctrine of Christ, by referring to his conviction that as we approach Omega we are not merging with the impersonal but with the "superpersonal." What we have in this last passage is perhaps the most revealing of all his Christological statements. *We are not just moving ahead, we are also being carried forward*. There is, of course, a sufficient mystery and wonder about the future, so that we cannot always be clear-sighted about the path ahead. It is far easier to look backward, and Teilhard's arguments for a continuing future all originate from past evidence: "We recognize ourselves in our childhood; but our childhood would neither have foreseen nor understood our maturity. Such is the law of all growth."[57] To be sure, we have learned that we are moving ahead and that this movement must be free—that is, it must be our own. Still, there is an energy in the process that seems greater than our own, a wisdom that we did not know we had until we look backward. Teilhard's Christology is an acknowledgment that the whole process of evolution is always something more than we know or can see. He calls Christ "the principle of universal vitality" and often refers to the upward evolution of the cosmos, through the transformation of death, its "Christification." It is not as though we alone are alive and struggling upward against blind obstruction; instead, it is that we are waking up in a vibrantly alive universe, every fibre of which is directed toward Omega. Thus Teilhard can speak ecstatically of our existing, not in a lifeless universe, but in a *divine milieu*, or he can quote with considerable feeling Paul's *in eo vivimus, et movemur, et summus*, often translated as: God is that being "in whom we live and move and have our being."

This is a view reminiscent of the strange Platonic teaching that the universe is a living being. In Teilhard that teaching is revived, but this time on the basis of evidence offered by modern science and by the Christian doctrine of the Incarnation. And yet, the doctrine may seem as strange in Teilhard as it does in Plato, and the modern reader may well want to know what actual data, what concrete experience, will lead one to the belief that we are being Christified as evolution proceeds through us, and through our death toward Omega. What Teilhard offers here is not evidence, but a way of "seeing" the evidence; not an argument, but a vision. He saw the divine presence in the cosmos as a sort of "sensible radiance." "Their perception of the divine omnipresence is essentially a seeing, a taste, that is to say a sort of intuition bearing upon certain superior qualities in things." It is not something one comes to through reasoning or analysis; it is something that appears, and appears so brilliantly it is a wonder we do not see it at once: "we could say that the great mystery of Christianity is not exactly the appearance, but the transparence, of God in the universe."[58] God is not just apparent, he is "diaphanous"; that is, we can see through and into him. One does not think one's way into the divine, one simply beholds; *the divine is supremely visible to those who can see*.

With this last formulation we have returned to the point at which Teilhard himself preferred to begin: with the phenomenon of *seeing*. We remember his exclamation that the whole of life lies in that verb. We can see now how intensely he meant that. If we see the cosmos properly as that out of which we could have arisen with our gift of sight, and if we can see in ourselves the continuity between that sight and the cosmos, then we are carried on into the vision of a future convergence of the world and sight—or consciousness. Death for Teilhard is certainly real, but it is real as a threshold across which we move, by way of vision, into a mode of being that lies beyond all mortality, that is in fact nothing less than pure vision itself.

Many questions remain. No doubt many readers will want a far more detailed use of scientific data than one can find in Teilhard's works; some will want clearer definitions of such key terms as seeing, time, and reflection; and others may simply be numbed by the apparent comfort with which he combines material from such disparate conceptual treasuries. No effort will be made here to address these difficulties. It is sufficient if what has emerged here is a provocative attempt to draw the boundary of mortality even wider in order that the boundary of life may seem wider still.

There is, however, one question against which we must weigh Teilhard's thought, a question that will gain greater critical significance as we move ahead in this study. The question has to do with Teilhard's treatment of evil. In the previous chapter we examined, though briefly, the thought of another singular thinker, Jakob Boehme. It was Boehme who dared push the doctrine of freedom so far that it seemed to precede God himself, with the consequence that God had to contend with the possibility of evil as ineradicable—to him and to us. The universe for Boehme was therefore both dramatic and tragic. In the Neoplatonic tradition, in general, the universe is finally comic, since evil, which is simply nonbeing, will vanish like the darkness when the light penetrates it. How ineradicable is evil for Teilhard? It is clear that he felt the raw force of human suffering, that he saw the gifts of nature and culture distributed with great injustice. "The problem of evil," he wrote, "that is to say the reconciling of our failures, even the purely physical ones, with creative goodness and creative power, will always remain one of the most disturbing mysteries of the universe for both our hearts and our minds."[59] Moreover, we should remember the degree to which Teilhard insisted on human freedom. Although he does not propose anything so extreme as the Behmenist notion of a freedom that precedes God (or succeeds Omega), he does enunciate a view that comprehends an exceedingly vast range of human freedom. He says of each person participating in the march of orthogenetic history:

> *He makes his own soul* throughout all his earthly days; and at the same time he collaborates in another work, in another *opus*, which infinitely transcends, while at the same time it determines, the perspectives of his individual achievement: the completing of the world.[60]

We recall that the work of "making our souls" was suggested in the writing of the young Renaissance genius Pico della Mirandola, who said that God created us without forms, leaving us freely to decide how we should exist. But what would have been unthinkable to Pico was the additional claim that we are also free to collaborate in the building of the world itself.

Finally, however, for all his undeniable seriousness about the problem of evil, and for all his emphasis on radical human freedom, it is not to be denied that Teilhard's evolving cosmos is a comedy, albeit a sublime comedy. All creatures within that cosmos must endure the risk that they will fall prematurely, or suffer unjustly, because of the still "imperfect ordering of the manifold, in them and around them." Moreover,

> because the final victory of good over evil can only be completed in the total organization of the world, our infinitely short individual lives could not hope to know the joy, here below, of entry into the Promised Land. We are like soldiers who fall during the assault which leads to peace. God does not therefore suffer a preliminary defeat in our defeat because, although we appear to succumb individually, the world, in which we shall live again, triumphs in and through our deaths.[61]

Death, which Teilhard says "is *evil* itself," is then the very means of triumph. Far from being ineradicable, evil will in the end be utterly eradicated. The ultimate absence of evil in Teilhard's completed cosmos may seem like a remote and none too serious speculation, but in truth it masks a more serious problem in his thought as a whole: *in this perfect comedy neither death nor freedom exist.* We noted that Teilhard introduced the radical suggestion that evolution will continue only if we wish it to continue, that it depends utterly on our free decision to seize the tiller of the world. This also implies that it may *not* continue if we choose to end it. But Teilhard buries that implication under his vision of the radiant omnipresence of God. Such a choice will not be made since we shall all awake to find ourselves living in the divine milieu, proceeding forward by way of the "principle of universal animation"—that is, Christ himself.

And where there is neither death nor freedom, there is no selfhood. In this sense, Teilhard's thought attains an extreme we can only regard as instructive. He went further than Jung and the Neoplatonists in his conception of mortality. Where in Jung the agent of death is natural instinct, and in the Neoplatonists it is the material necessity (irrationality) of the disunified world, for Teilhard it is the universe in its full space-time reality—or evolution. By introducing time into his universe it became developmental, not a *collection* or a *hierarchy* of things, but a *sequence* of things—each of which has an absolute beginning and an absolute end. The universe consists entirely of discontinuous phenomena. To embrace this discontinuity is to take hold of the beginning and the end of the whole sequence. The spontaneity of the free person is that which has evolved out of this sequence to take command of evolution. Evolving out of time it becomes eternal in its time. Jung's universe is basically synchronous; that is, it all occurs at once. The unconscious is eternal; it knows no time. The ego, however, is a diachronous holdout; that is, it is sequential, still dwelling in history. It is this history that Jung refuses to give up to the synchronous psyche. Plotinus, however, wants to abandon the diachronous ego utterly. His universe is synchronous without exception. Teilhard's universe is simultaneously synchronous and diachronous. Where Jung's approach to eternity always keeps one foot in history, and where Plotinus attains eternity by leaping free of history, Teilhard achieves eternity by way of history. For Teilhard the struggle is to become so perfectly historical that one *becomes* history. This is what he means by taking hold of the tiller of the world.

If we magnify our picture, we can see in Teilhard the problem with all threshold thinkers: their vision of continuity is so inclusive that it finally suffers no opposite. To use somewhat more technical language, we could say that they have no capacity for transcendence; ultimately, all otherness is immanent. That is, there must always be some unbroken, continuous link between the self and its Other. As we observed, the Jungians finally refuse to let go of an *observer* for their "impersonal" realm of the archetypes. The psyche's images may have their origin in those archetypes, but they must be *seen* by someone in space and time. Neither will the Jungians put the ego in a world that is utterly strange; nor will they have a world without an ego to behold it. Theirs is the assumption that if the light of eternity is so perfect that it cannot be seen, it cannot be light. Plotinus required such continuity in his system that the One had no Other at all—and as a result could not even be self-aware and, indeed, could not even be said to be. Only from the lower, less perfect perspective of the separate soul can the One even be spoken or thought of. But this is a separation that must be overcome as quickly and as completely as possible.

The conception of death's discontinuity as a threshold seeks fundamentally to eliminate all otherness. The Jungians, Neoplatonists, Hermetics, Romantics, and such singular *magi* as Teilhard, all cannot endure their isolation in the universe, their alienation from its very matter, much less from other minds and souls. But to overcome all alienation is to achieve a final silence, an unknowing blindness. These philosophies, in brief, are sublime expressions, not of the *triumph of the soul over death*, but of the *triumph of grief over the soul*. They are eloquent justifications for the stupor we experience in the face of death, or the terrible speechlessness that seizes us when all meaning has been lost. They do not, therefore, deal with the irreversible losses death brings, but so strip us of the temporal and spatial qualities of life that there is nothing further to be lost. Like all forms of acute grief, they deal with death by existing in the mode of death.

We learn from them that the problem of dealing with death's discontinuity is the problem of dealing with Otherness. That is, if death is to be a true discontinuity it must always appear in the form of something truly and irreconcilably alien. If death is a threshold, we pass beyond it by making it a part of our experience. We must "die with life" Jung said. We do so by way of vision or knowledge. Death is therefore something comprehended, something known. But, then, as we have seen, since that vision constitutes a direct connection between the knower and the known, whatever we have seen as death ceases to be death—and life ceases to be life. Therefore death must confront us as something unknown and unknowable. It cannot be an abstract or casual unknown. It is not like knowing whether there is life on another planet or whether civilization will survive its present century. It is a far more intimate unknown. It is precisely that which threatens my own knowledge. We can "know" death only by confronting the unsurpassable boundaries of our own experience and knowledge—boundaries that forever limit their scope, but boundaries without which there can be neither experience, nor knowledge, nor selfhood. Death does not confront us as *an* Other, but as *my* Other; it is an Other I could never become, but without which I could never be.

We turn then to those thinkers for whom the problem of Otherness has become the problem of human existence.

Notes

1. Philip Hefner, *The Promise of Teilhard*.
2. Quoted by Christopher Mooney, *Teilhard de Chardin and the Mystery of Christ*, pp. 196 ff.
3. *The Promise of Teilhard*, p. 14.
4. *The Phenomenon of Man*, p. 31.
5. *The Divine Milieu*, p. 46.
6. *The Phenomenon of Man*, p. 29.
7. Ibid., pp. 257 ff.
8. *The Divine Milieu*, p. 58.
9. *Writings in Time of War*, p. 118.
10. *The Phenomenon of Man*, p. 44.
11. Ibid., p. 45.
12. Ibid., p. 44.
13. Ibid., p. 46.
14. *Timaeus*, pp. 30,32.
15. *Divine Milieu*, p. 59.
16. Quoted in *Teilhard de Chardin and the Mystery of Christ*, p. 72.
17. "The Mysticism of Science," *Human Energy*, pp. 168 ff.
18. Ibid., p. 168.
19. *The Phenomenon of Man*, p. 52.
20. Ibid., p. 144.
21. Ibid., p. 145.
22. *The Vision of the Past*, p. 22.
23. *The Phenomenon of Man*, p. 52.
24. Ibid., p. 57.
25. Ibid., p. 57.
26. *The Vision of the Past*, p. 72.
27. *The Phenomenon of Man*, pp. 64 ff.
28. Ibid., p. 163.
29. Ibid., p. 165.
30. Ibid., p. 221.
31. Ibid., p. 250.
32. *The Appearance of Man*, p. 254.
33. *The Phenomenon of Man*, p. 224.
34. Quoted by Henri de Lubac, *The Religion of Teilhard de Chardin*, p. 47.
35. *The Divine Milieu*, p. 82.
36. *The Phenomenon of Man*, p. 273.
37. Ibid., p. 231.
38. Ibid., p. 232.
39. *The Future of Man*, p. 302.

40. *The Phenomenon of Man*, p. 272.
41. *Science and Christ*, p. 57.
42. *The Divine Milieu*, p. 88.
43. Ibid., p. 89.
44. "Mass on the World," *Hymn of the Universe*, p. 31.
45. *The Phenomenon of Man*, p. 220.
46. Ibid., p. 259.
47. *The Future of Man*, p. 127.
48. Ibid., p. 123.
49. *The Phenomenon of Man*, pp. 261 ff.
50. Ibid., p. 262.
51. Ibid., p. 262 ff.
52. *Writings in the Time of War*, p. 145.
53. *The Divine Milieu*, p. 46.
54. Ibid., p. 103.
55. Ibid., p. 102.
56. *The Phenomenon of Man*, p. 294.
57. "The Mysticism of Science," *Human Energy*, p. 165.
58. *The Divine Millieu*, p. 131.
59. Ibid., p. 85.
60. Ibid., p. 61.
61. Ibid., p. 83.

Bibliography

H. James Birx, *Pierre Teilhard de Chardin's Philosophy of Evolution* (Springfield: 1972).

Claude Cuenot, *Science and Faith in Teilhard de Chardin*, tr. Noel Lindsay (London: 1967).

Philip Hefner, *The Promise of Teilhard* (Philadelphia: 1970).

Henri du Lubac, *Teilhard de Chardin, the Man and his Meaning*, tr. René Hague (New York: 1965).

———— *The Religion of Teilhard de Chardin*, tr. René Hague (New York: 1967).

Christopher F. Mooney, *Teilhard de Chardin and the Mystery of Christ* (London: 1966).

Teilhard de Chardin, *The Appearance of Man*, tr. J. M. Cohen (New York: 1965).

———— *Christianity and Evolution*, tr. René Hague (New York: 1971).

———— *The Divine Milieu*, tr. Bernard Wall (New York: 1965).

———— *The Future of Man*, tr. Norman Denny (New York: 1969).

———— *Human Energy*, tr. J. M. Cohen (New York: 1970).

———— *Hymn of the Universe*, tr. Simon Bartholomew (New York: 1965).

────── *The Making of a Mind: Letters from a Soldier-Priest 1914–1919*, tr. René Hague (New York: 1965).

────── *Man's Place in Nature*, tr. René Hague (New York: 1966).

────── *The Phenomenon of Man*, tr. Bernard Wall (New York: 1965).

────── *Science and Christ*, tr. René Hague (New York: 1968).

────── *The Vision of the Past*, tr. J. M. Cohen (New York: 1966).

────── *Writings in Time of War*, tr. René Hague (New York: 1968).

NINE
DEATH AS POSSIBILITY
—*POWER*

---

12 G.W.F. HEGEL

The desire of the Romantics and their Neoplatonic predecessors to achieve a perfect continuity between the human and the natural, between the soul and its universe, inevitably raises the question as to what it was they dreaded in an alienation of the human from the natural. The curious place of Jakob Boehme in that tradition is very revealing. Strongly influenced by the Hermetic philosophers of the Renaissance, Boehme nonetheless discovered in his own spiritual journeys that each ultimate reality is coeval with its opposite Other. It is the same discovery that Blake offers in his poetry, or Goethe in his Mephistopheles. We find it surfacing, even if trivially, in the fascination of the occult with darkness, danger, and evil.

It is a mistake to consider this obscure rival to the One, or this ultimate obstacle to unity, in the Neoplatonic/Romantic tradition something a consistent thinker could eliminate. Instead, it is something the deepest thinkers could not escape, in spite of their declaration of the connectedness of the self with nature; however, it is not surprising that this coeval Other lay hidden under a veil of symbols or was ignored altogether. The dangers in affirming the Other are self-evident. It threatens the very nature of thought itself. The discovery that there is an Other that thought cannot envision destroys the confidence of thinkers that thought they could know the world. To the degree that they cannot know the Other they cannot control it, opening themselves to the indifference and caprice of a nature that suffers no opponents to itself, that takes all things into its blind necessity. (We are still haunted in the thought of the Romantics by Plato's perception that necessity is fundamentally irrational.) Nature, in other words, wears the face of death. To reconcile the human and the natural is not only to pacify and domesticate the powers of nature; it is to rob death of its adventitious sting and perhaps even of its reality. At one level, where the vision of unity has seized the imagination, death is unthinkable to the Romantics; but at another level, where the insuperable Otherness of nature breasts the paper swords of the imagination, the Romantics could scarcely think of anything but death.

The supreme threat of death is *its ability to make me into an Other, but an Other with which I have no connection.* And yet, death is not just *anybody's* death, it is not some abstract condition; it is *my* death. It is a state in which I become a stranger to myself, in which I am alienated from myself. This is the real issue in freedom, as Jakob Boehme saw. If I have a genuine choice, I could go in the direction of life as well as death—toward what I am as well as what I am not. It is a direction in which I go. I am not forced by something exterior to my will. If death is an enemy, it must therefore lodge within my own freedom. If it does not, I am not really free. If not free, I am not alive. To be at all, therefore, is to *be* in the form of acute danger to myself, to have the power of becoming my own Other.

It is in this respect that death is the very thing that thought cannot take into itself. The threat of discontinuity, coming from within in this form, is doubly stupefying; I refuse to think about it. And still, just because it is in this form, we are compelled to think about. It stands directly in the path of all thought. There is no way of going around it. Thought is itself the manifestation of our freedom, and if death lodges in freedom, it is always at the door of thought.

The Romantics and Neoplatonists stopped in the doorway. They thought they could tear the mask of death from nature and find a perfect Oneness behind it. They thought they could cross that threshold by way of vision, but as we have seen, the vision was essentially a retreat away from freedom and, therefore, life. Their vision was a work of grief. If freedom is taken seriously death is no mask; it is the guarantor of freedom.

We shall now examine a body of thought that attempts to take freedom seriously in this fundamentally Behmenist sense. We can say in a preliminary way that the thinkers we shall now study understand that the crisis of Otherness—or transcendence, to use its more common philosophical term—originates from within. They regard the threat of death as a threat of self-alienation, our becoming strangers to ourselves. In one sense, this view of death has already been developed in Christian thought. When Paul spoke of the "resurrection body" and Luther of our *vita extranea*, they meant dying in such a way that we are ourselves and something alien to ourselves. Christians, however, as we have seen, conceived this alien existence antihistorically. The Otherness of death lifts us into a different mode of temporality that has no continuity with worldly history. Jews, however, understood that in our encounter with Otherness we are reconciled not out of history but into it. This view is only implicit in the structure of rabbinical Judaism, for the most part, and is not developed philosophically. The body of thought we now examine attempts to make this insight explicit. These thinkers have taken on the task of meeting the threatened discontinuity of death *by way of history*, and not *by overcoming history*. To put it in the most succinct formula, they seek to show that *the transcendent is not eternal but temporal*.

It is simply mistaken to claim that Boehme's vatic, oracular, but strangely uncouth, writings have themselves introduced the problem of the transcendence of the Other into modern thought. Boehme has the distinction of offering an insight into the problem, but the problem itself received its philosophical shape elsewhere: in the appearance of Descartes' *Meditations* in 1641. Boehme has the greater insight, but Descartes has a much greater philosophical influence. It is in Descartes' idiom, not Boehme's, that the problem is addressed.

Not without justification, the publication of the *Meditations* is often considered as the birth of modern thought. Descartes, distressed by the lack of substantial grounding in all previous philosophy, decided he would start anew. He did not consider all that preceded him as false, only as inadequately verified. He sought first, therefore, a method by which one might arrive at self-evident, certain truth. He began by rigorously subjecting all philosophical propositions to radical doubt, refusing to accept any truth that could not withstand his scrutiny. This was a daring attempt to drive all Otherness out of the mind—and not only from the mind, out of personal existence altogether. This was daring in the sense that Descartes took the risk of arriving at a permanently crippling doubt that would have left the self unable to protect itself from Otherness. Indeed, initially, there is no reason to believe that the mind is to be excused from the attack of doubt. He might well have stripped the self of such content that it would have nothing of its own, and consequently be helpless before, even indistinguishable from, the indifferent universe. He came close. Extending his doubt to include even the possibility that his merest sensory impressions of the world are the results of a deceiving *malin génie*, an evil genius, Descartes arrived at the indubitable conclusion that he was still thinking—even if his thoughts were only doubts—and, therefore, *there must be something thinking*. Or in the familiar expression: I think, therefore I am (*cogito ergo sum*).

This was all he needed. He knew from his thinking that he existed, that he was not therefore simply a *thing*, but that he was a *thinking thing*. On this foundation he could erect, by the careful use of reason, a new and veritable edifice of knowledge. What then happens to the Other? Descartes was careful to insist that the Other is not eliminated by this emboldened philosophical method. On the contrary, he could acknowledge that the Other persistently exerts its influence over the mind, giving shape to its thoughts in ways the mind would not. That is, the world, by way of our experience of it, makes impressions on thought in a manner impossible to reason, but not hostile to reason, since the results of experience can all be neatly integrated into the structures of knowledge. Reason cannot determine what we will experience, but it can always make use of what we have experienced. In summary, Descartes affirmed the reality of the Other from within his system, but the daring use of methodological doubt allowed him to meet the Other with confidence that Otherness can always be managed by thought and managed rationally.

Descartes' metaphysics proved to have serious problems, particularly in his untroubled certainty that he could subdue the Other to reason; but his method to find a self-evident, indubitable point of departure for knowledge would become an emulated philosophical style. What makes Descartes *modern* is his forthright refusal to accept the authority of the past. If what Plato or Aristotle said is true, it is not because they said it, but because we can discover the same truth by the use of reason—without even knowing that Plato or Aristotle had ever existed. Of course, not all subsequent thinkers would follow Descartes in believing that the *cogito* was the obvious place to begin, but they were essentially unanimous in their modernity—that is, in their refusal blindly to accept the authority of past thinkers and in their insistence on an indubitable and self-evident point of departure. The empiricists, for example, took sensory experience as the only adequate starting point, and as a result they seem to have lost Descartes' irreducible *cogito* along the way. It was as though they had thrown the *cogito* to the senses where it was swallowed whole. On the other side of the fence, the idealists did begin with the *cogito*, but could find no good reason to assert the reality of the world's independent Otherness. It was as though the *cogito* had rubbed away all the boundaries between itself and the Other.

At the end of the eighteenth century Immanuel Kant rose to meet the conflict between idealists and empiricists by declaring both sides seriously wanting, though he certainly did not urge a return to Descartes. Kant's attack was directed at the hitherto uncritical use of reason. Without denying the existence of either the self or its Other, Kant argued that the pure use of reason can give us the content of neither. Like Descartes he thought the *cogito* is self-evident, but unlike Descartes he did not think the self could be found *in* its thinking. The self is always prior to, or transcendent to, its own thought; it cannot then be the subject of knowledge. Kant's transcendent self could not know itself any more than light could illumine itself, or the ear hear itself. In the same way, the objective world was not to be denied, but neither could reason take us into its entities, providing knowledge of what things are in themselves. Like the self, the world is transcendent.

In one important respect Kant does sustain one aspect of the Cartesian philosophy: its methodological doubt. In Kant, however, the doubt is permanent. There is no way we can ever arrive at knowledge of the transcendent ego or the transcendent thing-in-itself. The Other lies eternally beyond the grasp of knowledge. However, Kant resolved this dilemma for himself, but not for all his successors, by saying that the metaphysical knowledge we are unable to attain by way of *pure* reason (primarily, the existence of God, the freedom of the will, and the immortality of the soul) is accessible in a different way—by the use of *practical* reason. We can never *know* whether there is a world there, or a God, or a free and immortal soul, but it is nonetheless reasonable to act as if these particular metaphysical claims are true.

Scarcely a generation had passed before Kant's solution came under vigorous attact from another giant of modern thought, G. W. F. Hegel. Where Kant emptied both sides of the Cartesian philosophy of their content—that is, the *cogito* and its Other—then tried to have it all back by fleeing from thought to practice, Hegel wanted not only to affirm both the *cogito* and the Other, he wanted also to bring them together. He wanted to take the Other into the very heart of the self-certain *cogito*, so that the self (in Hegel's thought, Spirit, or *Geist*) would simultaneously *have* an Other and *be* its Other in a perfectly reconciled unity. Hitherto the problem had been that the boundary between the self and the Other had not been drawn firmly enough, so that the one would collapse into its opposite, or had been drawn too firmly, isolating each from the other. The consequence of this dilemma in relation to death has two sides: according to the idealist view, the self cannot die; according to the empiricists, it cannot live. Hegel, determined to avoid both sides of this dilemma, kept the boundary between self and

Other firm, but brought the Other with its boundary into the Self, or Spirit. Hegel wanted to deal with discontinuity, but would not eliminate it nor establish some continuity of his own and thrust it defiantly, but irrationally, before the face of the threatening discontinuity. He brought discontinuity into the Spirit, tirelessly reminding his readers and students that it remains as discontinuity.

Hegel is the first, in other words, to attempt to take death into the center of life, to see the living not as the not-dead, or the not-yet-dead, but as *mortal*.

The reader may be doubtful concerning this last claim. Hasn't human mortality been widely affirmed in other traditions and by other thinkers, even by some of those discussed previously in this work? It has. What is novel in Hegel is not the attempt to bring thought to a recognition of the fact of death, but the attempt to bring death *into* thought itself. We have seen, most notably in Judaism and Christianity, how the fact of death brings the speculative mind to perfect silence. This has led neither tradition to maintain silence with respect to *life*. Christians express wonder at the fact that there is life at all. Jews know that the silence of death challenges the living to continue the conversation that keeps history open. Hegel's gigantic ambitions for philosophy are not to go beyond Christianity and Judaism, nor to replace them with something of his own invention—they are simply to show that what the Christians call faith and the Jews discourse is what the philosopher calls truth.

The issue here is a subtle one and easily misunderstood. If death cannot somehow be taken into thought, thought acquires something of a deathless quality and establishes a region immune to mortality. This was exactly how Plato understood the nature of thought. This has the consequence of closing the doors of meaningful reflection to the experience of anticipated discontinuity in the face of death. *Not only could we not think about death, but all thinking would have the nature of a flight from death.* But, as we have attempted to make clear, it is death that has impelled us into thought. If thought cannot develop the capacity to integrate death into itself, it becomes a kind of sleep from which no one can be awakened by the question of existence. Hegel wanted to rouse us to thought and, in doing so, to make thinking equivalent to living.

Like Descartes, Hegel disregards the authority of previous thinkers and looks for his own self-evident place to begin. However, his point of departure is much more modest than Descartes'; he starts with mere *sense-certainty.* In its purest form sense-certainty is nothing but the rise of Otherness, the first manifestation of a flaw in the perfect but opaque wholeness in which all things are indistinguishable from each other. At first, Otherness is not even constituted by other *things*, just the recognition that there is Otherness—like the first light of dawn, which is enough to make seeing possible but not enough to distinguish what is seen. Once the mind is awakened it is not satisfied with mere Otherness; it soon begins restlessly to distinguish one object from another. Otherness is now other *things*. The viewer then moves from sense-certainty to what Hegel calls *perception.* But the viewer cannot stop here either. The perceived things, in the rising light of knowledge, appear now not as a mere collection of things, but a relatedness of things. When the mind turns from distinct objects to the relations between them, perception has given way to *understanding.*

In our discussion of Hegel's thought as it pertains to death, we shall examine two large areas: Understanding and Reason. Following the custom of many scholars of Hegel, we shall capitalize these two terms only to indicate that Hegel has very special uses for them that only vaguely overlap with their ordinary use. At the outset we can say that it is through the *Understanding* that the problem of death arises, and through the *Reason* that it is resolved. So far, then, all we know is that Hegel's starting point—sense-certainty—quickly gives way to Understanding.

What is not yet apparent is that the movement from sense-perception through perception to Understanding contains within itself the fundamental logic of the whole of being, or the Absolute, as he prefers to call it. These first steps upward from his self-evident starting point, which seem to give increasing distinctiveness to the Other, are but the initial moments in a ceaseless to-and-fro that will not end until absolutely all Otherness has become identical to the subject on whom the dawn of knowledge originally broke. It is therefore necessary that we look more closely at these first simple moves.

Any attempt to identify an object, simply to know it *as* an object, requires that we distinguish it from other objects. As we do this we no longer pay attention to the object as such, but only to its relations. We know what something is only in relation to something else. I know what rain is because I know it to be cold and wet—in contrast to the shower, which is warm and wet, or the sunlight, which is warm and dry. Each of these terms—coldness, warmth, dryness—are relational. Nothing is cold or dry in itself, but only in relation to something that is warm or wet. What is essential for Hegel at this point is that none of these relational terms are found *in* the objects that we know by way of their relations. All of these terms are *universals*; that is, they can be made use of in knowing any number of objects, and not just *this* object or *that* one. Does this mean that we cannot know particular objects in their concrete uniqueness through the use of such universals? We cannot *understand* them except through the universals and the rules by which the universals are applied. Without using these relational terms we can have only the vaguest awareness of Otherness, a mere collection of indistinguishable things, by no means a *world*.

This brings us to a considerable dilemma. What the mind has as its object in Understanding cannot therefore be the things that are understood, but only the relations between them, or the universals, and the rules for applying them. The universals, however, can only be in the Understanding. This is equivalent to saying that the object of the Understanding can only be itself. It is this moment in the to-and-fro between the mind and Otherness that self-consciousness appears; *in Understanding the mind knows itself*. For most thinkers the arrival at self-consciousness represents a terminus, an unsurpassable level of human development. Hegel is unable to accept self-consciousness as unsurpassable because he finds an intolerable contradiction in it.

Self-consciousness is contradictory in the sense that in it all Otherness seems to vanish. In knowing myself I certainly do not know the Other. And yet, Hegel will not let us forget that it was our sense-certainty of the Other that began the process that leads to Understanding and self-consciousness. If our sense-certainty of the Other is denied, we cease to be conscious of ourselves. Here then is the essence of the great Hegelian contradiction: *we must preserve the world in sense-certainty in order to cancel it out in Understanding.* Hegel sometimes formulates this as a longing on the part of self-consciousness to possess the Other. Its contradictoriness then appears in the fact that if it succeeded in having what it lusted after—that is, if it could take the Other into itself—it would cease to exist altogether, since it is before the Other that it comes to self-consciousness. It is this contradictoriness that is the key to understanding the whole, or the Absolute, according to Hegel's philosophy.

Through the Understanding we have come to self-consciousness, but self-consciousness embodies a contradictory quality that causes it irresistibly to transform itself into successively higher levels. As we noted, it is through the Understanding that the problem of death emerges, subsequently to be solved by the Reason. Hegel's account of the unfolding of self-consciousness is one of the most admired parts of his philosophy. It has had a formative influence on a great many later thinkers in such diverse schools as Marxism, phenomenology, and existentialism. We shall follow the path of his thought here as briefly as possible.

The first stage in the development of self-consciousness consists in a "life-and-death" struggle with other selves. Just how and why these other selves appear Hegel does not explain; but it seems reasonable to say that when the self first confronts its own compelling desire to overcome Otherness it will take the simplest strategy of *finding itself in the Other*, thus eliminating Otherness altogether. If it can see itself as the Other, there is in effect no Other there. But if it is looking for itself in the Other it will find not simply an object, but another self-consciousness. This other self-consciousness seeks the same goal of eliminating *its* self-conscious Other. This means that each self-consciousness becomes increasingly aware that it not only *has* an Other, but *is* an Other—but it is an awareness that rises in antagonism, a struggle to the death between each self and its Other. It is significant that Hegel puts the matter in terms of a murderous *struggle* between opposing selves, and not in the mere desire to kill the Other. Unless there is some reciprocity, unless the Other can strike back, it is not a true Other but only a thing that can be swept into the Understanding without the least remainder. "The process then is absolutely the double process of both self-consciousnesses. Each sees the other do the same as itself; each itself does what it demands on the part of the other, and for that reason does what it does, only so far as the other does the same."[1] There must then be a contest, an *agon*, in which two selves view each other simultaneously as the threat and the possibility of their own existence. We must note that the importance of death to Hegel's thought is announced at once, in the most primitive stages of self-consciousness. Unless we risk our own life, subject it to mortal danger in a struggle with another conscious life, we cannot have it for ourselves. At the very beginning death is an ingredient in our self-consciousness: "it is solely by risking life that freedom is obtained; only thus is it tried and proved that the essential nature of self-consciousness is not bare existence, is not the merely immediate form in which it at first makes its appearance, is not its mere absorption in the expanse of life."[2] It is that which is definitively limited by an insuperable Other. But, still, the contradictoriness has not been done away with in this "trial by death." There is too much risk in it. We may die in it, or, what has the same effect for self-consciousness, we may kill the Other in our struggle with it. In each case we lose the very thing we are trying to preserve—our self-consciousness.

Is there, then, some other way of reducing the risk by, say, *overcoming the Other* while *still having it as an Other,* but without causing the physical death of either opponent? The attempt to achieve this goal brings us to the next stage, which Hegel calls the master-servant relationship. In the previous stage the pure self-consciousness *for itself* that first evolves in Understanding is not eliminated, but finds in its contest with the Other that it is also consciousness *for the Other*. This division of the self into two modes of consciousness has its *external* manifestation in the dual roles of master and servant: "The master is the consciousness that exists *for itself*,"[3] and the servant is the consciousness that exists as the master wishes it, *for the master* or for the Other. This will also not succeed in overcoming the contradiction for either the master or the servant. The master faces the dilemma of attempting to achieve an independent consciousness by requiring that the servant be dependent on him, but the master is in turn dependent on the servant's recognition of the master's independence, which is the contradiction in another form. To the degree that the servant has done what the master desires, the servant too is dependent.

But, surprisingly, Hegel considers the place of the servant to be superior to that of the master. The servant's self-consciousness first develops in relation to what the servant perceives to be the master's independence. Insofar as the master is absolutely powerful over the servant, the latter's existence is totally at the mercy of the former. The servant's consciousness now feels an acute danger. It is a consciousness that recognizes death as its "sovereign master." As a servant standing before the master I am as nothing. The merest gesture on the part of the Other can mean my death. There is no possibility of a struggle here. The opposed pair is not the master's life and my life—but my life and my death. My life, for the first time, is to be understood as that which takes the possibility of death into itself, but not idly, not through occasional moments of self-doubt; instead, death is perceived through a "complete perturbation" of my entire consciousness. It is not as though I should now and then be conscious of my death, but that my self-consciousness rest completely on the possibility of death. The master got the thing desired: a servant who continues physically to live, but has died internally. This interiorization of death, however, this capitulation to the master, has a surprising and ironic consequence. What the servant has done is simply to have achieved a self-consciousness that is independent of the Other. Since death is not something that is done to my physical body by something external to it, but is *my death*, internalized as the end of *my life*, my self-consciousness has oriented itself entirely around an Otherness which is *my* Otherness—that is, myself as a dead Other.

Previously death was represented as the external boundary of my existence, limiting me to my own self-consciousness. Now in the master-servant relationship, I am not locked in mortal struggle with the master but have taken the master's view of my dispensability into myself. This means that I am no longer limited *to* my self-consciousness, but am limited *by* my self-consciousness. I am not *made* mortal by a hostile Other, but *am* mortal as an Other to myself. *This is exactly the point in our long narrative where mortality is first described as part of the structure of selfhood.* No philosopher prior to Hegel had attained such a conception. The agency of death had always been viewed as external. Even in Freud, where for a moment it seemed he would say that as we die by choice we could also live by choice, we do not find a conception of mortality anywhere near this complete—chiefly because Freud's monistic materialism allowed no capacity finally for an irreducibly internalized Other. Freud's Other, in the form of the superego, finally reduces to the same instinct by which the whole self is moved.

In terminology used earlier, we can say that Hegel has here succeeded in finding a continuity for life that does not take all discontinuity totally into itself, thereby wiping away all sense of its own meaning, but joins itself to discontinuity in such a way that each requires the other.

Hegel, however, is not yet satisfied with this account of self-consciousness, for it brings a new contradiction to light. Because the very structure of the servant's selfhood is mortal, we have reached a high level of freedom within the servant's consciousness, but only at the price of a new bondage *without*. Hegel reminds us that the independent self-consciousness of the servant is, after all, the self-consciousness of a *servant*. The freedom achieved by the servant is not a freedom *from* servitude, but *in* servitude. The servant *as servant* is not free to alter the structure of the *world* except by identifying with the *objects* of labor. This can only mean that the servant is closed in by the actual things of the world.

The intolerability of this bondage eventually leads to another stage of consciousness, in which one ignores the world of external things and withdraws into thought: "In thinking I am free, because I am not in an other, but remain simply and solely in touch with myself; and the object which for me is my essential reality, is in undivided unity my self-existence; and my procedure in dealing with notions is a process within myself." Hegel calls this stage *Stoicism* and means by it exactly what was attempted historically by the classical Stoics—a key to the fact that Hegel understands each of these stages to have their manifestations in human history.

In one respect the Stoics are successful. That they had overcome the master-servant relationship utterly is shown by the fact that two of the greatest Stoics were Marcus Aurelius, Emperor of Rome, and Epictetus, a Roman slave. But in another respect, the Stoics find that same persistent contradiction at the very center of their resolution. They had sought to eliminate the Other by retreating into thought; they succeeded only in making thought into an Other, but an Other "that lacks the concrete filling of life." What the Stoics have found is "merely the notion of freedom, not living freedom itself."[4] To put it in slightly different terms, what the Stoics wanted to do was negate the Other by negating the objects of the external world, but this move was inadequate, its intentions too limited. The Stoics were not finally concerned with the act of negation, but with the idea of negation.

This becomes obvious in the next stage, which Hegel historically identifies with the Sceptics: "*Scepticism* is the realization of that of which Stoicism is merely the notion, and is the actual experience of what freedom of thought is; it is in itself and essentially the negative, and must so exhibit itself."[5] But Scepticism is no more able to hold the contradiction of consciousness from the door of thought than Stoicism. It is, in fact, directly self-contradictory. It announces the negation of all things, but that negation itself still exists: "It announces the nullity of seeing, hearing, and so on, yet *itself* sees and hears."[6]

The failure of Scepticism throws us into the stage of the *Unhappy Consciousness*. The historical period corresponding to this stage of consciousness is the Christian Middle Ages. The Unhappy Consciousness, like Stoicism and Scepticism, does not attempt to resolve the self-contradiction of consciousness by identifying Otherness with the external world or its contents. If there is any advance of medieval Christians over Stoics and Sceptics it is that they take the world seriously. They neither disregard nor deny it; they do, however, disavow it. Where the Stoics directed their negativity toward the world as such, and the Sceptics toward thought, the Unhappy Consciousness is negative toward both at the same time, adopting a strategy of asceticism in relation to the world and hope in an afterlife in relation to the soul. But ascetics and otherworldly persons also fall victim to contradiction inasmuch as the content of their lives is that which they *have not* and that which they *are not*.

We should take particular note of the fact that death has been driven back out of consciousness in this latest stage. The Unhappy Consciousness can no longer embrace its finitude within itself, but struggles to overcome it by continuing into an *after*life. The rich sense of mortality present in the servant is now gone, replaced by an uncertain otherworldliness. In one sense this is a descent from the servant's stage of self-consciousness, but it is an inescapable descent. The servant could not remain a servant—for the contradiction of self-consciousness at that stage is intolerable and impels one toward a new form of consciousness. But in another sense, the emergence of the Unhappy Consciousness is exceedingly significant, because *it definitively exposes us to the poverty of the Understanding.*

The Understanding, as we noted, has the function of seizing on the distinctions between objects. It is ever alert to the differences between things. We understand what something is by seeing what it is not. Consciousness dawned from the Understanding when we saw that we are not the Other. Understanding is therefore busy establishing discontinuity: Otherness. It is in the service of transcendence, holding things eternally apart. This is why the problem of death emerges by way of Understanding—because we come to see ourselves irreversibly alienated from every form of Otherness, including finally our own minds. The Unhappy Consciousness is the point at which the Understanding has at last become alienated from even itself. It is so run through by its own quality of seeing distinctions that it can no longer be *what* it is or *where* it is—thus an *other*world where it cannot be, and an *after*life that it cannot be. Understanding in its highest form is *grief*—a state of such complete alienation that neither life nor death is a genuine possibility. *The task therefore is to find a way of conceiving death as a possibility.*

Although darkness has closed in on the Understanding by way of the medieval Unhappy Consciousness, a new form of knowledge is preparing itself. "The owl of Minerva spreads its wings only with the falling of dusk," Hegel declared in a celebrated line.[7] The Middle Ages comes to an end with the appearance of the Renaissance. For Hegel this shift of historical epochs corresponds to the passage from *Verstand* to *Vernunft*, Understanding to Reason. The historical move is only a token of an inner move that occurs in the Self (*Geist*). Reason, like the Understanding, evolves out of the Self's own structure, with the same apparent necessity as the passage from one age of world history to another.

We indicated that Hegel has his own definition of Reason. If Understanding seizes on the distinction between objects, that is, the way in which one thing is not another, *Reason leaps beyond to seize the identity of those objects just separated by the Understanding.* Hegel is quite careful, however, not to allow Understanding to be replaced by Reason. There are quite obvious regions of human life where Understanding is required. In the sciences, for example, it would be foolish, even dangerous, to ignore the distinction between such objects as atoms and molecules, or microbes and antibodies, or mass and velocity. In putting on our clothes, crossing the street, eating lunch—in all such areas of ordinary human existence—Understanding is indispensable to life itself. Nonetheless, Understanding has its acute limitations: since we can only know what things *are not*, we cannot know what they truly *are*. Each object of the Understanding can be known only in its relatedness—that is, only relatively. There are no absolute objects for the Understanding, that is, objects complete in themselves. We are, therefore, simply drifting on a sea of ever-changing forms, with no possibility of a firm anchorage, much less any fixed points for navigation. It is as though we would be forced to live in Kant's world of ineradicable doubt, where both the subject and the object are transcendent and thus beyond knowledge.

Hegel's intention is, therefore, both to preserve understanding *and* go beyond it, to affirm complete relativity *and* the Absolute. He does this by giving Reason the task of taking the opposition of things into itself. It is an act of Reason not to determine *which* objects are truly distinguished and therefore proper objects of knowledge, but to see that this entire set of objects belongs to the same region of relatedness—or oppositeness. Thus, the objects of Reason are not opposed to each other, but are the regions within which opposition is able to exist. In Hegel's dynamic view of reality we remember that when one object is thought to be distinct from another it is not as though they simply are two objects existing alongside of, or independently of, each other— they are directly contradictory; they seek to destroy the other, to overcome the Otherness of the other. The ever-changing sea of consciousness is not to be thought of as *unceasing movement*, but *unceasing conflict*. The whole of reality is in the grip of a deadly reciprocity. Finitude, destruction, and death everywhere characterize the existence of individual objects. Now, from the perspective of Reason we can see that what keeps the whole of being from destroying itself is that this contradictoriness is contained within it as the very principle of being. It is Reason that has the capacity to grasp the whole according to the principle of its self-contradiction. It is here that Hegel introduces the famous notion of the *dialectic*. Two objects are dialectically related when each is viewed as the antagonistic Other of its opposite. Reason is inherently dialectical; it sees wholes only in terms of their self-contradictoriness. Hegel put the essence of this way of thinking most succinctly in his early writings with the claim that through the use of Reason we can arrive at the "identity of identity and non-identity," a claim one might well consider as the central idea of the Hegelian system.[8]

If the objects of Reason are themselves absolute, we might briefly examine one such absolute object. Hegel offers as examples the reigning concepts of traditional metaphysics: the world, the soul, freedom, God, and the Spirit. Consider the world, for example. If we view the world nondialectically, through the Understanding, we will not only be able to distinguish its contents from one another, we will also distinguish the world as a whole apart from objects or realities outside itself, perhaps other worlds. In this case, the world is not absolute, but relative and therefore vulnerable to that which it is not. If we view the world dialectically, through Reason, we will see it as the very being that exists to contain contradiction within itself, but is contradictory to nothing else. It is entire in itself and needs nothing else to exist. In viewing the world dialectically, the world ceases to be an object of the Understanding. The empirical sciences, that is, that kind of knowing that depends on the rules of opposition inherent in Understanding, cannot know anything absolute; they can have no knowledge of the soul, of freedom, of God, or of the Spirit. The sciences can have no knowledge of the higher unity that makes the oppositeness of their respective subject matters possible.

Hegel makes another distinction here that is useful to our comprehension of his thought. The objects of Reason are infinite, and by infinite he does not mean without end, but complete in itself. The open-ended infinity of, say, a sequence of numbers is not a true infinity. He refers to it in fact as a "bad infinity." The reason for this is that insofar as there could always be something more to the series there is always some kind of limitation. He admits that there are instances of infinity in the Understanding, but he insists that they are in every case forms of bad infinity. The truly infinite can exist only for the Reason.

The two forms of the infinite can be distinguished in another way. The true infinite always takes its Other into itself; the bad infinite is never able to swallow the sea onto which it has begun its endless voyage. Bad infinity can be pictured as a line without an end; true infinity as a circle without an outside. This distinction returns us to the essential place of death in Hegel's thought. Since bad infinity cannot even take the Other into itself, it can never contain its own death. Indeed, it is precisely bad infinity that is involved in the theory of the immortal soul; this soul survives the destruction of the body and lives on indefinitely. Hegel's contemptuous term for such a theory is *Dogma*, that is, the presumption of the Understanding that it possesses the objects of Reason. Understanding cannot affix a definite end to life, anymore than it can to the world; there is always something more, something afterwards, something remaining. The theory of immortality grows out of this perversion of the Understanding.

True death, however, is not a dogma. While it is absolutely absurd to the Understanding, it is absolutely required by the Reason. *Reason can comprehend nothing except that which has death within it*; that is, Reason sees each object, each person, in terms of itself and its opposite, its existence and its destruction. And that is equivalent to saying that the infinite is truly infinite only if it has taken death into itself as essential to its very being. Even more decisively: *whatever has taken death into itself is truly infinite*.

To perceive the true impact of this view of death we would do well to pause a moment to note a crucial difference between Hegel and Kant. Hegel was concerned to show that Kant was in error in his claim that the thing-in-itself could not be known. His unhappiness with Kant on this point appears frequently enough that we can conclude that something important was at stake in it for Hegel. There is, to be sure, great force in Kant's idea that knowledge does not have the capacity to enter into the inside of things; we sense something admirably modest about this. For Hegel, however, this modesty was really a masked arrogance. Among the many objections Hegel leveled against Kant on this question was the charge that he quite obviously could not have *discovered* the thing-in-itself, for then he would have known it; but to say that we could not know it is to say that he knows it is there. The thing-in-itself, in other words, is a mere invention of knowledge, not an obstruction to it. Thus, far from being an Other, it is simply an extension of the subject into bad infinity.

What is at stake for Hegel in this issue is the genuine power of the Other. *The Other cannot be an invention of knowledge*; it must be a true Other that forces itself on the knower, but persists in remaining Other. In turn, we see the power of Reason. Kant wanted to clip the wings of Reason to prevent its speculative soaring; Hegel makes use of Reason to put the whole of being into flight. There is, however, no flight, no movement, no life without death. Death as such is not an object of knowledge—that is, it cannot be understood—but since it is dialectically embraced by Reason, there can be no knowledge without death.

Here we can see how effectively Hegel has conjoined freedom and death. We noted that the emergence of Reason occurs in the Self (*Geist*), it is an ingredient in the structure of the Self. This means that the dialectical reconciliation of the Self and its opposite occurs within the Self. If it were the case, as in the Understanding, that the subject could be reconciled with its object only by something outside itself, it would not even be a subject, but an object for the reconciling agent. If I find myself deeply alienated from another person, unable to overcome the hostility on either side, and then am reconciled by a common friend, I am not the subject but the object of the reconciling action. In common discourse we might say we have "come to an understanding" and are now able to accept our differences. If I were the subject of the reconciliation, it could only be cause I have out of my own existence been able to take my differences with the Other into my relation with the Other. "Let us reason together," we might say.

This is all the more critical when that opposition to myself *is* myself—which is the crisis death causes in me. If I regard my mortality as the inevitable demise imposed on my physical existence by an external agent, even if it is nature itself, and if I struggle against it in the attempt to extend my natural life indefinitely, I am in conflict with myself. I want to be something else, something that lasts indefinitely; therefore, I exist in the form of not wanting to be who I am. If I then seek to be reconciled through the offices of another—as, say, by the grace of God expressed in the sacraments of the church—I would only have traded my freedom for a more acute self-alienation. We are genuinely free only when we embrace in the dialectic of Reason both our existence and nonexistence as though they belonged together.

This is the greatest strength in Hegel's thinking, but it is also its most serious flaw, for having given Reason the task not of making distinctions, but reconciling them, he finds no way—or wishes to find no way—of stopping Reason from reconciling all distinctions whatsoever. The restless to-and-fro that begins with the merest awakening of sense-certainty in the Spirit builds to a thundering crescendo in the dialectic of the Reason that cannot cease until it has taken all things into itself.

We noted earlier that for Hegel all the objects of rational knowledge—such as the world, God, and the Spirit—are infinite. We must now take notice of the fact that each of these infinite realities is identical to all the others, since none of them could have left the others out. This has the startling conclusion that the very Spirit that first awoke to the dawn of sensory knowledge can itself have no Other and is therefore nothing less than God himself. This runaway inclusiveness on Hegel's part allows the observation that the knowledge of the world that can be found in any existing personal self is but a manifestation of the Absolute Spirit's knowledge of itself. Each event, however minute or glorious, is only a moment in this single act of the Spirit's self-knowledge. Therefore, every act of knowledge on my part is nothing less than the knowledge of God (or the Spirit)—that is, knowledge that is both about God and by God. Thus Hegel can say of his *Logic* that it is "the account of *God* as he is in his eternal essence before the creation of nature and any finite spirit."[9] History is not the serial appearance of individual persons only, but also the way in which the Spirit unfolds its infinitude out of its very being. Indeed, the Spirit posits those persons, along with every other finite thing, only in order to unfold its own infinitude.

Hegel succeeded in placing mortality at the very center of human existence, an achievement no previous thinker could have claimed; however, the method he designed proved to have an appetite that was not to be satisfied until it had swallowed every discrete manifestation of the Spirit into the whole. *Hegel succeeded in finding a place for death in the structure of thought, but in doing so he left no place for the individual.*

We observed earlier in the concluding remarks concerning the Unhappy Consciousness that Hegel was faced with the task of showing how death is a human possibility—something Understanding could not grasp. It is only through Reason that death is a possibility for me, or is *my* possibility, as an option for my existence; it is a possibility I carry with me at all times as part of the very structure of my Selfhood. But the very means of reaching this point has left no discrete Self capable of dying. In Hegel's theory death is possible, but there is no one there to die.

Notes

1. *The Phenomenology of Mind*, p. 230.
2. Ibid., p. 233.
3. Ibid., p. 234.
4. Ibid., p. 245.
5. Ibid., p. 246.
6. Ibid., p. 250.
7. *The Philosophy of Right*, para. 13.
8. Cf. Taylor, *Hegel*, pp. 48 ff.
9. Quoted in Soll, *An Introduction to Hegel's Metaphysics*, p. 137.

Bibliography

Emil Fackenheim, *The Religious Dimensions in Hegel's Thought* (New York: 1965).

Murray Greene, *Hegel on the Soul: A Speculative Anthropology* (The Hague: 1972).

G. W. F. Hegel, *The Phenomenology of Mind*, tr. J. B. Baillie (New York: 1967).

———— *The Philosophy of Right*, tr. T. M. Knox (Oxford: 1942).

Jean Hyppolite, *Studies on Marx and Hegel*, tr. John O'Neill (New York: 1969).

Nathan Rothenstreich, *From Substance to Subject: Studies in Hegel* (The Hague: 1974).

Ivan Soll, *An Introduction to Hegel's Metaphysics* (Chicago: 1969).

Charles Taylor, *Hegel* (Cambridge: 1975).

13 JEAN-PAUL SARTRE

In 1933, Jean-Paul Sartre, then in his twenty-ninth year, won a fellow-ship to study at the Institut Francais in Berlin. The year he spent there had a decisive role in shaping his thought. For the first time he was exposed to three German philosophers then largely overlooked in French education: Hegel, Husserl, and Heidegger. The principal dynamic in Sartre's thought has consistently been his interior and aggressive discussion with the prevailing ideas in these three philosophers. The most important influence in Sartre's education to that point had been Descartes and the Cartesian philosophy that still flourished in the French schools and universities. That is, the *cogito* was still the intellectual center of gravity for formal thought. It is an index to Sartre's skill as a thinker that he was able in this year to master—in a foreign tongue—three philosophical systems of fabled complexity, but not only to master them, to recast their fundamental ideas into an enormous work that bears the stamp of his own originality.

The first sentence of his work, *Being and Nothingness*, written in the decade between his year in Germany and its publication in 1943, provides a precise summary of the influence German philosophy had on him: "Modern thought has realized considerable progress by reducing the existent to the series of appearances which manifest it."[1] There is a clear echo here of Hegel's rejection of the Kantian thesis that existence is hidden behind its appearance. This immediate reference to appearance also indicates that he intends to initiate his discussion of the nature of being within that area of philosophical labor known as *phenomenology*, whose leading representatives are Husserl and Heidegger.

It had already become clear from earlier published work that Sartre had put considerable critical distance between himself and Husserl. In his essay, *The Transcendence of the Ego*, he rejected Husserl's notion that there is a transcendent ego nestled behind the accumulation of received phenomena in the mind, but an ego that does not offer a phenomenon of itself. This is a view similar to Kant's, and Sartre preferred a much more dynamic, and by no means stationary, center of consciousness. It is clear in *Being and Nothingness* that Sartre has set Husserl aside by denying the validity of another crucial phenomenological procedure. In studying the nature of the mind and its ideas Husserl had insisted that the question of existence must be removed from philosophical consideration, for it contributes nothing to the clarity of our analysis of the way in which the mind seizes on appearances of things. Sartre quite obviously has agreed with Heidegger that suspending the question of existence is impossible and that, on the contrary, *the question of the existence of the appearance* is itself the premier philosophical question. *Being and Nothingness*, as we shall see, is an extended treatment of that question.

What is less obvious in that opening sentence is Sartre's departure from a central insight of Cartesian philosophy. While he does not tamper with the "modern" thinker's attempt to ground philosophy in the self-evident rather than in the authoritative subject matter of the past, and while he seems determined to begin with the *cogito*, he makes a subtle but all-important shift from knowledge to consciousness. When Descartes stressed the importance of doubt, it was the *dubiousness of knowledge* that he had in focus; when he concluded that he exists because he thinks, it was *existing in knowledge* that he meant. He did not find himself in his consciousness, but in the knowledge of which he was conscious.

By making the shift from knowledge to consciousness as the basis of philosophy, Sartre is following the path Hegel had already outlined. We do not need to read very far into Sartre to discover that Hegel is by far the most influential force in his intellectual development. As will become increasingly clear, he was persuaded that Hegel's treatment of the problem of the Other was a significant advance over the dualistic dilemmas that had arisen in the centuries since Descartes, which we discussed briefly above. At the same time, however, he also saw the dreadful flaw in Hegel's thought. Sartre could see that Hegel's inexhaustible dialectic first related the self to its Other but then caused the individual to disappear. Although Sartre apparently had not read

Kierkegaard he was familiar with the latter's reintroduction of the individual back into the universe, which Hegel's absolute had taken into itself. Our interest in Sartre here arises from the clarity of his perception of the problem of the Other, which has developed in modern thought since Descartes, and from the accuracy with which he has understood both the triumph and the failure of Hegel. As we characterized Hegel's dilemma, it was that he had succeeded in integrating death into thought, but then forced the individual to fall away. We shall examine Sartre to see if he can hold on to Hegel's integration of Otherness into selfhood (that is, sustain a workable conception of human mortality), without losing the individual to thought. Can Sartre, in brief, offer a description of existence that is both personal and mortal?

Although it is usually distorting to characterize a system as intricately constructed as Sartre's as growing organically around a single informing insight, it still seems to be the case that it is one feature of consciousness in particular that supplies the vital nerve of Sartre's thought. If this particular feature can be taken hold of clearly at the outset, what follows will certainly appear in the deep consistency all careful readers of Sartre know his thought to have. Here is that feature: *Consciousness is always consciousness of* . . . . Properly speaking, I may not even say that my consciousness *has* an object; consciousness is always *of* an object. There is nothing I have that could be called consciousness and that I could attach to this object or that object; either I am conscious *of* this or that, or I am not conscious at all. This gives consciousness the peculiar quality of being oriented toward that which is beyond itself. Consciousness cannot simply be itself, isolated from objects, as knowledge can be itself. It must always be *of* something that it cannot *be*.

This idea is not original with Sartre. It appears first in the philosophy of Hegel and constitutes the very heart of Husserl's phenomenology. Sartre borrows Husserl's term *intentionality* to describe this aspect of consciousness. Intentionality has the useful nuance of introducing a kind of willfulness into consciousness, conveying the sense that consciousness is not something that happens to me but something I am actively engaged in doing or being. Consciousness is not something I *have*, as a possession, but something I *am*. The fact that I have not noticed the flowers on the table between us until we have almost finished dinner is not that the flowers have been witholding themselves from my attention, but, to use the rather awkward formulation of the phenomenologists, I have not *intended them*. It is not that I intended them out of existence by not seeing them, nor into existence by noticing them for the first time; I was simply present in such a way that there were no flowers there for me. That has to do with the way I have been there; not the way the flowers have been there.

Important to the notion of intentionality is the *positional* nature of consciousness. To become aware of the flowers between us is not to place the flowers on the table, but to place myself in relation to the flowers, to take a position with reference to them. To be conscious is thus to be some*where*. When I take notice of the flowers I am for the first time seated *where* the flowers are on the table between us. It is true that I have not physically moved, but the *where* has nonetheless been changed. It is just this refinement of the concept of intentionality that allows Sartre to carry his readers into reflections that well exceed the limits of strictly phenomenological interests. It is by way of the notion of the positionality of consciousness that Sartre introduces self-consciousness and freedom into the analysis of human existence, and, what is more, introduces it in such a way that it does not become a mere moment in the dialectical self-unfolding of Hegel's Absolute Spirit.

Sartre asks us to examine the positional nature of consciousness by considering a most ordinary example: counting cigarettes.[2] "If I count the cigarettes which are in that case, I have the impression of disclosing an objective property of this collection of cigarettes: *they are a dozen.*" Now, should it happen that someone asks what I am doing, I could reply at once that I am counting. I am, in other words, conscious of the fact that I am counting. Counting is itself, of course, a conscious activity; therefore, when I answer, "I am counting," it is because I am conscious of a kind of consciousness. This is what most persons call ordinary self-consciousness, and do so without feeling a need to continue their analysis. Sartre is by no means finished with his analysis. He wants to draw our attention at once to a most unusual situation. We have just seen that to be conscious is to be positional; when I am counting I am positioned in a certain way in relation to the cigarettes. *However*, when I am conscious of consciousness, positionality vanishes. How could I be some*where* with relation to my consciousness of counting? I am aware that the flowers are between us, but where am I in relation to that awareness? Quite obviously, when it comes to *self*-consciousness I am not existing positionally; or, I am not *anywhere*.

It cannot be exaggerated how much purchase Sartre sees in this apparently simple idea. To begin with, we must note that all positional consciousness presupposes self- or non-positional consciousness: "This self-consciousness we ought to consider not as a new consciousness, but as *the only mode of existence which is possible for a con-*

sciousness of something."³ The force of this point will be more apparent if we turn back to the example of counting the cigarettes and introduce a variation into it. If someone should ask me what I am doing with those cigarettes and I should reply, honestly, "I haven't the faintest idea," I am in fact doing nothing with them. Unless I am conscious of counting, I am not counting; and if I am consciously counting, I can *always* be conscious of that consciousness, or self-conscious. Now, it is also the case that while I am conscious of the fact that I am counting, I cannot continue the counting. I cannot explain to someone what I am doing *and* keep track of the number of cigarettes. The obvious reason for this is that since I *am* conscious I cannot be conscious with part of my being. My *whole* being is taken into the consciousness *of* Sartre refers to the kind of consciousness that is not interrupted with self-consciousness as the "pre-reflective consciousness." Absolutely everything we do is therefore prereflective in this sense, else we are not doing it; thus there is nothing we can do in such a way that we cannot ever be aware of it. As we shall see, it is on this basis that Sartre draws his famous conclusion that we are responsible for everything that happens to us. He will even express his agreement with the extreme claim that "there are no innocent victims."⁴

In addition to the fact that self-consciousness always lurks beneath the surface of whatever it is we are doing, there is the fact that self-consciousness, so conceived, is *Absolute*. It is here that Sartre erects his dam across Hegel's raging dialectic, containing the entire to-and-fro of consciousness within the individual. Hegel placed his individual as an alien before the Otherness of the universe, but then conceived of consciousness as a way of overcoming that alienation; unfortunately, it overcame the individual as well. Sartre's individual is no less an alien, but an alien whose very consciousness is constituted by an irreconcilable alienation. It is with the absoluteness of self-consciousness that we first come across the individual condemned to be a stranger in his or her own universe.

The simplest way to state the absolute nature of consciousness is to stress that in self-consciousness consciousness is identical with itself. This has to do with the reason why "consciousness of consciousness is not positional; it is because it is one with the consciousness of which it is consciousness." This self-identity has the effect of sealing consciousness in on itself. It can have no motivation outside itself, for then it would be the effect of something of which it is not conscious; therefore, it could not be completely conscious of itself—that, as we have just seen, is impossible: "consciousness is consciousness through and through. It can be limited only by itself." The essential characteristic of consciousness is that it is determined by itself; however, even here we must carefully watch our language for it is distorting to say that consciousness *causes itself* since that presupposes it is somehow prior to itself, which it cannot be. It has no "before." "It would be more exact to say very simply: The existence of consciousness comes from consciousness itself."[5] Even with this remark, Sartre cautions us from assuming that what is meant here is that consciousness therefore comes from nothing. "Consciousness is prior to nothingness," Sartre adds, though just how this could be the case is not yet fully evident.[6]

It is worth noting here that Sartre's definition of consciousness has succeeded in achieving what Hegel called the "true infinite," namely, that which is limited only by itself. This has the clear advantage of making it unnecessary, indeed impossible, for consciousness to enlarge itself beyond the individual—how could the infinite enlarge itself? But it presents Sartre with a serious dilemma at the same time: *by making self-consciousness absolute has he not also caused the Other to vanish*? This is the most critical problem in Sartre's philosophy. His treatment of this problem constitutes the most original and valuable contribution of his thought.

Before we describe the way in which Sartre attempts to preserve the Other while maintaining the integrity of the individual in his or her absolute self-consciousness, it would be well briefly to retrace the path we have followed to this point and indicate which sections still lie before us. We are attempting to see whether Sartre can preserve Hegel's achievement of integrating death into a definition of human existence, without subsequently losing it to the deluge of the Hegelian dialectic. Sartre, with a clear view of this problem in Hegel, nonetheless follows Hegel rather than Descartes in preferring consciousness to knowledge as the point of departure for his analysis of human existence. Like Hegel and the phenomenologists, Sartre emphasizes the intentionality of consciousness, that is, the fact that it is always consciousness *of*. Intentionality implies positionality, it means being some*where*; but paradoxically it also implies the nonpositionality of self-consciousness. Self-consciousness is never oriented to *this* object or *this* place, but can always instruct us that object and place are what they are *only* for consciousness. We are therefore in the world, but radically free from it or, to use the somewhat more negative expression, always an alien within it. This alienation, however, derives from the fact that consciousness can come only from itself. We are therefore threatened by the possibility that having preserved the individual in its absolute freedom, Sartre has lost the Other.

If, as we indicated above, the vital nerve of Sartre's system is the notion of intentionality, it is also the case that the most serious threat to that system is the disappearance of the Other beyond the boundaries of absolute consciousness. It is in meeting this threat that we can see how serious Sartre is about the *of* in *consciousness of.* "This definition of consciousness," he explains, "can be taken in two very distinct senses: either we understand by this that consciousness is constitutive of the being of its object, or it means that consciousness in its inmost nature is a relation to a transcendent being." If we take the definition in the former sense it proves to be contradictory, for we are asking consciousness to oppose itself in the form of an object, which is precisely what it *cannot* do in its absolute self-identity. In the latter sense of the definition we are to take particular note of the term "transcendent."[7] This was the term Kant used for the thing-in-itself that lay beyond knowledge, as well as for the ego that preceded knowledge as the knower. If it is contradictory for consciousness to posit *the presence of something*, must it not then be the case that consciousness is a relation to a transcendent being in the form of the *absence of something*? At this juncture in his reflection Sartre offers an extremely daring solution: if consciousness is a way of being, then the transcendent object cannot present itself to consciousness as *another being*, for then consciousness would only be opposing itself; the object can be transcendent to consciousness only if it is present as *non-being*. "Thus the being of the object is pure non-being. It is defined as a *lack*. It is that which escapes, that which by definition will never be given, that which offers itself only in fleeing."[8]

This puts us in the strange position of having to conclude that consciousness can be only if it is conscious of that which it cannot be; that is, its being is supported by non-being: "consciousness is born *supported by* a being which is not itself."[9] We can see here that once he had shown the absolute nature of consciousness Sartre had not utterly discarded Hegel's dialectic, but had rather integrated the dialectic into the very heart of consciousness. For being to be supported by non-being means that to be is always to be in question. Descartes had restricted doubt to knowledge in a way that spared him from questioning existence itself. Sartre's remarkable move here has thrust doubt into the structure of existence so firmly that it is impossible to exist except in the mode of doubt. This reemergence of the dialectic brings Sartre to a more complete definition of consciousness: "*consciousness is a being such that in its being, its being is in question in so far as this being implies a being other than itself.*"[10]

But in what way is this a solution to the problem of the Other? If the Other appears in the form of its absence, or non-being, how could it possibly appear at all? Why would it not be the case that as we looked around us we do not see ciphers, mere empty spaces, pockets of void, rather than things? This latter question contains in itself the very misunderstanding that has led many a critical reader of Sartre to drop *Being and Nothingness* in despair, before even getting out of the introduction—which, like the notorious preface to Hegel's *Phenomenology*, is the most difficult and important part of the entire volume. The reason there is a misunderstanding in this question is that it presumes that we are looking at something as at an object that exceeds the limits of our vision and therefore misses the force of the nature of consciousness *of*. Looking at something is being conscious of it; it is the very form consciousness has taken—not in reference to the thing but in itself. This is not to say, however, that consciousness simply stretches itself about into an assortment of shapes. Its shaping is always a pointing toward that which it is not and cannot be. Its object is therefore something that will not allow itself to be absorbed into consciousness. We are therefore conscious of its solid resistance; it is entirely resistant to the viewer. We see it as something that can only be seen. Sartre uses the term "massive" for this; it is merely a mass, a solidity. It has no inside, no secrets. If there is an inside, or something hidden, we are either conscious of it and it is no longer secret, or we are not conscious of it and therefore it appears as though it were completely exposed to our view of it. But since consciousness can never be truly moved from without, the object has no power over consciousness; it is simply there *for* consciousness. Like consciousness it is completely identified with itself. Sartre's collective term for that kind of being of which we are conscious is *being-in-itself (être-en-soi)*. It is also, for the same reason, unnecessary, superfluous, or to use the common French term, *de trop*.[11]

The most effective evocation of this view of being as in-itself occurs in Sartre's first important literary work, *Nausea* (1938). The narrator Roquentin is seated in a park where his gaze falls on the roots of a chestnut tree at his feet: "I was sitting, stooping forward, head bowed, alone in front of this black knotty mass, which frightened me. Then I had a vision. It left me breathless." The vision was simply of the root, disconnected, merely there

> in such a way that I could not explain it. Knotty, inert, nameless, it fascinated me, filled my eyes, brought me back unceasingly to its

own existence. In vain to repeat: "This is a root"—it didn't work any more. I saw clearly that you could not pass from its function as a root, as a breathing pump, *to that*, to this hard and compact skin of a sea lion, to this oily, callous, headstrong look. The function explained nothing: it allowed you to understand generally that it was a root, but not *that one* at all.[12]

To employ the language of *Being and Nothingness*, which Sartre had begun to write about at the time of this novel, Roquentin suddenly had a vision of an object in-itself *as* in-itself. It was a moment when self-consciousness crept back into the wakefulness of the viewer, unable to disengage the viewer from his vision, destroying its positionality altogether and making all connections unnecessary, or superfluous. Roquentin seemed to be drifting through a sea of superfluous objects—so disconnected it did not even make sense to say they were "absurd"—inducing in him precisely the kind of nausea one might experience in a boat that had lost its mooring and rudder.

We are to remember that the relationship between consciousness and its object is dialectical, that the in-itself is not simply there, but there for consciousness that is not, and cannot be, in-itself. If the in-itself is a massive, solid being through and through, consciousness must then be its opposite: divided against itself, but thoroughly connected nonetheless; it is not superfluous but necessary. For consciousness conceived as the dialectical opposite of the in-itself Sartre uses the term *for-itself (être-pour-soi)*. In perfect contrast with the massiveness of the in-itself the for-itself constitutes a void, a nothingness that "lies coiled in the heart of being—like a worm."[13] The for-itself is a *nihilation* of being, the introduction of a nothingness into its very center in such a way that it allows it to stand in opposition to an in-itself, which it is not. Unless nothingness inserts itself consciousness is not possible.

Sartre's widely cited example of the necessity of nothingness to consciousness is the account of waiting for Pierre at a designated time in the cafe. Pierre has not appeared. We are conscious of his absence. But how could his absence appear? There is nothing in the cafe itself that announces Pierre's absence, and yet the cafe as a whole appears to us as the place where Pierre is not. The cafe "is a fullness of being," there is no space in it that could be filled only by Pierre; it is in-itself, solid, without mystery. The non-being of Pierre does not then come from the cafe in-itself. On that basis I could never say that my friend is *not* here. There must be quite another basis then for being conscious of an absence: "The necessary condition for our saying *not* is that non-being be a perpetual presence in us and outside of us, that nothingness haunt being."[14] We can extend this point to say that whenever we are conscious *of* anything, it is always non-being or absence that excited our consciousness. Imagine that Pierre suddenly appears. Are we no longer conscious now that his absence has been filled with being? Any consciousness of Pierre's presence must itself rise from a new absence—what will happen now that Pierre has arrived? What will he have to say about his delay? Is there something wrong with him? In every instance of consciousness there must be eruptions of nothingness that impel it forward in this manner.

Here, then, we have the *terms* of the dialectical nature of consciousness—the opposition of the for-itself to the in-itself, or non-being to being—but *what precisely is the energizing factor that sustains the continuing movement of the dialectic*? We are pressing Sartre here to offer the ground conception of his entire system. We have already indicated that the notion that consciousness is always consciousness *of* is the vital nerve of his thought; we are now asking what really is the vitality in that nerve. If this is the *way* consciousness works, we now want to know why it works at all. Sartre does have an answer for this question, an answer that reveals another though unacknowledged impact Hegel has on his thought. We recall from Hegel that a dialectical relationship does not consist in the mere fact that one thing is different from another, but in the fact that the related entities stand in active opposition to each other. In Hegel's inventive formulation of this relationship this relationship comes to be understood as one of *desire* (even yearning, or lust: *Begierde*), for each longs to eliminate the Other as Other by taking it into itself. Similarly, when Sartre divides being into the for-itself and the in-itself, it is not as though he now have two halves of a whole, or two separate entities; the two are opposed to each other as non-being and being, as we have seen. Therefore, Sartre reasons, the nothingness that appears in being is a "lack," *it is the loss of something that belongs there.*

Nothingness is an act on the part of being to separate itself from itself: "The for-itself is the in-itself losing itself as the in-itself in order to found itself as consciousness."[15] What propels consciousness forward toward the in-itself is therefore the hunger, or desire, of the for-itself to take the in-itself back and therefore eliminate the nothingness "coiled" within it. It is this dynamic self-separation that brings Sartre to declare: "Fundamentally man is *the desire to be*, and the existence of this desire is not to be established by an empirical induction; it is the result of an *a priori* description of the for-itself, since desire is a lack and since the for-itself is the being which is to itself its own lack of being."[16] As we shall see a bit later on, the assertion that primordial desire is the energizing element in consciousness has fateful consequences for Sartre's understanding of freedom.

What does the dialectical relationship of the for-itself and the in-itself, described in this manner, add to our understanding of the problem of the Other? We had observed earlier that the Other appears to consciousness as that which consciousness is not and cannot be; that is, the Other appears in the form of non-being. We then raised the question as to how we could actually relate to that which is not. This question brought us to the fact that consciousness can be *of* only those things that steadfastly refuse to give up their isolated existence to consciousness. We then perceive them as solid, self-identified, disconnected, superfluous. Sartre considers them in the mode of being in-itself. Now, since the inner structure of consciousness is dialectical, the in-itself can exist for it only insofar as it finds its opposite in the for-itself. The for-itself comes into existence when being "secretes" nothingness into its very center; the for-itself *is* that nihilation of being by itself. Consciousness is then the desire of the for-itself to obliterate its nothingness by filling it with the in-itself. It is for this reason that consciousness everywhere sees being in terms of that which is absent within it, like one sees the cafe as the place where one's friend is absent. The cafe comes into view *as something* only to the degree that it resists our desire to fill in the nothingness of Pierre's absence. We are conscious of the cafe as though it belongs to us, as though it is what we lack; but it nonetheless refuses to yield to us, leaving us with our preliminary, existential desire unfulfilled.

Otherness, in sum, is then the object we desire to take into ourselves as a way of extinguishing the coiled worm of nothingness within us. But the fact that we are related *dialectically* to that Otherness means that it appears as Other only to the degree that we are our nothingness. Kill the worm and consciousness dies with it; if there is no consciousness, there is no Other. But so long as there is consciousness there is an insatiable, restless, longing after Otherness.

We are now able to come to a preliminary conclusion concerning Sartre's contribution to our analysis of the problem of death. Throughout this book we have argued that death meets human existence in the form of perceived discontinuity. By way of this threatening perception we are challenged to discover a vision of continuity. In the modern discussion (that is, the tradition that begins with Descartes) the crisis of discontinuity is understood in terms of the self and its Other; that is, it is a crisis of transcendence. To die is to become discontinuous—or, to become an Other which I am not; to become transcendent to myself. At the same time, while discontinuity, or Otherness, is threatening, we have also discovered that the threat of death has its chilling opposite: if there is *only* continuity, or only self without Otherness, and no transcendence, there can be no life. What we have learned, in other words, is that the fact of death challenges us to find a way in which the self can be related to an Other, which is *its own Otherness*, without either canceling it out or vanishing into it. We have learned that we cannot know what it is to be human until we know what it is to be mortal.

In the light of these reflections we can see why Sartre's treatment of the problem of transcendence commends itself. To check the disappearance of the self into the Other that occurs in Hegel's use of the dialectic, Sartre confines the dialectic to the self's individual existence in the form of consciousness. Where consciousness was taken into the dialectic by Hegel as a mere moment in the self-unfolding of Absolute Spirit, Sartre argues forcefully that consciousness *is* the dialectic. It is the dialectic in the sense that it is an unceasing and unfulfilled longing after Otherness. In other words, *consciousness is an unrelieved lust after death*. And if it is consciousness that constitutes freedom, this is equivalent to saying that it is the nature of freedom to seek its own destruction. We must then see if Sartre can rescue us from this paradox.

We have already observed that Sartre's individual lives as an alien in the universe, a stranger whose connection with the whole of being does not consist in an ability to find a unity with being but to annihilate it. Sartre's individual is not at home in the world, belongs in no place, is nowhere. Such was the experience of Roquentin in *Nausea*. In the brief passage from that novel, quoted earlier, the narrator says of his peculiar vision of the superfluity of things that it was frightening: "It made me breathless." Why does alienation involve fright? Actually, Sartre has more than fright in mind here. He is, in fact, concerned to show that freedom induces anxiety (*angoisse*) in each of us; and since we are absolutely free, we are never rid of anxiety. The constant presence of anxiety is therefore always a kind of reminder of our freedom.

The nature of anxiety, and its inescapability, are most obvious when we consider the fact that nothingness, which makes consciousness possible, cannot come from something outside—for then it would be something intruding into our existence. Nothingness can only arise from within the absoluteness of our personal being. It arises with the act of putting our being into question—not in terms of knowledge, as in Descartes, but in terms of our entire existence. It is this radical doubt that constitutes anxiety; it is the dread that we might become nothing, not by the agency of something else, but by our own free act.[17]

It is, of course, only on the basis of self-consciousness that this kind of self-questioning occurs; in fact, it is self-consciousness that makes self-questioning certain. We have noted that self-consciousness demolishes our positionality in a spatial sense (it shows us to be nowhere); it also makes it impossible to be temporally positioned. This is a difficult but important point in Sartre. It is here that we will show how in freedom we are also free even from our own past. It is of course the case that we have a past, but it is a past only for consciousness; it is a past only so far as we are conscious that it is no longer present. The past is not a series of moments now existing in another mode of time outside the limits of consciousness, for then it would not be a past for anyone; it would be no one's past. It is possible therefore through consciousness to see myself *now* as I have been but no longer am. This, in fact, constitutes what Sartre calls my *essence*, borrowing a similar concept from Hegel which the latter had expressed in an elegant play of words: *Wesen ist was gewesen ist* (Essence is what has been). To the degree that I consider myself a teacher of these particular students, a friend of those persons, a father, this woman's husband, I am viewing myself according to what I have been. I cannot therefore be those things in the present; *I can only be them in terms of no longer being them.*[18] Having a past that I can no longer be is another form of human freedom: "Freedom is the human being putting his past out of play by secreting his own nothingness."[19]

This somewhat abstract point has long-range and decisive consequences, both positive and negative. Consider the negative consequences first. In the anxiety that attends the discovery of my own freedom, I begin looking for a way of canceling out that freedom, merely to escape the anxiety. The most accessible route of escape is into my essence, to become what I have been—to overlook the fact that I am no longer a teacher, and a father, and to begin to believe that I am in fact each of these things. Sartre's term for this attempt to take flight from freedom is *bad faith*.[20] He uses the term "faith" here because in order to be my essence I must actively *believe* it. Belief, he argues, always involves consciousness: I quite obviously cannot believe without knowing that I believe. If belief is therefore conscious, I am perfectly aware that I am believing something to be true that is not—that I am viewing myself as someone I am no longer. What is more, belief *as such* is self-contradictory: "To believe is to know one believes, and to know that one believes is no longer to believe."[21] I am therefore without excuse. I can blame my bad faith on no one. I am completely responsible for my actions. If I am an author, or an industrialist, or a mortician, it is not because anyone designated me as one of these, but because I chose them. I can only be *what* I am freely—and that always means being what I am in the mode of not being it. Another way of expressing this is to say that bad faith occurs when the for-itself abandons itself and takes flight into the in-itself. The in-itself always presents itself as past, as something that *has been*. Inasmuch as I understand myself to *be* that which I have been, I have become in-itself. This is a way of vacating the incessant dialectic of consciousness that keeps turning one back on one's own nothingness.

If the negative side of this freedom with reference to the past is bad faith, what is the positive side? If I have put the past out of play by secreting my own nothingness, the past then has no power over me. I am not compelled to be what the past has determined. Indeed, the past cannot determine anything. There is no predestination, no historical inevitability, no victimization of one generation by the preceding, no crippling or inhibiting heritage whether psychological or cultural. If there is no one but myself to blame for bad faith, it is also the case that the past cannot be blamed for anything at all. In his play *The Flies*, written during the Nazi occupation of France, certainly a time when history had seemed to overwhelm its children, Sartre offers an example of such freedom in the play's hero, Orestes. When in defiance of the gods Orestes has slain his mother Clytemnestra and her lover Aegisthus, Zeus pursues him with the flies (furies) as symbolic torment for his crime, but seeing that the flies have no effect, roars in defeat: "over a free man not even the gods have any power."[22] Orestes is not subject to the actions of the gods, in this case equivalent to the action of history, because he chose not to be what he was but what he *is*.

This absolute freedom with reference to the past, the fact that the past has power over us only to the degree that we make it ours, allows Sartre to go so far as to deny there are "innocent victims." Consider the following: "there are no *accidents* in a life; a community event which suddenly bursts forth and involves me in it does not come from the outside. If I am mobilized in a war, this war is *my* war; it is in my image and I deserve it. I deserve it first because I could always get out of it by suicide or by desertion; these ultimate possibles are those which must always be present for us when there is a question of envisaging a situation. For lack of getting out of it, I have *chosen* it."[23] These claims are not rare in Sartre's work. In one of his earliest published philosophical works,[24] he boldly argues that we are free even over our emotions; we choose even to faint in the presence of extreme danger.[25]

It seems here that he has gone far beyond himself in the overuse of a good idea. We might ask him whether we are free before our past with reference, say, to our racial heritage, or the period of time into which we are born. Why could I not decide to become a Persian woman in a medieval village? Sartre is ready for this objection to his doctrine of absolute freedom, and his answer is simple but effective. We are not free to do *to* our essence whatever we want, but we are free to do *with* it whatever we want. We cannot change the past, but we can change its meaning; there is no end to the number of changes we can make concerning the consequences of that past for the future. Sartre is careful here not to fall into Hegel's "bad infinity" by asserting that this sort of freedom means simply going on and on, making one change after another interminably. Instead, *it is that there is no situation in which we are not free to do something—even if there are some things that cannot be done.* I cannot change my race or my sex, but neither my racial past nor my gender can so crowd me into my self that I can do nothing with them: "Therefore there is no privileged situation. We mean by this that there is no situation in which the *given* would crush beneath its weight the freedom which constitutes it as such—and that conversely there is no situation in which the for-itself would be *more free* than in others."[26]

It is this latter point, the true infinity of freedom, that provides a strangely firm connection with the world about me, or what Sartre consistently calls my "situation." My freedom does not consist in my agility in eluding the oncoming forces of history, of staying ahead of disaster by my resourcefulness in always having an alternative escape. On the contrary, this sort of freedom means that we are always "responsible" for whatever occurs to us, even for the war which has fallen upon us with practically no warning: "I can no longer distinguish at present the choice which I make of myself from the choice which I make of the war. . . . In this war, which I have chosen, I choose myself from day to day, and I make it mine by making myself. If it is going to be four empty years, then it is I who bear the responsibility for this."[27]

There is still something vague here: what exactly is it I choose when I choose myself—as, for example, in the case of war? We have already seen that I cannot choose my essence, which is what I have been, for that throws me into the contradictory pose of bad faith. Strictly speaking, I cannot choose the present; I can only choose *in the present.* What I choose therefore is the future; I project a present into the future in the form of a possibility that is distinctly *my* possibility. Sartre refers to this as a "fundamental project." It is an end toward which I am directing my present actions. If I do not have an end, if there is no intentionality in my actions, they are not actions at all, but simply movements.[28] Insofar as I am acting I have a fundamental project, even though I may not be directly conscious of it. Ends cannot be imposed upon me; nothing can give me my intentionality. There is no inner nature to human existence that determines its ends: "It chooses them and by this very choice confers upon them a transcendent existence as the external limit of its projects."[29]

But my fundamental project does more than simply direct my actions. Sartre explains that the choice of an end causes the world to reveal itself "across our conduct." What he means by this is that once I have projected an end, say, establishing myself as a famous neurosurgeon, the world will then appear to me *as the place where* I pursue that end. If I should suffer an accident in which the tendons in my hand have been severed, I might consider that my world has come to an end. The experience is common. We find ourselves cut off from our dreams, our plans are in ruins due to some unforeseen disaster. The fact that our end was freely chosen may for a while be obscured by the disorienting character of this experience. This is particularly the case in acute grief when someone deeply and intimately associated with our own lives has died; bereft, we may perceive that our world is destroyed, perhaps even uninhabitable. No matter how severe a shock this might be, no matter how grave the loss, it is still the case that it *is* a shock; it *is* a loss only because we had freely chosen the end that gave prominence to that part of my world. And because I chose that end to begin with, I can choose another. Sartre wants to push this point even harder: these sudden turns in my affairs are not truly surprises, they are not even accidents, for I have put myself—freely—in the place where they could happen. I am therefore completely responsible for them, and in no case can use them as excuses for inaction.

It is in the notion of the fundamental project that we have the most complete view of Sartre's conception of life as absolute freedom. We noted above that the choice of an end confers on human existence an "external limit." Is this a limit we *must* live within? No. It is a limit we *do* live within, but only because we choose to. Whenever I wish I may push the limit back or draw it tighter. What is most remarkable about this freely chosen limit, which Sartre says has a "transcendent existence," is that however spacious or constricting I have projected the transcendent limits of my conscious existence, I cannot go beyond them, in fact, *I cannot even reach the limits of my existence.* I am, in other words, a captive in my own freedom: "I am condemned to be free. This means that no limits to my freedom can be found except freedom itself or, if you prefer, that we are not free to cease being free."[30]

Occasionally Sartre seems to be suggesting that there is one area in which my freedom is restricted, and that is in my relation to the Other in the form of an Other consciousness. In one of the most frequently cited passages of *Being and Nothingness*, Sartre vividly describes the experience of falling under the gaze of another person, particularly the experience of shame before the Other. The force of this long, but eminently readable and even entertaining, discussion is to indicate that when I become conscious of another person looking at me I find myself confronted with a different kind of being than the transcendently solid in-itself. I am suddenly in the presence, not of an "Other-as-object," but an "Other-as-subject."[31] I am aware of myself as I am being seen by another, as though I am seeing myself but from another subject. It is quite like beholding my own essence, which I am not, by another person, which I am not. Sartre appeals convincingly to the common experience of feeling sharply limited by the gaze of another. He offers the example of being caught eavesdropping through a keyhole. When the door is opened and I am discovered kneeling before it, I have the experience of being abruptly and helplessly defined by the vision of the person standing above me.

There is the suggestion in this situation that when the transcendent limit of my existence is a *fundamental project* in the form of the in-itself, which I have freely chosen, it is in effect endlessly changeable; but when it is another subject, another for-itself, I am powerless before it, and my freedom is consequently compromised. Sartre introduces this discussion, however, not to expose a flaw in the absoluteness of freedom, but to guarantee its absoluteness. To be conscious of the Other-as-subject is still a form of consciousness, and as such it is still haunted by the nonpositionality of self-consciousness. Even limited by the gaze of the Other as I kneel in the open doorway, I am at least conscious I am ashamed. This has the effect, then, not of limiting my freedom, but of making it all the more obvious, because in the acute self-consciousness that belongs to shame it is inescapably apparent that I cannot be the one ashamed *and* the one looking. If I am limited by the consciousness (freedom) of the other person it can only be because I have freely limited myself. Indeed, it is I who have spontaneously caused there to be an Other-as-subject. The consequence of introducing the problem of the relationship of consciousness to the transcendent Other-as-subject is only to seal more perfectly the imprisonment of human existence in its own freedom.*

---

*Sartre pointedly argues that the presence of the Other-as-subject is not an *ontological*, but a *contingent*, fact. That is, we cannot infer the existence of other persons from the structure of personal existence. It just *happens* that there are other persons. This point may seem unimportant in the present discussion, but, as we shall see, it is here that Sartre's thought, and particularly the consequences of his theory of freedom, most decisively departs from Heidegger's.

It is precisely at this point that we can begin to feel the grip of the paradox, described above, as it tightens on Sartre's claims for absolute freedom. That paradox is the desire of freedom to seek its own destruction—a desire it strangely is not free to achieve. By borrowing Hegel's dialectic to deal with the problem of the Other, and by limiting that dialectic to the individual in the form of consciousness, Sartre has defined freedom as the individual's self-opposition. Freedom is the desire of consciousness endlessly to drive itself out of existence.

It is true that as free persons we may (in fact *must*) set the limits within which we live and that we may alter those limits at any time; that is, we are absolutely free in the sense that nothing and no one can ever impose limits on us from without. However, we are not to lose sight of the fact that they are still *limits*; they stand forever as proof that human freedom is self-opposed limitation. In Sartre's conception freedom may never be understood as the capacity to live without regard to limits. We are free because we are against ourselves.

The self-opposition of consciousness may not, on the face of it, seem problematical, but as we look more deeply into it we find it has a devastating impact on Sartre's philosophy as a whole, but particularly on his understanding of death. *The self-opposition of consciousness has the effect of sealing us off from all Otherness.* Sartre's extravagant claims that we *choose* the war, even that in a certain sense we "*choose being born*," derive from his deep philosophical conviction that there is nothing whatsoever that can compromise human freedom.[32] We recall that he describes this freedom as our ability to choose our "fundamental project," that is, the end toward which we are moving and in light of which the world appears as world. While we might not experience a broad range of freedom *within* our fundamental project (there are only a few things I can fail to do if I wish to become a distinguished neurosurgeon), we can *always* select another fundamental project, even under the most exigent circumstances. But using such examples as the war and my birth backfires, for it also has the impact of saying that *nothing*, not even the terrors of war or the accident of birth, can force its Otherness into our consciousness. *Otherness arises only from within.* Because of the absolute self-opposition of consciousness, there is nothing that can oppose consciousness except consciousness itself. This utterly vacates the meaning of freedom. Freedom, by this conception, is only a movement in a vacuum, a furious gesture that has no object, a tornado that can move nothing but itself. It is a freedom to do nothing.

What has caused Sartre, "the philosopher of freedom," to paint himself into this isolated corner is, ironically, the very thing that constitutes his most daring philosophical strategy: to limit the dialectic to the existing *individual*. He did this to preserve the individual's true freedom in existential relation to Otherness. Hegel did not stop with the individual, but showed how the dialectical flow of consciousness continued to carry away all its restraining banks until it had eliminated every form of Otherness bringing the whole of being into the fully reconciled Absolute Spirit. Absolute Spirit is utterly free because there is nothing to oppose it, but, of course, this means that the dialectic has come to an end—there is no Otherness still to be overcome. When Sartre, in contrast, identifies the dialectic with the consciousness of the existing individual, it can have only itself as an Other and is therefore "condemned" to be consuming itself endlessly like the mythic serpent Ouroboros that circles the creation as it simultaneously feeds on and gives birth to itself. Unable to eliminate its Other and to move on to a higher opposition, Sartre's dialectical freedom is the very model of contradiction: *if freedom is our deepest yearning to become the Other, we shall either fail in that desire, in which case we are not free, or succeed, in which case we cease altogether to exist.*

Remarkably, Sartre seems neither oblivious to this contradiction, nor disturbed by it. He states it himself in a somewhat different, but characteristically imaginative, way: The desire that constitutes our freedom is a desire to become God. His point here is not that God is an incomparably greater being than we and therefore beyond our capacities, but that it is impossible that God exist. Sartre asserts the impossibility of God's existence by a clever forensic flourish. He cites the medieval definition of God, first formulated by Thomas Aquinas, as that being whose essence is existence. According to Sartre's definition of these terms this conception of God is flatly contradictory: essence is what *has been*; existence is what *is*; therefore, this formula represents God as a being that *is what it was*.

In what way is the existential desire of human existence the desire to become God? We recall that what being seeks to do is to fill in its nothingness with the in-itself, making it solid, immune to time, changeless—like God. But this is the desire precisely to become our essence, that which we were. As we noted above, this is what Sartre calls "bad faith." But it is also what we have described in our analysis of his theory of dialectical freedom: a desire to do that which it cannot do.

It is evident that Sartre's well-known atheism is not a mere idiosyncracy, a strong personal bias. It emerges from the very center of his thought. Just as consciousness cannot become the Other, it is impossible for God to exist. But this does not discourage the desire to become God. Since Sartre wants to rest his commitment to absolute freedom on this thoroughly contradictory desire, we should not be surprised if his final portrait of human existence is drawn in dismal tones. It is, he writes, "by nature an unhappy consciousness with no possibility of surpassing its unhappy state."[33] It is this inevitable frustration of our deepest longing that brings Sartre to conclude the main text of *Being and Nothingness* with the famous statement: "Man is a useless passion."[34]

How then are we to describe Sartre's final contribution to our understanding of the problem of death? Earlier, we came to the preliminary conclusion that consciousness is an unrelieved lust after death. We subsequently learned that this yearning harbors a contradiction that "condemns" it to a freedom in which it can do nothing but oppose itself. Does it then make any sense to speak of conscious persons dying? Sartre's answer is astonishing.

In the section of *Being and Nothingness* entitled "My Death," he observes that death is commonly thought of as a kind of boundary. It is the nature of boundaries that they face in two directions: *outward* toward the unknown and foreign, and *inward* toward that which is known and familiar. Sartre finds the metaphor of the boundary faulty, for death makes no sense whether we look at it from the outside or the inside. Those who consider death a boundary that looks outward toward the "nonhuman" Sartre calls the *realists*. For them death is the moment when we go silently into Dylan Thomas' "dark night," or Hamlet's "distant bourne from which no traveler ever returns." The problem with the metaphor here, Sartre states, is that "the very concept of the non-human is man's concept."[35] Those who take death as a boundary facing inward—the *idealists*—see it as that which "is the final phenomenon of life and is still life." The idealists believe death completes life, rounds it out: "Death becomes the meaning of life as the resolved chord is the meaning of the melody."[36] The error in this view lies in the assumption that we can somehow point ourselves toward this last moment, preparing for it in such a way that it will be a profound statement of the meaning of our lives. This assumption does not allow for the fact that death comes when *it* wills, and not when *we* will. Sartre suggests that the human condition is more accurately described if we "compare ourselves to a man condemned to death who is bravely preparing himself for the ultimate penalty, who is doing everything possible to make a good showing on the scaffold, and who meanwhile is carried off by a flu epidemic."[37]

The metaphor of the boundary obscures the basically *absurd* character of death. It is absurd chiefly because it comes by chance, without any relation to the purposefulness of life. Death is not the kind of limit to my life I could throw myself against, but an event that imposes itself out of some secret intentionality of its own: "Thus death is not *my possibility of no longer realizing a presence in the world, but rather an always possible nihilation of my possibles which is outside my possibilities.*"[38] Death is not something I could deal with in my freedom, something I could freely struggle with, or even freely accept, because it is that which comes without warning and deprives me of freedom. It is not a possibility for me, but that which eliminates all my possibilities. Since "death does not appear on the foundation of our freedom, it can only *remove all meaning from life.*"[39]

In this discussion Sartre is adamant to stress the fact that it is freedom that makes life meaningful. The meaning of life is that it has a future; it is a looking forward, a waiting for that which is to come. Life is precisely the freedom to keep "the account" from being closed. Life is therefore a kind of waiting, a "not yet," in contrast to which death is an "*all done.*" What we are waiting for, in each case, is not an end to our life, but a new moment of life that will in turn be a "not yet." "Thus it is necessary to consider our life as being made up not only of waitings but of waitings which themselves wait for waitings."[40]

Has Sartre brought a revived concept of freedom back into play in this discussion? It certainly seems as if the freedom we described as self-contradictory is being used here as the basis for the meaning of life. But does it work? We have described death as that which takes us without warning; it does not present itself as something I can cope with in my freedom. Sartre's use of freedom here plainly suggests that it is a kind of flight forward, with death snapping at its heels; it is the attempt to keep the account open, to follow one "not yet" with another "not yet." What has suddenly vanished is any sense of consciousness freely projecting its limits ahead of itself, as in the "fundamental project." Death is not something we can deal with by way of our fundamental project. We cannot calculate death as a risk, or plan to die heroically or in martyrdom—not because the flu might carry us off first, but because death is something that cannot be chosen.

What then *is* death? Sartre's answer: "nothing but the *given.*"[41] And what is the given? The in-itself. Essence. That which has been. Death, the in-itself, is absurd because it robs me of my possibilities, my not-yet. What is meaningful, then, is simply to be alive, to be moving forward. But toward what? Toward an end at which we cannot arrive. The force of this conception is that life is mere flight from the past. There can be no other purpose for it. It can go nowhere in particular, because it cannot arrive. It can only keep going. Life, therefore, has no more pattern to it than the track of its terrified escape through the contingent thickets of its own particular history. Such a life can scarcely be considered meaningful. A "useless passion" is the more appropriate term.

I offered the opinion earlier that Sartre's understanding of death is astonishing. We can now see why. *Death for Sartre can only be that which has happened. In no sense is death in our future.* That is why we cannot choose it. That is why consciousness, which is a longing for death (the past), is *condemned* to failure in its longing. If it gets what it wants, it cannot be what it is. So long as we are free, that is, so long as we have succeeded in preventing Otherness from fixing our feet in the concrete of a past that is no longer even ours, there can be nothing ahead of us. But this is no sort of freedom.

Sartre does not deny that death is ahead of us "within time," but, by what we have seen, it can only be ahead of us as that which is behind us (essence, the *given*) and, therefore, something we can never become. For this reason, just as human existence can never encounter the limits of its own freedom, it also cannot "discover its own mortality."[42] Just as I am not free to cease being free, I am not "free to die," although, Sartre adds inexplicably, "I am a free mortal."[43] It is this last phrase that seems most doubtful. It is true that I am mortal in the sense that eventually everything will be past, but the past cannot, by definition, claim *me* as an existing person. In Sartre's own words: "Since death escapes my project because it is unrealizable, I myself escape death in my very project. Since death is always beyond my subjectivity, there is no place for it in my subjectivity."[44] *To be conscious, in other words, is to be immortal.*

We saw that Sartre's doctrine of freedom got itself so helplessly tangled in the dialectic that it could no longer be considered freedom. We are then brought inescapably to the conclusion that *for Sartre human existence is neither free nor mortal.*

Our intention in studying Sartre was to ascertain whether in his skillful and critical use of Hegel he could capitalize on Hegel's success in introducing Otherness (or death) into the very center of selfhood, while avoiding his failure in the loss of the individual. Now we can see that where Hegel succeeded in finding a place for death in the structure of thought but left no place for the individual, Sartre succeeded in locating the individual in thought, but at the cost of making death unthinkable. Hegel showed that death was possible, but could not find anyone to die. Sartre's theory has rescued the discrete self, but then denied it the possibility of dying.

If, as we have described it in this study, the challenge death presents each of us is overcoming grief—or the deathlike response of life to anticipated discontinuity—Sartre has provided an unforgettable portrait of consciousness as grief itself and of human existence as an immortal and self-aware bereavement. We are not only condemned to freedom, but to unrelieved grief.

Sartre's failure is enormously useful to our longer account of the problem of death. It is, after all, a brilliant failure. Primarily we learn that the most acclaimed attempt of modern thought to deal with the problem of the irreducible Other—Hegel's dialectic—will not work. It can only affirm death at the price of the individual, or the individual at the price of death. Hegel and Sartre are thinkers of such consummate facility that we may not look for solutions to these problems in preceding thinkers. We are driven forward to those persons whose thought displays both the need to develop a cogent view of human mortality and the impossibility of doing so in the manner of Sartre and Hegel.

It is certainly to Sartre's credit that he sensed this failure himself in the years following the publication of *Being and Nothingness*, particularly when he had reflected on the terrible human cost of World War II. "There is a sweep of events," he admitted, "which cracks the dam of individualism."[45] No longer could he place the individual serenely above the terrible force of history, which "wears out the men she uses and kills them under her as though they were horses. She chooses the actors and transforms them, right to the marrow of their bones, by the role she imposes on them; then, at the slightest change, she dismisses them and takes on others who are completely fresh."[46]

Sartre subsequently abandoned his existentialist analysis of human affairs in favor of Marxism. His intention was plainly to account for the actual power the Other has over the lives of human persons. There is no space here to assess the success of this shift in focus, except to say that Sartre still has not abandoned the dialectical method—which Marx himself had taken from Hegel. And while the favored side of the dialectic is now the objective Other instead of the conscious subject, there is still the self-opposition of the dialectical to-and-fro that cannot permit the self and the Other to be integrally related without one taking the Other into itself.

We must therefore look to other thinkers. The requirements are clear. Since the root concept of Sartre's thought was the "intentionality" of consciousness (that is, the fact that consciousness is always *consciousness of*) that led him into the cul de sac of unavoidable immortality, but an immortal bereavement, we must find a thinker whose self-evident point of departure is something prior to consciousness.

Moreover, since Sartre's freedom is finally viewed as a headlong flight into an empty future from a pursuing mortality that is always in the form of the past, we must find a thinker who allows the existing person the freedom to move toward a future in which death exists as one's own free possibility.

Notes

1. *Being and Nothingness*, p. xlv.
2. Ibid., pp. lii, liv.
3. Ibid., p. liv.
4. Ibid., see pp. 554 ff.
5. Ibid., p. liv ff.
6. Ibid., p. lvi.
7. Ibid., p. lx.
8. Ibid., p. lxi.
9. Ibid., p. lxi.
10. Ibid., p. lxii.
11. Ibid., p. 84.
12. *Nausea*, pp. 177, 174.
13. *Being and Nothingness*, p. 21.
14. Ibid., p. 11.
15. Ibid., p. 82.
16. Ibid., p. 565.
17. Ibid., p. 29.
18. Ibid., see p. 117.
19. Ibid., p. 28.
20. Ibid., see especially pp. 47–70.
21. Ibid., p. 69.
22. *The Flies*, Act II, Scene 2.
23. *Being and Nothingness*, p. 554.
24. *The Emotions: Outline of a Theory*.
25. The same argument appears in *Being and Nothingness*, p. 445.
26. *Being and Nothingness*, p. 549.
27. Ibid., p. 555.
28. Ibid., p. 477.
29. Ibid., p. 443.
30. Ibid., p. 439.
31. Ibid., pp. 256 ff.
32. Ibid., p. 556.
33. Ibid., p. 90.

34. Ibid., p. 615.
35. Ibid., p. 533.
36. Ibid., p. 532.
37. Ibid., p. 533.
38. Ibid., p. 537.
39. Ibid., p. 539.
40. Ibid., p. 538.
41. Ibid., p. 547.
42. Ibid., p. 546.
43. Ibid., pp. 547 ff.
44. Ibid., p. 548.
45. Quoted by McMahon, *Humans Being*, p. 25.
46. Quoted, Ibid., p. 27.

Bibliography

Hazel Barnes, *Sartre* (New York: 1973).

Joseph Fell, *Emotion in the Thought of Sartre* (New York: 1965).

Marjorie Grene, *Sartre* (New York: 1973).

Thomas M. King, *Sartre and the Sacred* (Chicago: 1974).

Anthony Manser, *Sartre: a Philosophical Study* (London: 1966).

Joseph H. McMahon, *Humans Being: The World of Jean-Paul Sartre* (Chicago: 1971).

Iris Murdoch, *Sartre* (New Haven: 1953).

Arne Naess: *Four Modern Philosophers: Carnap, Wittgenstein, Heidegger, and Sartre*, tr. Alastair Hannay (Chicago: 1968).

Maurice Natanson, *A Critique of Jean-Paul Sartre's Ontology* (The Hague: 1973).

Jean-Paul Sartre, *Being and Nothingness: An Essay on Phenomenological Ontology*, tr. Hazel Barnes (New York: 1956).

—— *The Emotions: Outline of a Theory*, tr. Bernard Frechtman (New York: 1948).

—— *Existentialism*, tr. Bernard Frechtman (New York: 1948).

—— *Nausea*, tr. Lloyd Alexander, (Norfolk: n.d.).

—— *No Exit and Three Other Plays*, tr. Stuard Gilbert (New York: 1955).

—— *Situations*, tr. Benita Eisler (Greenwich: 1965).

—— *Transcendence of the Ego*, tr. Forrest Williams and Robert Kirkpatrick (New York: 1957).

—— *What is Literature?* tr. Bernard Frechtman (New York: 1949).

—— *Words*, tr. Bernard Frechtman (New York: 1964).

14 FRIEDRICH NIETZSCHE

In a previous chapter we discussed the way Hegel integrated the discontinuity of death into human existence. By appealing to the structure of consciousness he was able to show that it was the reality of death that made consciousness possible at all. He did this by bringing Otherness or discontinuity into consciousness. In order to contain the discontinuity within consciousness, however, he had to propose the dialectic, a continuing process of reconciling opposites. Hegel's failure, as the existentialists and other philosophers have frequently indicated, is his inability to set limits against the all-consuming appetite of the dialectic—like a river that eventually displaces everything but itself, it finally becomes a single global sea. This final state, which Hegel called the Absolute, leaves no place for the individual.

Sartre saw both the great strength and the great weakness of Hegel's thought and endeavored to correct it by defining the individual consciousness in such a way that the dialectic would be contained within it. Sartre has been justly praised for his own philosophic adroitness and ingenuity, but, as we observed in the last chapter, while he protected the individual against the dialectic, he was unable to integrate the fact of death into his description of human existence. The reason for this is perhaps obvious: having confined the dialectic to individual consciousness, Sartre found it impossible to describe any direct contact between the individual and true Otherness. Consciousness has no opposition to itself, except what originates in itself. This does indeed give Sartre license to declare a philosophy of absolute freedom for the individual, but, ironically, it is a freedom incapable of doing anything to any Other but itself. It is a complete freedom, but also completely without power. It does not even have the power of eliminating itself. One is "condemned to freedom," to use his famous phrase. We are quite prepared then to agree with him that, for this reason, "man is a useless passion."

As we continue our examination of modern Western thought on the subject of death, we have come to the question of whether it is possible to describe individual human existence in such a way that it can be seen as free *and* powerful, and still *mortal*. We have long since seen that that which is not free cannot be said to be alive—and ipso facto cannot die. But to be free without power over an Other (Sartre) is to be unable to die, and to be free with unlimited power over the Other (Hegel) is necessarily to sublate the Other and with it one's own individuality. In this chapter, and the one following, we shall argue that Nietzsche and Heidegger offer a significant advance over Sartre's thought on death, in spite of the fact that both precede him historically.

We had noted briefly that Sartre's philosophical interests fell under the decisive influence of three German thinkers—Hegel, Husserl, and Heidegger. From Hegel he took the dialectical structure of consciousness as the central problem of human existence, and from Husserl he took the phenomenological method. Heidegger's influence on Sartre is more complicated. His grasp of Heidegger's thought, in spite of the painfully involuted style in which Heidegger chose to express it, is exceptionally keen. There is no doubt that Heidegger's *Being and Time* was constantly before Sartre as he wrote his own *Being and Nothingness*, scarcely more than a decade later. It is therefore all the more surprising that he treats so lightly the central thrust of Heidegger's thought. Sartre quickly and accurately saw that Heidegger had set aside all philosophic importance to the phenomenon of consciousness, with exclusive priority to the question of Being. Sartre simply is unable to see how the question of Being could be prior to the question of our consciousness of Being. The reason for this is likely that Sartre, living and writing in the Cartesian atmosphere of formal French thought, was unable to see that Heidegger's own philosophy was written against a very different background. The intellectual air that Heidegger was breathing had little Cartesianism in it; instead, it was the chill mountain storms of Nietzsche's thought that in the end had the most telling impact on him. Heidegger's debt to Nietzsche is acknowledged toward the end of his career by a long essay and a two-volume study of Nietzsche's thought. Since there is little evidence that Sartre had read Nietzsche at all, or was even vaguely familiar with the prevailing themes of his thought, we should not expect him to understand that when Heidegger spoke of Being it was in light of Nietzsche's thorough and radical attack on the whole of Western thought. Although Heidegger claimed that his concept of Being can be found in such ancient thinkers as Parmenides and Heraclitus, it can nonetheless be shown that no one has hitherto spoken of Being in a manner similar to Heidegger. And certainly no one has made a closer association between Being and death than Heidegger. We shall enter this discussion through Nietzsche's thought—particularly those aspects of Nietzsche that illumine the problem of human mortality in light of the question to which our analysis has brought us: *is it possible to describe individual human existence as free and powerful—and yet mortal?*

We noted in the previous chapter that the informing center of Sartre's thought was his firmly held belief that consciousness is always *consciousness of*. We can find a similarly powerful organizing concept in Nietzsche's thought. Quite simply, it is *resentment*. Resentment is the difficulty of allowing the past to be past, the inability to forget. We can best see the place resentment takes in Nietzsche's thought by examining his relentless critique of morality—of which we can give here only an abbreviated account.

In his *Genealogy of Morals* he calls to task the "historians of ethics." In their attempt to locate the origin of morality "they have all been quite deserted by the true spirit of history. They all, to a man, think unhistorically, as is the age-old custom among philosophers."[1] Their most serious error is that they have looked "for the genesis of the concept *good* in the wrong place: the judgment *good* does not originate with those to whom the good has been done. Rather it was the 'good' themselves, that is to say the noble, mighty, highly placed, and high-minded who decreed themselves and their actions to be good. . . ."[2] Nietzsche, by training a philologist, claims authority for this view from the etymology of the word "good." He found from his own study that in various languages "good" can always be read as "*noble* in the hierarchical, class sense, and from this has developed, by historical necessity, the concept *good* embracing nobility of mind, spiritual distinction. This development is strictly parallel to that other which eventually converted the notions *common, plebeian, base* into the notion *bad*."[3]

What is important in this analysis is not Nietzsche's dubious etymological scholarship but his introduction of history *into* morality. The notion that morality is in itself historical not only implies that morals are relative, but that they are expressions of a given age, of an actual people. Each moral system can be read as a "type of involuntary and unaware memoir" of its originator. That Nietzsche does not intend to speak of timeless moral principles as they appear in history is clearly indicated in the title of his book. To speak of the genealogy of morals is to emphasize their historical origin and developmental character. It is Nietzsche's intention to rob morality—and much more, as we shall see—of any claim to universality.

This attack on the universality of morals does not spring only from Nietzsche's "scholarly" discovery that the universals are false, but also from his radical conviction that morality is the "negation of the will to life," it "is the very *instinct of decadence*, which makes an imperative of itself. It says 'Perish!' It is a condemnation pronounced by the condemned."[4] "Insofar as we believe in morality," he wrote, "we pass sentence on existence."[5] The reason for this is *resentment*, the inability to forget or the failure to exercise what Nietzsche called the "faculty of oblivion."[6]

Returning to the history of morality we can see, from Nietzsche's, account, how resentment takes its enormous toll. Originally the nobles did not consider themselves *good*, as though distinct from the ignoble or *bad*. It was of their nature simply to say *Yes!* to their own instincts, to act out of their high animal spirits without the least concern for the consequences of those acts. This original goodness was spontaneous, expansive, and joyful. It happened, however, that not all persons were noble, or "good," in this sense. There were also the weak, the deformed, the sick and the craven, who repeatedly found themselves the victims of the nobles' exuberant good health and unrestrained passion. Some of the most outrageous passages in Nietzsche's entire body of work concern these original relations between the nobles and their hapless plebeian victims. He fondly uses the infamous term "blond beast" to describe these more noble persons, though he hardly had in mind the Nazi's preference for the fair, Nordic appearance. Nietzsche intended no racial distinction whatsoever. The term is, in fact, a euphemism for "lion" and is used only to invoke the animallike energies of the nobles and their utter lack of conscience. They have "the innocence of wild animals: we can imagine them returning from an orgy of murder, arson, rape, and torture, jubilant and at peace with themselves as though they had committed a fraternity prank. . . . Deep within all these noble races there lurks the beast of prey, bent on spoil and conquest."[7] He finds evidence of blond beasts in every culture: "The noble races have everywhere left in their wake the catchword 'barbarian.'"[8] He elsewhere characterizes them as cruel, without pity, criminal, solitary, and always inclined toward lying and deception.[9] These citations are common enough in Nietzsche's writing that we cannot write them off as singular instances of rare churlishness. We cannot write them off at all, but we must interpret them carefully, for they offer an essential clue to Nietzsche's understanding of human mortality.

It is necessary to note that while it is altogether true that the weak are shamelessly abused by the strong, Nietzsche's philosophy, taken as a whole, distinctly underlines the fact that no one is condemned to weakness by external forces. *The weak are weak by choice.* They are not weak because the strong have victimized them. The strong also victimize each other. *The weak are weak because they resent what has been done to them by the strong.* They cannot forget it. It is not their lack of strength as such, but their recourse to resentment that constitutes their weakness. "It is a sign of strong, rich temperaments that they cannot for long take seriously their enemies, their misfortunes, their *misdeeds*; for such characters have in them an excess of curative power, and also a power of oblivion."[10] The weak and rancorous person, by contrast, has a long memory: "His soul squints."[11]

It is the hatred of the strong by the weak, their long-smoldering resentment, that gives rise to what Nietzsche calls the "slave revolt in morals." There is "an inversion in values," in which the capricious, spontaneous, destructive actions of the barbarian are declared *evil.* The victims, the sufferers, the "innocent" become *good.* Good, by this strange turn of events, has come simply to mean weak or powerless. What is important to remember here is that this inversion of values was imposed on no one; it is the willful invention of "slaves," that is, those who *become* slaves because they call weakness "good" and strength "evil." Nietzsche, in fact, seems to suggest that in the natural state the faculty of oblivion is more powerful than memory. The slaves, the weak, the base must *will* to remember the harm done them; theirs is "an active not wishing to be done with it, a continuing to will what has once been willed . . . ."[12]

Resentment, then, is more than the inability to forget. It is a free choice to live in the past. Because the slaves do not forget what was done to them, they still suffer it as though it were happening now. But it is not happening now. Since the past exists only in a willed remembering of it, the slaves can only be doing it to themselves. Their hatred of others is then a form of self-hatred; they become "expert in self-humiliation."[13] Since self-hatred focuses entirely on the past—on what has been done to one—it cannot be corrected any more than the past can be changed. Resentment, for this reason, becomes an exceedingly effective self-constructed trap for the free spirit. Nietzsche's term for this hateful caging of oneself is *conscience.*

Since the creation of the conscience so completely disturbs the natural order, it can only be achieved through a "long history of trans-formations." But this centuries-long attempt to "create a memory for the human animal" includes nothing that could be considered delicate. In fact, the most terrible episodes in early human history involved the evolution of conscience, for it was early discovered that the past could be retained only by fixing it with pain: "A thing is branded on the memory to make it stay there; only what goes on hurting will stick." This is the ancient psychological axiom that all the refined cultures have followed. "Whenever man has thought it necessary to create a memory for himself, his effort has been attended with torture, blood, sacrifice. The ghastliest sacrifices and pledges, including the sacrifice of the first-born; the most repulsive mutilations, such as castration; the cruelest rituals in every religious cult (and all religions are at bottom systems of cruelty)—all these have their origin in that instinct which divined pain to be the strongest aid to mnemonics."[14]

We should not mistake this kind of cruelty and blood-letting, how-ever, as similar to the joyful energies of the strong, for it has the inten-tion not of expressing one's freedom, but of turning freedom in on itself. The purpose of the repeated punishment is to convince oneself that the Other is in every case the cause of one's distress. But since the Other has vanished into the past, all attempts to strike back succeed only in striking oneself. As the "higher" cultures became more skillful in the cruel creation of memory, "man began rending, persecuting, terrifying himself, like a wild beast hurling himself against the bars of its cage." Having turned his own interior selfhood into a wilderness, "this fool, this pining and desperate prisoner, became the inventor of 'bad conscience.'"[15]

All conscience for Nietzsche is bad conscience, because it is the consequence of the self-hating recreation of the past. But it is more than self-inflicted pain that he is concerned with here. Having trapped themselves in their own memory, the weak have turned away from life itself. They have abandoned their own spontaneity by orienting them-selves entirely toward an Other, on whom they have taken no more than an "imaginary vengeance."

> All truly noble morality grows out of triumphant self-affirmation. Slave ethics, on the other hand, begins by saying no to an "out-side," an "other," a non-self, and that no is its creative act. This reversal of direction of the evaluating look, this invariable looking outward instead of inward, is a fundamental feature of rancor. Slave ethics requires for its inception a sphere different from and hostile to its own. Physiologically speaking, it requires an outside stimulus in order to act at all; all its action is reaction.[16]

We initiated this exploration of Nietzsche with the question as to whether it is possible to describe human existence as both free and powerful, but also mortal. Nietzsche's distinctive answer has begun to take shape: freedom is closely identified with life itself, and what is inherently good in human existence is the powerful manifestation of life. Power, of course, is a relational term. Someone or something is not simply powerful, but always powerful in relation to something or someone else. Power presupposes otherness; it is in relation to an Other that one is powerful. What we have seen thus far in Nietzsche is that when one person has fallen under the influence of another's vital presence a relationship of power develops. But it is a relationship in which the powerful can say either *yes* or *no* to life; that is, they can either manifest their freedom in relation to the Other, or they can freely cage themselves in "bad conscience." We must observe that the latter, though Nietzsche calls them "weak," are not truly powerless. It is simply that they have turned themselves into the Object for their own power. *All power is relational, but in the case of the bad conscience it is self-relational. To be self-relational is to say NO to life.*

It is evident then that we have before us a most rare understanding of the nature of both power and life. Nietzsche has plainly not taken over a mechanical sense of the nature of power; he is not speaking of blind forces striking one another with greater or lesser quanta of energy. Such a conception of power leaves no space for freedom; instead, it is a vision of reality in which a static balance of opposing forces is being sought. Nietzsche's novel conception paradoxically *combines* power with freedom. This means that there is nothing like a given amount of power either in a single object or in a collection of objects. When power is combined with freedom its quantity is not fixed, but variable: the greater the freedom, the greater the power. This turns the other conception of power on its head, for previously it was thought one could be free only to the extent that one was already powerful. It also introduces an extraordinary effervescence into human existence. Where the ordinary view understands the power relationship as the search for balance, for *stasis*, Nietzsche understands it as the search for novelty, chaos, increasing complexity.

To this singular vision Nietzsche has given the widely misinterpreted term "will-to-power." Before we look more closely at what is contained in this rich conception, it would be helpful to look back briefly and appraise the distance we have already come from Sartre's view of human existence. Sartre thought that the one indispensable given of human existence was the phenomenon of consciousness—in which one becomes an object for oneself. What Sartre showed quite convincingly is that in this self-relatedness one can never relate to oneself as *something that is in-itself*, but always to that which one is not and cannot be. What Nietzsche introduces into the notion of consciousness is not just self-relatedness, but also self-hatred. Sartre, moreover, thought that we were "condemned" to consciousness. Nietzsche has shown that consciousness is a choice; it is a free disposition of power, a self-opposed labor, a desperate struggle to suppress one's own vitality. Sartre's despairing insight that we are hopelessly doomed to our own impotence is, in Nietzsche's philosophy, a characteristic view of the slave mentality. In this sense, Sartre is not the "philosopher of freedom," but the "philosopher of weakness."

We also observed that Sartre strangely found it impossible to describe how one could choose to die. Since one is condemned to life, one is not free to end it. It would appear that Sartre is precisely that sort of philosopher whose morality has, in Nietzsche's phrase, "passed sentence on existence." As we look ahead into Nietzsche's thought, we must then attempt to discern how he integrates mortality into the paradoxical conjunction of freedom and power. We shall do so by way of a more careful examination of his "will-to-power."

We had suggested that the central informing concept in Nietzsche's thought is resentment, or the inability to allow the past to be past. We have seen how this guided his critique of morality, where the term resentment seems to have a natural home. But Nietzsche argues that resentment is the fundamental logic of many other pursuits: politics, art, religion, and philosophy. We have the space here to consider only a single example of his lengthy critique of these disciplines.

Nietzsche is especially contemptuous of that philosophical tendency to locate a subject behind the phenomenon, in the same way that "popular superstition divorces the lightning from its brilliance, viewing the latter as an activity whose subject is the lightning." In some respect this might sound as though he has moved on to familiar Kantian territory, drawing doubt on our ability to find the real thing behind the appearance of the thing. But Nietzsche's intentions are more radical than this by far. Unlike Kant he wants utterly to deny the existence of an agent "behind" the action: "no such agent exists; there is no 'being' behind the doing, acting, becoming; the 'doer' has simply been added to the deed by the imagination—the doing is everything."[17]

This position seems implausible to us; it is in fact unthinkable to most persons that there could be a deed without a doer, that there could be acts but with no agents to do them. Nietzsche says this seems impossible to us partly because we have been led astray by language. Ordinary grammar requires each sentence to have a subject and an object connected by an action. When a philosopher analyzes the expression "I think" he comes to the conclusion that "there is a something which performs thinking; that thinking is an activity and an effect of a creature which is thought of as its cause; that there exists an 'I' . . . ."[18] Nietzsche regards this conclusion as plainly false: "A thought comes when 'it' will and not when 'I' will. It is thus a *falsification* of the evidence to say that the subject 'I' conditions the predicate 'think.' It is thought, to be sure, but that this 'it' should be that old famous 'I' is, to put it mildly, only a supposition, an assertion."[19]

There is something more serious in this matter than the mere seduction of our thinking by the grammatical structure of language. It is Nietzsche's claim that the "repressed and smoldering emotions of vengeance and hatred have taken advantage of this superstition" to provide an "excuse" for their weakness. Even if the weak have chosen not to act freely in the presence of the powerful Other, they still possess a subject, or soul, that exists independently of their action or inaction— and that they can consider good in itself.

> We can hear the oppressed, downtrodden, violated whispering among themselves with the wily vengefulness of the impotent, "Let us be unlike those evil ones. Let us be good. And the good shall be he who does not do violence, does not attack or retaliate, who leaves vengeance to God, who, like us, lives hidden, who shuns all that is evil, and altogether asks very little of life—like us, the patient, the humble, the just ones."[20]

This retreat from the dynamic and vital exchange of animal energies to a belief in a subject that exists secretly and unseen behind it all has spawned a great swarm of errors. Contrary to the claim of philosophers, belief in the subject is not the consequence of their discovery of an unchanging *substance*, which is present behind the unstable appearance of things. On the contrary: "The concept of substance is a consequence of the concept of the subject: not the reverse! If we relinquish the soul, 'the subject,' the precondition for 'substance' in general disappears." The concept of the subject, sprung as it were from resentment, has in fact become the model for many other philosophical "fictions." Among these is *causation*. Since we know that the subject is a fiction and therefore can have no causal influence, "then belief also disappears in effective things, in reciprocation, cause and effect between those phenomena that we call things." Another error is *materiality*: when one has done away with substance, with the "thing in itself," there is no possibility of belief in the "eternity and immutability of matter."[21]

Nietzsche's collective name for these errors is *Platonism*. It is Plato's creation of a transcendent and changeless world of ideas that most typically exresses the thinker's flight from life. Nietzsche sees in this a genuine abhorrence of the dynamism and growth that is the essence of life: "Philosophers are prejudiced against appearance, change, pain, death, the corporeal, the senses, fate and bondage, the aimless."[22] It is their inability to endure the suffering that goes with all of this that presses them into the creation of timeless ideas: "to imagine another, more valuable world is an expression of hatred for a world that makes one suffer. . . .[23] Nietzsche thought that hints of Platonism can be found in all forms of civilized life. Ideas of the state, the philosophy of beauty, and religion are all dominated by the belief in timeless verities. Nietzsche often refers to Christianity as the present form of Platonism, particularly in its antagonism to the body and in its assertion of a "world beyond." In his words, "General insight: it is the instinct of life-weariness, and not that of life, which has created the 'other world.' Consequence: philosophy, religion, and morality are *symptoms of decadence*."[24]

We have argued that Nietzsche's objection to "Platonism," or this enormous accumulation of superstitions, is based on his belief that they are all expressions of resentment. Let us look at this more closely. We have observed that resentment involves a kind of looking backward, a willed remembering of the past so effective that we continue to experience it as though it were present. We have also noted that the object of one's resentment cannot be the Other, since the abuse one suffered from the Other is now past; the object is therefore oneself. Resentment, in other words, appears to be hostility toward the world, but in truth it is nothing more than self-hatred—experienced in the form of conscience. Finally we have seen that resentment is life-denying; it is an active avoidance of the dynamic openness of human existence. Therefore, all Platonists—or moralists of any sort—display the characteristics of a preoccupation with the past, hatred of self that takes the form of hatred of the world, and a flight from life.

In the terms of this study it is now evident that what Nietzsche means by Platonism we have called the negative reaction to death's discontinuity, or *grief*. Confronted with the hazardous character of life—its pain, misery, and death—we are tempted to pull back into something exempt from history; thus, we create the "I," or "substance," or a realm of timeless realities. To fly from both life and death, this is the characteristic reaction of grief.

We can begin to grasp the form freedom would take to confront this sort of grief by considering Nietzsche's model philosopher, Zarathustra, who avoids all inclinations toward an absorption in the past: "Verily, I do not want to be like the ropemakers: they drag out their threads and always walk backwards."[25] Zarathustra is drawn deliberately in contrast to Socrates, against whom Nietzsche releases a surprisingly virulent attack: "Is the irony of Socrates an expression of revolt? Of plebeian *resentment*? Does he, as one oppressed, enjoy his own ferocity in the knife-thrusts of his syllogisms? Does he *avenge* himself on the noble people whom he fascinates? . . . Is dialectic only a form of *revenge* is Socrates?"[26] That aspect of resentment, which takes the form of life-denial, is most vividly described in Nietzsche's use of the term "Egypticism," a term for what philosophers do. When they deal with any subject they first "de-historicize" it, "they turn it into a mummy. All that philosophers have handled for thousands of years have been concept-mummies; nothing real escaped their grasp alive."[27]

This wholesale condemnation of philosophy brings us to Nietzsche's infamous sneer at the possibility at arriving at truth of any kind. After discussing the impossibility of words—which after all are only "nerve stimuli"—to carry us to things in themselves, Nietzsche asks, "What, then, is truth?" His memorable answer is worth quoting at length: "A mobile army of metaphors, metonyms, and anthropomorphisms—in short, a sum of human relations which have been enhanced, transposed, and embellished poetically and rhetorically, and which after long use seem firm, canonical, and obligatory to a people: truths are illusions about which one has forgotten that this is what they are: metaphors which are worn out and without sensuous power; coins which have lost their pictures and now matter only as metal, no longer as coins."[28] It would be a mistake to interpret this statement to mean that Nietzsche has adopted the self-canceling view that there is no such thing as truth whatsoever—or, worse, that all statements are false. The point of this statement is subtler. Nietzsche is attacking his old enemy, Platonism, by arguing that its timeless verities are nothing more than words and have therefore no more value than the mere sound of their utterance.

What lies behind his attack on "truth" is the belief that this way of thinking is life-negating, a fruit of resentment. He often characterizes truth as "inertia," a way of making the "smallest expenditure of spiritual force."[29] Truth-seekers are simply avoiding any expression of energy or power whatsoever—an opinion that leads Nietzsche frequently to praise the tendency toward lying and deception simply because it is more energetic and complicated. "The falseness of a given judgment does not constitute an objection against it," Nietzsche declares in a manner most uncharacteristic of philosophers. "The real question is how far a judgment furthers and maintains life, preserves a given type, possibly cultivates and trains a given type."[30] Thus, *what Nietzsche is seeking is not living truths, but living thinkers.* There is no power in truth as such; indeed, it is likely there is much weakness. There is power only in the free exercise of expansive and dynamic vitality. Nietzsche is not making a case for falsehood, only an appeal for heightened vitality. Truth, in fact, is an enemy of living thinkers. It is the refuge of the grief-stricken who want to cease thinking.

In spite of himself, however, Nietzsche does offer us what is in effect a metaphysical account of the world—or, at least a consistent account of the way things are. His universe is infinite in time, without beginning or end. There is no reason for its existence. There is no aim, no final state.[31] The earth is nothing but "a star on which clever animals invented knowledge. . . . After nature had drawn a few breaths the star grew cold, and the clever animals had to die."[32] If there is no reason *for* this universe, neither is there any reason *within* it: "In the great whirlpool of forces man stands with the conceit that this whirlpool is rational and has an aim: an error!"[33] If there is a truth for Nietzsche it is that nature deceived us by the invention of consciousness, then promptly "threw away the key" to prevent any access to an accurate view of our state, for we would doubtless find ourselves "hanging in dreams, as it were, on the back of a tiger."[34]

Nietzsche's most distinctive term for this chaotic state is "becoming," a word he intends to stand opposed to "being." Being is the static and timeless world of the Platonists, the refuge of the weak and rancorous. The force of Nietzsche's thought is unmistakable: he is summoning his readers to the bracing life of the strong that does not resist but rather joyously duplicates the chaotic "becoming" of the universe. There are passages in which this duplication seems to be a passive yielding to the blind fate of aimless nature. His preference for instinct over consciousness and knowledge, as well as his frequent celebration of frenzy, suggests a loss of control over one's own mind and body and, therefore, a loss of individuality—as though one were merely to be swept along in nature's "whirlpool of forces." But in the full context of his thought this is quite evidently not his intention. In one of his most wonderfully exultant passages his invented sage Zarathustra declares: "I say unto you: one must have chaos in oneself to be able to give birth to a dancing star. I say unto you: you still have chaos in yourselves."[35]

We have come to the most difficult facet of Nietzsche's thought, the point at which he introduces his will-to-power. What we must see in this concept is its double aspect—how instinctual frenzy can be creative, how the chaos within us can give birth to dancing stars. In the notions of frenzy and instinct Nietzsche is invoking the absolute primacy of the will. He frequently attempts to relieve us of the burden of thinking that the will is a kind of inner mechanism we can use as we wish, as though we have aims or intentions prior to our willing. Aims and intentions are themselves willed. To say that the will follows a wish or intention is to say that the will has a will or that the will is the effect of something other than itself, in which case it is no longer a will. Whatever is willed is willed freely and out of itself. This puts Nietzsche in the rather extreme position of arguing that, if nothing precedes the will as a cause, all events, whether human or natural, inasmuch as they are manifestations of energy, are without cause and are therefore to be understood as though they too are will. Assuming we could trace our entire instinctual life to the will-to-power, "we should be justified in defining *all* effective energy unequivocally as *will-to-power*. The world seen from within, the world designated and defined according to its 'intelligible character'—this world would be *will-to-power* and nothing else."[36]

One half of this double aspect of the will-to-power presents a view of the unity between individual existence and the universe. Nietzsche repeatedly cites this unity. "Remain faithful to the earth," Zarathustra exhorts his friends. "Lead back to the earth the virtue that flew away, as I do—back to the body, back to life, that it may give the earth a meaning, a human meaning."[37] This identity of the earthly with the human has its most exaggerated form in Nietzsche's praise of the ancient rites of Dionysian drunkenness: "In nearly every case these festivals centered in extravagant sexual licentiousness, whose waves overwhelmed all family life and its venerable traditions; the most savage natural instincts were unleashed," with their "horrible mixture of sensuality and cruelty."[38]

But the Dionysian is only one aspect of the will-to-power; there is also the other half of this famous duality: the Apollonian, the essence of which is not ecstatic drunkenness but fantasy and dreaming. If the Dionysian represents the self-immolating, cruel, frenzied, and animalistic yearning for the dark consanguinity of flesh and earth, the Apollonian stands for the brilliant dream projection, the sun-drenched appearance of the creative individual: "we might consider Apollo himself as the glorious divine image of the *principium individuationis*, whose gestures and expression tell us of all the joy and wisdom of 'appearance,' together with its beauty."[39] This is the side of the will-to-power that is inherently creative. We must be careful here not to confuse the heavenward flight of the Apollonian imagination with the "other-wordliness" of Platonism. *The Apollonian is not seeking truth but appearance.* It is the instinct of sheer inventiveness, of playing at deception.

The theme of deception runs strong through Nietzsche's literature. We have already seen how lying is superior to truth inasmuch as it requires more life to sustain. But this is not because there is any attempt to "get away with something," or especially not a desire to project an "untrue" reality as though it were "true." Since there is no true reality, the inventions of the imagination will be thrown off with a genuine modesty, with the knowledge that no image can capture its maker. A great man, Nietzsche says, "when not speaking to himself wears a mask. He rather lies than tells the truth: it requires more spirit and *will*. There is a solitude in him that is inaccessible to praise or blame, his own justice that is beyond appeal."[40] Elsewhere: "Everything deep loves masks; the deepest things have a veritable hatred of image and likeness. Might not *contrareity* be the only proper disguise to clothe the modesty of a god?"[41] We are not dealing here with a recommended falseness, but with a profound understanding of the distinction between the image, caught for a brilliant moment in the full light where for an instant it seems real, and the restless fire, in which it was fashioned. It is not only then that deep thinkers love masks, but that "around every deep thinker a mask constantly grows, thanks to the consistently wrong, that is, superficial, interpretations of his every word, his every step, his every sign of life."[42]

The notion of deception, of course, always has something of a scandalous quality, and no doubt Nietzsche is exploiting that for the sheer effect on his reader. In fact, however, in Nietzsche's philosophy lying and deception are no different from interpretation. One lies because there is no fixed and permanent reality to be truthful about, because there can be no factual basis for knowledge as such. The "reality" of the Platonists is not, as they think, some eternal region of being that exists prior to the will; it is not even separate from the will—it *is* what the Platonists will. Knowledge, too, must be willed, for the simple reason that *there is nothing to be known*. Knowledge is not seeing something that is there, but is sheer invention, or interpretation: "Against that positivism which stops before phenomena, saying 'there are only *facts*,' I should say: no, it is precisely facts that do not exist, only interpretations . . . ."[43] This makes interpretation and, indeed, all knowledge more like sheer invention or art than mere description or explanation. But this scarcely counts against it, in Nietzsche's opinion: "Art and nothing but art! It is the great means of making life possible, the great seduction to life, the great stimulant of life."[44]

We are discussing the second aspect of the will-to-power that we have characterized as the "creative" aspect in distinction to the "frenzied" aspect. We might wonder why, if Nietzsche is concerned primarily with creativity, he should have used the term "power." We observed earlier that the kind of power of which he speaks is most definitely not the kind of mechanical force that exists in quantifiable amounts, but is an expansive energy that is free within itself. He is, however, quite definite in his attachment to the notion of power. In fact, he often speaks of the will-to-power as a kind of *commanding*.[45] The reason for this is that Nietzsche has never lost his view of the Other. Hegel and Sartre could discuss the Other only in terms of consciousness, thereby rendering the question of power meaningless. Since Nietzsche rejects consciousness as the refuge of the weak who refuse (freely, of course) to acknowledge that the will is prior even to consciousness, the Other remains truly Other. The will-to-power is not a mode of creativity in which the imagination simply throws its own products defiantly against the void; instead, it is a creativity whose true object is the Other. Nietzsche expresses it this way: "The will-to-power can manifest itself only against resistances; therefore it seeks that which resists it."[46] This means, quite simply, that *the will can be a will only if it is opposed by another will*. But such opposed willing does not command out of resentment or some other inner need: the strongest and most spiritual persons "rule not because they want to but because they *are*."[47]

This is precisely why the Apollonian is referred to as the *principium individuationis*. Where the Dionysian seeks a merger with the whirlpool of nature's blind forces, the Apollonian seeks to command the Other with its illusions. It is this latter characteristic of willing that makes human existence possible at all. If there were no opposition of wills, there would be no way of distinguishing one's creativity from the flow of nature. But note: *it is not just the existence of the Other, but the opposition of the Other, that makes it possible for me to be an individual. Moreover, without this opposition life itself could not exist:* "To refrain from wounding, violating, and exploiting one another, to acknowledge another's will as equal to one's own," this can be proper behavior in certain limited circumstances.

> But as soon as one wants to extend this principle, to make it the *basic principle of society*, it shows itself for what it is: the will to negate life, the principle of dissolution and decay .... Life itself is essential assimilation, injury, violation of the foreign and the weaker, suppression, hardness, the forcing of one's own forms upon something else, ingestion and—at least in its mildest form—exploitation.[48]

Again, we must be reminded that Nietzsche is not describing an attempt merely to *overpower* the Other. Life does not overcome opposition in order that it may simply survive; the very essence of life is growth, the *increase* of power;[49] therefore, life needs opposition to increase its potency. Thus, the opposition of wills is not a competition, but a manner of growth. Nietzsche clearly does not mean *domination* of one will by another, for in this case the opposition of the other will is crushed—and this means life itself is crushed. For this reason strong and vital persons even have a preference for tragedy and suffering, "*for questionable and terrifying things*," Nietzsche writes with his own emphasis. "It is the *heroic* spirits who say Yes to themselves in tragic cruelty: they are hard enough to experience suffering as a *pleasure*."[50] As an example of this heroism he offers the Jews, who "are beyond doubt the strongest, toughest, and purest race now living in Europe; they know how to assert themselves in the midst of the worst possible conditions (better, in fact, than under more favorable ones)."[51]

What Nietzsche has achieved in his concept of the will-to-power is an extraordinarily dynamic picture of life that is not threatened by, but requires, genuine and powerful Otherness. Where other philosophers have speculated at length on the doubtfulness of even knowing whether there are other minds, for example, Nietzsche, by giving primacy to the will in his typically radical fashion, has swept all this aside as mere words and has shown that the fact that there is willing already implies other wills. Where other philosophers or assorted social theorists have attempted to design ways of eliminating the opposition to life by reducing the danger of Otherness, Nietzsche has embraced danger and risk as the highest form of life: "believe me, the secret of the greatest fruitfulness and the greatest enjoyment of existence is: to *live dangerously*! Build your cities under Vesuvius! Send your ships into uncharted seas! Live at war with your peers and yourselves!"[52]

In spite of his claim that history has no aim but what we give it, he does outline a type of historical *progressus* in which the powerful, creative persons play something of a messianic role. Ancient Greece was a kind of golden age; other cultures had their golden ages. But the noble barbarians were gradually undermined by the resentful and the weak—particularly the priests, "the greatest haters in history—but also the most intelligent haters."[53] The erosion of true greatness, and the rise of the Platonists and moralists, seems to have run its course, however. The values and the ideals they have offered as truths are about to collapse into mere sound. Nihilism, "the uncanniest of all guests," stands waiting at the door.[54] Nietzsche is by no means distressed by this threatened entrance of nihilism, for it can only show the falsehood of all existing values and prepare the way for a genuine transformation. This transformation may not be far off. At some future time "the true Redeemer will come, whose surging creativity will not let him rest in any shelter or hiding place, whose solitude will be misinterpreted as a flight from reality . . . ."[55] Just who this is, or how his work is to be accomplished, Nietzsche does not speculate. However, he often calls for the advent of a "higher person," an *Übermensch*, who does not seem to be a particular Redeemer, but a collective phenomenon like the dawning of a new age. The Übermensch has not yet come, though we are on the way toward the arrival of this superior being. Elsewhere, less apocalyptically, he declares that we must seek *"new philosophers*, spirits strong or original enough to give an impulse to opposing valuations, to transvalue and turn upside down the 'eternal values'; we must seek heralds, men of the future, who will now tie the knot and start the pressure that shall force the will of milleniums to run *new* orbits. Men who will teach man that man's future is man's *will*. . . ."[56]

These new philosophers combine both sides of the will-to-power: the instinctive and the creative. They say *Yes* to life; they do not hide behind their abstractions, nor hesitate before suffering and pain. Their strength of will is shown in their ability to "do without meaning in things . . . ."[57] Such a philosopher, Nietzsche says, "lives 'unphilosophically' and 'unwisely' and above all un-shrewdly. He feels the burden and duty to take up the hundreds of experiments and temptations of life; he constantly risks *himself* . . . ."[58]

To risk *themselves* in all the experiments and temptations of life— this is what the self-haters, the priests, the old philosophers will not do. Where these new barbarians, these warrior philosophers, exuberant Zarathustras, say Yes to the Other in *action*, the slavish herd says No in *reaction*. The slaves turn inward capturing themselves in their own freedom, driven in their resentment to quarrel with a past that no longer exists. The new philosophers turn outward aiming their creativity at other wills, giving words their meanings and compelling others to use them,[59] joyously shaping and reshaping the world,[60] the world which Others also inhabit: *"the real philosophers are commanders and legislators.* They say, 'It *shall* be thus!' They determine the 'whither' and the 'to what end' of mankind. . . . Their 'knowing' is *creating*. Their creating is legislative."[61] Unlike the herd, they have freed themselves from the past by refusing to see themselves as its victims, as the crippled inheritors of former injustices. They have been "redeemed" by their ability to "recreate all 'it was' into a 'thus I willed it.'"[62]

However, these new philosophers do not live this way simply to preserve themselves; they are always acting in the interest of increasing life. Nietzsche occasionally but briefly envisions a society fashioned by persons for whom all desire for punishment, all preoccupation with indebtedness, all attempts to establish a rigid social order have disappeared. "It is possible to imagine a society flushed with such a sense of power that it could afford to let its offenders go unpunished. What greater luxury is there for a society to indulge in?"[63] There would be an elevation of "the general feeling of life" if "together with the belief in guilt we could also get rid of the ancient instinct of revenge," even pronounce a blessing over our enemies and benefit "those who have harmed us."[64] Nietzsche is not hinting that when criminals are released or go unpunished they will cease being criminals out of gratitude, or cease being criminals at all. This would only be a subtler form of domination, a way of crushing the criminal's will. Instead, he is underscoring the powerful human appetite for danger.

What is most important to grasp in this messianic vision of the redemptive new philosophers is that their creative and commanding power is never separable from the chaotic condition of becoming. The Apollonian dreamer is always bound in a "primal unity" to the Dionysian ecstatic. To be joyously creative is simultaneously to be torn apart in the "atomic whirl of egoisms" that constitutes human history. *To choose life is to choose tragedy.* The strong cannot say Yes to life without opening themselves to injury, pain, meaninglessness, and death—without making life itself a risk and a danger. They must embrace their finitude, their vulnerability, and their mortality in order to embrace life itself. It is the desire of the strong *to die at the right time.* "Of course, how could those who never live at the right time die at the right time?" To live at the right time is to be the sole master of one's existence, to be willing it directly. "My death I praise to you," Zarathustra exclaims, "the free death which comes to me because *I* want it." He condemns that death which takes us from behind, when we have lost control over our lives, when cowardice has kept us on the branch too long and we have begun to rot.[65] What Nietzsche is counseling here is not the famous Stoic preference for suicide, but the attitude that life always constitutes danger, and when we have begun to seek security, when we have started to long for survival, we have effectively ceased to live. This is most perverse when we begin to believe we can survive death itself; when we think that life may *in the end* not be tragic. The belief in immortality, he says, "has so far been the greatest, most malignant, attempt to assassinate *noble* humanity."[66]

Placing death at the very creative center of life leads Nietzsche to draw a sharp distinction between the death of Dionysus and the death of Jesus. The fact that Jesus was "Crucified as the innocent one" means that his death "counts as an objection to this life, as a formula for its condemnation." But Dionysus' death demonstrates the conviction that "Life itself, its eternal fruitfulness and recurrence, creates torment, destruction, the will to annihilation." For Nietzsche the issue is whether suffering and death have a "Christian meaning or a tragic meaning. In the former case, it is supposed to be the path to a holy existence; in the latter case, being is counted as *holy enough* to justify even a monstrous amount of suffering."[67]

We discovered in the discussion of the Christian view of death that the tragedy of life is overcome by the resurrection, by a transformation into another, though mysterious, mode of existence. Nietzsche has consistently and passionately chosen the tragic instead of the Christian understanding of death, because mortality, in his vision, is the very path into the center of *this* life. Because Nietzsche's deepest conviction is that life is not a state or a condition, but a dynamic process which he called "becoming," he seized on the tragic not because it is pessimistic, and not because it is antilife, but, on the contrary, because it offers the way "to be *oneself* the eternal joy of becoming."[68]

We can most usefully summarize Nietzsche's understanding of death by quickly glancing back over the territory we covered in order to arrive at his thought. We had seen that in the modern philosophical discussion (since Descartes) the problem of death was inseparable from the problem of Otherness (or transcendence). The threat of death is the threat of becoming an Other, of becoming alien or strange to oneself. Hegel attacked the problem by the daring philosophical move of bringing the transcendent, in the form of an opposed Otherness, into the mind—where it takes the form of self-consciousness. In self-consciousness we are alienated from ourselves. This represented the first attempt to describe selfhood as *inherently mortal*. Hegel's famous solution produced an appropriately famous dilemma. To prevent the self from being destroyed by its own Otherness, Hegel had to invent a novel form of dialectical Reason that is able to reconcile the difference between the self and its Other. This results in an elevated form of consciousness, which then has an equivalently higher object, with which it must consequently reconcile itself. This process continues until it reaches Absolute Spirit, which has no Other transcendent to itself. Absolute Spirit is absolutely immanent, that is, identical to itself. Sartre, believing that Hegel's loss of the individual to the dialectic could be prevented by restricting the dialectic to individual self-consciousness, composed a virtuosic description of human existence in which the person is absolutely, even necessarily, free. We found two difficulties with this description. The first is that Sartre's theory of freedom is meaningless, for according to it freedom has only the power to transform itself in reaction to the Other. It is not a freedom to do anything. The second difficulty is that Sartre's freedom is so complete within itself it cannot even admit the possibility of death; it has no power to become an Other—for all Otherness is Other only for consciousness, and without consciousness there can be no Other. The self remains an immortal captive of its own impotent consciousness.

We entered into Nietzsche's thought by asking whether he could describe human existence as free *and* powerful in relation to the Other and yet describe it as still genuinely mortal. We noted that Nietzsche had abandoned the category of consciousness since it sprang from self-hatred, the product of one's resentment for what was done to one in the past, but not genuinely released to the past. Nietzsche appealed instead to the primacy of the will as the key to human existence. Nothing is prior to willing, not even consciousness—not even the events of nature, which constitute a "whirlpool of forces" with no aim or shape. In the individual's willing there is no essential distinction between his or her actions and the chaotic rush of natural events, the condition Nietzsche called "becoming." So far, however, this identification of willing and becoming wipes away all the distinguishing features of individual existence. Nietzsche addresses this dilemma by arguing that real willing must always be a kind of comanding; it cannot exist unless there is something to resist it. What resists it must be another will. Therefore, the very phenomenon of willing presupposes, even demands, the existence of the Other. By insisting on the primacy of willing Nietzsche has preserved the absolute freedom Sartre described, but by showing the necessity of the Other he combined freedom with power. The power in this case is not the desire to eliminate the Other, neither is it what he sneeringly calls "will-to-existence"[69] or self-preservation; it is a desire for the increase of life. But since the individual is never released from the eternal flux of becoming, the freely willed increase in life can come only at the price of suffering and death—a tragic view, to be sure, but in Nietzsche's vision the true response to tragedy is to identify *oneself* with "the eternal joy of becoming." It is by no means *resignation* as it is in Sartre and in countless other philosophers and sages. "The free man," Nietzsche exclaims, "is a *warrior*."[70] Compare this image to Sartre's Orestes in *The Flies*. Orestes walks away from the scene of his crime a free man, but only because he has resigned himself to the punishing vengeance of the past, not because he vigorously steps forward ready for battle again, prepared to throw his life away in an instant. The free man is always ready to "die at the right time."

We described the challenge to modern thought as the task of showing that the threatened discontinuity of death can be met by *way of history* and not by *overcoming history*, showing, that is, that *the transcendent is temporal.* It would appear that Nietzsche, through his understanding of life as opposed wills and the consequent joy of eternal becoming, has successfully met this challenge. It is in Heidegger that we learn that in one crucial detail Nietzsche's thought falls short of the goal. We can see this shortcoming most clearly by comparing, in a roundabout way, Nietzsche's thoroughly Western thought with a thoroughly Eastern counterpart—Buddhism—with which Nietzsche's thought has an astonishing likeness.

He did, in fact, admire Buddhism above all other religions, chiefly for its lack of resentment. Buddhists deal with the discontinuity of death by absolutizing discontinuity. In our earlier discussion we emphasized this tendency by referring to Buddhism as the "religion of becoming," in distinction to Hinduism as the "religion of being." As we have seen, Nietzsche's preference for becoming over being is a major theme in his thought. In this important respect his metaphysics very closely resembles Buddhism. When he says, for example, that a thought comes when *it* will, and not when *I* will, or that this little "I" is a mere grammatical mistake, he has walked directly into the most powerful argument of Buddhist philosophy: the existence of a thought does not presuppose a thinker, an act does not presuppose a doer. Nietzsche's fondness for deception, appearance, and interpretation, as well as his insistent denial that there are any real "facts," sounds very much like the Buddhist teaching that human existence (and therefore death) is a fiction; it is not an *illusion* that masks something real, but a *fiction* that is only a mask with nothing real behind it.

Yet, in at least one decisive respect, Nietzsche is not a Buddhist and, in fact, is an infinite distance from Buddhism. He does finally rest his whole system of thought on the actual existence of the creative, *individual* will, which he repeatedly celebrates in the messianic figure of the "new philosopher," the free warrior of thought. Our question is what warrant does Nietzsche have in his philosophy for holding fast to the real existence of an isolated and centered will.

Heidegger, who saw himself as a philosophical successor to Nietzsche, noted this strange holding back in Nietzsche's thought, this need to establish the originating will as a fixed point in the "eternal becoming," and ascribed it to an ironic twist. Heidegger writes, "Nietzsche understands his own philosophy as the countermovement to metaphysics, and that means for him a movement in opposition to Platonism." But as in all movements of opposition, Nietzsche's thought is "held fast in the essence of that over against which it moves."[71] Through his rejection of the suprahistorical Platonic "I," or of the theory that there must be a mind thinking the thought, he erected a suprahistorical "I" of his own. It is a willing "I" instead of a thinking "I," but it is an "I" all the same.

It is in this way that Nietzsche fails finally to meet the challenge of modern thought and to show the temporality of transcendence. We could state it as *his inability to show that the self is capable of dying.* Zarathustra speaks of a death that is free: "because *I* want it." In truth, Zarathustra does not *die,* but *risks death.* What sets aside the "new philosopher" from other persons is that they live dangerously, they risk being killed. The philosopher is not mortal by definition, but by demonstration. Mortality implies that one can be killed, but mortality is meaningful only when life is lived in such a way that murder is possible. This still requires an external agent, a dependence on the Other, and therefore a serious compromise of one's freedom.

Nietzsche's singular achievement is to have offered a philosophy that preserves both the individual and the individual's power in such a way that life cannot be life without an Other. But because he was unable, due to the undetected influence of Platonism, to carry becoming into the will itself, *life is always in the form of being against life.* We turn to Heidegger to see if mortality can be integrated into selfhood. Can one be an individual, free, powerful, and mortal in a way that is not against Others, but with Others?

Notes

1. *The Genealogy of Morals,* p. 159.
2. Ibid., p. 160.
3. Ibid., p. 162.
4. "Twilight of the Idols," *The Portable Nietzsche,* pp. 490 ff.
5. *The Will to Power,* #6.
6. *The Genealogy of Morals,* p. 189.
7. Ibid., p. 174.
8. Ibid., p. 175.
9. See especially *The Will to Power,* #962.
10. *The Genealogy of Morals,* p. 173.

11. Ibid., p. 172.
12. Ibid., p. 190.
13. Ibid., p. 172.
14. Ibid., pp. 192 ff.
15. Ibid., p. 218.
16. Ibid., pp. 170 ff.
17. Ibid., pp. 178 ff.
18. *Beyond Good and Evil*, p. 17.
19. Ibid., p. 18.
20. *The Genealogy of Morals*, p. 179.
21. *The Will to Power*, #552.
22. Ibid., #407.
23. Ibid., #579.
24. Ibid., #586.
25. "Thus Spake Zarathustra," *The Portable Nietzsche*, p. 184.
26. "Twilight of the Idols," p. 476.
27. Ibid., p. 478.
28. "On Truth and Lie in an Extra-Moral Sense," *The Portable Nietzsche*, pp. 46 ff.
29. *The Will to Power*, #537.
30. *Beyond Good and Evil*, p. 4.
31. *The Will to power*, #708.
32. "On Truth and Lie in an Extra-Moral Sense," p. 42.
33. Ibid., p. 50.
34. Ibid., p. 44.
35. "Thus Spake Zarathustra," p. 129.
36. *Beyond Good and Evil*, pp. 43 ff.
37. "Thus Spake Zarathustra," p. 188.
38. "The Birth of Tragedy," *Philosophies of Art and Beauty*, p. 503.
39. Ibid., p. 500.
40. *The Will to Power*, #962.
41. *Beyond Good and Evil*, p. 46.
42. Ibid., p. 47.
43. "Notes, 1888," *The Portable Nietzsche*, p. 458.
44. *The Will to Power*, #853.
45. See especially "Thus Spake Zarathustra," pp. 226 ff.
46. *The Will to Power*, #656.
47. "The Twilight of the Idols," p. 646.
48. *Beyond Good and Evil*, p. 201.
49. *The Will to Power*, #702.
50. Ibid., #852.
51. *Beyond Good and Evil*, p. 186.

52. "The Gay Science," *The Portable Nietzsche*, p. 97.
53. *The Genealogy of Morals*, p. 167.
54. *The Will to Power*, #1.
55. *The Genealogy of Morals*, p. 229.
56. *Beyond Good and Evil*, p. 114.
57. *The Will to Power*, #585.
58. *Beyond Good and Evil*, pp. 121 ff.
59. *The Will to Power*, #573.
60. Ibid., #495.
61. *Beyond Good and Evil*, p. 135.
62. "Thus Spake Zarathustra," p. 251.
63. *The Genealogy of Morals*, p. 205.
64. "Dawn," *The Portable Nietzsche*, p. 87.
65. "Thus Spake Zarathustra," p. 184.
66. "The Antichrist," *The Portable Nietzsche*, p. 619.
67. The Will to Power, #1052.
68. "The Twilight of the Idols," p. 463.
69. "Thus Spake Zarathustra," p. 226.
70. "The Twilight of the Idols," p. 542.
71. "The Word of Nietzsche: God is Dead," *The Question concerning Technology*, p. 61.

Bibliography

David B. Allison, ed., *The New Nietzsche* (New York: 1977).

Friedrich Nietzsche, *Beyond Good and Evil*, tr. Marianne Cowan (Chicago: 1966).

———— "The Birth of Tragedy," tr. Clifton Fadiman, *Philosophies of Art and Beauty*, ed., Albert Hofstadter and Richard Kuhns (New York: 1964).

———— *The Genealogy of Morals*, tr. Francis Golffing (New York: 1956).

———— *Philosophy in the Age of the Greeks*, tr. Marianne Cowan (Chicago: 1962).

———— *The Portable Nietzsche*, tr. and ed. Walter Kaufmann (New York: 1966).

———— *Schopenhauer as Educator*, trs. James W. Hillesheim and Malcolm R. Simpson (South Bend: 1965).

———— *The Will to Power*, trs. Walter Kaufmann and R. J. Hollingdale (New York: 1967).

15 MARTIN HEIDEGGER

We had noted earlier that where Sartre and Hegel had made *consciousness* the point of departure for their thought, Heidegger had taken *Being* as the center of his focus. Heidegger well knew that this would dismay and confuse most of his philosophical readers who generally considered Being one of the most notorious fictions of the metaphysical tradition. However, very few of his early readers were able to see that what he meant by *Being* was essentially what Nietzsche meant by *Becoming*. Heidegger insisted on using the term not out of some personal whim, defiant of the philosophical community, but out of respect for the philosophical tradition in its entirety. It is Heidegger's strongly held belief that philosophical thought in the West dawned with the question of Being. In its most rudimentary form that question is: "Why is there something rather than nothing?"[1] It is to this question that the great pre-Socratic philosophers, particularly Parmenides and Heraclitus, had addressed their thoughts.

This question, as it was originally framed, requires an utter openness of mind. Suppose, Heidegger says, we ask it of someone for whom the Biblical faith is normative. Even before the question is fully considered the Christian or Jew may be expected to answer that there are things rather than nothing because God created them. Such a person has not yet truly asked the question. In order genuinely to ask why there is something rather than nothing, one must set aside all beliefs, all presuppositions. One must open oneself to whatever course the inquiry will take.[2] It is this openness Heidegger expects of his readers; he expected it of himself. And for all its apparent self-conscious profundity his philosophy is exceedingly modest. He describes it as an attempt to listen to Being's own answer to this original question; it is an attempt to "let Being be" in and through himself, to put himself in the service of Being's "unconcealment" of itself.

Nietzsche's rejection of the term "being" in favor of "becoming," was not an error in itself; it is only evidence of the power of the Platonic philosophy in its distortion of the original question. When Plato identified the real with the realm of eternal, changeless ideas he abruptly broke with the older tradition, initiating what Heidegger has called "the forgottenness of Being." What Plato *called* Being was only evidence that he had already forgotten what the original question was about.

Nietzsche's durable insight is that the "being" of the Platonists has in it nothing of the dynamic of lived experience. *It has no time in it.* Becoming, in contrast, is a time-laded term, indicating something unfinished but continuing. It is Heidegger's understanding of the history of thought that this was the original conception of Being. He then recasts the question of Being "within the horizon of temporality." He wants to inquire into the meaning of Being, and from his study of the origins of thought in the West he wants to see precisely how time is related to the meaning of Being. His guiding insight from the first is the difficult notion that *time IS the meaning of Being*—a perplexing notion not because it is complicated in itself, but because centuries of active "forgetting" of the question have buried it under layers of misleading terminology and reasoning. Buried with the original understanding of Being is a view of death that, though simple in itself, we are likely to find most peculiar; it is especially important when we are told in advance that Heidegger has placed in bold type the statement that Being is FREEDOM TOWARDS DEATH, which is Heidegger's expression for what we have called the temporality of transcendence.

In order to make any sense of that claim we must briefly trace the path of Heidegger's thinking. If we remember that by Being he means something quite close to Nietzsche's becoming, we can see at once that he does not mean an eternal and changeless reality, nor certainly anything vague and empty. Just as it makes no sense to speak of becoming without reference to something in the process of becoming, it makes no sense to speak of Being except as the *Being of beings* (*das Sein des Seiendes*). It is well to examine a bit more closely this perplexing phrase. In German *Being* (*das Sein*) carries a much more active connotation. Some commentators have noted that it would be more accurate, though perhaps too awkward, to translate the term "the to-be." From the context of Heidegger's thought it is evident that he uses the term in this more active sense. "To be" does certainly have the sense of something happening—and something about to happen, as in "bride to be" or "father to be." We avoid this clumsy locution, however, and instead capitalize the word *Being* whenever it means *das Sein. Das Seiendes*, which we write as *being* with lower case "b," has much more the sense of *something that is*; in other words, the sort of objects or entities with which we are ordinarlly familiar. Thus, when Heidegger writes, "Being is always the Being of a being,"[3] he means that ordinary entities have a "to-be" that is itself not an entity and is therefore not to be viewed in the same way they are. In fact, if we were to look for Being as we might look for beings, we would find nothing whatsoever; and yet, if it were not for Being there could be no beings at all.

Since Being is always the Being of beings, we cannot begin to look for it somewhere else than where beings are. But where are beings? Heidegger points out that beings tend to be gathered into subject matters. We never really speak of just "things." We refer to the playthings of a child, the objects of art, the tools of a carpenter, the rules of atomic behavior in physics. The power of subject matter areas to cause things to stand out is seen in the fact that from different points of view the same objects are quite differently understood. A child, for example, might consider the carpenter's auger a most marvelous toy; an artist might consider it a masterpiece of design; a physicist could study it for its molecular composition. When we ask, But what is it *really*? we are confronted with a dilemma. Insofar as we are going to speak of it as a thing, a being, we are not going to be able to approach it except through a subject matter of some kind. The thing never simply stands there naked and self-defining, independent of all subject matters. What is primary, then, is not the thing but the subject area. If, for example, we ask the carpenter what in fact this thing is, he will likely show or explain what it is that an auger does when it is used by carpenters. If you were to press him further to tell you what it *really* is, he might become quite confused, even angry. He might, of course, speculate on its physical composition, but then he has ceased speaking *as a carpenter* and has entered into the area of the physicist.

There are several conclusions we can draw from this simple example. The first is that we can discover nothing from a subject area about the Being of beings. The playing child, the carpenter, the artist, and the physicist can speak about or use the things (beings) of their subject area quite intelligibly, but they have nothing to say about what these beings really *are*. The second is that since there are no beings except in subject areas the way to the question of the meaning of Being must be through the nature of the subject area and not its things. In other words, the original question, Why is there something rather than nothing? cannot be answered *within* a subject area, simply because we cannot inquire of things why there are things. The physicist might discover why there is evidence of crystallization in the bit of the auger, but she cannot discover from her physics why there is evidence of crystallization *instead of nothing*. As a physicist she cannot be concerned with the Being of the auger, but only its being as it relates to her work as a physicist. It is, in fact, completely meaningless in physics to ask why there is crystallization instead of nothing. Moreover, the physicist, speaking *as* a physicist, cannot tell you why there is physics. There is not the merest physical reason for the existence of physics. It seems then that if we are going to ask the original question of Being, we must step back far enough to ask why there are subject areas at all, like physics and carpentry and art.

What we have then is two ways of asking questions. One can inquire of an object from within an area, or one could inquire into the existence of the area itself. The one is a question of being: Why do you use the auger this way rather than that way? The other is a question of Being: Why do you use the auger rather than doing nothing? Heidegger calls the first class of questions *ontic*, and the second *ontological*. Ontic questions concern beings; ontological questions concern Being. *Why is there something rather than nothing?* is the archetypal ontological question.

If one must stand within a subject area to deal with ontic questions, where does one stand to ask the ontological question? Is there a region of thought that is somehow superior to all ordinary areas like child's play and carpentry? Heidegger is quite emphatic that there is not. This was the presumption of the old metaphysicians who thought they could sit in their study and offer an adequate explanation of the way things are—quite as though they were not limited by a subject area that confined them to their own "beings." Nietzsche forever overturned this presumption. An illustration of Heidegger's philosophical modesty is his refusal to delineate a privileged region of knowledge. We cannot stand outside all subject areas, he taught, but we can nonetheless *look* at a subject area while standing in it. This looking from within Heidegger called "fundamental ontology."

If "fundamental ontology" seems technical and specialized, we might add that Heidegger insists we start our inquiry into the meaning of Being simply by looking to see where we are in our "average everydayness."[4] In the most obvious and ordinary sense it must be said at the beginning of our inquiry that we are beings *in a world*. The world makes its most immediate appearance to us as a collection of things. We seem to be beings in the midst of beings. We have already seen that these beings all appear to us out of one or another subject area. Let us look more closely at this.

Our glance falls on the carpenter's auger. In the tradition that Heidegger (and Neitzsche) have rejected, serious thinkers might have begun with the question, How do we know this is an auger? or, How do we know there is something there in-itself? Heidegger waves aside all such questions and steps further back (or, as he would prefer to say it, steps closer) and asks why our glance fell on the auger to begin with. We do not even look at all, Heidegger says, unless we are looking *for* something. We cannot look *for* something unless we already know roughly what we want, and what we want to do with it. Perhaps we need a harbor for our wooden ships, positioned on the living room carpet, or an example of primitive design among early twentieth-century toolmakers. When the child or the art historian come across the auger they certainly are aware that they were not looking for *this* auger, but, on the other hand, this object will serve their purposes splendidly. What the child and the historian see in the auger is nothing that belongs to the auger in-itself; what they see is a series of *potential* uses for the auger. In fact, they see quite beyond the auger. The child wants to hide his ships from the enemy approaching around the sofa so that he can ambush them, destroy them completely, and have the sea to himself. The historian wants to read a paper to a society of art historians in order to establish herself as an authority on American crafts. We never look quite *at* the object, or being, itself; we look around it and beyond. But the beyond does not belong to the being; the beyond is in our seeing and is something we bring to the being.

Heidegger concludes from this manner of thinking that we have learned something about the Being of beings. One of the reasons there is something rather than nothing is that *we are in the world in a mode of being ahead of ourselves*. But, one might ask, isn't this a rather subjective matter? What does this have to do with the *world*? Heidegger's answer to this query is taken again from what I have called his philosophical modesty, although it is one of the more difficult ideas we find in his body of work. He points out that since we are already in some sense ahead of the beings that come into our view, and are therefore bringing the beyond to them, we are actually *involved with them* on our way toward what follows. The art historian does not simply make the auger a part of her list of examples as an isolated thing; she becomes involved in a description of it that points in the direction she wishes to go. She cannot get where she wants to go except through an involvement with it. But that involvement then leads to another, and another. However, this does not mean that the sequence of involvements fades into the infinite of an indefinite future. There is what Heidegger calls a "totality of involvements." That is, our art historian is not involved with the auger simply to be involved with something beyond it; what carries her forward is not her interest in involvement as such. She becomes involved *for the sake of* something other than mere involvement. For the sake of what? We can answer this provisionally by saying that it is for the sake of her own existence. But this will need more clarification.

If we return to the example of the child at play—an example, albeit a simple one, that will serve at present for all of human existence—what soon becomes obvious is that the child has designed his play as a unified totality of involvements. He harbors his wooden ships with a view to destroying the enemy. His intention, however, is not mere destruction. By way of that destruction he plans still further moves, perhaps even the introduction of a new enemy, that will have the effect of maintaining the viability of his present play. There appears to be a curious circularity here. We could say that the child plays for the sake of the play. The historian anticipates a sequence of involvements that will guarantee the consequentiality of what she is undertaking at present; her history is for the sake of her history.

What we are to see in this example is that a "totality of involvement" leads us to an understanding of the nature of the world. The world is not the totality of involvements as such, but that wherein such a totality is possible. We must follow the path of Heidegger's thinking here very cautiously; one is easily lost. From a phenomenological point of view, the world *appears* to be the *place where* this totality occurs. But a totality of involvements is not an ontic phenomenon; that is, it is not a thing or being. It is an ontological phenomenon inasmuch as it has to do with the fact that there is something rather than nothing. In other words, there can be a totality of involvements only because we are the way we are, namely, ahead of ourselves for the sake of ourselves. If the world, then, appears to be the place where the totality occurs, *the world is our way of Being.*[5]

The historian and the child, the carpenter and the physicist—and anyone at all—are not *in* the world as, say, a chair is in the room or a cloud is in the sky. They *are* in such a way that their present totality of involvements exists in a world. The world is not a being; one cannot go out to find it. Instead, the world is where beings are in such a way that we can be involved with them. In this sense Being is prior to world; we can *have* a world only because we already *are.*

Of course, not every being has a world. The auger is in the carpenter's world, but does not have its own. Only humans can be in such a way that they have a world. Heidegger's term for human existence, particularly in his earlier writing, is *Dasein*, an ordinary German word meaning *existence*. He chooses to use this term in place of such alternatives as "man" or "self" or "soul" simply because he wants to distance himself from the errors that have accumulated around these terms in the long tradition of hiding Being behind beings. Dasein's distinctive mode of Being is referred to by Heidegger as *existence* (*Existenz*). Existence is the particular way Dasein is, in distinction to the way other beings are. Heidegger's way of characterizing the *existence* of Dasein is to say that other beings simply are while Dasein is in such a way that "Being is an issue for it." Dasein must always contend with Being, comport itself toward Being. Dasein must always decide *how* it will be. The auger simply is. It does not have to contend with its Being as an issue for itself. Dasein may, for example, choose to live in a world made of things, ignoring the fact that the world is not *there* but is Dasein's way of Being. In other words, Dasein could choose to live ontically rather than ontologically. A serious problem arises here, according to Heidegger, since even the choice to live ontically is a way of Being; thus there is a kind of contradiction within human existence, and Heidegger refers to it as "inauthenticity." It is as though Dasein in this case is choosing against itself. We shall return to the phenomenon of inauthenticity.

It may seem that we have left far behind the "modesty" we claimed for Heidegger's style of thought and have followed his path of "fundamental ontology" into a hopeless conceptual undergrowth. Perhaps it will help briefly to summarize. The most fundamental question before any thinker is, Why is there something rather than nothing? Heidegger understands this as the completely open question of the Being of beings. What is evident is that we cannot answer the (ontological) question of Being by (ontically) consulting beings, since they themselves only come to be in light of our own projected intentions and interests. These projections, by way of which we become involved with beings, do not lead endlessly on like Hegel's notion of "bad infinity," but always point toward a "totality of involvements" inasmuch as we undertake involvement with beings for the sake of our own existence. The fact that we always understand these involvements to occur in a world does not mean that we can ontically discover the world as a kind of open locus, but that the world can be understood only ontologically as one of our ways of Being.

Earlier we observed that Heidegger claimed to be conducting his "fundamental ontology" within the horizon of temporality. He wanted to recover the original relatedness of time and being. We can already see how he has succeeded in doing this. When he speaks of Being-in-the-world as Dasein's Being-ahead-of-itself he has introduced the future as a central element of Dasein's existential worldliness. Again, it is important to note that time is introduced ontologically and not ontically. Dasein does not *have* a future in the sense of a certain number of days and hours yet to be lived through. Dasein *is* ahead-of-itself; the future is part of its existential structure just as the world is. To use Heidegger's invented term, Dasein is "futural."

The future is undoubtedly the most important aspect of time for Heidegger, though he finds that the present and past also have their indispensable places in the ontological understanding of human existence. The present and past each have their own corresponding mode of Being.

The present appears in the following way. Each one of our involvements has something of a shared or public character.[6] The art historian would never take up the auger were there no one to whom she could address her thoughts concerning its design. The carpenter would only find a use for it if his work could take place in a community of other persons. We might, of course, say that the carpenter is merely building his own house; just as the child is playing his game in complete solitude. But the house is already an enormously complicated manifestation of human traditions; even it were constructed by a solitary builder completely out of the sight of others it would embody in itself ways of thinking and being that have been developing through many centuries of human history. The child could not play at all unless he could at least imaginatively project the existence of others. History, play, work, science—there is no region of human activity that does not require that in each of our involvements we be involved *with others*.

This is a matter of great importance to Heidegger, for he sees that we cannot be *with* others except ontologically. A stone is not with a tree, nor the auger with the tool bench. They might be in proximity inasmuch as we see them that way, but there is nothing in the nature of these things that permits them of themselves to be with any other being. *Being-with* is then one of Dasein's ways of Being. Dasein has an Other not merely because some other Dasein happens to be present—this would be an ontic Otherness—but only because Dasein is in such a way that to-be at all means to-be-with.[7] Otherness, then, is not a contingent or accidental fact about Dasein; it is part of Dasein's existential structure. We should be careful to note here that Heidegger is definitely not indicating any kind of an identity or unity between Dasein and its Other. To *be with* is not to *be* the Other. It is also quite distinct from

Nietzsche's position that, inasmuch as willing requires an opposed will, we are always against the other.

Just as Being-in-the-world is possible only because Dasein is futural, Being-with is possible because the *present* can be a part of Dasein's existential structure. This is evident in the use of the term "presence," which is used when another is *with* us in some way. True presence does not require physical or temporal proximity in an ontic sense. Someone may be standing directly before us, but not be present in the sense that we are not with that person. On the other hand, the carpenter in the building of his house will be in the "presence" of scores of unseen builders and dwellers *with whom* he is engaged in his labors.[8]

The ontological nature of the past is introduced in a surprising way: through state-of-mind, or mood. Again, attempting to stay as close as possible to our average everyday experience, Heidegger observes two striking characteristics of our state of mind. The first is that a mood is not something we *have*, but something we *are*. We do not have a depression or a rush of joy, say, as we might have a cold or a muscle cramp; we *are* depressed, we *are* joyful. Moreover, whatever state of mind we happen to be in has a direct relation to the way we understand our world. When we are depressed, the world is depressing. Thinking inauthentically and ontically, we are likely to suppose that it is the world in this case that is depressing us. Either way the world is as we find it in our mood, and we are never without a mood. Heidegger describes moods as the way we are "attuned" to the world.[9] Mood shows us the way the world "matters" to us.[10]

The second important feature of state of mind is that we seem to have no choice in the matter. "A mood assails us," Heidegger says. "It comes neither from 'outside' nor from 'inside,' but arises out of Being-in-the-world, as a way of such Being."[11] Since we *are* our mood, this "assault" is not truly against us as an object, but is a way of Being. Heidegger's well-known term for this way of Being is "thrownness" (*Geworfenheit*).[12] The world that matters to us in our mood is not, therefore, something we just happen to have come across; it is something into which we have been thrown. We exist in it as that which is being thrown. This means that we are always encountering the world and all our involvements within it as something that is already there; we always see ourselves as that which we have been. *What* we have been, and *what* we find the world already to have been, is what Heidegger calls "facticity," a term taken over by Sartre and given a prominent place in his thought. Sartre underlines the way facticity is a phenomenon of the past by quoting Hegel's "*Wesen ist was gewesen ist*," Essence is what has been. This certainly parallels Heidegger's view that what is *already there* when we are thrown into it is that mode of time we call the past.

There is one final feature of Heidegger's manner of understanding Being within the horizon of time we must examine before we can grasp the essential place death takes in his fundamental ontology. There is a powerful temptation, arising as a consequence of thrownness, to let the past take over our way of Being. Yielding to this temptation is what Heidegger calls "falling." The term is most appropriate for just as falling is something quite easy to do, almost as though we are *doing* nothing but letting ourselves go, we can fall existentially by taking on that kind of being that we already are. Instead of being a carpenter in the sense of being ahead of himself for the sake of himself with others, the carpenter may simply choose to turn away from the futural aspects of his Being present with others and see himself as one of *those* who are called carpenters. Heidegger invents a phrase to describe this movement: "das Man." The German word *man* is similar to the indefinite "one" or "they," as in, "What are *they* wearing at the beach this summer?" or, "What does *one* say when meeting the President?" It is a characteristic of this expression that it is so indefinite as to be neither singular nor plural. The "they" or "one" could mean anyone, but in fact means no one in particular. And yet it has a distinct power. "In polite society one never eats peas with a knife," we might whisper in rebuke to a visiting relative who will likely feel the sting of embarrassment and take up a spoon at once. *Fallenness* is the state of having become a They-self. Of course, since the They-self does not truly exist, it is not an authentic existential choice for Dasein. Therefore, it is a way of Being in which Dasein has turned away from Being.

Earlier, referring to Heidegger's choice of the term "existence" (*Existenz*) for Dasein's way of Being—in which its Being is an issue for itself—we observed that it is possible for Dasein to live in the world ontically. This is what happens in falling. Dasein understands itself as *someone* living in an external world of *somethings*. Heidegger refers to this condition as inauthenticity, the German word for which, *Uneigentlichkeit*, has the sense of not being one's own (*eigen*), as though one is in the mode of not being what one actually is.

The question is *why* Dasein might choose to be an inauthentic They-self. What is the temptation in falling? It is in the answer to this question that we can see the basic unity of all three modes of Being. Since Dasein is in the world in the futural mode of Being-ahead-of-itself, we can say that *Dasein is its not-yet*. Heidegger is quite concerned we understand this point. It does not mean, for example, that Dasein has an end, a final state which it has not yet reached, as the runner reaches the finish line, or the green fruit reaches a perfect state of ripeness. Dasein *is* its not-yet, since its own way of Being is *always* to be ahead of itself. This means that there can be no mode of existence in which Dasein can eliminate its not-yet and still be at all. This is equivalent to saying that there is no way Dasein could ever be *a* being, and whenever it so comports itself that it moves toward the attainment of such an end it has turned away from its own existential not-yet. It is as though the child will not be complete until he has become an art historian, and when he has he can simply be *what* he is.

This existential inability to reach an end, to become *a* being, to be *what* we are, means that the inescapable not-yet confronts us simply as a Not: we are Not a thing; we are no-thing. We have come face to face with the ineradicable Not in those moments when we have been seized by the state of mind Heidegger calls anxiety.[13] What is tempting about falling is that it seems to promise us protection from anxiety. If we could only become *some*one we would not have to contend with this incurable existential emptiness. The *They* presents us with a variety of someones that tempt us into taking flight from our anxiety and, therefore, from our *own* authentic Being.

We can see, then, that the futural mode of Being-in-the-world evokes anxiety by exposing our not-yet, thereby tempting us to take flight into the past, for the someones who are made available to us are, of course, *already there*. To become someone is to take over that which has been; it is to live in the past. Here we can see Heidegger's basic agreement with Nietzsche inasmuch as both feel the enormous life-denying power of the past—a power that does not belong to the past but that we have freely given it. The difference between the two appears most significantly in Heidegger's "Being-with," or understanding of the present. Where Nietzsche, thinking metaphysically and therefore ontically, saw willing as a mounting struggle with Other opposed wills, Heidegger sees Dasein's uniqueness in the fact that it must always be *with* and not *against*. Just as the tranquilizing flight into the past cuts one off from the future, it cuts one off from the present as well. The They-self is never *with* an Other; it is an Other that has no Other. In the They-self Dasein has utterly lost its uniqueness; it is incapable of true *presence*.

To complete this summary of that part of Heidegger's fundamental ontology that leads to his theory of death, I would only refer back to that existential characteristic of Dasein that Heidegger called the "totality of involvements." I cited Heidegger's formula, ahead-of-itself-for-the-sake-of-itself, acknowledging its apparent circularity. We should now be able to see that when one acts existentially for the sake of oneself, it is not a form of egotism or mere self-referentiality, for there is no ego or self present in the ordinary sense. To act for the sake of oneself is to act in such a way that one will sustain the not-yet at the very center of one's self-understanding. To do this is not only always to be creatively open to the future, but also to accept the past as past and to be authentically present with Others. Heidegger's most comprehensive term for Dasein's ontological status is potentiality-for-Being, literally, being able to Be. Where Nietzsche conceived power in relation to what we are able to do with our existence, Heidegger conceives it in relation to our ability to be.

We have seen that it is an existential impossibility for Dasein to be a *what*, a being in the ontic sense. To do so would be to obliterate the not-yet without which Dasein cannot *be* at all. It is precisely here that Heidegger introduces death into his description of human existence: "As long as Dasein is, there is in every case something still outstanding, which Dasein can be and will be. But to that which is thus outstanding, the 'end' itself belongs. The 'end' of Being-in-the-world is death."[14] There is no question that when Dasein has come to an end as a being, that is to say, ontically, its not-yet vanishes along with its existence. But—and here is the essence of Heidegger's view of death— *Dasein as such does not and cannot have its own ontic end, simply because Dasein is an ontological phenomenon.* Dasein as an ontic entity comes to an end, but this has no bearing on the ontological meaning of death—that is the way Dasein *is* toward its death. Heidegger even goes so far as to say that Dasein can *decease* "without authentically dying."[15] Speaking ontologically, we can say that Dasein takes its death into itself: "Death is a way to be, which Dasein takes over as soon as it [Dasein] is."[16] What does it mean to say death is a way to be?

If to-be is to be not-yet, and if it is impossible for Dasein ever to be something, then death is the absolute guarantee that Dasein will never be *something*. Death "gives Dasein nothing to be 'actualized,' nothing which Dasein, as actual, could itself *be*."[17] Inasmuch as Dasein resolves in the face of anxiety never to be some*one* or some*thing* actual, it has taken on its own end as part of the structure of its existence by *Being towards it*: "just as Dasein *is* already its 'not-yet,' and is its 'not-yet' constantly as long as it is, it *is* already its end too. The 'ending' that we have in view when we speak of death does not signify Dasein's Being-at-an-end, but a *Being-towards-the-end* of this being."[18] If to-be, then, is to be not-yet, it is also to be dying.

We can clarify Heidegger's view if we place his thought in the context of our preceding discussion concerning the *agency* of death. In

Hegel the agency of death is not something Other *to* the Self (*Geist*), but is the Self's Otherness to itself—a self-alienation it can sustain only by dialectically joining existence to its own ending through the office of Reason. Through the continuing dialectic of Reason, however, the Self not only ceases to be the agent of death, but ceases to be an agent altogether, since every form of Otherness has been eliminated. Sartre followed Hegel in bringing the agency of death into the self (*pour-soi*) through the self's fundamentally self-limiting character, but then he robbed this agency of its power so that, although he declared the self to be mortal, it is in fact unable to die. The limits that the self establishes for its own conscious existence are certainly established freely, but the self "*never encounters them.*"[19] Nietzsche succeeds in maintaining genuine individuality (in contrast to Hegel) and truly powerful agency (in contrast to Sartre); but while willfully creative persons are radically vulnerable and spiritually prepared to affirm life in tragedy, they cannot actually die—they can only kill or be killed. Because they injure or kill others out of their own healthy spontaneity, they do not regard their own opponents or murderers as *enemies*, or even as *hostile*, just exuberant. They do not die but *suffer death*, though with equanimity.

Heidegger acknowledges Nietzsche's success in finding a powerful agency in the self, but he sets aside Nietzsche's use of power as *commanding* in favor of power as *Being-with*. Being-with the Other does not mean that the object of one's power is the existence of the Other, but instead one's own existence. Dasein's existence is *potentiality-for-Being*, but in such a way that it includes Dasein's *not-yet*; or, put differently, to be with Others is to be dying—and not killing, or being killed. Dasein then is the agent of death. It is a powerful agency because it allows Being to be, and, because Being is always Being-with, it simultaneously allows the Other to be Other as one's own Other.

In falling, that is, in its inauthentic mode, Dasein will regard death as *something* externally caused that could happen to itself as someone, or "they." ("People who smoke heavily tend to die sooner; therefore, I have stopped smoking so I won't be one of them.") But this is not true death since the They cannot die, or even live; They cannot *be* at all except in Dasein's mode of not being what it is.

The agent of death is Dasein's own not-yet. When Dasein, threatened by discontinuity so close at hand, falls into the They, it is the flight from death that perfectly characterizes *grief*. The They is neither dead nor alive, it cannot act on its own; it is speechless and mindless. In place of genuine discourse, Heidegger says, the They has only "idle talk" in which nothing is said; in place of true understanding there is only curiosity in which nothing is known.

The agent of death, however, is both threatening and promising. It always holds before us the possibility of a greater continuity. If in Heidegger's terms the *negative* guarantee of death is that Dasein will never *actually* be something—or They—its *positive* guarantee is that Dasein will always exist in the mode of possibility. Death, for Dasein, is not only one of its possibilities, it is the one possibility that assures Dasein of all its other possibilities. To be dying in the existential sense is not therefore the anticipated loss of something actual, but the antici- pated openness of possibility that no one or no thing could close to us. There is something deeply freeing in this anticipation: it "discloses to existence that its uttermost possibility lies in giving itself up, and thus it shatters all one's tenaciousness to whatever existence one has reached."[20] In anticipation we can see how death cuts off all paths to the They-self, to the lifeless past into which we are strongly tempted to fall. Therefore, by taking our own death into ourselves in this existen- tial manner, our attention is always focused forward toward possibility. Quoting Nietzsche, Heidegger says that in this way Dasein "guards itself against 'becoming too old for its victories.'"[21]

But death extends its guarantee still deeper into human existence: it provides the ground for our individuality, our uniqueness. It is because of death that my existence is truly *mine*. It is death that forever makes it impossible to speak of existence in general, ontic terms. The only exis- tence I can speak of legitimately is my own. This, of course, means that all genuine speaking must be personal—or, in Heidegger's term, exis- tential. This is another central theme in Nietzsche: each philosophical expression must be regarded as the manifestation of the will of that philosopher who is speaking. Heidegger reaches that point through a different, and more controversial, route.

"Death does not just 'belong' to one's own Dasein in an undif- ferentiated way; death *lays claim* to it as an *individual* Dasein." Death shows us that our involvement with the world, and our Being-with Others, is of no help to us when our Being-ahead-of-ourselves is an issue. Neither our involvements nor Others can rescue us from the solitary possession of our own not-yet. In simpler terms, *no one can do our own dying for us*.

This view of death has been strongly challenged by several distin- guished philosophers. Sartre, for example, in *Being and Nothingness* strongly resists the connection of death with individuality. It may be true that no one can die for us, existentially speaking, but neither can anyone love for us, or eat for us. The fact that we are individual does not then derive from our mortality but from our simple ability to act, or to do anything at all. This significantly reduces the importance

Heidegger gives to death, Sartre argues, and even eliminates its existential character. Sartre then comes to regard death not as a part of the structure of human existence, but a contingent fact that, as we observed, is strangely unable to touch that existence itself.

What Heidegger's critics have overlooked is a most unusual, though clear enough, aspect of his thinking about death—an aspect we have already seen in part. In a close reading of Heidegger's analysis we find that, contrary to the ordinary way of thinking, it *is* possible that someone else do our loving, or our eating, or our thinking, or anything at all. *Someone else does our living for us when we have fallen into the They-self.* But, is it not possible to do these things without falling into them? We are inclined to say Yes at once to this, on the grounds that it is reasonable to think that, if one is able to love inauthentically, one is ipso facto able to love authentically. However, we are closer to the truth when we say that in every act of love—insofar as it is experienced as love—we are acting *as someone*; we are doing what lovers do and experiencing their emotions. We know that this is love only insofar as *they* say it is.

Dying, on the other hand, is precisely that which the They-self cannot do. Just as the They-self cannot really live, it cannot really die. *They* are always there. *They* have no real beginning and no real ending. *They* are somehow immune to time for we always find *them* in the temporal mode of already having been there. It is not that they are immortal; they are simply nonexistent and therefore have neither Being nor time.

We are left then with a strange but provocative conclusion: *if to-be is always to be dying, all of Dasein's authentic acts are essentially acts of dying.* It may well be that on any given occasion Dasein is demonstrating behavior, even giving testimony to feelings, that the They-self would know to be love, or housemaking, or selling used cars. But if these acts are authentic, if they originate in Dasein's own not-yet, they are resolutely understood by Dasein as acts of dying—and that for two reasons: because Dasein understands them entirely in the mode of possibility, and because Dasein understands them to be a way of Being that is entirely its own. Unless what Dasein is doing is an act of dying, what it is doing is neither free nor its own act.

When one rises to the challenge of death's discontinuity, thereby overcoming grief, it is a new freedom that is acquired. Death is powerful. To overcome grief means to be free enough to contend with this power. In Heidegger, since the power of death belongs to Dasein itself as its most authentic possibility, freedom takes the form of moving always in the direction of death, or of always choosing to be toward our own end. For this reason Heidegger describes Dasein's existence as

FREEDOM TOWARD DEATH, a phrase printed in exaggerated typeface in *Being and Time*. All along we have seen that *only that which is free can die*. In Heidegger this principle is carried so far that it can be stated: *only that which can die is free*. Now it is clear how he has achieved the goal described earlier—to show the temporality of transcendence. What is transcendent to Dasein is its own Being, but in the form of its not-yet. Dasein is potentiality-for-Being, always moving toward that which it is not. Since it is always moving *toward* its end, and is never *at* its end, it is thoroughly historical. The not-yet is the very heart of temporality. Dasein in its freedom toward death is not freed from history but in history.

We began this discussion of Heidegger by noting his desire in *Being and Time* to show that the meaning of Being is time. This goal was only partially realized in that volume, which was never completed. It is certainly evident from what we have seen so far that it is impossible to speak of Being except within the horizon of temporality. Dasein's basic futurality, its not-yet, and its potentiality-for-Being, all indicate the integral association of Being and time.

The place of time is important to our study since if one is truly free in one's response to the experienced discontinuity of death, and particularly if one is free to the extent Heidegger has claimed, it should make a difference *in time*. To be free is to be able to make decisions that have an effect. It is only out of freedom that history arises. Now we have seen that Dasein is historical through and through. By virtue of Heidegger's interpretation of Being as Being-with, everything Dasein does is not only done freely, but is affected by and affects Others. Heidegger's *tour de force* is to show that *because of death* Dasein is not only free but also completely unique *and* bound with Others.

It is significant, however, that the part of *Being and Time* that remained unwritten is the major division of the book dealing with time. In the long course of Heidegger's career (when all his writings have been published they will total more than 60 volumes) one can easily see that his early interest in time steadily diminished in favor of the question of Being, and, in fact, in the latter period of his writing, both time and death seem to have been forgotten. Throughout his work Heidegger has been concerned with the problem of transcendence—or Otherness—and in *Being and Time* he discusses both Being and time in these terms. As we move on through his work, however, we notice that Being is transcendent even to time. That is, it is Being that precedes time and not time Being. Where Hegel exalted Reason, Sartre freedom, and Nietzsche power, Heidegger gives the highest place to Being.

It is true that Being is always Being-with in his early work, but even there we can see that it is Being that precedes Otherness. The Others with whom Dasein is cannot be truly transcendent, for there can *be* Others only insofar as Dasein itself *is* in the mode of *Being-with*. In other words, Being is always prior to this kind of Otherness. Being is that which is truly transcendent. Of course, it is not transcendent to Dasein in the sense of Being separate, forever inaccessible like Kant's thing-in-itself. Being is transcendent to Dasein even as Dasein *is*. In *Being and Time* this transcendence is expressed chiefly through the temporal modes in which Dasein exists, principally the futural mode in which Dasein is always ahead of itself. If Being were not temporal Dasein would simply be identical to Being and would exist as an eternal presence, incapable even of experience, much less death. In *Being and Time* the discussion turns so exclusively on Dasein that the nature of Being as such is left unexplored—in spite of its acknowledged priority. Heidegger came to see that he had not fully plumbed the mystery of this priority. When he looked beyond Dasein toward Being itself, he realized that the original question—Why is there something rather than nothing?—had not been answered, only deepened. If Being is truly prior to Dasein, and to all else, why should it offer itself in it modes of temporality to Dasein? Why should it bother to enter history at all?

Heidegger finds no simple answer to this question, but he recognizes its importance to understanding the nature of human existence, and he spends the rest of his long and extremely productive career clarifying it and attempting to find a way one can live in full view of this mystery. We cannot follow the often serpentine and obscure lines of thought that Heidegger writes in the forty odd years following *Being and Time*, but we can suggest the general flow of his thinking.

In brief, what remained constantly before Heidegger's attention through these years was the wondrous fact that, in spite of its absolute priority, Being had nonetheless entered into time in and through human existence. Much of his writing is an attempt to recover this sense of wonder in the origins of Western thought. He finds that this is the prevailing insight behind the Greek's use of the term *physis*. When Latin thinkers translated the word into *natura*, giving the sense of something born, they distorted and lost the Greek's vision of *physis* as that which is eternally prior to all of its manifestations. Since *physis* never gives up its priority, each disclosure of itself, in what we consider the ordinary events of the world, bears the certain signs of that priority. That is to say, each time it opens itself to a new appearance it announces through that appearance that it remains concealed. There is always some reminder of the "ontological difference" between Being and beings in each natural or historical event.

One of the ways in which Heidegger addresses the diference between Being and beings is by way of the relation of "earth" to "world." The world is always erected on the earth; in fact, we must make use of the earth in assembling the beings of the world. The Greeks built their temples of stone; Beethoven wrote his quartets on paper. Although the earth is necessary for the world to be able to exist, the earth is not visible in the world. When we look at the temple we do not see the stone, but something of the way the Greeks lived with each other in their world. Even if we do look at the stone we see it not as mere earth but as that which was used in a world. There is no way we can look through our world at the earth that makes it possible; the earth is always hiden in it. And yet, the earth's presence does disclose itself in what Heidegger describes as a struggle between earth and world. The earth is forever reaching out to reclaim the world that was built on it, even against it. The earthiness of worldly things can never be utterly denied. However much we might consider them timeless or immortal, "Beethoven's quartets lie in the storerooms of the publishing houses like potatoes in a cellar."[22] They will turn to earthly dust just as the Greek temple will eventually crumble. "World" is obviously a temporal category here. It is not even a place; it is the way persons are with each other.

Heidegger does not make a direct association of earth with Being in this discussion, but instead suggests that Being is the struggle between the two. Being allows the world to rise on the earth and to struggle with it. It is not as though we are worldlings thrusting structures of our own making against the indifferent stuff of the universe. We do not exist first and have a world second. We do not "discover" the world of the Greeks in their temple; we see that accumulation of stone as a temple only because we are already in a world. We do not make our world, but only dwell in it. Where does the world come from? "The world worlds" (die Welt weltet)[23] is Heidegger's answer—his way of underlining the priority of Being. We do nothing to Being, for we already are in all that we do.

The priority of Being, then, means that it is not something which belongs to us, but that to which we belong. In some of his most recent writings Heidegger has alluded to this relationship between Dasein and Being in an analysis of the danger and the promise of modern technology. He insists that the real "danger consists in the threat that assaults man's nature in his relation to Being itself, and not in accidental perils."[24] The danger exists in our failure to see that what Being has provided us is inexhaustible possibility, and not some ideal state in which all human crises have been eliminated, in which death itself may be conquered. Taking his cue from the Greek word *techne*, which, by his analysis, means "letting something appear,"[25] Heidegger argues that what is truly valuable in technology is the way it has revealed the energy of what is "locked" into nature, and thus concealed in it. What happens in technology is that "the energy concealed in nature is unlocked, what is unlocked is transformed, what is transformed is stored up, what is stored up is, in turn, distributed, and what is distributed is switched about ever anew."[26] The priority of Being shows itself in technology by way of the fact that this energy does not belong to us, but we belong to it. It is already there, preceding us; it is always already there, never to be exhausted. We do not even control it; we only reveal its inexhaustibility. But even the revealing is something we do not originate, for we can reveal only that which has already disclosed itself *to us*. It is Being that has initiated this "unconcealment" of itself. In misunderstanding this priority we exalt ourselves "to the posture of the lord of the earth."[27] However, this is a posture in which we can never succeed: "Technology, whose essence is Being itself, will never allow itself to be overcome by men. That would mean, after all, that man was the master of Being."[28]

We see in this later writing of Heidegger's a subtle shift in his thinking about death. We described his earlier view in the phrase: to-be is to be dying. Dasein took death over as its way of Being, and, unless it was dying, it was incapable of existing. Now the focus has moved in the direction of Being. It is now not so much that Dasein needs death to exist, but Being needs Dasein's death to be at all. Dasein's death is a kind of seal, a guarantee of the priority of Being. Dasein must be thrown from the posture of lord of the earth; it is death that will do this in every case. Thinking in this way about death, Heidegger reaches out for such metaphoric descriptions as "the shrine of the Not" (*der Schrein des Nichts*) and the "mountain fastness of Being,"[29] by which he indicates that death is that very phenomenon that will drive Dasein out of its actuality in the interest of showing that Being comes before all beings.

Still, we must not think that Heidegger is demanding that we be broken on the rack of time *simply to give way to Being*. Even as death descends on us from its mountain "fastness," we nonetheless *are*. Our task as mortals is not directly to fall before the attack, but instead to take full stock of the fact that Being does "unconceal" itself in the form of

our own existence. Being has "ventured us," "flung us loose" as beings; and we are what is thus ventured, but also the venturing.[30] In
taking full stock we find the possibility of willing to "go with" the
venture,[31] in a way that plants and animals cannot, for they cannot die,
only "perish."[32] A great deal of Heidegger's later thought centers on the
way in which we may thus "let Being be" through our own existence,
describing this as a kind of sublime serenity (*Gelassenheit* from the
verb *lassen*, to let, or allow).

This increasing attention on the priority of Being over (Dasein's)
existence in Heidegger's later writing has its most provocative and
suggestive moments in his discussion of language. He sees that, just as
the priority of Being shows itself through natural energy by already
being there as an inexhaustible reserve, so does language precede our
speaking it. Heidegger says he prefers "saying" to "language," if only
because saying (like *techne*) has the sense of letting something appear,
or even shine.[33] This implies that there is something there, something
inexhaustible waiting to be said, preceding our saying it. For this reason language cannot be thought of as a tool we have; we are not animals
with the faculty of speech (as we have been described by the
metaphysicians).[34] Just as we do not possess Being but are possessed by
it, we are possessed by language: "Man acts as though *he* were the
shaper and master of language, while in fact *language* remains the
master of man."[35] We do not speak a language, but language speaks
through us.[36] To capture this characteristic of language Heidegger invents the most prominent metaphor of his later work: "Language is the
house of Being."[37] He is carried to this metaphor by the belief that
"Only where the word for the thing has been found is the thing a thing.
Only thus *is* it."[38] Elsewhere he argues that it is only because we can
dwell in language as the house of Being that we can reach whatever is
in this house: "When we go to the well, when we go through the
woods, we are already going through the word 'well,' through the word
'woods,' even if we do not speak the words and do not think of anything relating to language."[39]

When we overlook the priority of language, when we begin to think
we can master it as we would a tool, we fall into the same danger that
we noted with technology wrongly understood. Indeed, it is our failure
to understand language that has led to the death- and life-denying
tendency of technology. Who will pull us back from this danger? Only
the poets can save us, Heidegger exclaims. "Poetry," he tells us, comes
from the Greek word "poiesis," which means "making" or "creating."
It is poetry, the making of words out of soundlessness, that builds the
house of Being.[40] The true poet lets that soundlessness show through

the words, just as the earth shows through the Greek temple. We see in true poetry that words do not stand for things that already exist, but that things come into existence with the words. The poet then does not simply speak words that are already there, but speaks with words that "shine" and with the inexhaustibility of that which could be said. Heidegger therefore calls for poets who can "say more sayingly," who can in their language go with the "venturing" of beings by Being.[41]

The priority of Being shows through this discussion of language most distinctly in the fact that for Heidegger *listening* is prior to *speaking*. The poets can "say more sayingly" because they have opened themselves to the unspoken from which the spoken comes.[42] It is the poets *speaking* that always reflects the fact that language is prior to the world. To do this the poets must "listen" to the way in which language itself is granted, and in this way they make speech possible. When language has shown them its essential being, "the being of language becomes the language of Being."[43] Therefore, all that the poets have to say is what Being says—they have no words of their own.

There is a strange fading of the power of death once Heidegger has taken his thought into the "house of Being." Because Dasein can only *dwell* in the house of Being, and because language is already there with its inexhaustible ability to speak through Dasein, death no longer seems central to Heidegger's thought. We can see how death destroys the presumption that we can master the unlimited powers of nature, but it is difficult to see how death is required for the transformation of the *being of language* into the *language of Being*. In fact, Heidegger offers no rigorous examination of the place of death in the house of Being; and his references to death decrease sharply when we enter this discussion. We might assume, however, that he has not abandoned his earlier position, for he clearly insists that we dwell in this house as *mortals*.[44] What is more likely the case is that he has not—at least in his published essays—found a philosophically adequate way to integrate language and death. Indeed, in one late essay he says: "The essential relation between death and language flashes up before us, but remains still unthought."[45]

I would suggest that Heidegger's final insight into the nature of death—its essential relation to language—is difficult to integrate into the rest of his thought because it threatens utterly to undo the whole extraordinary edifice of his "philosophy of Being." Heidegger emphasized the priority of the listening *of* a speaker; he conspicuously ignored the matter of listening *to* a speaker. This has the effect of placing the meaning of the utterance prior to the utterance itself. It is this very priority that makes possible the priority of Being. It is also this priority that vacates the force of history. If the listening *of* a speaker comes first, then what can be spoken truly is only that which *already is*. Nothing can come of it that has any historical importance. When poets say more "sayingly" they do serve to "unconceal" Being in history, but not toward the end of making history *more* consequent, but *less*. What is most important is not that history points toward itself, but away from itself. History, which occurs when speakers listen to one another, is replaced by speakers listening to Being. To use the earlier terminology, Heidegger has come to see death ontologically rather than existentially; that is, as part of the structure of Being rather than as Dasein. It is not Dasein that achieves the higher continuity through contending with death, but Being. What Heidegger earlier described as Dasein's potentiality-for-Being is now understood as the power of Being.

I would suggest in conclusion that what drew Heidegger's philosophical attention from history to Being was his misunderstanding of the nature of language. It seemed absolutely clear to Heidegger that discourse is significant only when there is something to *say*, something that is there before the speaking. This is why language is the "house of Being." It might have been otherwise. He might have understood Being as the "house of language." Instead of saying we cannot go to the well before there is the word "well," he could have said we cannot be until we "are." Instead of insisting that we could not truly speak to the Other except as we listen to Being, he might have argued that we could not speak of Being except as we listen to the Other.

We shall conclude this study by examining two thinkers for whom death frees us for history when we understand it as "death."

Notes

1. *An Introduction to Metaphysics*, p. 1.
2. See Ch. One, Ibid.
3. *Being and Time*, p. 29.
4. Ibid., p. 38.
5. See especially ibid., p. 119.
6. Ibid., p. 153.
7. Ibid., p. 162.
8. Ibid., p. 156.
9. Ibid., p. 172.
10. Ibid., p. 176.
11. Ibid., p. 176.
12. Ibid., p. 174.

13. Ibid., pp. 232 ff.
14. Ibid., pp. 276 ff.
15. Ibid., p. 291.
16. Ibid., p. 289.
17. Ibid., p. 307.
18. Ibid., p. 289.
19. *Being and Nothingness*, p. 531.
20. *Being and Time*, p. 308.
21. Ibid., p. 308.
22. "The Origin of the Work of Art," *Poetry, Language, and Truth*, p. 19.
23. Ibid., p. 44.
24. "What are Poets for?", ibid., p. 117.
25. "Building Dwelling Thinking," ibid., p. 159.
26. "The Question concerning Technology," *The Question concerning Technology*, p. 16.
27. Ibid., p. 27.
28. "The Turning," ibid., p. 38.
29. "Building, Dwelling Thinking," p. 159.
30. "What are Poets for?" p. 101.
31. Ibid., p. 110.
32. "The Thing," *Poetry, Language, and Truth*, pp. 78 ff.
33. "A Dialogue on Language," *On the Way to Language*, p. 47.
34. "Language," *Poetry, Language, and Truth*, p. 189.
35. "Building Dwelling Thinking," p. 146.
36. "Language," p. 210.
37. "The Nature of Language," *On the Way to Language*, p. 63.
38. Ibid., p. 62.
39. "What are Poets for?" p. 132.
40. ". . . Poetically Man Dwells . . ." *Poetry, Language, and Truth*, pp. 214 ff.
41. "What are Poets for?" p. 141.
42. See "The Way to Language," *On the Way to Language*, p. 120.
43. "The Nature of Language," p. 72.
44. See "The Way to Language," p. 134.
45. "The Nature of Language," p. 107.

Bibliography

Martin Heidegger, *Being and Time*, tr. John Macquarrie and Edward Robinson (New York: 1962).

———— *Discourse on Thinking*, tr. John M. Anderson and E. Hans Freund (New York: 1966).

——— *Hegel's Concept of Experience,* (New York: 1970).

——— *Identity and Difference,* tr. Joan Stambaugh (New York: 1969).

——— *On the Way to Language,* tr. Peter D. Hertz (New York: 1971).

——— *Poetry, Language, Thought,* tr. Albert Hofstadter (New York: 1971).

——— *The Question Concerning Technology,* tr. William Lovitt (New York: 1977).

——— *What is Called Thinking?* tr. Fred D. Wieck and J. Glenn Gray (New York: 1968).

TEN
DEATH AS HORIZON
—DISCOURSE

16 SÖREN KIERKEGAARD

In his analysis of human existence, or what he preferred to call *Dasein,* Heidegger met the challenge of integrating death into existence by showing that transcendence is temporal, that we integrate the discontinuity of death by way of history—and not by way of rising above history. But, then, curiously, the momentum of his thought slowly, but definitely, caused him to back away from this achievement. As he increasingly turned his attention away from Dasein toward Being, he began to affirm the priority of Being over time. According to our judgment what led Heidegger to this shift was his understanding of the nature of language. More and more he came to see the importance of language to his analysis of Being, using the metaphor "house of Being" for language. Heidegger's crucial move was to give much more weight to the *saying* than to the *listening* of language. The speaker can say more "sayingly" only by first listening to language itself. What is spoken therefore is what is *already there.* The language precedes the speaker; the speaker is in the service of language.

This understanding of language allowed Heidegger to withdraw Being from history, to disengage transcendence from temporality. Death is still possible for Dasein, but the continuity Dasein established in the face of death, which Heidegger referred to as *freedom toward death,* now seems to have been lost. Death is now understood as Being's way of establishing its priority over Dasein.

What we find in Kierkegaard (1813–1855) is just the opposite view of language. What one listens to is not the language, but the speaker. What the speaker says is not what is there to be said, but what is heard.

Being is not prior to language. Being is not *something already there*, but *something said*. As we shall see, this understanding of language gives sure footing for Heidegger's earlier achievement of showing the temporality of transcendence.

Heidegger would have been surprised by the suggestion that Kierkegaard goes beyond him in this respect. *Being and Time* appeared shortly after the influence of Kierkegaard was first felt in Europe. He certainly was a major figure in the academic firmament under which Heidegger's own thinking developed. There are several references to Kierkegaard in *Being and Time*, all footnotes. In these Heidegger praises him for working out the question of Being in his own personal existence and for having written the most penetrating study of anxiety to date (*The Concept of Dread*), but faults him for having no genuine ontology and for ascribing to the ordinary understanding of time. These references are remarkable for, as any student of both thinkers can readily see, large conceptual areas of Heidegger's thought read as though he had been directly instructed by the nineteenth-century Dane.

In his *Concluding Unscientific Postscript*, Kierkegaard's pseudonymous author, Johannes Climacus, inquires into the difference between the "actual presence" of death "and the thought of it." The difference is important simply because of the uncertainty of its arrival: "suppose death were so treacherous as to come tomorrow!" This uncertainty means that one must be prepared: "It thus becomes more and more important for me to think it in connection with every factor and phase of my life; for since the uncertainty is there in every moment, it can be overcome only by overcoming it in every moment." But how *does* one think about death, if thinking about it is different from its arrival? There is something peculiar here for if "the actual being of death is a non-being, I should have to ask whether it follows as a consequence that death is only when it is not . . . ." It seems quite puzzling to have to think about something that only is when it is not, and yet if I cannot think about it, then "that which really comes is not that for which I prepared myself . . . ." After several pages of such reflection Climacus concludes: "When death thus becomes something to be related to the entire life of the subject, I must confess I am very far indeed from having understood it, even if it were to cost me my life to make this confession. *Still less have I realized the task existentially.* And yet I have thought about this subject again and again; I have sought for guidance in books—and I have found none!"[1]

Our *first* question in response to this passage has to do with what

Climacus could mean by the remark that he has not achieved the task of understanding death *existentially*. Insofar as Climacus has *not* succeeded in understanding death, Heidegger's criticism of Kierkegaard stands, for it is only in an understanding of death that one's ontology can properly be developed. But there is a *second* question that arises here—a question that completely changes the force of the first, and a question Heidegger apparently never asked of Kierkegaard: *who is Climacus?* Is Climacus Kierkegaard? Scarcely. His *Training in Christianity* is written by Anti-Climacus, an author with a manifestly different attitude toward religion. And other pseudonyms appear regularly throughout his writings, names such as Victor Eremita, Johannes de Silentio, Constantine Constantius, Frater Taciturnus, and Hilarius Bookbinder, each of them with a different personality, a different question to pursue, a different way of looking at the same issue. Indeed, in Climacus' *Postscript* there is a lengthy appendix inserted into the middle of the volume entitled "A Glance at a Contemporary Effort in Danish Literature," in which he reviews the work of each of the pseudonymous authors, clearly contrasting them. To compound the confusion a large number of writings appear under his own name. Kierkegaard's use of these imaginary personalities is often mixed with humor and irony, but it would be a mistake to think that his design is itself whimsical. In fact, the most important task in understanding Kierkegaard is to understand the role of the pseudonyms in his authorship as a whole.

It is evident they are not *noms de plume*, intended to give the author a screen behind which he can conceal his identity. Some of the names are so outrageous, and some of the literary tricks associated with their use so manifestly playful, that one immediately suspects pseudonyms at work. Moreover, *Concluding Unscientific Postscript* ends with "A First and Last Declaration" in which all the pseudonymous works are listed with their fictional authors, and in which Kierkegaard announces that he "has poetically produced the *authors*," along with their invented points of view. He also declares that, as with all "poetic production" taken as a whole, the meaning of these works "would be rendered impossible and unendurable if the lines must be the very words of the producer, taken literally." He then begs the reader "to cite the name of the respective pseudonymous author" when quoting from any of his writings.

What, then, is the reason for what he calls his "polynymity"? In 1859, four years after Kierkegaard's death at the age of 42, there appeared a small volume, written under his own name, intended for posthumous publication, the complete title of which is *The Point of View for my Work as an Author: A Report to History*. He had written this a decade earlier after the most important of his writings had been completed, having apparently become doubtful that his readers would come to understand the strategy of his pseudonyms and, therefore, of his "authorship" as a whole. Quite directly and plainly he declares that the contents of this little book affirm "what I truly am as an author, that I am and was a religious author, that the whole of my work as an author is related to Christianity, to the problem 'of becoming a Christian,' with a direct or indirect polemic against the monstrous illusion we call Christendom, or against the illusion in such a land as ours all are Christians of a sort."[2]

The *problem* in becoming a Christian, to put it in its most abbreviated form, arises from the confused identification of Christianity with Christendom. By Christendom Kierkegaard means all the cultural and historical institutions that have come to be understood as Christian. This not only includes the Church, and the Danish nation, but much of the Church's teaching as well. His polemical sword is unsparing. When he finished cutting away all that he considered either false or inessential, the "monstrous illusion" of Christendom had not been trimmed to its minimal skeleton; its very bone had been reduced to splinters. Not even the Bible was spared. Kierkegaard's purifying zeal is well evidenced in a remark Climacus makes: If the generation contemporary to Jesus had "left nothing behind them but these words: 'We have believed that in such and such a year God appeared among us in the humble figure of a servant, that he lived and taught in our community, and finally died,' it would be more than enough."[3]

The problem of becoming a Christian is then the difficulty of erecting an entire life of faith on nothing more than a vague and uncertain historical event. The problem is made all the worse by the fact that, since essentially everyone is under the illusion that Christianity is identical to Christendom, they are quite unable to see the adequacy of this event of which practically nothing need be, or even can be, known. It is obvious then that the first task is to relieve oneself of the "monstrous illusion." But this is no simple matter, for it is of the nature of illusions that they are taken to be truth. To know that one is living in an illusion is *ipso facto* to cease living in it. No one, therefore, can be directly instructed to set aside their illusions: "A direct attack only strengthens a person in his illusion, and at the same time embitters him."[4]

Kierkegaard then describes his strategy as a "religious author" as necessarily *indirect*:

> If it is an illusion that all are Christians—and if there is anything to be done about it, it must be done indirectly, not by one who

vociferously proclaims himself an extraordinary Christian, but by one who, better instructed, is ready to declare that he is not a Christian at all. That is, one must approach from behind the person who is under an illusion. Instead of wishing to have the advantage of being oneself that rare thing, a Christian, one must let the prospective captive enjoy the advantage of being the Christian, and for one's own part have resignation enough to be the one who is far behind him—otherwise one will certainly not get the man out of his illusion, a thing which is difficult enough in any case.

The religious writer must first "get in touch" with these persons precisely where they are. And where are they? "They live in aesthetic, or, at the most, in aesthetic-ethical categories."[5]

The terms "ethical" and "aesthetic" introduce us to Kierkegaard's distinctive conception of the "stages" persons must pass through from their present imaginary status to one that is genuinely religious. Most frequently he describes four stages: the aesthetic, the ethical, and two stages of religiousness that he designates simply as "A" and "B." A closer reading, however, will reveal that there are considerably more stages than this, perhaps as many as nine. We can leave this problem to the Kierkegaard scholar. What is important for our purposes is to note, first, that the successive stages represent an *ascent* from the aesthetic to the religious. It is certainly not altogether whimsical that Kierkegaard's major author is named *Climacus*, from the Greek word for ladder (*Klimax*). Second, we must remember that each stage is described not by Kierkegaard, but by one of his invented authors who usually is representative of the stage he speaks of. In other words, *the entire conception of the stages is nothing but an invention of Kierkegaard's indirect method of communicating with his readers.* It is not his intention to offer a comprehensive metaphysical account of the process of human development as one finds, for example, in the psychology of Erik Erikson. Scholars of Kierkegaard's work have given considerable attention to the proper characterization of the stages, asking whether they are merely autobiographical, or whether they are levels of consciousness similar to Hegel's famous discussion in the *Phenomenology*, or whether they somehow indicate stages in world history, and so forth. But this approach to Kierkegaard is simply caught in the snare of his irony; it misses the genuine comedy with which he saturated his writing. He would not only have been amused by such a "direct" reading of his literature; he would also have been somewhat pleased, for in such a misreading there is always the possibility that the reader will get the joke—that we will understand *why* he had to be so indirect, ironic, pseudonymous, in short, comical, with us. We will discover that he wanted to "get in touch" with us, and in a way that is surprisingly freeing *for us*.

We must take care to note, of course, that when he said the *problem* addressed in his authorship was "becoming a Christian" he was not speaking pseudonymously, but as himself. He is "directly" serious about that. *However*, what it means to *be* a Christian is by no means clear from what we have so far seen of his stated intention. All we can say at the outset is that to be a Christian has to do with "getting the joke" of his indirect method; it has to do with *the way we listen* to what he is saying and not at all to do with *what he is saying*. The most adequate way of understanding how Christianity is a way of listening is briefly to listen to his "comical" construction of the stages. There is insufficient space here to reconstruct each of the stages in anything resembling their complete detail, but with an eye backward as well as forward we shall quickly characterize each of them in terms of their distinctive orientation to time—and therefore to death. It will be immediately apparent that Heidegger was simply wrong in assuming that Kierkegaard had settled for a traditional view of time; and it will become clearer that the temporality Heidegger gave up to Being is quite powerfully felt in Kierkegaard's work.

What Kierkegaard's personae, and Kierkegaard himself, refer to repeatedly as the aesthetic stage is, in fact, two distinct stages; we could characterize them with the words "immediate" and "reflective." The basic design of both aesthetic categories is to achieve a maximum of enjoyment. *Immediate* enjoyment is that state where the desired object of pleasure has no distance whatsoever from the subject; there is not the slightest film of consciousness between the person and the source of pleasure, even though that source is external to the person. Kierkegaard's favored example is physical beauty, which the immediate aesthetic considers the highest good. "Now beauty is a very fragile good, and therefore, one seldom sees this view carried through. One encounters often enough a young girl (or maybe a young man) who for a brief time prides herself upon her beauty, but soon it deceives her."[6] This is said in the person of a civil magistrate, Judge William (whose last name we never learn), Kierkegaard's premier spokesman for the ethical stage. The judge's description of the aesthetic stage has, in this case, his implicit critique of it, namely, that the beauty will be lost. Each of us is living toward that moment in which all beauty fades, in which we are subject to the physical laws that are quite indifferent to all the sources of immediate pleasure. This description is written by the judge, and not the young beauty, simply because that person who is still taking delight in his or her own beauty does not have the conscious distance from it to see it as the judge, now in his later years, sees it.

It is possible, perhaps inevitable, that the young beauty will be carried into such reflection. When this happens a new phase of the aesthetic opens. It is far subtler than immediate enjoyment; in fact, it can embrace the most extravagant of long-range intentions. The *reflective* aesthetic, knowing the fragility of beauty, knowing moreover the fleeting quality of all immediate pleasure, has forestalled the immediate possession of the desired object and takes pleasure instead in *approaching* that moment. Kierkegaard's classic representation of the person in the reflective aesthetic stage is found in the anonymous "Diary of a Seducer," discovered accidentally by another anonymous author, whose own papers were also discovered accidentally by Victor Eremita, the first of Kierkegaard's pseudonyms.

The seducer, known to his diary only as Johannes, is carried by chance into the presence of a girl still innocent of a serious love affair. He resolves at once to lay the elaborate plans of a conquest. It is evident throughout that Johannes' pleasure is all in anticipation. "The moment is everything," he writes to himself, but does not for that reason seize it at once, for then it should lose all its interest. This requires a constant distance from the girl, a space sufficient to allow his manipulation of the affair, but also to savor the progress he is making by remaining an observer to it. He shapes her passion as though it were a work of art by carefully calculated moves such as entering into an engagement with her, then breaking it at the right moment, and making it again. "How interesting she is in this deep passionateness," he writes celebrating his success. "Everything is in movement, but in thess elemental storms I find myself precisely in my element."[7] On the eve of the seduction Johannes ecstatically thanks Nature who made the rare gift of her beauty and the human beings who kept her unsophisticated. "Her development was my handiwork—soon I shall enjoy my reward.—How much I have gathered into this one moment which now draws nigh. Damnation—if I should fail!" But he does not fail. The next day he enters into his diary the pained question, "Why cannot such a night be longer?" But an experienced aesthetic like Johannes knows that the moment cannot be sustained. "Still, it is over now, and I hope never to see her again."[8]

The temporal character of the two aesthetic stages is already evident in their respective orientation to the "moment." The "immediate" aesthetic is essentially *oblivious to the moment.* We cannot say that such a person lives *in* the moment, for the moment as such has not emerged; the immediate stage of the aesthetic is pretemporal. When reflection takes hold of the aesthetic, however, there is a poignant, almost desperate, sense of the effervescence of the moment; it is therefore suspended in the future. The "reflective" aesthetic lives *toward the moment.* The highest art of the aesthetic is not however to reach the moment; it is to move toward it as long as possible without reaching it. Although the aesthetic would scarcely admit it, the moment has already shown itself to be utterly empty, without meaning in itself. It is interesting only so far as it is being approached.

The death appropriate to the aesthetic stages has perhaps already been suggested. Whether immediate or reflective, in the aesthetic stage one is fundamentally *unable to die.* In a brief but vivid essay, "The Unhappiest Man," Victor Eremita evokes the fact that somewhere in England there is an empty grave marked by a tombstone that has only the inscription "The Unhappiest Man," and no name. Victor wonders why the grave is empty, and why even one would have bothered to look into it. He decides that what distinguishes the unhappiest person is not some sort of suffering that leads inevitably to death, but a kind of suffering that comes precisely from the fact that one cannot die. The unhappiest person cannot die for the very reason that that person has suspended time and exists outside all its dimensions: "In one sense of the word he cannot die, for he has not really lived; in another sense he cannot live, for he is already dead. He cannot love, for love is in the present, and he has no present, no future, and no past. . . . He has no time for anything, not because his time is taken up with something else, but because he has no time at all. He is impotent, not because he has no energy, but because his own energy makes him impotent."[9]

If one "has no time at all," one must be utterly without hope. If there is no genuine future, there is nothing to hope *for.* The term for this condition is "despair," which in Latin means "without hope." Kierkegaard's pseudonymous writings give a prominent place to expressions of despair, and in *The Sickness unto Death,* a work "written" by Anti-Climacus (who in constrast to the unbelieving Climacus *is* a Christian) and "edited by S. Kierkegaard," there is a famous analysis of despair. There we learn that the aesthetic person is in despair and that the form of that despair is "willing *not* to be oneself." This is a "sickness unto death" different from ordinary mortal diseases that end in death, for this is a sickness that seeks an end to itself in death, which it *cannot* achieve. The Christian knows, Anti-Climacus declares, that this particular sickness is far more horrible than death itself.[10] Despair is precisely what we have hitherto considered *grief.* It is an attempt to live in such a way that one is not truly living; it is an attempt to achieve a state of living death.

It is not only christians who understand despair in this way. Judge William, the archetypal ethicist, directly avers "that every aesthetic view of life is in despair, and that everyone who lives aesthetically is in despair, whether he knows it or not."[11] He would have quite enthusiastically endorsed the remark of Anti-Climacus that even the youth existing unconsciously in his beauty is in despair; indeed, "the dearest and most attractive dwelling-place of despair is in the very heart of immediate happiness."[12] As the judge offers his own view of the reason the aesthetic life inevitably leads to despair, the contours of the ethical stage come into sight. He exclaims emphatically that anyone *who says he wants to enjoy life always posits a condition which either lies outside the individual or is in the individual in such a way that it is not posited by the individual himself.*"[13] The difficulty here is that one therefore has no control over one's own life, but is dependent on accidental circumstances to provide the sought for enjoyment. Even if the external conditions are favorable, however, the situation is not improved, because what enjoyment the aesthetic person has found still comes by way of chance and not by way of that person's decision. What the aesthetic person has done by suspending the moment is to have suspended all decision. If the essence of the ethical is the *either/or,* seizing on either this option or another, the essence of the aesthetic is *neither/nor,* avoiding choice altogether.

The decision itself is what the judge places at the very center of life; in fact, he seems to equate decision *with* life: "I should like to say that in making a choice it is not so much a question of choosing the right as of the energy, the earnestness, the pathos with which one chooses."[14] At the same time, it makes little sense to speak of a *decision* or *choice* if there is nothing that is chosen. The judge is quite aware of this: "But what is it I choose? Is it this thing or that? No, for I choose absolutely, and the absoluteness of my choice is expressed precisely by the fact that I have not chosen to choose this or that. I choose the absolute. And what is the absolute? It is myself in my eternal validity." With the introduction of the term *eternal* we might suspect that what the judge has in view here is a kind of immortal soul that exists independently of our decision—whether we choose it or not. This, of course, could not be the case, for then we fall back into the aesthetic. It would be a way of depending on something we did not ourselves decide to have or be. The Judge continues: "But what, then, is this self of mine? If I were required to define this, my first answer would be: It is the most abstract of all things, and yet at the same time it is the most concrete—it is freedom."[15]

To choose myself in my eternal validity, in other words, is to choose my own freedom, the fact that I am responsible for all that I am. The judge is careful to say that "I do not create myself, I choose myself."[16] In choosing oneself "the individual thus becomes conscious of himself as this definite individual, with these talents, these dispositions, these instincts, these passions, influenced by these definite surroundings, as this definite product of a definite environment. But being conscious of himself in this way, he assumes responsibility for all this."[17] (The reader will recognize in this remark the character of existing which Heidegger calls "facticity" and Sartre "essence.")

Speaking temporally, Judge William has moved the moment of which the "immediate" person is oblivious, and the "reflective" person anticipatory, into the lived present. The ethical person lives *in the moment*. By way of the either/or the future is brought into the present as one's own, and by way of responsibly claiming one's own "facticity" the past is claimed as well. Past, present, and future are simultaneous in the moment. It is for this reason that the judge speaks of the self's "eternal validity."

The judge claims superiority of the ethical over the aesthetic not for the reason the aesthetic person expects; it is not because he prefers his eternal validity to aesthetic enjoyment, but because, the Judge insists, it is only in the ethical that such enjoyment can be found, and—what is more important—sustained. The ethical person is therefore saved from the despair that befalls the person in the aesthetic stage. What then does this say of death? Is the ethical person capable of dying where the aesthetic is not? Is the ethical stage free from the sickness unto death? Anti-Climacus' answer is No. There is a kind of despair from which the ethical cannot escape: if the aesthetic despaired at willing *not* to be oneself, the ethical despairs at willing *to be* oneself. We can clarify this point only by looking deeper into the argument of Anti-Climacus in *The Sickness unto Death*.

In what is likely the most difficult passage in all of Kierkegaard's literature, Anti-Climacus attempts his definition of the self—a definition far more subtle than Judge William's. Fortunately, it is not necessary for us to explicate this passage here (a most careful and clear interpretation of Anti-Climacus' definition of the self can be found in Mark Taylor's *Kierkegaard's Pseudonymous Authorship*, pp. 87 ff.), but we must restate it in terms that will place it in the context of our earlier discussion, particularly that concerning Heidegger's view of death and the self. For Anti-Climacus the decisive factor in the constitution of the self is the relation between what is actual in the self and what is possible. Anti-Climacus uses a perplexing phrase to describe this: "the self is not the relation but consists in the fact that the relation relates itself to its own self." A relation is not a passive condition created by the mere fact of its two terms; it is an active, spontaneous act that holds the terms in relation. The chair is related to the table inasmuch as it stands near it. But in this case it is not the relation that does the relating; it is some third term such as an observer. In the self it is the relation that does the relating. This means that the self is neither what is actual in it, nor what is possible in it, nor the fact that it stands between the actual and the possible; *the self is that which actively relates the actual to the possible without becoming either.*

Judge William, we recall, stressed the fact that the self chooses itself, but it does not create itself. Anti-Climacus agrees. Although the self is the source of its own activity in sustaining the relatedness of actual and possible, *it is not its own source:* "Such a relation which relates itself to its own self (that is to say, a self) must either have constituted itself or have been constituted by another." Anti-Climacus, who is an explicit Christian, utterly dismisses the possibility that the self constitutes itself, but says instead that in its relation to itself it is simultaneously related to that which constitutes it.[18]

We had noted previously that the kind of despair into which the ethical person falls is what Anti-Climacus describes as "willing to be oneself." In light of the latter remarks we can now see how this could take a variety of forms. In "choosing oneself absolutely," to use the Judge's brief description of the ethical, one might choose to be what one actually is (as "this definite product of a definite environment"), which, of course, is to choose what one *already is*—and therefore to choose the past. On the other hand, one might will to be what one *possibly* is, chosing to be one's possibilities. Each of these choices is in fundamental conflict with the very structure of the self. Willing to *live in the future,* or to *live in the past,* is the very essence of despair; willing to be *actively related to the past and future as one's own* is the eradication of despair.

There is still a deeper and more dreadful variety of the "sickness unto death": choosing to be the very Power that constitutes the self. If we could refer back to Heidegger's terminology for a moment, we can say that the self is related to its past and future in the existential mode of *Geworfenheit,* or "thrownness." According to Heidegger, Dasein discovers its thrownness by way of its states of mind that are always its own, but that it never really chooses. As we probed deeper into Heidegger's thought we saw that it was not Dasein that throws itself, but Dasein's Being that has thrown Dasein into time. So too with Anti-Climacus. As the self comes to see that it is constituted by a Power other than itself, and constituted in such a way that it can never choose to be what it actually is or what it possibly is (that is, it can never choose not to be a self), it can react in the despair of "defiance" and will to constitute itself. In this state a person "wills to tear his self away from the Power which constituted it. But notwithstanding all his despair, this he is unable to do, notwithstanding all the efforts of despair, that Power is the stronger, and it compels him to be the self he does not will to be."[19] The reason that this form of despair is the most dreadful is that willing *to be oneself* can be done only in defiance of the Power that constitutes oneself; it is therefore the willing *not to be oneself*. It is self-contradiction at its deepest level. It is the most intense longing after a death for the self one is, but a longing that can only fail.

The very essence of the ethical is, of course, free choice. If the ethical stage is superior to the aesthetic it is because it lives decisively, not toward a receding moment, but in the moment that has the character of eternal presence. But that eternal presence bears in itself the torment-ing quality of the deepest possible despair. As such, it is grief of the most intense sort: *the desire to exist in the form of not existing.* This does not mean that the next stage, the religious, does away with the ethical. Just as the ethical took the aesthetic into itself, so does the religious take the ethical into itself—along with the aesthetic. What the religious stage does is to take the despair, or grief, of the ethical into itself by way of a greater freedom. Our question is whether the religious stage can offer a *true* death.

Kierkegaard assigns the task of describing the two stages of the religious—A and B—to Johannes Climacus who "does not give himself out to be a Christian," but instead is content to describe himself as a "a humorist in private practice," as though to remind us that we are still being dealt with "indirectly" even in the discussion of the two reli-gious stages.

In his *Philosophical Fragments* Climacus sets himself to the task of answering the question: "How far does the Truth admit of being learned?" There would seem at first to be no problem here in that we assume that Truth is quite accessible to any inquirer. Not so, Climacus says. He cites as his authority in this matter Socrates who in the *Meno* offered his "pugnacious proposition" that if we do not know the Truth we do not know what to look for in our inquiry; if we do know what to look for, we already possess what we seek. This brings Socrates to the famed doctrine of *recollection*: the Truth is eternally known by the soul prior to death and is somehow forgotten or set aside in the experience of birth. This conception of the Truth gives the teacher a distinctive role: a teacher does not *have* the Truth in such a form that it can be *given* to the learner. Since the learner already has the Truth, the teacher can only provide the *occasion* for the learner to recollect it. This puts the teacher in the role of midwife, inasmuch as the teacher can only assist the learner in coming to possess what already has been conceived in the learner. It also puts the teacher in a reciprocal relationship with the learner, since the teacher must also have an occasion for recollecting the Truth and the learner can provide such an occasion.

There is, then, an eternality at the center of existence so conceived that it is essentially different from the "eternal validity" of the ethical. Climacus writes, "In the Socratic view each individual is his own center, and the entire world centers in him, because his self-knowledge is a knowledge of God."[20] There is not the faintest tendency in Socrates toward the despair of "defiance," that is, toward willing to be the very Power by which one is constituted. There is a serene equanimity in Socrates, an exceedingly rare quality of allowing the eternal to show through his historical existence. We have already seen how this conception of the Truth brought him to face his own death in high humor, with compassion for his friends and confidence that the Truth for which he had lived would not be affected in the least.

Socrates is Climacus' exemplary representative of religiousness A. He embodies perfectly all that belongs to this stage. As the immediate aesthetic is *oblivious to the moment*, the reflective aesthetic living *toward the moment*, and the ethical *in the moment*, existence in religiousness A is *above the moment*. "From the Socratic point of view the Moment is invisible and indistinguishable; it is not, it has not been, it will not come. Hence the learner is himself the Truth, and the moment of occasion but a jest, like a bastard title that does not essentially belong to the book."[21] It is true that Socrates is not in despair, that he does not suffer from the sickness unto death. The reason for this is not that he has integrated death into his self-understanding, but has eliminated death altogether. Socrates' equanimity with reference to his historical experience is actually due to his conviction that the soul, as the possessor of Truth, must be as immortal as the Truth itself. In the *Postscript* Climacus observes: "In religiousness A there is no historical starting-point. The individual merely discovers in time that he must assume he is eternal. The moment in time is therefore *eo ipso* swallowed up by eternity."[22]

In overcoming despair by eliminating death one pays a price far too high: the elimination of the self itself. The reason for this is already clear from the structure of the self. If the self is the self-choosing relatedness of the actual with the possible, emptying the actual (or the historical) of all of its significance has the effect of doing away with the self.

In spite of his great admiration for Socratic teaching, Climacus knows one cannot stop with this stage, but must ascend to the next—a stage he can describe but cannot attain. In religiousness B one has overcome despair, while still preserving the historical in its full actuality—including even the death of the self.

The move to religiousness B constitutes an abrupt rejection of the Socratic answer to the question as to how far the Truth admits of being learned. Suppose "things to be otherwise," Climacus asks us. Suppose, that is, we do not already have the Truth within us. If we reject the Socratic understanding of Truth "the seeker must be destitute of the Truth up to the very moment of his learning it; he cannot even have possessed it in the form of ignorance, for in that case the moment becomes merely occasional."[23] The role of the teacher is now given much greater importance, for the teacher must not only have the Truth about which the learner is in error, but must also be able to give the learner both the Truth and the "condition for learning it." Since the learner exists in the kind of error that excludes all trace of the Truth, cannot even be a seeker, and is therefore not even aware of being in error, the teacher can do nothing less than transform the learner into "*a new creature.*" But with this requirement "we have already far transcended the ordinary functions of a teacher." Such a teacher can only be God himself, and the learner only a disciple. Moreover, the Truth that the teacher offers the disciple cannot be something the disciple remembers, but only what has been learned for the first time; since it comes only with the disciple's transformation into a new creature, the moment in time in which this occurs has the greatest possible significance, for it is the moment in which the eternal entered history.

Climacus then asks why God has any interest in the disciple? It is clear that Socrates' relationship with the learner was reciprocal, and that he had as much to learn as he had to teach. "But God needs no disciple to help him understand himself, nor can he be so determined by any occasion that there is as much significance in the occasion as in the resolve." God needs neither learner, nor moment. If God acts to bring the disciple into the Truth, Climacus decides, it can only be because God *loves* the disciple. But it is an eternal love that cannot be determined from without, a love so perfect there can be nothing externally great enough to occasion it: "The Moment makes its appearance when an eternal resolve comes into relation with an incommensurable occasion."[24]

However, a new difficulty arises. It is not enough for God merely to resolve out of his own eternity to love the disciple. The disciple must actually *be loved;* God must reveal this eternal resolve to the disciple. But how can this be done? For God to take the disciple up into heaven, or to appear before the disciple in his full heavenly splendor, would be so overwhelming that the disciple's sense of historical identity would be swept away, and the person whom God loved would scarcely continue to exist. There is only one possible solution, Climacus decides. God must "appear in the form of a *servant.*" But this can be no mere external appearance; God must *become* the servant, setting aside all the prerogatives of divinity. It must be "his true form and figure. For this is the unfathomable nature of love, that it desires equality with the beloved, not in jest merely, but in earnest and truth." Climacus, the nonbeliever, gets swept into the rapture of this proposal: "Behold where he stands—God! Where? There; do you not see him? He is God; and yet he has not a resting-place for his head, and he dares not lean on any man lest he cause him to be offended." Inasmuch as he has emptied himself of his divinity, he has taken on true human vulnerability. "He must suffer hunger in the desert, he must thirst in the time of his agony, he must be forsaken in death, absolutely like the humblest—behold the man!"[25]

Climacus has quite obviously pursued his line of thought directly into the classical Christian doctrine of the Incarnation. But he scrupulously omits any mention whatsoever of the words "Christian" or "Christianity," even failing to give the name "Jesus" or "Christ" to the servant form of the incarnate God. There is some comedy in this—he says in the *Postscript* that he would like to give the old language a rest—but there is also something in this omission that is essential to his "indirectness." Climacus seems clearly to want us to take note of the features of this stage before we call it Christianity, since that term will doubtlessly blind us to much of what he has said of religiousness B.

What is most obvious is that the eternal Deity found in Socrates (religiousness A) has been scrapped. What may not be so clear is that this eternal Deity had all along been identified with our inwardness; our eternality was never distinct from God's. Now our inwardness is sharply limited to our own individuality. Moreover, the source of our delight—what Climacus here calls "eternal happiness"—is once more outside ourselves. This is the very flaw the judge found in the aesthetic stage; but now there is a difference. In the aesthetic stage the relation of the person to the source of pleasure is *immediate*—there is no insertion of consciousness between the self and its object. The youth *is* her beauty. In religiousness B the external object—that is, the Truth—to which the disciple is related is a *paradox*, and the relation is no longer immediate, and not even reflective, but *dialectical*. Let us briefly examine the terms *paradox* and *dialectical* as Climacus uses them.

In its simplest form the paradox refers to the appearance of the eternal in historical form. Eternity and history are contradictory terms, but in at least one moment they come together in the same event. Climacus, however, is not quite satisfied with the term "paradox"; it does not really capture the full breadth of the contradiction involved in the Incarnation. Instead, he prefers to call it the "Absolute Paradox." He puts the case as follows: "In order to be man's Teacher, God proposed to make himself like the individual man, so that he might understand him fully. Thus our paradox is rendered still more appalling, or the same paradox has the double aspect which proclaims it as the Absolute Paradox; negatively by revealing the absolute unlikeness of sin, positively by proposing to do away with the absolute unlikeness in absolute likeness."[26] But note carefully: Climacus is not satisfied merely to say that the eternal entered history. The eternal entered history because the beloved disciple was in a great error. And what was the error? That the disciple already possessed the eternal and was thereby exempt from history. The error was that the disciple had ceased being historical, had ceased to exist in time. *For that reason, the eternal gave itself up in order to restore the integrity of the historical.*

But there is still more—and this is where the Absolute Paradox brings us to the *dialectical*. God knew that he could not be the disciple's teacher until he had become like the disciple, *in order that he might understand the disciple.* It is not until we can see that we have been understood by God that we can be related to the paradox; in this case, the Absolute Paradox. Since the Absolute Paradox is a highly concentrated contradiction there is no possibility that we could relate to it by way of Reason, although Reason is surely tempted to clear up the conflicting terms of the paradox. "When the Reason takes pity on the Paradox, and wishes to help it to an explanation, the Paradox does not indeed acquiesce, but nevertheless finds it quite natural that the Reason should do this; for why do we have our philosophers, if not to make supernatural things trivial and commonplace?"[27] If not by way of the Reason, how is it that the learner comes to an understanding of this paradox? "It comes to pass when the Reason and the Paradox encounter one another happily in the Moment; when the Reason sets itself aside and the Paradox bestows itself." Reason and the paradox are brought together in this manner by a "happy passion to which we will now assign a name, though it is not the name that so much matters. We shall call this passion *Faith*." And then Climacus adds that *faith* is precisely that *condition* the disciple must receive from God before learning the Truth.[28]

What kind of a condition is faith? It is a thoroughly *dialectical* condition. The reason for this is that the believer and the paradox have their existence only in relation to each other. Faith is possible only if there is an object commensurable to it. That is, if its object were *only* a historical fact this "happy passion" would have no interest in suspending Reason. On the contrary, it is precisely with historical fact that the Reason concerns itself. The historical fact must be a paradox, else there can be no faith. Far more radical is the opposite implication: if the paradox cannot offer itself to faith, but has only the Reason as its object, it cannot appear at all. Thus it is that faith and the paradox come into existence simultaneously. *We can have an understanding of the paradox only insofar as we are understood by it.*

The dialectical nature of faith is not to be taken to mean that faith simply takes some fact from history and arbitrarily holds it up as the paradox. Climacus has in mind something far more radical than this. In sum, his argument is that unless the self has no corresponding paradox external to itself it can have no history; and without history there is no self. It is a serious mistake to look for the paradox in history; for unless there is already some dialectical understanding of the paradox there is no history.

Climacus gives hundreds of pages in the *Concluding Unscientific Postscript* to the clarification of this point. He takes it as a fact of great but ironic importance that the ordinary knowledge of history is inherently antihistorical. The reason for this is that one can have no historical knowledge without imposing some limitation of abstract order on original historical material; but "historical material is infinite, and the imposition of a limit must thereofre in one way or another be arbitrary." At best it is an "approximation." One cannot even begin to investigate history without first having such an approximating limitation on what one expects to find.[29] But it is not just a question of the *inadequacy* of historical knowledge, as though if one had more facts or a more comprehensive scheme one could get to the truth of historical matters. All abstract thought robs history of its reality; it omits the fact of its actual existence by transforming everything into thought. What's worse, it robs the thinker of concrete existence as well. "What is abstract thought? It is thought without a thinker. Abstract thought ignores everything except the thought, and only the thought is, and is in its own medium. Existence is not devoid of thought, but in existence thought is in a foreign medium." What Climacus seeks is a kind of thinking that preserves its concreteness, its genuine historical character. "What is concrete thought? It is thought with a relation to a thinker, and to a definite particular something which is thought, existence giving to the existing thinker thought, time, and place."[30]

Historical truth, in other words, is not a truth that can be found "out there" in an objective historical medium; it is a way of existing that is truly historical. For this reason, historical truth is always related to the existence of the thinker; *historical truth is the way the thinker preserves his or her own subjectivity.* Climacus' famous declaration is that "Truth is subjectivity!" But his cry is almost universally misunderstood. What his readers too often overlook is that by subjectivity he does not mean something Socratic, a state of existing that is immune to historical becoming; he means a method of existing in which one is intensely historical. We could just as well invert the previous claim and state with equal force that *subjectivity is the way the truth preserves its historical character.*

What we must keep in the center of our own view of Climacus' thought is the essential relation between subjectivity and the paradox. "When subjectivity, inwardness, is the truth, the truth becomes objectively a paradox; and the fact that the truth is objectively a paradox shows in its turn that subjectivity is the truth."[31] It is the paradox in its dialectical relation to faith that prevents reason from swallowing history utterly into itself, obliterating personal existence along with it. We observed above that, in distinction to the Socratic understanding, inwardness is strictly limited to the individual. What Climacus has shown is that the inwardness of the individual must correspond to the inwardness of history. Just as there is something in my own existence that forever remains resistant to reason, so also is there in history. It is that fact that makes history possible.

We can see now the temporal character of religiousness B: it is not *oblivious to* the moment, *toward* the moment, *in* the moment, or *above* the moment; *it is with the moment.* Climacus characterizes the genuinely subjective (that is, faithful) relationship to history as one of *contemporaneity.* To be dialectically related to the paradox is to exist *with* it in history. It is therefore irrelevant that 1843 years have passed between the Incarnation and the time Climacus is writing; there is still no reason why he cannot be a contemporary disciple of the teacher.

We might quickly pause here to offer a distinction between Climacus and Heidegger on this point. Heidegger spoke of *being with* as one of Dasein's ways of existing. There is a clear difference, however, between the "with" in each of these thinkers. The "with" in Heidegger originates in one's own Being; it is because Being can be *Being-with* that history is possible. The "with" in Climacus originates in history; it is because history is irreducible to Reason in at least one of its moments—the paradox—that personal existence is possible. In Heidegger it is my own Being that is transcendent to my experience; in Climacus it is the paradox that is transcendent. Heidegger is finally pushed to a form of self-transcendence that empties death of its force. Climacus has sustained the transcendence of the historical other and has left the self fully exposed to death.

Where, then, is the place of death in religiousness B? In religiousness A despair, or the sickness unto death, is overcome simply by eliminating death. The question now is whether Climacus can show how one can be cured of despair without being swallowed by immortality. He has already shown that when God sets aside his divinity to take on the servant form he will suffer the full range of human vulnerability—including death. Kierkegaard's most common expression for this mode of existence is *becoming*. Subjectivity and inwardness are essentially synonymous with becoming. To be a subjective thinker is to enter vigorously into the unending process of historical becoming: "While objective thought translates everything into results, and helps all mankind to cheat, by copying these off and reciting them by rote, subjective thought puts everything in process and omits the result; partly because this belongs to him who has the way, and partly because as an existing individual he is constantly in the process of coming to be, which holds true of every human being" who has not given into the deceptions of objective and abstract thinking.[32] "The incessant becoming," Climacus adds later, "generates the uncertainty of the earthly life, where everything is uncertain."[33] We opened this discussion of Kierkegaard with quotations from Climacus that described the uncertainty of death. It is precisely this uncertainty that guarantees the fact that human existence will remain in the state of becoming.

Death, for Climacus, is not what it was for Heidegger, a feature of the structure of Being; instead, death is something we cannot escape as genuinely historical persons. For this reason it is not a cruel trick of Nature or an unjust imposition of fate; there is no evil in death. In the true sense there is nothing final about death, for death is only an event in the "incessant becoming" of existence. Anti-Climacus writes,

> death is the last thing of all; and, humanly speaking, there is hope only so long as there is life. But Christianly understood, death is by no means the last thing of all, hence it is only a little event within that which is all, an eternal life; and Christianly un-

derstood there is in death infinitely much more hope than merely humanly speaking there is when there not only is life but this life exhibits the fullest health and vigor.[34]

If death is not the last thing because we can go beyond it, and if, at the same time, we are not immortal in the mode of Socrates, what does it mean to go beyond death and still be mortal? How, in other words, does Climacus or Anti-Climacus, or any of Kierkegaard's other authors, or Kierkegaard himself, propose to establish the continuity of life in death itself?

The very first question we raised in response to Climacus concerned his remark that, although death is something to be related to the entire life of the subject, he had still not understood it and, more importantly, had not realized the task "existentially." Climacus never does indicate *directly* how we can realize this task. The absence of such a discussion in Kierkegaard's literature has led many students of his thought to charge him with a serious distortion of Christianity: he exalts the Crucifixion by emphasizing the death of the incarnate God in history, but he omits altogether any impassioned appeal to the Resurrection as the final ground of the Christian's hope.

In a narrow theological sense, this is quite true. But such readers have read Kierkegaard only "directly." They have overlooked the rich suggestiveness that lies in Kierkegaard's "indirectness." They have failed to see that even religiousness B is a pseudonymous creation, still clothed in the humor of a nonbeliever. There is, in other words, a stage beyond religiousness B. It is a stage Kierkegaard never really described. Instead, he lived it. What this final stage is, we can begin to discern, however, by listening to prominent clues left by Climacus.

"The difference between subjective and objective thinking," Climacus writes, "must express itself also in the form of communication suitable to each. That is to say, the subjective thinker will from the beginning have his attention called to the requirement that this form should embody artistically as much of reflection as he himself has when existing in his thought."[35] Subjectivity and objectivity are not simply modes in which the individual can choose privately to exist— they are *forms of communication*. To be subjective or objective is simultaneously to bring that mode of thinking to expression. Climacus holds the terms in such simultaneity that he commonly speaks of "existence-communication."

Now one of the differences between the two modes is that subjective thinking always communicates itself indirectly, and objective thinking directly. "Precisely because he himself is constantly in process of becoming inwardly or in inwardness, the religious individual can never use direct communication, the movement in him being the precise opposite of that presupposed in direct communication. Direct communication presupposes certainty; but certainty is impossible for anyone in process of becoming, and the semblance of certainty constitutes for such an individual a deception."[36] The difference does not, then, have anything to do with the *content* of the communication. "*The objective accent falls on WHAT is said, the subjective accent on HOW it is said,*" Climacus emphatically declares. Therefore, the objective truth or falsehood of Christianity is quite beside the point; in fact, neither can be established in the least. Christianity is either a subjective existence-communication, or it is nothing at all. Objectively, Climacus exclaims, "Christianity has absolutely no existence."[37]

That subjectivity expresses itself through the *how* and not through the *what* means that it is primarily interested in the appropriation of its communication by the listener. Inasmuch as objective thinking is wholly indifferent to subjectivity it is "hence conscious only of itself, and is not in the strict sense of the word a form of communication at all, at least not an artistic form, insofar as artistry would always demand a reflection within the recipient, and an awareness of the form of the communication in relation to the recipient's possible misunderstanding."[38] The objective thinker is therefore quite oblivious to the listener; in fact, the highest goal in understanding such a thinker "is to become altogether indifferent to the thinker's reality." In contrast, Climacus describes the subjective thinker: "A believer is one who is infinitely interested in another's reality. This is a decisive criterion for faith, and the interest in question is not just a little curiosity, but an absolute dependence upon faith's object."[39] In other words, to be dialectically related to the paradox through faith is to be infinitely interested in the personal existence of the recipient of one's existence-communication. Interest in the other is not something one *may do with* one's inwardness, it *is* one's inwardness. If inwardness cannot be communicated it is not inwardness.

Let us look more closely at the manner of communication appropriate to subjectivity—or faith. There are obviously two poles to it: the inwardness of the communicator and the inwardness of the recipient. It is essential that what the faithful person communicates is not the *objective fact* of one's own inwardness, but that inwardness itself. The problem is "expressing this existentially in the medium of existence. It does not consist in testifying about an eternal happiness, but in transforming one's existence into a testimony concerning it."[40] As for the other pole of the communication, it is essential that the existing communicator adapt the communication to the understanding of the recipient; this means that one must understand the recipient as an existing person. Of course, the communication will not be a success if the recipient simply offers a nodding recognition that, yes, your inwardness shows—bravo! The infinite interest in the other is expressed only in the communication of genuine existential possibilities to the other, possibilities that the recipient can make his or her own.[41]

Climacus has brought us to a radical conclusion: *One is truly inward only to the degree that the other realizes the possibilities opened up by the existence-communication of one's inwardness.* We are genuinely subjective—that is, free, existing persons—only if someone else listens in such a way that they too become subjective and subsequently capable of their own existence-communication. It is here that we see most clearly how Kierkegaard, through Johannes Climacus, has shifted the nature of language from the saying of it (as in Heidegger) to the hearing of it. The meaning of our discourse does not exist prior to its utterance, but subsequent to it. Our entire existence, since it is an existence-communication, has its meaning ahead of itself in the future response of other living persons, and not prior to it in the mystery of our own Being.

It is also here that we can get a clear grasp of the temporal character of this stage beyond the stages. It is not *oblivious to* the moment, *toward* the moment, *in, above* it, or *with* it; *it is itself the living moment.* Although the future orientation of existence-communication seems to resemble the *toward* of the aesthetic stage, the differences are great. The subjective communicator is not aiming at an objective goal that one could be *immediately*, but rather at an endless openness that offers possibilities that will in turn lead to further possibilities. This openness is the very essence of becoming, and becoming is Kierkegaard's highest term for life.

We have now outlined enough of Kierkegaard's thought to see that the agent of death is *time* itself. From the beginning Kierkegaard has described each of the stages in terms of its temporality. Time presents itself in the form of the moment. The moment is always a terminus. It marks the end of something. It is an insuperable boundary. The *only* function of time is to impose limits. Time, like all agents of death, is exceedingly powerful; it cannot be compromised. The way in which each of the stages relates to the *moment* indicates the different ways time's power of establishing boundaries is avoided. Each stage has its form of despair, or hopelessness, and each reaction to the moment is one of grief. It is the attempt to avoid death by achieving a living form of death—a direct contradiction.

The contradiction of grief is broken only by an act of freedom that seizes the moment itself and becomes living time. Of course, if it is true freedom, our actions will make a difference to others; our actions will have a history. In this case, we become our own boundary for the sake of history. We exercise our power of freedom by *communicating* the living moment to others. *Death is what we freely suffer for the sake of communicating to others that we understand what it means for them to be historical.* We can only think what the consequences might have been if the incarnate God had spent his several years among us, undergoing all the uncertainties of human finitude, then blissfully withdrew into his own secure immortality, beckoning us to follow. This would have made us all enemies of history and, therefore, enemies of ourselves. These consequences need not be conjured by the free imagination—they can all be openly displayed in the phenomenon Kierkegaard called "Christendom." But Christendom is built on a colossal misunderstanding; it is a vast construct still in the process of being assembled by objective thinkers. They have yet to discover that their Lord has not withdrawn to a place of eternal authority where he protects an abstract meaning of history against the reality of history itself; but that he is truly dead and has left them with their own inwardness in a history that they can understand only by living it toward the open possibilities of their own successors. It is, in fact, the death of Jesus—freely offered—that gives all his other experiences their true human character. It was his death that made his life a teaching. To the degree that his so-called believers cannot see this they will continue willfully supporting their illusion; Christendom will continue to be a massive expression of the collective grief of an entire civilization.

Kierkegaard understood perfectly that he could not attack the outrageous distortion of Christianity by elevating himself into his own transhistorical authority. He understood himself first as a listener to a past that was waiting for its own existence-communication to be received, and second as a teacher whose method of instruction required him to show the marks of his learners' finitude on his own personal existence. "Instruction begins," he wrote in his posthumously published work *The Point of View for my Work as an Author*, "when you, the teacher, learn from the learner, put yourself in his place so that you may understand what he understands and in the way he understands it, in case you have not understood it before. Or if you have understood it before, you allow him to subject you to an examination so that he may be sure you know your part."[42] Kierkegaard's elaborate construction of the "stages on life's way" is not an objective attempt to fit an abstract limitation over history's infinities; it is a gleeful gesture in our direction, an attempt to show that he understood where we are, and by way of that understanding an attempt to free us to turn forward ourselves, so that having listened we too might be teachers. It is an invitation to go beyond our own death, not by denying it, but by being free to use it as a token which shows that we chose truly to live.

Was Kierkegaard in fact a Christian? Some of his most perceptive and favorable critics have offered their doubts. "In the hands of Kierkegaard's pseudonyms," Louis Mackey has written, "the mystery and the miracle of Christianity have degenerated to contradiction and nonsense. Christianity has become not difficult to believe, but completely incredible."[43] Mark Taylor concludes his careful scholarly investigation of Kierkegaard's thought by noting that because the "self's faith, as Jesus' divinity, is inward and cannot be outwardly expressed," Kierkegaard's Christianity removes its believers from the world-historical process, forcing them to "remain isolated individuals, closed in their own subjectivity."[44] In part, Kierkegaard can be defended against this latter charge. It is true, of course, that he disclaimed any world-historical significance for Christianity, although this is only because "objective world-history" is not history at all, but the triumph of abstract thought over actual existence. Taylor, however, may still be quite correct, even if for the wrong reason, in his implication that Kierkegaard has distorted Christianity. Christianity is itself existence-communication, he said, and what it communicates is not a world-historical phenomenon like Christendom, but inwardness. Because he defines Christianity as communication itself, and not the content of that communication, Mackey decides that Kierkegaard is most fittingly described as a poet. He offers a "verbal object" that reaches for a response from the reader. "Kierkegaard's work is poetry because it traffics in possibilities."[45]

Whether existence-communication is truly Christian need not be settled here. What we are concerned with is Kierkegaard's radical theory of language—which derives its meaning from *what is heard* and not from *what is said*—and its consequences for understanding the place of death in human existence. We must remind ourselves, to be sure, that by virtue of his own intense subjectivity Kierkegaard had little interest in offering a full, "objective" statement of his theory of language. Even his most thoroughly "philosophical" observations on the nature of communication are authored by Johannes Climacus and are therefore laced with enough humor and irony that it is essentially impossible to pick his theory clean of its dialectical frame.

As it happens exactly a century after Kierkegaard wrote his *Point of View*, a strikingly similar view of language and communication was given a brilliant philosophical debut in Ludwig Wittgenstein's *Philosophical Investigations*. We shall look at several features of Wittgenstein's thought in order that we might bring into higher relief Kierkegaard's understanding, *and use*, of language. Although Wittgenstein (1889–1951) offered most of his thought, particularly his early thought, in the medium of twentieth-century philosophy—a genre scarcely distinguished by its "subjective artfulness"—he was a remarkably inward person, greatly concerned with the effectiveness of his communication. His youthful *Tractatus Logico-Philosophicus* has a renowned stark and oracular quality, but it also has a self-consciously crafted texture that even possesses a kind of Kierkegaardian demurrer on the final page: Anyone who understands his propositions, he wrote, "eventually recognizes them as nonsensical" and must use them merely as steps to a higher view. "He must, so to speak, throw away the ladder after he has climbed up it."[46]

Wittgenstein's later work, particularly the *Philosophical Investigations*, is essentially conversational in style and conspicuously avoids technical philosophical language. Many of his most important arguments are left in the form of questions, as though inviting the reader's thoughtful response. "I should not like to spare other people the trouble of thinking," he writes in the preface to the *Investigations*. "But, if possible, to stimulate someone to thoughts of his own."[47]

Although, as with Kierkegaard, it is never completely clear whether we are to respond to the thinker or the thought, there is in Wittgenstein's writing the direct presentation of a theory of language—not always clear, but always provocative. He opens the *Investigations* with a quotation from Augustine, offering a theory of language—closely resembling his own earlier theory—in which words are taken to be the names of objects. We soon learn that he intends to reject this theory and offer another in its place. "Augustine, we might say, does describe a system of communication; only not everything we call language is this system."[48] In fact, practically no language functions this way. Even when objects do have names we need to know what to do with the name; it is not the names of objects that we communicate in our speaking, we communicate by way of names. This means that "an ostensive definition [connecting a name with its object] can be variously interpreted in *every* case."[49]

We discover that the meaning of a word is not the thing it names;

instead: "the meaning of a word is its use in the language."[50] This simple statement, perhaps the most frequently cited remark of the entire *Investigations*, immediately appears subtle and complicated. Wittgenstein does not have in mind here the use of a word as a kind of tool or instrument. We do not use words *to do something*, we use words *in doing something*. I do not employ language as a device to win your sympathy for a cause; I employ it in winning your sympathy for the cause. The difference appears slight, but, in fact, is crucial, for it emphasizes the contextual nature of language. I do not carry words around as devices I might use in one place or another, as I might carry a screwdriver or a pocket calculator. The words belong to the context and have no existence—as words—outside the context. They might have existence as sound, but this is analogous to saying that chess pieces exist in the form of walnut or ivory outside the game. In fact, chess pieces *are* chess pieces only because they are used *in playing* chess.

This observation has a double edge. Wittgenstein's statement observed that the meaning of a word is its use *in the language*. The word is meaningful not only because we use it in doing something, but because we also use it in the language. From this it follows that if the language cannot exist independently of its context, neither can the context exist independently of a language.

Wittgenstein's most common term for this context is "form of life." A form of life is not something we can move in and out of, as we might pass from one part of a house to another; it is itself a complete way of living. What we have in this conception is not, however, anything similar to Heidegger's Being, for it is central to Wittgenstein's thinking that one normally exists in a variety of forms of life, each more or less comprehensive than the others.

To learn the use of a language is really to learn one or another form of life; but to learn that form of life is also to learn a language. We find a persistent confusion among philosophers, professional and amateur; it is the belief that the words and sentences of language carry their meaning with them, irrespective of the form of life in which they are uttered or written. However, the word "expectation," for example, will mean one thing to parents in relation to their children, another to a politician seeking to please the electorate, and yet another to the social scientist who is describing societal patterns. We can go even further and say that the word "expectation"—indeed every word, and every sentence—has a distinct meaning in each case of its actual use.

If this is true, how is it ever possible to understand what is being said? One of Wittgenstein's most revealing discussions concerns the matter of understanding. He offers as an example a numerical progression (1, 5, 11, 19, 29, etc.) and asks when we can be said to have understood the progression. He wants to counter the view that understanding is some sort of a hidden process in the brain, as though we will understand the series of figures when the formula for its progression appears before our minds. It may well be that we will discover what the next number is and call out "41!" without having the faintest idea of what the formula is. On the other hand, it may be the case that I do know the formula but I sit in silence, perhaps only casually nodding. In the former instance it would be appropriate to say that a person has understood, but it would not in the latter. Wittgenstein's point is that understanding an expression or a language is equivalent to showing that *I know how to go on with it.*[51]

Wittgenstein often stresses that he is not denying the existence of a mental process in such an instance, but rather that the mental process cannot be the meaning of the expression "I understand," or "she understands." We use that expression only in those cases where someone plainly *shows* he or she can go on.

Of course, there is never simply one way of understanding, or knowing how to go on. One might understand the uttered series of numbers as, say, an example of a teaching method, or as the manifestation of an instinct of playfulness in the human species. But if they can say "I understand" in either of these ways, it is only because there are others who can see that, yes, they do indeed know how to go on. There must still be a form of life in which going on in this way is possible; or, to put it more strongly, there must be a form of life whose essence is to go on with something in this way. A community of persons that has always been isolated from Western civilization will doubtless feel that the visiting anthropologist has understood nothing about their lives if he has done nothing in response but write into a large notebook and take photographs at awkward moments. And, indeed, unless there is a body of persons, say, a Western academic audience, who can subsequently declare, "Well, he certainly knows what to do with *this* data," he will *not* have understood.

Understanding, then, not only does not consist in some sort of inner state—it does not even have primary reference to something that has already happened. Understanding points forward toward its consequences *with other persons.* Kierkegaard was quite aware that essentially no one knew how to go on with what he was saying in his own age, and that it may be a century before they did. But what is implied in this is that if no one ever learns to go on with what Kierkegaard or anyone else has said, they have said nothing. They themselves will not have shown anyone that they had understood what was said to them.

Kierkegaard's case is extreme. There are few persons indeed who have so deeply understood their own past that they could be confident that a subsequent age would understand how they had gone on with that past and in such a way that they could go on with their own in equivalent depth—that is to say, with an equivalent view forward. There is always risk in understanding, for it may be that no one will see how you have gone on. It is never a question of a *correct* understanding—for there is nothing there prior to the person which is to be understood—but only of a *powerful* understanding. Kierkegaard knew the risk, and that makes him all the more powerful. He knew that he offered his understanding of the past to a variety of forms of life, and, indeed, persons have gone on with his writings as though they belonged to the academic form of life, or the psychiatric, or the romantic, or the heroic. Kierkegaard, however, if we listen carefully, has shown how one leaps ahead of each of these. In none of them do we have Kierkegaard—we have only his laughter, and the invitation to look elsewhere.

Kierkegaard knew how to die. He utterly vacated himself from his language. He turned his discourse over to his readers without leaving the merest fragment of his own authority in it. He had no desire to place his books in our path as something we must contend with. He did not claim them to be eternally valid descriptions of reality, or of the mind. They were not offered as conclusions to thought, but as provocations to thought. "So then the book is superfluous," he wrote through Climacus at the end of his *Concluding Unscientific Postscript*, "let no one therefore take the pains to appeal to it as an authority; for he who thus appeals to it has *eo ipso* misunderstood it. To be an authority is far too burdensome an existence for a humorist. . . ."[52]

One of the most distinctive features of Wittgenstein's "form of life" is that it indicates a definable body of persons and comprehends them in the full range of their existence, but it also leaves their understanding open toward the future. The form of life is not something we speak or live in as though it were always prior to our existence, like Heidegger's Being. It is something that changes as we live in it. *It does not have fixed boundaries that keep all our definitions clear; it has an ever moving horizon that keeps all our definitions open.*

The fact that a form of life is horizonal, and not bounded, is made most evident in the way Wittgenstein, like Kierkegaard, has withdrawn his authority from his own philosophy. And, of course, the analysis of understanding we have just summarized is not an analysis of understanding at all, but of "understanding." Wittgenstein is not attempting to explain *what understanding is*, but *what we mean when we say*

"Now I understand." What has so frequently foiled the professional philosophers in their study of Wittgenstein is their inability to see that when Wittgenstein denies that pain is an inner process it is not pain he is speaking of, but "pain." They have wanted to offer counterarguments showing that an inner process—mental or physiological—*can* be accurately coordinated with the recognizable *experience* of pain, and so on. In doing so they have missed the laughter altogether; they have attempted to strengthen the boundaries of their own fixed forms of life, shoring the walls against any openness to the future.

We have said of Kierkegaard that this understanding of language shows he *knew how to die.* He knew that Kierkegaard could only be "Kierkegaard" to history. Had Kierkegaard insisted on being Kierkegaard, if he had sought to lodge his subjectivity in a firmly established objectivity, he would have become thoroughly antihistorical. He would not have invited us to "go on" with his discourse in a way that opens us to history through our own discourse. Climacus said death was the event that introduced such uncertainty into our lives that we could not transcend the mode of becoming. If we listen to Kierkegaard through Climacus—if we "throw away the ladder"—we hear the strong declaration that it is death that sweeps history clean of our presence, and with it all our authority to hold history where we want it. Death blows away the boundaries of life and establishes a horizon in their place. We never reach the horizon, for it goes on ever before us. But unless we go toward it there is no horizon. We go toward it by way of discourse—talk that seeks to be answered by further discourse. It is not the objective description of a bounded subject matter immune to time, but a conversation in which all subject matters can find their home, though it belongs to no subject matter; its only interest is to keep history open. Whether or not Kierkegaard is a Christian, he is in full accord with the firm belief of the ancient rabbis that it is only by way of their continued discourse that they can undo the attempts to bring history to an end.

To be sure, death also is finally to be understood as "death." When we speak of "death," therefore, we are not speaking of a biological event, and not even an event of history; we are speaking of the ways in which our forms of life are kept open to the future because they do not belong to us, because they do not belong to anyone, because it is not of the nature of a form of life to *belong* at all. A form of life can only be given. We live in them not insofar as we make them ours, but only insofar as we make them a gift to others.

When we convert death to "death" we have utterly relinquished all objective, factual grounds for human existence and have set it free into its own discourse. We are mortal because we can speak; we speak because we need the other in order to exist ourselves. To the degree that we have put death in the place of "death" we ground language in the inconsequential, rob it of meaning, and diminish our own existence. *I cannot die in an objective sense, but I can speak meaningfully of my death in a subjective sense.* I do so when I display my utter vulnerability to time. I am temporal through and through. That is why I cannot exist *as* what I am, or *in* what I do, but only *toward* the consequences of my discourse.

Wittgenstein said in his *Tractatus* that "Death is not an event of life; one does not experience death." Kierkegaard would have emphatically agreed. Death is not an objective event that occurs somehow within our subjectivity. Wittgenstein continues: "Our life is endless, in just the same way that our field of vision has no boundaries."[53] This brings us to the conclusion of our examination of Wittgenstein and Kierkegaard, a conclusion that must, appropriately enough, be expressed in a paradox: *We do not see death as the boundary of life when we look forward precisely because if it were not for death we could not look forward at all.*

Notes

1. *Concluding Unscientific Postscript*, pp. 148 ff. Italics mine.
2. *The Point of View*, pp. 5 ff.
3. *The Philosophical Fragments*, p. 87.
4. *The Point of View*, p. 25.
5. Ibid., pp. 24 ff.
6. *Either/Or Vol. II*, p. 185.
7. *Either/Or, Vol. I*, p. 419.
8. Ibid., p. 439.
9. Ibid., p. 224.
10. *The Sickness unto Death*, p. 145.
11. *Either Or, Vol. II*, p. 197.
12. *The Sickness unto Death*, p. 158.
13. *Either/Or, Vol. II*, p. 184.
14. Ibid., p. 171.
15. Ibid., p. 218.
16. Ibid., p. 220.
17. Ibid., p. 255.
18. *The Sickness unto Death*, p. 144.
19. Ibid., p. 153.

20. *The Philosophical Fragments*, p. 7.
21. Ibid., p. 41.
22. *Concluding Unscientific Postscript*, p. 508.
23. *The Philosophical Fragments*, p. 9.
24. Ibid., p. 18.
25. Ibid., pp. 24 ff.
26. Ibid., p. 37.
27. Ibid., p. 42.
28. Ibid., p. 47.
29. *Concluding Unscientific Postscript*, p. 134.
30. Ibid., p. 296.
31. Ibid., p. 183.
32. Ibid., p. 68.
33. Ibid., p. 79.
34. *The Sickness unto Death*, p. 145.
35. *Concluding Unscientific Postscript*, p. 68.
36. Ibid., p. 68n.
37. Ibid., p. 116.
38. Ibid., p. 70.
39. Ibid., p. 290.
40. Ibid., p. 353.
41. Ibid., p. 320.
42. *The Point of View*, p. 30.
43. *Kierkegaard: A kind of Poet*, p. 242.
44. Mark Taylor, *Kierkegaard's Pseudonymous Authorship*, p. 367.
45. *Kierkegaard: A kind of Poet*, page 289.
46. *Tractatus Logico-Philosophicus*, 6.54.
47. *The Philosophical Investigations*, p. x.
48. Ibid., #3.
49. Ibid., #28.
50. Ibid., #43.
51. Ibid., #146, #147, #148, #150.
52. *Concluding Unscientific Postscript*, p. 547.
53. *Tractatus Logico-Philosophicus* 6.4311.

Bibliography

Soren Kierkegaard, *Attack Upon Christendom*, tr. Walter Lowrie (Boston: 1956).

—— *The Concept of Dread*, tr. Walter Lowrie (Princeton: 1946).

—— *Concluding Unscientific Postscript*, trs. David F. Swenson and Walter Lowrie (Princeton: 1944).

—————— *Fear and Trembling* and *The Sickness unto Death*, tr. Walter Lowrie (Princeton: 1974).

—————— *Either/Or*, 2 vols., trs. David F. Swenson and Lillian Marvin Swenson (New York: 1959).

—————— *Philosophical Fragments or a Fragment of Philosophy*, tr. David F. Swenson (Princeton: 1952).

—————— *Purity of Heart is to Will One Thing*, tr. Douglas Steere (New York: 1956).

—————— *Repetition*, tr. Walter Lowrie (New York: 1964).

—————— *Training in Christianity*, tr. Walter Lowrie (Princeton: 1960).

Louis Mackey, *Kierkegaard: A Kind of Poet* (Philadelphia: 1971).

Mark Taylor, *Kierkegaard's Pseudonymous Authorship: A Study of Time and the Self* (Princeton: 1975).

Ludwig Wittgenstein, *Philosophical Investigations*, tr. G. E. M. Anscombe (New York: 1967).

—————— *Tractatus Logico-Philosophicus*, trs. D. F. Pears and B. F. McGuiness (New York: 1963).

CONCLUSION

When Socrates instructed his friends that philosophers, of all persons, should have no fear of death, he was appealing to an extreme view of the nature of human existence. He taught that the soul—or that which most truly constitutes the personhood of each of us—is all-knowing and timeless. It can be touched neither by change nor by ignorance. We may not know this because we may have fallen into the habit of thinking about ourselves in the way that we think about tangible objects. All such objects exist in the mode of becoming; they pass in and out of existence. Thus we may have mistakenly come to believe that we have a beginning and an end, that we will exist but a little while then perish utterly. Plato assigned philosophers to the task of curing us of this mistake. Philosophers know that ideas must be timeless and cannot therefore have a beginning or an end. They know also that the mind cannot be distinguished from its contents, and since its contents are timeless ideas the mind must be deathless.

What makes this an extreme position is that in no other thinker or tradition are life and death placed in such complete opposition. In Plato's view life and death are related to each other as the terms of a contradiction. Whatever is alive can in no way be capable of death. Since death means change everything that truly lives must exclude all change—or becoming—from itself.

I began this study with Plato and ended it with Kierkegaard in whom the opposite extreme appears. In almost every detail Kierkegaard has inverted Plato's thought concerning death—and since Plato described philosophy as preparation for dying, this is virtually the whole

466

of his thought. For Kierkegaard becoming is not the agent of death, it is the very essence of life. Whoever lives is in a state of constant becoming. It is not becoming that the living person excludes from existence, but permanence. It is not change, but changelessness, that stands in opposition to life.

If life and death relate to each other as the terms of a *contradiction* for Plato, they relate to each other as the terms of a *paradox* for Kierkegaard. For Plato it is life *or* death; for Kierkegaard life *and* death. Plato could not think of personal existence except in the category of immortality; Kierkegaard could describe life *only* in the category of mortality. For this reason an appeal to the eternality of knowledge has no foothold in Kierkegaard's thought. Indeed, the highest stage of human existence for him is reached only when one has set the timeless truths of reason aside and embraced the Absolute Paradox—the paradox that the eternal has come into history, and has given up every trace of timelessness. By this view one may not take flight from death by departing from history and seizing onto the changeless contents of the mind; this is precisely a flight from life. One lives most truly—most *passionately*, Kierkegaard would have preferred us to say—by affirming most completely one's mortality, or by existing most perfectly in the mode of becoming.

In the Introduction to this study I suggested that since we cannot experience death directly we come to know what death is through the radical discontinuities that appear in our lives by way of the death of others. The most powerful lesson in the death of others is not simply that *things are contingent*, but that *we are contingent*. We do not completely belong to ourselves. Our personhood is always fundamentally related to the personhood of others. But it is not a relation of complete dependence. Just as we are related to others, they are related to us. It is a dynamic interrelationship which is simultaneously composed of our dependence on, and freedom with, each other. Death reveals both that we have our personhood from others *and* that we can be persons only so far as we are free.

I suggested further that the grief we normally experience when important relationships have come to an end derives from the fact we do not belong to ourselves, and that the irreversible rupture in the pattern of our lives has the immediate effect of seeming to bring our own lives to an end. This presents us with the challenge of freely refashioning our vital relationships, for this alone can rescue us from the deathlike grip of continuing bereavement.

Plato and Kierkegaard offer quite distinct solutions to the problem of grief. Plato denies that death is real. The experience of discontinuity is, from his point of view, the result of our mistaking the nature of our own existence. The doctrine of immortality of the soul which developed out of the Platonic philosophy is a profound rejection of human freedom inasmuch as it leaves us without any choice concerning our own life and death. We could not, in fact, choose to die; by the same terms, we do not choose to live. Indeed, living has nothing to do with choice, for *whatever we do we cannot but continue living.*

In Kierkegaard the emphasis falls on the opposite side: living is only choice; *we do not live at all unless we freely will to do so.* Kierkegaard certainly does not deny the fact that we are dependent on others for the very existence of ourselves as persons, but he interprets this dependence in a very different way from Plato. Existence, for Plato, is something we *receive*; we have nothing whatsoever to do with the fact that we are. For Kierkegaard personal existence is, paradoxically, something we can only give to others. It is true that we have received it from others, but only as a gift that can be received in the mode of giving it on. We cannot receive it to keep it.

It is for this reason that *history* is so important in Kierkegaard's thought. History, for Kierkegaard, did not mean simply what is past, but the way in which the remembered past is constantly reinterpreted in light of an anticipated future. It is also for this reason that the paradoxical affirmation of the Christian faith appealed so deeply to Kierkegaard. As he interpreted it, when the eternal God desired to make a gift of life to his own children he did not lift them out of their histories, but became historical himself. Although this doctrine may be so singularly stressed by Kierkegaard that he departs from the traditional Christian understanding of it, and he may well not be a Christian himself, we can nonetheless identify it as a radical cure for grief.

Between Plato and Kierkegaard a number of alternative approaches to the problem of human mortality have appeared. We found in Epicureanism and modern scientific theory a rejection of Plato's immortal soul in favor of a belief that all things, including conscious human persons, are composed of tiny entities (atoms), all in motion, but governed by invariable laws. Epicurus succeeded in overcoming Plato's absolute contradiction between life and death by doing away with a dualism of mind and matter, but the result is that we can now find no distinction whatsoever between life and death. It is meaningless to say that human persons are either alive or dead.

Mystics and psychoanalytic theorists proposed an odd sort of dualism where the soul was regarded as isolated from its material ground—or from its spiritual ground—and seeking to return. Death has been understood in both bodies of literature as the soul's retreat from the realm of becoming into the serene origin of all things that is itself immune to all change. "Die before ye die," cried of the great Islamic mystics, as though the return of the spirit could precede the return of the flesh to its source.

Hindus, in at least one of their major traditions, suggested a method of coping with grief still more ambitious. Instead of affirming an immortal soul, as Plato had, the Upanishadic rishis found that the comprehending mind in each person is intimately connected with the Perfect Mind (Atman) that knows all things and is all things. The becoming from which Plato was in permanent flight seemed to the rishis to be nothing more than the playful illusoriness of that which alone is real (Brahman).

Buddhists rejected the Hindu doctrine of the Brahman/Atman, arguing that the transitoriness of which death is such a painful reminder is not an illusion, but the very nature of things. In place of the unbroken continuity of the soul with all that is, Buddhists respond to grief by affirming there is *nothing but* discontinuity, and that the soul will be freed from its preoccupation with suffering and death when it sees that it too is completely discontinuous, and nothing in itself.

Jews understood history as the continuing drama of a whole people—a drama that includes the death of all its members but no end in time to its ever-unfolding story. Christians also saw that God's promise to his people to rescue them from the pain and death that history brings means a renewed history, but in their case a history available to faith alone. Death is not denied by Christians—as Plato, or even as the Hindus and Buddhists, had denied it—but death is nonetheless overcome in each individual life inasmuch as each person has a life *in Christ.* The renewed history Christians have sought is a history of the resurrected believers who have their life elsewhere than in this world.

The Neoplatonists and their intellectual descendents, C. G. Jung and Teilhard de Chardin, regarded present historical existence as fragmentary, shadowy, but capable of moving inward toward the center of the psyche, or upward toward the center of the One, or onward toward the Omega or center of time, where it would lose all its darkness and become complete. Death, though real and occurring in time, is but a threshold on the soul's journey toward wholeness.

Hegel's achievement was to show for the first time that the self can be properly described as carrying the source of its own discontinuity within itself. Death occurs when and where the self becomes an irreconcilable Other to itself. Hegel, in his attempt to overcome death also overcame Otherness, ultimately describing the self as Absolute Spirit containing all things in itself. Sartre, resolved not to lose what

Hegel had gained in this conception, confined the category of Otherness to the individual's own consciousness. This had the ironic effect of not allowing the self the power to die, for its powerlessness to become its own Other is precisely what constituted selfhood for Sartre. Contrary to his intentions, Sartre indirectly proposed a theory of existential immortality.

Nietzsche, rejecting the category of consciousness as a form of impotence, focused on the vital will of the individual—an active, restless form of becoming which can exist only in the mode of power in relation to other wills. While in Nietzsche's thought we recover the sense of becoming that is lost in Sartre's, it is still the case that Nietzsche's identification of life *as* willfulness means that death cannot occur from within, but only from without. One does not die, in Nietzsche's view of it, one must be killed.

Heidegger, seeing that Nietzsche let the elusive category of becoming slip out of his thought, therefore offers in his own philosophy a way of understanding Being within the mode of time, thereby establishing human existence (Dasein) as the state of irreducible becoming. In his later thought when Heidegger turned more directly to Being—and away from Dasein—the category of becoming fell into the background. It is Being—birthless, deathless, timeless Being—that speaks through our mortality.

In Kierkegaard it is not Being but becoming that speaks through our mortality. Speech, in fact, is the very way our mortality makes itself evident—for speech is something we must first receive from others, and something we cannot truly receive until we speak ourselves. We do not truly speak, however, until we speak to the understanding of others— until, that is, we freely turn over to others what has been turned over to us. Kierkegaard saw that our ability to communicate reveals our mortal nature most completely. It is only because we are mortal that we can speak, and only because we can speak that we are free, and only because we are free that we can join with others in the creation of an open future that does not eliminate death but affirms life by affirming the reality of death.

Kierkegaard proposed that we overcome despair—the highest form of grief—not by attaining the changeless state of immortality (the very sickness unto death itself), but by taking death into our personal history in the act of turning the meaning of our lives over to others. Indeed, only in so dying can we live at all.

INDEX

DATE DUE